D0713431

Bibliography of Place-Name Literature

AMERICAN NAMES

I HAVE fallen in love with American names,
The sharp names that never get fat,
The snakeskin-titles of mining-claims,
The plumed war-bonnet of Medicine Hat,
Tucson and Deadwood and Lost Mule Flat.

Seine and Piave are silver spoons,
But the spoonbowl-metal is thin and worn,
There are English counties like hunting-tunes
Played on the keys of a postboy's horn,
But I will remember where I was born.

I will remember Carquinez Straits,
Little French Lick and Lundy's Lane,
The Yankee ships and the Yankee dates
And the bullet-towns of Calamity Jane.
I will remember Skunktown Plain.

• • • • • • • • • • • • • • • • • •

Rue des Martyrs and Bleeding-Heart-Yard,
Senlis, Pisa, and Blindman's Oast,
It is a magic ghost you guard
But I am sick for a newer ghost,
Harrisburg, Spartanburg, Painted Post.

• • • • • • • • • • • • • • • • • •

I shall not rest quiet in Montparnasse.
I shall not lie easy at Winchelsea.
You may bury my body in Sussex grass,
You may bury my tongue at Champmédy.
I shall not be there, I shall rise and pass.
Bury my heart at Wounded Knee.

Stephen Vincent Benét

From *Ballads and Poems* by Stephen Vincent Benét. Copyright 1931 by Stephen Vincent Benét. Copyright © 1959 by Rosemary Carr Benét. Reprinted by permission of Holt, Rinehart and Winston, Publishers.

Bibliography of Place-Name Literature

United States and Canada

Third Edition

By

Richard B. Sealock

Margaret M. Sealock

and Margaret S. Powell

AMERICAN LIBRARY ASSOCIATION

Chicago, 1982

Designed by Ellen Pettengell
Text composed by Caron Communications
in Bold Legal Statistical P.S.
Display type, Americana,
composed by Eddie Price, Inc.
Printed on Warren's 1854, a pH-neutral
stock, and bound in C-grade
Holliston cloth by Braun-
Brumfield, Inc.

Library of Congress Cataloging in Publication Data

Sealock, Richard Burl, 1907-
Bibliography of place-name literature.

Includes indexes.
1. Names, Geographical—United States—Bibliography.
2. Names, Geographical—Canada—Bibliography.
3. United States—History, Local—Bibliography.
4. Canada—History, Local—Bibliography. I. Sealock,
Margaret M. II. Powell, Margaret S. III. Title.
Z6824.S4 1982 [E155] 016.9173'01'4 81-22878
ISBN 0-8389-0360-6 AACR2

Copyright © 1982 by the American Library Association. All rights reserved except those which may be granted by Sections 107 and 108 of the Copyright Revision Act of 1976.
Printed in the United States of America.

CONTENTS

219007

PREFACE

The present Bibliography of Place-Name Literature—United States and Canada is a third edition of the Bibliography of Place Name Literature—United States, Canada, Alaska and Newfoundland, published by the American Library Association in 1948. It has been prepared to assist the librarian, the researcher, the historian, and the general reader interested in the location of information about place-names—local, state, provincial, or regional—in the United States and Canada. The third edition lists many new items published since 1946 and shows a continued important and gratifying increase in scholarly studies in the field of place-name literature.

The third edition includes the available published material in place-name literature, both books and periodical articles, and some manuscript compilations to be found in libraries. Following a national section, the material is arranged in two categories: by states for the United States and by provinces for Canada. Regional sections are included for the Mississippi Valley, New England, the Maritime Provinces and the Northwest Territories.

New editions are listed as main entries with notes giving information on the earlier editions. Reprints, which have restored the availability of numerous important books, are cited in notes under the latest edition of the work.

Although there is still no complete dictionary of place-names for either Canada or the United States, seemingly an impossible task considering the several million names to be listed in either case, two important works for the United States have been published since the second edition of this bibliography. Attention is called to the dictionary by George R. Stewart, American Place-Names, and to an Illustrated Dictionary of Place Names, United States and Canada, by Kelsie B. Harder. Although there has been an increase in the number of comprehensive guides to the origin and meaning of names in the states and provinces, the authors have found it necessary to include the many articles in little-known or ephemeral publications since these add unusual names and explain the possible origin and meaning of local names. Gazetteers have been included because of their usefulness in establishing the basic list of names for a given area and the dates when the names were in use. They also show variant forms and names no longer in use. No attempt has been made to include sections in county histories or other books limited to a specific locality since these publications seemed obvious sources.

Attention is called to the publications of the Québec Commission de Toponymie, which reflect the mandate of the August, 1977 Quebec charter of the French language, probably the instrument for the most extensive change in the place-names of a large region—the Province of Quebec.

For the convenience of the reader two indexes have been supplied: an author and personal name index and a subject index. The detailed subject index directs the reader to specific place-names, broad categories of names (such as rivers, mountains, etc.), foreign-language names (such as Celtic names, French names, etc.), and types of names (such as Indian). It does not attempt to include all the many individual place-names given in the annotations.

The goal of personally examining each item listed has become more difficult to achieve due to the general reduction of library book budgets. However, the greater reliance placed on general bibliographies has probably led to the discovery of additional items.

Some of the new material in the second and third editions has appeared in a frequent bibliographical feature in Names, the quarterly journal of the American Name Society, established in 1953. The authors wish to express their appreciation to the editors of the journal for their kind permission to reprint this material. The first editor of the journal, Erwin G. Gudde, not only requested the series, but also supported the project as well, and wrote a foreword to the second edition, herein reprinted, for which the authors are extremely grateful.

Throughout the work of gathering the items two contributors continuously sent in new entries many of which would have been missed. The late Mamie Meredith of Nebraska University and the late Gerald D. McDonald of the American History Division of the New York Public Library were responsible for the inclusion of many important and obscure articles. Others who have been helpful include Virgil J. Vogel, Northbrook, Illinois; Laurence E. Seits, Sugar Grove, Illinois; Douglas W. Tanner, Charlottesville, Virginia; Conrad M. Rothrauff, Potsdam, New York, recent editor of Names; and Kelsie B. Harder, Potsdam, New York, recent secretary of the American Name Society. Margaret M. Bryant, Brooklyn, New York, who deserves special mention for informing us of so many of those elusive but important master's theses, reviewed 25 years of onomastic study in the United States and Canada in 1976. This review proved to be a valuable aid in insuring the inclusion of important items. For many years Edward C. Ehrensperger has conducted a survey of work in progress on place-names, which has continuously furnished clues to items that should be searched. For this help we are deeply indebted.

The study of the literature has been carried on in numerous libraries. For this third edition we wish particularly to acknowledge the help received from the staff of the University of Toronto Library and the staff of the National Library of Canada. Also, Alan Rayburn kindly gave us access to the special collection on geographical names at the Department of Energy, Mines and Resources of Canada in Ottawa.

The first two editions were prepared in collaboration with the late Pauline A. Seely. The third edition, with the continuing heavy dependence on various libraries, has been compiled by three persons. This new edition recognizes the library research, preparation of French material, indexing, and general editorial work of the second author during the preparation of the second and third editions. Also, another librarian, cataloger, and now documents librarian at the College of Wooster has been added to help watch for pertinent publications. Margaret S. Powell, a member of the American Name Society, also helped edit the last three supplementary lists that appeared in Names.

ACKNOWLEDGMENTS

The author is indebted to the following authors from whose cited works he has drawn for quoted material in this edition:

Eckstorm, Fannie Hardy. Indian place-names of the Penobscot Valley and the Maine coast. Orono, Me., Printed at the Univ. Press, 1941. (see #1893, this edition)

Griffin, Grace Gardner. Writings on American history. 1906-1939/40 (various imprints, 1908-44), 33 vols.

Pilling, James Constantine. Bibliography of Algonquian languages. Washington, Govt. Print. Off., 1891.

Price, Esther Frances. Guide to material on place-names in the United States and Canada. Urbana, Ill., 1934. (see #436, this edition)

FOREWORD TO THE SECOND EDITION

In European countries the investigation into the origin and meaning of names is a recognized and assiduously studied branch of philology. The study of geographical terms has proved an invaluable help in the delineation of primeval periods of history for which no recorded documents are available. The names of rivers, lakes, mountains, and other features are often the only records of the onetime presence of a people whose language and culture have completely disappeared. For later periods, place-names show not only the migrations and the shifting of linguistic boundaries of the various sections of Europe, but also the presence or absence of plants, animals, natural resources, and cultural manifestations. The chief purpose of European place-name research is, therefore, the etymology and evolution of geographical terms. The editions of the English Place Name Society and similar, less voluminous publications in Germany, France, Scandinavia, and other countries have for many years disseminated the results of such studies.

Place-name research in the United States presents a different aspect. With the exception of the great number of native Indian names, and some smaller groups like the Aztec terms in the Southwest, names in this country present few problems to the etymologist. This does not mean that they are less interesting or less important. They are an intrinsic part of everyday life, and in them are reflected all phases of the nature of the country and the history and culture of the people. Interest in American geographical names goes back to the very beginning of the settlement of North and South America, and interpretations of certain names have not been lacking. But a systematic effort to put name research on a scholarly basis was not undertaken until the present generation.

A number of monographs and articles on regional nomenclature, especially on Indian names, had been published before then. Even a brave, though unsatisfactory, attempt to cover the place-names of the United States had been made by Henry Gannett, which appeared as a Bulletin of the U.S. Geological Survey in 1902. In the 1920s and 1930s a number of state surveys were published—for Arizona, Minnesota, Nebraska, Oklahoma, Oregon, Pennsylvania, South Dakota, and Washington—some of which were comprehensive and adequate. But it was the publication of Henry L. Mencken's The American Language in 1929, and its various supplements, that gave a dynamic impulse to the science, for the sage of Baltimore discussed the importance of names in his stimulating and provocative fashion.

A solid foundation for American name research was established in the decade following World War II. In 1945, George R. Stewart's Names on the Land appeared, representing the first attempt to treat geographical names in a scholarly and objective, yet sprightly and entertaining, manner. Three years later the American Library Association issued The Bibliography of Place Name Literature by Richard B.

Sealock and Pauline A. Seely—an indispensable tool for all future work in North American toponymy. In 1951, the American Name Society was founded in Detroit, and the first issue of Names, the official publication of this Society, appeared in March, 1953.

Since then the importance of and interest in the study of names have been growing steadily, and this branch of philology has begun to take root in the fertile soil of American culture. The new edition of Sealock and Seely's Bibliography is another important step in the right direction.

ERWIN G. GUDDE
Emeritus Associate Professor
University of California, Berkeley

UNITED STATES

GENERAL

1. Abbott, N. C. Lincoln: name and place. Nebraska State Historical Society. Publications 21:8-133. 1930.

Traces the origin of the name Lincoln to Celtic-Latin, with notes on all communities in the United States with the name Lincoln.

2. Aboriginal etymology. Olden time 1:325-29, July 1846.

The derivation and significance of some Indian names, such as Allegheny, Winnipee, and Ohio, as interpreted by the Reverend Timothy Alden in Allegheny magazine.

3. Aboriginal names. Southern literary messenger 7:477-78, July 1841.

Signed: G. S. M'K.

Emphasis on Indian names of rivers in the Middle West, including some that were no longer used in 1841.

4. Adkinson, Burton W. Some research problems on geographical names. Association of American Geographers. Annals 33:220-21, Dec. 1943.

A study of examples submitted to the U.S. Board on Geographical Names.

5. Alexander, Gerard L. Nicknames of American cities, towns, and villages, past and present. New York, Special Libraries Assoc., 1951. 74p.

Arranged by state, with an alphabetical index by place-name. Nicknames are given without explanation or history.

Review: Albert Keiser, Names 2:68-69, March 1954.

6. Alexander, Henry. The new advance in place name study. Queen's quarterly 33:194-201, Oct.-Dec. 1925.

First part is a discussion of the English Place Name Society, Introduction to the study of place names. Second, the peculiarity of American place-names is cited, with examples, and suggests that there is room for much investigation.

7. Alleghany—what is the meaning of this word. Historical magazine 4:184, June 1860.

The derivation and meaning of this word as applied to the river is "Cold water."

8. Allen, E. L. The devil's property in the United States. Outlook 126:246-47, Oct. 6, 1920.

The use of the word devil in place-names.

9. Allen, Harold B. Distribution patterns of place-name pronunciations. Names 6:74-79, June 1958.

The effect of native speech and the prestige factor on the pronunciation of local place-names. Examples drawn from The linguistic atlas project of the upper Midwest.

Comment on this article and the pronunciation of some of the place-names mentioned in it (Iowa, Omaha, Missouri, Chicago, Illinois) appeared in Omaha world-herald Nov. 3, 1958, p. 8, col. 2, taken from Chicago tribune.

10. Allen, Mary Moore. Origin of names of army and air corps posts, camps, and stations in World War II in the United States. Goldsboro, N.C., The Author, n.d. 352p.

Originally published in separate parts for each state.

11. American ghost towns. American notes and queries 3:152, 187-88, Jan., March 1944; 4:14, 63, April, July 1944.

12. America's Christmas postmarks. Good housekeeping 145:60, Dec. 1957.

A list of town names related to Christmas, such as Santa Claus, Ind.

13. America's inept place-names. Literary digest 53:790-91, Sept. 23, 1916.

Some of the place-names of the western states.

14. Andriot, John L. Township atlas of the United States. McLean, Va., Andriot Associates, 1979. 1184p. maps.

1st ed. 1977. 724p.

Counties and minor civil divisions index: p. 737-1032; Populated places index: p. 1033-1155; Urbanized areas index: p. 1157-1184.

Includes 43,294 entries to the named subdivisions of the 3067 counties in the United States.

15. Another view of town nomenclature. Nation 8:147-48, Feb. 25, 1869.

Discusses disagreeable place-names in this country, but suggests that association with men will dignify and endear what primarily is trivial or low.

16. Arnold, Pauline & Percival White. How we named our states. New York, Criterion Books, [1966]. 192p. maps.

Addressed to the teenage reader.

Review: Robert M. Rennick, Names 15:152-53, June 1967.

17. Ashley, James M. The naming of Montana. Montana magazine of history 2:65-66, July 1952.

Reprinted with comments in Names 4:176-77, Sept. 1956.

A letter to Judge William H. Hunt, dated April 28, 1892. James M. Ashley explained his choice of names for western territories while serving as chairman of the Committee on Territories (1863-69) in the House of Representatives. Those included are Montana, Arizona, and Wyoming in addition to others not named.

18. Ashton, J. W. Some folk etymologies for place names. Journal of American folklore 57:139-40, April-June 1944.

19. Ashton, William E. Names of counties and county seats. Names 2:14-20, March 1954.

Relationships between some counties and the seats thereof.

20. —— Presidential place-name covers. Weekly philatelic gossip 53:590-91, 622-23, 642, 654-55, 671, 822-23, 829, Jan. 12, 19, 26, March 1, 1952; 54:42-43, 52, 78-79, 94, 170-71, 202-03, 330-31, 374-75, 382, 490-92, 757-58, 761, 810-11, 825, March 15, 22, April 12, 19, May 17, 24, June 21, Aug. 16, 30, 1952; 55:42-45, 106-07, 338-40, 526-

27, 622, 692-93, 782, Sept. 13, 27, Nov. 15, Dec. 27, 1952, Jan. 17, 31, Feb. 21, 1953; 56:18-19, 181, 337-40, 500-01, 684-87, March 7, April 11, May 16, June 20, Aug. 1, 1953; 57:45-46, 430-31, 688-91, Sept. 12, Dec. 5, 1953, Jan. 30, 1954; 58:300-02, 461, 678, May 8, June 12, July 31, 1954; 59:464-65, 818-19, Dec. 11, 1954, Feb. 26, 1955; 60:182-83, 326-27, 522-23, April 9, May 14, June 25, 1955.

Author decided to collect covers with presidential stamps canceled at post offices named for the president. Includes origin of derivation of place-name from name of president.

21. Austin, Mary. Geographical terms from the Spanish. American speech 8:7-10, Oct. 1933.

In the Southwest.

22. Bailey, John. Hysterical history-state names. Saturday evening post 226:38, April 3, 1954; 226:40, May 1, 1954; 226:14, June 12, 1954; 227:38, Aug. 21, 1954; 227:46, Sept. 11, 1954; 227:44, Oct. 16, 1954; 227:38, Nov. 6, 1954; 227:40, Dec. 4, 1954; 227:38, Jan. 29, 1955; 227:40, Feb. 26, 1955; 227:38, April 2, 1955; 227:40, April 30, 1955; 227:40, May 28, 1955; 228:38, July 23, 1955; 228:38, Aug. 20, 1955; 228:42, Sept. 17, 1955.

23. Bakal, Carl. Town namer. Cosmopolitan 139:79, Sept. 1955.

Brief statement on the work of Meredith F. Burrill, Director of the Office of Geography.

24. Baker, Ronald L. Role of folk legends in place-name research. Journal of American folklore 85:365-73, Oct. 1972.

25. Ballas, Donald J. Place names as a teaching device in geography. Journal of geography 59:419-21, Dec. 1960.

Bibliography: p. 421.

26. Barbour, Philip L. Toponymy in the service of biography. Names 12:108-18, June 1964.

The place-names given by Captain John Smith, as seen on his maps, contribute to his biography and have effectively altered the entire picture of his life. The study illustrates how place-names can be an extremely valuable adjunct to biographical research.

27. Bastian, Robert W. Generic place-names and the northern-midland dialect boundary in the Midwest. Names 25:228-36, Dec. 1977.

A study based on generic terms for small streams and communities.

28. Bayer, Henry G. French names in our geography. Romanic review 21:195-203, July-Sept. 1930.

Names selected from his proposed work on French names.

A newspaper article on this proposed publication appeared in New York times Sept. 14, 1930, sec. 2, p. 1.

29. —— French place names in America. Légion d'honneur 3:115-20, Oct. 1932.

30. Beeler, Madison S. George R. Stewart, toponymist. Names 24:77-85, June 1976.

Introductory article to this issue, a Festschrift in honor of Prof. Stewart, compares his contributions to the work of others, particularly European scholars, and contrasts their concentration on languages with Stewart's interest in the process of naming, and in geography, history and folklore.

31. —— On etymologizing Indian place-names. Names 5:236-40, Dec. 1957.

32. Beer, William. The "Dixie bill." Magazine of history 20:1-3, Jan. 1915.
Offers possible origin of the word Dixie as applied to the extreme southern states.

33. Bell, Laura. Some geographical names and their significance. Geographical Society of Philadelphia. Bulletin 18:31-34, Jan.-April 1920.
Discusses in a general way the assignment of names to places.

34. Benagh, Christine L. 100 keys: names across the land [by] Christine Fletcher. Nashville, Abingdon Press [1973]. 288p.
Juvenile literature describing the history and legends associated with two names in each state.

35. Benét, Stephen Vincent. American names. Life 16:48-57, Jan. 31, 1944.
Poem, accompanied by editorial comment, and a list of odd and wonderful names.

36. Bentley, Harold Woodmansee. A dictionary of Spanish terms in English; with special reference to the American Southwest. New York, Columbia Univ. Press, 1932. 243p. (Columbia University studies in English and comparative literature)
A list of Spanish place-names in the United States arranged under each state, p. 221-36. A discussion of place-names, p. 16-18.

37. —— & M. Robert Snyder. Place names in the United States, a tentative bibliography. n.p., 1938. 8, 5p.
A brief list which was distributed at the 1938 meeting of the Modern Language Association.

38. Best, Katharine & Katherine Hillyer. Very funny name, Peculiar; history and whimsy go into the naming of our home towns, and the results are sometimes pretty weird. Coronet 37:75-78, Jan. 1955.

39. Birss, John Howard. Nicknames of the states; a note on Walt Whitman. American speech 7:389, June 1932.
Nicknames for the inhabitants of the various states.

40. Blakeslee, Alton L. How to find your friend's house—in 10 easy lessons. Chicago sun-times March 11, 1956, p. 40.
Description of a numbering system devised by Ambrose Ryder and set forth in a booklet Where is where.

41. Bonnell, Jesse W. Etymological derivation of the names of states and territories. Journal of education (Boston) 47:378, June 16, 1898.

42. Boorstin, Daniel Joseph. The Americans, the national experience. New York, Random House, c1965. 517p.
Names in profusion and confusion: p. 299-306.

43. Booth, George D. Indian names for towns. New York times Aug. 17, 1930, sec. 3, p. 2, col. 5.

44. Boyd, Stephen Gill. Indian local names, with their interpretation. York, Pa., The Author, 1885. 70p.
"Names of places in a number of Indian languages, among them the Abnaki, Delaware, Minsy, Algonkin, Powhatan, Lenape, Shawnee, and Chippewa."—Pilling.

45. Bradsher, Earl L. Some aspects of American place names. South Atlantic quarterly 13:174-88, April 1914.
The great varieties of names from "European and native white sources, and their

interest as a study in the history, the geography, the social customs, and the psychology of the people of our country."--Griffin.

46. Brainerd, Ezra. The significance of some familiar names of persons and places. Education 19:140-51, Nov. 1898.
Discussion of the factors involved in the forming of names.

47. Brant-Sero, J. Ojijateckha. Indian place names in Mohawk, collected by J. O. Brant-Sero and Chief Alexander Hill. Toronto, Ontario Provincial Museum. Annual archaeological report 1898:171-72.
A list of Canadian and American names with their Indian equivalents and meanings.

48. British towns greet American namesakes. New York times Feb. 6, 1938, sec. 4, p. 6.
More than 50 British towns maintain contact in various ways with more than 600 of their namesake towns in the United States.

49. Broche, Gaston E. Villes américaines de noms français. Société de Géographie et d'Études Coloniales de Marseille. Bulletin 63:73-89. 1944-47.

50. Brower, Jacob Vradenberg. The Missouri River and its utmost source; curtailed narration of geologic, primitive and geographic distinctions descriptive of the evolution and discovery of the river and its headwaters. [2d ed.] St. Paul, Minn. [The Pioneer Press], 1897. 206p.
Montana, Iowa, Nebraska, and Kansas; historical letters defining the true meaning and derivation of the names of several western states: p. 178-81.

51. Brown, Dee. Looking behind America's colorful place names. Baltimore sun, Sept. 11, 1938.

52. Brown, Frederic. Cardinal street names. American printer 119:48, Aug. 1944.

53. Brunn, Stanley D. & James O. Wheeler. Notes on the geography of religious town names in the United States. Names 14:197-202, Dec. 1966.
Comment on this article by Donald Baker and reply by the authors, ibid. 16:70-71, March 1968.

54. Bryan, J., 3d. A letter to 123 East 456th St. will always find me. Holiday 52:4, 8-9, Nov. 1972.
Discussion of both uninspired and unusual street names.

55. Bryant, Margaret M. After 25 years of onomastic study. Names 24:30-55, March 1976.
A survey of onomastic study in the United States and Canada during the first 25 years of the American Name Society.

56. Buchanan, Milton Alexander. Notes on Portuguese place-names in northeastern America; In Estudios hispánicos, homenaje a Archer M. Huntington. Wellesley, Mass., 1952. p. 99-104.
Principally Newfoundland; also Labrador, Nova Scotia, New England coast.

57. Bue, Conrad D. Principal lakes of the United States. Washington, 1963. 22p. map. (Geological Survey. Circular 476)
Bibliography: p. 21-22.
Lakes of ten square miles or more.

58. Burrill, Meredith F. The Board on Geographic Names. Military engineer 348:2, July-Aug. 1960.

Written by Meredith F. Burrill, Director of the Board, though not credited to him in the issue.

59. —— Generic terms in United States watercourse names. International Congress of Onomastic Sciences. 6th, Munich, 1958. v. 2, Report of Congress and section meetings. 1961. p. 175-80.

60. —— Localized toponymic generics. Association of American Geographers. Annals 47:156, June 1957.
Abstract of paper. Copy of the full paper is in the office of the U.S. Board on Geographic Names.

61. —— The new look in geographic name standardization. American Congress on Surveying and Mapping. Papers from the 29th annual meeting, March 9-14, 1969. p. 244-47.

62. —— Official standardization of geographic names in the United States. International Congress of Toponymy and Anthroponymy. 3d, Brussels, 1949. v. 2, Proceedings and transactions, 1951. p. 394-99.

63. —— Principles underlying domestic place name decisions in the United States. Revue internationale d'onomastique 1:197-212, Sept. 1949.
Abstract in Association of American Geographers. Annals 37:16, March 1947.

64. —— The reorganization of the United States Board on Geographical Names. Association of American Geographers. Annals 33:222-23, Dec. 1943.
Abstract of paper describing the program of the Board and its reorganization to handle increased work due to the war.

65. —— The reorganization of the United States Board on Geographical Names. Geographical review 35:647-52, Oct. 1945.

66. —— Stream terms in U.S. geographic names. Association of American Geographers. Annals 45:173, June 1955.
Abstract.

67. —— Toponymic generics. Names 4:129-37, 226-40, Sept., Dec. 1956.
An essay on generic names used in the geography of the United States.
"Gat and gut," comment by A. R. Dunlap on derivation of these generics as given in Burrill's article, ibid. 5:248, Dec. 1957.

68. —— & Edwin Bonsack, Jr. Use and preparation of specialized glossaries; In Conference on Lexicography, Indiana University, 1960. Problems in lexicography: report. Ed. by Fred W. Householder and Sol Saporta. Bloomington, 1962. p. 183-99. (Publications of the Indiana University Research Center in Anthropology, Folklore, and Linguistics, 21) (International journal of American linguistics, v. 28, no. 2, pt. 4, April 1962).

69. Burton, W. E. Derivation of names affixed to various places upon the American continent. Burton's gentleman's magazine 4:37-38, Jan. 1839.

70. Bye, John O. Why these names for rivers, creeks, buttes and mines; In his Back trailing in the heart of the short-grass country. Everett, Wash., Alexander Print Co., 1956. p. 367-68.

71. Byington, Steven T. On European and American river-names. American speech 2:425-28, July 1927.

The use and omission of the substantive river in connection with the names of rivers. Shows how the word river, although it duplicates the foreign term for the word, has gradually become widely used on maps and in speech.

72. Calkins, Ernest Elmo. Punxsutawney and points west. Good housekeeping 120:42, 105-08, Feb. 1945.
United States place-names.

73. Carlton, W. R. Podunk. American speech 13:174, Oct. 1938; 14:73-76, Feb. 1939.
In origin, an Algonquin Indian place-name or location.

74. Cassidy, Frederic Gomes. How to collect local place names. Indiana names 1:21-33, Fall 1970.

74a. —— Unofficial sectional city names. Verbatim 7:1-3, Autumn 1980.

75. Chamber of Commerce of the United States of America. Civic Development Dept. Origin and changes of names of American cities. n.p., 1925. 17p.
Comp. by Dorsey W. Hyde, Chief, National Civics Bureau.
Bibliography: p. 15-17.

76. Chapman, John. There is a Podunk! Ford times 59:36, May 1966.
An actual town in Massachusetts and other places in the United States. Origin of the expression for hick towns in general credited to George M. Cohan.

77. Childears, Lucille. An analysis of Indian place names in four Rocky Mountain states. Denver, 1949. 186p.
Thesis (M.A.) Univ. of Denver.

78. Chisholm, George Goudie. Note on the spelling of place-names with special reference to the United States; In American Geographical Society of New York. Memorial volume of the Transcontinental excursion of 1912 of the American Geographical Society of New York. New York, 1915. p. 47-48.

79. Chrisman, Lewis H. The romance of American place names. Education 50:173-78, Nov. 1929.

80. —— What's in a name? National Education Association. Journal 21:276, Nov. 1932.
The value of the study of place-names.

81. Clark, Ellery H., Jr. United States place names honoring the Navy. Annapolis, U.S. Naval Institute, 1948. p. 452-55.
Reprinted from the United States Naval Institute. Proceedings v. 74, no. 4, April 1948. p. 452-55.

82. Clark, Thomas L. A semantic class in the Great Basin. Names 26:48-57, March 1978.
Beginning with a brief note on work done on the theory of place-names, the results of a survey of the pah form in Shoshonean names are presented.

83. Clarke, James Freeman. On giving names to towns and streets. Christian examiner 86:19-29, Jan. 1869.

84. —— On giving names to towns and streets. Boston, Lockwood, Brooks & Co., 1880. 19p.
Proposes historic names.

85. Clepper, Henry. Trees and forests in American place names. American forests 83:20-22, Aug. 1977.

86. Coard, Robert L. The possessive apostrophe in names. American speech 33:176-79, Oct. 1958.
Includes place-names.

87. Colby, Frank. Romance in American place names. Omaha world-herald Nov. 4, 1945, p. 19-C.
One of a series of syndicated daily articles on language, entitled "Take my word for it."

88. Coltharp, Lurline H. A digital classification of place-names. Names 20:218-19, Sept. 1972.
The computer can be used profitably in onomastic research. An outgrowth of the author's work on the street names of El Paso, Texas.

89. Coulet du Gard, René. A comparison of toponomy between France and the United States. Canadian Society for the Study of Names. Onomastica no. 53:17-20, June 1978.
French version: p. 20-23.

90. —— Origins of French place names in the U.S.A.; In South Central Names Institute. Naughty names. Commerce, Tex., Names Institute Press, 1975. (Publication 4) p. 15-19.

91. —— & Dominique Coulet Western. The handbook of French place names in the U.S.A.: a tribute to the Bicentennial of the U.S.A., 1776-1976. Enl. and rev. 2d ed. n.p., Éditions des Deux Mondes, c1977. 296p.
1st ed. 1974. 234p. (Onomastica no. 51)
Bibliography: p. 276-87.
Review of 1st ed.: W. F. H. Nicolaisen, Names 24:134-36.

92. Counts, Dorothy Ayers. Naming the western states. Frontier times 37 (n.s. no. 24):47, 70-72, June-July 1963.
The names of 17 western states fall into four categories.

93. Coxe, A. Cleveland. American geographical names. Forum 4:67-77, Sept. 1887.
Urges use of historical and, if possible, aboriginal names in the United States.

94. Crane, William Ward. Our street-names. Lippincott's monthly magazine 60:264-66, Aug. 1897.

95. Cray, Ed. Ethnic and place names as derisive adjectives. Western folklore 21:27-34, Jan. 1962; 24:197-98, July 1965.

96. Cross, Marion Hood. Happy birthday, U.S.A.; a rhymed account of the origin of the names of the fifty states and of their year of entry into the Union. New York, Comet Press Books, 1960. 56p.

97. Crouch, Kenneth Elwood. Bedford and its namesakes; In Bedford County bicentennial, official program. 1954. p. 107.
Bedford, Va., and other Bedfords, with origin of the name for each.

98. —— Bedford and its namesakes. Annals of Wyoming 29:38-40, April 1957.
Discussion of the various places in the United States named Bedford. Traces migration of name.

99. —— "Kenneth Elwood Crouch." n.p., 1959. [9] p.
Places with the same names as the author's: Kenneth, Elwood, and Crouch.

100. —— Names of county post offices are popular throughout the United States. Altavista (Va.) journal July 30, 1959, p. 7.
The 12 post offices in Campbell County, Va., and the county itself have namesakes in 32 states of the United States.

101. —— Places named Bridgewater in the United States. U.S. Congress. Congressional record 106:A3462, April 21, 1960.
Reprinted: Bridgewater (Mass.) keynote May 19, 1960, p. 1, 6.
Extension of remarks of Hon. A. Willis Robertson in regard to the 125th anniversary of Bridgewater, Va.

102. —— Thurman named for 19th century Ohio senator. Sidney (Iowa) argus-herald June 11, 1959, p. 7, col. 1-3.
Places in Iowa, Ohio, New York, and Idaho named Thurman, and in West Virginia and South Carolina named Thurmond, for members of the Thurman family of Virginia.

103. Cushman, Horatio Bardwell. North American Indian names; In his History of the Choctaw, Chickasaw and Natchez Indians. Greenville, Tex., Headlight Print House, 1899. p. 592-607.

104. —— —— In his History of the Choctaw, Chickasaw and Natchez Indians. Ed. and with a foreword by Angie Debo. Stillwater, Okla., Redlands Press, 1962. p. 477-94.
Choctaw and Chickasaw ancient names of places, towns, villages, rivers, creeks, lakes, mounds, bluffs, etc., in the now states of Mississippi, Alabama, Georgia, Florida, Louisiana, and others, with the derivations, corruptions, originals, orthography, and significations.

105. Cutler, Charles L., Jr. The battle the Indians won. American history illustrated 6:20-27, Jan. 1972.
Popular article on Indian place-names.

106. Cutler, H. G. Romance of the map of the United States, how California was named. Magazine of American history 23:288-96, April 1890.
Gives the origin and meaning of the place-name, California, p. 290, besides other names which were applied to it.

107. Daly, Reginald A. The nomenclature of the North American cordillera between the 47th and 53d parallels of latitude. Geographical journal 27:586-606, June 1906.
Bibliography: p. 604-06.
A systematic nomenclature is needed for this vast mountain system so that the geology may be more adequately described. Various definitions used for the mountain ranges, systems, etc., are included.

108. A Defiant little town. Literary digest 54:648-49, March 10, 1917.
An amusing article which deals with the request of Oakland, Calif., that Oakland, Kan., change its name to avoid confusion; also Salem, Ore., and Salem, Mass.

109. De Ford, Miriam Allen. Two-state towns and cities. American notes and queries 4:64, July 1944; 5:112, Oct. 1945.

110. Derrickson, Lloyd. Wayoutsville, U.S.A. American mercury 91:134-36, Nov. 1960.
Brief comment on a variety of names.

111. Desert place names. Desert magazine v. 1-5, Feb. 1938-April 1942.
A regular monthly department. Earlier numbers compiled by Tracy M. Scott. Gives origin of names in Arizona, California, New Mexico, Nevada, and Utah.

112. De Voto, Bernard. The Indian all round us. Reader's digest 62:61-64, April 1953.
Includes place-names of Indian origin.

113. Dillon, Richard H. Name indexes in American libraries. Library journal 81:56, 58-60, Jan. 1, 1956.
Brings up to 1955 the status of card files of place-names in libraries throughout the United States as originally (1947) listed in Ireland, Norma Olin. Local indexes in American libraries.

114. —— Names on the land. Special libraries 62:405-12, Oct. 1971.
The study of America's geographic place-names offers an interesting commentary on the country's history.

115. Dingman, Lester F. Federal-state cooperation in geographic names. Surveying and mapping 26:635-38, Dec. 1966.
Describes the cooperation between the U.S. Board on Geographic Names and various state agencies.

116. —— Naughty names: geographic names--colorful or offensive?; In South Central Names Institute. Naughty names. Commerce, Tex., Names Institute Press, 1975. (Publication 4) p. 1-4.

117. Dobie, James Frank. The mustangs. Boston, Little, Brown, 1952. 376p.
American places named for wild horses: p. 330.

118. Donovan, Frank P., Jr. Named for railroad presidents. Railroad magazine Feb. 1965, p. 24-27.
Communities in the U.S. and Canada that were named for railroad presidents.

119. Dressman, Michael R. Names are magic: Walt Whitman's laws of geographic nomenclature. Names 26:68-79, March 1978.
A review of the many references in Whitman's writings on names, his approval both of Indian names for places in America and the naming of places for some natural peculiarity of water or earth, or for some event.

120. Duckert, Audrey R. Cottage Grove from coast to coast: the genealogy of a place name. Names 6:180-83, Sept. 1958.
The author finds no ties between the 11 towns with this name in all parts of the United States.

121. —— Gutter: its rise and fall. Names 4:146-54, Sept. 1956.
A proposal to change the name of Grassy Gutter Road, a street in Longmeadow, Mass., prompted this study of the use of the term Gutter in geographic terminology.

122. —— Names forever on the land. Names 24:124-27, June 1976.
Concerns the duplication of names, many of which are dull or unrelated to the places where they are found.

123. —— Place nicknames. Names 21:153-60, Sept. 1973.
A sampling of spontaneous nicknames applied to cities in the Midwest and New England.

124. Duffy, Thomas F. A controlled research project: American place names. New York, Holt, Rinehart and Winston, 1968. 78p. maps. (Aspects of English)
Bibliography: p. 14-17.
Describes a project for controlling the sources used by students in writing research papers, using a study of American place-names as an example. Contains a group of four general readings on place-naming practices and four readings dealing with place-names in Massachusetts and Virginia.

125. Dunlap, Arthur Ray. Corner Ketch. Names 11:71-73, March 1963.
Speculation on the origin of this place-name in Delaware, Maryland, and Pennsylvania.

126. —— English and American place-name studies; a contrast. American speech 31:119-21, May 1956.
In reviewing Simeon Potter's article on Cheshire names and David Lindsey's book, Ohio's Western Reserve, author indicates means of broadening American studies.

127. —— & E. J. Moyne. The Finnish language on the Delaware. American speech 27:81-90, May 1952.
Place names: p. 88-90.

128. Eastern names in the western world. Aramco world 5:6-7, Aug. 1954.
139 communities in the United States have names taken from the Middle East.

129. Eastman, Elaine Goodale. Indian names for country places. Country life in America 24:72, Oct. 1913.
Sioux words with their meanings.

130. Eberle, William. Humor zigzags through American town names. Plymouth traveler July-Aug. 1960, p. 20-21.

131. Editorial on origin of French and Indian names in the United States. New York times May 17, 1939, p. 22, col. 4.

132. Egan, Clifford L., editor. Joel Barlow's suggestion to rename the Columbia [River]. Oregon historical quarterly 24:268-70, Sept. 1973.
Barlow's ode, "On the discoveries of Captain Lewis," enclosed in his letter to Thomas Jefferson suggests the name Lewis River, with the principal branch to be Clarke.

133. Ellis, Erl H. That word "Idaho." Denver, Univ. of Denver Press, 1951. 35p. (Denver University. Publications. Studies in humanities, no. 2, i.e., 3)
A shortened version appeared in Western folklore 10:317-19, Oct. 1951, with title Idaho.
Bibliography: p. 33-35.
Traces the use of the word in various places in the West: the state; Idaho Springs, Colo., proposed for Colorado Territory, etc.

134. Ellis, William Donohue. Names on the land. Inland seas 30:242-65, Winter 1974.
Popular address with information on the Great Lakes area.

135. Emrich, Duncan. It's an old wild west custom. New York, Vanguard Press, 1949. 313p.
To name the land: p. 27-36; ...And the mines: p. 37-42.

136. Eno, Joel Nelson. Picture-like American geographical names. Journal of education (Boston) 82:73-74, 101-02, Aug. 5-12, 1915.

North and South American place-names, language from which derived and the meaning of the names.

137. Estrin, Herman A. Romance of American place names. Travel/holiday 151:28-30, Feb. 1979.

Unusual names with brief explanation of origin or meaning.

138. Fairclough, G. Thomas. Notes on some unusual street names in Nebraska City. American speech 34:70-71, Feb. 1959.

Use of Corsos in this city in Nebraska. Half the article lists unusual terms for streets found in the U.S. and requests information on their current use.

139. —— An onomastic miscellany. American speech 34:226-27, Oct. 1959.

Addendum to his article "The style of street names," and the articles mentioned under it (see no. 140).

The form which street names take in common speech; unique thoroughfare terms; city segments whose names are points of the compass.

140. —— The style of street names. American speech 33:299-300, Dec. 1958.

A note in reply to Allan F. Hubbell, ibid. 32:233-34, Oct. 1957, and Jerome Rhodes, ibid. 33:116-17, May 1958.

141. —— Toward a systematic classification of street name patterns in the U.S.A. and Canadian cities: a progress report; In South Central Names Institute. They had to call it something. Commerce, Tex., Names Institute Press, 1974. (Publication 3) p. 65-76.

142. —— A variant of "downtown." American speech 37:158, May 1962.

143. Faris, Rush C. American town names. Chautauquan 19:723-26, Sept. 1894.

On the repetition of names in America and some of the causes.

144. Farkas, Zoltan J. Hungarian city and county names in the United States. Names 19:141-43, June 1971.

145. Farnham, Amos W. The origin of some geographic names. Journal of geography 9:9-15, Sept. 1910.

The origin and meaning of topographic features in place-names.

146. Farquhar, Francis Peloubet. Naming America's mountains—the Cascades. American alpine journal 12:49-65. 1960.

Eight peaks selected because they are the dominant ones and the circumstances of their naming have historical significance: Adams, Baker, Hood, Jefferson, Olympus, Rainier, St. Helens, Shasta.

147. Fay, Charles E. Our geographical nomenclature. Appalachia 3:1-13, June 1882.

Suggests certain principles to follow in naming places.

Review: Nation 34:523, June 22, 1882.

148. Feipel, Louis Nicholas. American place-names. American speech 1:78-91, Nov. 1925.

Offers "a few prolegomena to the study" of United States place-names. Divided into types, as Indian; historical; from other languages; corrupted; from persons; religious; literary and patriotic; prosaic and artificial; and other arbitrary names.

149. —— More place-name words. American speech 1:395, April 1926.
Names for articles derived from American place-names.

150. Ferguson, De Lancey. Two queries about American place-names. American speech 18:309-10, Dec. 1943.
"What are the limits, in time and geography, of the Virginian practice of omitting the word 'county' in county names?" and the question of local pronunciation of imported names.
See the article by George Rippey Stewart, Some American place-name problems, no. 526.

151. Field, David Dudley. On the nomenclature of cities and towns in the United States. American Geographical Society. Bulletin 17:1-16. 1885.
Also published separately, New York, M. B. Brown, 1885. 15p.
An appeal for the use of Indian names.

152. —— Pleasant names for pleasant places. Address before the American Geographical Society. 1884; In his Speeches, arguments and miscellaneous papers. New York, Appleton, 1890. 3:352-62.
Suggests Indian names.

153. First-aid towns, U.S.A. Good housekeeping 146:111, Jan. 1958.
A list of names such as Pillow, Pa.; Hygiene, Colo.

154. Flanagan, John T. An early discussion of place names. American speech 14:157-59, April 1939.
Mentions interest of James Hall in place-names as demonstrated by material in his Letters from the West. 1828 (see no. 198).

155. Florin, Lambert. Ghost town album. Maps and drawings by David C. Mason. Seattle, Superior Pub. Co., 1962. 184p.

156. —— Ghost town El Dorado. Seattle, Superior Pub. Co., 1968. 192p. maps. (The western ghost town series)
Includes towns in eleven western states and in British Columbia.

157. —— Ghost town trails. Maps and drawings by David C. Mason. Seattle, Superior Pub. Co., 1963. 192p.
Bibliography: p. 190.
A roster of known ghost towns: p. 191-92.
Includes western states and British Columbia.

158. —— A guide to western ghost towns. Seattle, Superior Pub. Co., 1967. 96p. maps.
Includes more than 400 towns in the western states and Canada.

159. —— Western ghost towns. Maps and drawings by David C. Mason. Seattle, Superior Pub. Co., 1961. 174p.

160. Ford, Zillah. The pronunciation of Spanish place names in the southwestern United States.
Thesis (M.S.) Univ. of Oklahoma, 1947.

161. Franciscans, Saint Michaels, Ariz. An ethnologic dictionary of the Navaho language. Saint Michaels, Ariz., The Franciscan Fathers, 1910. 536p.
Names of places, p. 130-37.

162. —— A vocabulary of the Navaho language. Saint Michaels, Ariz., 1912. 2v. in 1.
v. 1. English-Navaho. v. 2. Navaho-English.
Geographical names: 1:226-28; 2:202-06.
Limited to the states adjacent to the Navaho reservation, i.e., Arizona, New Mexico, Colorado, and Utah.

163. Frazer, Robert Walter. Forts of the West: military forts and presidios, and posts commonly called forts, west of the Mississippi River to 1898. Norman, Univ. of Oklahoma Press, 1965. 246p.
Bibliography: p. 190-226.
Arranged alphabetically by present states. Includes origin of the post name and changes in name and location.

164. French on the map. Chicago tribune May 11, 1961, pt. 1, p. 16.
Pronunciation of some French place-names in the United States.

165. Freudenberger, Ruby W. Celtic elements in place names. Country life in America 29:80-82, April 1916.
"No element could be better suited as basic material for picturesque combinations than the Celtic as exemplified by this alphabetical list of such name elements with their meanings."—Price.

166. Froman, R. Who puts the names on maps? Science digest 27:77-80, April 1950.
Condensed from the Elks magazine Jan. 1950.
Concerning the work of the Board on Geographic Names.

167. Frugality, Pa. dropped; New Deal on postal map. New York times July 7, 1935, p. 2, col. 6.
Changes in Postal guide. New Deal, Mont., etc.

168. Furnas, J. C. The names we go by. Saturday evening post 230:36-37, 71, Dec. 28, 1957.
Popular article on personal and place-names, including towns, city streets, and developments.

169. Gandy, William E. The value of place etymology in the teaching of geography. Journal of geography 64:250-53, Sept. 1965.
Brief survey of common English, Slavic, and Chinese roots and of influences in America to support theory that geographic place-name etymology is of interest to students and an aid to understanding and retention.

170. Gannett, Henry. The origin of certain place names in the United States. 2d ed. Washington, Govt. Print. Off., 1905. 334p. (U.S. Geological Survey. Bulletin no. 258, Series F, Geography 45)
1st.: 1902. 280p. (Bulletin no. 197) Reprinted: Detroit, Gale Research Co. 1971. 280p.
Reprinted under title American names, a guide to the origin of place names in the United States. Washington, Public Affairs Press, 1947. 334p.; also reprinted under original title Baltimore, Genealogical Pub. Co., 1973. 334p.
Authorities: p. 10-14.
"Unfortunately it was chiefly the work of subordinates, and notable mainly for its inaccuracies."—George Rippey Stewart.

171. —— The work of the United States Board on Geographic Names. National geographic magazine 7:221-27, July 1896.

172. Gemmill, William Nelson. Romantic America. Chicago, Jordan Pub. Co., 1926. 143p.
Short lists of Spanish, French, English, and Indian names; also state names, Illinois counties, and Chicago street names.

173. Geographic Board wars on place names like Uz. New York times Jan. 23, 1937, p. 19, col. 2; editorial Jan. 26, 1937, p. 20, col. 4.
Changes made in freak names.

174. Geographic posers settled by Board. Nearly 1,000 queries answered during the past year. New York times Feb. 14, 1937, sec. 4, p. 12, col. 6-7.

175. Gerard, William R. The adopted Indian word "Poquosin." American anthropologist n.s. 1:586-87, July 1899.
A different interpretation of the derivation and meaning of the term Poquosin from that presented by W. W. Tooker in the Jan. and Oct. numbers of this same volume.

176. Gerke, Lucien. Sur une migration toponymique: le nom de Waterloo en Amérique. [Waterloo, Société d'Études historiques et folkloriques de Waterloo, Braine-l'Alleud et environs, 1965]. 23p.

177. Githens, Harry W. Animal towns. Nature magazine 47:463, Nov. 1954.
Towns with animal names.

178. —— Bird towns. Nature magazine 48:132, March 1955.
Towns with bird names.

179. —— Tree towns. Nature magazine 47:516, Dec. 1954.
A list of towns named for trees.

180. Gitman, Carolyn Lieberman. From these roots. New York, Vantage Press, 1971. 581p.

181. Goforth, Elena. What's in a state name? American mercury 79:125-28, Aug. 1954.
Meaning of the state names.

182. Granger, Byrd Howell. Handbook for establishing a state center for a survey of place names. [Tucson, Ariz., 1972?]. 25p.

183. —— National place name survey, a proposal. Tucson, Ariz., 1969. 20ℓ.
Adopted by the American Name Society, Dec. 30, 1969.

184. Grant, Bruce. American forts, yesterday and today. Illustrated by Lorence F. Bjorklund. New York, Dutton, 1965. 381p. maps.
Bibliography: p. 365-66.
Records over 1200 forts.

185. Gregg, Jacob Ray. What's in a name?; In his Pioneer days in Malheur County. Los Angeles, Privately printed by L. L. Morrison, 1950. p. 11-20.
Naming of some of the great rivers and smaller streams of the West.

186. Gregory, Herbert Ernest. Geographic terms, with table of geographic names in the Navajo country; In his The Navajo country, a geographic and hydrographic reconnaissance of parts of Arizona, New Mexico, and Utah. Washington, Govt. Print. Off., 1916. (U.S. Geological Survey. Water-supply paper 380) p. 189-97. Also in his

Geology of the Navajo country, a reconnaissance of parts of Arizona, New Mexico, and Utah. Washington, Govt. Print. Off., 1917. (U.S. Geological Survey. Professional paper 93) p. 149-55.

187. Grinnell, George Bird. Cheyenne stream names. American anthropologist n.s. 8:15-22, Jan.-March 1906.

A list of place-names alphabetically arranged, with pronunciation, derivation, and meaning, which were given by Cheyenne Indians to some of the rivers in the country over which they roamed.

188. —— Some Indian stream names. American anthropologist n.s. 15:327-31, April-June 1913.

The names bestowed on rivers by two Indian tribes: the Gros Ventres of the Prairie, and the Pawnees. Attention is also paid to pronunciation, source, and meaning.

189. Gudde, Erwin Gustav. Frémont-Preuss and the western names. Names 5:169-81, Sept. 1957.

A study of the place-names assigned and recorded on maps by John Charles Frémont and Charles Preuss on Frémont's expeditions between the Mississippi River and the Pacific Ocean.

190. —— Mohave and Mojave. Western folklore 7:169-71, April 1948.

Arizona and California.

191. —— Sugarloaf. Names 4:241-43, Dec. 1956.

A strange generic topographical term.

192. Hafen, LeRoy Reuben. Armijo's journal. Huntington Library quarterly 11:87-101, Nov. 1947.

Antonio Armijo, on Old Spanish Trail, 1829. Hafen's excellent place-name footnotes make this extremely valuable.

193. Hahn, Holly Jane. Place names in the high school classroom. Indiana Place-Name Survey. Newsletter 5:3-5, 1975.

194. Haines, Elijah Middlebrook. The American Indian (Uh-nish-in-na-ba). Chicago, Mas-sin-na-gan Co., 1888. 821p.

Indian geographical names, p. 704-806; Indian names by which localities here given were formerly known, p. 807-21.

195. Hale, Edward Everett, Jr. French place-names in the Far West. French review 2:500-10, May 1929.

196. —— Geographical terms in the Far West. Dialect notes 6:217-34, July 1932.

197. Hale, Ruth F. A map of vernacular regions in America.

Thesis (Ph.D.) Univ. of Minnesota, 1971. 321ℓ. map.

An attempt to identify the names commonly used to identify regions that are larger than counties but smaller than states; for example, in Kansas, the Flint Hills, or in Illinois, Little Egypt.

198. Hall, James. Letters from the West; containing sketches of scenery, manners, and customs; and anecdotes connected with the first settlements of the western sections of the United States. London, Henry Colburn, 1828. 385p.

Reprinted Gainesville, Fla., Scholars' Facsimiles & Reprints, 1967.

Names of places: p. 193-214.

199. Hand, Wayland D. Legends in place-name study. Indiana names 4:37-50, Fall 1973.

200. Hannant, Owen. Indian place-names, a beautiful heritage. Central States archaeological journal 2:15, July 1955.

201. Harder, Kelsie B. Illustrated dictionary of place names, United States and Canada. New York, Van Nostrand Reinhold Co., 1976. 631p.
Bibliography: p. 627-31.
An essential reference book of over 15,000 names for states, provinces, counties, towns, and physical features including those that are historically important, unique, of linguistic interest, or of Indian origin.
Review: Eugene B. Vest, Names 24:315-16, Dec. 1976; Manford Hanowell, Beiträge zur Namenforschung, neue Folge 12:303-05, 1977.

202. —— The names of TVA dams. Mississippi folklore register 11:131-41, Fall 1977.
Includes also data on other names related to or located near the dams.

203. Harper, Roland M. Pronunciation of certain place names. Journal of geography 16:255-58, March 1918.
Names of Indian origin, principally in the southern United States.

204. Harrington, John Peabody. American Indian place-names; abstract. Nature 142:960, Nov. 26, 1938.

205. —— The origin of our state names. Washington Academy of Sciences. Journal 34:255-59, Aug. 15, 1944.
Based on lengthy study of state and territory names—a preliminary, brief version of the ethnological and historical origin of the names.

206. —— Our state names. Smithsonian Institution. Annual report 1954:373-88.
Reprinted: Smithsonian Institution. Publication 4205. 1955.
Includes Canadian names of Indian origin: p. 387-88.

207. Harris, Clement Antrobus. The devil in place-names. Chambers's journal 7th ser. 13:84-87, Jan. 6, 1923.
"There are good reasons why some places should be associated in people's minds with the devil. Citing some examples in the United States and abroad, the author traces the connection between the term and the location."—Price.

208. Harrisse, Henry. The discovery of North America; a critical, documentary, and historic investigation, with an essay on the early cartography of the New World, including descriptions of two hundred and fifty maps or globes existing or lost, constructed before the year 1536; to which are added a chronology of one hundred voyages westward, projected, attempted, or accomplished between 1431 and 1504; biographical accounts of the three hundred pilots who first crossed the Atlantic; and a copious list of the original names of American regions, caciqueships, mountains, islands, capes, gulfs, rivers, towns, and harbours. London, H. Stevens and Son; Paris, H. Welter, 1892. 802p.
Reprinted: Amsterdam, N. Israel, 1961. 802p.
Geographical index, p. 751-84.

209. Harshberger, John W. Geographic names and terms of significance in plant geography and ecology. Geographical Society of Philadelphia. Bulletin 18:100-07, Oct. 1920; 19:14-22, 45-50. 1921; 20:32-46. 1922.
A compilation of geographic names and terms—physiographic, phytogeographic,

and ecologic—with significations. The vegetation of a place combined with physiographical features is very often responsible for its name. The author interprets the meaning of many such terms in general use.

210. Hart, Herbert M. Forts of the old West. Seattle, Superior Pub. Co., 1963-67. 4v.
Contents: v. 1 Old forts of the Northwest. 1963. 192p.; v. 2 Old forts of the Southwest. 1964. 192p.; v. 3, Old forts of the Far West. 1965. 192p.; v. 4 Pioneer forts of the West. 1967. 192p.

211. Hartesveldt, Richard J. & Jane Hartesveldt. The campsite finder. Cartoons by Marian Smith. San Martin, Calif., Naturegraph Co., 1957. 2v.

212. Haugen, Einar Ingvald. The Norwegian language in America; a study in bilingual behavior. Philadelphia, Univ. of Pennsylvania Press, 1953. 2v.
v. 1, chap. 9, Names in a new world, p. 222-32, concludes with an analysis of place-names in Norwegian communities in America.

213. Hecht, Arthur & William J. Heymen. Records and policies of the Post Office Department relating to place-names. Washington, National Archives and Records Service, 1975. 16p. (Reference information paper 72)

214. Heck, Henry J. State border place-names. American speech 3:186-90, Feb. 1928.
Examples from 26 states.

215. Heck, Lewis. Geographic names in the U.S. Coast and Geodetic Survey. Names 1:103-11, June 1953.
By the chief of the Geographic Name Section, Chart Division, of the Survey.

216. Hedblom, Folke. Place-names in immigrant communities: concerning the giving of Swedish place-names. Swedish pioneer historical quarterly 23:246-60, Oct. 1972.

217. Heflin, Thelma E. What's in a name? Palimpsest 57:82-85, May-June 1976.
Places named for Col. Isaac Shelby, hero of the battle at Point Pleasant, West Virginia, 1774, and the battle of the Thames, 1813, and governor of Kentucky.

218. Heier, Edmund. Russo-German place-names in Russia and in North America. Names 9:260-68, Dec. 1961.
Names resulting from the Russo-German immigration are discussed on p. 266-68.

219. Helfer, Harold. Ever been to Mugfuzzle Flat? American mercury 81:12-14, Oct. 1955.
A popular article on odd town names.

220. Hello! His hobby is "meatography." Saturday evening post 224:48, Oct. 6, 1951.
An advertisement of the American Meat Institute giving place-names that remind one of aspects of the meat business.

221. Hewes, Gordon W. American Japanese place names. American speech 21:100-05, April 1946.
Methods of treatment of American place-names which have passed into American/Japanese literary usage, with a table of Japanese equivalents for certain American place-names.

222. Hill, Robert T. Corruption of American geographic names. Science 10:143, Sept. 16, 1887.
Reasons for the origin of some place-names which are misnomers. Also considers factors that corrupt the original name.

223. Himes, George Henry. Nomenclature of Northwest mountains. Mazama 4:1-5, Oct. 1912.
Principal peaks in the Coast, Cascade, and Blue Mountain ranges.

224. Hinton, John Howard. The history and topography of the United States of America, ed. by John Howard Hinton assisted by several literary gentlemen in America and England. 4th ed., brought down to 1850. London, John Rallis and Co., n.d., 2v. maps.
1st ed.: London, R. Fenner, Sears & Co., 1830-32.
Origin of the names of the several [30] states: 2:753-54.

225. Hitchman, Robert. Onalaska, Washington. Western folklore 8:368-69, Oct. 1949.
Connection with towns of same name in Wisconsin, Arkansas, and Texas.

226. Hixon, Jerome C. Place names. Words 2:8-9, 13, 20-22, Sept. 1936; 2:14-15, Oct. 1936; 2:8-9, 20, Nov. 1936.
Readable, lengthy account of place-names of cities, towns, and states in the United States.

227. Hockett, Charles F. Reactions to Indian place names. American speech 25:118-21, May 1950.

228. Hodge, F. W. The name of Canadian River. Masterkey (Southwest Museum, Los Angeles) 23:91, May 1949.

229. Hoffman, Bernard G. Cabot to Cartier, sources for a historical ethnography of northeastern North America, 1497-1550. Toronto, Univ. of Toronto Press, 1961. xii, 287p. maps.
Bibliography: p. 229-63.
Complementary to, and an evaluation of, much the same material in William Francis Ganong's, Crucial maps in the early cartography and place-nomenclature of the Atlantic coast of Canada. Toronto, 1964.

230. Hoge, Thomas A. Streets of America. Service (Cities Service Company) July 1960, p. 12-15.

231. Hollis, C. Carroll. Names in Leaves of grass. Names 5:129-56, Sept. 1957.
Conclusions from an investigation of new manuscript evidence of Walt Whitman's concern with names, particularly place-names, presented with the explanation of his theory and practice.

232. Holmer, Nils Magnus. Indian place names in North America. Cambridge, Harvard Univ. Press, 1948. 44p. (American Institute in the University of Upsala. Essays and studies on American language and literature)
Reprinted: Nendeln, Kraus Reprint, 1973.

233. Holt, Alfred Hubbard. American place names. New York, Crowell, 1938. 222p.
Reprinted: Detroit, Gale Research Co., 1969. 229p.
Bibliography: p. 221-22.

A collection of general names giving pronunciation only.
Review: American speech 14:134, April 1939.

234. Homburg, Frederick. Names of cities. Journal of geography 15:17-23, Sept. 1916.
A study of the principles of forming place-names by combining prefixes or suffixes to indicate location with proper or scenic names.

235. Honest creeks, their names reflect rare quality of accuracy. Life 29:108, Aug. 21, 1950.
Letters to the editors, Sept. 11, 1950, p. 12, 16, contain readers' additions.

236. Horgan, Paul. The names of the Rio Grande; In his Great river: the Rio Grande in North American history. New York, Rinehart, 1954. 2:981.

237. How cities chose their names. American city 73:173, Aug. 1958.
Different factors that influence the choice of name, also names from famous places and famous persons.

238. How oil fields get their names. Sunray news Feb. 1954, p. 10-11.
The naming of new oil fields is usually casual, although must be approved in most states by the commission which administers oil and gas matters.

239. How to study place-names. Badger folklore 1:23-24, April 1948.

240. Hubbell, Allan F. Form of street addresses. American speech 32:233-34, Oct. 1957.
Variation in American usage regarding use or omission of street, avenue, road, and boulevard. For further information see article by Jerome Rhodes, ibid. 33:116-17, May 1958, and reply by G. Thomas Fairclough, ibid. 33:299-300, Dec. 1958.

241. Hull, Anthony Hardinge. Spanish and Russian rivalry in the North Pacific regions of the New World, 1760-1812. vi, 272ℓ. maps.
Thesis (Ph.D.) Univ. of Alabama, 1966. Dissertation abstracts 27:1757A, Dec. 1966.
Bibliography: l. 251-72.
Selected place-names, north Pacific region, showing present and past localities: l. 237-46.

242. Hyde, John. The National geographic magazine and the U.S. Board on Geographic Names. National geographic magazine 10:517-19, Nov. 1899.

243. In the driftway. Nation 124:421-22, April 20, 1927.
Some peculiar place-names that are to be found in the United States—particularly Long Island, N.Y.—and abroad are mentioned in this article.

244. Indian cuss words. Associated Press dispatch, Washington, D.C., Dec. 5, 1936. Printed in many newspapers.
"G. C. Martin of the U.S. Board on Geographical Names reveals that Indian expressions of irritation, misunderstood as place-names, were often preserved as such in America."—American speech.

245. Indian cuss words responsible for many strange place names. Cumberland (Md.) evening times Dec. 4, 1936.

246. Indian geographical names—Chillakothe. Magazine of American history 3:512, Aug. 1879.
Indicates the probable origin and application of the place-name Chillakothe found in several states.

247. Indian names of American states. Chambers's journal 4th ser. 15:663-64, Oct. 19, 1878.
Considers the source of aboriginal appellations of states.

248. The Indians said it first. Aramco world 11:13-15, Dec. 1960.
25 states bear Indian names. Origin of these and other state names.

249. Interesting post office names. Hobbies 63:99, Oct. 1958.
Examples of many different categories of post office names.

250. Interpretation of Indian names. Historical magazine 9:90-91, March 1865.
The derivation and meaning of a short list.

251. Interstate towns. School science and mathematics 21:24, Jan. 1921.
The names of towns which indicate that they lie partly in one state and partly in another, for example, Texarkana.

252. Iroquois names of places. Historical magazine 8:373, Nov. 1864.

253. Irving, Washington. National nomenclature, by Geoffrey Crayon. Knickerbocker 14:158-62, 203, Aug. 1839.
Reprinted in his Biographies and miscellanies, ed. by Pierre M. Irving. New York, Putnam, 1866. p. 522-30.

254. Isaacs, A. S. Towns with strange names. Harpers weekly 54:33, Oct. 1, 1910.
A general article about some of the unusual names in the United States.

255. Jacobs, Jane. Nombres de lugares de Estados Unidos. Revista geografica americana 35:257-66, junio 1953.
Popular article in Spanish on place-names in the United States.

256. Jaeger, Edmund C. Names of desert things and places. Desert magazine 22:22-23, March 1959.
On borrowed desert names, such as vada, barranca, mesa.

257. Jenks, Albert Ernest. Influence of wild rice on geographic nomenclature; In his The wild rice gatherers of the upper lakes. U.S. Bureau of American Ethnology. Annual report v. 19, pt. 2, p. 1115-26. 1897-98.

258. Jennings, Gary. Naming names—and backgrounds. Denver post Oct. 29, 1961, Roundup, p. 31.
Condensed in Reader's digest 79:114-16, Dec. 1961 under title Why did they call it that?
General article on names in the United States.

259. Jensen, Andrew. Origin of western geographic names, associated with the history of the "Mormon" people. Utah genealogical and historical magazine 10:1-16, 81-85, 120-28, 181-90, Jan.-Oct. 1919; 11:34-40, 82-91, 141-44, 170-77, Jan.-Oct. 1920; 12:41-48, 125-30, 188-92, Jan., July, Oct. 1921; 13:38-43, Jan. 1922.
A list of place-names in Utah, Idaho, Montana, Oregon, Nevada, California, Wyoming, Colorado, New Mexico, and Arizona—also Alberta, Can., and Mexico—that have had Mormon settlements.

260. Johnson, Amandus. Indian geographical names; In Lindeström, Peter Martensson. Geographia Americae. Philadelphia, Swedish Colonial Society, 1925. p. 299-408.
Sources for the location, meaning and derivation of the words: p. 291-98.
Includes names in the Delaware Basin.

261. Johnson, E. Gustav. The study of American place-names of Swedish origin. Chicago, 1946. 16p.
Reprinted from Covenant quarterly Nov. 1946.

262. Jones, Nathan W. A brief account of Chinese voyages to the north-west coast of America, and the interpretation of 200 Indian names. New York, C. A. Alvord, 1869. 26p. (Indian bulletin, no. 2, 1868)

263. Kane, Joseph Nathan. The American counties: origins of names, dates of creation and organization, area, population, historical data, and published sources. 3d ed. Metuchen, N.J., Scarecrow Press, 1972. 608p.
1st ed. 1960. 500p.; 2d ed. 1962. 540p.

264. —— & Gerard L. Alexander. Nicknames and sobriquets of U.S. cities, states, and counties. 3d ed. Metuchen, N.J., Scarecrow Press, 1979. 429p.
1st ed. 1965. 341p.; 2d ed. 1970. 456p.
A ready reference tool but not a scholarly work. No sources are given. Includes 10,000 listings.
Review of 1st ed.: Virgil J. Vogel, Names 14:61-64, March 1966.
Review of 2d ed.: Paul H. Spence, College and research libraries 32:55, Jan. 1971; Kelsie B. Harder, Names 18:321, Dec. 1970.

265. Katz, Sol. Rainbow hued streets. American city 61:115, April 1946.
Suggests scheme for using names of colors in street nomenclature.

266. Kellogg, David Sherwood. Early mention of some events and places in the valley of Lake Champlain. A paper read before the Vermont Historical Society, in the hall of the House of Representatives, Oct. 30, 1902. Vermont Historical Society. Proceedings 1901-02:51-64.

267. Kelly, Francis J. Towns on state borders go by interesting names. Austin (Tex.) statesman Aug. 27, 1953, p. B-12.
A.P. story, also in Omaha world-herald Aug. 16, 1953.

268. Kelton, Dwight H. Annals of Fort Mackinac. Ruggles edition. Detroit, Detroit Free Press Print. Co., 1888. 144p.
Earlier edition: Island edition. Detroit, 1884. 158p.
Ancient names of rivers, lakes, etc.: p. 117-21; Indian and French geographical names: p. 145-58.

269. —— Indian names of places near the Great Lakes. Detroit, Detroit Free Press, 1888. 55p.
Most of the names are derived from the Ojibway, Cree, and Delaware languages.
Review: A. S. Gatschet, Journal of American folklore 2:69, Jan.-March 1889; D. G. Brinton, American antiquarian 11:68, Jan. 1889.

270. Kenny, Hamill. Adena [ədínə]. Names 15:240, Sept. 1967.
Name for the culture of North American prehistoric mound-builders derived correctly from Greek "enough, plenty" can also be derived easily from Algonquian word for mountain and is found in place-names Katahdin, Massanutten, and Pasadena.

271. —— Introduction [to special issue on Indian names]. Names 15:157-65, Sept. 1967.

272. —— Place-names and dialects: Algonquian. Names 24:86-100, June 1976.
A significant analysis by this noted authority relying on the Proto-Algonquian, a common ancestral language reconstructed by Leonard Bloomfield.

273. Ker, Edmund Thomas. River and lake names in the United States. New York, Woodstock Pub. Co., 1911. 47p.

274. Kilpatrick, Jack Frederick. An etymological note on the tribal name of the Cherokees and certain place and proper names derived from Cherokee. Journal of the Graduate Research Center 30:37-41, April 1962.

275. King, Edith Morgan. No namee. New Yorker 20:55-57, Aug. 26, 1944.
A modest research in the field of house and estate names.

276. Kinneman, John A. Nationalism in names of counties. Education 51:483-90, April 1931.
"A comparative study of states to determine which national names are oftenest used for county names."—American speech.

277. Kolin, Philip C. Jefferson Davis: from President to place-name. Names 25:158-73, Sept. 1977.
A limited number of place-names is found generally in the South with a few in the West. Use of the name for buildings and other developments exceeds use as a place-name.

278. —— Place-names, naming, and folklore. Mississippi folklore register 11:72-75, Fall 1977.
The introduction to a special issue devoted to place-names and naming.

279. —— State names used as city and county names. Mississippi folklore register 11:164-73, Fall 1977.

280. Krahn, Cornelius. Mennonite names of persons and places. Mennonite life 15:36-38, Jan. 1960.
In North and South America.
For a complete list of Mennonite villages, see article "Villages" in v. 4 of Mennonite encyclopedia. 1959.

281. Kramer, Fritz L. Andover moves West. Names 1:188-91, Sept. 1953.
Traces the name Andover across the Atlantic and westward through the United States.

282. —— More on "Idaho." Western folklore 12:208-10, July 1953.
Mentions items that are missing or treated insufficiently in Erl H. Ellis, That word "Idaho" (see no. 133).

283. —— Place names: a note on the literature. Journal of geography 56:374-76, Nov. 1957.

284. Krapp, George Philip. The English language in America. New York, Century, for the Modern Language Assoc. of America, 1925. 2v.
The chapter on Proper names treats of place-names in the United States, 1:169-200.

285. Kratkiĭ slovar′ russkoĭ transkript͡sii geograficheskikh naimenovaniĭ Soedinennykh Shtatov Ameriki. Moscow, Izdatel′stvo Inostrannoĭ Literatury, 1950. 558p.

286. Krueger, John R. A pronunciation standard for place names of the Pacific Northwest. American speech 37:74, Feb. 1962.
Local pronunciations of some tribal names and place-names.
Further comments by C. F. Voegelin, ibid. 37:74, Feb. 1962.

287. —— Whitwell's nomenclature: an 1826 zip code. Names 13:139-42, June 1965.
Stedman Whitwell of the New Harmony, Ind., community devised a system whereby every place would have a unique name. The name was to be derived from the latitude and longitude of the location, according to a standard chart of equivalences for letters and numbers.

288. Kuehne, Oswald Robert. Place names in the United States as an incentive to foreign language study. Modern language journal 25:91-107, Nov. 1940.
Classification of European-language place-names by languages and by parts of speech or their combinations within languages.

289. Kuethe, J. Louis. Pocosin. Modern language notes 52:210-11, March 1937.
Meaning marsh or swamp, Pocosin is now used in southern states, but appears in Rent rolls of Baltimore County, Md. in 1700.

290. Lanos, J. M. What's in a name? Queen's quarterly 17:44-57, July-Sept. 1909.
A plea for regeneration in the practice of name-giving in the United States and Canada. Article deals largely with place-names in western Europe, showing how beautiful and appropriate is the terminology used by the Anglo-Saxons, Northmen, and Celts.

291. Lanouette, William J. How Smackover, Ark., got that way. National observer Jan. 8, 1977.
Emphasizes variety found in names of places in the United States and the need for a comprehensive national inventory.

292. Large, Arlen J. Naughty Girl Meadow by some other name is known and loved, but Niggerhead Mountain, Vt., is found offensive enough to ban from federal maps. Wall Street journal April 3, 1972, p. 1, 15.
The work of the U.S. Board on Geographic Names.

293. Laurent, Joseph. Etymology of Indian names by which are designated certain tribes, towns, rivers, lakes, etc.; In his New familiar Abenakis and English dialogues. Quebec, Printed by L. Brousseau, 1884. p. 205-22.

294. Lawrence, Frederick W. The origin of American state names. National geographic magazine 38:105-43, Aug. 1920.

295. Lawson, James. Handbook of Indian place names in America (population 2,500 or more). [Wisconsin Dells, Wis., 1970]. 32p.
By state. Gives tribe and meaning.

296. Leigh, Rufus Wood. Naming of the Green, Sevier, and Virgin Rivers. Utah historical quarterly 29:137-47, April 1961.
Adapted from his full-length book manuscript, Indian, Spanish, and government survey place-names of the Great Basin and Colorado plateaus.

297. Leighly, John. Biblical place-names in the United States. Names 27:46-59, March 1979.

298. Lewis, Oscar. George Davidson: pioneer west coast scientist. Berkeley, Univ. of California Press, 1954. 146p.
Place names: p. 89-98.
Includes places named by Davidson and for him.

299. Longstreth, Joseph & John Ludwig. 48 plus 1: Washington, and the District of Columbia; the story of how the forty-eight states and their capital cities got their names. New York, Abelard-Schuman, 1957. 176p.

300. Loomis, C. Grant. Names in American limericks. Names 2:229-33, Dec. 1954.
The rhymes used in limericks give some indication of early pronunciation of some place-names.

301. Ludwig, John Warner. City names, our forgotten memorials. American city 70:242-45, March 1955.

302. Lyman, William D. Indian myths of the Northwest. American Antiquarian Society. Proceedings n.s. 25:377-79, Oct. 1915.
Aboriginal names of rivers, mountains, etc. used in the northwestern part of the United States are mentioned in connection with myths.

303. Lyra, Elzbieta & Franciszek Lyra. Polish place-names in the U.S.A. Geographical polonica 11:29-39, 1967. maps.

304. McAdoo, William Gibbs. American geographical nomenclature. Address to the associated alumni of East-Tennessee University, at Knoxville, Tenn. June 20th, 1871. Milledgeville, Ga., Federal Union Book and Job Office, 1871. 24p.

305. McClelland, M. K. Towns with a sense of humor (I hope). American Motors news illustrated 3:4, Feb. 1960.
Places the author would like to visit because of their intriguing names.

306. McClung, Quantrille D. Bent, Boggs, and Carson place names. Colorado genealogist 28:35-36, June 1967.
Place-names derived from three surnames throughout the United States.

307. McConnell, Raymond. Where is the "Middle West"? Lincoln (Neb.) evening journal April 30, 1956.
Part of the column More or less personal.

308. McCutcheon, John T., Jr. A line o' type or two. Why is "street" in disfavor? Chicago tribune May 11, 1954, p. 20; May 12, p. 24; May 13, p. 18.
"The term 'street' in names of streets is being supplanted by other terms, for which etymologies are given."—American speech.

309. McDavid, Raven I., Jr. Linguistic geography and toponymic research. Names 6:65-73, June 1958.
The relationship between these two disciplines and a plea for cooperation among the students of the two fields.

310. McDermott, John Francis. Madame Chouteau's grandchildren. Names 9:108-11, June 1961.
Place-names derived from the family, illustrating the spread of the family's activities.

311. —— William Clark's struggle with place names in Upper Louisiana. Missouri Historical Society. Bulletin 34:140-50, April 1978.

312. McDonald, Gerald Doan. Doane place names. Doane Family Association of America. Report of proceedings. Reunion 1953. n.p., 1955. p. 3-11.

313. MacFarlane, James. An American geological railway guide, giving the geological formation at every railway station, with altitudes above mean tide-water, notes on interesting places on the routes, and a description of each of the formations. 2d ed., rev. and enl. New York, D. Appleton, 1890. 426p. map.
Useful for its lists of places on the railroads in the United States and Canada in the 1880s.

314. McMillan, James B. A further note on place-name grammar. American speech 27:196-98, Oct. 1952.

A rejoinder to George R. Stewart in American speech 25:197-202; supplements the author's article in American speech 24:241-48.

315. —— Observations on American place-name grammar. American speech 24:241-48, Dec. 1949.

316. McMullen, Edwin Wallace. The term prairie in the United States. Names 5:27-46, March 1957.

True and false generics. The result of a preliminary study of names containing the word prairie on 773 topographical maps.

317. Mahr, August C. Aus praktischen Gründen gebildete Fluss- und Ortsnamen der algonkischen Indianer in Nordamerika. Rheinisches Jahrbuch fur Volkskunde 11:212-32. 1960.

318. —— Practical reasons for Algonkian Indian stream and place names. Ohio journal of science 59:365-74, Nov. 1959.

319. Mallery, Richard D. Place names in America; In his Our American language. Garden City, N.Y., Halcyon House, 1947. p. 91-122.

320. Marckwardt, Albert Henry. American English. New York, Oxford Univ. Press, 1958. 194p.

The names thereof: p. 151-66.

"A summary statement. Treatment is sound, although he is able to include little that will be of interest to the specialist in Onomastics."--Review, David W. Reed, Names 6:246, Dec. 1958.

321. Marshall, James Leslie. Santa Fe town names; In his Santa Fe, the railroad that built an empire. New York, Random House, 1945. p. 351-59.

Names on the Santa Fe lines, from Illinois to California. Lists of Indian and Spanish names with meanings, and places named for officials and employees of the railroad.

322. Marshall, Orsamus Holmes. The historical writings of the late Orsamus H. Marshall relating to the early history of the West; with an introduction by William L. Stone. Albany, J. Munsell's Sons, 1887. 500p. (Munsell's historical series, no. 15)

Besides Indian material, this book contains his Niagara frontier, p. 275-320, and a valuable Index rerum, p. 343-468, which includes many references to place-names in various early works and maps, the most important and accessible of which is the Jesuit Relations.

323. —— The Niagara frontier, embracing sketches of its early history, and Indian, French, and English local names. Read before the Buffalo Historical Club, February 27th, 1865. Buffalo, N.Y., J. Warren & Co., 1865. 46p.

Also published in Buffalo Historical Society. Publications 2:395-429. 1880. Also reprinted from the Publications of the Society, Buffalo, 1881. 37p. Also in his Historical writings. Albany, Munsell, 1887. p. 275-320.

A history with information of many place-names. An appendix contains lists of Seneca names with meanings and location, and early names applied to the Great Lakes and rivers, and to some of the prominent localities.

324. Martin, Lawrence. The dates of naming places and things for George Washington; In U.S. George Washington Bicentennial Commission. History of the George Washington bicentennial celebration. Literature series. Washington, 1932. 3:308-12.

325. Matthews, Brander. On the poetry of place names. Scribner's magazine 20:22-28, July 1896.
Also in his Parts of speech (New York, Scribner, 1901), p. 271-91.

326. Matthews, Constance Mary Carrington. Place-names of the English speaking world. London, Weidenfeld & Nicolson, 1972. xi, 369p. map.
Also published: New York, Scribner [c1972].
The New World, p. 163-231: includes chapters on the American colonies, the United States, and Canada.
Review: Kelsie B. Harder, Names 21:112-14, June 1973.

327. Maurer, David W. Underworld place-names. American speech 15:340-42, Oct. 1940; 17:75-76, Feb. 1942.
A list of place-names used by criminals for cities of the United States.

328. Meanings of state names often lost. Baltimore sun, July 31, 1937.

329. Mencken, Henry Louis. The American language; an inquiry into the development of English in the United States. 4th ed., cor., enl., and rewritten. New York, Knopf, 1936. 769p.
1st ed. 1919; 2d ed. 1921; 3d ed. 1923.
Place-names: p. 525-54.
Indicates the variety of the names found in the United States and includes street names, appellations applied to the residents of a particular place, and the joke towns such as Podunk.

330. —— The American language; an inquiry into the development of English in the United States. Supplement II. New York, Knopf, 1948. 890p.
Place-names: p. 525-75; State nicknames: p. 596-642.

331. —— The American language; an inquiry into the development of English in the United States. The 4th ed. and the two supplements, abridged, with annotations and new material, by Raven I. McDavid, Jr., with the assistance of David W. Mauer. New York, Knopf, 1963. 777p.
Place names: p. 642-701.
The material reorganized, and considerably rewritten.
Review: Audrey, Names 12:123-26, June 1964.

332. —— American street names. American speech 23:81-88, April 1948.

333. —— Names for Americans. American speech 22:241-56, Dec. 1947.
Names for residents of the United States and of the states.

334. —— Postscripts to the American language: the Podunk mystery. New Yorker 24:75-81, Sept. 25, 1948.
Additional note, unsigned, Oct. 16, p. 26-27, on Podunk River, tributary of Connecticut River.

335. —— Some opprobrious nicknames. American speech 24:25-30, Feb. 1949.
For residents of states and cities.

336. —— What the people of American towns call themselves. American speech 23:161-84, Oct. 1948.

337. Meredith, Mamie. "Chicagonese," "Buffalonians," "Manhattaniten," "Omahogs," and other name lore. American speech 14:77-80, Feb. 1939.
Form of city name given to its residents.

338. —— A crack in the track. American speech 10:236, Oct. 1935.
A variant for Podunk.

339. —— Indian place-names as viewed by a Scotch noblewoman. American speech 4:364-67, June 1929.
Notes taken from Amelia M. Murray, Letters from the United States, Cuba and Canada, 1856. New York, G. P. Putnam, 1856.

340. —— Language mixture in American place names. American speech 5:224-27, Feb. 1930.
Examples of combinations of geographic names when Anglicized and the changes which words undergo as they are interpreted in turn by the Indians, the French and the English.

341. —— Local discolor. American speech 6:260-63, April 1931.
American Indian names.

342. —— "Mail box," "Flag-station," "Hell on wheels," and other synonyms for "Podunk." American speech 12:320-21, Dec. 1937.

343. —— "Miracle miles" in the U.S.A. American speech 31:230-31, Oct. 1956.
A new name for an out-of-city shopping center, first noted in Lincoln, Neb.
See additional article by Homer Aschmann, Miracle mile, ibid. 32:156-58, May 1957.

344. —— Picturesque town names in America. American speech 6:429-32, Aug. 1931.
"In different eras towns are named according to the popularity of some particular vogue at the time."—Price.

345. Mickelsen, John. Origin of the names of towns on the Northern Pacific Railway.
The origin of the names of the towns on this railroad line. There are about 1520 towns on the system.
An unpublished manuscript by a member of the Railroad's Engineering Department.

346. Millward, Celia M. Universals in place-name generics. Indiana names 3:48-53, Fall 1972.
Includes examples from Rhode Island.

347. Minkel, Clarence W. Names in the mapping of original vegetation. Names 5:157-61, Sept. 1957.
Analyzes and evaluates the place-name method of reconstruction of the original vegetation patterns in areas where the original plant cover has been greatly altered. Uses Minnesota as a testing ground.

348. Missouri Pacific Railroad Company. The empire that Missouri Pacific serves. St. Louis, Von Hoffman Press, 1956? 352p.
Origins of the names of most of the communities served by the Missouri Pacific lines.

349. Momsen, Richard. Similarities in settlement names of Brasil and the United States. Coimbra. Universidade. Centro do Estudos Geograficos. Boletim v. 3, no. 19, p. 41-55. 1962.
Résumés in Portuguese and French, p. 55.
Some general parallels in the derivations of the names of their settlements, arranged as Descriptive, Proper, Mining, Pseudo-classical, etc.

350. Monteiro, George. And still more ethnic and place names as derisive adjectives. Western folklore 27:51, Jan. 1968.

351. Mooney, James. The Siouan tribes of the East. Washington, Govt. Print. Off., 1894. 101p. (U.S. Bureau of American Ethnology. Bulletin no. 22)
Local names from Siouan tribal names in Virginia and Carolina: p. 87-88; some notes on names, p. 46-47.

352. Moore, M. V. Did the Romans colonize America? Magazine of American history 12:113-25, 354-64, Aug., Oct. 1884.
Correlations between American place-names and Latin words, such as Tennessee and Tenassy, Mississippi and Messisapa.

353. —— North and South American aboriginal names. Popular science monthly 44:81-84, Nov. 1893.
Many names of natural features in North America have their counterparts in South America, indicating that the languages of the people of the two continents had similar words and meanings.

354. —— Southern rivers. Names 3:38-43, March 1955.
A poem on the colorful names of the rivers of the South, which first appeared in Harper's new monthly magazine of Feb. 1883.

355. Moyer, Armond & Winifred Moyer. The origins of unusual place-names. Emmaus, Pa., Keystone Pub. Assoc., 1958. 144p.
Review: A. R. Duckert, Names 7:265-267, Dec. 1959.

356. Murray, J. Franklin. Jesuit place names in the United States. Names 16:6-12, March 1968.
Names of places for which European Jesuit missionaries are in some way responsible.

357. Mussey, June Barrows. Tied for first in the hearts of his countrymen. New York Public Library. Bulletin 54:55-60, Feb. 1950.
A summary of place-names found in J. D. B. De Bow's Statistical view of the United States . . . being a compendium of the seventh census.

358. The Name game. All aboard for Big Shanty. Denver post Nov. 24, 1963, Roundup, p. 9.
Unusual town names in the United States.

359. The Name of your town. Ladies home journal 30:3, Sept. 1913.
The origin of the names of some of the places in the East explained by historical legends.

360. Names and places. Western folklore (formerly California folklore quarterly) v. 4- . 1945- .
A department containing articles and brief notes on place-names and inquiries about them.

361. Names of American towns run the gamut of variety; many Washingtons and Lincolns may be found but Zipp and Author are not repeated. New York times Feb. 23, 1930, sec. 8, p. 17, col. 2-3.
Zipp and Author in Indiana.

362. Names of places in the United States. Chambers's Edinburgh journal n.s. 4:217-18, 254-56, Oct. 4, 18, 1845.

Names used in the United States include many from ancient times, from Europe, and from literature.

363. Names of topographic features in the United States. American Geographical Society. Bulletin 39:103-06, Feb. 1907.
Authoritative decisions handed down by the U.S. Geographic Board as to the extent of the region to which certain names of mountains apply.

364. Names of towns in the United States. Knickerbocker 9:19-25, Jan. 1837.
Signed: A. B. C.

365. National Geographic Society. U.S. town-city names spell enchantment, surprises too. Washington, D.C., 1955. 6p.

366. Nature names in America. Journal of geography 5:476-80, Dec. 1906.
A general article on the meanings of the words creek, freshet, swamp, etc. which now have different meanings in England and the United States.

367. Naughton, William A. What's in a name? Américas 16:27-31, Dec. 1964.
Names given during the exploration, conquest, and settlement of the Western Hemisphere. Mostly in Spanish America, but includes some in the United States.

368. Nestler, Harold. Poughkeepsie, as a place name. Dutchess County Historical Society. Year book 35:64-66. 1950.
In New York, Indiana, Arkansas, and Colorado.

369. New names for old streets. New York times magazine Oct. 28, 1930, p. 24.
Based on Pittsburgh's newest roadway called KDKA Blvd.

370. New York, Washington, Philadelphia. New York times Jan. 26, 1969, sec. x, p. 29.
Short article on small English towns bearing same name as the major United States cities.

371. Nichols, Maynard. Berlin, U.S.A. New York times magazine Oct. 22, 1944, p. 36.
An article on odd names in the United States inspired by attempts to secure change of one of the cities named Berlin to Distomo, a Nazi-destroyed Greek city.
cf. Letters to the editor, ibid. Nov. 12, p. 51; Nov. 26, p. 50.

372. Nicknames of the states. Current literature 24:41, July 1898.
Reprinted from the Philadelphia evening bulletin.

373. Nicknaming the states. Mentor 14:64, Jan. 1927.
A popular article which gives the significance of the nicknames attached to the states.

374. Nicolaisen, W. F. H. Onomastic dialects. American speech 55:36-45, Spring 1980.

374a. —— Onomastics—an independent discipline? Indiana names 3:33-47, Fall 1972.

375. Numbers as street names. Notes and queries 178:12, 174-75, 286, Jan. 6, March 9, April 20, 1940.
The practice of using numbers and letters for street names in America.

376. O'Callaghan, Edmund Bailey. Indian names of localities and their derivations. Historical magazine 3:84-85, 189-90, 278, 367, March-Dec. 1859.

A list of Algonquin and other Indian place-names in the East giving the origin and meaning.

377. —— Indian names of places with definitions. Historical magazine 6:30, 133, Jan., April 1862.
"This list of Indian place-names which belong to the Algonquin family gives the possible origin and meaning."—Price.

378. Och, Joseph Tarcisius. Der deutschamerikanische Farmer; sein Anteil an der Eroberung und Kolonisation der Bundesdomane der Ver. Staaten, besonders in den Nord Centralstaaten; nebst Wurdigung der kulturellen Bedeutung des deutschen Farmers, und Wertung der deutschen Auswanderung und deutschen Kolonisationsarbeit in Amerika vom amerikanischen und deutschen national-politischen Standpunkt. Eine statistische und volkswirtschaftliche Untersuchung. Columbus, Ohio, Heer Print. Co., 1913. 248p.
Verzeichnis deutscher Staedte- und Ortsnamen in den Ver. Staaten: p. 228-35.

379. Odd names adorn American cities and towns. Geographic news bulletin Nov. 11, 1932, p. 1-3.
Prepared as a news release by the National Geographic Society.

380. Oddities in postmarks, such as Odd, W.Va., fill Massachusetts collector with glee. New York times Oct. 3, 1937, sec. 2, p. 8, col. 2-3.
Fred G. Richardson claims to have oddest collection of postmarks in the country.

381. Ogden, Herbert G.; Gustave Herrle; Marcus Baker, & A. H. Thompson. Geographic nomenclature. National geographic magazine 2:261-78. 1890.
Need for standardization of names by the newly formed Board on Geographic Names.

382. Olson, James C. "Trace" and "trail." American speech 26:137, May 1951.
Question regarding use.

383. On the streets where we live. Aramco world 9:6-7, Sept. 1958.
Systems of forming addresses in many countries including the United States.

384. O'Neill, Jennie Lamb. On the street, lane, circle, or drive where you live. American home 71:40, Winter 1968.
Fancy street names given by developers.

385. Origin of names of projects and project features in reclamation territory. Reclamation era 30:63-65, 144-48, 179-81, 241-42, 253-57, 294-99, March-June, Aug.-Oct. 1940.
Deals with states in the West.

386. Orth, Donald J. Domestic geographic names activity in federal mapping. Surveying and mapping 24:603-06, Dec. 1964.
Presented at the 23d annual meeting of the American Congress on Surveying and Mapping, Washington, D.C., March 26-29, 1963, by a member of the Geographic Names staff, U.S. Geological Survey.

387. —— Geographic names and the public interest. Surveying and mapping 29:651-54, Dec. 1969.
Name standardization is in the public interest for economic and scientific reasons.

388. —— The nature of topographic terms. Indiana names 3:5-18, Spring 1972.
A study of topographic terms in general, including a short survey of terms used in Indiana.

389. —— Place names and computers: a new challenge. Indiana names 2:2-12, Spring 1971.
Automatic data processing equipment offers a new and valuable tool for place-name research. Discusses the application for place-name work in the U.S. Geological Survey.

390. Our classical belt. Nation 85:203-04, Sept. 5, 1907.
Some of the classical names in the United States.

391. Our Indian names. New York times July 28, 1937, p. 18, col. 3-4.
Meaning of Indian names of states as set forth by the Smithsonian Institution.

392. Our station names—their family trees. Louisville and Nashville magazine 25:18-19, May; 18-19, June; 20-21, July; 14, Aug.; 14-16, Sept.; 14-15, Oct.; 14-16, Nov.; 16-17, Dec. 1949; 26:16-17, Jan.; 34-35, March; 23, July 1950.

393. Our town nomenclature. Nation 7:499-500, Dec. 17, 1868.
The author regrets that, in this country, place-names have not had time to grow up. The people of this country have been compelled "to invent place names and impose them, without regard to appropriateness, upon places."

394. P.O. nomenclators. New York times Feb. 28, 1938, p. 14, col. 2; letter March 13, sec. 4, p. 9, col. 7.
Changes in Feb. supplement of U.S. postal guide.

395. Pace, G. B. Linguistic geography and names ending in <i>. American speech 35:175-87, Oct. 1960.
Focuses attention on pronunciation of Missouri and Cincinnati.

396. Paige, H. W. American names, American places. America 130:112-13, Feb. 16, 1974.

397. Palmer, C. B. O death! O misery! New York times magazine Jan. 30, 1955, p. 69.
Place-names in the United States and other countries taken from disasters.

398. Pap, Leo. The Portuguese adstratum in North American place-names. Names 20:111-30, June 1972.
A survey of Portuguese influence on the formation of place-names in the United States and Newfoundland, Labrador, and Nova Scotia, presented as a linguistic contribution to the investigation of naming processes.

399. Parry, Albert. Russian names for American towns. Russian review 3:30-43, Spring 1944.

400. Pearce, Thomas M. Animal place names in the West. Western folklore 13:203-05, July 1954.

401. —— Chicarica, Chico Rico, Sugarite: a puzzle in place naming. Western folklore 14:124-25, April 1955.

402. —— The lighter side of place naming. Western folklore 11:118-21, April 1952.

403. —— Names and places. Western folklore 8:157, April 1949.
The writer succeeded E. G. Gudde as editor of this regular column, and reviews the situation in the West.

404. —— Place-name pronunciation guides for western states. Western folklore 10:72-73, Jan. 1951.
Project of National Association of Radio News Directors.

405. —— Spanish place name patterns in the Southwest. Names 3:201-09, Dec. 1955.

406. —— Three Rocky Mountain terms: Park, Sugan, and Plaza. American speech 33:99-107, May 1958.

407. —— Western place name sketches. Names 2:272-74, Dec. 1954.
The status of work on place-names in the western states and the work of the Western Place Name Committee.

408. Pei, Mario. Faraway places with strange sounding names. Saturday review 51:64-65, Feb. 10, 1968.
Examples of colorful American and British place-names, river names, state line town names, and New Jersey place-names.

409. Peirce, Neal R. Cancel the two-letter state postal codes. Cleveland plain dealer Jan. 2, 1979, p. 21-A.
Decries the use of these in place of normal abbreviations or full name if short.

410. Pence, Monroe Conger. A history of Pence place names and early Pences in America, with genealogies. Mountain View, Calif., 1961. 31p.
Pence family place-names arranged geographically.

411. Pennsylvania Railroad Company. Alphabetical and geographical list of bituminous and anthracite coal mines on the Pennsylvania Railroad and lateral lines with names and post office address of operators. Philadelphia, 1956. 68p.

412. Perkins, Franklin. Geographical names. Journal of education (Boston) 45:367, 403. 1897.
Prefixes and suffixes used in compounding place-names.

413. Perrin, Noel. Rod-Island is real, but I'll never believe in Wisconsin. New Yorker 38:48-51, Nov. 24, 1962.
Place-names that foreigners change into their own language (e.g., Filadelfia on a Spanish map) illustrate the First Law of Geographical Reality, which is: The places in any country that seem authentic to the people of any other country may be determined by observing which place-names the other country changes.

414. Phelps, Dawson A. & Edward Hunter Ross. Place-names along the Natchez Trace. Journal of Mississippi history 14:217-56, Oct. 1952.

415. Pierce, Phillip. Ghost town directory of the West. Cheyenne, Wyo., Pierce Pub. Co., 1964. 36p.

416. Pioneers got place names often mixed. Cumberland (Md.) evening times Nov. 13, 1935.
A summary of a National Geographic Society bulletin.

417. Pizer, Vernon. Ink, Ark., and all that: how American places got their names. New York, Putnam, c1976. 123p.
Written for children, the stories present some unusual American place-names such as Embarrass, Minnesota, Tensleep, Wyoming, and Why Not, North Carolina.

418. The Place Name Committee. American speech 14:136-38, 212-14, April, Oct. 1939.
The appointment of a committee by the Present-day English Section of the Modern Language Association to further the study of place-names in the United States. Oct. issue includes comment by Prof. Max Forster.

419. Place name study aids in the classroom; educator says hobby provides adventure for history and geography students. New York times Nov. 9, 1932, p. 23, col. 7.
An interview with Lewis H. Chrisman.

420. Place-name study in the United States. Geographical review 24:659-60, Oct. 1934.

421. Place-Name Survey of the United States. Newsletter no. 1-3. Ed. by Robert M. Rennick. Prestonburg, Ky., 1972-74.

422. Place-names masquerade in strange disguises. Geographic news bulletin Nov. 13, 1935, p. 1-3.
A news release of the National Geographic Society.

423. Plank, Robert. Projection in topographic names. Names 6:80-87, June 1958.
A study of the psychological principle of "projection" in descriptive place-names.

424. Poast, Florence Maude. Indian names, facts and games for Camp Fire girls. Washington, James William Bryan Press, 1916. 78p.
Contains list of Indian names, with pronunciation and meaning, suitable for camps, country homes or bungalows, and boats.

425. Podunk was Indian name. Pennsylvania archaeologist 5:71, Oct. 1935.

426. Popular names of the states. Magazine of history 23:27-30, July 1916.
This alphabetical list contains most of the states with their nicknames and reasons for such terms. There is also a list of popular names applied to the inhabitants of some states.

427. Porter, Kenneth. Still more ethnic and place names as derisive adjectives. Western folklore 25:37-40, Jan. 1966; 26:189-90, July 1967.

428. Porter, P. W. Thanks to readers, Polecat Hollow is in the same orbit as Mars. Cleveland plain dealer May 5, 1958.
An additional article, April 24.
Odd place-names.

429. Porter, Philip. Porter on odd names. Cleveland plain dealer Sept. 13, 1958.
An editor of this paper lists odd place-names sent in by readers of his column. Similar lists appeared in the April 24 and May 5 issues.

430. Postal, Bernard. Jews on the map: geographical places named for Jews. Jewish digest 15:37-40, July 1969.
Condensed from Pioneer woman Sept.-Oct. 1968.
93 places in the United States are named for Jews, more than a third of them in the South.

431. Pound, Louise. "Gag" towns. American speech 26:137, May 1951.
Kalamazoo, Peoria, etc.

432. —— The locus of Podunk. American speech 9:80, Feb. 1934.

433. A Pretty idea at least. New York times July 20, 1923, p. 12, col. 5.
Editorial on abbreviations for state names, citing plan of Richmond times-dispatch to write out Virginia.

434. Preuss, Charles. Exploring with Frémont; the private diaries of Charles Preuss, cartographer for John C. Frémont on his first, second and fourth expeditions to the Far West; trans. and ed. by Erwin G. and Elisabeth K. Gudde. Norman, Univ. of Oklahoma Press, 1958. 162p. (The American exploration and travel series, no. 26)
The editors pay special attention to place-names and comment on them in numerous footnotes.
Review: Fritz L. Kramer, Names 6:187-88, Sept. 1958.

435. Price, Edward T. A geography of color. Geographical review 54:590-92, Oct. 1964.
Includes chromotoponyms, names in which a color is used, giving evidence of the importance of color to observers.

436. Price, Esther Frances. Guide to material on place-names in the United States and Canada. Urbana, Ill., 1934. 250p.
Thesis (M.A.) Univ. of Illinois, 1934.

437. Prucha, Francis Paul. A guide to the military posts of the United States, 1789-1895. Madison, State Historical Society of Wisconsin, 1964. 178p.
Includes an alphabetical catalog of more than 475 military posts of every description: forts, camps, barracks, and cantonments.
Review: Russell W. Fridley, Minnesota history 39:254, Summer 1965.

438. Quigg, Doc. American towns pose problem for writer. Austin (Tex.) statesman Oct. 4, 1957, p. 14.
Humorous names of American towns.

439. Quimby, Myron J. Scratch ankle, U.S.A.: American place names and their derivation. South Brunswick, N.J., A. S. Barnes, 1969. 390p.
A popular work on a limited number of unusual names.

440. Raup, Hallock Floy. Center vs. Centre. Names 1:259-61, Dec. 1953.
Are the variations in spelling due to fads in naming places?

441. —— Tivoli: a place-name of special connotation. Names 22:34-39, March 1974.
A geographical name used throughout the western world connoting entertainment and pleasure for both place and commercial names.

442. Read, Allen Walker. The basis of correctness in the pronunciation of place-names. American speech 8:42-46, Feb. 1933.
Fails to find a basis for correctness in legislative action, in etymology, in spelling, or in the so-called authorities.

443. —— The challenge of place-name study. Elementary English 48:235-36, April 1971.
Activities for students, grade school to college, on place-names. Emphasizes the interdisciplinary nature of such study.

444. —— Derivative forms from place-names; the contrast between England and America.
Paper read before the Dec. 1941 meeting of the American Dialect Society.

445. —— The pronunciation of place names on the frontier, 1829-1830. American speech 13:263-67, Dec. 1938.
Information from the correspondence of Joseph Emerson Worcester.

446. —— The prospects of a national place-name survey for the United States. Names 18:201-07, Sept. 1970.
A paper given before the 13th National Conference on Linguistics, March 9, 1968.

447. —— The rationale of "Podunk." American speech 14:99-108, April 1939.
Adopted by the early settlers from the Indians for places in Connecticut, Massachusetts, and New York and then used in a series of humorous letters of 1846.

448. —— The rivalry of names for the Rocky Mountains of North America. In International Congress of Onomastic Sciences, 10th. Vienna, 1969. Proceedings. 1:207-22.
Bibliography: p. 221-22.
Traces the names applied to the mountain system from earliest records until the present designation became fixed.

449. Read, William Alexander. A few American place-names. Journal of English and Germanic philology 22:242-44. 1923.
Study of the pronunciation of a few chosen names.

450. —— Research in American place names, 1920-1926. Zeitschrift für Ortsnamenforschung 4:185-91. 1928.
"Bibliographical account of recent publications relating to American place names, which the writer divides into 3 classes—investigations of the geographic and historical significance of place names, articles and books of a popular character, and scientific studies of Indian names."—Griffin.

451. —— Research in American place-names since 1928. Zeitschrift für Ortsnamenforschung 10:222-42. 1934.

452. Reade, John. The testimony of names of places. Rose-Belford's Canadian monthly 1:602-04, Nov. 1878.
The source of some of the names in North America.

453. Remington, Frank L. How it got that name. Think (International Business Machines Corporation) 17:14-15, Oct. 1951.
Some unusual American place-names.

454. —— Please write in ink. Surveying and mapping 13:185-87, April-June 1953.
Reprinted through the courtesy of Pen, March 1953.
Stories concerning the choice of unusual names for places in the United States.

455. Rennick, Robert M. The role of oral history in place-name research. Indiana names 3:19-26, Spring 1972.

456. Rice, Charlie. Fireman, name my street! This week magazine Jan. 26, 1963, p. 14.
Street names in developments.

457. Richardson, Charles F. The pronunciation of American names. Critic n.s. 2:73-74, Aug. 16, 1884.

458. Richmond, W. Edson. The value of the study of place names. Indiana names 1:1-10, Spring 1970.
The study leads directly to an understanding of the culture which created the names.

459. Richthofen, Erich von. The Spanish toponyms of the British Columbia coast, with sideglances at those in the states of Washington, Oregon and Alaska. Winnipeg, Ukrainian Free Academy of Sciences. Onomastica 26:1-22. 1963.

460. Ristow, Walter W. A covey of names. In U.S. Bureau of Sport Fisheries and Wildlife. Birds in our lives. Alfred Stefferud, editor. Washington, Govt. Print. Off., 1966. p. 68-77.

461. Robertson, Robert S. Long Island Indians. Magazine of American history 2:370-71, 501, June, Aug. 1878.
The interpretation and derivation of some Indian place-names.

462. Roe, Frank Gilbert. Buffalo place-names; In his The North American buffalo. Toronto, Univ. of Toronto Press, 1951. p. 817-28.
Also miscellaneous references in index: Place-names.

463. Rogers, P. Burwell. Inland ports. American speech 35:203-05, Oct. 1960.
Influence of inland streams and canals on use of ports, harbors, and havens in town names.

464. Romero, B. A. Origin of state names. New York times Sept. 19, 1937, sec. 4, p. 9, col. 6.
Believes many names of states and places could be traced back to Spanish words.

465. Rostlund, Erhard. The geographic range of the historic bison in the Southeast. Association of American Geographers. Annals 50:394-407, Dec. 1960.
Place names: p. 403-05.

466. Rothsteiner, John M. On the study of place-names. Mid-America 12:58-62, July 1929.
Discusses the relation of place-names to history.

467. Rouillard, Eugène. À propos de Jolliet. Société de Géographie de Québec. Bulletin 11:354-55, Nov. 1917.
Concerns the orthography of the name. The State of Wisconsin officially decided on Jolliet.

468. Rupert, William W. The significance and importance of geographical names. American Bureau of Geography. Bulletin 1:316-27, Dec. 1900.
Treats of names in the United States, some that were given by explorers, others which came into being in colonial times.

469. Russ, William A., Jr. The export of Pennsylvania place names. Pennsylvania history 15:194-214, July 1948.
On the transplanting of Pennsylvania names to the South and West, as a result of the Delaware migration (ca. 1765).

470. Russell, Israel C. The names of the larger geographical features of North America. Geographical Society of Philadelphia. Bulletin 2:55-69, Nov. 1899.
A discussion of topographical terms with a suggested nomenclature for the larger geographical features.

471. Rutherford, Phillip R. Pitfalls in place name study; In South Central Names Institute. Ethnic names. Commerce, Tex., Names Institute Press, 1978. (Publication 6) p. 31-35.

472. Ryan, Jack. What's in a name? Family weekly magazine Sept. 16, 1956, p. 2.
"Humorous names of American towns."—American speech.

473. Sadler, J. D. Classical U.S. cities. Classical bulletin 46:27-28, 32, 41-43, 91-92, 95-96, Dec. 1969, Jan., April 1970; 47:13-15, Nov. 1970.
"There is a richness of names, but a mixing-up of names that are classical in origin, classical in inspiration, Romance in origin, and classical in accidental appearance."—Rosen.
Review: Karl M. D. Rosen, American Name Society, Bulletin no. 22:9-11, June 1971.

474. Sage, Evan T. Classical place-names in America. American speech 4:261-71, April 1929.
From the standpoint of their linguistic interest, regardless of any sociological or historical inferences that might be based upon them.

475. Salmon, Lucy Maynard. Place-names and personal names as records of history. American speech 2:228-32, Feb. 1927.
A collection and arrangement of common nouns, adjectives, and verbs derived from proper nouns. Emphasis is placed on words derived from the names of persons and places of every nationality that have been identified with inventions, discoveries, and manufactures. Their significance is shown in geographic nomenclature.

476. Salomon, L. B. Lucifer's landholdings in America. Names 16:89-94, June 1968.
United States terrain features in either the Devil's or in Hell's name.

477. Sanborn, J. L. American town names. Kansas magazine 3:158-67, Feb. 1873.
Deplores the lack of taste in many town names, with examples.

478. Sandham, William R. Patrick Henry, orator, statesman and patriot for whom Henry County, Ill. was named. Illinois State Historical Society. Journal 18:1039-48, Oct. 1925.
Biographical account of Patrick Henry, prefaced and concluded by a few paragraphs on number of counties and towns named for him.

478a. Scheetz, George H. Peoria, U.S.A.; In North Central Names Institute. Papers, ed. by Lawrence E. Seits. Sugar Grove, Ill., Waubonsee Community College, 1980. p. 54-63.
The origin of the name from the Peoria tribe and its distribution, including variants in the United States, and with comments on the humorous use of the name.

479. Schele De Vere, Maximilian. Americanisms; the English of the New World. New York, Scribner, 1872. 685p.
Sections of the chapters The Indian, and Immigrants from abroad, treat of Indian and foreign influence in place-names. In the chapter New words and nicknames is a list of nicknames of states and cities.

480. Schoolcraft, Henry Rowe. Mohegan language and geographical names. Knickerbocker, or New York monthly magazine 10:214-16, Sept. 1837.
Emphasis on names in New York.

481. Schorr, Alan Edward. A brief history of the United States Board on Geographic Names. Special Library Association. Geography and Map Division. Bulletin 96:18-20, June 1974.

482. The "Science" of street names. American city 75:7, Nov. 1960.
Editorial on systems of naming streets.

483. Sealock, Richard Burl. Place names in genealogy. Indiana historical bulletin 23:69-75, Jan. 1946.

484. Settlers imprint left on town names. Wisconsin geographer points out how American places reflect characteristics. New York times Aug. 18, 1929, sec. 2, p. 23, col. 5.
R. H. Whitbeck, the geographer.

485. Shankle, George Earlie. American nicknames: their origin and significance. 2d ed. New York, H. W. Wilson Co., 1955. 524p.
1st ed. 1937. 599p.
Includes places.

486. —— State names, flags, seals, songs, birds, flowers and other symbols; a study based on historical documents giving the origin and significance of the state names, nicknames, mottoes, seals, flags, flowers, birds, songs, and descriptive comments on the capitol buildings and on some of the leading state histories, with facsimiles of the state flags and seals. Rev. ed. New York, H. W. Wilson Co., 1941. 524p.
1st ed. 1934. 512p.; rev. ed. 1938. 522p.
Reprinted: Westport, Conn., Greenwood Press, [1970]. 522p.; St. Clair Shores, Mich., Scholarly Press, 1972. 522p.

487. Shea, John G. Indian names. Historical magazine 10:58, Feb. 1866.
A list of several Mohawk aboriginal place-names with their meanings.

488. Shelton, William E. Town and station names on the Illinois Central. Illinois Central magazine 44:21, Nov. 1955.
Groups of Bible, presidential, feminine, masculine, and curious names.

489. Sherwin, Reider Thorbjorn. The Viking and the red man: the Old Norse origin of the Algonquin language. New York, Funk & Wagnalls, 1940-48. 5v.
Algonquin place names: 1:254-310; 2:162-78; 3:155-61; 4:172-208; 5:170-99.
Bibliography of principal sources of Algonquin place names: 1:331; 2:191.

490. Short names for long ones. New York times Nov. 4, 1928, sec. 3, p. 4, col. 6.
Editorial on protest in San Francisco on shortening of Spanish names with mention of Filly and K. C. Another editorial against nicknames for cities appeared June 8, sec. 3, p. 6, col. 6.

491. Short (Va.) Story (Ark.), U.S.A. Good housekeeping 146:143, Feb. 1958.
A list of unusual town names.

492. Shulman, David. Nicknames of the states and their inhabitants. American speech 27:183-85, Oct. 1952.

493. Smelser, Marshall. Poets and place names. Names 1:15-19, March 1953.
Some comments on the English poet Robert Southey's concern over place-naming in America as evidenced in his review in the Quarterly review 12:317-68, Jan. 1815, of Lewis and Clark's Travels to the source of the Missouri River.

493a. Smith, Chester M., Jr., & Alan Petera. U.S. postal history: primary source, secondary sources, and problems with both. American philatelist Jan. 1979, p. 19-26.
A bibliographical guide to the lists and histories of post offices which can be so important in establishing the dates of names and their continuing use.

494. Smith, Elsdon Coles. Bibliographia onomastica. United States. 1951- . Onoma v. 3- . 1952- .
An annual bibliography of place-name literature.

495. The Soul of places. New York times Oct. 23, 1934, p. 18, col. 4.
Editorial on strange names.

496. Soulas, Jean. Toponymie nord-américaine. Annales de geographie 50:22-36, janv.-mars 1941.
An attempt by a French geographer to rationalize the seeming vagaries and incongruities of the pattern of North American place-names by a system of classification. Certain inaccuracies in this study illustrate some of the pitfalls for the unwary interpreter of place-names.

497. Spain. Ejército. Servicio Geográfico. Cartografía de ultramar. Carpeta II. Estados Unidos y Canadá. Toponimia de los mapas que la integran relaciones de ultramar. Madrid, Imprenta del Servicio Geográfico del Ejército, 1953. 598p.
A list of maps of the United States and Canada of the 17th and 18th centuries, with lists of place-names on the maps.

498. Speaking of pictures; tourist visits Europe's big cities without leaving U.S. Life 26:10-11, Jan. 10, 1949.
A trip through cities with foreign names in New York and Pennsylvania, with pictures showing some connection with each city's namesake.

499. Spelling of geographical names. American Geographical Society. Bulletin 34:155. 1902.
Maintains that certain rules should be followed in assigning new names to places.

500. Spiegelman, Julia. Map of America is dotted with names from Holy Land and Bible. Kansas City times Dec. 31, 1962, p. 24.

501. Spofford, Ainsworth Rand. American historical nomenclature. American Historical Association. Annual report 1893:33-42.
The composition of American place-names, the use many times over of imported names, and a summary of the types of names which might be used in the future.

502. Sprague, Marshall. The great gates: the story of the Rocky Mountain passes. Boston, Little, Brown, 1964. 468p. maps.
Bibliography: p. 356-64.
A roster of passes: p. 371-456. A list including altitude, location, and in many cases, origin of name.

503. —— Many "President" towns. New York times Oct. 10, 1937, sec. 12, p. 2, col. 2.
Towns named for presidents.

504. Sprague, Roderick. The meaning of Palouse. Idaho yesterdays 12:22-27, Summer 1968. maps.
Condensed from a segment of the author's doctoral thesis in anthropology.
North Idaho and eastern Washington, and a creek in Oregon.

505. Springer, O. Ortsnamen in der Neuen Welt. Germanisch-Romanische Monatsschrift 21:125-46, March-April 1933.
"Concerning American Indian place-names."—American speech.

506. Stanford, Annabella. The names of the states. American antiquarian and oriental journal 29:305-08, Sept.-Oct. 1907.
"The author's discourse is confined to the source and meaning of early names that were suggested or applied to the states and their reasons for being applied and why they were not retained."—Price.

507. Staples, Hamilton Barclay. Origin of the names of the states of the Union. American Antiquarian Society. Proceedings n.s. 1:366-83, Oct. 1881.
Also issued separately, Worcester, C. Hamilton, 1882. 25p.

508. State names and origins. Louis Allis messenger Jan.-Feb. 1953, p. [28-29].

509. States have Indian names; original designations range from Alibamu to Massawadschuasch. New York times Jan. 12, 1930, sec. 11, p. 6, col. 2.

510. States perpetuate Indian words. Kansas City star Sept. 29, 1960, p. 11.

511. Steel, William Gladstone. Place names. Steel points, junior v. 1, no. 4, Jan. 1928. 23p.
Includes short biography of Henry Gannett, upon whose work this is probably based.

512. Stegner, Wallace. C. E. Dutton—explorer, geologist, nature writer. Scientific monthly 45:82-83, July 1937.
Refers to his use of architectural names, particularly oriental, in national parks of the Southwest.

513. —— Powell and the names on the plateau. Western humanities review 7:105-10, Spring 1953.
Later published as a section in his book Beyond the hundredth meridian. Boston, Houghton Mifflin, 1954. p. 191-98, Notes p. 395-96.
The relationship of Major John Wesley Powell to some place-names in Utah, Wyoming, Colorado, and Arizona.

514. Stevenson, Andrew. Many towns named in honor of Santa Fe men. Santa Fe magazine 22:55-56, Aug. 1928.
From Illinois to California, but greatest number are in Kansas.

515. Stewart, George Rippey. American place-names: a concise and selective dictionary for the continental United States of America. New York, Oxford Univ. Press, 1970. xl, 550p.
Primary focus is upon the names, rather than on individual places. Provides the meaning and derivation of each name, and often such information as the date and occasion of naming and the namer. Includes some 12,000 entries.
Review: John Hollander, The babble of American place-names, Harper's magazine 242:22-23, 26-27, Jan. 1971; John Seelye, Placing names & naming places, New Republic 164:26-28, Feb. 13, 1971; McCandlish Phillips, All aboard for tour of place names! New York times Sept. 18, 1970, p. 32, col. 1; Frederic Gomes Cassidy, Names 20:141-46, June 1972.

516. —— A classification of place names. Names 2:1-13, March 1954.
Postulates nine classes of names.

517. —— From Cape Cod to Dragon Rocks: explanation of animal names for geographic areas. American history illustrated 9:34-41, July 1974.

518. —— Further observations on place name grammar. American speech 25:197-202, Oct. 1950.

519. —— Leah, Woods, and deforestation as an influence on place-names. Names 10:11-20, March 1962.

520. —— The names; In his U.S. 40, cross section of the United States of America. Boston, Houghton, Mifflin, 1953. p. 303-09.

521. —— Names of wild animals for natural features in the United States and Canada. Revue internationale d'onomastique 12:282-92, déc. 1960.
Estimated 40,000 natural features in the United States bear the names of wild animals; in Canada, about 10,000.

522. —— Names on the land: a historical account of place-naming in the United States. 3d ed. Boston, Houghton Mifflin, 1967. 511p.

1st ed. New York, Random House, 1945. 418p.; Rev. ed. Boston, Houghton Mifflin, 1958. 511p.

Revised editions contain a few minor changes, plus new chapters on Alaska, Hawaii, and current affairs, 1944-1958, and a valuable section of Notes and references, p. 442-82.

The process of place-naming is treated chronologically with definite trends and fashions noted: the unselfconscious names given by the early settlers, the influence of various national groups, the use of Indian names, and the names resulting from important historical events.

Review of 1st ed.: Harold W. Bentley, American speech 20:285-88, Dec. 1945; Raye R. Platt, Geographical review 35:659-64, Oct. 1945; H. L. Mencken, New York herald tribune weekly book review April 22, 1945, p. 5; George L. Trager, International journal of American linguistics 12:108-10, 1946.

Review of rev. ed.: D. J. Georgacas, Names 8:89-94, June 1960.

523. —— "Names on the land," Virginia, Susquehanna, Chicago, Roanoke, Massachusetts, Des Moines, Red Dog, the Bronx: American names come from hills and streams, Indians, and white men, history, and whimsy. Life 19:47-57, July 2, 1945.

524. —— Place name patterns. Names 4:119-21, June 1956.

A further discussion of the classification of place-names, in answer to Thomas M. Pearce, Spanish place name patterns in the Southwest, ibid. 3:201-09, Dec. 1955.

525. —— Place names; In Anderson, Wallace Ludwig & Norman C. Stageberg. Introductory readings in language. 4th ed. New York, Holt, Rinehart and Winston, [c1975]. p. 154-63.

526. —— Some American place-name problems: a letter from Professor Stewart. American speech 19:289-92, Dec. 1944.

Discussion of practice of omitting County in county name, and local pronunciations of imported names, questions raised in article by De Lancey Ferguson, Two queries about American place-names, ibid. 18:309-10, Dec. 1943.

527. —— Toward a new country; In Spectorsky, Auguste C., ed. The book of the earth. New York, Appleton-Century-Crofts, 1957. p. 3-7.

From the author's Names on the land. 1945.

528. —— What is named—towns, islands, mountains, rivers, capes. California. University. Publications in English 14:223-32. 1943.

An essay on the principles of naming places, with illustrations drawn chiefly from the naming of the territory of the United States.

529. —— Where's that again? American heritage 21:116, Oct. 1970.

A few diverting examples of place-names from the author's American place-names. 1970.

530. Still, James A. Place names in the Cumberland Mountains. American speech 5:113, Dec. 1929.

Names found in the vicinity of Cumberland Gap.

531. Straubenmuller, Gustave. Meaning of geographical names. Journal of school geography 3:332-37. 1899.

"The author has written in a popular style an interesting article about the definitions of topographical words."—Price.

532. Straw, H. Thompson. Geographical gazetteers and the Board on Geographic Names. Geographical review 46:274-75, April 1956.

A statement on the work of the Board, especially the series of gazetteers which eventually will achieve world-wide coverage.

533. Survivances françaises en Amérique du Nord: carte des villes et lieux géographiques qui ont conservé des noms français. Illustration 196:389, avril 10, 1937.

534. Swanton, John Reed. Early history of the Creek Indians and their neighbors. Washington, Govt. Print. Off., 1922. 492p. (Smithsonian Institution. Bureau of American Ethnology. Bulletin no. 73)

The author contributes information about many place-names.

535. —— Indian names in historical documents. Mississippi Valley Historical Association. Proceedings 3:341-46. 1909-10.

536. Swartz, George. The Tennessee River's name. A letter to Mrs. Howard Jones from Capt. George Swartz. Arrow points 15:12, Aug. 1929.

537. Tanner, Henry Schenck. An alphabetical index to the four sheet map of the United States. Philadelphia, Rackliff and Jones, 1836. 99p.

538. —— Memoir on the recent surveys, observations, and internal improvements, in the United States, with brief notices of the new counties, towns, villages, canals, and rail roads, never before delineated. Intended to accompany his New map of the United States. Philadelphia, The Author, 1829. 108p.

Lists of new counties and of new towns for each state and territory included.

539. Tarpley, Fred. Principles of place-name studies outlined. Humanities in the South, newsletter of the Southern Humanities Conference, 32:[3-4], Fall 1970.

Texas names are used as illustrations in the list of ten broad categories of origins of place-names.

540. Taylor, Allan. Communique from C. A. P. N. New York times magazine Nov. 6, 1955, p. 34, 36.

A member of the Connoisseurs of American Place Names warns that changes in our native nomenclature can go too far.

Reply: Robert Sonkin, ibid. Nov. 20, 1955, p. 5.

541. Taylor, Balma C. Towns, poets, and mythology. In South Central Names Institute. Of Edsels and Marauders. Commerce, Tex., Names Institute Press, 1971. (Publication 1) p. 58-65.

Place-names derived from ancient Greek and Roman mythology.

542. Taylor, Isaac. Words and places; or, Etymological illustrations of history, ethnology, and geography. 4th ed. rev. and compressed. London, Macmillan, 1873. 375p.

The chapter Names of recent origin deals with American place-names. Also part of the chapter Onomatology, or, The principles of name giving.

543. Territory of Lanniwa. U.S. Congress. Congressional globe, 37th Congress, 2d session, 1861-62, p. 1678, 2495, 2912; 37th Congress, 3d session, 1862-63, p. 25, 915.

A bill to organize the Territory of Lanniwa, a territorial government in the Indian Territory, was tabled.

544. Territory of Shoshone. U.S. Congress. Congressional globe, 37th Congress, 3d session, 1862-63, p. 403.

James M. Ashley's efforts on behalf of a bill to provide a temporary government for the Territory of Shoshone apparently failed.

545. Thomas, George Francis. Legends of the land of lakes; or, History, traditions and mysteries, gleaned from years of experience among the pioneers, voyageurs and Indians; with descriptive accounts of the many natural curiosities met with from Lake Huron to the Columbia River; and the meaning and derivation of names of rivers, lakes, towns, etc. of the Northwest, by George Francis [pseud.]. Chicago, G. F. Thomas, 1884.
pt. 1. Lake Superior and surroundings. pt. 2. Wisconsin.

546. Thomas, N. O. & G. E. Harbeck, Jr. Reservoirs in the United States. Washington, Govt. Print. Off., 1956. 99p. (U.S. Geological Survey. Water supply paper 1360-A)

547. Titular tour. Atlantic monthly 154:639-40, Nov. 1934.
Curious American place-names.

548. Tolchin, Martin. More changes in place names urged as Kennedy memorials. New York times Nov. 30, 1963, p. 13.

549. Tooker, William Wallace. The adopted Algonquian term "Poquosin." American anthropologist n.s. 1:162-70, 790-91, Jan., Oct. 1899.
The derivation and meaning of the word Poquosin, low land or swamp, and its effect on place-names.

550. —— Algonquian names of some mountains and hills. Journal of American folk-lore 17:171-79, July-Sept. 1904.

551. —— The Algonquian terms Patawomeke (Potomac) and Massawomeke, with historical and ethnological notes. New York, F. P. Harper, 1901. 62p. (The Algonquian series, VIII)
From the American anthropologist 7:174-85, April 1894.

552. —— The name Susquehanna; its origin and signification. American antiquarian and oriental journal 15:286-91, Sept. 1893.

553. The names Susquehanna and Chesapeake, with historical and ethnological notes. New York, F. P. Harper, 1901. 63p. (The Algonquian series, no. 3)
First printed in the Virginia magazine of history and biography 3:86-88, July 1895.

554. Toomey, Thomas Noxon. Proper names from the Muskhogean languages. St. Louis, Hervas Laboratories, 1917. 31p. (Hervas Laboratories of American Linguistics. Bulletin 3)
Literature: p. 31.
Based on a systematic survey of all present-day names of Indian origin in the territory south of Tennessee and South Carolina and east of Texas. Includes a section on personal names.

555. Torok, Lou. On the street where I live. Saturday review 54:4, Aug. 28, 1971.
An analysis of street names in the U. S. Post Office Zip code directory listing most repeated names and some unusual ones. Also lists synonyms used for street in street names e.g., alley, path, terrace, way, etc.

556. Town names show settlers' whims, map reveals that religious and patriotic instincts were invoked by them. New York times Aug. 3, 1930, sec. 8, p. 11, col. 2-4.

557. Towns protest U.S. changes in place names. Citizens petition Board on Geographic Names in long, stubborn fights. New York herald tribune Feb. 27, 1949.

558. Townsend, Malcolm. U.S.: an index to the United States of America, historical, geographical, and political. A handbook of reference combining the "curious" in U.S. history. Boston, Lothrop, 1890. 482p.

Principal lakes: p. 49-50; Principal rivers: p. 51-52; Derivation of names of states and territories: p. 53-65; Nicknames of the states: p. 66-74; Nicknames applied to the people of the states: p. 75-81; Derivation and signification of geographical names: p. 82-130; Glossary of geographical terms: p. 131-58.

559. A Treatise on the art of naming places. Southern literary messenger 4:257-61, April 1838.

"In this article some unknown writer shows the prevailing practice in assigning names to places in America. He points out the disadvantages and proposes a better method."--Price.

560. Trumbull, James Hammond. The composition of Indian geographical names, illustrated from the Algonkin languages. Connecticut Historical Society. Collections 2:1-50. 1870.

Also issued separately, Hartford, Case, Lockwood & Brainard, 1870. 51p.

A basic essay on place-name study. This work marks the beginning of sound scholarship in place-name study.

561. —— Pembina. Magazine of American history 1:47-48, Jan. 1877.

Proposed name of a new territory in the Northwest. Name is a corruption of the Cree name Nipiminan.

562. U.S. Army. Corps of Engineers. Report of an examination of the Upper Columbia River and the territory in its vicinity in September and October, 1881, to determine its navigability, and adaptability to steamboat transportation. Made by direction of the commanding general of the Department of the Columbia, by Lieut. Thomas W. Symons. Washington, Govt. Print. Off., 1882. 135p. (U.S. 47th Congress, 1st session. Senate. Ex. doc. no. 186)

The geographical nomenclature of the Columbia River region: p. 125-33.

563. U.S. Board on Geographic Names.

History of the Board is as follows:

U.S. Board on Geographic Names.

Established by Executive order Sept. 4, 1890.

U.S. Geographic Board.

Change of name, Aug. 10, 1906.

Abolished by Executive order April 17, 1934 and functions transferred to Dept. of the Interior.

U.S. Board on Geographical Names.

Created by Departmental order no. 1010 of the Dept. of the Interior Dec. 10, 1935.

Abolished by the law of July 25, 1947.

U.S. Board on Geographic Names.

Established by law in the Dept. of the Interior July 25, 1947. Congressional action leading to the establishment of the present Board will be found in U.S. Congress. Congressional record v. 93, 80th Congress, 1st session, 1947, as follows:

H. R. 1555:
p. 711, Jan. 30—Introduced by Mr. Welch and referred to the Committee on Public Lands.
p. 5227, May 13—Committee report submitted; with amendments. Report no. 366. (see no. 570)
p. 9554-55, July 21—Laid on the table. S. 1262 passed in lieu of it. Copy of the bill included.

S. 1262:
p. 4847, May 9—Introduced by Mr. Cordon and referred to the Committee on Public Lands.
p. 5779, May 26—Committee report submitted; without amendment. Report no. 205. (see no. 573)
p. 7008, June 16—Passed the Senate.
p. 9554-55, July 21—Passed the House (in lieu of H.R. 1555). Copies of both H.R. 1555 and S. 1262 are included.
p. 9926, July 24—Examined and signed by President pro-tempore of the Senate.
p. 9982, July 24—Presented to the President of the United States.
p. 10290, July 26—President of the United States approved and signed on July 25. It became Public Law no. 242. (see no. 574)

564. —— Decisions. no. 4301- July 1943- . Washington, Dept. of the Interior.
Frequency varies: the earlier issues were mostly monthly or quarterly; July 1950-Dec. 1958, cumulative; 1959- , three issues a year, each covering the quarter period.
Following the series of annual pamphlets which ended with June 30, 1943, the Board has published a series of numbered pamphlets containing miscellaneous lists of decisions.
Title varies slightly. Contents vary: 1943-55, most of the issues included, or consisted entirely of, foreign names; 1957- , limited to the United States, with some issues including Puerto Rico and/or the Virgin Islands.
Many issues contain lists of changes from earlier decisions.
The following numbers contain material on names in the United States (for those which also contain material on Alaska and Canada, see entries under Alaska and Canada): 4301-4303 (July-Dec. 1943); 4401-4403, 4405, 4408 (Jan.-March, May, Aug. 1944); 4501-4512 (1945); 4601-4609 (Jan.-Sept. 1946); 4701-4709 (Jan.-Sept. 1947); 4801-4812 (1948); 4903, 4905-4912 (March, May-Dec. 1949); 5003, 5006 (Jan.-March, April-June 1950); 5401 (July 1950-May 1954); 5701 (May 1954-March 1957); 5901 (April 1957-Dec. 1958); 5902-5904 (1959); 6001-6003 (1960); 6101-6103 (1961); 6201-6203 (1962); 6301-6303 (1963); 6401- (1964-).

565. —— 75th anniversary, 1890-1965. Washington, Govt. Print. Off., 1965. 8p.

566. —— Sixth report. 1890 to 1932. Washington, Govt. Print. Off., 1933. 834p.
Reprinted: Detroit, Gale Research Co., 1967.
Supersedes all previous reports. Earlier reports published 1892, 1901, 1906, 1916, 1921, and Index and supp. 1924.
Many of the earlier decisions were published in National geographic magazine v. 11-18, 1900-07.
The Sixth report is supplemented by Decisions, no. 19-41, May 4, 1932-May 2, 1934; and annual issues 1934-35 to 1941-43. In July 1943 a new series of Decisions was started, numbered 4301- (see no. 564).
A brief administrative report of the Board has appeared in U.S. Dept. of the Interior. Annual report, 1934-date.
Reviews of the earlier work of the Board are in American Geographical Society. Bulletin 22:531-32, 651-56. 1890; 24:162-64, 267-69. 1892; 30:156-57. 1898; Journal of education (Boston) 67:697-98, June 18, 1908.
Review of 1933 ed.: New York times Feb. 19, 1934, p. 15, col. 3-4; Geographical review 25:150-51, Jan. 1935.

567. —— Special decision list no. 1. Commemorative domestic names approved between Sept. 1950 and Feb. 1951. Washington, 1951. 2p.

568. U.S. Bureau of American Ethnology. Circular of information regarding Indian popular names. Washington, Govt. Print. Off., 1915. 8p.
Camp names: p. 5-6.

569. U.S. Bureau of the Census. Geographic identification code scheme; United States censuses of population and housing, 1960. Washington, Govt. Print. Off., 1961. v. p.
"United States P H C (2)-1."

A system of codes to identify all the political and statistical subdivisions for which data are tabulated. Each state divided into two sections: the Geographic Identification code scheme, which lists all the areas within the state, in alphabetic sequence by county, minor civil division, and place; and an alphabetical list of place names, which lists all the places within the state, in alphabetic sequence.

570. U.S. Congress. House. Committee on Public Lands. Promoting uniformity of geographic nomenclature in the federal government. May 13, 1947 . . . Report to accompany H.R. 1555. 13p. (U.S. 80th Congress, 1st session. House. Report no. 366)

571. —— —— Committee on Public Works. Subcommittee on Flood Control. Flood control projects, authorizing name changes. No. 87-24. Hearings on H.J. Res. 417, H.R. 9243, H.R. 9320, May 9 and 10, 1962. Washington, Govt. Print. Off., 1962. 8p.
To designate the lake formed by Terminus Dam on the Kaweah River in California as Lake Kaweah; to designate the reservoir created by the John H. Kerr Dam (Virginia and North Carolina) as Buggs Island Lake; change in name of the Beardstown, Ill., Flood Control Project, to the Sid Simpson-Beardstown Flood Control Project.

572. —— —— —— Subcommittee on Rivers and Harbors. Project designation and name change legislation. Hearing. 91st Congress, 2d session. December 1, 1970. Washington, Govt. Print. Off., 1970. 59p.
Reservoirs, locks, dams, lakes. Includes the 18 bills having to do with naming of projects after important people with supporting statements of members of Congress and others.

573. —— Senate. Committee on Public Lands. Providing a central authority for standardizing names for the purpose of eliminating duplication in standardizing such names among the Federal departments. May 26 (legislative day, April 21), 1947 . . . Report to accompany S. 1262. 4p. (U.S. 80th Congress, 1st session. Senate. Report no. 205)

574. U.S. Laws, statutes, etc. An act to provide a central authority for standardizing geographic names for the purpose of eliminating duplication in standardizing such names among the Federal departments, and for other purposes. Public law 242. (United States statutes at large. 80th Congress, 1st session. 1947. v. 61, pt. 1, p. 456-57, Chapter 330)
Establishes Board on Geographic Names and abolishes Board on Geographical Names in the Dept. of the Interior created by Departmental order. Membership of the new Board includes one representative from each of the Depts. of State, War, Navy, Post Office, Interior, Agriculture, and Commerce; from the Government Printing Office; and from the Library of Congress.

575. U.S. Map Information Office. Named peaks of the continental U.S. including Alaska in order of altitude above sea level of 14,000 feet or over. Rev. ed. Washington, 1955. 3ℓ.

576. U.S. town-city names spell enchantment and surprise. Omaha world-herald April 17, 1955, p. 18G, 19G.
Based on the release by the National Geographic Society (see no. 365).

577. U.S. town urged to take the name of Distomo, destroyed by Nazis with 1,100 residents. New York times Aug. 31, 1944, p. 19, col. 5.

578. Utley, Francis Lee. From the Dinnsenchas to Proust: the folklore of place names in literature. Names 16:273-93, Sept. 1968.
Also includes numerous United States place-name folk etymologies for New England, Ohio, Oklahoma, and Wisconsin.

579. —— The linguistic component of onomastics. Names 11:145-76, Sept. 1963.
This paper was read in much abridged form at Cambridge in Aug. 1962. See the abstract in Preprints of papers for the Ninth International Congress of Linguists (Cambridge, Mass. 1962), p. 105.
"Onomastics has many components; the question at issue is whether certain of these, like history, logic and etymology, have tended to obscure and overwhelm the potential linguistic component." "American onomastics needs much more linguistic rigor than it has yet acquired." The author makes a plea for a planned national project on place-names for the whole United States, similar to that of the British Isles.

580. —— Mountain nomenclature in the United States. International Congress of Onomastic Sciences. 10th, Vienna, 1969. Proceedings 3:34-54.

581. —— A survey of American place names. International Congress of Onomastic Sciences, 9th, London, 1966. Proceedings. p. 455-63.
Also published in Onoma 14:196-204, 1969.

582. Utter, Gus. She finds fun on the map. Cleveland plain dealer April 29, 1962.
Anne Celene Solomon has made a hobby of collecting U.S. names.

583. Vlasenko-Boitsun, Anna Mariia. Ukrains kl nazvy u ZSA.
Українські назвиу у ЗСА: та інші праці з назвознавства й історично-літературного дослідження А. Власенко-Бойцун; упорядкував Іван Овечко.—Бісмарк: Вид. ювілейного комітету з нагоди 60-річчя авторки, 1977.
Added title page: Ukrainian place names in the United States.
Summary in English.

584. Vogel, Virgil J. Names that come in pairs. In North Central Names Institute. Papers, ed. by Lawrence E. Seits. Sugar Grove, Ill., Waubonsee Community College, 1980. p. 9-21.
An introduction to the author's collection of paired place-names "which have the same meaning in different languages," including pairings of English-Indian, and French-Indian.

584a. —— The origin and meaning of "Missouri." Missouri Historical Society. Bulletin 16:213-22, April 1960.
An examination of the early sources of the name of the Indians and the river.

585. Wagner, Henry Raup. The cartography of the northwest coast of America to the year 1800. Berkeley, Univ. of California Press, 1937. 2v.
Reprinted: Amsterdam, N. Israel, 1968. 2v. in 1.
List of maps: 2:273-364.
Place names still in use: 2:371-422.
Obsolete place names: 2:423-525.
Bibliography: 2:527-43.

586. —— Quivira, a mythical California city. California Historical Society quarterly 3:262-67, Oct. 1924.
Traces the appearance of the name Quivira in various locations on early maps of the northwestern part of America, far from the actual location--northeast of New Mexico—of the city Coronado called Quivira.

587. Wagner, Leopold. More about names. London, Unwin, 1893. 287p.
Popular definitions of Nicknames of American states and people, p. 23-27, and Pet names of American cities, p. 243-47.

588. Wagner, Rudolph F. & Marney H. Wagner. Stories about place names. Portland, Me., J. W. Walch, 1963. 80p.
Bibliography: p. 73.

589. Wallis, Richard P. Names on the lakes. Inland seas 14:15-25, Spring 1958.
Supplement, by Janet Coe Sanborn, ibid. 14:150-51, Summer 1958.
Great Lakes region.

589a. Walls, David S. On the naming of Appalachia. Appalachian journal 4:56-76. 1977.
Origins of the word and later use of it in various social studies.

590. Walsh, W. H. No passport needed. Service (Cities Service Company). April 1949, p. 14-15, 18.
Names of places in the United States that suggest foreign cities.

591. Walton, Ivan H. Origin of names on the Great Lakes. Names 3:239-46, Dec. 1955.
Names of the lakes and their connecting waterways, with some mention of surrounding territory.

592. Watkins, Arthur Vivian. Western place names from Virginia sources; extension of remarks of Hon. Arthur V. Watkins of Utah in the Senate of the United States. U.S. Congress. Congressional record 103:A5009-11, June 24, 1957.
Includes reprint of articles, Bedford-born Mormon bishop gave names to Idaho towns, from the Bedford (Va.) democrat, April 18, 1957, and Settlement of Bedford 80 years ago, told in bicentennial feature by Kenneth E. Crouch, from the Star Valley independent, Afton, Wyo., March 22, 1957.
Bedford, Va., and other Bedfords, and the naming of places in the intermountain area.

593. Weidhaas, Walther E. German religious influences on American place names. American German review 23:32-34, Aug.-Sept. 1957.

594. Wells, David M. Stress and spelling in certain two-element place-names in the U.S. Names 25:5-7, March 1977.

595. Wells, Helen T., Susan H. Whitely & Carrie E. Karegeannes. Origins of NASA names. Washington, Scientific and Technical Information Office, National Aeronautics and Space Administration, 1976. 227p. map. (NASA SP-4402)
NASA installations: p. 136-60.
Twelve major places, a number of which were named for prominent space scientists.

596. Wells Fargo & Company. Express directory. List of principal points in territory occupied by Wells Fargo & Co., showing the proper express offices for way-billing or making rate to, and distance from same. Also list of the Company's offices, location, and means of communication therewith. San Francisco, 1880. 150p. map.
Valuable for its listing of early western names.

597. Welty, Eudora. Place-names and our history. New York times book review May 8, 1945, p. 1.

598. Weslager, Clinton Alfred. The Delaware Indians, a history. New Brunswick, N.J., Rutgers Univ. Press, [c1972]. xix, 546p. map.
Some attention, especially in Chapter 2: The homeland of the Delawares, p. 31-49, to place-names of Indian origin attributable to the Delawares and surviving in Delaware, Pennsylvania, Ohio, Indiana, Missouri, Kansas, and Oklahoma.

599. West, Robert C. The term "bayou" in the United States; a study in the geography of place names. Association of American Geographers. Annals 44:63-74, March 1954.
Abstract in its Annals 43:197-98, June 1953.

600. Wexler, Mark. Naming (and misnaming) of America: from Buffalo Creek and Cape Cod to Goose Lake and Baldy Mountain, wildlife has had a lot to do with the nation's nomenclature. National wildlife 16:13-16, Aug.-Sept. 1978.
Reprinted: U.S. Dept. of the Interior, Geological Survey. Washington, Govt. Print. Off., 1979. 11p.

601. What's in a name? American magazine 144:82, Nov. 1947; 144:80, Dec. 1947; 145:130, Jan. 1948; 145:132, Feb. 1948; 145:128, March 1948; 145:65, April 1948.

602. What's in a name? Bermudian 33:19, Nov. 1962.
Popular article on meaning of names of the states.

603. What's in a name? Nation 108:315, March 1, 1919.
A popular article about some of the freakish names in the United States.

604. What's in a name? Omaha world-herald Nov. 3, 1958, p. 8, col. 4.
Lists a few names of places that make interesting combinations when followed by their state abbreviations: High, Mass.; Bless, Me.; Pigs, Penn.

605. What's in a name? Some doubt as U.S. changes 436 for maps. New York times July 10, 1960, p. 44.
Brief report on the standardization of 436 place-names throughout the country by the Dept. of the Interior.

606. What's in a name? Worry! Outlook 134:449, July 25, 1923.
A brief article on the troubles of the post office with the duplication of place-names.

607. Whitbeck, Ray Hughes. Geographic names in the United States and the stories they tell. National geographic magazine 16:100-04, March 1905.

608. —— The meaning of the names of places. Independent 72:444-46, Feb. 29, 1912.
Historical effects on place-names in the United States.

609. —— Regional peculiarities in place names. American Geographical Society. Bulletin 43:273-81, April 1911.
"A study of the place-names of New England, New York, New Jersey, Pennsylvania, Virginia and the mountains of Kentucky and Tennessee and their significance, historical, etc."—Griffin.

610. White, Eliot. Sonorous names of states destroyed by abbreviations; our habit of saving time often takes beauty and romance from historical titles. New York times Aug. 24, 1930, sec. 3, p. 2, col. 3-4.

611. White, William. Walt Whitman, "Western nicknames": an unpublished note. American speech 36:296-98, Dec. 1961.
Names for people of a state, as Buckeye.

612. Whitney, Josiah Dwight. Names and places; studies in geographical and topographical nomenclature. Cambridge, Mass., Univ. Press, 1888. 239p.
Contents: Appalachian and Cordilleran. Oregon and Pend' Oreilles. Topographical nomenclature.

613. Why map makers go mad. Antiquarian bookman 20:1343, Oct. 28, 1957.
Name changes and some origins.

614. Wilkins, Ernest Hatch. Arcadia in America. American Philosophical Society. Proceedings 101:4-30, Feb. 15, 1957.
A well-documented study tracing the use of the name Arcadia and all its various spellings from earliest maps and journals to place-names in the United States, Canada, and South America today. All derive from the name of a novel, Arcadia, by Jacopo Sannazzaro, written ca. 1485.

615. Wilson, Herbert M. A dictionary of topographic forms. American Geographic Society of New York. Bulletin 32:32-41, July 1900.
A list of definitions intended to include all those terms employed popularly or technically in the United States to designate the component parts of the surface of the earth.

616. Wilson, P. W. Far-gathered names of our cities; the world's geography and history have contributed to the stories they tell. New York times magazine April 9, 1933, p. 18.

617. Wolk, Allan. The naming of America: how continents, countries, states, counties, cities, towns, villages, hamlets, & post offices came by their names. Nashville, Tenn., Thomas Nelson, c1977. 192p.
Popular, highly selective listing by categories: e.g., classical, people's, inspired, or lighthearted names.
Review: Kelsie B. Harder, Names 27:149-50, June 1979.

618. Wolle, Muriel Vincent Sibell. The bonanza trail, ghost towns and mining camps of the West. Bloomington, Indiana Univ. Press, 1953. 510p.

619. —— From "Sailors' Diggings" to "Miners' Delight." (How mining towns are named) Western folklore 13:40-46, Jan. 1954.

620. Wraight, A. J. Field work in the U.S. C. and G. S. Names 2:153-62, Sept. 1954.
How the Coast and Geodetic Survey carries out its field work on geographic names.

621. Wrenn, C. L. The name Bristol. Names 5:65-70, June 1957.
A study of the English origin of the name.

622. Wright, John Kirtland. The study of place names, recent work and some possibilities. Geographical review 19:140-44, Jan. 1929.
Most American studies have been of the accumulative or collective type rather than the ecological in which "investigation is made into the nature of the geographical nomenclature in the large and more especially in its relation to the environment, past and present, physical and human."

623. The Wrong state. New York times Jan. 13, 1940, p. 14, col. 4; Jan. 17, p. 20, col. 4.
Arkansas City, Kan., and other state names used for cities.

624. You name it! Home life Jan. 1955, p. 12-13.
Popular article on names in the United States.

625. Yount, W. H. Origin of the name Ozark Mountains. Missouri historical review 20:587-88, July 1926.
A brief article which also appeared in the Barnard bulletin March 18, 1926, on the derivation of the name.

626. Zelinsky, Wilbur. Classical town names in the United States: the historical geography of an American idea. Geographical review 57:463-95, Oct. 1967.
Traces the spread of classical place-names geographically and chronologically and relates it to American culture patterns.

627. —— Generic terms in the place-names of the northeastern United States: an approach to the demarcation of culture areas. Association of American Geographers. Annals 44:288-89, Sept. 1954.
Abstract.

628. —— Some problems in the distribution of generic terms in the place-names of the northeastern United States. Association of American Geographers. Annals 45:319-49, Dec. 1955.

GAZETTEERS

629. Alcedo, Antonio de. Diccionario geográfico-histórico de las Indias Occidentales ó América: es á saber: de los reynos del Perú, Nueva España, Tierra Firme, Chile, y Nuevo reyno de Granada. Madrid, En la impr. de B. Cano, 1786-89. 5v.

630. —— The geographical and historical dictionary of America and the West Indies. Containing an entire translation of the Spanish work of Colonel Don Antonio de Alcedo, with large additions and compilations from modern voyages and travels, and from original and authentic information. By G. A. Thompson. London, Printed for J. Carpenter, 1812-15. 5v.
Atlas to Thompson's Alcedo. London, Printed by G. Smeeton, 1816.
Descriptions of Jamaica, Newtown and Flushing, N.Y. and others are strangely reminiscent of Jedidiah Morse, The American gazetteer (see no. 653).

631. Allen, William Frederick. Gazetteer of railway stations in the United States and the Dominion of Canada. Designating telegraph, express, post, and money-order offices, with the population. Also, a list of the counties and county towns of the several states, with the date at which the several courts are held, together with much other valuable statistical information. Comp. from information obtained from official sources. Philadelphia, National Railway Publication Co., 1874. 412p.

632. The American gazetteer. Containing a distinct account of all the parts of the New World: their situation, climate, soil, produce, former and present condition; commodities, manufactures, and commerce. Together with an accurate account of the cities, towns, ports, bays, rivers, lakes, mountains, passes and fortifications. London, Printed for A. Millar, 1762. 3v.
Translation published: Il Gazzettiere americano. Livorno, M. Coltellini, 1763. 3v.

633. Baldwin, Thomas & J. Thomas. A new and complete gazetteer of the United States; giving a full and comprehensive review of the present condition, industry, and resources of the American confederacy. Philadelphia, Lippincott, Grambo & Co., 1854. 1364p.

634. Bradstreet, J. M. & Son. Gazetteer of the manufactures and manufacturing towns of the United States, containing a full and comprehensive review of the extent and condition of the manufacturing interests and resources of the United States, including a large amount of valuable geographical, geological, topographical, historical and statistical information, carefully comp. from recent reliable and original sources to the present date. New York, J. M. Bradstreet & Son, 1866. 172p.

635. Chapin, William. A complete reference gazetteer of the United States of North America; containing a general view of the United States, and of each state and territory, and a notice of the various canals, railroads and internal improvements. New York, T. & E. H. Ensign, 1843. 371p.
Earlier editions published 1838, 1839, 1840, 1841.

636. Colange, Leo de. The national gazetteer; a geographical dictionary of the United States, comp. from the latest official authorities and original sources. Cincinnati, J. C. Yorston & Co.; Philadelphia, G. Barrie, 1884. 1125p.
Also published London, Hamilton, Adams & Co. 1884.

637. Darby, William & Theodore Dwight. A new gazetteer of the United States of America, including geographical, historical, political, and statistical information; with the population of 1830. 2d ed. rev. Hartford, E. Hopkins, 1834. 608p.
1st ed. 1833. 630p. The 2d ed. reprinted 1835.

638. Davenport, Bishop. A history and new gazetteer, or geographical dictionary, of North America and the West Indies. Comp. from the most recent and authentic sources. A new and much improved ed. New York, S. W. Benedict & Co., 1842. 592p.
Earlier editions published in Baltimore, Philadelphia and Providence, 1832, 1833, 1835, 1836, 1838 under title A new gazetteer.

639. —— A pocket gazetteer, or Traveller's guide through North America and the West Indies; containing a description of all the states, territories, counties, cities, towns, villages, seas, bays, harbors, islands, capes, railroads, canals, &c. connected with North America, and the West Indies, to which is added a large amount of statistical information, relating to the population, revenue, debt, and various institutions of the United States. Comp. from the most recent and authentic sources. Baltimore, Plaskitt & Co., 1833. 468p.
Also published in Trenton, N.J.
Other editions published 1834, 1838.

640. Disturnell, John. Alphabetical list of post offices and postmasters in the United States, with a supplement containing the names of new post offices, counties and county seats and tables of distances from Washington, D. C. together with rates of postage, money-order offices, etc.; also a list of post offices in the Dominion of Canada. Rev. & cor. Philadelphia, W. B. Zieber, 1872. xxii, 259p.
Editions published 1863, 1865, 1866, and 1867.

641. Fanning's illustrated gazetteer of the United States, with the population and other statistics from the census of 1850. Illus. with seals and thirty-one state maps in counties and fourteen maps of cities. New York, Phelps, Fanning & Co., 1853. 400p.

642. Fisher, Richard Swainson. A new and complete statistical gazetteer of the United States of America, founded on and comp. from official federal and state returns, and the census of 1850. New York, J. H. Colton & Co., 1855. 960p.
Also published 1852, 1853.

643. Gannett, Henry. A dictionary of altitudes in the United States. 4th ed. Washington, Govt. Print. Off., 1906. 1072p. (U.S. Geological Survey. Bulletin no. 274) (Subject series F, Geography 47)
Issued also as House doc. no. 207, 59th Cong., 1st sess.
1st ed. 1884. 325p. (Bulletin no. 5); 2d ed. 1891. 393p. (Bulletin no. 76); 3d ed. 1899. 775p. (Bulletin no. 160)
Arranged by states, except 2d ed. which is in a single alphabetic arrangement.
Included for its gazetteer value.

644. —— The mountains of the United States. Washington, Map Information Office, Board of Surveys and Maps, 1928? 37p.

645. A Gazetteer: containing a general view of the United States and the several states and territories; with an accurate account of the internal improvements throughout the Union; also, a table of the counties, cities, towns, villages, &c. in the same; together with a table of the rivers, exhibiting their length and termination, to which is added a table of all the post offices in the United States, and their nett [sic] proceeds in 1841. The whole compiled from public documents and other popular works. Akron, Ohio, Manning & Darby, 1843. 409p.

646. Haskel, Daniel & J. Calvin Smith. A complete descriptive and statistical gazetteer of the United States of America with an abstract of the census and statistics for 1840, exhibiting a complete view of the agricultural, commercial, manufacturing, and literary condition and resources of the country. New York, Sherman & Smith, 1850. 770p.
Also published 1843, 1844, 1845.

647. —— Vollständiges Orts-Lexikon der Vereinigten Staaten von Nordamerika. Nach amtlichen und zuverlässigen Quellen. Hildburghausen, Druck und Verlag des Bibliographischen Instituts in Hildburghausen, 1852. 1108p.
"Based on the 1845 ed. of the above, with new material added to bring the work down to the year 1850."--L.C. card.

648. Hayward, John. A gazetteer of the United States of America to which are added valuable statistical tables, and a map of the United States. Hartford, Case, Tiffany, & Co., 1853. 861p.

649. Heck, Lewis. The problem of a national gazetteer. Names 1:233-38, Dec. 1953.

650. Logan's post-office, census, express, telegraph, railroad and river directory of the entire West & South, containing the names of all post-offices with a supplement complete to June, 1875. St. Louis, N. Orleans, Logan Pub. Co., 1875. 100, 30p.

651. Mitchell, Samuel Augustus. An accompaniment to Mitchell's reference and distance map of the United States: containing an index of the various counties, districts, parishes, townships, towns, etc., and an index of the rivers; together with a geographical description of every state and territory in the Union; also an accurate synopsis of the population in the year 1840, according to the sixth census, and a synopsis of the new postage law. Philadelphia, S. A. Mitchell, 1845. 302, 208p.
Also published 1834, 1835, 1836, 1839, 1840.

652. Morse, Jedidiah. An abridgement of the American gazetteer. Exhibiting, in alphabetical order, a compendious account of the states, provinces, counties, cities, rivers, bays, harbours on the American continent, and its appendant islands; particularly the West Indies. To which is annexed an accurate table of all the post-offices in the United States. Pub. according to act of Congress. Printed at Boston, by Thomas & Andrews. Sold by them, by E. Larkin, and other booksellers, in Boston; by I. Thomas, Worcester; by Thomas, Andrews & Penmiman, Albany; and by Thomas, Andrews & Butler, Baltimore, June 1978. 388p.
Also published in London, 1798.

653. —— The American gazetteer, exhibiting a full account of the civil divisions, rivers, harbors, Indian tribes, &c. of the American continent: also of the West-India and other appendant islands: with a particular description of Louisiana. Comp. from the best authorities. Illus. with maps, and accompanied by a new and elegant general atlas of the world. 3d ed. rev. and cor. Boston, Thomas & Andrews, 1810. 600p.
1st ed. Boston, 1797; 2d ed. Boston, 1798, London, 1798, Charleston, 1804.
The decision to compile and publish this was reached in 1786 while Morse was traveling for the purpose of collecting material for his American geography. The gazetteer was delayed by the work of revising the geography. Capt. Thomas Hutchins, Geographer General of the United States, had started a similar project, but upon learning of Morse's intention turned over to him all of his material. Morse said also, "After all it is but proper here to observe, that a very considerable part of the matter of this volume has been selected and alphabetically arranged, under the proper heads, from The American universal geography." cf. Preface, London ed. 1798, dated Charleston, June 1, 1797.
cf. also note under Joseph Scott, The United States gazetteer, no. 659.

654. —— & Richard C. Morse. The traveller's guide; or, Pocket gazetteer of the United States; extracted from the latest ed. of Morse's Universal gazetteer. With an appendix. 2d ed. enl., rev., and cor. New Haven, S. Wadsworth, 1826. 336p.
1st ed. New Haven, N. Whiting, 1823. 323p.
Review: United States literary gazette 4:305-06, July 1826.

655. The North-American and the West-Indian gazetteer. Containing an authentic description of the colonies and islands in that part of the globe, shewing their situation, soil, produce, and trade; with their former and present condition. Also an exact account of the cities, towns, harbours, ports, bays, rivers, lakes, mountains, number of inhabitants, &c. Illus. with maps. 2d ed. London, G. Robinson, 1778. 218p.
1st ed. London, G. Robinson, 1776. 220p.

656. Rand McNally geographical handbook. Chicago, Rand McNally, 1942. 128p.
On cover: A keyed index of the United States. All counties, all cities and towns of over 100 population.
Also published 1932.

657. Rowell, George P. & Co. Geo. P. Rowell & Co's gazetteer, containing a statement of the industries, characteristics, population and location of all towns in the United States and British America, in which newspapers are published. New York, G. P. Rowell & Co., 1873. 243p.

658. Scott, Joseph. A geographical dictionary; of the United States of North America. Containing a general description of each state. With a succinct account of Indiana, Michigan, and upper and lower Louisiana territories. Philadelphia, Printed by Archibald Bartram, for Jacob Johnson, & Co., 1805. 584p.

659. —— The United States gazetteer: containing an authentic description of the several states. Their situation, extent, boundaries, soil, produce, climate, population,

trade and manufactures. Together with the extent, boundaries and population of their respective counties. Illus. with nineteen maps. Philadelphia, Printed by F. & R. Bailey, 1795. 292p.

Although said to be the first gazetteer of the United States, Jedidiah Morse, in the Preface to his The American gazetteer, dated Charleston, June 1, 1797, says, "From this work [The American universal geography, by Morse], Mr. Scott, author of the Gazetteer of the United States, derived no small part of the information contained in his book, though he has not been candid enough to acknowledge it in his preface."—p. v, London ed. 1798.

660. Smith, Charles. The American gazetteer; or, Geographical companion. New York, Printed by A. Menut for C. Smith, 1797. [53]p. map.

"Containing a general and concise account, alphabetically arranged, of the states, principal cities, post towns, ports of entry, harbours, rivers, bays, capes, lakes, &c. of the American union."

661. Steinwehr, Adolph Wilhelm August Friedrich von. The centennial gazetteer of the United States. A geographical and statistical encyclopaedia of the states, territories, counties, townships etc. in the American union. Philadelphia, Cincinnati, Ziegler & McCurdy, 1873. 1016p.

Reprinted 1874.

662. U.S. Map Information Office. Principal lakes in the United States. Preliminary ed. Washington, 1929. 4p.

663. U.S. Post Office Dept. Directory of post offices. Washington, 1955-70.

Replaces U.S. official postal guide, Part 1, Domestic.

1955-56 kept up to date by loose-leaf pages; 1957-70, revised annually, kept up to date by changes in the Postal bulletin, which was published weekly.

Includes military installations with post offices. Lists post offices discontinued and names changed.

664. —— Post offices by counties. Washington, 1955-56. 2v.

Replaces the county list formerly contained in the U.S. official postal guide, Part 1. Was to have been revised and reissued annually as of July 1, but only two issues were published.

665. —— Street directory of the principal cities of the United States, embracing letter carrier offices established to April 30, 1908. Rev. in the Division of Dead Letters under the direction of P. V. De Graw, Fourth Assistant Postmaster-General. 5th ed. Washington, Govt. Print. Off., 1908. 904p.

1st ed. 1881; 2d ed. 1884; 3d ed. 1891; 4th ed. 1894.

Reprinted: Detroit, Gale Research Co., 1973.

Review: G. Thomas Fairclough, Names 24:211-12, June 1976.

666. —— United States official postal guide. Washington, U.S. Govt. Print. Off., 1874-1954.

Various official and unofficial editions were published, 1800-1873.

Includes list of post offices, and shows changes in names made by the Department over the years.

667. —— Zip code directory. Washington, [Govt. Print. Off., 1963-64]. 52v. (POD publication SD1-SD52)

A separate volume for each state plus one for Washington, D.C., and one for Puerto Rico and the Virgin Islands.

668. United States Postal Service. Directory of post offices (with zip codes). Washington, 1970-1978.
Published by U.S. Post Office Dept. 1955-1970.
Included in National zip code and post office directory. 1979- .

669. —— National zip code and post office directory. 1979- . Washington, Govt. Print. Off. (Publication 65)
Supersedes the National zip code directory published by the U.S. Post Office Dept. 1965-1968, and by the United States Postal Service 1969-1978, and the Directory of post offices published by the U.S. Post Office Dept. 1955-1970, and by the United States Postal Service 1970-1978.

670. Upham, Warren. Altitudes between Lake Superior and Rocky Mountains. Washington, Govt. Print. Off., 1891. 229p. (U.S. Geological Survey, Bulletin no. 72)
By places along railway lines, including supplementary lists, with indexes for Hills and mountains; Lakes; and Towns and stations.

671. White, Robert C. National gazetteers of the United States. Names 18:9-19, March 1970.
A review of those published, and the future outlook.

672. Worcester, Joseph Emerson. A gazetteer of the United States, abstracted from the Universal gazetteer of the author; with enlargement of the principal articles. Andover, Mass., Printed for the author by Flagg & Gould, 1818. 358p.

THE NAME UNITED STATES

673. Allers, Dale. What's in a name? Letter. Américas 16:44, Dec. 1964.
Questions American as nationality label for United States citizens.
Responses to this letter include the following:
Nubla, Roberto. What's in a name? Letter. Américas 17:48, March 1965.
Proposes "Ustatsian" as alternative to American.
Walton, L. L. What's in a name? Letter. Américas 17:48, March 1965.
Defends use of American.
Wood, Lois. What's in a name? Letter. Américas 17:48, March 1965.
Proposes Yankee or Usian as alternative to American.

674. American names. Democratic review 11:475-81, Nov. 1842.
Primarily concerned with the name United States, which should be changed because of its ambiguous nature.

675. Barnes, Homer Francis. Charles Fenno Hoffman. New York, Columbia Univ. Press, 1930. 361p. (Columbia University studies in English and comparative literature)
p. 160-65 describe the controversy over the name Alleghania proposed by a committee of the New York Historical Society, of which Hoffman was a member.

676. Boggs, Ralph Steele. The baffling designation "American." American speech 24:312-13, Dec. 1949.
Use for residents of the United States.

677. Burnett, Edmund C. The name "United States of America." American historical review 31:79-81, Oct. 1925.
"Some early instances of the use of the name, showing how it gradually became the official name."—American speech.

678. Douglass, C. H. J. Our national name--what does it mean? New Englander 40:629-34, Sept. 1881.
History and meaning of the name United States of America.

679. Dunlap, Leslie Whittaker. American historical societies, 1790-1860. Madison, Wis., Privately printed, 1944. 238p.
On p. 117-19 the author tells of the proposal made in 1845 by the New York Historical Society to change the national name of the country from America to Allegania.

680. Fitzpatrick, John C. The "United States of America" and the "U.S.A." Daughters of the American Revolution magazine 54:17-20, Jan. 1920.
Also in his The spirit of the Revolution (Boston, Houghton Mifflin, 1924), p. 228-36.
Congress decided that kegs of gunpowder be inspected and marked U.S.A. if acceptable, 1776.

681. Heslin, James J. The Republic of Allegania, an adventure of the New York Historical Society. New York Historical Society. Quarterly 51:24-44, Jan. 1967.
An early 19th-century proposal for a change in the name of the United States.

682. Irving, Washington. National nomenclature, by Geoffrey Crayon. Knickerbocker 14:158-62, 203, Aug. 1839.
Reprinted in his Biographies and miscellanies, ed. by Pierre M. Irving. New York, Putnam, 1866. p. 522-30.
Includes remarks on a national name for the United States.

683. Jones, Joseph. Hail Fredonia! American speech 9:12-17, Feb. 1934; 11:187, April 1936.
The lack of a suitable name for the United States and the attempt to introduce Fredonia about 1804-12. Takes Samuel Latham Mitchill's article Generic names. . ., which is reprinted here in full, too seriously.

684. Maclellan, W. E. America. Dalhousie review 7:523-24, Jan. 1928.
Application of the title Americans to the people of the United States justified.

685. Mitchill, Samuel Latham. An address to the Fredes, or people of the United States on the 28th anniversary of their independence. New York, G. & R. Waite, 1804. 8p.
Poem in which author asserts "that Fredonia is a cant phrase which certain 'small scribblers or prosaic poets' would have the nation adopt." Courtney Robert Hall, A scientist in the early republic (New York, Columbia Univ. Press, 1934), p. 116.

686. —— Generic names for the country and people of the United States. Monthly anthology 1:342-45, June 1804.
Originally published in the New York daily advertiser.
Reprinted in Monthly magazine, or British register 23:242-44, April 1807. Submitted by John Coakley Lettsom.
Reprinted also in article by Joseph Jones, Hail Fredonia. American speech 9:12-17, Feb. 1934.
Suggests the use of Fredonia; perhaps an attempt at humor in the eyes of the editor of the Monthly anthology.

687. Moore, George H. The name "Columbia." Massachusetts Historical Society. Proceedings 2d ser. 2:159-65, Dec. 1885.
Traces the use of the name Columbia for America, both in England and in the United States.

688. New York Historical Society. Report of the Committee on a National Name; In its Proceedings 1845:18-22, 115-24, 209-29.

Also published separately and sent to historical societies and prominent individuals.

Includes resolution calling for the selection of a specific name, and that Allegania be recommended as the best. The society voted in the negative. The committee included David Dudley Field, Henry Rowe Schoolcraft, and Charles Fenno Hoffman.

Massachusetts Historical Society. Proceedings 2:310-11, 315-17, April-May 1845, notes receipt of the New York report, with reply that there is no reason for discarding United States of America.

689. Nörrenberg, Constantin. Aussprache über America--U.S. America. Petermanns Mitteilungen aus Justus Perthes' geographischer Anstalt 63:306-09, Oct. 1917.

690. Proposal of a general name for the United States. Monthly anthology 1:217-18, March 1804.

Signed: "A National man."

Discussion of Jedidiah Morse's suggestion (in The American gazetteer) that the name be Fredonia.

691. Read, Allen Walker. Is the name United States singular or plural? Names 22:129-36, Sept. 1974.

692. Stovall, Benjamin F. Now we U-S-ians. Literary digest 124:2, Nov. 13, 1937.

"Suggests 'Uessian' (U-S-ian) instead of 'American' since 'American' rightly belongs to any person in North or South America."--American speech.

693. Tudor, William. Concerning a name for the United States. Monthly anthology 1:293-97, May 1804.

Letter to editor conveying Tudor's article was signed "Aconteus." Article dated Dec. 1799.

Proposes use of Columbia.

694. Tyler, Moses Coit. The historic name of our country. American Historical Association. Papers 3:176-78. 1889.

Abstract.

America should be the name, not the United States of America.

695. Willson, Beckles. Must we be Americans. University magazine 13:59-67, Feb. 1914.

Since the terms America and American have been appropriated by the United States, they should be restricted to that nation and not applied in a broader sense to include Canadians and South Americans.

696. Zabriskie, George A. Why we are called Americans. New York Historical Society. Quarterly bulletin 27:79-86, Oct. 1943.

Includes also a note on a national name, as Republic of Washington, Columbia, or Allegania.

ALABAMA

697. Adams, John D. Coosa County; present day place names showing aboriginal influence. Arrow points 2:73-75, April 1921.

698. Alabama county names. Magazine of history 25:54-59, Aug. 1917.

699. Bibb, J. Porter. Montgomery County; present day place names showing aboriginal influence. Arrow points 2:14-17, Jan. 1921.

700. Bonner, Jessie Lee. Where Oak Hill got its name. Arrow points 12:23, March 1926.
Legendary account of the place-name.

701. Brame, J. Y. Lowndes County; present day place names showing aboriginal influence. Arrow points 2:55-56, March 1921.

702. Brannon, Peter A. Aboriginal towns in Alabama; showing locations by present county boundary lines. Arrow points 4:26-28, Feb. 1922.

703. —— Alabama postoffice and stream names, 1922; a study of the etymology of the names of the state's present postoffices and streams. Arrow points 6:3-7, Jan. 1923.
Detailed account of locations having aboriginal significance followed by a list giving the modern post offices in their present spellings and a parallel list giving their aboriginal nationalities. Further list gives rivers and 25 of the largest streams still called by their native names.

704. —— Barbour County. Arrow points 5:32-37, Aug. 1922.
Present day place-names showing aboriginal influence.

705. —— Certain place names in Choctaw County. Arrow points 11:8-12, July 1925.

706. —— Clay County; present day place names showing aboriginal influence. Arrow points 3:56-58, Oct. 1921; 4:96-98, May 1922.

707. —— County names in Alabama history. Arrow points 6:33-34, Jan. 1923.

708. —— Elmore County; present day place names suggesting aboriginal influence. Arrow points 4:46-51, March 1922.

709. —— Jackson County place-names; a study of the names, suggesting the aboriginal history of the county. Arrow points 13:9-11, Sept. 1928.

710. —— Macon County; present day place names suggesting aboriginal influence. Arrow points 5:5-9, July 1922.

711. —— Monroe County; some sketches of its places. Arrow points 8:39-42, March 1924.

712. —— The name "Alabama." Arrow points 10:19-21, Jan. 1925.
Through etymological and historical analysis of the state name, discredits the traditional and poetic translation, "Here we rest."

713. —— Name places affected by the Indian war of 1813-14. Alabama historical quarterly 13:132-35. 1951.

714. —— Pike County; present day place names suggesting aboriginal influence. Arrow points 3:18-19, Aug. 1921.

715. —— Place names in Clarke County. Arrow points 6:103-07, June 1923.

716. —— Russell County place names; present day names perpetuating aboriginal and early historic points in the county. Alabama historical quarterly 21:96-103. 1959.

Embodies in a measure a paper very similar and published in Arrow points v. 1, Oct. 5, 1920. Apparently a reprint of the article as published in Arrow points 8:5-12, Jan. 1924.

On p. 104 of Alabama historical quarterly v. 21, 1959: Origin of county name. This is about Gilbert Christian Russell, reprinted from Heitman, Historical register, U.S. Army, v. 1, p. 853.

717. —— Tallapoosa County; present day place names suggesting aboriginal influence. Arrow points 3:46-49, Sept. 1921; 5:104-08, Dec. 1922.

718. Brown, Virginia Pounds & Jane Porter Nabers. The origin of certain place names in Jefferson County, Alabama. Alabama review 5:177-202, July 1952.

719. Chase, Carroll & Richard McP. Cabeen. The first hundred years of United States territorial postmarks, 1787-1887. Alabama Territory. American philatelist 55:78-82, Nov. 1941.

Includes list of post offices, 1817-19, with notes on origin of some names.

720. —— The first hundred years of United States territorial postmarks, 1787-1887. Mississippi Territory. American philatelist 55:220-26, Jan. 1942.

Includes list of post offices, 1803-17, with notes on some names.

721. Crenshaw, Mrs. William. Origins of Butler County place names. Butler County Historical Society. Publications 2:1-13, March 1966; 2:1-5, June 1966.

722. Danton, Emily Miller. Alabama place names, a selection. Alabama review 9:68-69, Jan. 1956.

Includes towns and communities, rivers and creeks. Omits Indian names.

723. Edwards, Thomas H. Lee County; present day place names showing aboriginal influence. Arrow points 2:112-14, June 1921.

724. Elmore, Frank H. Baldwin County; present day place names showing aboriginal influence. Arrow points 4:13-15, Jan. 1922.

725. Foscue, Virginia Oden. The place names of Sumter County, Alabama. University, Ala., Univ. of Alabama Press, c1978. 75p. map. (American Dialect Society. Publication no. 65)

Sources: p. [68]-75.

726. —— Sumter County place-names: a selection. Alabama review 13:52-67, Jan. 1960.

Abstracted from M.A. thesis, Univ. of Alabama, Dept. of English. Aug. 1959.

727. Gatschet, Albert Samuel. Towns and villages of the Creek Confederacy in the XVIII. and XIX. centuries. Alabama History Commission. Report 1:386-415. 1900.

Reprinted separately.

Rev. and largely supplemented from the list in his A Creek migration legend (Philadelphia, 1884), 1:120-50.

728. Halbert, Henry Sale. Choctaw Indian names in Alabama and Mississippi. Alabama Historical Society. Transactions 3:64-77. 1898-99.

729. Harris, W. Stuart. Dead towns of Alabama. University, Ala., Univ. of Alabama Press, c1977. 165p.

Bibliography: p. 135-44.

A study of three classes of former towns, Indian villages, fort sites, and colonial, territorial, and state towns, of which little or no trace remains.
Review: Kelsie B. Harder, Names 26:118-21, March 1978; Hugh C. Bailey, Alabama review 31:230, July 1978.

730. Hoppen, Harry E. Randolph County; present day place names showing aboriginal influence. Arrow points 2:86-87, May 1921.

731. Jenkins, William H. Some Alabama "dead" towns. Alabama review 12:281-85, Oct. 1959.

732. Kay, Carol McGinnis & Donald Kay. A preliminary survey of British-received place names in Alabama. Alabama review 28:282-85, Oct. 1975.
British names are second to those of Indian origin.

733. Lastelic, Joe. Unnamed lake on the Chattahoochee. Kansas City times Nov. 21, 1966, p. 16.
Body of water on the Chattahoochee River behind the Walter F. George Dam in Alabama and Georgia.

734. McNeel, Allen. Escamba County; present day place names showing aboriginal influence. Arrow points 2:32-35, Feb. 1921.

735. Maxwell, Thomas. Tuskaloosa, the origin of its name, its history, etc. A paper read before the Alabama Historical Society, July 1, 1876. Tuskaloosa, Office of the Tuskaloosa gazette, 1876. 86p.

736. Meaning of the Creek Indian name Eufaula. Chronicles of Oklahoma 40:310-11, Autumn 1962.
A city in Alabama and Oklahoma.

737. Names in Alabama. New York times March 16, 1929, p. 18, col. 5.
Notes beauty in Alabama river names.

738. Nelson, Mildred N. Folk etymology of Alabama place-names. Southern folklore quarterly 14:193-214, Dec. 1950.

739. Owen, Thomas McAdory. Alabama: state name, boundaries, capitol, executive mansion, seal, flag, holidays, song and flower. Montgomery, Brown Print. Co., 1915. 11p. (Alabama. Archives and History Dept. O.S.R. separate no. 1)
Reprinted: Alabama. Dept. of Archives and History. Alabama official and statistical register 1915:7-15.

740. —— Jefferson County; present day place names showing aboriginal influence. Arrow points 3:10-11, July 1921.

741. Read, William Alexander. Indian place-names in Alabama. Baton Rouge, Louisiana State Univ. Press, 1937. 84p. (Louisiana State University studies, no. 29)
Bibliography: p. 80-84.
Supplemented in American speech 13:79-80, Feb. 1938.
"Deals with the origin and meaning of Indian geographical names in Alabama. It does not include a detailed history either of aboriginal place-names in Alabama or of the tribes that inhabited the state. Its primary aim is linguistic."—Review by J. R. Swanton, American speech 12:212-15, Oct. 1937.

742. —— Ten Alabama place names. American speech 13:79-80, Feb. 1938.

743. Rich, John S. The place-names of Greene and Tuscaloosa counties, Alabama. 660p.
Thesis (Ph.D.) Univ. of Alabama, 1979. Abstract: Dissertation abstracts international 40:4576-77A. 1980.

743a. Robertson, Ann Eliza Worcester. Some Choctaw names. Arrow points 19:15-16, Aug. 1931.

744. Scaife, Walter Bell. Was the Rio del Espiritu Santo of the Spanish geographers the Mississippi? In his America: its geographical history, 1492-1892. Baltimore, Johns Hopkins Press, 1892. p. 139-72.
An examination of maps and early writings convinced the author that "the Mississippi was not discovered by Pinedo, and that the early Spaniards did not know that river under the name Espiritu Santo; but . . . they applied this name, generally, if not exclusively, to the stream which now bears, in its different parts, the names Coosa, Alibama, and Mobile."

745. Street, O. D. Cherokee towns and villages in Alabama. Alabama History Commission. Report 1:416-21. 1900.

746. U.S. 88th Congress, 1st session. House. A bill to designate the lake formed by the Walter F. George Lock and Dam, Alabama and Georgia, as "Lake Chattahoochee." H.R. 2127. Jan. 17, 1963. Washington, 1963. 1p.
Introduced by Mr. Forrester and referred to the Committee on Public Works.

747. —— Senate. A bill to designate the lake formed by the Walter F. George Lock and Dam, Alabama and Georgia, as Lake Eufaula. S. 454. Jan. 23 (legislative day, Jan. 15), 1963. Washington, 1963. 1p.
Introduced by Mr. Hill and Mr. Sparkman and referred to the Committee on Public Works.
An identical bill was introduced in the House as follows:

U.S. 88th Congress, 1st session. House. A bill to designate the lake formed by the Walter F. George Lock and Dam, Alabama and Georgia, as Lake Eufaula. H.R. 3163. Jan. 31, 1963. Washington, 1963. 1p.
Introduced by Mr. Andrews and referred to the Committee on Public Works.

ALASKA

748. Alaska. Bureau of Vital Statistics. Community gazetteer of Alaska, including geographic coordinates and latest population figures. Issued jointly by Office of the Governor, Department of Health & Welfare, Department of Labor, Alaska Legislative Council. Juneau, Alaska, 1964. [69]p.

749. Alaska. State Geographic Board. Annual report. 1966/67- . Juneau, 1967- .

750. Alaska rites to honor Reps. Boggs and Begich. New York times Oct. 6, 1977, sec. IV, p. 16.
Mountain peaks in Chugach Mountains to honor Representatives Hale Boggs and Nick Begich who disappeared on a flight Oct. 16, 1972.

751. Alaska town's name changed by colonists. New York times May 20, 1935, p. 17, col. 2.
Palmer, Alaska, changed informally to Valley City, by a group of Minnesota colonists.

752. Alaskan and Canadian nomenclature. American Geographical Society. Bulletin 29:439-40. 1897.
The U.S. Board on Geographical Names has imposed artificial spelling on points in the Upper Yukon region in case of Indian names.

753. Baker, Marcus. Alaskan geographic names. U.S. Geological Survey. Annual report 21:487-509. 1899-1900.
Also published separately.

754. —— Geographic dictionary of Alaska. 2d ed. Prepared by James McCormick. Washington, Govt. Print. Off., 1906. 690p. (U.S. Geological Survey. Bulletin no. 299)
Issued also as House doc. no. 938. 59th Cong., 1st sess.
1st ed. 1902. Bulletin no. 187.
Includes obsolete and current names.

755. Balcom, Mary Gilmore. Ghost towns of Alaska. Chicago, Adams Press, [1965]. viii, 80p. maps.
Bibliography: p. 79.
Reprinted with additions: 1973. 87p.

756. Bergsland, Knut. Place names. In his Aleut dialects of Atka and Attu. American Philosophical Society. Transactions n.s. v. 49, pt. 3, p. 17-55. 1959. maps.

757. Bilbao, Pedro. When Spaniards sailed the north Pacific. Américas 15:13-18, Jan. 1963. map.
Historical background on place-names of Spanish origin along the British Columbian and Alaskan coasts.

758. Bockstoce, John R. & Charles F. Batchelder. A gazetteer of whalers' place-names for the Bering Strait region and the western Arctic. Names 26:258-70, Sept. 1978.
Includes obsolete and obscure names with some in Siberia.

759. Bohn, Dave. Glacier Bay, the land and the silence. San Francisco, Sierra Club, 1967. 165p., map.
Place names: p. 156-58.
Glacier Bay National Monument.

760. Bojcun, Anna M. Ukrainian place names in Alaska. In Canadian Society for the Study of Names. Onomastica. No. 51:1-6, June 1977.

761. Chase, Carroll & Richard McP. Cabeen. The first hundred years of United States territorial postmarks, 1787-1887. Alaska Territory. American philatelist 55:82-85, Nov. 1941.
Includes list of post offices, 1867-87.

762. Clark, John Drury & L. Sprague De Camp. Some Alaskan place names. American speech 15:60-61, Feb. 1940.

763. Coolidge settled dispute, decided lakes and peaks called after explorers in Alaska should stand. New York times Jan. 22, 1928, p. 19, col. 1-3.
Decision two years earlier in regard to names in Valley of Ten Thousand Smokes which overruled U.S. Geographic Board in favor of National Geographic Society.
Editorial ibid. sec. 3, p. 4, col. 5 outlines U.S. Board's rule against naming places for living persons.

764. Davidson, George. Origin of the name "Cape Nome." National geographic magazine 12:398, Nov. 1901.

Illustrates the manner in which a permanent place-name will result from a series of mistakes due to misinterpretations.

765. DeArmond, R. N. Some names around Juneau. Sitka, Sitka Print. Co., 1957. 48p.
An alphabetical list of 123 names for 142 places or geographic features in Juneau and its immediate vicinity, plus some 70 obsolete or seldom-used names mentioned in the text. Locates the place and gives origin of the name.

766. Duncan, Tom, David L. Geesin and Kathryn Jensen. Alaska place name pronunciation guide. [Fairbanks], Elmer E. Rasmuson Library, Univ. of Alaska, 1975. 29 ℓ. map. (The Elmer E. Rasmuson Library occasional papers no. 4)

767. Farquhar, Francis Peloubet. Naming Alaska's mountains, with some accounts of their ascents. American alpine journal v. 11, no. 2, p. 211-32. 1959.

768. Forbes, H. A. Gazetteer of northern Canada and parts of Alaska and Greenland. Ottawa, Geographical Bureau, 1948. 75 l.

769. Holmer, Nils Magnus. The native place names of arctic America. Names 15:182-96, Sept. 1967; 17:138-48, June 1969.
Confined to Eskimo and Aleutian toponymy, which predominates in the region. Concludes that even in the toponymy the peoples of arctic America reveal themselves as speakers of typical Amerindian languages and that Eskimo and Aleutian place-names should not be excluded when dealing with the native names of America.

770. Jacobin, Louis. Guide to Alaska and the Yukon. 11th ed. Los Angeles, Guide to Alaska Co., 1957.
The towns and villages—how they got their names: p. 51.
This same list, with slight variations, has appeared in each edition.

771. Kennedy name to city in Alaska. Kansas City times Dec. 27, 1963.
Bay City changed to John Fitzgerald Kennedy City effective Dec. 20, 1963.

772. Kiska to be known as Narukam and Attu as Atsuta. New York times June 26, 1942, p. 7, col. 2.
Japanese broadcast said renamed by Japs, after landing there June 7, 1942.

773. Kodiak not Kadiak. National geographic magazine 12:397-98, Nov. 1901.
With the reversal of a decision by the U.S. Board on Geographic Names, Kadiak became Kodiak.

774. Lake named Rose Teed by army in Alaska; engineers mapping area find one with an hour-glass figure. New York times Nov. 29, 1942, p. 32, col. 3.
On Kodiak Island.

775. Leffingwell, Ernest de Koven. The Canning River region, northern Alaska. Washington, Govt. Print. Off., 1919. 250p. map. (Geological Survey professional paper 109)
Geographic nomenclature, with alphabetical list of names: p. 87-100.

776. Little, C. H. Alaskan place names. North 16:37-43, Sept.-Oct. 1969.
Account of Russian, Spanish, and English explorations responsible for place-names.

777. Mount Isto, Alaska peak named after late engineer. Denver post Dec. 18, 1966, sec. 1.
Mountain in Brooks Range named after Reynold E. Isto of the U.S. Geological Survey.

778. The Naming of Seward in Alaska. Alaska journal 8:51, 92, Winter 1978.
Reprinted from Washington historical quarterly v. 1, April 1907.
Correspondence between the chief engineer, C. M. Anderson of the Alaska Central Railway Company, and Edmond S. Meany, who suggested Seward in place of Vituska, derived from Vitus Bering, the Dane who discovered Alaska for Russia.

779. New names on the International Boundary. Geographical journal 62:234-35, Sept. 1923.
A glacier and several peaks.

780. Orth, Donald J. Dictionary of Alaska place names. Washington, Govt. Print. Off., 1967. 1084p. (Geological Survey professional paper 567)
Selected bibliography: p. 1072-84.
"Names in current use, as well as many names formerly in use, have been assembled . . . into a new and greatly enlarged edition of the geographic names dictionary [by Marcus Baker published in 1902 and 1906]." Reports all known information concerning the origin and meaning of each name.
Review: Edward C. Ehrensperger, Names 16:190-93, June 1968; John C. Reed, Arctic 21:210-11, Sept. 1968.

781. Phillips, James Wendell. Alaska-Yukon place names. Seattle, Univ. of Washington Press, [c1973]. 149p. map.
Bibliography: p. 147-49.
A short list with origins and meanings of city, town, and a sampling of remote native (both Eskimo and Indian) village names and name sources for historical or currently significant geographical features.
Review: Robert M. Rennick, Names 22:78-80, June 1974; C. F. Stevenson, Canadian geographical journal 89:44-45, Dec. 1974; Ted C. Hinckley, Montana, the magazine of western history 24:72, Winter 1974; Claus-M. Naske, Pacific Northwest quarterly 65:149, July 1974.

782. —— Name origins: Prudhoe Bay and Duke Island. Alaska journal 4:149-52, Summer 1974.
Both named to honor an English family, the Percys of Northumberland, the bay for Captain Algernon Percy, 1st Baron of Prudhoe, and the island for Sir Hugh Percy, the Duke of Northumberland. Includes other names given by Sir John Franklin, the explorer.

783. Putnam, G. R. Geographic names in Alaska. U.S. Coast and Geodetic Survey. Annual report 1902-03:1011-16.
List of native names for localities on St. George Island, Bering Sea. Russian or Aleut origin indicated as well as meaning.

784. Ransom, Jay Ellis. Alaxsxaq—where the sea breaks its back. Alaska journal 8:199, Summer 1978.
Breaking down the Aleut word gives the literal sense "the object toward which the action of the sea is directed," i.e., Alaska means "where the sea waves break upon themselves."

785. —— Derivation of the word "Alaska." American anthropologist n.s. 42:550-51, July-Sept. 1940.
Philological study of the word in Aleut.

786. Ransome, Alfred L. & William H. Kerns. Names and definitions of regions, districts and subdistricts in Alaska (used by the Bureau of Mines in statistical and economic studies covering the mineral industry of the territory). Washington, U.S. Bureau of Mines, 1954. 91p. (U.S. Bureau of Mines. Information circular no. 7679)

787. Ray, Dorothy Jean. Eskimo place-names in Bering Strait and vicinity. Names 19:1-33, March 1971.
Eskimo names for places with English names [a list]: p. 31-33.

788. Ricks, Melvin Byron. Directory of Alaska postoffices and postmasters. Ketchikan, Alaska, Tongass Pub. Co., 1965. 72p.

789. Schorr, Alan Edward. Alaska place names. Fairbanks, Elmer E. Rasmuson Library, Univ. of Alaska, 1974. 32p. (The Elmer E. Rasmuson Library occasional papers no. 2)
Names that have been listed in the U.S. Board on Geographic Names, Decision lists, no. 6601-7301, 1966-73.

790. Sorvo, Paul J. Pedro, Livengood, and Tanana; a study of place-names near Fairbanks, Alaska. Names 18:185-90, Sept. 1970.
A comparative study of the geographic names of a small area in the central part of Alaska.

791. Stewart, George Rippey. The name Alaska. Names 4:193-204, Dec. 1956.
Presents the general outlines of the process by which Alaska has become a notable name; some details of the process remain to be filled in.

792. Sullivan, Walter. A move to change name of Mount McKinley is gaining support. New York times Oct. 14, 1975, p. 14.
Proposal to make its Indian name, Denali, meaning The Great One, official.
Letter of Marshall Ackerman opposing the change appeared, ibid. Oct. 21, p. 36.

793. Thalbitzer, William. Eskimoiske stednavne fra Alaska til Grønland set i arkâeologieno lys. Geografisk tidsskrift 35:137-55. 1932.
"Eskimo place names in Alaska and Greenland in the light of archaeology. Summary in English."--Griffin.

794. U.S. Board on Geographic Names. Decisions. Washington, Dept. of the Interior.
Alaska is included in the following Decision lists: 4301 (July-Oct. 1943); 4401-4402, 4404, 4408 (Jan.-Feb., April, Aug. 1944); 4501-4503, 4510-4512 (Jan.-March, Oct.-Dec. 1945); 4601-4609 (Jan.-Sept. 1946); 4704-4707 (April-July 1947); 4801-4812 (1948); 4903, 4905-4912 (March, May-Dec. 1949); 5003, 5006 (Jan.-June, 1950); 5401 (July 1950-May 1954); 5701 (May 1954-March 1957); 5901- (April 1957-).

795. —— Decisions on names in Alaska. June 1952. Washington, Dept. of the Interior, 1952. 16p. (Its Decision list no. 5204)
"In effect as of May 1952."

796. —— Decisions on names in Alaska, Saint Lawrence Island. March 1951. Washington, Dept. of the Interior, 1951. 25p. (Its Decision list no. 5102)
"Comprises all decisions rendered for Saint Lawrence Island, Alaska, and associated features."

797. U.S. Board on Geographic Names. American Geographical Society. Bulletin 22:326-32. 1890.
Reports formation of the Board, and announces project to prepare Alaskan name list.

798. U.S. Map Information Office. Named and best known mountain peaks in Alaska, 10,000 feet or over. Washington, 1955. 2ℓ.

799. U.S. Work Projects Administration. Pennsylvania. Geographic names in the coastal areas of Alaska. Comp. under the supervision of the Coast and Geodetic Survey by personnel of Works [sic] Projects Administration, Project OP-765-23-3-7, in the city of Philadelphia, Pa., 1939-40. Washington, 1943. 133p.

800. Wagner, Henry Raup. The cartography of the northwest coast of America to the year 1800. Berkeley, Univ. of California Press, 1937. 2v.
List of maps: 2:273-364.
Place names still in use: 2:371-422.
Obsolete place names: 2:423-525.
Bibliography: 2:527-43.

801. Ward, D. & P. Craig. Catalogue of streams, lakes and coastal areas in Alaska along routes of the proposed gas pipeline from Prudhoe Bay, Alaska to the Alaskan Canadian border, prepared by Aquatic Environments Limited. [Calgary], Canadian Arctic Gas Study Ltd.; [Anchorage], Alaska Arctic Gas Study Co., 1974- . 1v. (Biological report ser. v. 19)

802. Zeusler, F. A. Alaskan names. United States Naval Institute. Proceedings 67:1428-31, Oct. 1941.

ARIZONA

803. Arizona. Development Board. Historical markers in Arizona. Phoenix, 1958? 2v.
Information on place-names scattered throughout.

804. Barnes, William Croft. Arizona place names. Tucson, Univ. of Arizona, 1935. 503p. (Arizona. University. General bulletin, no. 2) (University of Arizona bulletin, v. 6, no. 1)
Bibliography: p. 502-03.
Review: American literature 7:489-90, Jan. 1936; Mary Abbott, A million dollars worth of fun: Will Barnes' Arizona place names. Journal of Arizona history 20:239-54, Summer 1979.

805. —— Arizona place names. Rev. and enl. by Byrd H. Granger. Illus. by Anne Merriman Peck. Tucson, Univ. of Arizona Press, 1960. 519p.
Bibliographies: p. 397-407.
This edition is expanded from the original 2900 place-names to 7200.
Review: William Bright, Journal of American folklore 75:77-78, Jan. 1962; T. M. Pearce, Names 8:99-100, June 1960.

806. —— Arizona place names. A compilation of the names of Arizona's cities, villages, and settlements, early stage and modern railroad stations, its mountains and canyons, lakes and streams, springs and desert water holes, long forgotten mining towns, military posts and camps; their origin, meaning and history. Arizona historical review 5:286-301, Jan. 1933.
Reprinted as the first part of his book, Arizona place names, 1935.

807. Barney, James M. How Apache Leap got its name. Arizona highways 11:6-7, 20-21, Aug. 1935.

808. Brandes, Ray. Frontier military posts of Arizona. Globe, Ariz., D. S. King, 1960. 94p.
Descriptions and data relating to the name, origin, and existence of military posts in Arizona. Includes a listing of temporary camps, settlers' forts, and place-names which imply military origin.

809. —— A guide to the history of the U.S. Army installations in Arizona, 1849-1886. Arizona and the West 1:42-65, Spring 1959.
Includes list and name information.

810. Brophy, Frank Cullen. In the classical tradition; Of names and places; In his Arizona sketch book. Phoenix, Arizona-Messenger Print. Co., 1952. p. 147-51, 289-96.

811. Chapman, H. H. Why the town of McNary moved. American forests and forest life 30:589-92, 626, Oct. 1924.
The town of McNary, La., was abandoned and all the inhabitants moved to Cooley, Ariz., rechristened McNary, because of the depletion of the timber stand in Louisiana.

812. DeHarport, David L. Origin of the name, Cañon del Muerto. El Palacio 67:95-97, June 1960.

813. Dellenbaugh, Frederick S. Naming the Grand Canyon. Science n.s. 77:349-50, April 7, 1933.

814. Dike, Sheldon Holland. The territorial post offices of Arizona. Albuquerque, N.M., 1958. [31]ℓ.
A listing of 648 post offices covering the period to Feb. 14, 1912. Includes dates of establishment, discontinuance, re-establishment, and name changes.

815. Dobyns, Henry F. Pioneering Christians among the perishing Indians of Tucson. Lima, Peru, Editorial Estudios Andinos, 1962. 36p.
Indian origin of the name Tucson, p. 3.

816. —— Tubac: where some enemies rotted. Arizona quarterly 19:229-32, Autumn 1963.
An English borrowing of a Hispanicized form of an original Northern Piman designation.

817. Donovan, H. George. Ghost towns and camps of Arizona. The Westerners brand book, Chicago Corral, 20:57-59, 63-64, Oct. 1963.
Lists ghost mining camps in the southern half of Arizona.

818. Feather, Adlai. Origin of the name Arizona. New Mexico historical review 39:89-101, April 1964.

819. Fontana, Bernard L. Arizona place names. Arizona highways 36:2-5, March 1960.

820. Forrest, Earle Robert. Missions and pueblos of the old Southwest. Cleveland, Arthur H. Clark Co., 1929. 2v.
Spanish mission names in Arizona and New Mexico, with their English equivalents, 1:333-35.

821. Fox, Theron. Arizona treasure hunters ghost town guide. Includes 1881 fold-in map of Arizona, with glossary of over 1200 place names, 1868 map of Arizona. San Jose, Calif., 1964? 24p.

822. Freeman, Merrill P. "Arizona," its derivation and origin. Tucson, 1913. 11p.

823. Goldwyn is honored; Arizona governor names village for film producer. New York times Nov. 15, 1939, p. 18, col. 3.
Goldwyn, Ariz., will be a motion-picture set.

824. Granger, Byrd Howell. Early Mormon place names in Arizona. Western folklore 16:43-47, Jan. 1957.

825. —— Grand Canyon place names. Illus. by Anne Merriman Peck. Tucson, Univ. of Arizona Press, 1960. 26p.
A section from William Croft Barnes, Arizona place names, 1960 (see no. 805).

826. —— Influences on place names of the inverted mountains of the Grand Canyon of Arizona; In International Congress of Onomastic Sciences, 10th, Vienna, 1969. Proceedings. Vienna, Verlag der Wiener medizinischer Akademie, n.d. 2:17-23.

827. —— Methodology used in the revision of Arizona place names. Names 10:265-73, Dec. 1962.

828. Hinton, Richard Josiah. 1000 old Arizona mines; with a gallery of old photographs. [Photos from the Rose-Bartholomew collection] Toyahville, Tex., Frontier Book Co., 1962. facsim. (100p.), 101-126p. of illus.
Reproduction, newly paged, of chapters 4 and 5 (p. 72-167) of The hand-book of Arizona. San Francisco, Payot, Upham, 1878.
Includes lists of names of mines with their location, etc.

829. Honor Claude Birdseye's memory. Kansas City times March 1, 1965, p. 2.
Claude Birdseye Point.

830. Jett, Stephen C. An analysis of Navajo place-names. Names 18:175-84, Sept. 1970.
Many official place-names in northeastern Arizona, northwestern New Mexico, and southeastern Utah are of Navajo origin, either by anglicization of the Navajo names or by translation. Most Navajo place designations describe features of the natural landscape.

831. Kelley, Edward J. Early mine names were descriptive of events. Arizona highways 7:6-7, April 1931.

832. King, Dale S. Desert garden; will Congress change Organ Pipe Cactus National Monument to Arizona Desert National Park? Arizona highways 26:28-35, April 1950.

833. Kitt, Edith O. & T. M. Pearce. Arizona place name records. Western folklore 11:284-87, Oct. 1952.

834. Lesure, Nancy. Far-out place names dot Arizona. Denver post Nov. 17, 1968, Roundup, p. 9.
With Arizona place names, the actual is often more unusual than the fictional.

835. Lloyd, Elwood. Arizonology (knowledge of Arizona); a compilation of more than two thousand names found on the maps of Arizona, together with information concerning their meaning, history, and many other interesting facts about this wonderful state. Flagstaff, Coconino sun, 1933. 92p.

836. Marston, O. Dock. Who named the Grand Canyon? Pacific historian 12:4-8, Summer 1968.
Refutes Frederick S. Dellenbaugh's claim that Major John W. Powell named it when he referred to it as Grand Canon [sic] in 1869, by showing that the name had been used earlier.

837. Miller, Joseph. Arizona names and places. Arizona highways 19:20-23, 48-49, Sept.-Oct. 1943.

838. Mirkowich, Nicholas. A note on Navajo place names. American anthropologist n.s. 43:313-14, April-June 1941.
Lists Navajo names still in use for a few places in Arizona and New Mexico.

839. Navajo Tribe of Indians, petitioners. Before the Indian Claims Commission. The Navajo Tribe of Indians, petitioners, v. The United States of America, defendant. Proposed findings of fact in behalf of the Navajo Tribe of Indians in area of the overall Navajo claim (Docket 229), v. VI Appendices. [Window Rock, Ariz., Navajo Printing Section, 1967].
Appendix A-1: Alphabetical index of Navajo place names relative to the Navajo land claim. xxiv p.
Appendix A-2: Alphabetical list of English and Spanish place names (including those ordinarily anglicized from Indian names). vi p.

840. Newton, Charles H. The reason why place names in Arizona are so named. Phoenix, C. H. Newton Pub. Co., 1954. 47p.

841. Place names in Arizona. Southern Arizona Genealogical Society. Bulletin 4:6-8, Dec. 1968.
A rather full report of a speech made by Dr. Byrd Howell Granger.

842. Schilling, Frank A. Military posts of the old frontier: Arizona, New Mexico. Historical Society of Southern California. Quarterly 42:133-49, June 1960.
Includes origin and changes of names.

843. Sherer, Lorraine M. The name Mojave, Mohave: a history of its origin and meaning. Southern California Quarterly 49:1-36, March 1967.
Concerning the Indian tribal name and such geographic features bearing the name, derived from it, as Mojave River, Mojave Desert, Mojave Mountains, Mojave Valley Lake Mojave.
An addendum: ibid. 49:455-58, Dec. 1967.

844. Sherman, James E. & Barbara H. Sherman. Ghost towns of Arizona. Maps by Don Percious. Norman, Univ. of Oklahoma Press, 1969. 208p. maps.
Bibliography: p. 201-02.
An alphabetical listing of 130 towns, including county in which located and date when first post office was established and when it was discontinued.
Review: Fred & Harriet Rochlin, Journal of the West 8:647-48, Oct. 1969.

845. Smith, Gusse Thomas. Arizona names, their origin and meaning. Progressive Arizona and the great Southwest 6:34, 36, Jan. 1928; 6:27-30, 34, March 1928; 6:33-36, April 1928; 6:35-36, June 1928.

846. —— Priceless names of Arizona. Progressive Arizona and the great Southwest 6:21-22, 34, Jan. 1928.

847. Stephen, Alexander M. Hopi journal of Alexander M. Stephen; ed. by Elsie Clews Parsons. New York, Columbia Univ. Press, 1936. 2v. maps. (Columbia University contributions to anthropology v. 23, pt. 1-2)
Place names and references: 2:1152-69. A list in Hopi and English, with location and identification, meaning, and references to occurrence of the name in the book, in the text and on the maps.

848. The Stories of two Arizona place names: How the Hassayampa River got its name; and How the Colorado River turned red. New Mexico folklore record 4:33. 1949-50.
Collected by Walter N. Simons from Tom Larison.

849. Theobald, John & Lillian Theobald. Arizona Territory post offices & postmasters. Phoenix, Arizona Historical Foundation, 1961. 178p.
Pre-territorial post offices: p. 75-77.
Post offices, 1863-1912: p. 78-138.
These lists include some origins and changes of name.

850. Thornton, William. What's in a name? Desert 3:20-21, May 1968.
Arizona's place-names related to its history.

851. Tourist query serves as town name. Kansas City star April 22, 1965, p. 16.
Why, Arizona.

852. U.S. Board on Geographic Names. Decisions. No. 19- . Decisions rendered May 4, 1932. Grand Canyon National Park, Arizona. Washington, Govt. Print. Off., 1932. 16p.

853. Van Valkenburgh, Richard F. & Frank O. Walker. Old placenames in the Navaho country. Masterkey (Southwest Museum, Los Angeles) 19:89-94, May 1945.
Contains a list giving the popular, Spanish, and Navaho names; location; etc.

854. Warner, Robert C. The fortified spring; a good shot gave Pipe Spring its odd name. Denver post July 16, 1961, Empire magazine, p. 25.

855. Way, W. John. Ghosts and ghost towns: southeastern Arizona. Sketches by I. S. Painter. Tucson, Ariz., Livingston Press, 1966. 56p.

856. Willson, Roscoe G. The origin of Arizona's name. Arizona highways 31:2-5, March 1955.

ARKANSAS

857. Allsopp, Frederick William. Arkansas place names; In his Folklore of romantic Arkansas. New York, Grolier Society, 1931. 1:59-107.

858. Arkansas. History Commission. The Arkansas handbook, 1949-50. By Dallas Tabor Herndon. Little Rock, The Commission, 1950. 157p.
Arkansas counties, how they got their names: p. 144-45.

859. Arkansas. Laws, statutes, etc. Acts and resolutions of the General Assembly. 1881:216-17.
"Concurrent resolution declaring the proper pronunciation of the name of the state."
It should be pronounced in 3 syllables, with final "s" silent, the "a" in each syllable with the Italian sound, and accent on first and last syllables.
Also in Arkansas. Office of Secretary of State. Biennial report 1925-26:29-30. A short article entitled Arkansas or Arkansaw, including brief summary of the controversy and copy of Concurrent resolution declaring the proper pronunciation of the name of the state.

860. —— General acts and joint and concurrent resolutions and memorials and proposed constitutional amendments of the 44th General Assembly. 1923:803-04.
Senate concurrent resolution 2. Approved Jan. 26, 1923. Adopting popular name The Wonder State, and declaring The Bear State to be a misnomer.
Also in Arkansas. Office of Secretary of State. Biennial report 1925-26:12. A short article entitled Arkansas called "The Wonder State," which includes a copy of Senate concurrent resolution no. 2, 1923.

861. Arkansas. State Highway Dept. Places in Arkansas in alphabetical order. Little Rock, 1948. Unpaged.
Lists all towns, villages, and communities.

862. Arkansas divided by two. New York times Feb. 28, 1945, p. 13, col. 6-8.
Arkansas House rejects resolution to fix Ark-an-saw-yans as official pronunciation for residents of the state.

863. Bailey, W. E. How Enola got its name. Faulkner facts and fiddlings 9:93, Fall 1967.
A different version from that mentioned by Shipley, ibid. 6:22-23, Spring 1964. For relation with Enola, Pa., see article by Denton, ibid. 9:113-14, Winter 1967.

864. Blair, Mrs. Herbert. Names of many prominent families given to streets in Batesville. Independence County chronicle 2:34-39, Oct. 1960.

865. Branner, John Casper. Some old French place names in the state of Arkansas. Arkansas historical quarterly 19:191-206, Autumn 1960.
Reprinted from Modern language notes 14:33-40, Feb. 1899.
Also published separately, Baltimore, Md., 1899. 7p.
Review: American Geographical Society. Bulletin 31:94-95. 1899.
cf. article by Raoul Renault, no. 885.

866. Bryson, Fred R. The spelling and pronunciation of Arkansas. Arkansas historical quarterly 4:175-79, Autumn 1945.
Originally appeared in the Sunday magazine section of the Arkansas gazette, May 13, 1945, under title We call it "Arkansas."

867. Caldwell, Norman W. Place names and place name study. Arkansas historical quarterly 3:28-36, Spring 1944.
The author describes the work he has done on a study of place nomenclature in Arkansas. Suggests that the magnitude of the undertaking requires some form of cooperation to carry the study to completion.

868. Campbell, Tom W. The naming of Greene County. Craighead County historical quarterly 2:6-8, Winter 1963-64.
From the files of the Arkansas gazette May 6, 1945.
Named for Gen. Nathaniel Greene, of American Revolution fame.

869. Carter, Deane G. History in street names. Flashback v. 16, no. 1, 20p., Feb.; v. 16, no. 2, 12p., May 1966.
Gregg, Lafayette, Ida, Leverett, Storer, Whitham, and Lindell, in Fayetteville, Ark.

870. Chase, Carroll & Richard McP. Cabeen. The first hundred years of United States territorial postmarks, 1787-1887. Arkansas Territory. American philatelist 55:147-57, Dec. 1941.
Gives a list of post offices in the area of the present state of Arkansas and six in what became eastern Oklahoma, 1819-36, with notes on some names.

871. Cross County Historical Society. Naming a Confederate county, Cross County, Arkansas, 1862-1873. Wynne, Ark., 1973. 18p. illus.

872. Cypert, Eugene. Origin of the names of White County townships. White County heritage 2:15-16, Jan. 1964.
First published in Searcy daily citizen Aug. 18, 1924.

873. Denton, W. O. How another Enola was named. Faulkner facts and fiddlings 9:113-14, Winter 1967.
Origin of the name of Enola, Pa., which may have been the source of the name of Enola, Ark.

874. Eclectic Society of Little Rock, Ark. Proceedings of the Legislature and of the Historical Society of the State of Arkansas, and the Eclectic Society of Little Rock, Ark., fixing the pronunciation of the name Arkansas. Little Rock, Eclectic Society, 1881. 16p.
Reprinted: In relation to the pronunciation of the name "Arkansas." Arkansas Historical Association. Publications 2:462-77. 1908, with footnote: "Prepared in 1880 by a joint committee from the Eclectic Society and the old members of the then defunct Arkansas Historical Society. Issued at the time in pamphlet form. Because of its value it is reprinted here for permanent preservation."

875. Fenno, Cheryl Barnwell. The place names of Benton County, Arkansas. 401 ℓ.
Thesis (Ph.D.) Univ. of Arkansas, 1978. Abstracted in Dissertation abstracts, no. 3553A, 1978.
Bibliography: 389-401.
A dictionary of 2400 names with historical and statistical analysis.

876. Folklore in Ozark place names. Ozark visitor Feb. 1966, p. 6.

877. France, Isabel. Fascinating folk names of our hills and hollows. Ozarks mountaineer May 1959, p. 5.

878. Gazetteer and business directory of the new Southwest. Embracing all of that region of country—including counties, towns and cities—contiguous to the St. Louis and San Francisco Railway, its divisions and branches, located in southwest Missouri, southeastern Kansas, the eastern portion of the Indian country, and the northwest section of Arkansas. In which is included an abridged directory of leading business houses of St. Louis. St. Louis, United States Directory Pub. Co., 1881. 224p.

879. Hill, Robert T. The pronunciation of "Arkansas." Science 10:107-08, Aug. 26, 1887.

880. Martel, Glenn. Origin of Columbia's place names reviewed. Arkansas historical quarterly 11:1-14, Spring 1952.
Reprinted from Magnolia, Ark., Daily banner June 30, 1951.
Columbia County.

881. Miller, E. Joan Wilson. The naming of the land in the Arkansas Ozarks: a study in culture processes. Association of American Geographers. Annals 59:240-51, June 1969. maps.
The analysis of 2500 names reveals that the process of naming was both a folk and an official one.

882. Murdock, John. The pronunciation of "Arkansas." Science 10:120, Sept. 2, 1887.

883. The Name "Texarkana." American speech 2:113, Nov. 1926.

884. The Naming of Jamestown. Independence County chronicle 1:16-18, April 1960.
Includes a letter signed J. S. Trimble, which appeared in the North Arkansas times June 26, 1869.

885. Renault, Raoul. Some old French place-names in the state of Arkansas. Modern language notes 14:191-92, March 1899.
Some corrections of material in article by John Casper Branner (see no. 865).

886. Shelpman, Mrs. Bob. Desha named for distinguished soldier, Franklin W. Desha. Independence County chronicle 2:30-33, Oct. 1960.

887. Shipley, R. Sam. Enola and cross roads communities. Faulkner facts and fiddlings 6:22-23, Spring 1964.
Includes reference to origin of name of Enola.

888. Smackover, Arkansas. Times-picayune, New Orleans, Jan. 7, 1951, Dixie, p. 23.
One of a series on unusual place-names in lower Mississippi Valley region.

889. Stuck, Charles A. Timber names in Craighead County. Craighead County historical quarterly 1:37-38, Winter 1962-63.
Eighteen names which have a direct connection with timber.

890. Underwood, Eugene. Place name pronunciation in White County, Arkansas. In South Central Names Institute. The scope of names. Commerce, Tex., Names Institute Press, 1979.

891. U.S. 88th Congress, 1st session. House. A bill to provide that the Bull Shoals Dam and the Bull Shoals Reservoir, White River Basin in Missouri and Arkansas shall hereafter be known as the "Harry S. Truman Dam" and the "Harry S. Truman Reservoir." H.R. 1094. Jan. 9, 1963. Washington, 1963. 2p.
Introduced by Mr. Hull and referred to the Committee on Public Works.

892. U.S. 88th Congress, 2d session. House. A bill to designate the lake created by the Dardanelle Dam in the State of Arkansas as Lake David D. Terry in honor of the late David D. Terry. H.R. 9748. Jan. 27, 1964. Washington, 1964. 1p.
Introduced by Mr. Mills and referred to the Committee on Public Works.

893. Whaley, Storm. They call it; a guide to the pronunciation of Arkansas place names. n.p., Associated Press, 195?. 48p.

CALIFORNIA

894. Abbott, A. L. California ghost town guide. Anaheim, Calif., Abbott & Abbott, 1963. 21p.
An alphabetical list, containing 145 names.

895. Alegría, Fernando. Nombres españoles en California. Atenea 100:217-27, marzo 1951.

896. —— Trail of names. Américas 3:33-34, Nov. 1951.
Spanish geographical names in California. Translation of the article above in Atenea marzo 1951.

897. Ames, Richard Sheridan. Verdict on California names. Westways 26:20-21, 38-39, Dec. 1934.
Based on the Sixth report of the U.S. Geographic Board.

898. Applegate, Richard B. Chumash place names. Journal of California anthropology 1:186-205, 1974.
Names from the language of the Chumash Indians of southern California.

899. Aram, Mary. We call it Lake Tahoe. Pacific historian 18:11-15, Fall 1974.
Lake Bigler, named for a governor of California, was changed to more popular Lake Tahoe in 1945.

900. Archbald, John. Why "California"? Overland monthly 2:437-41, May 1869.
Various derivations considered etymologically.

901. Asbill, Frank M. Place naming in the Wailaki country. Western folklore 8:252-55, July 1949.

902. Aschmann, Homer. Miracle mile. American speech 32:156-58, May 1957.
Name for the commercial district on Wilshire Blvd., Los Angeles.
In response to article by Mamie Meredith, "Miracle miles" in the U.S.A. (see no. 343).

903. Austin, Herbert D. New light on the name of California. Historical Society of Southern California. Annual publication 12:29-31. 1923.

904. Austin, Mary Hunter. Regional place names; In her The land of little rain. Photographs by Ansel Adams; introduction by Carl Van Doren. Boston, Houghton Mifflin, 1950. p. 113-24.
The editors attempt to identify places the author mentions, some disguised.

905. Bailey, Gilbert Ellis. The history, origin and meaning of some California towns and places. Overland monthly 44:89-93, 199-204, 356-61, 468-78, 558-67, July-Nov. 1904.
Names classified in more than 50 categories, such as church, water, location, color, local peculiarities, soils, trees, animals, minerals, and others.

906. Bailey, Richard C. Kern County place names, [Bakersfield, Calif.] 1967. 28p. map.

907. Ballenger, Hersh. Kingdom of virgins. Westways 26:26-27, 40, Sept. 1934.
Recounts the story of Queen Calafia as told in the Spanish romance which is the source of the name California.

908. Bancroft, Hubert Howe. History of California. San Francisco, History Co., 1886. 1:142-46.
A list of places between San Diego and San Francisco as named in Crespi's diary of the first exploration of the California coast by land, with distances, bearings, and latitudes. The present name of each place is noted.

909. Barrett, Samuel Alfred. The ethno-geography of the Pomo and neighboring Indians. Berkeley, University Press, 1908. 332p. (University of California. Publications in American archaeology and ethnology, v. 6, no. 1)
"Includes the locations of the various ancient and modern villages and camp sites. The glossary contains a list of Indian terms from which place-names are derived. The bibliography includes a list of published works in which mention is made of the aboriginal names of peoples or places within the territory under investigation."—Price.

910. Beeler, Madison S. California oronym and toponym Montara. Romance philology 20:35-39, Aug. 1966.
Montara is both a mountain and a town.

911. —— Hueneme. Names 14:36-40, March 1966.
An etymology for the name Hueneme, which is attached to a point, a canyon, and a town, Port Hueneme, on the Pacific coast in Ventura County.

912. —— Inyo. Names 20:56-59, March 1972.
Discredits the widely accepted etymology of the name for a mountain range, a county, and a national forest in east-central California and offers an alternative suggestion.

913. —— Inyo once again. Names 26:208, June 1978.

914. —— Sonoma, Carquinez, Umunhum, Colma: some disputed California names. Western folklore 13:268-77, Oct. 1954.

915. —— Yosemite and Tamalpais. Names 3:185-88, Sept. 1955.

916. Block, Eugene B. The immortal San Franciscans for whom the streets were named. San Francisco, Chronicle Books, [1971]. 244p.

917. Bowman, J. N. Blucher. Western folklore 6:179, April 1947.
A land grant in Sonoma County.

918. —— The elusive Rio Jesus Maria. Western folklore 6:73-78, Jan. 1947.

919. —— The meaning of the name "Sonoma." California folklore quarterly 5:300-02, July 1946.

920. —— The names of land grants in provincial California. Names 7:122-26, June 1959.

921. —— The names of the California missions. The Americas: a quarterly review of inter-American cultural history 21:363-74, April 1965.

922. —— The names of the California missions. Historical Society of Southern California. Quarterly 39:351-56, Dec. 1957.

923. —— The names of the Los Angeles and San Gabriel rivers. Historical Society of Southern California. Quarterly 29:93-99, June 1947.

924. —— Place names from private land grant cases. Western folklore 6:371-75, Oct. 1947.

925. —— "Quesesosi." Western folklore 7:171-73, April 1948.
Supplement to Dorothy H. Huggins's article on the same name, ibid. 6:82, Jan. 1947, with additional note by Erwin G. Gudde p. 173.

926. —— Rio Ojotska—American River. Western folklore 6:177, April 1947.
In the early 1830s, Rio Ojotska was a name for the American River.

927. —— Schoolhouse Creek. Western folklore 8:64, Jan. 1949.
In north Berkeley.

928. —— Spring Valley. California folklore quarterly 5:199, April 1946.
San Francisco.

929. —— Tamalpais. Western folklore 6:270-71, July 1947.
Marion County peak.

930. Breeden, Marshall. California place names defined; In his The romantic southland of California. Los Angeles, Kenmore Pub. Co., 1928. p. 184-207.

931. Brentwood, R. G. D. The names of Lake "Taho." Grizzly bear 7:5, Oct. 1910.

932. Brewer, William H. The naming of Mount Tyndall. Sierra Club bulletin v. 12, no. 4, p. 443-44. 1927.

933. Brierly, A. A. Dead Horse Meadow. Western folklore 8:65, Jan. 1949.

934. Bright, William. Karok names. Names 6:172-79, Sept. 1958.
Analysis and classification of 117 Karok village names.

935. —— Some place names on the Klamath River. Western folklore 11:121-22, April 1952.
Names from the Karok Indian language.

936. Brown, Alan K. Place names of San Mateo County. San Mateo, San Mateo County Historical Association, 1975. 118p. map.
An earlier partial version appeared in Names 12:154-84, Sept.-Dec. 1964.
Bibliography: p. 116-18.
Review: George R. Stewart, Names 24:63-64, March 1976.

937. Brown, Thomas Pollok. Colorful California names, their history and meaning; with a foreword by Nancy Newhall. San Francisco, Wells Fargo Bank American Trust Co., 1957. 45p.
1st ed. 1934, 28p., with title: California names; rev. eds.: 1935, 28p.; 1954, 44p.; 1955, 44p.

938. Budd, Louis J. The naming of Altruria, California. Western folklore 10:169, April 1951.

939. Budge, Belva Adele. A source unit on the origin and meaning of California place names: original studies drawn from the period of the Spanish missions. 59p.
Thesis (M.A.) Stanford Univ., 1941.

940. Bumpass Hell is official. Board on Geographic Names says California approves it. New York times Oct. 31, 1948, sec. 1, p. 60.

941. Bunnell, Lafayette H. Origin of names in the Yosemite Valley; In Biennial report of the Commissioners to ManageYosemite Valley and the Mariposa Big Tree Grove, 1889-90, p. 9-13. (California. Legislature. Appendix to the Journals of the Senate and Assembly. 29th session, v. 2, doc. 5. 1891)
Portion of a manuscript rejected by Century magazine because it disproved their case regarding Yosemite.

942. California. Division of Highways. California city and unincorporated place names. Sacramento, 1971. Unpaged.

943. California. Legislature. Senate. Select Committee on the Derivation and Definition of the Names of Counties of California. Informe de la Comision Especial sobre la derivacion y definicion de los nombres de los diferentes condados del estado de California, &c. [San José], H. H. Robinson, [1850]. 20p.

944. —— Report on the derivation and definition of the names of the several counties of California, by Mr. Vallejo. [San José], H. H. Robinson, [1850]. 16p.
Translated from the original by Joseph H. Scull.

945. California. Mining Bureau. Origin of the name California; In its Sixth annual report, 1885-86, pt. 1, p. 8-10. (California. Legislature. Appendix to the Journals of the Senate and Assembly. 27th session, v. 4, doc. 2. 1887)
Quotes from a Spanish romance published in 1521 in which the name California appears. Refutes idea that this could be the origin of the name.

946. California is restless; her southern cities seek new names, and a special war rages about Hollywood. New York times June 13, 1937, sec. 10, p. 14, col. 1-2.
Proposed change of Culver City to Hollywood City and of South Pasadena to San Pasqual.

947. California names with their pronunciation and definition. Pasadena, Wood & Jones, 1924. 16p.

948. Carlisle, Henry C. San Francisco street names; sketches of the lives of pioneers for whom San Francisco streets are named. San Francisco, American Trust Co., 1954. 26 ℓ.
Limited to names of pioneers who were in San Francisco before 1850.

949. Carranco, Lynwood & Andrew Genzoli. California redwood empire place names. Journal of the West 7:363-80, July 1968.

950. Cerf, Bennett. [Streets named for literary folk, San Diego.] Saturday review 39:6, June 23, 1956.
In the Trade winds column.

951. Chapman, Charles Edward. The name "California"; its origin and application. Grizzly bear 26:3-5, Dec. 1919.

952. —— New light on origin name "California." Grizzly bear 18:5, March 1916.

953. Chase, Carroll & Richard McP. Cabeen. The first hundred years of United States territorial postmarks, 1787-1887. California Territory. American philatelist 63:561-67, April 1950.
Includes list of post offices.

954. Coast area to vote on an African name. New York times April 4, 1968, p. 43, col. 4.
Municipal Council proposes change of name from East Palo Alto to Nairobi, after the capital of Kenya, as a means of making the area's black Americans feel a sense of belonging to America.
Later reports on this proposal follow:
New name defeated for East Palo Alto. New York times Nov. 26, 1968, p. 26, col. 5.
Voters, predominantly Negro, reject the proposed change.
Renaming of town divides Negroes on Coast. New York times Dec. 26, 1968, p. 17, col. 1.
Young Negro militants press drive to change name, score older residents' disinterest.

955. Coester, Alfred. Names on the land: the name Carquinez. Western folklore 6:81-82, Jan. 1947.

956. Colorful place names of northern California. [Rev. ed.]. [San Francisco], Wells Fargo Bank, [1969]. 31p.

957. Conner, E. Palmer. Lost street names of Los Angeles. Touring topics 22:57, July 1930.

958. Conrad, Dale. Street names; In Conrad, Barnaby. San Francisco: a profile with pictures. New York, Viking Press, 1959. p. 214-24.
Includes a list of typical street names in San Francisco, plus information about them.

959. Cordary, N. J. Off with the old! On with the new! But let's not apply the slogan to street names. Los Angeles realtor 10:11, 33-34, June 1931.
Los Angeles street names.

960. The Correct name of Lassen Peak. Geographical review 2:464-65, Dec. 1916.

961. Couro, Ted & Christina Hutcheson. Dictionary of Mesa Grande Diegueño. Banning, Calif., Malki Museum Press, Morongo Indian Reservation, 1973. 118p.
Includes a discussion of about 50 place-names in the territory of the Mesa Grande dialect and the Diegueño language.
Review: Madison S. Beeler, Names 22:137-41, Sept. 1974.

962. Cray, Ed. Ethnic and place names as derisive adjectives. Western folklore 21:27-34, Jan. 1962.
Glossary of pejorative terms collected in southern California which reflect tensions between ethnic groups or between different sections of the country.

963. Cretser, Emory C. Pudding from Put-In? Western folklore 8:64, Jan. 1949.

964. Curletti, Rosario Andrea. Pathways to pavements, the history and romance of Santa Barbara Spanish street names; illus. by Peter Wolf. Santa Barbara, County National Bank & Trust Co., 1950. 87p.

965. Cutter, Donald C. Sources of the name "California." Arizona and the West 3:233-44, Autumn 1961.

966. Davidson, George. The origin and the meaning of the name California, Calafia the queen of the island of California, title page of Las Sergas. San Francisco, F. F. Partridge Print., 1910. 50p. (Transactions and proceedings of the Geographical Society of the Pacific. v. 6, pt. 1. ser. 2)
Also published separately.

967. —— Voyages of discovery and exploration on the northwest coast of America from 1539 to 1603. Washington, Govt. Print. Off., 1887. (U.S. Coast and Geodetic Survey. Report, 1886. Appendix no. 7)
The name "California" (extracted from Coast pilot of California, Oregon and Washington. 4th ed. 1886): p. 156-57.

968. —— Why San Francisco Bay was so named; In his The discovery of San Francisco Bay. Geographical Society of the Pacific. Transactions and proceedings 2d ser. 4:5-6. 1907.

969. De Ford, Miriam Allen. American ghost towns. American notes and queries 4:75-76, Aug. 1944.
Sutterville, California.

970. Denison, Don & Thomas Winnett. Sierra Nevada place name guide; an index to the USGS topographic maps in the High Sierra region. Berkeley, Wilderness Press, 1969. 86p. map.

971. Dickison, Roland. Onomastic amelioration in California place names. Names 16:13-18, March 1968.
A sampling of place-name changes, with examples drawn from the Mother Lode country, primarily El Dorado and Placer counties.

972. Diller, J. S. The basis for the official designation of Lassen Peak. Geographical review 4:56-58, July 1917.

973. Douglas, Edward Morehouse. California mountain passes. Washington, Board of Surveys and Maps, Map Information Office, 1929. 3p.

974. —— Gazetteer of the mountains of the State of California. Preliminary (incomplete) ed. Washington, Map Information Office, Federal Board of Surveys and Maps, 1929. 63p.

975. Drake, C. M. California names and their literal meanings, also other primary geography names and their meanings; a book for teachers and other curious people. Los Angeles, Jones Book & Print. Co., 1893. 80p.

976. Dressler, Albert. How some of the mining towns and diggings derived their names; In his California's pioneer mountaineer of Rabbitt Creek. San Francisco, A. Dressler, 1930. p. 35-36.

977. An Early day romance. Grizzly bear 32:6, Jan. 1923.
Contains personal recollections on the origin and meaning of some California names.

978. Edwards, Clinton R. Wandering toponyms: El Puerto de la Bodega and Bodega Bay. Pacific historical review 33:253-72, Aug. 1964; 35:345, Aug. 1966.

979. El Capinero. Western folklore 8:370, Oct. 1949.
Signed: E. R. F.
Tulare County.

980. Eldredge, Zoeth Skinner. The beginnings of San Francisco, from the expedition of Anza, 1774 to the city charter of April 15, 1850. San Francisco, Z. S. Eldredge, 1912. 2v.
The streets of San Francisco: 2:732-48. Lists about 130 streets with their historical significance.

981. Enochs, Elizabeth. A study of place names in the American River drainage system, 1848-1854. 1957.
Thesis (M.A.) Sacramento State College, 1957.

982. Evans, Oscar. What's in a name? Western folklore 6:174-76, April 1947.
Names of physical features.

983. Farquhar, Francis Peloubet. A footnote on the name California. California Historical Society quarterly 6:167-68, June 1927.
Contains an excerpt from Notes and queries 3:289, 519, April 11, June 27, 1857, on the possibility of the name California being an ingredient used in the making of fireballs or combustibles.

984. —— Naming America's mountains—the Sierra Nevada of California. American alpine journal v. 14, no. 1, p. 131-58. 1964.

985. —— Place names of the High Sierra. San Francisco, Sierra Club, 1926. 128p. (Sierra Club. Publications no. 62)
Enlarged from the Sierra Club bulletin 11:380-407; 12:47-64, 126-47. 1923-25.

986. Faull, Harry A. From pathways to freeways, a study of the origin of street names in the city of Pomona. Historical Society of Southern California. Quarterly 34:133-46, June 1952.

987. Frickstad, Walter Nettleton. A century of California post offices, 1848-1954. Oakland, 1955. 395p.
A Philatelic Research Society publication.
Part I presents an abstract of the official records of the establishment, discontinuance, and change of name of all post offices operated in California from 1848 to the end of 1954.
Part II consists of 20 official and unofficial lists published on various dates between 1849 and 1859, reporting the offices then operating in California.

988. Friis, Leo J. California place names. California herald 11:4-5, 13, Feb.; 3, April; 15, Aug. 1964; 12:5, Nov.; 5, 13, Dec. 1964; 13, Jan.; 2, 10, Feb.; 2, 15, April 1965.
A continuing series through June 1966.

989. "Frisco" is now conceded as a term of affection. New York times Dec. 2, 1945, p. 12, col. 4.
San Francisco.

990. Gamble, Thomas S. How the cities of southern California were named. Overland monthly and Out West magazine 2d ser. 91:57, April 1933.

991. —— The unsung romance of California. Overland monthly and Out West magazine 2d ser. 91:39-40, March 1933.
Origin and meaning of various place-names.

992. Gannett, Henry. Place names for application in the Sierra Nevada. Sierra Club bulletin 4:239-41, Feb. 1903.
Ideas regarding selection of place-names in the Sierra Nevada.

993. Garber, Elaine K. Hueneme: origin of the name. Ventura County Historical Society. Quarterly 12:11-15, June 1967.
Includes discussion of its pronunciation.

994. Gardner, J. E. The flag of freedom. California folklore quarterly 5:199, April 1946.
Freedom, formerly Whiskey Hill, Santa Cruz County.

995. Gill, R. Bayley. $200.00 for a name. Western folklore 6:375, Oct. 1947.
Tecopa, Inyo County.

996. Girgich, Henrietta. Sniktaw Creek. Western folklore 7:175, April 1948.
Watkins reversed.

997. Goethe, Charles Matthias. Sierran cabin, from skyscraper; a tale of the Sierran piedmont. Sacramento and San Francisco, Keystone Press, 1943. 185p.
Place names [of ghost towns]: p. 109-17.

998. —— "What's in a name." Tales, historical or fictitious, about 111 California Gold Belt place names. Sacramento, Calif., Keystone Press, c1949. 202p.
Review: Aubrey Drury, Western folklore 9:175-76, April 1950.

999. Goulet, Lucien. Another Dardanelles. Western folklore 6:178, April 1947.
Whittaker's Dardanelles, rocky peaks.

1000. —— The Dardanelles once more. Western folklore 6:79-81, Jan. 1947.

1001. Green, Allan W. C. Alteration of place names. Western folklore 30:56-57, Jan. 1971.

U.S. Forest Service and U.S. Geological Survey are quietly and systematically changing place-names in Northern Mines area of Mother Lode country of Sierra Nevada Mountains.

1002. Gregoire, Henri. La Chanson de Roland en l'an 1085. Baligant et Californe ou l'etymologie du mot "Californie." Academie Royale de Belgique. Classe des lettres et des sciences morales et politiques 5ième sér. 25:211-73. 1939.

1003. Gregory, Tom. How Santa Rosa received its name. Grizzly bear 9:2, Oct. 1911.

1004. Gudde, Elisabeth K. Mocho Mountain. Names 5:246-48, Dec. 1957.
A typical example of the processes involved in establishing a name of foreign origin, from the papers of George Davidson.

1005. Gudde, Erwin Gustav. The buttes of California. Western folklore 6:265-66, July 1947.

1006. —— California gold camps: a geographical and historical dictionary of camps, towns, and localities where gold was found and mined, wayside stations and trading centers. Edited by Elisabeth K. Gudde. Berkeley, Univ. of California Press, c1975. 467p. maps.
Glossary and bibliography: p. 382-429.
Includes 3500 sites, 1848-1900, with brief historical information.
Review: Kenneth M. Johnson, Journal of the West 15:144, April 1976; Otis E. Young, Southern California quarterly 58:255, Summer 1976; Margaret M. Bryant, Names 24:224-27, Sept. 1976.

1007. —— California place names: the origin and etymology of current geographical names. Rev. and enl. [3d] ed., with maps and reference list of obsolete names. Berkeley, Univ. of California Press, 1969. 416p. maps.
1st ed. 1949. 431p.; [2d] ed. 1960. 383p.
Glossary and bibliography: p. 374-99.
Review of 1st ed.: T. M. Pearce, Western folklore 9:82-83, Jan. 1950.
Review of 2d ed.: William Bright, Journal of American folklore 75:78-82, Jan. 1962: Kemp Malone, More about place names, American speech 35:210-11, Oct. 1960; E. Wallace McMullen, Names 12:58-64, March 1964; George R. Stewart, California Historical Society quarterly 39:364-66, Dec. 1960; Fritz L. Kramer, Cahier de géographie 10:350, sept. 1966.

1008. —— Dunderberg, not Dunderberg Peak. Western folklore 6:375, Oct. 1947.

1009. —— Hoopa from Whoop-ah? Western folklore 6:179, April 1947.
Valley and Indian reservation, Humboldt County.

1010. —— Literary echoes in California place names. Book Club of California. Quarterly news-letter v. 14, no. 2. 1949.
Reprinted in Lewis, Oscar, comp. Second readings: selections from the Quarterly news-letter, 1933-1963. San Francisco, Book Club of California, 1965. p. 61-67.

1011. —— The name California. Names 2:121-33, June 1954.

1012. —— The name of our state. California. Secretary of State. California blue book 1958:651-52.

1013. —— The names in Death Valley. Western folklore 8:160-61, April 1949.

1014. —— The names of California counties. California. Secretary of State. California blue book 1958:653-61.
Earlier issues of the California blue book contained the Vallejo report (see no. 944) and Prentiss Maslin's Origin and meaning of the names of the counties of California (see no. 1090). Gudde's account is based on the results of scholarly research obtained since Maslin published his article.

1015. —— One thousand California place names: their origin and meaning. 3d ed. Berkeley, Univ. of California Press, 1969. 96p.
1st ed. 1947; rev. ed. 1949; 2d rev. ed. 1959.
A popular edition based on the author's California place names.

1016. —— Paradise or Pair o' Dice. Western folklore 6:178, April 1947.
Butte County.

1017. —— Place names in the San Francisco Bay counties; In California. Dept. of Natural Resources. Division of Mines. Geologic guidebook of the San Francisco Bay counties. San Francisco, 1951. (Its Bulletin 154) p. 31-38.

1018. —— The solution of the Islay problem. California folklore quarterly 5:298-99, July 1946.
Islais Creek.

1019. —— [Topographic nomenclature]. California Historical Society quarterly 28:184-85, July 1949.
Report of talk at Society's meeting.

1020. Gudde Ridge. Names 19:33, March 1971.
A ridge near Oakland dedicated to Erwin G. Gudde, co-founder of the American Name Society, and first editor of Names.

1021. Guinn, James Miller. The passing of our historic street names. Historical Society of Southern California. Annual publication v. 9, pts. 1-2, p. 59-64. 1912-13.
Street names of Los Angeles.

1022. —— The plan of old Los Angeles and the story of its highways and byways. Historical Society of Southern California. Annual publication v. 3, pt. 3, p. 40-50. 1895.
Plan of early streets, origin of street names, changes in names, etc.

1023. —— Some California place names (their origin and meaning). Historical Society of Southern California. Annual publication 7:39-46. 1906.

1024. Hale, Edward Everett. The name of California. American Antiquarian Society. Proceedings April 1862, p. 45-53.
Also in Historical magazine 6:312-15, Oct. 1862.

1025. Hanna, Phil Townsend. The dictionary of California land names. Rev. and enl. ed. Los Angeles, Automobile Club of Southern California, 1951. 392p.
1st ed. 1946. 360p.
Originally published serially in Westways v. 31-38, Jan. 1939-March 1946, under title California names—a gazetteer.
Review: W. W. Robinson, Pacific historical review 16:196, May 1947; Mamie Meredith, Names 1:284-86, Dec. 1953.

1026. —— The origin and meaning of some place names of the Death Valley region. Touring topics 22:42-43, 54, Feb. 1930.

1027. Harrington, John Peabody. A tentative list of the Hispanized Chumashan place-names of San Luis Obispo, Santa Barbara, and Ventura counties, California. American anthropologist n.s. 13:725-26, Oct.-Dec. 1911.

1028. Harrison, William Greer. Romance of the word "California." Overland monthly 68:443-44, Dec. 1916.

1029. Hart, James D. San Francisco streets. Overland monthly and Out West magazine 88:49, 59, Feb. 1930.

1030. Hartesveldt, Richard J. Place names of Yosemite Valley. Yosemite National Park, Calif., Yosemite Natural History Assoc., 1955. 21p.

Special issue, v. 34, no. 1, Jan. 1955, of Yosemite nature notes, the monthly publication of the Yosemite Naturalist Division and the Yosemite Natural History Association..

Includes the names shown on the U.S. Geological Survey's Yosemite Valley special sheet and a few other local names.

"Does not measure up to our standards of popular onomatology."—Erwin G. Gudde, Names 3:194, Sept. 1955.

1031. Heck, Lewis. California. Congrès international de sciences onomastiques. 5ième, Salamanca, 1955. Programme et communications. p. 47.

Résumé of paper on the name California.

1032. Hill, Archibald A. California place-names from the Spanish. American speech 7:317-18, April 1932; 8:75, April 1933.

Criticism of article by Joseph B. Vasche (see no. 1185).

1033. Hine, Robert V. The naming of California's utopias. Western folklore 12:132-35, April 1953.

1034. Hisken, Clara. Tehama—Indian or Aztec? Western folklore 8:62-63, Jan. 1949. Supplemented by information from Dorothy H. Huggins, ibid. p. 63-64.

1035. Hoy, William J. Chinatown devises its own street names. California folklore quarterly 2:71-75, April 1943.

Ten streets and alleys in Chinatown in San Francisco are known by native names other than the legal ones bestowed on them by the city fathers.

1036. Hubbard, Harry D. Vallejo. Ed. by Pauline C. Santoro. Boston, Meador Pub. Co., 1941. 374p.

Naming of important geographical points: p. 75-83.

The discovery of, and the origin of the name, California: p. 165-73.

1037. Hudson, Thomas. Three paths along a river: the heritage of the valley of the San Luis Rey. Palm Desert, Calif., Desert-Southwest Publishers, 1964. 245p.

Romance in names: p. 159-61.

1038. Huggins, Dorothy H. Batiquitos and San Elijo lagoons. Western folklore 6:376, Oct. 1947.

San Diego County.

1039. —— Butano. Western folklore 9:157, April 1950.

San Mateo County. A request for information.

1040. —— Carquinez, the strait of the Mud People. California folklore quarterly 5:104-07, Jan. 1946.

George R. Stewart disagrees in his article Carquinez again, ibid. 5:302-03, July 1946.

1041. —— More Dardanelles. California folklore quarterly 5:303, July 1946.
Tuolumne County.

1042. —— Nicasio and Novato. Western folklore 6:270, July 1947.
Marin County.

1043. —— The oldest names in new California. California folklore quarterly 5:197-98, April 1946.
Mugu Laguna and Mugu Point, Ventura County.

1044. —— Place names from the Portola pilgrimage; In Essays for Henry R. Wagner. San Francisco, Grabhorn Press, 1947. p. 65-80.

1045. —— Puente. Western folklore 6:269-70, July 1947.
Los Angeles County.

1046. —— "Quesesosi" or "Guesesosi." Western folklore 6:82, Jan. 1947.
Land claim. cf. J. N. Bowman's article on the same name, ibid. 7:171-77, April 1948.

1047. Hutchinson, W. H. The naming of Cohasset. Western folklore 6:266-69, July 1947.
Butte County.

1048. Ide, Arthur Frederick. San Diego, the saint and the city. Journal of San Diego history 22:21-25, Fall 1976.

1049. Index to California place names. California. State Library, Sacramento.
Continuing.

1050. Island's name changed to Wake. New York times April 26, 1942, p. 33, col. 3.
Mullet Island changed for duration of war.

1051. Iventosch, Herman. Orinda, California; or, The literary traces in California toponymy. Names 12:103-07, June 1964.

1052. James, George Wharton. The various names of Lake Tahoe; In his The lake of the sky, Lake Tahoe. Chicago, C. T. Powner, 1956. p. 56-62.
First published 1915. 2d ed. 1921. Rev. ed. 1928.

1053. Jones, Joseph. Street-names of Palo Alto, California. American speech 7:273-77, April 1932.
"Names of colleges, authors, trees, prominent citizens, some Civil War generals, and feminine given names serve as headings under which the street names are listed."—Price.

1054. Karpenstein, Katherine. Amboy to Goffs. California folklore quarterly 5:200, April 1946.

1055. —— California place name records. Western folklore 12:129-32, April 1953.

1056. Kelly, Isabel T. Ethnography of the Surprise Valley Paiute. California. University. Publications in American archaeology and ethnology v. 31, no. 3, p. 74-75. 1932.
Indian names of the Valley and their meaning.

1057. Klar, Kathryn A. Pismo and Nipomo: two northern Chumash place-names. Names 23:26-30, March 1975.

1058. Kniffen, Fred B. Achomawi geography. California. University. Publications in American archaeology and ethnology v. 23, no. 5, p. 297-322. 1928.

Discussion of the areas occupied by different tribes and the meaning of some of the Indian place-names.

1059. Koenig, George. Ghosts of the gold rush; being a wayward guide to the Mother Lode country. Glendale, Calif., La Siesta Press, 1968. 72p. maps.

Ghost towns listed by current highway routes. Includes origin and changes of name.

1060. Kroeber, Alfred Louis. California place names of Indian origin. California. University. Publications in American archaeology and ethnology v. 12, no. 2, p. 31-69. 1916.

1061. —— The ethnography of the Cahuilla Indians. California. University. Publications in American archaeology and ethnology v. 8, no. 2, p. 29-39. 1908.

"Two parallel lists of place-names in the Cahuilla Indian language; one, the original place-name, and second, the present name, or, this being impossible, the location of the name."--Price.

1062. —— Karok towns. California. University. Publications in American archaeology and ethnology v. 35, no. 5, p. 29-38. 1936.

Towns along the Klamath River.

1063. —— Place names; In his Handbook of the Indians of California. U.S. Bureau of American Ethnology. Bulletin 78:892-97. 1925.

1064. Kruse, Rhoda E. Mystery man of Ocean Beach. Journal of San Diego history 23:58-68, Fall 1977. maps.

Naming the streets in some pre-1900 subdivisions.

1065. Krutch, Joseph Wood. The forgotten peninsula; a naturalist in Baja California. New York, Sloane, 1961. 277p.

Brief mention of place-names in Baja California, and origin of the name California, p. 56-60.

1066. Lassagne, Art. California pioneer towns. Volume 1: The northern Mother Lode. Alama, Calif., Gold Bug Pub. Co., c1968. 51p.

Includes six northern counties and place names in each.

1067. LeConte, J. N. Identification of the great peaks of the southern Sierra. Sierra Club bulletin 11:244-54. 1922.

Includes origin of names.

1068. Leland, J. A. C. Cohasset—well named. Western folklore 6:377, Oct. 1947.

1069. —— Eastern tribal names in California. California folklore quarterly 5:391-93, Oct. 1946.

1070. —— Gualala again. Western folklore 7:175, April 1948.

Additional note to the Harriet B. Titus article. Walhalla-Gualala, ibid. 6:271, July 1947.

1071. —— The origin of the name "Sequoia." Western folklore 6:269, July 1947.

1072. —— Some eastern Indian place names in California. California folklore quarterly 4:404-08, Oct. 1945.

1073. Lloyd, Elwood. Californology (knowledge of California), a compilation of more than fifteen hundred Spanish, Indian and unusual names found on the maps of California, together with information concerning their meaning, pronunciation and history. Hollywood, Hartwell Pub. Corp., 1930. 55p.

1074. The Local name of Lassen Peak. Geographical review 3:148, Feb. 1917.

1075. Locker, Zelma Bays. From Aspin to Zanzibar Street, names in San Diego's Mission Beach. Journal of San Diego history 21:41-48, Spring 1975.

1076. —— Whatever happened to Izard Street? Pacific Beach and its street names. Journal of San Diego history 22:20-30, Spring 1976.

1077. Lodian, L. History of the name Kalifornia (California). Coal trade journal 40:998, Dec. 4, 1901.
Also in Book-lover 3:142, May-June 1902, with title Meaning of the name Kalifornia (California).

1078. Loud, Llewellyn L. Ethnogeography and archaeology of the Wiyot territory. California. University. Publications in American archaeology and ethnology v. 14, no. 3, p. 284-98. 1918.
Gives "the chief Wiyot settlements and their sites, minor settlements and camp sites in 1850; places abandoned previous to 1850; places of mythological interest; and lists of geographical names with maps."--Price.

1079. Lovejoy, Ora A. A study of southern California place names. Historical Society of Southern California. Annual publications v. 11, pt. 1, p. 44-50. 1918.

1080. Lynch, Frank E. Counties of California; In his The pathfinder of the great western empire. Los Angeles, Gem Pub. Co., 1920. p. 15-37.
Derivation of the name is included in the description of each county.

1081. McAbee, Forrest L. How Yorkville was named. Western folklore 6:177, April 1947.

1082. McKenney, J. Wilson. He named Lake Cahuilla. Desert 13:11-13, March 1950.

1083. McKeon, Thomas J. Some conjectures on place names in Marin County. Grizzly bear 57:3, Oct. 1935.

1084. McNary, Laura Kelly. California Spanish and Indian place names, their pronunciation, meaning and location. Los Angeles, Wetzel Pub. Co., 1931. 77p.
References: p. 77.

1085. Make Japan St. Colin Kelly St. New York times Feb. 10, 1942, p. 4, col. 5.
San Francisco.

1086. Maloney, Alice Bay. Shasta was Shatasla in 1814. California Historical Society quarterly 24:229-34, Sept. 1945.

1087. Marcou, Jules. Notes upon the first discoveries of California and the origin of its name. U.S. Engineer Dept. Annual report, 1877-78, pt. 3, Appendix NN, p. 1648-51.
"Describes some of the old maps of California and treats of the seventeenth century controversy as to whether California was an island or part of the mainland. Gives various names by which some of the places were known."--Price.

1088. Marshall, Martha Lebeaud. A pronouncing dictionary of California names in English and Spanish. San Francisco, French Book Store, 1925. 40p.

1089. Maslin, Prentiss. Counties in California; In McGroarty, John Steven. California, its history and romance. Los Angeles, Grafton Pub. Co., 1911. p. 309-22.
Data concerning the names and the origin of the counties of California prepared and published officially by direction of the state legislature in accordance with an act approved Feb. 12, 1903.

1090. —— Origin and meaning of the names of the counties of California. California. Secretary of State. California blue book 1907:275-81; 1909:338-44.

1091. Masson, Marcelle Saylor. How Dunsmuir was named. Western folklore 6:377, Oct. 1947.

1092. Mathes, W. Michael. The Puerto de Don Gaspar: a note on an erroneous California place-name. Journal of San Diego history 20:30-32, Spring 1975.
On the name Drakes Bay.

1093. Maule, William M. Buckeye Creek. Western folklore 8:65, Jan. 1949.

1094. —— Fales Hot Springs. Western folklore 7:174-75, April 1948.

1095. —— Folger Peak. Western folklore 6:376, Oct. 1947.

1096. —— Montgomery Peak. Western folklore 6:178, April 1947.

1097. —— Why Disaster Peak was so named. Western folklore 6:270, July 1947.
Alpine County.

1098. Meadows, Don. Historic place names in Orange County. Balboa Island, Calif., Paisano Press, 1966. 141p.
Review: C. E. Parker, California Historical Society quarterly 46:86-87, March 1967; Maurice A. Mook, Names 16:187-89, June 1968.

1099. Merriam, Clinton Hart. Cop-eh of Gibbs. American anthropologist n.s. 31:136-37, Jan.-March 1929.
"Points out the excusable error of George Gibbs in identifying 'Cop-eh' with the stream 'Putes Creek.' "—Price.

1100. —— Source of the name Shasta. Washington Academy of Sciences. Journal 16:522-25, Nov. 18, 1926.
Peter Skene Ogden gave name to river now known as Rogue River, and to mountain at head of it, now known as Mount Pitt. Due to break in continuity of local knowledge of the region, name has been transferred to features remote from those upon which originally bestowed. Great mountain and river to which name was transferred are still within or bordering on the territory of the Shasta tribe.

1101. —— Village names in twelve California mission records. Assembled and ed. by Robert F. Heizer. Berkeley, Univ. of California Archaeological Research Facility, Dept. of Anthropology, 1968. 175p. (Reports of the University of California Archaeological Survey, no. 74)

1102. Miers, Allan. Bogus in Siskiyou. Western folklore 6:376-77, Oct. 1947.

1103. Miller, Guy C. College Terrace. Western folklore 6:78-79, Jan. 1947.
In Palo Alto.

1104. —— Palo Alto. Western folklore 7:284-88, July 1948.

1105. Moore, Edwin R. Spanish and Indian names in California and the Southwest pronounced and defined. South Pasadena, Vance Print. Co., 1924. 18p.

1106. Moreno, Henry Manuel. Moreno's dictionary of Spanish-named California cities and towns; comp. from the latest U.S. postal and parcel zone guides; California blue book; Velazquez dictionary; Southern Pacific & Union Pacific maps and authentic sources. An accurate, ready reference for all schools, newspaper offices, etc. Chicago, Donohue, 1916. 95p.

1107. Morley, S. G. Carquinez Straits once more. Western folklore 6:271-72, July 1947.
Differs with Alfred Coester, ibid. p. 81-82.

1108. Mott, Gertrude. A handbook for Californiacs; a key to meaning and pronunciation of Spanish and Indian place names; with foreword by Herbert E. Bolton. San Francisco, Harr Wagner Pub. Co., 1926. 104p.
Also published under title Handbook for Californians.
Authorities consulted: p. 104.
"Earlier and more nearly correct pronunciation of these many place-names along with an explanation of the meaning of each."--Review, American speech 1:562-63, July 1926.

1109. Mountain nicknamed. Baldy is popular name used for peak in California. New York times Aug. 20, 1959, p. 22.
Real name Mount San Antonio, probably for St. Anthony of Padua.

1110. [Mountain peak in Yosemite National Park to be named for Amelia Earhart] Zontian 47:14, Spring 1967.

1111. Murbarger, Nell. The ghost towns of Inyo. The Westerners. Los Angeles Corral. Brand book 11:1-18. 1964.

1112. Nadeau, Remi A. Ghost towns and mining camps of California. Los Angeles, Ward Ritchie Press, 1965. 278p.
Bibliography: p. 271-74.
Much of the text material appeared in the author's The ghost towns of California, Los Angeles, Fortnight Magazine Press, 1954, compiled from Fortnight magazine. It appears here in revised and expanded form. Material was also drawn from articles in Westways and American heritage.

1113. Names, full of meaning, alone remain of early day gold camps. Grizzly bear 38:4, March 1926.

1114. Names of old places in Valley Springs region; Names of old places around West Point. Las Calaveras (Quarterly bulletin of the Calaveras County Historical Society) 5:[1-2], July 1957.

1115. Names on the land: Hobo Hot Springs. Western folklore 6:176-77, April 1947.
Near Bakersfield.

1116. New place names approved. Sierra Club bulletin 35:10, Jan. 1950.
Sierra names approved by U.S. Board on Geographic Names.

1117. Nomland, Gladys Ayer & A. L. Kroeber. Wiyot towns. California. University. Publications in American archaeology and ethnology v. 35, no. 5, p. 39-48. 1936.
Along Eel River, Mad River, and on Humboldt Bay.

1118. Norton, Arthur Lauren. How California received her name. Los Angeles County employee 4:10-12, 45-46, Oct. 1931.

1119. Not funny, at home. Cucamonga thinks it's time for a name change. Kansas City star Oct. 6, 1958, p. 3.
A.P. release.
Considering among other names Arpege, after the perfume.

1120. Old meanings of Indian place names overturned. Grizzly bear 20:5, Dec. 1916.
Based on Alfred Louis Kroeber, California place names of Indian origin (see no. 1060).

1121. Olmsted, Frederick Law. Place names for California. Landscape architecture 13:40-42, Oct. 1922.
Suggests ways of forming an English place-name, and mentions some names that have local characteristics and English terminations that could be applied in the vicinity of Berkeley.

1122. Origin and meaning of the names of the counties of California, with county seats and dates upon which counties were created; In California. Constitution. Constitution of the state of California. 1945-1946, p. 467-79.

1123. Oswalt, Robert L. Gualala. Names 8:57-58, March 1960.
A note on the origin of the name Gualala for a small coastal town in Mendocino County and for the river at whose mouth the town lies.

1124. Palmer, Theodore Sherman. Place names of the Death Valley region in California and Nevada. Los Angeles, Dawson's Book Shop, 1948. 80p.
Result of National Park Service project.
Review: Katherine Karpenstein, Names 1:62-63, March 1953.

1125. Patton, Annaleone Davis. California Mormons by sail and trail. Salt Lake City, Utah, Deseret Book Co., 1961. 197p.
Mormon names in early California; Geographic names associated with or named by early Mormons: p. 189-90.

1126. Peaks in the Sierra named. Sierra Club bulletin 34:16, Feb. 1949.
Five features on east slope of Sierra Nevada named by U.S. Board on Geographic Names.

1127. Pearce, Thomas M. Maggie's Peak. Western folklore 8:370, Oct. 1949.
Napa and Sonoma counties. Request for information.

1128. Pioneer Dean tells how Tahoe got its name. Grizzly bear 26:5, Feb. 1920.

1129. Place-name card index. San Diego Public Library.
Continuing.

1130. Place-name file. Los Angeles Public Library.
A collection of notes on the origin and meaning of California place-names compiled by the Library School of the Los Angeles Public Library under the supervision of Charles Fletcher Lummis.

1131. Powers, Stephen. Tribes of California, Yosemite. Contributions to North American ethnology 3:361-68. 1877.
Indian names of places in the Yosemite Valley with their meaning, and some legends connected with the names.

1132. Pronunciation of "Los Angeles." American speech 25:75, Feb. 1950.
Signed: H. S.

1133. Putnam, George Palmer. Death Valley and its country. New York, Duell, 1946. 231p.
The name: p. 10-15.

1134. Putnam, Ruth & Herbert I. Priestley. California: the name. California. University. Publications in history 4:293-365. 1917.

1135. Rambo, F. Ralph. Almost forgotten; [cartoon pen and inklings of the old Santa Clara Valley] written, drawn, and hand-lettered by F. Ralph Rambo. Santa Clara? Calif., 1964. 48p. map.

1136. Raup, Hallock Floy. Modern California cartography, aids for the map compiler. Pacific historical review 15:77-84, March 1946.
Sources for place-names.

1137. —— Place names of the California gold rush. Geographical review 35:653-58, Oct. 1945.
Also reprinted.
827 place-names in Trinity, Amador, and Calaveras counties were studied "to ascertain tendencies in geographical nomenclature among the early miners."

1138. —— & William B. Pounds. Northernmost Spanish frontier in California as shown by the distribution of geographic names. California Historical Society quarterly 32:43-48, March 1953.

1139. Raymenton, H. K. San Diego's street names. San Diego Historical Society. Quarterly 10:24-25, April 1964.

1140. Ricard, Herbert F. Place names of Ventura County. Ventura County Historical Society quarterly 17:1-104, no. 2, 1972.

1141. Richards, Elizabeth W. Guideposts to history: concerning origins of place and street names in San Bernardino County. San Bernardino, Santa Fe Federal Savings and Loan Association, 1966. [110]p.

1142. Rivera, Adolfo G. Along the highways, meaning of the words you see. Los Angeles County employee v. 10, Oct. 1937-Jan. 1938.
A series of articles. Mostly Spanish words.

1143. Rodriguez de Montalvo, Garci. The Queen of California; the origin of the name of California, with a translation from the Sergas of Esplandian, by Edward Everett Hale. San Francisco, The Colt Press, 1945. 46p. map. (Colt Press series of California classics, no. 4)
The present text was published in Edward Everett Hale's His level best, and other stories, Boston, Roberts Bros., 1872, p. 234-78; an earlier variation appeared in the Atlantic monthly, 13:265-78, March 1864.
Hale's translation includes only those parts of Montalvo's Las sergas de Esplandian relating to the Queen of California.

1144. Russell, Richard Joel. Basin Range structure and stratigraphy of the Warner Range, northeastern California. California. University. Publications. Bulletin of the Dept. of Geological Sciences 17:387-496. 1928.
Some material on place-names in northeastern California, p. 392-94.

1145. Sanchez, Louis A. "El Capinero" twice more. Western folklore 9:155-56, April 1950.
Includes notes by S. G. Morley.

1146. Sanchez, Nellie Van de Grift. The name of our beloved California, was it given in derision? Grizzly bear 18:8, April 1916.

1147. —— Origin of "California." Motor land 33:7, 13, Sept. 1933.
A popular article on the origin of the name in the old Spanish tale, Las sergas de Esplandian.

1148. —— Spanish and Indian place names of California, their meaning and their romance. San Francisco, Robertson, 1930. 343p.
Earlier editions: 1914. 445p.; 1922. 454p.
Reprinted: New York, Arno Press, 1976. (The Chicano heritage)
Review of 1914 ed.: Charles A. Kofoid, Dial 57:497-98, Dec. 16, 1914.

1149. —— Spanish Arcadia. Los Angeles, Powell Pub. Co., 1929.
Principal Spanish place names of California--pronunciation, p. 390-91.

1150. Schulz, Paul E. Stories of Lassen's place names. The origins and meanings of the place names in Lassen Volcanic National Park, with relevant annotations. Mineral, Calif., Lassen Volcanic National Park, 1949. 62p.

1151. Schwartz, J. K. L. List of Ventura County post offices. Ventura County Historical Society quarterly 10:2-5, May 1965.

1152. Scott, Fred N. Pronunciation of Spanish-American words. Modern language notes 6:435-36, Nov. 1891.

1153. Shafer, Robert. The pronunciation of Spanish place names in California. American speech 17:239-46, Dec. 1942.

1154. Sherer, Lorraine M. The name Mojave, Mohave: a history of its origin and meaning. Southern California quarterly 49:1-36, March 1967.
Concerning the Indian tribal name and such geographic features bearing the name, derived from it, as Mojave River, Mojave Desert, Mojave Mountains, Mojave Valley, Lake Mojave.
An addendum: ibid. 49:455-58, Dec. 1967.

1155. Shulman, David. Derivation of California. New York times Nov. 20, 1938, sec. 4, p. 8, col. 5-6; reply by Howard W. Vernon, ibid. Nov. 27, 1938, sec. 4, p. 9, col. 6.

1156. Sierra County changes name. Sierra Club bulletin 35:11, Jan. 1950.
Names of rivers changed by Sierra County Board of Supervisors.

1157. Sierra or Sierras? Sierra Club bulletin 32:32, Nov. 1947.
Refers to Sierra Nevada.

1158. Sokol, A. E. California, a possible derivation of the name. California Historical Society quarterly 28:23-30, March 1949.

1159. The Spanish confusion. How to ask directions in and around southern California without getting laughed at. Sunset 157:54-61, Oct. 1976.
Pronunciation problems with local names.

1160. Steger, Gertrude A. Place names of Shasta County. Revision by Helen Hinckley Jones. Rev. ed. Glendale, Calif., La Siesta Press, 1966. 71p. maps.
1st ed.: Bella Vista, The Author, 1945. 75p.

1161. Stein, David Allen. Los Angeles: a noble fight nobly lost. Names 1:35-38, March 1953.
The pronunciation of Los Angeles.

1162. Stein, Lou. San Diego County place-names; they had to call it something. San Diego, Tofua Press, c1975. xv, 163p. map.
Bibliography: p. 157-60.
Review: Neil Morgan, Journal of San Diego history 22:64-65, Spring 1976; Robert M. Rennick, Names 26:295-96, Sept. 1978.

1163. Stephenson, Terry Elmo. Names of places in Orange County. Orange County Historical Society. Orange County history series 1:45-54. 1931; 2:107-17. 1932.

1164. Stercula, Beverly M. Riverside place names and the organization of the towns. Lost leaves from Southern California trails 2:38-39, 64-65, 90-91, March, June, Sept. 1965.
The origin of the names in the county.

1165. Stewart, George Rippey. Caribou as a place name in California. California folklore quarterly 5:393-95, Oct. 1946.

1166. —— More on the name California. Names 2:249-54, Dec. 1954.

1167. —— Nomenclature of stream-forks on the west slope of the Sierra Nevada. American speech 14:191-97, Oct. 1939; 16:312, Dec. 1941.

1168. —— Place names; In his Donner Pass and those who crossed it. San Francisco, California Historical Society, 1960. p. 89-90.
Various types of names in the Donner Pass area.

1169. —— Three Mendocino names. Western folklore 9:154-55, April 1950.

1170. Stockton, Calif. Chamber of Commerce. Ghost towns and relics of '49. Stockton, 193? 32p.
The ghost towns, including some origins of the names, in the Mother Lode or southern mines area from Mariposa to Placerville.

1171. Stories behind California's names. I. Indian names. II. Spanish names. III. American names. California historical nugget 1:39-43, 59-66, 79-87, March-May 1924.

1172. Sykes, Godfrey. How California got its name. Out West magazine 41:225-30, June 1915.

1173. Tamony, Peter. Sailors called it "Frisco." Western folklore 26:192-95, July 1967.
Discussion of the nickname for San Francisco.

1174. Teeter, Karl V. Notes on Humboldt County, California, place names of Indian origin. Names 6:55-56, March 1958.
Addenda, ibid. 7:126, June 1959.

1175. Terrill, Nate. The etymological history of a clam. Western folklore 9:264-65, July 1950.
Pismo Beach.

1176. Thompson, Betty. Once Hangtown—now Placerville. Mining world 10:42, Feb. 1948.

1177. Titus, Harriet B. Walhalla-Gualala. Western folklore 6:271, July 1947.
Sonoma County. cf. J. A. C. Leland's article, Gualala again, ibid. 7:175, April 1948.

1178. To vote on becoming Distomo. New York times Dec. 3, 1944, p. 24, col. 3.
Linda Vista, Calif.

1179. Treutlein, Theodore E. Los Angeles, California: the question of the city's original Spanish name. Southern California quarterly 55:1-7, Spring 1973.

1180. Turk, Henry W. Place names along the emigrant trail. Grizzly bear 56:5, Feb. 1935; 56:2, March 1935.

1181. U.S. Board on Geographic Names. Decisions. Place names, Sequoia National Park, California. Oct. 3, 1928. Washington, Govt. Print. Off., 1928. 11p.

1182. —— Decisions. No. 30, June 30, 1932. Yosemite National Park, California. Washington, Govt. Print. Off., 1934. 29p.

1183. U.S. Work Projects Administration. Pennsylvania. Geographic names in the coastal areas of California, Oregon and Washington. Comp. under the supervision of the Coast and Geodetic Survey. Washington, 1940. 94p.

1184. Utley, Francis Lee. Onomastic variety in the High Sierra. Names 20:73-82, June 1972.

1185. Vasché, Joseph B. Trends in the pronunciation of the Spanish place-names of California. American speech 6:461-63, Aug. 1931.
cf. article by Archibald A. Hill, no. 1032.

1186. Vasquez, Pablo. Place names on the coast. La Peninsula, journal of the San Mateo County Historical Association v. 10, no. 4, p. [16-18], Feb. 1960.
From the foot of the San Pedro Mountain, north of Spanish Town, to the Santa Cruz line on the south.

1187. Wagner, Henry Raup. The discovery of California. California Historical Society quarterly 1:36-56, July 1922.
Has sections on By whom was the name given and to what was it applied? and The derivation of the name California as applied to the island or peninsula so called.

1188. —— The names of the Channel Islands. Historical Society of Southern California. Annual publication v. 15, pt. 4, p. 16-23. 1933.
The islands now known as San Miguel, Santa Rosa, Santa Cruz, and Anacapa.

1189. —— Saints' names in California. Historical Society of Southern California. Quarterly 29:49-58, March 1947.

1190. Wakefield, Lucy. Hangman's tree. Grizzly bear 7:9, June 1910.
Origin of name Hangtown.

1191. Walsh, Martin. Can you pronounce the name of your town correctly? Touring topics 25:12, 40-41, Sept. 1933.

1192. —— Name pronunciation contest: prize-winning lists of correctly-pronounced California names. Touring topics 25:33, Oct. 1933.

1193. Wannamaker, Jim. Tail of the dog. Frontier times 32 (n.s. no. 2):27, Spring 1958.
Account of how White River in Tulare County got its nickname of Tailholt.

1194. Wardlaw, Muriel. Early history of Fresno County: place names. Ash tree echo 4:153-61, Oct. 1968.
Includes a list of some of the place-names in the Fresno County of the past century.

1195. Waterman, Thomas Talbot. The village sites in Tolowa and neighboring areas in northwestern California. American anthropologist n.s. 27:528-43, Oct.-Dec. 1925.
The names of the Indian villages with their English meanings. Includes some Oregon material.

1196. —— Yurok geography. California. University. Publications in American archaeology and ethnology v. 16, no. 5, p. 177-283. 1920.
Contains several thousand primitive place-names of the Yurok Indians.

1197. Weber, Francis J. El Pueblo de Nuestra Señora de Los Angeles; an inquiry into early appellations. Los Angeles, 1968. 17p.

1198. Wells, Harry Laurenz. California names; words, phrases and place names in common use in the Golden State, spelled, pronounced, defined and explained. Los Angeles, Kellaway-Ide Co., 1940. 96p.
1st ed. 1934. 94p.

1199. White, Lynn Townsend. Changes in the popular concept of "California." California Historical Society quarterly 19:219-24, Sept. 1940.
Briefly traces mention of name California in literature from the 12th century on.

1200. Whiting, Joseph Samuel & Richard J. Whiting. Forts of the State of California. [Seattle], 1960. 90p.
Descriptions and data relating to the name, origin, and existence of military and semimilitary establishments in the State of California which have been designated or referred to as forts. Also includes place-names with the word Fort as a part of the name but which are neither military nor semimilitary establishments.

1201. Why Little Ovens? Western folklore 8:65, Jan. 1949.
Hornitos, Mariposa County.

1202. Wishart, Helen Collier. Elsinore—Danish not Spanish. California folklore quarterly 5:198-99, April 1946.
Influence of the Shakespeare play.

1203. Wood, Beatrice Dawson. Gazetteer of surface waters of California. Prepared under the direction of John C. Hoyt, in cooperation with the State Water Commission and Conservation Commission of the State of California. Washington, Govt. Print. Off., 1912-13. 3v. (U.S. Geological Survey. Water-supply paper 295-297)
A list of all lakes and streams, based on the topographic atlas, the Land Office map, and the official county maps.

1204. Wood, Raymond F. The origin of the name of Fresno. Fresno past and present 2:2-3, Oct. 1960.

1205. Wyatt, Roscoe D. Names and places of interest in San Mateo County with pronunciation, history and traditions. Redwood City, Pub. by the San Mateo County Title Co. for the San Mateo County Historical Assoc., 1936. 30p.

1206. —— & Clyde Arbuckle. Historic names, persons and places in Santa Clara County. San Jose, Calif., San Jose Chamber of Commerce for the California Pioneers of Santa Clara County, 1948. 42p.

COLORADO

1207. Arps, Louise Atkinson Ward & Elinor Eppich Kingery. High country names: Rocky Mountain National Park. 2d rev. ed. Estes Park, Colo., Rocky Mountain Nature Association, 1977. 212p. maps.

1st ed.: Louise A. W. Arps, Denver, Colorado Mountain Club, 1966; rev. ed.: Estes Park, Rocky Mountain Nature Association, 1972.

Review of 1st ed.: R. A. Mohl, Names 16:52-54, March 1968.

1208. Baker, Fred. The town of Dinosaur. Denver post Dec. 19, 1965, Empire magazine p. 18-19.

The name of Artesia was changed to Dinosaur and its street names to those of prehistoric reptiles, because of proximity to Dinosaur National Monument and to foster tourist business.

1209. Baskette, Floyd. Pronunciation guide: Colorado. Comp. by Floyd Baskette, College of Journalism, Univ. of Colorado, with the cooperation and assistance of Colorado broadcasters. [n.p., 1951?]. 11p.

Inlcudes counties, cities and towns, mountain peaks, lakes and reservoirs, mountain passes, rivers, national parks, and national forests.

1210. Bauer, William H., James L. Ozment & John H. Willard. Colorado postal history: the post offices. [Crete, Neb., J-B Pub. Co., c1971]. 248p.

1211. Bean, Luther E. Place names of the San Luis Valley; In his Land of the blue sky people; a story of the San Luis Valley. Monte Vista, Colo., Monte Vista Journal, 1962. p. 96-97.

1212. Block, Augusta Hauck. Old Burlington. Colorado magazine 19:15-17, Jan. 1942.

History of a ghost town of Colorado Territory.

1213. Brandes, T. Donald. Military posts of Colorado. Fort Collins, Colo., Old Army Press, 1973. 77p.

19 forts, posts and cantonments.

Review: James E. Sefton, Arizona and the West 16:195. 1974.

1214. Brown, Robert Leaman. Colorado ghost towns—past and present. Illus. with photos. Caldwell, Idaho, Caxton Printers, 1972. xxvii, 322p. map.

Bibliography: p. x-xi.

1215. —— Ghost towns of the Colorado Rockies. Caldwell, Idaho, Caxton Printers, 1968. 401p. map.

59 towns included.

1216. —— Jeep trails to Colorado ghost towns. Caldwell, Idaho, Caxton Printers, 1963. 239p.

57 settlements representing a sampling, typical of the various kinds of ghost camps.

1217. Cairns, Mary Lyons. Origin of names of points of interest; In her The olden days. Denver, World Press, 1954. p. 235-39.
Around Grand Lake.

1218. Calhoun, Raymond. The naming of Pikes Peak. Colorado magazine 31:98-105, April 1954.
Condensed from his thesis, a historical study of Pikes Peak.

1219. Carson, J. Nevin. Naming Denver's streets. The Westerners. Denver Posse. Brand book 20:3-24. 1964.

1220. Cattle crippled crossing creek gave Cripple Creek its name. Denver post July 6, 1952, p. 2A.
Names of places, mines, and streets in the district.

1221. Chase, Carroll & Richard McP. Cabeen. The first hundred years of United States territorial postmarks, 1787-1887. Colorado Territory. American philatelist 55:362-72, 456-64, 467, March-April 1942.
Includes list of post offices, 1861-78, with notes on some names.

1222. Cline, Platt. Some place names of Mesa Verde. Mesa Verde notes (U.S. National Park Service) 6:11-13, Aug. 1935.

1223. Colorado ghost towns. n.p., n.d. [208]ℓ.
Manuscript in Denver Public Library. Western History Dept.

1224. Colorado place names file. State Historical Society of Colorado.
A comprehensive guide to Colorado's mountains, streams, lakes, settlements, and other geographical points in the Society's library. Compiled by James Grafton Rogers. The cards have been microfilmed to ensure preservation.

1225. Crocchiola, Stanley Francis Louis. The grant that Maxwell bought, by F. Stanley, pseud. [Denver, World Press, 1952]. 256p.
Living towns of the Grant: p. 159-201.
Ghost towns of the Grant [including rivers, canyons, parks, mesas, lakes, ranches]: p. 203-35.
Includes origins of some names.

1226. Crofutt, George A. Crofutt's grip-sack guide of Colorado. A complete encyclopedia of the state. Resources and condensed authentic descriptions of every city, town, village, station, post office and important mining camp in the state. 2d ed. Omaha, Neb., Overland Pub. Co., 1885. 174p.
1st ed. 1881. 183p.; reprinted: [Golden, Colo., Cubar Associates, 1966]. 264p.

1227. Davidson, Levette J. Colorado cartography. Colorado magazine 32:178-90, 256-65, July, Oct. 1955.
From work of earliest explorers to date. Many place-name notes.

1228. —— Colorado place-name studies. Western folklore 12:204-08, July 1953.
Also reprinted separately.

1229. —— Street-name patterns in Denver. Names 2:46-50, March 1954.

1230. —— Two Colorado place names. Western folklore 11:41-42, Jan. 1952.
Fairplay and Cripple Creek.

1231. —— & Olga Hazel Koehler. The naming of Colorado's towns and cities. American speech 7:180-87, Feb. 1932.
Names grouped according to nationality, physical characteristics, slang phrase, etc.

1232. Dawson, John Frank. Place names in Colorado. Why 700 communities were so named. 150 of Spanish or Indian origin. Denver, J. F. Dawson Pub. Co., 1954. 52p.
Alphabetical. Includes earlier names of many places.
Review: Names 2:208-09, Sept. 1954.

1233. Denver. Public Library. Origin of Denver street names; comp. by Anna G. Trimble. 1932?. 15ℓ.
Typewritten.

1234. Denver. Public Library. Western History Dept. Place-name file on cards.
Supplemented by extensive clipping file of brief articles from newspapers; also clippings on ghost towns.

1235. Dike, Sheldon Holland. The territorial post offices of Colorado. Albuquerque, N.M., 1957. Unpaged.

1236. Dirty Woman's Creek. Colorado magazine 25:282-83, Nov. 1948.

1237. Eberhart, Perry. Guide to the Colorado ghost towns and mining camps. 4th rev. ed. [Chicago], Sage Books, [c1969]. 496p. maps.
1st ed. Denver, 1959. 479p.; 2d rev. ed. Denver, 1959 [i.e. 1961]. 479p.; 3d rev. ed. Denver, 1959 [i.e. 1965]. 479p.
Bibliography: p. 485-86.
Some 850 towns are mentioned, located in every important mountain-mining area of the state.

1238. Eichler, George R. Colorado place-names: communities, counties, peaks, passes, with historical lore and facts, plus a pronunciation guide. Foreword by W. E. Marshall, State Historical Society of Colorado. Boulder, Johnson Pub. Co., 1977. 109p.
Bibliography: p. 107.
Review: Robert M. Rennick, Names 27:141-43, June 1979.

1239. Excelsior! Time 63:63, May 3, 1954.
A mountain peak in Colorado to be named Colorado Mines, for the Colorado School of Mines.

1240. Farquhar, Francis Peloubet. Naming America's mountains—the Colorado Rockies. New York, American Alpine Club, 1961.
Reprinted from the American alpine journal v. 12, no. 2, p. 319-46. 1961.

1241. French, A. A. The why of our street names. Colorado genealogist 17:31-33, April 1956.
In Denver.

1242. Gannett, Henry. A gazetteer of Colorado. Washington, Govt. Print. Off., 1906. 185p. (U.S. Geological Survey. Bulletin no. 291)
Issued also as House doc. no. 839, 59th Congress, 1st session.

1243. Gilfillan, George R. & Ruth Gilfillan. Among the tailings; a guide to Leadville mines. Leadville, Colo., Herald democrat, 1964. 85ℓ.
A comprehensive list, giving historical and descriptive information.

1244. Greenhorn battle marker finds new home in park. Rocky Mountain news, Denver, March 11, 1968, p. 34.

Greenhorn Creek and valley named for Indian Chief Cuerno Verde, which means Greenhorn.

1245. Griswold, Don L. & Jean Griswold. Colorado's century of "cities." With illustrations from the Fred M. and Jo Mazzula collection. Denver, Smith-Brooks Print. Co., 1958. 307p.

Contains many references to changes of name, name forms, and "kiting"—the practice of adding a common word such as city to the specific name, like a tail to a kite.

1246. —— Names in the Leadville district. Carbonate chronicle Jan. 2, 1961, p. 7-10.

1247. Hafen, LeRoy Reuben. Colorado cities, their founding and the origin of their names. Colorado magazine 9:170-83, Sept. 1932.

1248. —— The counties of Colorado; a history of their creation and the origin of their names. Colorado magazine 8:48-60, March 1931.

1249. —— Ghost towns—Tarryall and Hamilton. Colorado magazine 10:137-43, July 1933.

1250. —— How Colorado got its name. Denver post Jan. 4, 1959, Empire magazine, p. 6-7.

1251. Hagerman, Percy. Notes on mountaineering in the Elk Mountains of Colorado, 1908-1910. Denver, Colorado Mountain Club, 1956. 28p.

Origin of the name of Buckskin Pass, p. 25, and Hagerman Peak, p. 27, with a suggestion that some peak in the Elk Mountains be named Clark Peak.

1252. Hart, John Lathrop Jerome. Fourteen thousand feet; a history of the naming and early ascents of the high Colorado peaks. 2d ed. By John L. Jerome Hart. A climber's guide to the high Colorado peaks, by Elinor Eppich Kingery. Denver, Colorado Mountain Club, 1931. 68p.

1st ed. 1925. 51p. Supplement to Trail and timberline June 1925; reprinted 1972. 48p.

Kingery's A climber's guide . . . appears in 1931 edition only.

1253. Hoskin, H. G. Kit Carson County's ghost towns. Colorado magazine 10:69-71, March 1933.

1254. Hutton, Tom. Wheat Ridge or Wheatridge? They seem agreed to differ. Denver post June 30, 1957, p. 19A.

1255. Idema, Jim. New streets, names, numbers slated for Littleton by June. Denver post Dec. 18, 1960, p. 24C.

A new street-naming ordinance goes into effect in 1961.

1256. Keeton, Elsie. The story of Dead Man's Canon and of the Espinosas. Colorado magazine 8:34-38, Jan. 1931.

Origin of the name of the canon as told by Henry Priest, pioneer.

1257. Kernochan, Mrs. E. L. List of Colorado towns. n.p., n.d. 15 ℓ.

Manuscript in Denver Public Library Western History Dept.

Emphasis on ghost towns.

1258. Knight, MacDonald B. & Leonard Hammock. Early days on the Eagle; a biographical history of pioneer life in Colorado's Eagle River Valley. Eagle?, Colo., 1965. 48p. map.
Text is a revision of M. B. Knight's M.A. thesis, 1953.
The communities: p. 17-32.
History of the early mining camps, with some origins and changes of name.

1259. Koehler, Olga Hazel. Place names in Colorado.
Thesis (M.A.) Univ. of Denver, 1930.

1260. Kregar, Lester & Helyn Kregar. Origins of Otero County town names. Rocky Ford (Colo.) daily gazette June 29, 1962, Rocky Ford history edition, p. [21].

1261. Lichtenstein, Grace. Pronounce it "Callaradda," son. American heritage 27:81-82, Oct. 1976.
Popular article on the Congressional decision on the name of the state, and a comment on current pronunciation.

1262. Logan, Donna. He has high hope on names. Denver post Dec. 21, 1964, p. 18.
Robert M. Ormes, Colorado College professor, researching the history of the state's mountains, complains of many commonplace names and will recommend names for the more than 200 mountain summits which should receive official names.

1263. Lowry, Maxine. 'X' marks the spot. Lady, how do you feel about Xenon, Xanadu, Xebec? Denver post July 19, 1959, p. 6D.
The problem of finding names that start with "X" to continue the practice of naming streets in alphabetical order in Denver and suburbs.

1264. McHendrie, A. W. Origin of the name of the Purgatoire River. Colorado magazine 5:18-22, Feb. 1928.

1265. Matthews, Ruth Estelle. A study of Colorado place names. Stanford Univ., 1940. 412p.
Thesis (M.A.) Stanford Univ., 1940.

1266. Mining claims. Gilpin County miner, Central City, Colo., July 13, 1939.
Reprinted in part in American speech 17:72, Feb. 1942.
Names of recorded mining locations.

1267. Page, Charles Albert. What's in a name? In the Gunnison country. Gunnison, Colo., Page Books, 1974. 76p.
Bibliography: p. 74-76.

1268. Places and names. Silver state record v. 1-4, no. 3, May 1963-July 1966.
A monthly column in the Silver state record devoted to Colorado history excerpted from old newspapers.

1269. Richie, Eleanor L. Spanish place-names in Colorado. American speech 10:88-92, April 1935.

1270. Ring, Edward. Silverheels. Colorado magazine 17:27, Jan. 1940.
Story of the naming of Mount Silverheels at Fairplay, Colo.

1271. Rizzari, Francis B. Notes on a few early towns of Jefferson County. The Westerners. Denver Posse. Brand book 21:235-55, 1965.

1272. Shoemaker, Len. Early days in Garfield County. The Westerners. Denver Posse. Brand book 21:307-31, 1965.
Early towns.

1273. —— National forests. Colorado magazine 21:182-84, Sept. 1944.
Changes in name and status of many national parks, particularly those in Colorado.

1274. Some of the lost towns of Kansas. Kansas State Historical Society. Collections 12:426-90. 1911-12.
Includes a list of incorporations, by Kansas men, of towns now within the boundaries of Colorado.

1275. Taylor, Morris F. Trinidad legends. Colorado magazine 41:154-57, Spring 1964.
"There is no good evidence to support the contention that the town was named after a daughter of Felipe Baca."

1276. Taylor, Ralph C. Colorado, south of the border. Denver, Sage Books, 1963. 561p.
Origin of names [southeastern Colorado]: p. 533-49.

1277. Territory of Colorado; In Bancroft, Hubert Howe. History of Nevada, Colorado and Wyoming. San Francisco, History Co., 1890. p. 401-13; also in U.S. Congress. Congressional globe, 36th Congress, 1st session, 1859-60, p. 1502; 36th Congress, 2d session, 1860-61, p. 639-40, 728-29, 763-66, 792, 833, 1003-05, 1012, 1205-06, 1248, 1274.
Inhabitants of the Pikes Peak region first tried to organize as a county of Kansas, called Arapahoe, Nov. 1858. After many petitions to Congress, a bill for the creation of a new territory was finally introduced and passed, becoming law Feb. 28, 1861. The names Colorado, Jefferson, and Idaho were all considered, but Colorado prevailed.

1278. Toll, Oliver W. Arapaho names and trails; a report of a 1914 pack trip. n.p., 1962. 43p.
Field notes on a pack trip with three Arapaho Indians through the Estes Park-Grand Lake region of Colorado, arranged in order to learn the Arapaho names for the area.

1279. Toll, Roger Wolcott. The mountain peaks of Colorado, containing a list of named points of elevation in the state of Colorado with elevations and topographic details. Denver, Colorado Mountain Club, 1923. 59p.
Supplement to Trail and timberline Jan. 1923.

1280. Trager, George L. Some Spanish place-names of Colorado. American speech 10:203-07, Oct. 1935.
To record the pronunciation of a number of Colorado place-names of Spanish origin in the mouths of native speakers of English.

1281. U.S. Board on Geographic Names. Decisions. No. 27—June 30, 1932. Rocky Mountain National Park, Colorado. Washington, Govt. Print. Off., 1934. 10p.

1282. —— Decisions. No. 37, Decisions rendered February 7, 1934. Mesa Verde National Park, Colorado. Washington, Govt. Print. Off., 1934. 7p.

1283. —— U.S. Writers' Program. Colorado. Place names of Colorado towns. Colorado magazine v. 17-20, Jan. 1940-May 1943.
An alphabetical series of some 3,000 town names, giving brief history of the name with source.

1284. Vivian, C. H. Ghost camps. Compressed air magazine 46:6474-79, July 1941.

Describes several towns that flourished for a time due to mines, but were later abandoned. Gives origin of some of the names.

1285. Volstad, Steve. A left-handed Indian: or, how Niwot got its name. Public Service Company of Colorado. Your home and community 32:[1-4], Feb. 1971.

A popular, general article on place-names in Colorado.

1286. Wallrich, William Jones. The village of Old San Acacio. Western folklore 8:367-68, Oct. 1949.

1287. Wells, Merle W. From western Kansas to Colorado: problems of naming a new mining territory. Journal of the West 16:63-65, Jan. 1977.

Traces the Congressional action in naming the Territory, 1861, with consideration of Osage, Jefferson, Idaho, and others.

1288. Wolle, Muriel Vincent Sibell. Stampede to timberline; the ghost towns and mining camps of Colorado. 2d ed., rev. & enl. Chicago, Swallow Press, 1974. 583p. maps.

1st ed.: Denver, Sage Books, c1949; reprinted 1965. 544p.

Published under the auspices of the University of Colorado, Boulder.

Includes place-name origin and history for many of the names.

CONNECTICUT

1289. Allen, Morse S. Connecticut place names. Connecticut antiquarian 15:20-24, Dec. 1963.

Deals with the problems the author and Arthur H. Hughes encountered in compiling a book of Connecticut place-names.

1290. —— Place-names in Salisbury, Connecticut. Names 6:97-111, June 1958.

1291. Ashley, Leonard R. N. New England looks like olde England in the place-names of Connecticut. Connecticut onomastic review 1:1-22, 1979.

1291a. Caulkins, Frances Manwaring. History of New London, Connecticut. New London, The Author, 1852. 680p.

"A chapter of names, English and aboriginal, p. 118-25, contains a list of geographic names in the Pequot or Mohegan territory."--Pilling.

1292. Connecticut. General Assembly. Centennial Committee. The one hundredth anniversary of the first meeting of the General Assembly, under the present constitution and the second general legislative reunion. The Capitol, Hartford, Wednesday, May 7, 1919. Comp. by William Harrison Taylor, secretary of the Centennial Committee. Hartford, Pub. by the State, 1919. 188p.

"Connecticut towns in the order of their establishment since 1819; with the origin of their names: p. 177-78."--Griffin.

1293. Dexter, Franklin Bowditch. The history of Connecticut, as illustrated by the names of her towns. Worcester, Mass., Press of C. Hamilton, 1885. 30p.

Reprinted from the American Antiquarian Society. Proceedings n.s. 3:421-48, April 1885.

Also in his A selection from the miscellaneous historical papers of fifty years (New Haven, Tuttle, 1918).

1294. Eno, Joel Nelson. Ancient place-names in Connecticut. Connecticut magazine 12:93-96, Jan.-March 1908.

The nomenclature of familiar localities with the derivation and interpretation from the Indian language.

1295. —— The nomenclature of Connecticut towns. Connecticut magazine 8:330-35, Dec. 1903.

Three types of names: historical, geographical, and biographical.

1296. Gannett, Henry. A geographic dictionary of Connecticut. Washington, Govt. Print. Off., 1894. 67p. (U.S. Geological Survey. Bulletin no. 117)

Issued also as House miscellaneous doc. v. 57, 53d Congress, 2d session.

1297. Hawley, Charles W. Old names of Connecticut towns. Stamford Genealogical Society. Bulletin 3:61-63, Feb. 1961.

A compilation which translates obsolete place-names into their present-day geographical identity. Includes only Fairfield County.

1298. Hughes, Arthur H. Connecticut place names ending in "—ville." Connecticut Historical Society. Bulletin 35:40-64, April 1970.

An alphabetical list giving location, origin of name, and indication if post office. Includes names no longer in use.

1299. —— & Morse S. Allen. Connecticut place names. [Hartford] Connecticut Historical Society, 1976. xx, 907p.

Bibliography: p. 773-803.

Series of appendices giving lists of names in categories including Connecticut town names in Vermont, Connecticut place names in Ohio, and town names rare in the United States.

Review: Kelsie B. Harder, Names 25:44-48, March 1977.

1300. Martin, Stanley. Indian derivatives in Connecticut place-names. New England quarterly 12:364-69, June 1939.

"Contains an extensive list of the more frequent prefix and suffix components which enter in the formation of local place names of Indian origin."—American speech.

1301. Nine new nicknames pondered by Norwalk. New York times July 26, 1960, p. 24, col. 1.

Residents asked to pick a new name to replace Clamtown, which is neither complimentary nor accurate.

1302. Pease, John Chauncey & John Milton Niles. A gazetteer of the States of Connecticut and Rhode-Island. Written with care and impartiality, from original and authentic materials. Consisting of two parts. With an accurate and improved map of each state. Hartford, Printed and pub. by William S. Marsh, 1819. 389p.

1303. Prindle, Paul W. The 169 towns of Connecticut. Stamford Genealogical Society. Bulletin 8:110-17, May 1966.

Gives present and former name, date of first settlement, date when made a town, where settled from, and what set off from.

1304. Pronunciation across the seas. Christian Science monitor Oct. 31, 1955, p. 11.

Pronunciation of Greenwich.

1305. Republican town erasing "Roosevelt." Stratford, Conn. pushes plan to change name of park. New York times Jan. 1, 1940, p. 25, col. 4.

1306. Sanford, Irvin Wilbur. History and explanation of Indian names in Salisbury, Conn.; In Rudd, Malcolm Day. An historical sketch of Salisbury, Connecticut. New York, 1899. p. 19-23.

1307. Sellers, Helen Earle. Connecticut town origins. Stonington, Conn., Pequot Press, [1964?]. 96p. (Connecticut booklet, no. 10)
Reprint of the author's Origins of the names of the Connecticut towns; In Connecticut. Secretary of State. Register and manual 1942:358-438.

1308. Speck, Frank Gouldsmith. Geographical names and legends at Mohegan. U.S. Bureau of American Ethnology. Annual report 43:253-59. 1925-26.
Appendix to his Native tribes and dialects of Connecticut, a Mohegan-Pequot diary. A record of names in the old Mohegan community on the Thames River.

1309. Trumbull, James Hammond. Indian names of places etc., in and on the borders of Connecticut: with interpretations of some of them. Hartford, Case, Lockwood & Brainard Co., 1881. 93p.
Reprinted: [Hamden, Conn.] Archon Books, 1974.
Review: Nation 32:424-25, June 16, 1881.

1310. Tyler, Clarice E. Topographical terms in the seventeenth century records of Connecticut and Rhode Island. New England quarterly 2:382-401, July 1929.
"These terms provide some interesting illustrations of changes in the English language."—Griffin.

DELAWARE

1311. Dunlap, Arthur Ray. Another Welsh tract. Names 13:258-62, Dec. 1965.
Describes a Welsh tract and the place-names in it a few miles below the present Delaware-Pennsylvania boundary, a tract south of the one described by Ruth L. Pearce in her Welsh place-names in southeastern Pennsylvania, ibid. 11:31-43, March 1963.

1312. —— Dutch and Swedish place-names in Delaware. Newark, Del., Pub. for the Institute of Delaware History and Culture by the Univ. of Delaware Press, 1956. 66p.
A collection of some 132 names of Dutch or Swedish origin, with a discussion of each, based on researches on 17th century maps and documents.
Review: C. A. Weslager, Names 5:182-83, Sept. 1957.

1313. —— An example of dialect in Delaware place names. American speech 25:71-72, Feb. 1950.
Hecklebirnie, dialect word for "hell," and Hackley Barney, both formerly found in Delaware.

1314. —— More light on "Catenamon." Archaeological Society of Delaware. Bulletin 6:1-5, April 1954.

1315. —— Names for Delaware. Names 3:230-35, Dec. 1955.

1316. —— & C. A. Weslager. Indian place names in Delaware. Wilmington, Archaeological Society of Delaware, 1950. 61p.
Review: J. A. C. Leland, Names 1:59-61, March 1953; James B. McMillan, American speech 27:190-91, Oct. 1952.

1317. —— Toponomy of the Delaware Valley as revealed by an early seventeenth-century Dutch map. Archeological Society of New Jersey. Bulletin 15-16:1-13, Nov. 1958.
Bibliography: p. 5-6.

1318. Gannett, Henry. A gazetteer of Delaware, Washington, Govt. Print. Off., 1904. 15p. (U.S. Geological Survey. Bulletin no. 230, Ser. F, Geography 38)
Reprinted as A gazetteer of Maryland and Delaware. Baltimore, Genealogical Pub. Co., 1976. 84, 15p.

1319. Gritzner, Janet H. Seventeenth century generic place-names: culture and process on the Eastern Shore. Names 20:231-39, Dec. 1972.
Summarizes the results of a study to identify the various cultural processes involved in naming all of the peninsula east of Chesapeake Bay.

1320. Heck, L. W. & others. Delaware place names. Washington, U.S. Govt. Print. Off., 1966. 124p. maps. (U.S. Geological Survey. Bulletin no. 1245)
Prepared by the Geological Survey, U.S. Dept. of the Interior, and the Coast and Geodetic Survey, U.S. Dept. of Commerce.
Bibliography: p. 123-24.
A gazetteer of the known places and features of Delaware. All known variant names and spellings are listed alphabetically. Includes some information on name derivation but no attempt was made to do any original name study.

1321. Weslager, Clinton Alfred. The Delaware Indians, a history. New Brunswick, N.J., Rutgers Univ. Press, [c1972]. xix, 546p. map.
Bibliographical footnotes.
Some attention, especially in Chapter 2: The homeland of the Delawares, p. 31-49, to place names of Indian origin attributable to the Delawares, and surviving in Delaware, Pennsylvania, Ohio, Indiana, Missouri, Kansas, and Oklahoma.

1322. —— Dutch explorers, traders, and settlers in the Delaware Valley, 1609-1664. In collaboration with A. R. Dunlap. Philadelphia, Univ. of Pennsylvania Press, 1961. 329p.
Dutch maps and geographical names: p. 215-32.

1323. —— An early American name puzzle. Names 2:255-62, Dec. 1954.
Origin of the name Hoere-kil.

1324. —— Hockessin: another Delaware place-name puzzle. Names 12:10-14, March 1964.

1325. —— New Castle, Delaware—and its former names. Names 24:101-05, June 1976.

DISTRICT OF COLUMBIA

1326. Anthropological Society of Washington. Geographic nomenclature of the District of Columbia. A report. Washington, 1893.
James Mooney, chairman of the committee.
From the American anthropologist 6:29-53, Jan. 1893.
A system for naming the streets.

1327. Capital street named for MacArthur. New York times March 6, 1942, p. 6, col. 1.
President Roosevelt signed bill renaming Conduit Road, Washington, D.C., MacArthur Blvd.

1328. Edwards, Richard. Statistical gazetteer of the State of Maryland, and the District of Columbia. To which is appended a business directory of the federal metropolis and suburbs. Baltimore, J. S. Waters; Washington, W. M. Morrison & Co., 1856. 328p.

1329. Hagner, Alexander Burton. Street nomenclature of Washington City. Columbia Historical Society. Records 7:237-61. 1904.
Suggests names and methods for naming the streets to take the place of the system in use—designation by letters.

1330. Hodgkins, George W. Naming the capitol and the capital. Columbia Historical Society. Records 60-62:36-53. 1960-62.

1331. Maine Avenue again on Washington maps. New York times May 15, 1938, sec. 4, p. 6, col. 6.
Congress moves to change name of Water St. to Maine Ave.

1332. Martin, Joseph. A new and comprehensive gazetteer of Virginia, and the District of Columbia. To which is added a History of Virginia from its first settlement to the year 1754: with an abstract of the principal events from that period to the independence of Virginia, written expressly for the work by a citizen of Virginia [W. H. Brockenbrough]. Charlottesville, J. Martin, 1836. 636p.
Also published 1835, and at Richmond without date under title A comprehensive description of Virginia and the District of Columbia.

1333. Mooney, James. Indian tribes of the District of Columbia. American anthropologist 2:259-66, July 1889.
Concerning aboriginal place-names and the current names for the same localities.

1334. Tindall, William. Naming the seat of government of the United States; a legislative paradox. Columbia Historical Society. Records 23:10-25. 1920.

1335. Tooker, William Wallace. On the meaning of the name Anacostia. American anthropologist 7:389-93, Oct. 1894.

1336. Weekley, Larry. McAuley Park streets perpetuate nuns' names. Washington post Feb. 6, 1965, sec. E, p. 1.

FLORIDA

1337. Applegate, Roberta. What's in a name? History in our parks. Miami herald June 24, 1962, sec. E, pt. II, p. 17.
In Miami area.

1338. Bloodworth, Bertha Ernestine. Florida place-names. Gainesville, Univ. of Florida, 1959. 260ℓ.
Thesis, Univ. of Florida.
Bibliography: 256-59.

1339. Boone, Lalia. Florida, the land of epithets. Southern folklore quarterly 22:86-92. 1958.
Nicknames of place-names.

1340. Boyd, Mark F. Mission sites in Florida; an attempt to approximately identify the sites of Spanish mission settlements of the seventeenth century in northern Florida. Florida historical quarterly 17:255-80, April 1939.
Includes list of names as given in old manuscripts and maps.

1341. Chardon, Roland. Notes on south Florida place names: Norris Cut. Tequesta 37:51-61, 1977.
Until 1905 Norris Cut was the principal waterway into Biscayne Bay and Miami.

1342. Chase, Carroll & Richard McP. Cabeen. The first hundred years of United States territorial postmarks, 1787-1887. Florida Territory. American philatelist 56:246-59, Jan. 1943.
Includes list of post offices, 1821-45, with notes on some names.

1343. Corse, Herbert M. Names of the St. Johns River. Florida historical quarterly 21:127-34, Oct. 1942.
Bibliographical footnotes.
Four centuries of history are reflected in the changing names of the St. Johns River.

1344. Craig, James C. Origins of street names. Jacksonville Historical Society. Papers 3:7-11. 1954.
Jacksonville, Fla.

1345. Dau, Frederick W. Indian and other names in Florida, their meaning and derivation; In his Florida old and new. New York, Putnam, 1934. p. 336.

1346. Drew, Frank. Some Florida names of Indian origin. Florida Historical Society quarterly 4:181-82, April 1926; 6:197-205, April 1928.

1347. Drew, Shelley. Place names in ten northeastern counties of Florida. American speech 37:255-65, Dec. 1962.

1348. Enumeration of Florida Spanish missions in 1675, with transcript of documents by Mark F. Boyd. Florida historical quarterly 27:181-85, Oct. 1948.

1349. Florida. Department of Agriculture. The seventh census of the State of Florida, 1945. Nathan Mayo, Commissioner of Agriculture. [Tallahassee, 1946?]. 141p.
Origin and names of Florida counties: p. 7-8.

1350. Florida. Division of Water Resources and Conservation. Florida lakes. Tallahassee, Florida Board of Conservation, 1969. 3v.
v. 3: Gazetteer.

1351. —— Gazetteer of Florida streams. Tallahassee, 1966. 88p.

1352. Florida law restores Cape Canaveral's name. New York times May 30, 1973, p. 79.
Florida law, signed May 29, 1973, restored the name Cape Canaveral to the area which President Johnson renamed Cape Kennedy on Nov. 29, 1963. The John F. Kennedy Space Center name was not changed. Selected related articles follow:
Renaming of Cape Kennedy is backed. New York times Nov. 25, 1969, p. 33.
Report of a Senate hearing on the return to the centuries-old name, proposed in the Senate Joint Resolution, no. 133.
U.S. 91st Congress, 1st session. Senate. Joint resolution to redesignate the area in the State of Florida known as Cape Kennedy as Cape Canaveral. S.J. Res. 133. July 10, 1969. Washington, 1969. 2p.
Introduced by Mr. Holland and Mr. Gurney and referred to the Committee on Interior and Insular Affairs.
Cape's name restored by Florida Legislature. New York times May 19, 1973, p. 24.
U.S. Board on Geographic Names. Decisions. 7304:4, Oct.-Dec. 1973.
ANS Bulletin 33:12, Dec. 1973.
Summary and partial listing of press coverage:
[U.S. Board on Geographic Names consideration]. Morning advocate. Baton Rouge, Oct. 4, 1973.
Kennedy, Edward M. Letter to the editor of the Miami herald accepting restoration of the original name. Cape Cod standard times Oct. 20, 1973.

1353. Hawkins, Benjamin. A sketch of the Creek country, in the years 1798 and 1799. Georgia Historical Society. Collections v. 3, pt. 1, 1848. 88p.
An explanation of Creek and Seminole Indian place-names in Georgia and Florida.

1354. Hawks, John Milton. The Florida gazetteer, containing also a guide to and through the state; complete official and business directory; state and national statistics. New Orleans, Printed at the Bronze Pen Stfam [sic] Book and Job Office, 1871. 214p.

1355. How did the Keys get names? Key West citizen Nov. 15, 1964, p. 6E.

1356. McMullen, Edwin Wallace. Cape Canaveral and Chicago. Names 12:128-29, June 1964.
Report on discussion of the name change of Cape Canaveral to Cape Kennedy at the meeting of the American Name Society in Chicago, Dec. 1963.

1357. —— English topographic terms in Florida, 1563-1874. Gainesville, Univ. of Florida Press, 1953. 227p.
Also published as doctoral thesis, Columbia Univ. and on microfilm, Ann Arbor, University Microfilms, 1950. Publication no. 1877. Abstracted: Microfilm abstracts 10:204-05.
Dictionary of topographic terms found in Florida, with bibliography, preceded by an interesting introduction.
Review: Margaret M. Bryant, Names 2:142-43, June 1954; Raven I. McDavid, Jr., American speech 30:53-54, Feb. 1955.

1358. —— The origin of the term Everglades. American speech 28:26-34, Feb. 1953.
A revised article taken from his doctoral dissertation, above.
cf. James B. McMillan, To the editor. American speech 28:200-01, Oct. 1953.

1359. Morris, Allen Covington. Florida place names. Coral Gables, Univ. of Miami Press, 1974. 160p. maps.
Bibliography: p. 155-60.
General work includes alphabetical list of incorporated towns of 1000 or more population.
Review: Margaret M. Bryant, Names 23:117-19, June 1975; Pat Dobson, Florida historical quarterly 54:95-96, July 1975.

1360. Phillips, Cabell. Canaveral Space Center renamed Cape Kennedy. New York times Nov. 29, 1963, p. 1, 20.
References to other newspaper articles on this name change follow:
Protests are mounting on renaming Canaveral. New York times Dec. 5, 1963, p. 35.
Cape's name change declared official. New York times Dec. 6, 1963, p. 18.
Federal group supported L. B. J. in retitling Cape Canaveral. Kansas City star Dec. 6, 1963.
Wright, C. E. Cape Kennedy. Space Center is renamed but city and port retain name Canaveral. New York times Dec. 8, 1963, sec. XX, p. 5.
Fail to block "Cape Kennedy"; despite residents' historical pleas, new name is likely to stick; dates from the 1500s. Kansas City star Dec. 8, 1963, p. 4AA.
Random notes from all over: Canaveral renamed in a hurry; "Kennedy" approval reported in 3 hours by Udall—old name lasted centuries. New York times Dec. 9, 1963, p. 14.
Kennedy's name to Cape in 3-hour rush request. Kansas City times Dec. 12, 1963.

1361. Read, William Alexander. Caxambas, a Florida geographic name. Language 16:210-13, July 1940.

1362. —— Florida place-names of Indian origin and Seminole personal names. Baton Rouge, Louisiana State Univ. Press, 1934. 83p. (Louisiana State University studies, no. 11)

Bibliography: p. 80.

Review: John R. Swanton, American speech 9:218-20, Oct. 1934; James A. Robertson, Florida Historical Society quarterly 13:111-12, Oct. 1934.

1363. —— The Hitchiti name of Silver Springs, Florida. Modern language notes 53:513-14, Nov. 1938.

The Indian name may be freely translated as "wells of light."

1364. Simpson, James Clarence. Middle Florida place names. Apalachee 1946:68-77.

Indian names.

1365. —— A provisional gazetteer of Florida place-names of Indian derivation, either obsolescent or retained, together with others of recent application. Ed. by Mark F. Boyd. Tallahassee, 1956. 158p. (Florida. Geological Survey. Special publication no. 1)

Review: E. Wallace McMullen, Names 4:249-52, Dec. 1956; John W. Griffin, Florida historical quarterly 35:194, Oct. 1956.

1366. Tongue-twisting name to stay. Lincoln (Neb.) evening journal and Nebraska State journal Aug. 1, 1962, p. 2.

Pilaklakaha Ave. in Auburndale, Fla.

1367. Utley, George Burwell. Origin of the county names in Florida. Magazine of history 8:77-81, Aug. 1908.

Reprinted in Florida Historical Society. Publications quarterly 1:29-35, Oct. 1908.

1368. Wilkinson, Herbert James. The Florida place name "Jupiter." American speech 13:233-34, Oct. 1938.

GEORGIA

1369. Algeo, John. From classic to classy: changing fashions in street names. Names 26:80-95, March 1978.

The early nineteenth century commemorative names are contrasted with the decorative, artificial, and slick names of post-1960 in Athens, Georgia.

1370. Brinkley, Hal E. How Georgia got her names. Rev. ed. [Atlanta, The Author, 1973]. 196p.

Alphabetical listing of more than 4,000 names.

Review: Robert M. Rennick, Names 24:318, Dec. 1976.

1371. Cohen, Hennig. On the word Georgian. Georgia historical quarterly 37:347-48, Dec. 1953.

Use of the word from 1735.

1372. Ee places in Georgia. Sun, New York, March 30, 1938.

Most of those discussed end in -hatchee, meaning river in the Seminole-Creek language.

1373. Georgia. Department of Archives and History. Georgia's official register.

Each issue has section County data, which includes origin of the name of the counties.

1374. Godley, Margaret W. Georgia county place-names.
Thesis (M.A.) Emory Univ., 1935.

1375. Goff, John Hedges. The beaverdam creeks. Georgia mineral newsletter 7:117-22, Fall 1954.
Streams in Georgia that now have or formerly had beaver in their name.

1376. —— The buffalo in Georgia. Georgia review 11:19-28, Spring 1957.
Georgia place-names which contain the word buffalo.

1377. —— The Creek village of "Cooccohapofe" on Flint River. Georgia mineral newsletter 14:34-35, Spring 1961.
Concerning its location and derivation.

1378. —— The derivations of Creek Indian place names. Georgia mineral newsletter 14:63-70, Summer-Fall 1961.

1379. —— The devil's half-acre. Georgia review 9:290-96, Fall 1955.
Reprinted in Georgia mineral newsletter 12:27-29, Spring-Summer 1959.
Deals with Georgia appellations containing the words devil and hell, like Devil's Elbow, Hell's Half Acre.

1380. —— Hog Crawl Creek. Georgia mineral newsletter 7:38-40, Spring 1954.
A study of the name.

1381. —— The "Hurricane" place names in Georgia. Georgia review 18:224-35, Summer 1964.

1382. —— Old Chattahoochee town, an early Muscogee Indian settlement. Georgia mineral newsletter 6:52-54, Summer 1953.
The name and site of the town.

1383. —— Placenames of Georgia; essays of John H. Goff, edited by Francis Lee Utley and Marion R. Hemperley. Athens, Univ. of Georgia Press, c1975. xxxviii, 495p. map.
Review: Allen Morris, Florida historical quarterly 55:104-05, July 1976; John E. Talmadge, Georgia historical quarterly 60:68-69, Spring 1976; Robert M. Rennick, Names 24:321-23, Dec. 1976.

1384. —— The poor mouthing place names. Georgia review 12:440-50, Winter 1958.
Republished in Georgia mineral newsletter 12:65-68, Fall 1959.
Place-names that reflect poverty.

1385. —— Short studies of Georgia place names. Georgia mineral newsletter 7:87-88, 124-28, 163-64, Summer-Winter 1954; 8:22-26, 78-81, 122-25, 158-60. 1955; 9:32-36, 75-80, 105-08, 136-40. 1956; 10:32-35, 56-60, Spring-Summer 1957; 11:31-35, 54-59, 131-32, Spring-Summer, Winter 1958; 12:63-65, Fall 1959; 13:35-42, 102-06, 129-38, Spring, Summer, Fall 1960; 14:30-34, Spring 1961; 15:31-33, 95-101, Spring-Summer, Fall-Winter 1962; 16:45-53, 88-97, Spring-Summer, Fall-Winter 1963; 17:55-73. 1964-65.

1386. —— Some old road names in Georgia. Emory University quarterly 14:30-42, March 1958.
Republished in Georgia mineral newsletter 11:98-102, Autumn 1958.

1387. —— Ty Ty as a geographic name. Georgia mineral newsletter 7:36-38, Spring 1954.

1388. Hawkins, Benjamin. A sketch of the Creek country, in the years 1798 and 1799. Georgia Historical Society. Collections v. 3, pt. 1, 1848. 88p.
An explanation of Creek and Seminole Indian place-names in Georgia and Florida.

1389. Hemperley, Marion R. Indian place names in Georgia. Georgia historical quarterly 57:562-79, Winter 1973.

1390. Irvine, William Stafford. Governor Wilson Lumpkin and the naming of Marthasville. Atlanta historical bulletin 2:46-56. 1937.

1391. —— Terminus and Deanville, local names of long ago, of the site of Atlanta. Atlanta historical bulletin 3:101-19. 1938.

1392. Jones, Billie Walker. Origin of the name Dry Branch, Georgia. Georgia mineral newsletter 10:69, Summer 1957.

1393. Krakow, Kenneth K. Georgia place-names. Macon, Ga., Winship Press, 1975. 272p. maps.
Bibliography: p. 267-72.
A dictionary of more than 5000 names with historical data for many, and with a note on Militia Districts, Georgia being the only state with such divisions of counties.
Review: Robert M. Rennick, Names 23:306-07, Dec. 1975; Pat Dobson, Florida historical quarterly 54:95-96, July 1975; William Tate, Georgia historical quarterly 59:460-62, Winter 1975.

1393a. —— Georgia place names with South Carolina derivations. Names in South Carolina 22:17-24, Winter 1975.

1394. Lagoudakis, Charilaos. Greece in Georgia. Georgia historical quarterly 47:189-92, June 1963.
Place-names with Greek derivations.

1395. Lanman, Charles. The falls of Tallulah. Magazine of history 19:249-53, Dec. 1914.
Meaning of Tallulah, also of Deer Leap, Hawthorn's Pool, and Hanck's Sliding Pool.

1396. Lastelic, Joe. Unnamed lake on the Chattahoochee. Kansas City times Nov. 21, 1966, p. 16.
Body of water on the Chattahoochee River behind the Walter F. George Dam in Alabama and Georgia.

1397. McDavid, Raven I., Jr. & Virginia McDavid. Cracker and Hoosier. Names 21:161-67, Sept. 1973.
Relationship and geographical spread of the two nicknames.

1398. Mitchell, Eugene M. Queer place names in old Atlanta. Atlanta historical bulletin 5:22-31, April 1931.

1399. Moore, Violet. What's in a name? Plenty for some Georgia towns. Mercer toponomist studies Georgia. Atlanta journal Jan. 29, 1970.
Describes Kenneth K. Krakow's work on the place-names of Georgia, with some general material on the names.

1400. Read, William Alexander. Indian stream-names in Georgia. International journal of American linguistics 15:128-32, April 1949; 16:203-07, Oct. 1950.

1401. Sherwood, Adiel. A gazetteer of Georgia; containing a particular description of the state; its resources, counties, towns, villages, and whatever is usual in statistical works. 4th ed., rev. and cor. Macon, Ga., S. Boykin; Atlanta, J. Richards; etc. etc., 1860. 209p.
1st ed. 1827; 2d ed. 1829; 3d ed. 1837 (two printings).

1402. —— A gazetteer of the State of Georgia, by Rev. Adiel Sherwood; biographical sketch by John B. Clark; foreword by President Spright Dowell, Mercer University. The present edition being a facsimile reprint of the original 1827 publication, with a map of Georgia from the 1829 edition and a portrait of the author. Athens, Ga., Univ. of Georgia Press, 1939. 143p.

1403. States or Staten; Ville remains same. Denver post July 18, 1965, p. 26.
The town will continue to be called Statesville popularly and Statenville officially.

1404. U.S. 88th Congress, 1st session. House. A bill to designate the lake formed by the Walter F. George Lock and Dam, Alabama and Georgia, as Lake Chattahoochee. H.R. 2127. Jan. 17, 1963. Washington, 1963. 1p.
Introduced by Mr. Forrester and referred to the Committee on Public Works.

1405. —— Senate. A bill to designate the lake formed by the Walter F. George Lock and Dam, Alabama and Georgia, as Lake Eufaula. S. 454. Jan. 23 (legislative day, Jan. 15), 1963. Washington, 1963. 1p.
Introduced by Mr. Hill and Mr. Sparkman and referred to the Committee on Public Works.
An identical bill was introduced in the House as follows:
U.S. 88th Congress, 1st session. House. A bill to designate the lake formed by the Walter F. George Lock and Dam, Alabama and Georgia, as Lake Eufaula. H.R. 3163. Jan. 31, 1963. Washington, 1963. 1p.
Introduced by Mr. Andrews and referred to the Committee on Public Works.

1406. Utley, Francis Lee. Hog Crawl Creek again. Names 21:179-95, Sept. 1973.

HAWAII

1407. Alexander, William DeWitt. Hawaiian geographic names. U.S. Coast and Geodetic Survey. Report 1901/02, Appendix 7, p. 367-425.
Includes a glossary of the words most frequently occurring in Hawaiian geographic names, p. 396-99.

1408. Boom, Robert & J. S. Christensen. Important Hawaiian place names. Rev. ed. Honolulu, R. Boom Co., 1971. 34p.
1st ed.: Honolulu, Star-Bulletin Print Co., c1969.

1409. Bryan, Edwin Horace. Hawaiian place names. Hawaiian annual 1947:255-74.

1410. Cartwright, Bruce. Place names in old Honolulu. Paradise of the Pacific 50:18-20, Jan. 1938.

1411. Coulter, John Wesley. A gazetteer of the Territory of Hawaii. Honolulu, Univ. of Hawaii, 1935. 241p. (University of Hawaii. Research publications, no. 11)
References on Hawaiian place-names: p. 238-39.

1412. The Flying trees of Lahaina, Maui. Paradise of the Pacific v. 61, Jan. 1949, Travel supp. p. 17.

1413. Helumoa. Paradise of the Pacific v. 61, April 1949, Travel supp. p. 22.
Name of coconut grove where Royal Hawaiian Hotel is located, also a street in Waikiki.

1414. Hogue, Charles Edward. Puowaina, consecrated hill. Paradise of the Pacific 61:6, 30, Oct. 1949.
From the Honolulu advertiser.
In Honolulu.

1415. Honolulu street names rich in lore and history. Paradise of the Pacific v. 59, Nov. 1947, Travel supp. p. 5.

1416. Hyde, C. M. Hawaiian poetical names for places. Hawaiian almanac and annual 1887:79-82.

1417. Judd, Henry Pratt. Place names on Oahu. Paradise of the Pacific 50:11-12, Feb. 1938.

1418. —— Pronouncing Hawaii's place names. Paradise of the Pacific 58:26, Dec. 1944.

1419. Kauai is island of many names. Paradise of the Pacific v. 61, Feb. 1949, Travel supp. p. 20-21.

1420. Kelsey, Theodore. The pronunciation of Hawaiian names. Paradise of the Pacific 42:25-30, Feb. 1929.

1421. Lindsey, Jessie Higbee. District and county guide of the Territory of Hawaii. Honolulu, 1947. 38p.
Typewritten.

1422. Lyons, C. J. History in Honolulu streets: highway names are full of meaning. Hawaiian annual 1932:74-76.
As told by C. J. Lyons in the P. C. advertiser March 3, 1902.

1423. —— The meaning of some Hawaiian place-names. Hawaiian almanac and annual 1901:181-82.

1424. [The Naming of the streets of Honolulu]. Hawaiian almanac and annual 1884:73.

1425. Oahu place names. Paradise of the Pacific v. 61, Feb. 1949, Travel supp. p. 28.

1426. Obsolete street names. Hawaiian almanac and annual 1897:88-89.
In Honolulu.

1427. Odd named localities. Hawaiian almanac and annual 1906:108.
In Honolulu.

1428. On Hawaiian duplicated place names. Hawaiian almanac and annual 1905:150-54.

1429. Pukui, Mary Wiggin, Samuel H. Elbert & Esther Mookini. Place names of Hawaii. Rev. and enl. ed. Honolulu, Univ. Press of Hawaii, c1974. 289p.
1st ed.: 1966. 53p.
References: p. 281-89.

Review of 1st ed.: Kelsie B. Harder, Names 16:63-64, March 1968.
Review of 2d ed.: Fred Tarpley, Names 24:136-38, June 1976.

1430. Sandwich vs. Hawaiian Islands. Hawaiian almanac and annual 1923:70-71.

1431. Stewart, George Rippey. Hawaii; In his Names on the land; a historical account of place-naming in the United States. Rev. and enl. ed. Boston, Houghton Mifflin, 1958. p. 412-23.

1432. Street name index. Honolulu Municipal Reference Library.
Card file—continuing.

1433. Taylor, Clarice B. & George H. Miranda. Honolulu street names. Honolulu star-bulletin Jan. 16-April 21, 1956.

1434. Thrum, Thomas George. Hawaiian place names; In Andrews, Lorrin. A dictionary of the Hawaiian language. Rev. by Henry H. Parker. Prepared under the direction of the Board of Commissioners of Public Archives of the Territory of Hawaii. Honolulu, Pub. by the Board, 1922. p. 625-74.

1435. U.S. Board on Geographic Names. Decisions. Washington, Dept. of the Interior.
Hawaii is included in various Decision lists through 1958. Beginning with list no. 5902, Jan. 1959, Hawaii is included in its alphabetical place with the other states.

1436. —— Decisions on names in Hawaii. July 1954. Washington, Dept. of the Interior, 1954. 50p. (Its Decision list, no. 5403)
Contains 966 decisions.

1437. —— Names approved by the United States Geographic Board on the recommendation of the Advisory Committee on Hawaiian Geographic Names; In its Fifth report. Washington, Govt. Print. Off., 1921. p. 362-90.

1438. U.S. Geological Survey. Water resources of Hawaii, 1909-1911. Prepared under the direction of M. O. Leighton by W. F. Martin and C. H. Pierce. Washington, Govt. Print. Off., 1913. 552p. (Water-supply paper 318)
Meaning of geographic names: p. 498.
Glossary of some geographic names: p. 498-505.
Principal watercourses, by islands: p. 506-09.
Gazetteer: p. 509-36.

1439. U.S. Hydrographic Office. Gazetteer (no. 4). Hawaiian Islands. Nov. 1943. Washington, Govt. Print. Off., 1944. 51p. (H. O. Misc. no. 884. Reprint Sept. 1944 of H. O. Misc. no. 10,884)

1440. U.S. Office of Geography. Hawaiian Islands; official standard names approved by the United States Board on Geographic Names. Washington, 1956. 89p. (U.S. Board on Geographic Names. Gazetteer no. 24)

1441. Westervelt, W. D. Legendary places in Honolulu. Hawaiian Historical Society. Annual report 1910:10-21.

1442. Wrestling with place names. Hawaiian almanac and annual 1922:82-87.

IDAHO

1443. Baker, Marcus. Survey of the northwestern boundary of the United States, 1857-1861. U.S. Geological Survey. Bulletin 174:58-61. 1900.

Indian names of camps, stations, rivers, etc., along the 49th parallel in Washington, Idaho, and Montana. Based on the work George Gibbs did for the Smithsonian Institution.

1444. Boise City's change of name. New York times Aug. 28, 1940, p. 18, col. 7.

1445. Boone, Lalia Phipps. Names of Idaho counties. Names 16:19-26, March 1968.

1446. Bridger, Clyde A. The counties of Idaho. Pacific Northwest quarterly 31:187-206, April 1940.
Bibliographical footnotes.
Notes on the creation of the counties, and their boundaries at different periods. Includes copies of acts of the first legislature establishing counties, a table of counties not now in Idaho, counties in Idaho, and a section on origin of county names.

1447. Chamberlain, Alexander F. Geographic terms of Kootenay origin. American anthropologist n.s. 4:348-50, April-June 1902.
"Concerned with names of places, camp-sites, and stations, along the 49th parallel in British Columbia, Washington, Idaho, and Montana. These names which seem to have been taken from the language of the Kootenay Indians of this region are mentioned in the reports on the boundary survey. The meanings and etymologies are given where possible."—Price.

1448. Elsensohn, Alfreda, Sister. Pioneer days in Idaho County. Caldwell, Idaho, Caxton Printers, 1947-51. 2v.
Name Idaho: 1:10-16; origin of other names scattered throughout.

1449. Ghost towns; In U.S. Federal Writers' Project. Idaho. The Idaho encyclopedia. Caldwell, Idaho, Caxton Printers, 1938. p. 98-114.

1450. Koch, Elers. Geographic names of western Montana and northern Idaho. Oregon historical quarterly 49:50-62, March 1948.

1451. Kramer, Fritz L. Idaho place name records. Western folklore 12:283-86, Oct. 1953.

1452. —— Idaho town names. Idaho. State Historical Dept. Biennial report 23:14-114. 1951-52.
Review: H. M. Lovett, Names 1:216-17, Sept. 1953.

1453. Landis, Robert L. Post offices of Oregon, Washington, and Idaho. Portland, Ore., Patrick Press, 1969. 89, 98, 55, 9p.
Includes post offices of the Railway Mail Service, 1906.

1454. New notes on the word "Idaho." Idaho yesterdays 2:26-28, Spring 1958.
Reprinted: Boise, Idaho Historical Society, 1959. [4]p. (Idaho historical series, no. 1)
Meaning of the word unknown.

1455. Origins of the name Idaho. Boise, Idaho Historical Society, 196? [4]p. (Idaho historical series, no. 13)
Summarizes the Colorado use of the name, the investigations in Idaho and the Pacific Northwest.
The Society has also published leaflets on other individual names in Idaho.

1456. Rees, John E. Idaho chronology, nomenclature, bibliography. Chicago, Conkey, 1918. 125p.
Includes the following item; also a section on Idaho nomenclature, p. 52-118.

1457. —— Idaho, its meaning, origin and application. Portland, Ore., Ivy Press, 1917. 12p.

Reprinted from the Oregon historical quarterly 18:83-92, June 1917; also included in no. 1456, p. 46-51.

1458. Sexton, Lena Anken. What's in a name? A story of Idaho landmarks and how they received their names. Scenic Idaho 6:17, 32-34, 3d quarter 1951.

1459. Talbert, Ernest W. Some non-English place names in Idaho. American speech 13:175-78, Oct. 1938.

1460. Territory of Idaho; In Brosnan, Cornelius James. History of the State of Idaho. New York, Scribner, 1918. p. 117-22; also in U.S. Congress. Congressional globe, 37th Congress, 3d session, 1862-63, p. 166, 884, 905, 914, 924, 951, 1509, 1513, 1525, 1530, 1542.

On March 3, 1863, the bill organizing the Idaho Territory was passed. There was considerable discussion about whether the name should be Montana or Idaho, but Idaho was finally chosen.

1461. Thompson, Albert W. Coeur d'Alene, the names applied to tribe and lake. Idaho yesterdays 21:11-15, Winter 1978.

1462. —— The early history of the Palouse River and its names. Pacific Northwest quarterly 62:69-76, April 1971.

1463. Todd, C. C. Origin and meaning of the geographic name Palouse. Washington historical quarterly 24:190-92, July 1933.

"A modification of the Indian tribal name Palloatpallahs."—Griffin.

1464. Twin Falls County Territorial Centennial Committee. A folk history of Twin Falls County, comp. and ed. by the History Publication Committee; illus. by Mrs. Donald Lambert. Twin Falls, Idaho, Standard Print. Co., 1962. 110p.

Historical names and how they came to be: p. 97-98.

1465. U.S. 88th Congress, 1st session. Senate. A bill to change the name of the Bruces Eddy Dam and Reservoir in the State of Idaho to the Dworshak Dam and Reservoir. S. 850. Feb. 19, 1963. Washington, 1963. 2p.

Introduced by Mr. Jordan and Mr. Church and referred to the Committee on Interior and Insular Affairs.

In honor of the late Senator from Idaho.

Subsequent documents relating to this bill were published as follows:

U.S. 88th Congress, 1st session. Senate. Changing the name of Bruces Eddy Dam and Reservoir, Idaho, to the Dworshak Dam and Reservoir. Report no. 268, to accompany S. 850. June 19, 1963. Calendar no. 249. Washington, 1963. 2p.

Submitted by Mr. McNamara, from the Committee on Public Works, without amendment.

—— [Reprint of the original bill, June 19, 1963, to accompany the report. Report no. 268 and Calendar no. 249 added] 2p.

U.S. 88th Congress, 1st session. House. An act to change the name of the Bruces Eddy Dam and Reservoir in the State of Idaho to the Dworshak Dam and Reservoir. S. 850. In the House of Representatives June 24, 1963. Washington, 1963. 2p.

Referred to the Committee on Public Works. Passed the Senate June 20, 1963.

— Changing the name of Bruces Eddy Dam and Reservoir, Idaho, to the Dworshak Dam and Reservoir. Report no. 569, to accompany S. 850. July 22, 1963. Washington, 1963. 2p.
Submitted by Mr. Davis, from the Committee on Public Works, without amendment.

— [Reprint of the act, July 22, 1963, to accompany the report. Report no. 569 and House Calendar no. 109 added]. 2p.

1466. U.S. Federal Writers' Project. Idaho. Idaho, a guide in word and picture. 2d ed. rev. New York, Oxford Univ. Press, 1950. 300p.
1st ed. 1937.
Origin of names: p. 279-86.

1467. Walgamott, Charles Shirley. South Idaho's names; In his Six decades back. Caldwell, Idaho, Caxton Printers, 1936. p. 349-58.

1468. Wells, Merle W. Origins of the name Idaho, and how Idaho became a territory in 1863; In Etulain, Richard W. & Bert W. Marley, The Idaho heritage; a collection of historical essays. [Pocatello], Idaho State Univ. Press, 1974. p. 30-45. maps.

ILLINOIS

1469. Ackerman, William K. The origin of names of stations on the line of the Illinois-Central Railroad Company; In his Early Illinois railroads. Chicago, Fergus Print. Co., 1884. p. 109-52.
Also published separately, 67p.

1470. Adams, James N. A list of Illinois place names. Illinois libraries 50:275-596, April-June 1968, Special sesquicentennial issue.
Reprinted as Illinois State Historical Society. Occasional publications no. 54, 1968. 321p.
13,948 entries based on Post Office Department records and county histories, atlases, and newspapers. Includes names no longer in existence. Completed in 1961.
Review: Eugene B. Vest, Names 20:214-15, Sept. 1972.

1471. Allen, John W. Legends & lore of southern Illinois. Carbondale, Southern Illinois Univ., Area Services Division, 1963. 404p.
Chap. 2, p. 40-51, deals with southern Illinois place-names.

1472. Barge, William D. Illinois county names. Magazine of history 9:273-77, May 1909.

1473. — The rejected Illinois county names. A paper prepared for the Illinois State Historical Society, and submitted at its annual meeting, Jan. 24, 1906. Chicago, 1906. 34p.
Also in Illinois State Historical Society. Transactions 1906:122-37 (Illinois State Historical Library. Publications 11:122-37. 1906)

1474. — & Norman W. Caldwell. Illinois place-names. Illinois State Historical Society. Journal 29:189-311, Oct. 1936.

1475. Beck, Lewis Caleb. A gazetteer of the states of Illinois and Missouri; containing a general view of each state, a general view of their counties, and a particular description of their towns, villages, rivers, &c., &c. With a map, and other engravings. Albany, Printed by C. R. and G. Webster, 1823. 352p.
Reprinted New York, Arno Press, 1975.

1476. Briggs, Harold E. Folklore of southern Illinois. Southern folklore quarterly 16:207-17, Dec. 1952.
The origin of the name Egypt, p. 208-09.

1477. Brown, Donald E. and Frank E. Schooley. Pronunciation guide for Illinois place names. Urbana, Univ. of Illinois, Division of Univ. Broadcasting, College of Journalism and Communications, 1957. 48p.

1478. Chase, Carroll & Richard McP. Cabeen. The first hundred years of United States territorial postmarks, 1787-1887. Illinois Territory. American philatelist 56:179-83, Dec. 1942.
Includes list of post offices.

1479. Custer, Milo. The name Bloomington, and the "ington" names. Bloomington, Ill., 1925. 6p. (Central Illinois Historical Society. Publications no. 3)
In general an analysis of the "ington" names; in particular an interpretation of the word Bloomington. Data apply to all Bloomingtons, of which there are several, author says. He often refers to "our Bloomington," meaning Illinois.

1480. Cutshall, Alden. Origin of our state and county names. Illinois bulletin of geography 6:[6-11], March 1944.

1480a. Graham, Fred B., Jr. Street names of Aurora; In North Central Names Institute. Papers, ed. by Lawrence E. Seits. Sugar Grove, Ill., Waubonsee Community College, 1980. p. 91-94.

1481. Griffith, Will. Egyptian place-names. Egyptian key 2:29-31, March 1947.
Some southern Illinois appellations are unusually interesting.

1482. Halpert, Herbert. "Egypt"--a wandering place-name legend. Midwest folklore 4:165-68, Fall 1954.
Reprinted in Richard Mercer Dorson, Buying the wind: regional folklore in the United States. Chicago, Univ. of Chicago Press, 1964. p. 295-99.
Discrepancies between the historical explanation of the name Egypt for southern Illinois and the legendary one.

1483. Harris, Jesse W. Illinois place-name lore. Midwest folklore 4:217-20, Winter 1954.

1484. —— The origin of Grand Tower; In his article, Myths and legends from southern Illinois. Hoosier folklore 5:14, March 1946.
Reported by Lydia Keneipp, Grand Tower.

1485. —— Wetaug--a place-name puzzle. Names 9:126-28, June 1961.

1486. Horton, Albert Howard. Water resources of Illinois, with an appendix on water power and drainage districts of Illinois. Prepared in cooperation with the United States Geological Survey. Springfield, Ill., 1914. 400p. (Illinois. Rivers and Lakes Commission. [Bulletin no. 14])
Gazetteer of Illinois streams: p. 326-57.
Includes nearly 500 streams.

1487. How Egypt got it's [sic] name. Egyptian key 2:31, March 1947.

1488. Hubbard, Anson M. A colony settlement, Geneseo, Illinois, 1836-1837. Illinois State Historical Society. Journal 29:403-31, Jan. 1937.
The origin of the name, p. 405-06.

1489. Hubbs, Barbara Burr. Egypt, the story of a name. Egyptian key 1:10, April-May 1943.
Egypt and other Egyptian names in southern Illinois.

1490. Illinois. Secretary of State. Official list of counties and incorporated municipalities of Illinois, 1955. Comp. by Charles F. Carpentier, Secretary of State. Printed by authority of the State of Illinois. n.p., n.d. 23p.
Gives many earlier names of places.

1491. Illinois state gazetteer and business directory, for the years 1864-5. Chicago, J. C. W. Bailey, 1864. 820p.

1492. Is Chicago "Skunk-town"? Masterkey (Southwest Museum, Los Angeles) 32:10, Jan.-Feb. 1958.
Signed: M. R. H.

1493. Is given new odor, meaning of "Chicago." Chicago daily news Dec. 29, 1955, p. 23.
Prof. Edward Taube stated in a paper read at the 4th annual meeting of the American Name Society that Chicago, meaning "cracked corn makers," stands as a memorial to the Illinois Indians who first occupied the area.

1494. Larsen, Carl. It's a stinking lie—a skunk didn't give Chicago its name. Chicago sun-times Dec. 29, 1955, p. 16.
Report on Prof. Edward Taube's paper, The name: Chicago, read at the annual meeting of the American Name Society.

1495. Lohmann, Karl B. Cities and towns in Illinois: a handbook of community facts. Urbana, Univ. of Illinois Press, 1951. 109p.
Appendix A. Origin of Illinois place names: p. 88-94.

1496. McCulloch, David. Old Peoria. Illinois State Historical Society. Transactions 1901:41-51 (Illinois State Historical Library. Publications 6:41-51)
Mention of early names scattered throughout this brief history of Peoria.

1497. McDavid, Virginia. Some observations on the pronunciation of Chicago and Illinois. Mississippi folklore register 11:93-100, Fall 1977.
Based on material assembled for a linguistic atlas of the north-central states.

1498. Meyer, Alfred H. & Norma Baumeister. Toponomy in sequent occupance geography: Calumet region. Indiana Academy of Science. Proceedings 54:142-59. 1945.
Reprinted separately, 1945.
"The systematic study of place names, in association with the physical and cultural elements of a region, is often helpful in relating and integrating geographic phenomena. Particularly is this true in a sequent occupance study in which the 'philological fossils,' as relicts of the landscape, may be instrumental in reconstructing the historical-geographic reality of a region. The sequent occupance toponomic technique is applied chorographically to the Calumet region of northwestern Indiana and northeastern Illinois."—Abstract.

1499. The Name of Illinois. Annals of Iowa 3:523-24, July 1865.
Source of the name is attributed to the French Isle [sic] aux Nois.

1500. Peck, John Mason. A gazetteer of Illinois, in three parts; containing a general view of the state, a general view of each county, and a particular description of each

town, settlement, stream, prairie, bottom, bluff, etc.; alphabetically arranged. 2d ed., entirely rev., cor., and enl. Philadelphia, Grigg & Elliott, 1837. 328p.
1st ed.: Jacksonville, R. Goudy, 1834. 376p.

1501. Peterson, Gordon E. Place names of Bond County, Illinois. Abingdon, Ill., 1951.
Unpublished manuscript.

1502. Professor sheds some new light on Indian origin of city's name. Chicago tribune Dec. 29, 1955, p. 4.
Edward Taube in a paper read at annual meeting of American Name Society offered as the meaning of the name Chicago "cracked corn makers," derived from an Algonquian tribal name.

1503. Sandham, William R. A lost Stark County town. Illinois State Historical Society. Journal 13:109-12, April 1920.
The story of Osceola and of its founder.

1504. —— The naming of a group of eight Illinois counties created at the same time. Illinois State Historical Society. Journal 25:120-23, April-July 1932.
States the source for the names of the counties and county seats.

1505. Schooley, Frank E. & Donald E. Brown. Pronunciation guide for Illinois towns and cities. Urbana, School of Journalism, Radio Station WILL, Univ. of Illinois, 1948. Unpaged.

1506. Smith, Grace Partridge. Speech currents in "Egypt." American speech 17:169-73, Oct. 1942.
Includes notes on place-names of southern Illinois, p. 169 and 173.

1507. —— They call it Egypt. Names 2:51-54, March 1954.
The nickname Egypt for the southern portion of Illinois.

1508. Smith, Hermon Dunlap. Des Plaines, Eau Plaine, or Kickapoo. Chicago, 1940. 3p.
Autographic reproduction of typewritten copy. In Newberry Library, Chicago, Ill.

1509. Steward, John Fletcher. Chicago, origin of the name of the city and the old portages. Illinois State Historical Society. Transactions 1904:460-66 (Illinois State Historical Library. Publication no. 9)
Also published separately.

1510. Syfert, Vernon A. The naming of Bloomington. Illinois State Historical Society. Journal 29:161-67, July 1936.

1511. Thompson, Joseph J. Chicagou—the grand chief of the Illinois. Illinois Catholic historical review 7:332-37, April 1925.
"Points out in an interesting discussion the meaning in various Indian languages of the protonym of the western metropolis."—Price.

1512. Vogel, Virgil J. Illinois' onion patch: the origin of Chicago's name. Illinois history 12:38-41, Nov. 1958.

1513. —— The Indian origin of some Chicago street names. Chicago schools journal 36:145-52, March-April 1955.

1514. —— Indian place names in Illinois. Springfield, Illinois State Historical Society, 1963. 176p. (Pamphlet series, no. 4)

Reprinted from Illinois State Historical Society. Journal 55:45-71, 157-89, 271-308, 385-458. 1962.

Review: Philip Wagner, Linguistic folklore. Journal of American folklore 79:386-87, April-June 1966.

1515. —— The mystery of Chicago's name. Mid-America 40:163-74, July 1958.

A detailed search of original sources and discussions.

1516. —— Some Illinois place-name legends. Midwest folklore 9:155-62, Fall 1959.

INDIANA

1517. Baker, J. David. The postal history of Indiana. Louisville, Leonard H. Hartmann, 1976. x, vi, 1061p. in 2v. maps.

Bibliography: p. 1055-61.

Includes list of Indiana post offices, 1800-1970, giving for each the date established or closed and changes in town names.

Review: Pamela J. Bennett, Indiana magazine of history 75:93-95, March 1979.

1518. Baker, Ronald L. Brown County place names. Midwestern journal of language and folklore 2:64-70, Fall 1976.

1519. —— County names in Indiana. Indiana names 2:39-54, Fall 1971. map.

Analyzes the names by categories. Concludes with a list of Indiana's 92 counties giving final date of organization and origin of the names.

1520. —— Indiana settlement names from foreign countries. Indiana Place-Name Survey. Newsletter 4:6-7, 1974.

A partial list from the more than 7 percent of foreign origin.

1521. —— Legends about lakes named Blue Hole. Indiana names 1:50, Fall 1970.

1522. —— Legends about the naming of Hymera, Indiana. Indiana names 4:62-63, Fall 1973.

1523. —— Locational and descriptive settlement names in Indiana. Indiana Place-Name Survey. Newsletter 5:6-8. 1975.

1524. —— Monsterville: a traditional place-name and its legends. Names 20:186-92, Sept. 1972.

An unofficial name applied to two different locales in southern Vermillion County, Indiana, is an example of a place-name derived from local legends.

1525. —— The role of folk legends in place-name research. Journal of American folklore 85:367-73, Oct.-Dec. 1972.

1526. —— The study of place names in Indiana. Onoma 18:572-75, no. 3, 1974.

1527. —— & Marvin Carmony. Indiana place names. Bloomington, Indiana Univ. Press, c1975. xxii, 196p. map.

Bibliography: p. 187-92.

2271 names in this study, with a brief section on pronunciation and on classification of names.

Review: Donald Zimmer, Indiana magazine of history 72:360-61, Dec. 1976; Arthur F. Beringause, Names 24:216, Sept. 1976.

1528. Bates, Roy M. Paper towns and ghost towns of Allen County. Old Fort news 6:1-12, Sept. 1941.

Towns that were platted but never developed, and towns that died leaving little trace of their existence.

1529. Beckwith, Hiram Williams. Indian names of water courses in the State of Indiana. Indiana. Dept. of Geology and Natural History. Annual report 12:37-43. 1882.

Reprinted in part in American naturalist 18:101, Jan. 1884.

Includes map, prepared by Daniel Hough, showing Indian names of lakes, rivers, towns, forts, etc., of Indiana.

1530. Bowers, John O. Dream cities of the Calumet. Gary, Calumet Press, 1929. 32p.

Published also in Lake County Historical Association. Publication 10:174-98, 1929.

Early towns that were planned, and in some cases started, but never reached maturity.

1531. Brewster, Paul G. A glance at some Indiana place-names. Hoosier folklore bulletin 2:14-16, June 1943.

Grouped into 12 categories.

Additional observations on Indiana place-names, ibid. 3:74-76, Dec. 1944.

1532. Brunvand, Jan. Some Indiana place-name legends. Midwest folklore 9:245-48, Winter 1959.

1533. Burns, Lee. Some vanished towns of pioneer days. Society of Indiana Pioneers. Yearbook 1940:7-12.

1534. Carmony, Marvin. Amateur radio and the Indiana place-name survey. Indiana Place-Name Survey. Newsletter 5:2-3, 1975.

1535. —— The Americanization of Terre Haute. Indiana names 2:13-18, Spring 1971.

On the origin and pronunciation of the name.

1536. Chamberlain, E. The Indiana gazetteer, or Topographical dictionary of the State of Indiana. 3d ed. Indianapolis, E. Chamberlain, 1850. 440p.

First issued 1849. p. 425-40 differ. Probably a 3d ed. of John Scott's The Indiana gazetteer (see no. 1592).

Gives origin of name of county in most instances.

1537. Cowen, M. V. B. The Indiana state gazetteer and shippers' guide for 1866-7. Lafayette, Rosser, Spring & Cowen, 1866. 428p.

1538. Daggett, Rowan Keim. The place-names of Chester Township, Wabash County, Indiana. Indiana names 4:4-30, Spring 1973.

1539. —— Upper Wabash Valley place names: Wabash and Miami counties, Indiana. 631p.

Thesis (Ph.D.) Indiana Univ., 1978.

1540. Dégh, Linda. Importance of collecting place-name legends in Indiana. Indiana names 1:34-39, Fall 1970.

1541. De la Hunt, Thomas James. History lessons from Indiana names. Indiana history bulletin 3:43, 49, March 1926.

1542. Dunn, Jacob Piatt. Glossary of Indian names and supposed Indian names in Indiana; In his Indiana and Indianans. Chicago, 1919. 1:86-97.
This alphabetical list gives the source and significance of the names in Indiana. Practically the same material is to be found in the author's True Indian stories.

1543. —— Indiana geographical nomenclature. Indiana magazine of history 8:109-14, Sept. 1912.
Offers corrections of article Indiana geographical nomenclature (see no. 1569).

1544. —— The meaning of "Tassinong." Indiana magazine of history 11:348-51, Dec. 1915.
Probably an original Indian place-name, not a corruption of the French tassement.

1545. —— True Indian stories, with glossary of Indiana Indian names. Indianapolis, Sentinel Print. Co., 1908. 320p.
Reprinted: 1964 by Lawrence W. Shultz.
Glossary: p. 253-320.
Manuscript notes on which Dunn based this and the revised glossary in his Indiana and Indianans are in the Indiana State Library. Indiana Division.
Review: American historical review 14:628, April 1909.

1546. —— The word Hoosier; In his Indiana and Indianans. Chicago, 1919. 2:1121-55.
Suggests a derivation from the word hoozer, also that it was imported by Cumberland Mountain settlers.

1547. —— The word, Hoosier, by Jacob Piatt Dunn; and John Finley, by Mrs. Sarah A. Wrigley. Indianapolis, Bobbs-Merrill, 1907. 37p. (Indiana Historical Society. Publications, v. 4, no. 2)
An earlier version appeared in Indiana magazine of history 1:86-96, June 1905.

1548. Ellis, Horace. Indiana's map of patriots. National republic 20:8-9, 47, July 1932.
"A discussion of place-names of Indiana which have been selected because of the popularity of noted men."—American speech.

1549. Feightner, Harold C. Indiana county government. Indiana history bulletin 9:262-63, March 1932.
A list of the counties, giving origin of name, date of organization, and present county seat.

1550. Fort Wayne. Public Library. Streets of Fort Wayne. Fort Wayne, 1953. 33p.

1551. Granger, Byrd Howell. Indiana and the Place-name Survey of the United States. Indiana names 2:55-59, Fall 1971.

1552. Green, Charlie. Tactic planned to gain O. K. of name change for Dunes. Cincinnati enquirer July 28, 1978, sec. C, p. 1.
Supporters of a move to change the name of the Indiana Dunes National Lakeshore have a plan to bypass Indiana senator's opposition to the name Paul H. Douglas Indiana Dunes National Lakeshore.

1553. Grissom honor urged. New York times June 11, 1960, p. 60. Representative Roush asked Congress to name Indiana Dunes National Lakeshore in honor of the late astronaut Lt. Col. Virgil I. Grissom.

1554. Guernsey, E. Y. Indiana; the influence of the Indian upon its history, with Indian and French names for natural and cultural locations. Indiana. Conservation Dept. Publication no. 122. 1933. map.

1555. Gutermuth, Clinton Raymond. Where to go in Indiana: official Indiana lake guide. [Indianapolis?] Division of Fish and Game, Indiana Dept. of Conservation, [1952]. 60p.
List of Indiana lakes: p. 9-16. Gives with the county location, all lakes of five acres or more; Official Indiana lake guide: p. 18-27, 32-58. List by counties of all lakes of five acres or more.

1556. Hahn, Holly Jane. The place-names of Brown Township, Montgomery County, Indiana. Indiana names 5:19-36, Spring 1974.
Bibliography: 35-36.

1557. Hand, Wayland D. Legends in place-name study. Indiana names 4:37-50, Fall 1973.

1558. Hartke, Vance. Hoosiers wear name with pride. Congressional record v. 21, pt. 15, p. 18983, June 16, 1975.
On the nickname Hoosiers, and including an article by Sydney J. Harris from the Chicago daily news June 3, 1975; also reprinting Vance Hartke's article, "Hoosier" a unique nickname, from the Congressional record of Feb. 26, 1966.

1559. Hixson, Jerome C. Some approaches to Indiana place names. Indiana names 1:11-18, Spring 1970.
Indicates some of the possible directions for a study of Indiana place-names.

1560. Hodgin, Cyrus Wilburn. The naming of Indiana. Richmond, Ind., Nicholson Print. Co., 1903. 16p. (Papers of the Wayne County, Indiana, Historical Society, v. 1, no. 1)
On the source and meaning of the name, and of the nickname Hoosier. Includes poem by John Finley, The Hoosier's nest.

1561. Hoffmann, Frank A. Place names in Brown County. Midwest folklore 11:57-62, Spring 1961.

1562. Hollar, Jean. Place-names of Fayette County, Indiana. Indiana names 5:43-70, Fall 1974.
List of both natural and artificial features, including variants, type of feature, pronunciation, date and degree of usage, type of name and circumstance of naming and surveyor's location.

1563. "Hoosier" (based on files in Indiana State Library). Indiana history bulletin 15:211-12, April 1938.

1564. Indiana. Laws, statutes, etc. A concurrent resolution concerning Indian names of streams and lakes, directing the State Highway Commission to erect suitable markers at all places in the state where state highways cross streams bearing Indian names, and providing for the education of the public in the use of such Indian names; In Indiana. Laws 1:1818-19. 1945.

1565. —— State Library. Indiana Division. Origin of Indiana counties.
Typewritten. Based on the work of Max Robinson Hyman, William S. Raymond, and, for Indian names, Jacob Piatt Dunn.

1566. —— State Planning Board. Gazetteer of Indiana cities, towns and villages. 1936.
Typewritten. Rev. ed., 1939?, typewritten.

1567. Indiana Board on Geographic Names. Findings. May 1961/June 1962- . Indianapolis. v. 1- .
Also published July 1963/June 1965.

1568. Indiana county names. Magazine of history with notes and queries 2:420-23, Dec. 1905.

1569. Indiana geographical nomenclature. Indiana magazine of history 8:70-83, June 1912.

Taken from Henry Gannett, The origin of certain place names in the United States (see no. 170). Cf. article by Jacob Piatt Dunn, Indiana geographical nomenclature, no. 1543.

1570. Indiana Historical Society. Notes on sources of information concerning lost towns.

Card file in the Society Library. Supplemented by special card index in the Indiana State Library. Indiana Division.

1571. Indiana names. v. 1-5, Spring 1970-Fall 1974. Terre Haute, Indiana State Univ., Dept. of English.

A journal devoted to Indiana names and onomastic theory and methodology.

Succeeded by Midwestern journal of language and folklore (v. 1- Spring 1975-) which includes place-name material.

1572. Indiana Place-Name Survey. Newsletter v. 1- Summer 1971- Terre Haute, Indiana State Univ., Dept. of English.

Designed to report progress on the Indiana Survey and to publish notes and news dealing with place-names.

1573. Kleber, Albert. The naming of Troy, Indiana. Indiana magazine of history 44:178-80, June 1948.

The original county seat of Perry County, named ca. 1847.

1574. Lanahan, Margaret. "Silopanaidni." Outdoor Indiana Dec. 1950, p. 17-18.

The derision which the name Indianapolis met at first, and the suggestion of the Vincennes sentinel editor that the name, later copied elsewhere, be spelled backward.

1575. Lockridge, Ross F. Indian names of Indiana streams. Indiana teacher April 1945, p. 215-16.

1576. McCoy, Angus C. The streets of Fort Wayne. Old fort news 9:3-25, Dec. 1945.

Origin of the names.

1577. McDavid, Raven I., Jr. Word magic, or would you want your daughter to marry a Hoosier? Indiana English journal 2:1-7, 1967.

Originally published in Indiana State University alumni magazine.

1578. —— & Virginia McDavid. Cracker and Hoosier. Names 21:161-67, Sept. 1973.

Relationship and geographical spread of the two words.

1579. McKesson, Jon. Most counties named to honor men who helped make history. Indianapolis star April 17, 1966, sec. 2, p. 5.

1580. Meyer, Alfred H. & Norma Baumeister. Toponymy in sequent occupance geography: Calumet region. Indiana Academy of Science. Proceedings 54:142-59, 1945.

"The systematic study of place names, in association with the physical and cultural elements of a region, is often helpful in relating and integrating geographic phenomena. Particularly is this true in a sequent occupance study in which the 'philological fossils,' as relicts of the landscape, may be instrumental in reconstructing the historical-geographic reality of a region." The technique is applied chorographically to the Calumet.

1581. Miner, Virginia Scott. Indiana names. Indiana names 1:[11], Fall 1970.
Poem reprinted from Saturday review of literature Nov. 21, 1942, p. 24.

1582. Names of Indiana streams. Indiana history bulletin 9:543-45, Aug. 1932.
The naming of streams in Indiana.

1583. Nicholson, Meredith. The Hoosiers. 2d ed. New York, Macmillan, 1915. p. 29-36.
Traces the origin of the term to a date earlier than the use of it in John Finley's poem, "The Hoosier's nest," a New Year's address for the Indianapolis journal 1830.

1584. Orth, Donald J. The nature of topographic terms. Indiana names 3:5-18, Spring 1972.
A study of topographic terms in general, including a short survey of terms used in Indiana.

1585. Osterhus, Grace Buzby. Names of northern Indiana counties reflect pioneer thinking. Society of Indiana Pioneers. Yearbook 1943:12-18.

1586. Place-names index.
On cards, Indiana Historical Society Library. Indexes variant forms of names as found on old maps, in books, etc. Gives location, derivation of name, origin of name, other names for, etc. About 1000 cards.

1587. Preston, Dennis R. Southern Indiana place-name legends as reflections of folk history. Indiana names 4:51-61, Fall 1973.

1588. Redfield's Indiana railway gazetteer, traveler's guide, and express and shippers' directory, embracing a complete alphabetical gazetteer and travelers' guide, designating express and telegraph offices, railway stations and routes, and giving location, population and full traveling and shipping directions to all points in the state. Indianapolis, D. A. Redfield, 1865. 94p.

1589. Rennick, Robert M. The folklore of place-naming in Indiana. Indiana folklore 3:35-94, Fall 1970.
Bibliographical notes: p. 84-94.
On the traditional accounts of the origin of some of the more colorful and unusual community names in the state.

1590. —— Place-name derivations are not always what they seem. Indiana names 2:19-28, Spring 1971.

1591. Richmond, Winthrop Edson. Library resources for the study of place names in the State of Indiana. Indiana names 1:41-49, Fall 1970.
Book list: p. 44-49.

1592. Scott, John. The Indiana gazetteer, or Topographical dictionary; containing a description of the several counties, towns, villages, settlements, roads, lakes, rivers, creeks, and springs, in the State of Indiana. 2d ed. carefully rev., cor., and enl. Indianapolis, Douglass & Maguire, 1833. 200p.
1st ed., by John Scott, published in Centreville by John Scott and W. M. Doughty, 1826. 143p. Reprinted: Indianapolis, Indiana Historical Society, 1954. 129p. (Indiana Historical Society. Publications, v. 18, no. 1)
2d ed. published anonymously. Introduction states that the publishers had purchased copyright of John Scott's gazetteer. The Indiana gazetteer by E. Chamberlain (see no. 1536) is probably a 3d ed. of Scott's.

1593. Seits, Laurence E. Using maps in place-name research. Indiana names 2:29-33, Spring 1971.

Selected bibliography of useful Indiana maps and atlases (in chronological order): p. 32-33.

1594. Short, Oscar D. 'Origin of the term "Hoosier." Indiana magazine of history 25:101-03, June 1929.

1595. Skinner, Hubert M. An echo from the era of the tassements. Indiana magazine of history 12:84-88, March 1916.
Skinner upholds his theory of the French derivation of Tassinong as opposed to Jacob Piatt Dunn's.

1596. That word "Hoosier" again. Indiana history bulletin 35:88-89, July 1958.
Reprinted from the Indianapolis journal with editorial comment.
Includes letter of John Vawter printed in the Franklin democratic herald Jan. 19, 1860.

1597. Town balks at its own name. New York times Aug. 21, 1937, p. 17, col 8.
Petitions ask community name be changed from William Williams Corner to Billville.

1598. Tucker, Glenn. Was "Hoosier" a headgear? Indiana history bulletin 35:141-42, Oct. 1958.
Suggests derivation of name from those who wore hats made by Hosier Brothers at the site of Clarksburg, now Rocklane.

1599. Turner, Timothy Gilman. Gazetteer of the St. Joseph Valley, Michigan and Indiana, with a view of its hydraulic and business capacities. Chicago, Hazlitt & Reed, printers, 1867. 166p.

1600. Wells, George Y. Visit to Mecca (Ind.). Little town keeps its name as a reminder of Moslem settlement many years ago. New York times Aug. 31, 1952.

1601. Wood, Mary Elizabeth. French imprint on the heart of America; historical vignettes of 110 French-related localities in Indiana and the Ohio Valley. Evansville, Ind., Unigraphic, 1976. xxxi, 304, 20p.
Bibliography: p. 295-304.

1602. Yeager, Lyn Allison. Our county's namesake: John Allen. Old fort news Fall 1972.
Allen County.

IOWA

1603. Andrews, L. F. The word "Iowa"--what it means. Annals of Iowa 3d ser. 2:465-69, July 1896.

1604. Barnes, Arthur M. Pronunciation guide to names of places and state officeholders in Iowa. Prepared in cooperation with the Iowa Radio-Telegraph News Association. 2d ed. Iowa City, State Univ. of Iowa, 1959. 12p.
1st ed. 1948.

1605. Briggs, John Ely. Along the Old Military Road. Palimpsest 51:265-76, June 1970. map.
Includes discussion of name origins for towns: Anamosa, Wapsipinicon, Monticello, Cascade, etc.

1606. Casady, P. M. The naming of Iowa counties. Annals of Iowa 3d ser. 2:195-202, July-Oct. 1895.
Abstract of paper read before the Pioneer Lawmakers' Association of Iowa, Feb. 15, 1894.

1607. Chase, Carroll & Richard McP. Cabeen. The first hundred years of United States territorial postmarks, 1787-1887. Iowa Territory. American philatelist 57:582-86, 798-803, May, Aug. 1944.
Includes list of post offices, with notes on some names.

1608. Childs, C. C. Names of Iowa counties. Iowa historical record 4:32-37, Jan. 1888.

1609. Cook, Pauline. Classical place names in Iowa. Classical journal 41:323-24, April 1946.

1610. Counties and county names; In Iowa. Secretary of State. Iowa official register 1909-10:687-716.
Also in Iowa. Secretary of State. Census of Iowa for 1880. Des Moines, 1883. p. 381-421.

1611. Curtis, Samuel Prentis. I-O-W-A. Annals of Iowa 10:286-87, Oct. 1872.
A plea that some one, properly qualified, explain the real meaning of the word Iowa.

1612. Denny, Robert R. & LeRoy G. Pratt. Historical highlights of Polk County, Iowa. n.p., 1973. 73, 22p.

1613. Des Moines—origin and meaning. Iowa historical record 4:40, Jan. 1888.
"Father Kempker in his 'History of the Catholic church in Iowa' gives his reasons for interpreting Des Moines as 'river of monks.'"—Price.

1614. Des Moines River. Annals of Iowa 3d ser. 10:342, Jan.-April 1912.
An article quoted from the Iowa advocate and half-breed journal, Montrose, Iowa, Aug. 16, 1847, discussing the origin of the name.

1615. Dubuque County place names. Dubuque telegraph-herald Sept. 7, 1930.

1616. The Early names of Council Bluffs. Annals of Iowa 3d ser. 2:480, July 1896.
A letter from D. C. Bloomer gives an account of early names of Council Bluffs, especially that of Kanesville.

1617. Eriksson, Erik McKinley. The name of Odebolt. Palimpsest 10:432-41, Dec. 1929.

1618. Fitzpatrick, Thomas Jefferson. The place-names of Appanoose County, Iowa. American speech 3:39-66, Oct. 1927.

1619. —— The place-names of Des Moines County, Iowa. Annals of Iowa 3d ser. 21:56-73, 127-40, 535-52, 604-40, July, Oct. 1937, Jan., April 1939.
Bibliography: p. 635-40.

1620. —— The place-names of Lee County, Iowa. Annals of Iowa 3d ser. 17:13-58, July 1929.
Bibliography: p. 57-58.

1621. —— The place-names of Van Buren County, Iowa. Annals of Iowa 3d ser. 18:12-41, 87-116, July, Oct. 1931.
Bibliography: p. 113-16.

1622. Fulton, Alexander R. Iowa Indian nomenclature; In his The red man of Iowa. Des Moines, Mills & Co., 1882. p. 421-34.

1623. Garver, Frank Harmon. Boundary history of the counties of Iowa. Iowa journal of history and politics 7:3-129, Jan. 1909.
In alphabetical order, the counties of the state are listed with historical data and the old names of those counties with changes.

1624. Glass, Remley J. Iowa-Minnesota townsite towns. Annals of Iowa 3d ser. 28:69-70, July 1946.
Wheelerwood, Hanford, Cartersville, and Dougherty, platted by Iowa and Minnesota townsite company along the railroad right of way in Cerro Gordo County in 1898-99. Includes origin of names.

1625. The Hawk-eye. Hawk-eye and Iowa patriot, Burlington, v. 1, no. 14, p. 2, Sept. 5, 1839.

1626. "Hawkeye" the nickname for Iowans. Annals of Iowa 3d ser. 31:380-81, July 1952.

1627. Hildreth, W. H. The name "Iowa." Annals of Iowa 1:268-69, April 1864. From the Davenport gazette April 1860.

1628. Hills, Leon Corning. History and legends of place names in Iowa; the meaning of our map. 2d ed. Omaha, Omaha School Supply Co., 1938. 90p.
1st ed. 1937. 78p.
Key to references in various books consulted and quoted in the book: p. 89-90.

1629. Hoffman, M. M. The first gazetteer on Iowa. Annals of Iowa 3d ser. 18:383-90, July 1932.
Contains information about Jedidiah Morse, The American gazetteer, 1797 (see no. 653), with excerpts of Iowa material.

1630. Honest to goodness, Iowa has real Podunk Center. Des Moines (Iowa) Sunday Register April 14, 1963, Iowa sec., p. 1, 3.
Podunk Center consists of one small building that houses a grocery store, cafe, and family of five; not on the Madison County maps or in the postal guide.

1631. Howe, Samuel Storrs. A memoir of Indian names in Iowa. Annals of Iowa 2d ser. 1:3-28, Jan. 1882.

1632. I-O-W-A. Annals of Iowa 10:234-35, July 1872.
Meaning of the name.

1633. Iowa. University. School of Journalism. Pronunciation guide to Iowa place names, prepared by Arthur M. Barnes. Iowa City, 1948. 2, 8 ℓ.

1634. An Iowa editor gives a nickname. Hawk-eye v. 5, no. 34, Jan. 18, 1844.
James G. Edwards, quoting his own editorial in the Fort Madison patriot, March 24, 1838, suggests the name Hawk-eyes, suggested to him by the title of Chief Black Hawk.

1635. Iowa—its original meaning. Iowa historical record 1:135-37, July 1885.
A letter from William Phelps to L. F. Ross is quoted, giving his opinion on the derivation of the name.

1636. Iowa state gazetteer, embracing descriptive and historical sketches of counties, cities, towns and villages to which is added a shippers' guide and a classified business directory. Comp. and ed. by James T. Hair. Chicago, Bailey & Hair, 1865. 722p.

1637. Irish, C. W. Iowa. Iowa historical record 1:13-25, Jan. 1885.
The history of the state serves as a background for the evolution of the name.

1638. Johnson, Ava. Choosing a place-name. Annals of Iowa 3d ser. 31:538-42, Jan. 1953.

1639. Keyes, Charles R. Des Moines River, and origin of the name. Annals of Iowa 3d ser. 3:554-59, Oct. 1898.
Introduces several possible interpretations concerning the source of the name, with reference to historical maps.

1640. Lathrop, H. W. The naming of Lee County. Iowa historical record 9:505-08, July 1893.
Credit for this name in Iowa has usually been ascribed to Charles Lee, but the author discusses the possibility that it may have been named after other persons.

1641. Lea, Albert Miller. The book that gave to Iowa its name, a reprint. Iowa City, State Historical Society of Iowa, 1935. 53p.
Also reprinted in Annals of Iowa 3d ser. 11:115-67, July-Oct. 1913.
Includes reprint of title page of original: Notes on Wisconsin Territory by Lieutenant Albert M. Lea. Philadelphia, H. S. Tanner, 1836. And of cover-title: Notes on the Wisconsin Territory; particularly with reference to the Iowa District, or Black Hawk purchase.

1642. Ludwig, Mary Culbertson. Namer of towns. Palimpsest 29:161-73, June 1948.
Article on John I. Blair, railroader, who named numerous towns for friends and relatives.

1643. Mawrer, Oscar Edward. "I'oway, my I'owa-a-ay." Atlantic monthly 147:42 (2d pagination), June 1931.
Concerning the pronunciation of Iowa.

1644. Mereness, Newton D. Early post offices established in Iowa. Iowa journal of history and politics 28:34-35, Jan. 1930.

1645. Mott, David Charles. Abandoned towns, villages, and post offices of Iowa. [Council Bluffs, Iowa, J. W. Hoffman & S. L. Purington, 1973]. 178p.
Reprinted from Annals of Iowa 3d ser. 17:435-65, 513-43, 578-99; 18:42-69, 117-48, Oct. 1930-Oct. 1931; 18:189-220, Jan. 1932.

1646. Mott, Frank Luther. Pronunciation of Iowa. Palimpsest 38:100-05, March 1957.
Reprinted from ibid. 5:373-77, Oct. 1924.

1647. —— The pronunciation of the word Iowa. Iowa journal of history and politics 23:353-62, July 1925.

1648. Murdock, Samuel. Origin of the name of Iowa. Iowa historical record 12:458-62, April 1896.
Gives credit for the name to William Brown and Henry R. Schoolcraft, who, as a committee, brought before the legislature of Michigan a bill to organize the County of Iowa, a name derived from an Indian tribe, the Kiowas, meaning "across the river."

1649. The Name "Ottumwa." Annals of Iowa 3d ser. 29:503, Jan. 1949.
From Ottumwa courier Aug. 7, 1948.

1650. The Naming of Floyd County. Annals of Iowa 3d ser. 2:398-400, April 1896.
Material assembled by P. M. Casady.

1651. The Naming of Henry County. Annals of Iowa 3d ser. 2:364, April 1896.
Condensed from the Iowa capital, Des Moines, Nov. 6, 1895.

1652. Naming of Iowa counties. Annals of Iowa 3d ser. 36:395-400, Summer 1962.
From Iowa official register, 1909-1910.

1653. The Naming of the city of Davenport. Annals of Iowa 3d ser. 2:243-44, July-Oct. 1895.
Mrs. Maria Peck argues, in the columns of the Davenport democrat, Dec. 1894, that the city was named after Col. George Davenport.

1654. Naming of Wisconsin and Iowa. Annals of Iowa 3d ser. 27:323-24, April 1946.
Naming of the territories described in a letter from Sen. George W. Jones, Iowa, to Charles Aldrich, curator of the Iowa Historical Department, in 1896.

1655. Odd stories disclose how Iowa towns got named. Annals of Iowa 3d ser. 36:71-72, Summer 1961.
From Des Moines register April 27, 1959.

1656. Old Military Road—Dubuque to Keosauqua. Palimpsest 51:281, June 1970.
A list of post offices along the road, mostly pre-Civil War, with dates and first postmasters.

1657. Organizing the County of Iowa. Annals of Iowa 3d ser. 3:224-25, Oct. 1897.
Copy of an act, passed by the legislature of the Territory of Michigan, Oct. 9, 1829, said by Hon. T. S. Parvin to be the first official publication in which the name Iowa appeared.

1658. Origin of some Iowa place names. Des Moines tribune May 4, 17, 1940.

1659. Parvin, Theodore Sutton. The name Iowa. Iowa historical record 12:388-89, Jan. 1896.

1660. Petersen, William J. Naval namesakes of Iowa cities. Palimpsest 34:481-512, Nov. 1953.

1661. —— A town of many names. Palimpsest 45:324-30, Sept. 1964.
Reprinted from ibid. 20:349-54, Oct. 1939.
Muscatine.

1662. Pratt, LeRoy G. Iowa's counties and courthouses: an introduction. Annals of Iowa 43:459-75, Fall 1976.
Includes information on the names.

1663. Price, Eliphalet. The origin and interpretation of the names of the rivers and streams of Clayton County. Annals of Iowa 4:707-11, 753-59, July, Oct. 1866; 5:794-800, 842-47, Jan., April 1867.
The sources of some of the names of the rivers and streams are discussed.

1664. Read, Allen Walker. "Liberty" in Iowa. American speech 6:360-67, June 1931.
"Historical summary of use of 'Liberty' as a place name."—Griffin.

1665. —— Literary place names. Palimpsest 9:450-57, Dec. 1928.
Regarding place-names in Iowa derived from literature, from which something may be learned of the character of the reading matter of the pioneer Iowan.

1666. —— Observations on Iowa place names. American speech 5:27-44, Oct. 1929.

1667. —— Study of Iowa place names selected from counties A through F. Thesis (M.A.) Univ. of Iowa, 1926.

1668. Shambaugh, Benjamin F. The naming of Iowa. Palimpsest 16:81-86, March 1935.
His shorter article, The naming of Iowa, was published in Palimpsest 5:370-72, Oct. 1924. It includes a paragraph on the use of Hawkeye.

1669. —— The naming of Iowa. Palimpsest 38:97-99, March 1957.

1670. —— The origin of the name Iowa. Annals of Iowa 3d ser. 3:641-44, Jan. 1899.
Bibliography of the name Iowa: p. 644.

1671. —— The territorial capital is named. Palimpsest 20:139-45, April 1939.
Iowa City.

1672. Signification in 1854 of Iowa and other Indian names. Annals of Iowa 3d ser. 15:541-42, Jan. 1927.
Mr. Le Claire, an Indian interpreter of the government, translates several Indian place-names in Iowa. He declares that Iowa means "a place of retreat" rather than "beautiful." The article is from the Iowa City journal, reprinted in the Democratic union, Keosauqua, Iowa, July 29, 1854.

1673. Soland, Martha Jordan. Iowa mirrors the American Revolution. Daughters of the American Revolution magazine 108:424-27, May 1974.
Places named for Revolutionary War heroes.

1674. U.S. 88th Congress, 1st session. House. A bill to designate the dam being constructed and the reservoir to be formed on the Des Moines River, Iowa, as the Red Rock Dam and Lake Red Rock. H. R. 1135. Jan. 9, 1963. Washington, 1963. 2p.
Introduced by Mr. Smith and referred to the Committee on Public Works.
Subsequent documents relating to this bill were published as follows:

U.S. 88th Congress, 1st session. House. Designating the dam being constructed and the reservoir to be formed on the Des Moines River, Iowa, as the Red Rock Dam and Lake Red Rock. Report no. 618, to accompany H. R. 1135. July 30, 1963. Washington, 1963. 3p.
Submitted by Mr. Davis, from the Committee on Public Works, without amendment.

—— [Reprint of the original bill, July 30, 1963, to accompany the report. Report no. 618 and House Calendar no. 115 added]. 2p.

U.S. 88th Congress, 1st session. Senate. An act to designate the dam being constructed and the reservoir to be formed on the Des Moines River, Iowa, as the Red Rock Dam and Lake Red Rock. H. R. 1135. In the Senate Aug. 6, 1963. Washington, 1963. 2p.
Referred to the Committee on Public Works. Passed the House of Representatives Aug. 5, 1963.

—— Designating the dam being constructed and the reservoir to be formed on the Des Moines River, Iowa, as the Red Rock Dam and Lake Red Rock. Report no. 453, to accompany H. R. 1135. Aug. 23, 1963. Calendar no. 429. Washington, 1963. 3p.
Submitted by Mr. McNamara, from the Committee on Public Works, without amendment.

—— [Reprint of the act, Aug. 23, 1963, to accompany the report. Report no. 453 and Calendar no. 429 added] 2p.

1675. Vizetelly, Frank. Pronunciation of Iowa. Atlantic monthly 147:62 (2d pagination), April 1931.
Traces the spelling of the name of the Indian tribe, 1689-1905.

1676. Willcockson, Mrs. Edwin. History of the origin of county names of the state of Iowa. Sigourney, Iowa, 1957. 18 ℓ.
Typewritten. Copies at Newberry Library, Chicago, D.A.R. Library, Washington, D.C., Iowa Historical Society Library, Des Moines, and State Historical Society Library, Iowa City.

1677. Williams, Ora. Camels gave a name to Iowa. Annals of Iowa 3d ser. 32:51-54, July 1953.
Indianola.

1678. Zwart, Elizabeth Clarkson. How Iowa towns were named. Des Moines register Oct. 14, 1934.

KANSAS

1679. Adams, F. G. County names. Daily commonwealth, Topeka, June 17, 1875.

1680. Admire, William Woodford. Origin of name, location of county seat and date of organization of each county; In his Admire's political and legislative hand-book for Kansas, 1891. Topeka, Crane, 1891. p. 200-14.

1681. Asks Breidenthal name for Tuttle Reservoir. Kansas City star March 30, 1960, p. 2.
For Willard J. Breidenthal.

1682. Atchison, Topeka & Santa Fe Railway Company. Statement of origin of names and stations on Panhandle Division of the Atchison, Topeka & Santa Fe Railway Company. Amarillo, Tex., Office of Assistant General Manager, 1936. 40p.

1683. Barry, Louise. The renaming of Robidoux Creek, Marshall County. Kansas historical quarterly 18:159-63, May 1950.
Previously named Vermillion Creek or West Fork, of Black Vermillion River.

1684. Baughman, Robert Williamson. Kansas in maps. Topeka, Kansas State Historical Society, 1961. 104p.
Includes a brief study of the origin and orthography of the name Kansas during various periods (p. 5-6), and the earliest appearances of the name on maps.

1685. —— Kansas post offices, May 29, 1828-August 3, 1961. Topeka, Kansas Postal History Society, 1961. 256p.
Three major parts: (1) Alphabetical list, every known Kansas post office, past and present; (2) Territorial list, limited to those established before Kansas became a state, Jan. 29, 1861, including pre-territorial offices created before May 30, 1854; (3) County list, all post offices that ever existed within each county.
Includes name changes.

1686. Beachy, E. B. Dykes. Famous men and heroic deeds recalled by the names of counties in Kansas. Kansas City times Dec. 6, 1951, p. 34.

1687. —— Indians have left their marks on Kansas in unusual and musical names of towns. Kansas City star Feb. 23, 1950, p. 22.

1688. —— Names of Kansas rivers reflect some of the history made on their banks. Kansas City times Jan. 17, 1950, p. 22.

1689. —— Railroad men gave their names to towns which grew on Kansas prairie. Kansas City star March 9, 1950, p. 26.

1690. Campbell, W. M. Many mixups occur in Kansas counties; towns and counties of the same names sometimes are found hundreds of miles apart. Topeka capital May 4, 1930.

1691. Carney, Alfred. The christening of a Kansas town, Herndon, Kansas. Aerend 5:174-75, Summer 1934.

1692. Carruth, W. H. Origin of Kansas names—Foreign settlements. Kansas State Historical Society. Transactions 4:257-58, 1886-88.

1693. Chaffin, J. W. How White Woman Creek got its name; In Lawson, O. S., History of Scott County, Kansas, thesis (M.A.) Colorado State College of Education, 1936. p. 25-26.

1694. Chase, Carroll & Richard McP. Cabeen. The first hundred years of United States territorial postmarks, 1787-1887. Kansas Territory. American philatelist 58:616-20, May 1945; 59:57-74, Oct. 1945.
Includes a list of post offices.

1695. Clark, Richard C. Place names of German origin in Kansas. Beiträge zur Namenforschung N.F. 5:371-404, Heft 4, 1970. maps.

1696. Cobb, Glenn. Fort Scott place names. Fort Scott daily tribune-monitor June 4, 1917.

1697. Connelley, William E. Origin of the name of Topeka. Kansas State Historical Society. Collections 17:589-93, 1926-28.

1698. Cooper, F. A. It happened in Kansas, Kansas origin of county names and date of organization. Kansas business 7:5, May 1939.

1699. Corley, Wayne E. County and community names in Kansas; how the 105 counties and over 1000 of the communities got their names. Denver, The Author, 1962. 83 ℓ.

1700. Cory, Charles Estabrook. Place names of Bourbon County, Kansas; streams, towns, deserted villages, local place names, townships, etc. Fort Scott, Whiteside Pub. Co., 1928. 63p.

1701. County was named for Indian tribe. Arkansas City (Kan.) daily traveler Oct. 25, 1955.
Arapahoe County.

1702. Cover, Anniejane Hicks. Some place names of Kansas. Heritage of Kansas v. 4, no. 4, Nov. 1960. 63p.
Origin of names in lists under various categories.

1703. Dallas, Everett Jerome. Early-day post-offices in Kansas. Kansas State Historical Society. Transactions 7:441-46, 1901-02.
Includes date established, changes of name, and date abolished.

1704. Declare 49 Kansas counties named for military chieftains; two changed after officers had joined rebels. Wichita eagle Jan. 6, 1931.

1705. Diller, Aubrey. Origin of the names of tributaries of the Kansas River. Kansas historical quarterly 21:401-06, Summer 1955.

1706. "Flint Hills" misnomer; a Kansas statistician would call them "Blue Stem." Kansas City (Mo.) star April 14, 1929.

1707. Forgotten counties of Kansas; with past and present names of counties. Wichita eagle March 27, 1927.

1708. Gamble, Mary Brewer. Kansas and its counties. Treesearcher 8:133-40, Oct. 1966; 9:15-22, Jan. 1967. maps.
A list of counties created before 1868 in v. 8; from 1868 to 1893 in v. 9. Includes origin of names.

1709. Gannett, Henry. A Gazetteer of Kansas. Washington, Govt. Print. Off., 1898. 246p. (U.S. Geological Survey. Bulletin no. 154)

1710. Gazetteer and business directory of the new Southwest. Embracing all of that region of country—including counties, towns and cities—contiguous to the St. Louis and San Francisco Railway, its divisions and branches, located in southwest Missouri, southeastern Kansas, the eastern portion of the Indian country, and the northwest section of Arkansas. In which is included an abridged directory of leading business houses of St. Louis. St. Louis, United States Directory Pub. Co., 1881. 224p.

1711. Geographical names. 2v.
Mounted newspaper clippings in Kansas State Historical Society Library.

1712. Gill, Helen Gertrude. The establishment of counties in Kansas. Kansas Historical Society. Transactions 8:449-72. 1903-04.
Thesis (M.A.) Kansas Univ., 1903.
Includes origin of names that have disappeared.

1713. Hardeman, Nicholas P. Camp sites on the Santa Fe trail in 1848 as reported by John A. Bingham. Ed. by Nicholas P. Hardeman. Arizona and the West 6:313-19, Winter 1964.

1714. Have old names; creeks near Topeka got designations from Indians; "Shunganunga" meant "The race course" in Indian tongue. Topeka state journal Sept. 4, 1926.

1715. Hay, Robert. Kaw and Kansas, a monograph on the name of the state. Kansas State Historical Society. Transactions 9:521-26. 1905-06.

1716. Hickman, Russell K. The name of Topeka. Shawnee County Historical Society. Bulletin 25:3-7, June 1956.

1717. Hill, W. A. Robbers Roost Creek. Aerend 8:45-48, Winter 1937.
Includes names of other streams in Rooks County.

1718. Honig, Louis O. Origin of Kansas place-names. n.d. 16p.
Manuscript in the Kansas State Historical Society Library.

1719. How Cawker City got its name. n.p., n.d. Broadside 15 x 23 cm.
"The naming the new town was settled by a poker game, with E. Harrison Cawker holding the winning hand, hence Cawker City."

1720. Howes, Cecil. Ghost towns of Shawnee County. Shawnee County Historical Society. Bulletin 1:25-31, Dec. 1946.

1721. —— How counties got their names. Kansas teacher 58:46-48, April 1950.

1722. ——Nearly half the Kansas counties named in honor of war heroes. Kansas City (Mo.) times Nov. 8, 1939.

1723. —— They tried to spell "Kansas." Kansas magazine 1945, p. 98-99.

1724. —— What about the name, Topeka? Shawnee County Historical Society, Bulletin 1:104-08, Sept.-Dec. 1947.

1725. Indian names. Sumner County press, Wellington, Jan. 29, 1874.

1726. Indian names in Leavenworth County and their origin. Leavenworth times Sept. 14, 1911.

1727. Ingleman, Anna A. Indian place names of Kansas. n.p., 1929. 386 ℓ.
Thesis (M.A.) Kansas Univ., 1929. Microfilm copy in Kansas State Historical Society Library.

1728. Inman, Henry. Counties of Kansas. Topeka commonwealth Jan. 12, 1886.

1729. Kansas. University. William Allen White School of Journalism. A pronunciation guide to Kansas place names. Lawrence, 1955. 23p.

1730. Kansas counties. 1939. 15p.
Manuscript in Kansas State Historical Society Library.

1731. Kansas counties named for military men. Kansas. Adjutant General. Biennial report 28:63-64. 1931-32.

1732. Kansas county names. Magazine of history with notes and queries 7:343-47, June 1908.

1733. Kansas, its power and its glory, ed. by Peg Vines. Topeka, J. R. Peach, 1966. 312p.
City index guide to Kansas: p. 89-233. An alphabetical list of cities and towns with gazetteer information on each and with longer articles on some.

1734. Kurious Kansas. Kansas abstracter 16:12, Nov. 1942.

1735. Letters regarding the origin of the names Monravia, Farmington, Arrington, and Hawthorne.
Manuscript file in the Kansas State Historical Society Library.

1736. Lyman, William A. Origin of the name "Jayhawker," and how it came to be applied to the people of Kansas. Kansas State Historical Society. Collections 14:203-07, 1915-18.
Dates from 1859, and was applied then to a Linn County band organized in opposition to Missouri proslavery ruffians.

1737. McCandlish, J. Vernon. The organization dates of the counties of Kansas with information about whom the counties were named. Kansas City, Kan., March 1, 1955. 9ℓ.
Manuscript in Kansas State Historical Society Library.

1738. McCoy, John Calvin. Indian names of certain Kansas rivers. Kansas State Historical Society. Transactions 4:305-06. 1886-90.
Information in regard to the significance of the names is incorporated in a boundary survey made by the author.

1739. —— Name of Solomon River and names of other Kansas streams.
Letter on file in the Kansas State Historical Society Library.

1740. Main origin of Ottawa County names. Tescott news Dec. 26, 1940.

1741. Many counties are named for non-Kansans. Topeka journal Jan. 28, 1942.

1742. Mead, James Richard. Origin of names of Kansas streams. Kansas Academy of Science. Transactions 18:215-16, 1901-02.

1743. —— The Wichita Indians in Kansas. Kansas State Historical Society. Transactions 8:171-77, 1903-04.
Place-names which originated during the occupancy of this tribe are mentioned on p. 173-75.

1744. Meanings of Topeka, Wakarusa, and Shunganunga. Topeka mail and Kansas breeze May 22, 1896, p. 43.

1745. Mechem, Kirke. The mythical jayhawk. Topeka, Kansas State Historical Society, 1944. 12p.
A delightful fantasy tracing the mythical bird, the jayhawk.

1746. Montgomery, Mrs. Frank C. Fort Wallace and its relation to the frontier. Kansas State Historical Society. Collections 17:195-200, 1926-28.
Origin of place-names along the Smoky Hill route.

1747. Moore, Ely. The naming of Osawatomie, and some experiences with John Brown. Kansas State Historical Society. Collections 12:338-46, 1911-12.
Brief mention of the naming of the town by the author's father.

1748. Murdock, Victor. When the country around Wichita was Peketon County. Wichita eagle magazine Aug. 29, 1926.
Includes other place-names which have disappeared.

1749. Myers, C. Clyde. Salem: a town that bloomed, then faded. Kansas State Historical Society. Collections 17:384-88, 1926-28.

1750. The Name "Kansas." Kansas historical quarterly 20:450-51, May 1953.
Variant forms beginning with Kansa Indian village shown on Marquette's map, about 1673-74. Includes Kansas City.

1751. Names of Ford County's communities preserve for all time the names of pioneers whose efforts founded them. Dodge City journal Oct. 22, 1936.

1752. Names of Kansas towns duplicated. Lawrence journal world Oct. 13, 1937.

1753. Names of Kansas towns from many sources. Topeka capital July 30, 1916.

1754. The naming of Pittsburg. Pittsburg headlight Nov. 18, 1955.
Also in Pittsburg sun Nov. 19, 1955.

1755. The Naming of the different counties. Kansas. State Board of Agriculture. Annual report 4:185-437. 1875.

1756. Nomenclature of Kansas counties. The Kansas official Feb.-April 1921.

1757. Old county names. Daily commonwealth, Topeka, April 13-14, 1875, p. 2.

1758. Origin of county names; origin of city names. Kansas State Historical Society. Transactions 7:472-86. 1901-02.
Prepared by the Kansas State Historical Society for the Geographer of the United States Geological Survey.

1759. Origin of Doniphan County names. Atchison daily globe May 24, 1907.

1760. Origin of Doniphan County names. Troy chief May 5, 1932.

1761. Origin of names of Bourbon County's streams reveals interesting sidelights. Fort Scott tribune, Anniversary ed., May 30, 1942, p. 68-69.

1762. Origin of names of the stations on the L. K. & W. Leavenworth times Jan. 5, 1912.

1763. Peterson, Karl L. Legendary frontier names identify growing list of Midwestern reservoirs. Kansas City star June 28, 1964, p. 2G.
Map on p. 1G.

1764. Place-names of Kansas towns.
File of postal cards in Kansas State Historical Society Library, received in response to queries regarding origin of names, 1901-02.

1765. Poetic Indian names remembered by Henry Trinkle. Kansas State Historical Society. Collections 16:652-53. 1923-25.
Reprinted from La Cygne weekly journal June 21, 1895.
The location and source of the Indian names Nop-shin-gah and Ach-a-pon-gah.

1766. Remsburg, G. J. Many Shawnee County names are derived from Indians and from early settlers. Topeka capital July 2, 1922.

1767. —— Origin of Central branch names. Atchison daily globe Jan. 27, 1909.

1768. —— Origin of names of county places. Leavenworth times Jan. 24, 1907.

1769. —— Origin of Nemaha County names. Sabetha herald Jan. 28, 1909.

1770. Richards, Walter Marvin. Some ghost towns of Kansas. Heritage of Kansas v. 5, no. 1, Feb. 1961. 32p.

1771. Rosen, Karl. Classical place names in Kansas. Heritage of Kansas 8:31-35, 1975.

1772. —— Community names from personal names in Kansas: post offices. Names 21:28-39, March 1973.
A study of the 368 post offices that were named after their first postmaster.
Supplemented by the author's article: Kansas places with postmasters' names: a master list. ANS bulletin 36:3-16, Sept. 1974.

1773. Rumpf, Dan B. What's in a Kansas name? Kansas business magazine 5:4, March 1937.

1774. Rydjord, John. Indian place-names: their origin, evolution, and meanings, collected in Kansas from the Siouan, Algonquian, Shoshonean, Caddoan, Iroquoian, and other tongues. Norman, Univ. of Oklahoma Press, 1968. xi, 380p.
Bibliography: p. 347-68.
Includes a wide variety of interpretations, even contradictory ones.
Review: Virgil J. Vogel, Names 17:235-37, Sept. 1969; William N. Fenton, Pacific historical review 39:108-09, Feb. 1970.

1775. —— Kansas place-names. Norman, Univ. of Oklahoma Press, 1972. xiii, 613p. maps.
Bibliography: p. 564-94.
Definitive work on Kansas place-names, including not only current names but also those of earlier times and of places no longer in existence. In topical arrangement including rivers, lakes, landforms, towns, and counties.
Review: Richard J. Loosbrock, Journal of American history 60:1143-44, March 1974: Francis Lee Utley, Names 21:262-67, Dec. 1973; Homer E. Socolofsky, Journal of the West 12:189, Jan. 1973.

1776. Scheffer, Theodore H. Geographical names in Ottawa County. Kansas historical quarterly 3:227-45, Aug. 1934.

1777. Schmidt, Henry. Ashes of my campfire; historical anecdotes of old Dodge City. Dodge City, Kan., Journal, Inc., publishers, 1952- . v. 1- .
Ghost city of Hess named for a child: 1:59-62.

1778. Schoewe, Walter H. Name of river. Kansas Academy of Science. Transactions 54:269-71, 275-76, 281, 309-29, Sept. 1951.
Names of Kansas streams; Kansas River and Missouri River, with a list of Kansas streams based on Henry Gannett, A Gazetteer of Kansas, 1898 (see no. 1709).

1779. Seek to name a city. Kansas City star May 1, 1959, p. 6B.
Postcard returns favor Overland Park as the name for the new city to be formed from the Mission urban township in Johnson County.
References to later newspaper articles follow:
Tanquary, E. A. "Kansas City South, Kansas"? Kansas City star May 1, 1959, p. 14D.
White, Mary W. Oh, please! Kansas City star May 6, 1959, p. 12D.
Suggests the name Johnson city.
Overland Park is name of new city. Kansas City star May 8, 1959, p. 1.
Johnson cities set boundaries for 12. Kansas City star May 13, 1959, p. 1.

1780. Sibley, George Champlain. Big John's Spring, Council Grove, Diamond of the Plain; In Hulbert, Archer Butler. Southwest on the Turquoise Trail. Colorado Springs, Stewart Commission of Colorado College, 1933. p. 111-13.

1781. Some "misplaced" cities; many of the same name as counties located in other counties. Topeka journal Nov. 23, 1935.

1782. Some of the lost towns of Kansas. Kansas State Historical Society. Collections 12:426-90, 1911-12.
Includes a list of incorporations, by Kansas men, of towns now within the boundaries of Colorado; also, Extinct geographical locations: p. 471-90.

1783. Station names. Missouri Pacific lines magazine 25:9, Feb. 1952; 26:11, Aug. 1952.
Station names along the Missouri Pacific lines in Kansas.

1784. Stevenson, Andrew. Many towns named in honor of Santa Fe men. Santa Fe magazine 22:55-56, Aug. 1928.
From Illinois to California, but the greatest number are in Kansas.

1785. Stewart, Ora T. Names of Kansas towns reveal romance. Jayhawk, the magazine of Kansas 2:5-6, 29, Jan. 1929.

1786. There are many queerly named towns in Missouri and Kansas. Kansas City star Aug. 1, 1937.

1787. Three towns in Atchison County named for Indian chieftains. Atchison globe June 13, 1916.

1788. Tilghman, Zoe A. Origin of the name Wichita. American anthropologist n.s. 43:488-89, July-Sept. 1941.
Reply by Mary R. Haas, ibid. n.s. 44:164-65, Jan.-March 1942 refutes Tilghman's theory that the name derives from the Creek language.

1789. U.S. 86th Congress, 2d session. House. A bill to designate the Tuttle Creek Reservoir, Kansas, as the Willard J. Breidenthal Reservoir. H. R. 11400. March 28, 1960. Washington, 1960. 2p.
Introduced by Mr. George and referred to the Committee on Public Works.
Same, 87th Congress, 1st session. House. H. R. 1741, Jan. 4, 1961. 1p. Introduced by Mr. Breeding and referred to the Committee on Public Works.

1790. U.S. 88th Congress, 1st session. House. A bill to designate the Perry Dam and Reservoir, Delaware River, Kansas, as the Ozawkie Dam and Reservoir. H. R. 7645. July 18, 1963. Washington, 1963. 1p.
Introduced by Mr. Avery and referred to the Committee on Public Works.
An identical bill was introduced as H. R. 7653, July 18, 1963, by Mr. Ellsworth and referred to the Committee on Public Works.

1791. What's in a name? Progress in Kansas 1:27-28, March 1935.
Origin of names of some Kansas towns, based on a radio talk by Prof. Allen Crafton, Kansas University.

KENTUCKY

1792. Anderson, James Lee. The house that named the town. American motorist 24:3, Jan. 1956.
Story of the Owings house in Owingsville, Ky.

1793. Bryant, Thomas Julian. Bryant's Station and its founder, William Bryant. Missouri historical review 5:150-73, April 1911.
Arguments to prove that the name of the pioneer Kentucky fort and of its founder was Bryant, not Bryan.

1794. Casey Jones. New York times Oct. 16, 1938, sec. 4, p. 8, col. 1-2; letter Oct. 30, sec. 4, p. 9, col. 7.
Pronunciation of Cayce, Ky.

1795. Cleaves, Mildred P. Kentucky towns and their mark. In Kentucky 11:39, Winter 1948.

1796. Counties in Kentucky and origin of their names. Kentucky State Historical Society. Register 1:34-37, Jan. 1903.
Published by courtesy of the geographer of the Smithsonian Institution.

1797. Creason, Joe. What was that name again? Louisville courier-journal, Nov. 20, 1955, Magazine, p. 7-10.
Kentucky place-names.

1798. Davis, T. N. Of many things. America 112:407, March 27, 1965.
General comments on names in Kentucky.

1799. Field, Thomas Parry. A guide to Kentucky place names. In cooperation with Dept. of Geography, University of Kentucky. Lexington, College of Arts and Sciences, Univ. of Kentucky, 1961. 264p. (Kentucky. Geological Survey. Series X. Special publication 5)
Review: Helen Carlson, Names 10:190-92, Sept. 1962.

1800. —— The Indian place names of Kentucky. Names 7:154-66, Sept. 1959.
Reprinted in Filson Club history quarterly 34:237-47, July 1960.

1801. —— Religious place-names in Kentucky. Names 20:26-46, March 1972. maps.
A study of the 261 religious place-names in the state, including their areal distribution, their proportion of the total of the place-names, their origin in the Old and New Testaments of the Bible and saints' names, etc.

1802. Grubbs, Millard Dee. Origin of historic place names; In his The 4 keys to Kentucky. Louisville, Slater & Gilroy, 1949. p. 227-50.

1803. Haber, Tom Burns. "Gulliver's travels" in America. American speech 11:99-100, Feb. 1936.
Lulbegrud Creek in Kentucky named from the "Travels" according to a record made by Daniel Boone.

1804. Halpert, Herbert. Place name stories of Kentucky waterways and ponds, with a note on bottomless pools. Kentucky folklore record 7:85-101, July-Sept. 1961.

1805. Halpert, Violetta Maloney. Place name stories about west Kentucky towns. Kentucky folklore record 7:103-16, July-Sept. 1961.

1806. Hardy, Emmet Layton. An introduction to the study of the geographic nomenclature of Kentucky's counties, cities, and towns. Lexington, 1949. 119p.
Thesis (M.S.) Univ. of Kentucky.

1807. —— Place names in old Kentucky. Louisville courier-journal Dec. 4, 1949, Roto-sec., p. 14; Dec. 18, Roto-sec., p. 28; Jan. 15, 1950, Roto-sec., p. 31; March 12, Roto-sec., p. 14; April 30, Roto-sec., p. 41.

1808. Hazelip, Pauline. Tales of Glasgow Junction: a town is named. Kentucky folklore record 6:1-3, Jan.-March 1960.
Names of Glasgow Junction.

1809. Hewitt, John Napoleon Brinton. The name "Kentucky." American anthropologist n.s. 10:339-42, April-June 1908.
A thorough treatise on the derivation and meaning of the name.

1810. Huddleston, Eugene L. Place names in the writings of Jesse Stuart. Western folklore 31:169-77, July 1972.
Includes many that can be verified on maps of this area in Kentucky.

1811. Kay, Donald. British influence on Kentucky municipal place names. Kentucky folklore record 20:9-13, Jan.-March 1974.
Parallel listing of Kentucky names and British equivalent names.

1812. Keglertown. Lincoln (Neb.) evening journal and Nebraska state journal Dec. 12, 1962.
Derived its name from the game of bowls.

1813. Kentucky proud of unique town names. Cumberland (Md.) evening times Sept. 18, 1935.

1814. Ladd, Bill. Boaz is Bohz, Bouty Bow-ti and there's no T in Egypt. Louisville courier-journal Dec. 7, 1949, sec. 1, p. 9.

1815. Mahr, August C. Shawnee names and migrations in Kentucky and West Virginia. Ohio journal of science 60:155-64, May 1960.
The migration of the western half of the Shawnee nation from the Cumberland River eastward through the wilderness later called Kentucky can be traced by place-names of Shawnee origin.

1816. Plummer, Niel. Guide to the pronunciation of Kentucky towns and cities. Lexington, Univ. of Kentucky, Dept. of Journalism, 1949. 52p.

1817. Rothert, Otto A. Origin of the names Beargrass Creek, The Point, and Thruston Square. History quarterly 2:19-21, Oct. 1927.
"Regarding these sections of Louisville."--Griffin.

1818. Scomp, H. A. Kentucky county names. Magazine of history with notes and queries 7:144-54, March 1908.

1819. Spence, Dorothy Clark. How Tolu, Kentucky, got its name. Kentucky folklore record 7:119-20, July-Sept. 1961.

1820. Stratton, Margaret Barnes. Place-names of Logan County, and oft-told tales. 3d ed. Russellville, Ky., News-democrat, 1950. 76p.

1821. Swift, Lucie. "Who'd a thought it" and other Paducah place names; ed. by Herbert Halpert. Kentucky folklore record 7:117-19, July-Sept. 1961.

1822. Thompson, Lawrence S. The meaning of Kentucky. American notes and queries 7:68-71, Jan. 1969.
Summarizes the main lines of speculation about the origin and etymology of Kentucky, an Indian word, but of what language?

1823. Treadway, C. M. City of Irvine was named for brothers who were among early settlers in state. Lexington leader April 4, 1957, p. 3.

1824. Trout, A. M. When it comes to naming streets, sky's the limit. Louisville courier-journal June 2, 1960, sec. 1, p. 7.

1825. Trout, Allan. Unusual place names in Kentucky. Louisville courier-journal March 2, 1950, sec. 2, p. 15; Jan. 11, 1951, sec. 2, p. 15; April 12, sec. 2, p. 17.

1826. —— What inspired--name of Monkey's Eyebrow? Louisville courier-journal Feb. 21, 1951, sec. 2, p. 15; Feb. 28, sec. 2, p. 15; March 21, sec. 2, p. 13; April 16, sec. 2, p. 11.

1827. U.S. Board on Geographic Names. Decisions. No. 31--February 1, 1933. Mammoth Cave National Park, Kentucky. Washington, Govt. Print. Off., 1934. 6p.

1828. U.S. Congress. House. Committee on Interior and Insular Affairs. Abraham Lincoln Birthplace National Historic Site, Hodgenville, Ky. August 24, 1959 . . . Mrs. Pfost submitted the following report. To accompany H.R. 5764. Washington, 1959. 3p. (U.S. 86th Congress, 1st session. House. Report no. 986)

The Committee recommends the enactment of H.R. 5764, with amendments to change the proposed name from Abraham Lincoln's Birthplace to Abraham Lincoln Birthplace National Historical Site.

1829. —— Senate. Committee on Interior and Insular Affairs. Abraham Lincoln Birthplace National Historic Site. August 4, 1959 . . . Mr. Murray submitted the following report. To accompany S. 1448. Washington, 1959. 2p. (U.S. 86th Congress, 1st session. Senate. Report no. 617. Calendar no. 617)

Recommends that the bill pass, with amendments to change the proposed name from Abraham Lincoln's Birthplace to Abraham Lincoln Birthplace National Historic Site.

1830. U.S. 88th Congress, 1st session. House. A bill to designate Fishtrap Reservoir, to be created by the dam authorized to be constructed on the Levisa Fork, in Pike County, Kentucky, as "Kennedy Lake" in honor of the late President John F. Kennedy. H. R. 9524. Dec. 19, 1963. Washington, 1963. 2p.

Introduced by Mr. Perkins and referred to the Committee on Public Works.

1831. —— Senate. A bill to change the name of the lake formed by Kentucky Dam. S. 462. Jan. 23 (legislative day, Jan. 15), 1963. Washington, 1963. 2p.

Introduced by Mr. Kefauver and Mr. Gore and referred to the Committee on Public Works.

To change the name from Kentucky Lake to Tennessee-Kentucky Lake.

An identical bill was introduced in the House as follows:

U.S. 88th Congress, 1st session. House. A bill to change the name of the lake formed by Kentucky Dam. H.R. 4254. Feb. 26, 1963. Washington, 1963. 2p.

Introduced by Mr. Murray and referred to the Committee on Public Works.

1832. U.S. Laws, statutes, etc. An act to change the name of the Abraham Lincoln National Historical Park at Hodgenville, Kentucky, to Abraham Lincoln Birthplace National Historic Site. Public law 86-231. (United States statutes at large. 86th Congress, 1st session. 1959. v. 73, p. 466)

S. 1448 was approved Sept. 8, 1959.

1833. Wilson, Gordon. Place names in the Mammoth Cave region. Kentucky folklore record 14:8-13, Jan.-March 1968.

Also in his Folklore of the Mammoth Cave region. Ed. by Lawrence S. Thompson, with a foreword by Frederic G. Cassidy. Bowling Green, Kentucky Folklore Society, 1968. p. 27-32. (Kentucky folklore series no. 4)

All the names found on the maps of the park and the area within a mile of its boundaries. Nearly all came from some distinctive feature of the surroundings or from the names of the owners of the land.

1834. Woodbridge, Hensley C. Place names; In his A tentative bibliography of Kentucky speech. American Dialect Society. Publication 30:31-33, Nov. 1958.

A bibliography of items on place-names in Kentucky.

1835. Woods, Robert E. Heroes of the War of 1812 for whom Kentucky counties are named. Jeffersontown, Ky., 1937. 6p.
Address given at the state meeting of the Daughters of 1812 in Louisville, Ky.

LOUISIANA

1836. Alleman, Elise A. The legend and history of place names of Assumption Parish. 104p.
Thesis (M.A.) Louisiana State Univ., 1936.

1837. Banta, Anna. How Louisiana bayous got their names. Colonists nearly exhausted own vocabularies and then called on Indians. Times-picayune, New Orleans, March 11, 1928, p. 2.

1838. Berry, Nora. Place names of Natchitoches Parish. 133p.
Thesis (M.A.) Louisiana State Univ., 1935.

1839. Bonham, Milledge Louis. Clear reference to word "Istrouma" found by Bonham, former L.S.U. professor, during research in Paris. State times, Baton Rouge, April 10, 1930.

1840. —— Notes on place names. American speech 1:625, Aug. 1926.
In South Carolina and Louisiana.

1841. Bushnell, David Ives. The Choctaw of Bayou Lacomb, St. Tammany Parish, Louisiana. Washington, Govt. Print. Off., 1909. 37p. (Smithsonian Institution. Bureau of American Ethnology. Bulletin no. 48)
Place names in St. Tammany Parish: p. 6-7.

1842. Chapman, H. H. Why the town of McNary moved. American forests and forest life 30:589-92, 626, Oct. 1924.
The town of McNary, La., was abandoned and all the inhabitants moved to Cooley, Ariz., rechristened McNary, because of the depletion of the timber stand in Louisiana.

1843. Chase, Carroll & Richard McP. Cabeen. The first hundred years of United States territorial postmarks, 1787-1887. Orleans Territory. American philatelist 55:721-25, Aug. 1942; 56:177-79, Dec. 1942.
Includes list of post offices, 1804-12, with notes on some names.

1844. Chase, John Churchill. Frenchmen, Desire, Good Children, and other streets of New Orleans, in words and pictures. New Orleans, R. L. Crager, 1949. 246p.
Reprinted: New Orleans, Robert L. Crager & Co. 1960.
New Orleans street names related to history.

1845. Detro, Randall A. Generic terms in Louisiana place names: an index to the cultural landscape. 395ℓ.
Thesis (Ph.D.) Louisiana State Univ., 1970.

1846. Douglas, Lillian. Place-names of East Feliciana Parish. 38p.
Thesis (M.A.) Louisiana State Univ., 1930.

1847. Ficklen, John Rose. Origin of the name Louisiana. Louisiana historical quarterly 2:230-32, April 1919.

1848. Fitzpatrick, William H. Odd plantation names hint at comedy, tragedy of era living only in memory. Times-picayune, New Orleans, Aug. 28, 1938, p. 3.

1849. Gill, Donald Artley. Louisiana place names of arboreal origin; In South Central Names Institute. Labeled for life. Commerce, Tex., Names Institute Press, 1977. p. 55-57. (Publication 5)

1850. —— Louisiana place names with a touch of the unusual; In South Central Names Institute. They had to call it something. Commerce, Tex., Names Institute Press, 1974. p. 83-92. (Publication 3)
References: p. 90-92.

1851. —— The onomastics of Louisiana river names; In South Central Names Institute. Naughty names. Commerce, Tex., Names Institute Press, 1975. p. 5-13. (Publication 4)
Bibliography: p. 11-13.

1852. —— Place names of Bienville Parish, Louisiana; In South Central Names Institute. The scope of names. Commerce, Tex., Names Institute Press, 1979. p. 7-11. (Publication 7)

1853. Grima, Edgar. Les noms géographiques français en Louisiane. Société de Géographie de Québec. Bulletin 8:267-69, sept. 1914.

1854. Halbert, Henry Sale. Bvlbancha, Choctaw word for the town of New Orleans. Gulf States historical magazine 1:53-54, July 1902.

1855. Hearn, Lafcadio. The curious nomenclature of New Orleans streets; In his Occidental gleanings, sketches and essays now first collected by Albert Mordell. New York, Dodd, 1925. 1:263-75.

1856. Italian names displaced. New York times June 16, 1940, p. 34, col. 5.
Street names in Bossier City changed unofficially as result of anti-Italian sentiment.

1857. Jeff street has new name. Times-picayune, New Orleans, Nov. 19, 1967.
Name of a street in Metairie to be changed to Melvil Dewey Drive on the occasion of the completion of a new library headquarters for Jefferson Parish.

1858. Kaltenbaugh, Louise P. A study of the place names of St. Bernard Parish, Louisiana. 100ℓ.
Thesis (M.A.) Louisiana State Univ., 1969.
A historical and linguistic record of some 500 local names.

1859. Krumpelmann, John T. The renaming of Berlin Street and Berlin streets. American speech 26:156-57, May 1951.
New Orleans.

1860. Laurent, Lubin F. Origin of certain place names. Louisiana historical quarterly 7:327-31, April 1924.
From the parish of St. John the Baptist, the author has procured names of towns and villages for the purpose of studying their source.

1861. Leeper, Clare D'Artois. Louisiana places; a collection of the columns from the Baton Rouge Sunday advocate, 1960-1974. Baton Rouge, Legacy Pub. Co., 1976. 264p. maps.
1975 supplement, 265-96p.
Review: Robert M. Rennick, Names 25:39-40, March 1977.

1862. Linton, Albert C. New Orleans street names record history. Illinois Central magazine 32:5-6, March 1944.

1863. Lorio, E. C. Place-names of Pointe-Coupée Parish. 68p.
Thesis (M.A.) Louisiana State Univ., 1932.

1864. Louisiana. Dept. of Public Works. Directory of Louisiana cities, towns, and villages. [Baton Rouge], 1971. 167p.
Earlier edition: 1969.

1865. McDavid, Raven I. Berlin Street in New Orleans. American speech 24:238, Oct. 1949.
Changed to General Pershing Street.

1866. —— & Raymond K. O'Cain. Louisiana and New Orleans: notes on the pronunciation of proper names. Mississippi folklore register 11:76-92, Fall 1977. maps.
Based on material assembled for the linguistic atlas of the middle and south Atlantic states.

1867. Maxwell, Cordelia. A place-name study of Washington Parish. Louisiana studies 10:170-86, 1971.

1868. Mitchiner, Nantelle. Place names in Louisiana, extraordinary, survey reveals, Bible and literature culled. Morning advocate, Baton Rouge, Sept. 4, 1938, p. 16.

1869. —— What's in a name? Many strange place names are found in Louisiana. Louisiana tourist (Louisiana Dept. of Commerce and Industry) 1:6, Nov. 1938.

1870. Parkerson, Codman. Those strange Louisiana names; a glossary. Baton Rouge, Claitor's Book Store, 1969. 22p.

1871. Read, William Alexander. Geographical names; In his Louisiana-French. Baton Rouge, Louisiana State Univ. Press, 1963. p. 152-201.
1st ed. 1931.
Includes lists under the headings: Indian, French, Spanish, and The Ouachita region in 1797.

1872. —— Istrouma. Louisiana historical quarterly 14:503-15, Oct. 1931.
The Indian word Istrouma, meaning "red post," is the source of the name Baton Rouge.

1873. —— Louisiana place-names of Indian origin. Baton Rouge, Louisiana State Univ., 1927. 72p. (Louisiana State University. University bulletin n.s. v. 19, Feb. 1927)
Bibliography: p. x.
A list of addenda and corrigenda in Louisiana historical quarterly 11:445-62, July 1928. Also published separately.

1874. Reynolds, Jack Adolphe. Louisiana place-names of romance origin. 566p.
Thesis (Ph.D.) Louisiana State Univ., 1942.

1875. Scroggs, William Oscar. Origin of the name Baton Rouge. Historical Society of East and West Baton Rouge. Proceedings 1:20-24. 1916-17. (Louisiana State University. Bulletin n.s. v. 8, no. 8, Aug. 1917)

1876. Shampine, William J. Gazetteer of Louisiana lakes and reservoirs. Baton Rouge, Louisiana Dept. of Public Works, 1970. 31p. maps. (Louisiana. Dept. of Public Works. Basic records report, no. 4)
Prepared by U.S. Geological Survey in cooperation with Louisiana Dept. of Public Works.
Bibliography: p. 4.

1877. Sternberg, Hilgard O'Reilly. The names "False-River" and "Pointe Coupée," an inquiry in historical geography. Louisiana historical quarterly 31:598-605, July 1948.

1878. Turner, Sarah Anne. Place-names of Webster Parish. A linguistic, historical study. 93p.
Thesis (M.A.) Louisiana State Univ. 1935.

1879. Villiers du Terrage, Marc, Baron de. La Louisiane, histoire de son nom et de ses frontières successives (1681-1819). Paris, Adrien-Maisonneuve, 1929. 74p. (Publications de la Société des Américanistes de Paris)

1880. Walker, Norman M. The geographical nomenclature of Louisiana. Magazine of American history 10:211-22, Sept. 1883.

1881. Whitbread, Leslie George. Louisiana place names: some preliminary considerations. Louisiana studies 7:228-51, Fall 1968.
Aim of the present notes is to enlist support and establish possible guidelines for a systematic and comprehensive record of Louisiana place-names, past and present.

1882. —— Place names of Jefferson Parish, Louisiana, an introductory account. Gretna, La Pelican Press, 1975. Unpaged. (Jefferson historic series no. 1)

1883. Woods, William S. L'abbé Prévost and the gender of New Orleans. Modern language notes 66:259-61, April 1951.
Reply by Leo Spitzer, ibid. 66:571-72, Dec. 1951.
Concerning the gender of New Orleans in French.

1884. Wurzlow, Helen Emmelin. There's more than meets the eye in names of bayous. Times-picayune, New Orleans, Dec. 12, 1943, p. 11.

MAINE

1885. Ambitious names of Maine towns. New York times magazine June 24, 1928, p. 20.

1886. Andrews, L. A. Squeaker Guzzle. Rudder 63:18-19, 68, Nov. 1947.
Concerning this island's name and other Maine names.

1887. Attwood, Stanley Bearce. The length and breadth of Maine. Orono, Univ. of Maine, 1973. 279, 12, 30p. (Maine studies no. 96)
Reprint of 1st ed., 1946, and the 1949 and 1953 supplements.
Alphabetical list of place-names: p. 95-279, with special lists for counties, townships, discontinued names of townships, proposed names of ponds, lakes, and streams, and other miscellaneous lists.

1888. Ballard, Edward. Geographical names on the coast of Maine. U.S. Coast Survey. Report 1868:243-59.
Also issued separately, 1871.
"Full of errors, because Dr. Ballard, though painstaking, relied upon incompetent information."—Eckstorm.

1889. Beck, Horace P. The folklore of Maine. New York, Lippincott, 1957. 284p.
Names on the sea: p. 1-24. Coastal names.

1890. Chadbourne, Ava Harriet. Maine place names and the peopling of its towns. Portland, Me., Bond Wheelwright Co., 1955. 530p.

"An excellent example of sound historical research based on geographical names."—E. K. Gudde.

Review: Elisabeth K. Gudde, Names 4:185, Sept. 1956.

1891. Coffin, F. Parkman. Indian names on the Piscataqua River, Great Bay and its tributary streams. New Hampshire archeologist no. 11:5-8, Oct. 1962.

1892. Eckstorm, Fannie Hardy. The Indian names of two Maine mountains. New England quarterly 9:132-42, March 1936.

Sowbungy, or Sourbungy, Mountain, and Sowangas Mountain were given Indian names of the golden eagle.

1893. —— Indian place-names of the Penobscot Valley and the Maine coast. Orono, Me., Printed at the Univ. Press, 1941. 272p. (University of Maine studies. Second series, no. 55) (The Maine bulletin, v. 44, no. 4, Nov. 1941)

The Appendix (p. 237-41) includes a reproduction of Joseph Nicolar's articles on Penobscot place-names which appeared originally in the Old town herald, of unknown date.

Bibliography: p. 242-54.

Review: New England quarterly 16:503-07, Sept. 1943.

1894. —— Is Kokadjo Indian? Sprague's journal of Maine history 13:95-97, April-June 1925.

Kokadjo (an Indian word) is the name of Little Spencer Mountain but is not desirable as a name replacing the old, established names of First, Second, and Third Roach ponds.

1895. Fobes, Charles B. Indian names for Maine mountains. Appalachia 34:521-29, June 1963.

Includes alphabetical list with meanings for 41 mountains.

1896. Gatschet, Albert Samuel. All around the Bay of Passamaquoddy, with interpretation of its Indian names or localities. Washington, Judd, 1897. p. 16-24.

Reprinted from National Geographic magazine 8:16-24, Jan. 1897.

Supplemented by an article in the Eastport sentinel Sept. 15, 1897.

1897. Gentler place names along Maine's coast. New York times magazine Oct. 12, 1930, p. 18.

Replace robust and expressive names given by early settlers.

1898. Greenleaf, Moses. Indian place-names; Indian names of some of the streams, islands, etc., on the Penobscot and St. John rivers in Maine, taken from a letter from M. Greenleaf, esq., to Rev. Dr. Morse. Bangor, Me., Privately printed, 1903. 12p.

Reprinted from American Society for Promoting Civilization and General Improvement of the Indian Tribes of the United States. Report. New Haven, 1824.

Also reprinted in Edgar Crosby Smith, Moses Greenleaf, Maine's first map-maker (Bangor, Printed for the De Burians, 1902).

1899. Hayward, John. A gazetteer of the United States, comprising a series of gazetteers of the several states and territories. Maine. Portland, Me., S. H. Colesworthy; Boston, B. B. Mussey, 1843. 92p.

1900. Hubbard, Lucius Lee. Woods and lakes of Maine; a trip from Moosehead Lake to New Brunswick in a birch-bark canoe, to which are added some Indian place-names and their meanings, now first published. New and original illustrations by Will L. Taylor. Boston, J. R. Osgood & Co., 1884. 223p.

Reprinted: Boston, Ticknor, 1888. This edition reprinted with a foreword by Edmund S. Muskie. Somersworth, New Hampshire Pub. Co., 1971. 223p.

Some Indian place-names in northern Maine: p. 192-216.

1901. Kennebunkport keeps name. New York times March 8, 1938, p. 21, col. 2; letter March 20, 1938, sec. 4, p. 9, col. 2.
Proposal to change to its original name of Arundel defeated.

1902. Lacasse, Jean-Paul. Limochoronymie de la frontière Québec-Maine; In Canadian Society for the Study of Names. Onomastica 52:1-5, Dec. 1977.

1903. McKeon, Ed. Ever hear of K'chi Mugwock? Bangor area abounds in Indian names. Bangor daily news Feb. 12, 1959, p. 7.

1904. Maine. Fishery Research and Management Division. Maine lakes; index of lake surveys completed through 1969. [Augusta, Dept. of Inland Fisheries and Game, 1970]. 83p.
An inventory of lakes and ponds, with township in which located.

1905. —— State Water Storage Commission. Gazetteer of the rivers and lakes of Maine. Waterville, Sentinel Pub. Co., 1914. 323p. (Fourth annual report, 1913)
Arranged alphabetically by drainage basins.

1906. Matthews, Albert. Origin of the name of Maine. Cambridge, J. Wilson and Son, 1910. 366-82p.
Reprinted from the Colonial Society of Massachusetts. Publications 12:366-82. 1909.
P. 380-82, note on the name Mariana, the name intended by John Mason for the territory between the Naumkeag and the Merrimac, granted to him in 1621-22.

1907. Maurault, Joseph Pierre Anselme. Histoire des Abenakis, depuis 1605, jusqu'à nos jours. [Sorel, Qué.], Imprimé à l'atelier typographique de la "Gazette de Sorel," 1866. 631p.
A list of place-names in Maine and Canada, with significations, in Introduction p. ii-vii.

1908. Meaning of the Indian names Penobscot and Kennebec. Ladies' repository 24:631, Oct. 1864.
Signed: H. Y. W.

1909. Placentia Islands. Historical magazine 10:321, Oct. 1866.
Possible derivation of the name.

1910. Potter, Chandler Eastman. Appendix to the "Language of the Abnaquies" [By William Willis]. Maine Historical Society. Collections 4:185-95. 1856.
More on Abnaki names of geographic features in Maine.
Cf. William Willis, The language of the Abnaquies, or eastern Indians, no. 1925.

1911. Randel, William Peirce. Saco names for Indians. New York times Nov. 14, 1937, sec. 4, p. 9.

1912. —— Town names of York County, Maine. New England quarterly 11:565-75, Sept. 1938.
Bibliographical footnotes.

1913. Rutherford, Phillip Roland. Censorship and some Maine place names; In South Central Names Institute. Of Edsels and Marauders. Commerce, Tex., Names Institute Press, 1971. p. 47-50. (Publication 1)
Examples of some names that have been "cleaned up."

1914. —— The dictionary of Maine place-names. Freeport, Bond Wheelwright Co., 1970. 283p.

Lists approximately 20,000 names alphabetically under counties. Limited to names that appear on the latest set of United States Geological Survey maps. Origins supplied by local inhabitants.

1915. —— Maine place names of Indian origin; In South Central Names Institute. Labeled for life. Commerce, Tex., Names Institute Press, 1977. p. 47-54. (Publication 5)

1916. —— Tragedy in Maine place names; In South Central Names Institute. They had to call it something. Commerce, Tex., Names Institute Press, 1974. p. 77-81. (Publication 3)

Names given for people who met a tragic death.

1917. Sands, Donald B. The nature of the generics in island, ledge, and rock names of the Maine coast. Names 7:193-202, Dec. 1959.

Deals with the four groups into which the generics fall and the problem of when elements of binomial toponyms can be considered lexical evidence.

1918. Shaw, Justin H. Kittery, Devon. Devon and Cornwall notes and queries 9:48-49, April 1916.

Question concerning origin of name. Had been referred to in Everett Schermerhorn Stackpole, Old Kittery and her families (Lewiston, Me., Press of Lewiston Journal Co., 1903) as derived from Kittery Point near Dartmouth, England.

1919. The Strangest things happen in Maine. Christian Science monitor May 25, 1962, p. 4.

"On town names, especially the cosmopolitan—Norway, Belfast—and the abstract—Unity, Freedom."—American speech.

1920. Thoreau, Henry David. The Maine woods, arranged with notes by Dudley C. Lunt, illus. by Henry Bugbee Kane. New York, Norton, 1950. 340p.

Appendix, p. 336-40: A list of Indian words; including a short list from William Willis, The language of the Abnaquies. Maine Historical Society. Collections 4:93-117. 1856.

Also in other editions.

1921. True, Nathaniel Tuckerman. Indian names on the Androscoggin. Historical magazine 8:237-38, July 1864.

45 names of geographic features in the Abnaki language.

1922. U.S. Board on Geographic Names. Decisions. No. 39--Decisions rendered April 4, 1934. Acadia National Park, Maine. Washington, Govt. Print. Off. 1934. 3p.

1923. Varney, George Jones. A gazetteer of the State of Maine. Boston, B. B. Russell, 1881. 611p.

1924. Whipple, Joseph. A geographical view of the District of Maine, with particular reference to its internal resources, including the history of Acadia, Penobscot River and Bay, with statistical tables, shewing the comparative progress of the population of Maine with each state, list of the towns, their incorporations, census, polls, etc. Bangor, P. Edes, printer, 1816. 102p.

1925. Willis, William. The language of the Abnaquies, or eastern Indians. Maine Historical Society. Collections 4:93-117. 1856.

Includes Indian names applied to portions of the state, with definitions, p. 103-17.

Some of these names were included in Henry David Thoreau, The Maine woods (see no. 1920).

For additional material, see Chandler Eastman Potter, no. 1910.

1926. Wright, Walter W. Norway, Maine. Norwegian-American studies and records 15:219-22, 1949.

Origin of the name; answers the speculations of Dr. Halvdan Koht in v. 13, and his articles in Nordisk tidends Sept. 3, 1942 and Decorah-posten Sept. 4, 1942.

MARYLAND

1927. Associated Stamp Clubs of the Chesapeake Area. Postal markings of Maryland, 1766-1855. [The Maryland postal history catalog] Ed. Roger T. Powers. Baltimore, 1960. 100p.

More than 600 names, with period of operation, of Maryland offices.

1928. Babcock, W. H. Notes on local names near Washington. Journal of American folklore 1:146-47, July-Sept. 1888.

The origin and changes of several place-names around Washington.

1929. Baltimore's quaint local names are being lost. Baltimore American Feb. 4, 1923.

1930. Barbour, Philip L. The earliest reconnaissance of Chesapeake Bay area: Captain John Smith's map and Indian vocabulary. Virginia magazine of history and biography 79:280-302, July 1971.

Bibliography: p. 283-84.

The Indian place-names recorded by Smith in his writings and on his map are listed, roughly located, and analyzed where possible. Most are in the language called Powhatan. Names are mainly in Virginia and Maryland, with a few in Delaware and Pennsylvania.

1931. Berkley, Henry J. Extinct river towns of the Chesapeake Bay region. Maryland historical magazine 19:125-34, June 1924.

1932. Bevan, Edith Rossiter. Some Maryland towns have odd place names. Maryland gardener 6:6, 19-20, May 1952.

1933. Bigbee, Janet H. 17th century place names: culture and process on the Eastern Shore.

Thesis (M.S.) Univ. of Maryland, Dept. of Geography, 1970.

1934. Bouton, E. H. A competition in street naming. Landscape architecture 9:125-28, April 1919.

The winning plan for naming the streets at Sparrows Point.

1935. Bump, Charles Weathers. Indian place-names in Maryland. Maryland historical magazine 2:287-93, Dec. 1907.

1936. Collitz, Hermann. Baltimore—what does the name mean? Johns Hopkins alumni magazine 22:133-34, Jan. 1934.

1937. Conowingo known in Indian lore. Sunday sun, Baltimore, March 28, 1926, Magazine sec., p. 9.

1938. Coyle, Wilbur F. Few original names of estates in Baltimore have survived. Baltimore news Jan. 22, 1922.

1939. Craig's business directory and Baltimore almanac for 1842. Baltimore, Craig, 1842. 145p.

Post offices in Maryland: p. 56-57.

1939a. Duckson, Don W., Jr. Toponymic generics in Maryland. Names 28:163-69, Sept. 1980.
It is impossible to expect that a single standardized connotation can be identified for each toponymic generic, but use of morphometric properties provides a means for arriving at regional, if not standard, connotations.

1940. Edwards, Richard. Statistical gazetteer of the State of Maryland, and the District of Columbia. To which is appended a business directory of the federal metropolis and suburbs. Baltimore, J. S. Waters; Washington, W. M. Morrison & Co., 1856. 328p.

1941. Filby, Vera Ruth. From Forest to Friendship. Maryland historical magazine 71:93-102, Spring 1976.
Abridged version appeared in the Anne Arundel County history notes, 1974.
Anne Arundel County names in the vicinity of Friendship airport, now Baltimore-Washington International, the airport named originally for Friendship Methodist Church which stood in the middle of the site.

1942. Fisher, Richard Swainson. Gazetteer of the state of Maryland, comp. from the returns of the seventh census of the United States, and other official documents. To which is added, A general account of the District of Columbia. New York, J. H. Colton; Baltimore, J. S. Waters, 1852. 122p.

1943. Forgotten names "Below the deadline." Baltimore American Feb. 11, 1923.
South Baltimore.

1944. Gannett, Henry. A gazetteer of Maryland. Washington, Govt. Print. Off., 1904. 84p. (U.S. Geological Survey. Bulletin no. 231)
Also in Maryland. Bureau of Industrial Statistics. Report 1908:415-523.
Reprinted as A gazetteer of Maryland and Delaware. Baltimore, Genealogical Pub. Co., 1976. 84, 15p.

1945. Gilliam, Charles Edgar. The Potomac debate. Extracts from his letter, September 1966. Names 15:242, Sept. 1967.
Disagrees with the meaning "place of trade" or "emporium" especially if trade was in buffalo skins or steatite.

1946. Gordon, Douglas H. Hero worship as expressed in Baltimore street names. Maryland historical magazine 43:121-26, June 1948.

1947. Gritzner, Janet H. Seventeenth century generic place-names: culture and process on the Eastern Shore. Names 20:231-39, Dec. 1972.
Summarizes the results of a study to identify the various cultural processes involved in naming all of the peninsula east of the Chesapeake Bay.

1948. Harris, William H. How it got that name. Upper Chesapeake Bay and tributaries. Salem, N.J., n.d. 4p.
Folder issued by Mr. Harris, 127 Seventh St., Salem, N.J., giving information about names of places along Chesapeake Bay and requesting additional information to be published in the Salem (N.J.) standard and jerseyman (about 1938).

1949. Heckewelder, John Gottlieb Ernestus. Names given by the Lenni Lenape or Delaware Indians to rivers, streams and places in the now states of New Jersey, Pennsylvania, Maryland, and Virginia. Pennsylvania German Folklore Society. Publications 5:1-41. 1940.
Published also in American Philosophical Society. Transactions 4:351-96. 1834; Historical Society of Pennsylvania. Bulletin 1:121-35, 139-54, June, Sept. 1847; Moravian Historical Society. Transactions 1872:275-333; published separately: Bethle-

hem [Pa.], H. T. Claude, printer, 1872. 58p.; and in his A narrative of the mission of the United Brethren among the Delaware and Mohegan Indians. Cleveland, Burrows Bros., 1907. p. 523-66.

1950. How well are you up in Easton history? Easton (Md.) star-democrat Feb. 2, 1945.
Talbot County names.

1951. Hoye Crest name given highest peak. Glades star (Garrett County Historical Society) 2:160, June 30, 1952.

1952. Island's name changed; Potomac Park redesignated to honor architects. New York times July 13, 1960, p. 53.
Name of Falls Island changed to Olmsted Island.

1953. Johnson, Gerald W. Place-names. Baltimore evening sun July 2, 1931.

1954. —— What's in a name? Baltimore sun Oct. 31, 1929.

1955. Kenny, Hamill. Alias Pangayo. Names 15:238-39, Sept. 1967.
An alias of Zekiah Swamp, Charles County, southern Maryland.

1956. —— Baltimore: new light on an old name. Maryland historical magazine 49:116-21, June 1954.
Its Irish provenance and American history and meaning.

1957. —— The origin and meaning of the Indian place-names of Maryland. College Park, Md., 1950, i.e., 1951. 2v.
Thesis (Ph.D.) Univ. of Maryland.

1958. —— The origin and meaning of the Indian place names of Maryland. Baltimore, Waverly Press, 1961. 186p.
Bibliography: p. 161-175.
Review: C. A. Weslager, Maryland historical magazine 56:311-14, Sept. 1961; V. J. Vogel, Names 10:65-69, March 1962; A. R. Dunlap, American speech 37:55-57, Feb. 1962.

1959. —— Place-names from surnames: Maryland. Names 18:137-54, Sept. 1970.
Of the 3,183 entries in Gannett's A gazetteer of Maryland (1904), 1,731 (54 percent) are probably derived from surnames. Many of these surnames, in turn, were derived from English place-names. Therefore, the author has classified the Maryland place-names by the Anglo-Saxon place-name elements in them.

1960. Kerney, Ellen. American ghost towns. American notes and queries 4:32, May 1944.
Snowhill, and Furnace, Md.

1961. Kuethe, J. Louis. A list of Maryland mills, taverns, forges and furnaces of 1795. Maryland historical magazine 31:155-69, June 1936.

1962. —— Maryland place names. Baltimore sun Sept. 8, 1940, sec. 2, p. 3.

1963. —— Maryland place names have strange origins. Baltimore sun May 23, 1937, sec. 2, p. 2; March 24, 1940.

1964. —— Runs, creeks and branches in Maryland. American speech 10:256-59, Dec. 1935.

1965. McDavid, Raven I., Jr., & Raymond K. O'Cain. Some notes on Maryland and Baltimore. American speech 55:278-87, Winter 1980.
On the pronunciation of the two words.

1966. Marye, William Bose. Place names of Baltimore and Harford counties. Maryland historical magazine 25:321-65, Dec. 1930; 53:34-57, 238-52, March, Sept. 1958.

1966a. —— The several Indian "Old Towns" on the upper Potomac River. Maryland historical magazine 34:325-33, Dec. 1939.

1967. —— Some Baltimore city place names. Maryland historical magazine 54:15-35, 353-64, March, Dec. 1959; 58:211-32, 344-77, Sept., Dec. 1963; 59:52-93, March 1964.
Part 2 has subtitle: Huntington or Huntingdon, the two Liliendales and Sumwalt Run; Parts 3-4 (Sept. 1963-March 1964) have title and subtitle: Baltimore city place names: Stony Run, its plantations, farms, country seats and mills.
Supplementary note by the author, ibid. 54:437-38, Dec. 1959.

1968. Maryland. Board of Public Works. Maryland as it is. A good land to live in and raise a family. Opportunities for settlers. Varied resources of land and water. Baltimore, Sun Job. Print. Off., 1903. 168p.
Indian names, county names, towns and localities: p. 113-21.

1969. —— State Planning Commission. Gazetteer of Maryland. Prepared jointly by Maryland State Planning Commission and Department of Geology, Mines and Water Resources. Baltimore, Johns Hopkins Press, 1941. 242p. (Maryland. Geological Survey. Reports v. 14)
Issued also as its Publication no. 33.
"Assistance in the preparation of this report was furnished by the Work Projects Administration project no. 651-25-2089."
Sources of information: p. 237.

1970. —— State Planning Department. Maryland manual of coordinates. New ed. Baltimore, 1962. 168p. maps. (Publication no. 120)
Earlier edition published in 1947 by Maryland State Planning Commission under title: Manual of coordinates for places in Maryland.
Embodies a simple method for locating some 12,000 places within the state. An alphabetical listing of places, giving county and grid coordinate numbers according to the system of the United States Coast and Geodetic Survey.

1971. Morris, Clay Louise. You take the high road: a guide to the place names of colonial Eastern Shore of Maryland. [Easton, Md., Easton Pub. Co., c1970]. 48p.

1972. The Name "Accident." Glades star (Garrett County Historical Society) v. 2, p. 85-87, June 30, 1951.

1973. Names. Eastern Shore magazine v. 1, Dec. 1937, p. 5; Feb. 1938, p. 4.
Peculiar names found on the Eastern Shore.

1974. Names of neighborhoods in old Baltimore town. Baltimore sun Jan. 20, 1907.
On the names of the villages absorbed into Baltimore.

1975. A New name needed for Swastika Road. Kansas City star Feb. 5, 1960, p. 8.
A 1920 name in Frederick, Md.

1976. Norris, Walter B. More Maryland place names: "Maryland Point." Maryland and Delaware genealogist 1:63, March 1960.

1977. —— Origin of some interesting Maryland place names. Maryland and Delaware genealogist 1:16, Sept. 1959.

1978. The Origin of many of Talbot's geographical names. Easton (Md.) star-democrat Dec. 11, 1931.

1979. Robb, Kenneth A. Names of grants in colonial Maryland. Names 17:263-77, Dec. 1969.
Broad classes of names, based on study of 2,401 names listed in rent rolls for Baltimore, Anne Arundel, and Dorchester counties.

1980. Rubincam, Milton. Queen Henrietta Maria: Maryland's royal namesake. Maryland historical magazine 54:131-48, June 1959.
Biography of the member of the royal family for whom Maryland was named.

1981. Stewart, Richard D. Baltimore day by day. Baltimore news-post Nov. 21, 25, 1944.
Other material on place-names appeared from time to time in this column, signed Carroll Dulaney, and also appeared on Sundays in the Baltimore American.

1982. Touch of London recurs in old local names. Baltimore American Feb. 18, 1923.
Names in old Baltimore.

1983. Truitt, Alfred. They left many mementoes. Baltimore sun Feb. 10, 1929.
Indian place-names.

1984. U.S. Post Office, Baltimore, Md. Alphabetical list of streets served by the following Maryland post offices: Cockeysville, Ellicott City, Fullerton [and others]. William F. Laukaitis, Postmaster. [Baltimore, 1960]. 16ℓ.

1985. —— Alphabetical listings of streets in Baltimore City, Anne Arundel, Baltimore, & Howard counties; for use by city & county officials, builders, & developers. Baltimore, 1960. 65ℓ.

1986. Weird names given estates on city sites centuries ago. Baltimore sun Jan. 23, 1927.
Baltimore place-names.

1987. What's in a name in Maryland. Baltimore evening sun Oct. 6, 1944.
Origin of about 40 Maryland place-names.

1988. Wright, Esther Clark. The naming of Monkton Mills. Maryland historical magazine 52:248-50, Sept. 1957.
After a Nova Scotia township name.

MASSACHUSETTS

1989. Amory, Thomas C. Report on the names of streets. Massachusetts Historical Society. Proceedings 6:24-40, June 1862.
Street names of Boston. In answer to a letter from the New England Historic Genealogical Society, Proceedings 6:4-5, April 1862.

1990. Asks Cambridge to drop name of Harvard Square. New York times June 29, 1939, p. 8, col. 4.
Proposal to change name to George Washington Square.

1991. Banks, Charles Edward. Capowack. Is it the correct Indian name of Martha's Vineyard? New England historical and genealogical register 52:176-80, April 1898.
Algonquin name.

1992. —— Martin's or Martha's—What is the proper nomenclature of the Vineyard? New England historical and genealogical register 48:201-04, April 1894.

1993. Barrows, Charles Henry. An historical address delivered before the citizens of Springfield in Massachusetts at the public celebration, May 26, 1911, of the two hundred and seventy-fifth anniversary of the settlement; with five appendices, viz: Meaning of Indian local names, The cartography of Springfield, Old place names of Springfield, Unrecorded deed of Nippumsuit, Unrecorded deed of Paupsunnuck. Springfield, Mass., Connecticut Valley Historical Society, 1916. 100p.

1994. Baylies, Francis. The original of local and other names, a letter from Hon. Francis Baylies to Hon. P. W. Leland. Brooklyn, 1879. 24p. (Elzevir Club series, no. 1)
Reprinted: New York, Burt Franklin, 1969.
Most of the names are of Massachusetts.

1995. Boston streets well-named. Magazine of history 17:93, Aug.-Sept. 1913.

1996. Budgar, Esther L. The second-longest name in the English language. New York times April 4, 1971, sec. XX, p. 40.
Lake Chargoggaggoggmanchauggagoggchaubunagungamaugg, near Webster, Mass.

1997. Captain Gosnold's Martha. New York herald tribune Sept. 14, 1947.
Origin of name Martha's Vineyard.

1998. Chase, George W. List of dates of incorporation of the towns in Massachusetts, and their historical origin; In Massachusetts. Abstract of the Census of Massachusetts, 1860. Boston, Wright & Potter, 1863. p. 215-37.
Includes many Indian names of places before incorporation under present form.

1999. De Costa, B. F. Cago de baxos: or, The place of Cape Cod in the old cartology. New England historical and genealogical register 35:49-59, Jan. 1881.
A study of the various names for Cape Cod appearing on old maps.

2000. Dexter, Ralph W. The relationship of natural features to the place names of Cape Ann, Massachusetts. Essex Institute. Historical collections 88:141-49, April 1952.

2001. Dudley, Myron Samuel. Indian names of Nantucket. Nantucket, 1894. 1p.
Names found in the various records of Nantucket and adjacent islands as designations of persons and places.

2002. Fay, Joseph Story. Letters on the origin of names prevailing on Vineyard Sound. Massachusetts Historical Society. Proceedings 12:334-35, Feb. 1873.

2003. —— The track of the Norseman, a monograph. Boston, C. C. Roberts, 1876. 7p.
Reprinted in Magazine of American history 8:431-34, June 1882.
Some place-names that author considers of Norse origin and favors supposition that Hole in such names as Wood's Hole, Holmes's Hole, etc. is a corruption of a Norse word, holl, meaning hill.

2004. Fish tales can't beat lake name. Rocky Mountain motorist 31:4, May 1961.
The lake name with 45 letters: Chargoggaggoggmanchauggagoggchaubunagungamaugg.

2005. Freeman, Nathaniel. Indian places within, or near the county of Barnstable. Massachusetts Historical Society. Collections 1:230-32, 1792.

2006. Gahan, Laurence K. Methods of translating Indian place names. Massachusetts Archaeological Society. Bulletin 21:46-47, April-July 1960.

2007. Gannett, Henry. A geographic dictionary of Massachusetts. Washington, Govt. Print. Off., 1894. 126p. (U.S. Geological Survey. Bulletin no. 116)
Issued also as House miscellaneous doc. v. 27, 53d Cong., 2d sess.

2008. Geographical gazetteer of the towns in the Commonwealth of Massachusetts. Boston, Greenleaf & Freeman, 1784-85. 98p.
Issued in parts, appended to the monthly numbers of the Boston magazine Oct. 1784-Dec. 1785. Includes only Suffolk County (p. 1-90) and part of Middlesex County (p. 91-98). "The publisher informs his customers that he is obliged to suspend the publication of the gazetteer for the present."—Note in Boston magazine 2:442, Dec. 1785. It was never completed nor issued as a separate work and was without a separate title page.
Edited probably by Rev. James Freeman. The Society for Compiling a Magazine in the Town of Boston voted Aug. 20, 1784, "That a committee be appointed to prepare proposals for collecting a complete geographical gazetteer of the several towns in the Commonwealth, to be inserted in the magazine." cf. Manuscripts of the Society for Compiling a Magazine, in the collection of the Massachusetts Historical Society.

2009. Green, Eugene. The American Revolution and the names of towns in Massachusetts. Connecticut onomastic review 1:41-51. 1979.

2009a. —— Place-names and images of Jamaica Plain, Massachusetts. Names 24:106-23, June 1976.

2010. —— & Rosemary M. Green. Place-names and dialects in Massachusetts: some complementary patterns. Names 19:240-51, Dec. 1971.

2011. Green, Samuel Abbott. Observations on the names of certain villages in Massachusetts and New Hampshire. Massachusetts Historical Society. Proceedings 2d ser. 10:465-67, Feb. 1896.
Use of Harbor away from the coastline. Includes Townsend Harbor, Mass.

2012. —— Remarks on Nonacoicus, the Indian name of Major (Simon) Willard's farm at Groton, Mass. Massachusetts Historical Society. Proceedings 2d ser. 8:209-12, May 1893.

2013. —— The town of Becket. Cambridge, 1890. 2p.
Remarks by Dr. Green at a meeting of the Massachusetts Historical Society, Jan. 9, 1890.

2014. Harding, William B. Origin of the names of the towns in Worcester County. Worcester, C. Jillson, 1883. 21p.

2015. Hayward, John. A gazetteer of Massachusetts, containing descriptions of all the counties, towns and districts in the commonwealth; also, of its principal mountains, rivers, capes, bays, harbors, islands, and fashionable resorts. To which are added, statistical accounts of other useful information. Rev. ed. Boston, J. P. Jewett & Co., 1849. 452p.
Earlier editions: 1846. 444p.; 1847. 444p.

2016. Holly, H. Hobart. Wollaston of Mount Wollaston. American neptune 37:5-25, Jan. 1977.
Now a part of Quincy, it was named for Capt. Richard Wollaston.

2017. Hommel, Rudolf. American ghost towns. American notes and queries 4:45-46, June 1944.
Dogtown, Mass.

2018. Horsford, Eben Norton. The Indian names of Boston, and their meaning. Cambridge, J. Wilson & Son, 1886. 26p.
Originally published in New England historical and genealogical register 40:94-103, Jan. 1886.

2019. Kinnicutt, Lincoln Newton. Indian names of places in Plymouth, Middleborough, Lakeville and Carver, Plymouth County, Massachusetts, with interpretations of some of them. Worcester, Commonwealth Press, 1909. 64p.

2020. —— Indian names of places in Worcester County, Massachusetts, with interpretations of some of them. Worcester, Commonwealth Press, 1905. 59p.
Names of the Nipmuck tribe.

2021. Lake with a long name. New York times June 12, 1938, sec. 11, p. 20, col. 1-2.
Origin of lake name with 45 letters, Chaubunagungamaug for short.

2022. Leland, P. W. Algonquin, or Indian terms as applied to places and things. Old Colony Historical Society. Collections 3:83-103. 1885.

2023. Lucas, J. Landfear. The Mary Ann Rocks, U.S.A. Notes and queries 154:280, April 21, 1928.
The author's supposition about the origin of the name of the rocks near Cape Cod was subsequently challenged by Albert Matthews in the May 26, 1928, number of the same magazine, p. 372.

2024. Martha's Vineyard. New England historical and genealogical register 12:33, Jan. 1858.

2025. Massachusetts. Secretary of the Commonwealth. Historical data relating to counties, cities and towns in Massachusetts. Prepared by the Secretary of the Commonwealth, Division of Public Records. Boston, Wright & Potter Print. Co., 1920. 73p.

2026. —— Historical data relating to counties, cities and towns in Massachusetts. Prepared by Frederic W. Cook. n.p., 1948. 92p.
Part 1. Counties, containing a list of counties with date of incorporation; Part 2. Existing cities and towns; Part 3. Extinct places.

2027. Massachusetts Geodetic Survey. Massachusetts localities. A finding list of Massachusetts cities and towns; and of villages, certain lesser localities, railroad stations, and post offices whose location is not localized within the appropriate cities and towns by their names, and other generally related material. Arranged for quick reference within one alphabet. Boston, Dept. of Public Works, Offset Print. Division, 1962. 53p. (Massachusetts. Dept. of Public Works. Publication no. 90)
Reprinted 1963. 51p.
Originally published 1938, 78p., as Massachusetts WPA project no. 16565, sponsored by Massachusetts Dept. of Public Works.

2028. Matthews, Albert. The naming of Hull, Massachusetts. Boston, Press of D. Clapp & Son, 1905. 12p.
Reprinted from New England historical and genealogical register 59:177-86, April 1905.

2029. Meigs, Peveril. The cove names of Walden. The Thoreau Society bulletin 104:5-7, Summer 1968. map.
Names for five otherwise unnamed coves of Walden Pond found in Thoreau's writings.

2030. Mood, Fulmer. Why the "Vineyard"? New England quarterly 6:131-36, March 1933.
Bibliographical footnotes.
Speculations on the origin of the word Vineyard in the name Martha's Vineyard.

2031. Nason, Elias. A gazetteer of the State of Massachusetts. Rev. and enl. by George J. Varney. Boston, B. B. Russell, 1890. 724p.
1st ed. 1874. 576p.

2032. Palmer, Charles James. Berkshire County. Its past history and achievements. n.p., n.d. 24p.
Origin of the names of the towns and villages of Berkshire County: p. 11-24.

2033. Poore, Alfred. Groveland localities and place-names. Essex Institute. Historical collections 46:161-77, April 1910.
Compiled in 1854.

2034. Reed, Donald. Rockport names. Essex Institute historical collections 114:24-31, Jan. 1978.
Coastal place-names with derivation if known.

2035. Spofford, Jeremiah. A historical and statistical gazetteer of Massachusetts, with sketches of the principal events from its settlement; a catalogue of prominent characters, and historical and statistical notices of the several cities and towns, alphabetically arranged. 2d ed. rev., cor., and a large part rewritten. Haverhill, E. G. Frothingham, 1860. 372p.
1st ed. published under title A gazetteer of Massachusetts. Newburyport, C. Whipple, 1828. 348p.

2036. Stilgoe, John R. Place-names in the wilderness: Scituate, Massachusetts, 1634-1700. Places 2:20-22, July 1975.

2037. Tolman, Adams. Indian relics in Concord. Concord Antiquarian Society. Publications v. 10, n.d.
Place-names, p. 4-13.

2038. Tooker, William Wallace. The name Massachusetts. Magazine of New England history 1:159-60, July 1891.
The derivation and meaning of the place-name. Opposes idea in note, ibid. 1:13, Jan. 1891, and states article by James Hammond Trumbull (see no. 2039) is best.

2039. Trumbull, James Hammond. Letter on the name Massachusetts. American Antiquarian Society. Proceedings Oct. 21, 1867, p. 77-84.
With remarks by Edward Everett Hale.

2040. U.S. Writers' Program. Massachusetts. The origin of Massachusetts place names of the state, counties, cities, and towns, comp. by workers of the Writers' Project of the Work Projects Administration in Massachusetts. Sponsored by the state librarian of the Commonwealth of Massachusetts. New York, Harian Publications, 1941. 55p.
Bibliography: p. 54-55.

2041. Waugh, William. A sketch of Wappanucket. Middleborough antiquarian 10:4-5, May 1968.
Includes origins of village's early name Walnut Plain, of its present name, and of roads in the village.

2042. Whitmore, William Henry. An essay on the origin of the names of towns in Massachusetts, settled prior to A.D. 1775. To which is prefixed An essay on the name of the town of Lexington. Boston, Press of John Wilson & Son, 1873. 37p.
Reprinted from Massachusetts Historical Society. Proceedings 12:269-76, 393-419, Oct. 1872, Feb. 1873.
With James Hammond Trumbull's The composition of Indian geographical names (see no. 560), marks the beginning of sound scholarship in place-name studies.

2043. Winship, A. E. Massachusetts names. Journal of education (Boston) 48:109-10, 142-43, Aug. 18, Sept. 1, 1898.

2044. Wright, Harry Andrew. Indian deeds of Hampden County, being copies of all land transfers from the Indians recorded in the county of Hampden, Massachusetts, and some deeds from other sources, together with notes and translations of Indian place names. Springfield, Mass., 1905. 194p.
Includes also records of the counties of Hampshire, Worcester, Berkshire, and Franklin, Mass. At the end of each deed, notes are given regarding the meaning or the source of the aboriginal names.

2045. —— Some vagaries in Connecticut Valley Indian place-names. New England quarterly 12:535-44, Sept. 1939.
"Discusses various causes of corruption in Indian place-names."--American speech.

MICHIGAN

2046. Applebaum, Emanual. Biblically influenced place names in Michigan. Michigan Jewish history 2:6-10, Jan. 1962.
Contains a list of names that may refer to biblical places and Hebrew names and words.

2047. Armitage, B. Phillis. A study of Michigan's place-names. Michigan history magazine 27:626-37, Oct.-Dec. 1943.
Extracted from a paper written for a course in Michigan history at Western Michigan College.
Bibliography: p. 636-37.

2048. Arneson, Winfield H. Henry Dearborn: city's namesake. Dearborn historian 7:3-16, 43-51, 71-83, Winter-Autumn 1967.

2049. Blois, John T. Gazetteer of the State of Michigan, in three parts, with a succinct history of the state, from the earliest period to the present time, with an appendix, containing the usual statistical tables, and a directory for emigrants, &c. Detroit, S. L. Rood & Co., 1840. 418p.
Editions published also in 1838, 1839.
Reprinted: New York, Arno Press, 1975.

2050. Brotherton, R. A. Meaning of Escanaba. Inland seas 4:210-11, Fall 1948.

2051. Brown, Claudeous Jethro Daniels. Lake names. Ann Arbor, Michigan Dept. of Conservation, 1944. 26p. (Michigan. Institute for Fisheries Research, Ann Arbor. Miscellaneous publication no. 2)

2052. Bunker, Norman & Victor F. Lemmer. How Little Girl's Point got its name. Michigan history 38:169-73, June 1954.

2053. Butler, Albert F. Rediscovering Michigan's prairies. Michigan history 31:267-86, Sept. 1947; 32:15-36, March 1948; 33:117-30, 220-31, June-Sept. 1949.

2054. Carpenter, C. K. Squaw Island—how it received its name. Michigan Pioneer and Historical Society. Historical collections 13:486-88. 1889.
An island in Orion Lake.

2055. Catlin, George B. Biography and romance in Detroit's street names. Michigan history magazine 11:604-20, Oct. 1927.

2056. Change of names of counties. Pioneer Society of the State of Michigan. Pioneer collections 1:94, 1877.
A table of changes made by legislative acts, followed by the acts in a section. Reports of counties, towns, and districts, p. 94-518.

2057. Chaput, Donald. A plea for moderation in place-name controversies. Michigan history 49:68-72, March 1965.
Based on the attempts to change Indian names in Michigan.

2058. —— Pronunciation of Algonquian place names. Inland seas 21:322-24, Winter 1965.

2059. Clapp, A. B. Sault Ste. Marie and its names. n.p., n.d. 23p.
Bibliography: p. 7-23.

2060. Davies, Florence. Six Michigan towns (Reading, Plymouth, Bath, Rochester, Manchester, and Oxford) invited to meet "grandmas." Detroit news Sept. 18, 1932.
Namesake town association sponsored by the English-speaking Union to encourage exchange of visits between representatives of the cities in the Old and the New World.

2061. Doty, Mrs. W. G. Ann Arbor. Michigan history magazine 7:192-98, July-Oct. 1923.
Origin of the name.

2062. Dustin, Fred. Isle Royale place names. Michigan history magazine 30:681-722, Oct.-Dec. 1946.

2063. —— Some Indian place-names around Saginaw. Michigan history magazine 12:729-39, Oct. 1928.
Reprinted: Michigan archaeologist 14:117-25, 1968.

2064. Dykstra, Lillian. The founding and naming of Ann Arbor. Michigan history 40:419-32, Dec. 1956.

2065. Foster, Theodore G. Indian place names in Michigan. Totem pole 28:3-4, Jan. 1952; 29:1-6, Aug. 1952.

2066. —— More Michigan place names. Totem pole 33:1-3, Nov. 1953; 35:1-6, Feb. 1955.

2067. —— Place-names of Ingham County. Michigan history magazine 26:480-517, Autumn 1942.

2068. —— Some Michigan place-names honoring the Navy. Inland seas 6:166-68, Fall 1950.

2069. —— Townships in Michigan, an alphabetical list. Lansing, Michigan State Library, 1948. 16p.

2070. —— The Vermont ancestry of some Michigan place names. Vermont Historical Society. News and notes 11:55, 62, March, April 1960.

2071. —— What's in a name. Lansing state journal.
A series that appeared ca. 1954. Similar series in Jackson citizen patriot, Kalamazoo gazette, and Grand Rapids press, each dealing with names in the particular paper's circulation area.

2072. Fox, George R. Place names of Berrien County. Michigan historical magazine 8:6-35, Jan. 1924.

2073. —— Place names of Cass County. Michigan history magazine 27:463-91, Summer 1943.

2074. Gagnieur, William F. Indian place-names. Michigan history magazine 9:109-11, Jan. 1925.
Corrections and additions to articles on Indian place-names which appeared in the Michigan history magazine in July 1918 and July 1919.

2075. —— Indian place-names in the Upper Peninsula, and their interpretation. Michigan history magazine 2:526-55, July 1918.

2076. —— Ketekitiganing (today Lake Vieux Desert). Michigan history magazine 12:776-77, Oct. 1928.
A supposition concerning the origin of the Indian place-name Ketekitiganing.

2077. —— Some place names in the Upper Peninsula of Michigan and elsewhere. Michigan history magazine 3:412-19, July 1919.

2078. —— Tahquamenon. Michigan history magazine 14:557, July 1930.
The possible significance of the old Indian name.

2079. Gerard, William R. Kalamazoo. American anthropologist n.s. 13:337-38, April-June 1911.
Gives the derivation and meaning of the word Kalamazoo.

2080. Hamilton, Charlotte. Chippewa County place names. Michigan history magazine 27:638-43, Oct.-Dec. 1943.

2081. Harrington, John Peabody. From Majiigan to Michigan. Michigan conservationist 25:14, Jan.-Feb. 1956.
A brief note reprinted from the U.S. Bureau of American Ethnology, Annual report, 1954.

2082. Hennig, Marciana, Sister. Post offices of Michigan. Hastings, Mich., Hastings Commercial Printers, 1976. 995p.
Michigan's 843 post offices, listed by town, with historical information on each.

2083. Hinsdale, Wilbert B. Archaeological atlas of Michigan. Ann Arbor, Univ. of Michigan Press, 1931. 38p. (University Museums, University of Michigan. Michigan handbook series, no. 4)
Sources: p. 1-3.
Includes lists of villages, etc.

2084. Indian names. Pioneer Society of the State of Michigan. Pioneer collections 7:136. 1884.

From the Detroit gazette Dec. 6, 1882.
The original Indian names and their significance are given in a brief note for Saginaw, Shiawassee, and Tittibawassa, Mich.

2085. Inkster prospers. Lincoln (Neb.) star Dec. 5, 1959, p. 5.
Residents being polled on their reaction to changing the name of Inkster (Detroit suburb) to Cherry Hill Heights or Dearborn Hills.

2086. It wasn't always called Dearborn. Dearborn historian 7:21-22, Winter-Spring 1967.
Other names attached to both the east and west ends of present Dearborn before 1929.

2087. Jenks, William L. History and meaning of the county names of Michigan. Michigan Pioneer and Historical Society. Historical collections 38:439-78. 1912.
Alphabetical list compiled from this in Michigan history 10:646-55, Oct. 1926.

2088. Johnson, William W. Indian names in and about the County of Mackinac. Pioneer Society of the State of Michigan. Historical collections 12:375-81. 1887.
Translation of the names, and location of the places.

2089. Kaups, Matti Enn. Finnish place-names in Michigan. Michigan history 51:335-47, Winter 1967.

2090. Kelton, Dwight H. Indian names and history of the Sault Ste. Marie Canal. Detroit, Detroit Free Press Print. Co., 1889. 32p.

2091. Langenfelt, Gösta. "Michigander." American speech 29:295-96, Dec. 1954.
Supplement to the Hans Sperber article, ibid. 29:21-27.

2092. —— "Michigander": an addendum. American speech 31:238, Oct. 1956.

2093. Lanman, James Henry. Indian topographical terms; In his History of Michigan. New York, E. French, 1839. p. 260-61.
Chippewa Indian names with English definitions, obtained from Henry Connor, and supervised by H. R. Schoolcraft.

2094. Leestma, Roger A. Origin of Dutch place names in Allegan and Ottawa counties, Michigan. Michigan Academy of Science. Papers 34:147-51. 1948.

2095. McCormick, William R. Indian names in the Saginaw Valley. Pioneer Society of the State of Michigan. Pioneer collections 7:277. 1884.
List of the original names, with their meanings, for places and rivers in the Saginaw Valley.

2096. McMullen, Edwin Wallace. Prairie generics in Michigan. Names 7:188-90, Sept. 1959.
The author gives more attention to the Indian names listed in this article, as a result of a communication from Virgil J. Vogel, in More information on Michigan prairie names, ibid. 8:53-56, March 1960.
Addendum, by Virgil J. Vogel, ibid. 8:186, Sept. 1960.

2097. Marckwardt, Albert Henry. Naming Michigan's counties. Names 23:180-89, Sept. 1975.

2098. —— Wolverine and Michigander. Michigan alumnus quarterly review 58:203-08, Spring 1952.
Early history of these names.

2099. May, George S. The meaning and pronunciation of Michilimackinac, general introduction. Michigan history 42:385-90, Dec. 1958.
This article introduces the following:

Greenman, Emerson F. The meaning of Michilimackinac. p. 391-92.
Originally published by Michigan Historical Commission. Information series no. 97.
Smith, Emerson R. Michilimackinac, land of the great fault. p. 392-96.
Dever, Harry. Back the attack! It's Mackinac! p. 396-99.
Kelsey, William Kline. Mackinac, not Mackinaw. p. 400-01.
Originally appeared in his column, The Commentator, Detroit news Nov. 5, 1957.
Rankin, Ernest H. What is the proper pronunciation of Mackinac? p. 402-05.
Originally appeared in Mining journal, Marquette, March 5, 1958.
Marckwardt, Albert Henry. The history of the pronunciation of Mackinac. p. 405-13.

2100. Michigan. Dept. of Conservation. Geological Survey Division. Committee on Geographic Names. Lake gazetteer, Gogebic County, Michigan. Lansing, 1952, i.e., 1954. 50, 27p.

2101. —— Historical Commission. Names of places of interest on Mackinac Island, Michigan, established, designated and adopted by the Mackinac Island State Park Commission and the Michigan Historical Commission. Descriptive and explanatory notes by Rt. Rev. Monsignor Frank A. O'Brien, president, Michigan Historical Commission. Lansing, Wynkoop, Hallenbeck, Crawford Co., 1916. 86p. (Bulletin, no. 5)

2102. —— State University. Department of Resource Development. Michigan lakes and ponds. East Lansing, 1965. var. p. maps. (Water bulletin no. 12-13, 15-17)
Alphabetical index of lakes and ponds.

2103. Michigan lakes and streams directory. Lansing, Mich., R. J. McCarthy, n.d. Unpaged. maps.

2104. Mikado, Mich. may vote to be Marion Claire. New York times Feb. 1, 1942, p. 33, col. 2.

2105. Monette, Clarence J. Some copper country names and places. [Lake Linden, Mich.], Monette, [c1975]. 54p.
Includes Baraga, Houghton, and Keweenaw counties.

2106. Noggle, Fred D. Origin of the name "Chicaming." Totem pole 24:4-5, Jan. 2, 1950.
Berrien County.

2107. The Origin and meaning of the name Michigan. Michigan. Historical Commission. Information series no. 3, June 20, 1957. 1p.

2108. Origin and orthography of some of the proper names in the Lake Superior district; In U.S. General Land Office. Report on the geology and topography of a portion of the Lake Superior land district, in the State of Michigan. Washington, Govt. Print. Off., 1851. 2:396-400.

2109. Peters, Bernard C. Relic names on the landscape: the prairies of Kalamazoo County. Names 20:60-61, March 1972.
As the pioneer landscape disappeared so did many of the names associated with it. Only three of the original prairie place-names remain, used now in a different context.

2109a. —— Voyageur place names in the Great Lakes with emphasis on Michigan's Upper Peninsula. In North Central Names Institute. Papers, ed. by Lawrence E. Seits. Sugar Grove, Ill., Waubonsee Community College, 1980. p. 64-76. maps.

2110. Purcell, J. M. "Michigander." American speech 31:303-04, Dec. 1956.

2111. Quaife, Milo Milton. [Wolverine]. Michigan history magazine 22:338-39, Summer 1938.
Name Wolverine for people of Michigan not due to presence or abundance of wolverines.

2112. —— Wolverine. American notes and queries 3:181-82, March 1944.
Why is Wolverine applied to the people of Michigan?

2113. Rankin, Ernest H. Michilimackinac. Inland seas 14:270-76, Winter 1958.
Proper pronunciation: Mackinaw.

2114. —— Some place names in the Upper Peninsula. Harlow's wooden man 3:3-5, Summer 1967.

2115. Romig, Walter. Michigan place names; the history of the founding and the naming of more than five thousand past and present Michigan communities. Grosse Pointe, Mich. [1973?] 673p. map.
Bibliography: p. 620-27.

2116. Rosalita, S. M. Detroit, the story of some street names; illus. by Charles Acker, ed. by Joe L. Norris. Detroit, Wayne Univ. Press, 1951. 20p.

2117. Russell, John Andrew. The geographical impress of the races in the making of Michigan; In his The Germanic influence in the making of Michigan. Detroit, Univ. of Detroit, 1927. p. 358-61.
Influence of the French, English, American, and German inhabitants on the place-names in Michigan.

2118. Sault Ste. Marie, Mich. Sault Junior High School. On the streets where we live. Sault Ste. Marie, 1968. 37p.
A history of the streets and avenues of Sault Ste. Marie.

2119. Scott, Irving Day. Inland lakes of Michigan. Lansing, Wynkoop, Hallenbeck, Crawford Co., 1921. 383p. (Michigan. Geological and Biological Survey. Publication 30. Geological series 25)

2120. Sidetracked no longer by its name. Kansas City star March 29, 1960, p. 3.
From Detour to De Tour Village to prevent misunderstanding of highway signs.

2121. Smith, C. Henry. Place names: Metamora. Michigan history magazine 28:319-20, April 1944.

2122. Smith, Kenneth G. How White Lake was named. Michigan history magazine 6:273-76. 1922.

2123. Sperber, Hans. Words and phrases in American politics: Michigander. American speech 29:21-27, Feb. 1954.
Traces the state nickname to its origin as a personal nickname for Gen. Cass, meaning "the gander from Michigan."

2124. The Story of a river name. Michigan Archaeological Society. News 2:17-21, Dec. 1956.
Shiawassee.

2125. Teaboldt, Elizabeth. History of street names in Ypsilanti. Ann Arbor, 1947.
Thesis (M.A.) Univ. of Michigan.

2126. Thundiyil, Zacharias & Barry L. Knight. Missionaries and place names in the Upper Peninsula; In South Central Names Institute. They had to call it something. Commerce, Tex., Names Institute Press, 1974. p. 93-101. (Publication 3)
Sources consulted: p. 100-01.

2127. Tongue twisters are made easier. Detroit free press June 4, 1939.
Pronunciation of ten tongue-twisting Michigan names.

2128. Turner, Timothy Gilman. Gazetteer of the St. Joseph Valley, Michigan and Indiana, with a view of its hydraulic and business capacities. Chicago, Hazlitt & Reed, printers, 1867. 166p.

2129. Turrell, Archie M. Some place names of Hillsdale County. Michigan history magazine 6:573-82. 1922.

2130. Verwyst, Chrysostom. Geographical names in Wisconsin, Minnesota and Michigan having a Chippewa origin. Wisconsin. State Historical Society. Collections 12:390-98. 1892.
"Cites distortions of names and the source and significance of the correct terminations."—Price.

2131. —— A glossary of Chippewa Indian names of rivers, lakes, and villages. Acta et dicta 4:253-75, July 1916.
These names are mostly of the Chippewa language, though a considerable number of them are from other Algic dialects.

2132. Wahla, Ed J. Mackin-aw or Mackin-ac? Totem pole 24:1-2, Feb. 6, 1950.

2133. Walton, Ivan H. Indian place names in Michigan. Midwest folklore 5:23-34, Spring 1955.

2134. Washtenaw County. Pioneer Society of the State of Michigan. Pioneer collections 4:393-94. 1881.
R. V. Williams's interpretation of the name is supplemented by further comments by the editor.

2135. "Wolverine." American speech 24:301, Dec. 1949.
Signed: W. G.
Question concerning origin. Refers to note in Michigan alumnus March 26, 1949, p. 302.

2136. Wood, Edwin Orin. Historic Mackinac; the historical, picturesque and legendary features of the Mackinac country; illus. from sketches, drawings, maps, and photographs, with an original map of Mackinac Island, made especially for this work. New York, Macmillan, 1918. 2v.
Michilimackinac--application of name and various spellings: 2:563-66.
Indian names in the Mackinac country (taken from Dwight H. Kelton's Indian names of places near the Great Lakes): 2:624-40.

2137. Yost, Fielding H. The Wolverine. Michigan history magazine 27:581-89, Oct.-Dec. 1943.

2138. —— The Wolverine state. Michigan history magazine 27:337-39, Spring 1943.
Two popular articles on the question of Michigan's nickname.

MINNESOTA

2139. Baker, James H. Chippewa origin of the name "Minnesota." Minnesota Historical Society. Collections 3:337-38. 1870-80.
A discussion of the name's meaning, possibly of Chippewa origin.

2140. Berthel, Mary W. Place names of the Mille Lacs region. Minnesota history 21:345-52, Dec. 1940.

2141. Blegen, Theodore Christian. That name "Itasca." Minnesota history 13:163-74, June 1932.

2142. Brower, Jacob Vradenberg. Nomenclature of Itasca State Park. Minnesota Historical Society. Collections 11:271-79. 1904.
Similar to the author's article ibid. 7:282-89. 1893.

2143. Brown, Calvin L. Some changes in local boundaries and names in Minnesota. Minnesota history bulletin 4:242-49, Feb.-May 1922.

2144. Chase, Carroll & Richard McP. Cabeen. The first hundred years of United States territorial postmarks, 1787-1887. Minnesota Territory. American philatelist 58:287-97, 420-35, Jan., March 1945.
Includes list of post offices, with notes on some names.

2145. Culkin, William E. North Shore place names. St. Paul, Scott-Mitchell Pub. Co., 1931. 95p.
"This treatise undertakes to give the origin of the place names along the North Shore of Lake Superior between Fond du Lac in Duluth on the southwest and the Pigeon River at the Canadian boundary on the northeast."—p. 13-14.

2146. Davis, Edward W. Taconite: the derivation of the name. Minnesota history 33:282-83, Autumn 1953.
The geological term taconite, used for the iron formation of the Mesabi Range, came from an Indian geographic name in Massachusetts.

2147. Edgar, Marjorie. Northern Minnesota is rich in musical Finnish names. Carlton County vidette June 25, 1942.

2148. Empson, Donald. The street where you live: a guide to the street names of St. Paul. St. Paul, Witsend Press, 1975. xi, 181p.
Includes date and significance of the names and an important introduction regarding street naming.
Review: P. Burwell Rogers, Names 24:214-15, Sept. 1976.

2149. Explorer names on the land. Gopher historian 11:9, Fall 1956.

2150. Explorers, Indians, old country places gave names to sites. New Ulm (Minn.) journal June 26, 1962.
Renville County names.

2151. Flandrau, Charles E. Reminiscences of Minnesota during the territorial period. Minnesota Historical Society. Collections 9:212-15, 219-21. 1898-1900.
"From reminiscences and his knowledge of the Sioux language, the writer gives his own interpretations of the significance of geographical names, some of which are sinking into oblivion, and the origin of the word Itasca."—Price.

2152. Forrest, Robert J. Mythical cities of southwestern Minnesota. Minnesota history 14:243-62, Sept. 1933.

An exposé of forgeries in census reports and voting tabulations, and of cities that existed only on the plat books in the speculators' offices.

2153. Fritzen, John. Historic sites and place names of Minnesota's North Shore. Duluth, St. Louis County Historical Society, 1974. 35p.
Bibliography: p. 34-35.

2154. Gale, Edward C. The legend of Lake Itasca. Minnesota history 12:215-25, Sept. 1931.
"The author connects the name with two Indian legends, neither of which is known to-day to the Indians or white inhabitants of the region. Nevertheless, he explains the probability of the relationship."—Price.

2155. Gilfillan, Joseph A. Minnesota geographical names derived from the Chippewa language. Minnesota. Geological and Natural History Survey. Annual report 15:451-77. 1886.
A list of 439 names of rivers, lakes, etc., in Minnesota, and some in the adjoining territories of Dakota and Manitoba, and the State of Wisconsin, in the Ojibwa or Chippewa language. The meanings and the English names are given.

2156. Grant, Evelyn Bolles. Afton road names. Minnesota history 44:75-76, Summer 1974.
Afton Township.

2157. Hart, Irving H. The origin and meaning of the name "Itasca." Minnesota history 12:225-29, Sept. 1931.
An independent study made by an Iowan, published with the Gale article (see no. 2154) under general title Itasca studies, since they supplement each other in unusual fashion.

2158. Hiebert, John M. Historic names of Minnesota counties. Gopher historian 9:14-17, Fall 1954.

2159. Jones, Jefferson. A check list, the territorial post-offices of Minnesota. Bozeman, Mont., The Author, 1949. 16p.

2160. Kaups, Matti Enn. Finnish place names in Minnesota: a study in cultural transfer. Geographical review 56:377-97, July 1966.
Abstract: Association of American Geographers. Annals 55:625, Dec. 1965.

2161. Minnesota. Department of Drainage and Waters. Gazetteer of meandered lakes of Minnesota. n.p., 1928. 183p.

2162. —— Division of Game and Fish. Minnesota lakes: an index and guide. St. Paul, Minnesota Dept. of Administration, Division of Central Services, 1963. 101p.
List of lakes and streams, by county, p. 8-28.

2163. —— State Drainage Commission. Gazetteer of Minnesota streams; In its Report of the water resources investigation of Minnesota, 1909-10. St. Paul, McGill-Warner Co., 1910-12. 1:318-43; 2:566-94.

2164. —— State Geographic Board. Minnesota geographic names.
Manuscript file in the Minnesota Historical Society Library, started by the Federal Writers' Project.

2165. —— Waters Section. An inventory of Minnesota lakes. St. Paul, Division of Waters, Soils, and Minerals, Minnesota Conservation Dept. 1968. 498p. maps. (Bulletin no. 25)
15,292 Minnesota lakes of ten acres or more, arranged by counties.

2166. Minnesota. Something about the names of its counties. St. Cloud journal-press Jan. 31, 1878.

2167. Minnesota to rename lakes. New York times June 6, 1937, p. 17, col. 3.
The newly created State Geographic Board will rename the lakes with duplicate names in the Long lakes and Rice lakes.

2168. Moyle, John B. Indian names on a Minnesota map. Conservation volunteer (Minnesota Dept. of Conservation) 25:27-31, Jan.-Feb. 1962.
A condensation under the title The origin of names appeared in Over the years 2: [4], April 1962.
Nearly all of Chippewa and Dakota (or Sioux) origin.

2169. Neufeld, Jean. Indian names of Minnesota counties. Gopher historian 8:15-16, Spring 1954.

2170. Nicollet, Joseph Nicolas. Joseph N. Nicollet on the plains and prairies; the expeditions of 1838-39 with journals, letters, and notes on the Dakota, translated and edited by Edmund C. Bray and Martha Coleman Bray. St. Paul, Minnesota Historical Society Press, 1976. 294p.
Includes a great deal of information on Dakota Indian place-names in Minnesota, North and South Dakota, and Nebraska.

2171. —— The journals of Joseph N. Nicollet; a scientist on the Mississippi headwaters, wtih notes on Indian life, 1836-37. Trans. from the French by André Fertey. Ed. by Martha Coleman Bray. St. Paul, Minnesota Historical Society, 1970. 288p. maps.
Names of lakes and streams: p. 225-41.
An alphabetical list of modern names for lakes and rivers with, in columns opposite each, the name as found in the Journal, on the 1836 and 1837 maps, on the 1843 map, and in other Nicollet notes.
Review: Raphael N. Hamilton, Wisconsin magazine of history 54:223-24, Spring 1971.

2172. Nute, Grace Lee. Posts in the Minnesota fur-trading area, 1660-1855. Minnesota history 11:353-85, Dec. 1930. map.
Also in Minnesota archaeologist 15:61-79, July 1949.
Describes 132 posts. Includes southern Manitoba.

2173. Ojibway-Dakota Research Society of Minnesota. Ojibway and Dakota place names in Minnesota. Ed. by Karen Daniels Petersen. Minnesota archaeologist 25:5-40, Jan. 1963.

2174. Potter, Alan H. Sioux names on the Minnesota map. Gopher historian 20:26-27, Winter 1965-66.

2175. Rossman, Laurence A. Naming Itasca's lakes. Grand Rapids, Minn., 1931. 10p.

2176. The Route of the Dan Patch Line and Dakota County waystations. Over the years 2: [5], April 1962.
Route and stations reproduced from a timetable of a half-century ago. Many of the names do not remain.

2177. St. Louis County, Minnesota Dept. of Highways. County road names and numbers. April 1964. Unpaged.

2178. Street names: for St. Anthony and Minneapolis; shown on an early map, what they are called today. Hennepin County history 18:8-10, Spring 1959.

2179. Swanson, Roy W. Scandinavian place-names in the American Danelaw. Swedish-American historical bulletin 2:5-17, Aug. 1929.

"A study of place-names of Scandinavian origin in Minnesota, the Danelaw of America."—Griffin.

2180. U.S. Work Projects Administration. Minnesota. Alphabetical index of Minnesota lakes and streams showing identification numbers. Prepared under the direction of the hydrologist of the Division of Water Resources and Engineering of the Department of Conservation by the Work Projects Administration. St. Paul, 1941. 115p.

2181. Upham, Warren. Minnesota county names. Magazine of history with notes and queries 8:152-59, 215-18, 285-92, Sept.-Nov. 1908.

2182. —— Minnesota geographic names, their origin and historic significance. With an introd. by James Taylor Dunn. Reprint ed. [St. Paul], Minnesota Historical Society, 1969. xxiv, 788p.

Reprint of the 1920 edition. 735p. (Collections of the Minnesota Historical Society, v. 17)

The introduction has been added, and two supplements list communities incorporated since 1920 and decisions on place-names made by the Minnesota and United States Geographic Boards from 1890 to July, 1969. The names of streets and parks in Minneapolis, St. Paul, and Duluth are included.

Review of 1st ed.: M. R. Gilmore, Minnesota history bulletin 3:448-49, Aug. 1920.

Review of reprint ed.: Robert E. Hoag, Minnesota history 42:36-37, Spring 1970; Edward C. Ehrensperger, Names 18:121-24, June 1970.

2183. —— The place names of St. Paul and Ramsey County. Saint Paul, 1920. p. 611-42, 436-44 [sic].

Reprinted from the author's Minnesota geographic names. 1920.

2184. Verwyst, Chrysostom. Geographical names in Wisconsin, Minnesota and Michigan having a Chippewa origin. Wisconsin. State Historical Society. Collections 12:390-98, 1892.

"Cites distortions of names and the source and significance of the correct terminations."—Price.

2185. —— A glossary of Chippewa Indian names of rivers, lakes and villages. Acta et dicta 4:253-74, July 1916.

These names are mostly of the Chippewa language though a considerable number of them are from other Algic dialects.

2186. Williams, John Fletcher. Origins of Minnesota county names. St. Paul daily pioneer March 13, 1870.

2187. Williamson, Andrew W. Minnesota geographical names derived from the Dakota language, with some that are obsolete. Minnesota. Geological and Natural History Survey. Annual report 13:104-12. 1884.

2188. Zumberge, James H. The lakes of Minnesota, their origin and classification. Minneapolis, Univ. of Minnesota Press, 1952. 99p. (Minnesota. Geological Survey. Bulletin no. 35)

Lists of lakes, p. 85-94.

MISSISSIPPI

2189. Alford, Terry L. An interesting American place-name. Mississippi folklore register 2:76-77, Fall 1968.
An account of the change of Powderhorn, Mississippi, to Indianola, one of seventeen United States towns thus named.

2190. Bass, Mary Frances. A study of place names of Clarke County, Mississippi. Thesis (M.A.) Univ. of Alabama, 1941.

2191. Boswell, George W. A selection of Mississippi place names. ANS bulletin 45:4-11, March 9, 1976.
A tentative list taken from the work of students in the Folk Literature class at the University of Mississippi.

2192. Brinegar, Bonnie. Choctaw place-names in Mississippi. Mississippi folklore register 11:142-50, Fall 1977.

2193. Cain, Cyril E. The first hundred years of post offices on the Pascagoula River. Journal of Mississippi history 11:178-84, July 1949.
Jackson and Greene counties, 1821- .

2194. Chase, Carroll & Richard McP. Cabeen. The first hundred years of United States territorial postmarks, 1787-1887. Mississippi Territory. American philatelist 55:220-26, Jan. 1942.
Includes list of post offices, 1803-17, with notes on some names.

2195. Gannett, Henry. The origin of certain place names in the State of Mississippi. Mississippi Historical Society. Publications 6:339-49, 1902.

2196. Halbert, Henry Sale. Choctaw Indian names in Alabama and Mississippi. Alabama Historical Society. Transactions 3:64-77. 1898-99.

2197. —— Origin of Mashulaville. Mississippi Historical Society. Publications 7:389-97. 1903.
An American village that has grown on the site of an ancient Indian village and named for the Indian chief Moshulitubee.

2198. Kay, Donald. British influence on Mississippi municipal place names. Journal of Mississippi history 36:269-72, Oct. 1974.

2199. Mississippi. Dept. of Archives and History. The official and statistical register. 1904- . Nashville, Tenn.
Each issue contains a list of the counties, with date of establishment and origin of name; also article on the meaning of Mississippi; also in 1917:446-47, Indian names of Mississippi, an article condensed from the paper by H. S. Halbert (Dept. reports, 1896-97).

2200. Note on the origin of Natchez. Louisiana historical quarterly 14:515, Oct. 1931.

2201. Oakley, Bruce C. A postal history of Mississippi stampless period, 1799-1860. Baldwyn, Miss., Magnolia Publishers, 1969. 290p. maps.
Embracing a record of the establishment and discontinuance of the post offices of the Mississippi Territory and State of Mississippi.

2202. Richardson, Thomas J. Current place-names of Jasper County, Mississippi. Mississippi folklore register 11:101-30, Fall 1977.

2203. Riley, Franklin L. Extinct towns and villages of Mississippi. Mississippi Historical Society. Publications 5:311-83. 1902.

2204. Seale, Lea Leslie. Indian place-names in Mississippi. Louisiana State University and Agricultural and Mechanical College. Publications n.s. v. 32, no. 1, Jan. 1940. The Graduate School abstracts of theses, session of 1938-1939, p. 5-7.
Thesis (Ph.D.) Louisiana State Univ., 1939.

2205. Smith, Jack Alan. The Mississippi place-name repository. Mississippi folklore register 2:19-25, Spring 1968.
Describes operations of the repository: carded records, filing and limitations on the study of each place name.

2206. —— A study of place-names in Forrest County. Mississippi. [Ann Arbor, Mich., University Microfilms], 1969. viii, 181ℓ. map.
Thesis (Ph.D.) Auburn University. Dissertation abstracts 30:709A, Aug. 1969.
Bibliography: 173-79.

2207. Spiro, Robert H. Place names in Mississippi. Mississippi magazine 1:6-8, Jan. 1955.

2208. Thigpen, Samuel Grady. Next door to heaven. [Picayune? Miss.; Kingsport, Tenn., Kingsport Press, 1965]. 247p.
The romance of names, of Hancock County, p. 10-17.

MISSISSIPPI VALLEY

2209. Berger, Vilhelm. Amerikanska ortnamm af svenskt ursprung. New York, 1915. 12p.
Swedish names in Minnesota, Iowa, Nebraska, Kansas, and the Dakotas.

2210. Bragg, Marion. Historic names and places on the lower Mississippi River. Vicksburg, Mississippi River Commission, 1977. 282p. maps.
At head of title: Dept. of the Army, Corps of Engineers, U.S. Army.
Includes the area south of the juncture of the Ohio and Mississippi rivers with origin of many of the names.

2211. Chase, Carroll & Richard McP. Cabeen. The first hundred years of United States territorial postmarks, 1787-1887. The District of Louisiana, The Territory of Louisiana and Missouri Territory. American philatelist 55:572-78, 636-40, June-July 1942.
Includes list of post offices, 1804-21, with notes on some names.

2212. —— —— Indiana Territory. American philatelist 56:80-86, Nov. 1942.
Includes list of post offices, with notes on some names.

2213. —— —— Michigan Territory. American philatelist 56:722-30, Aug. 1943; 57:137-43, Nov. 1943.
Includes list of post offices, with notes on some names.

2214. —— —— The territory northwest of the River Ohio (usually known as Northwest Territory). American philatelist 55:775-82, Sept. 1942.
Includes list of post offices, with notes on some names.

2215. —— —— Wisconsin Territory. American philatelist 57:301-05, 387-402, Jan.-Feb. 1944.
Includes list of post offices, with notes on some names.

2216. Conclin, George. A book for all travelers. Conclin's new river guide; or, A gazetteer of all the towns on the western waters: containing sketches of the cities, towns, and countries bordering on the Ohio and Mississippi rivers and their principal tributaries. Cincinnati, U. P. James, 1855. 128p.

Earlier editions 1848, 1849, 1850, 1851. For later editions, see Uriah Pierson James, James' river guide, no. 2228.

2217. Connelley, William E. Origin of Indian names of certain states and rivers. Ohio archaeological and historical quarterly 29:451-54, Oct. 1920.

The derivation and meaning of the names of the states of Iowa, Missouri, Mississippi, Ohio, and Kentucky and the rivers Ohio, Mississippi, Missouri, and Neosha.

2218. Craig, Isaac. The Shawanese name for the Ohio. Magazine of American history 8:363-64, May 1882.

The author gives the origin of the name and denounces the interpretation of Col. John Johnston in Henry Howe's Historical collections of Ohio (Cincinnati, Derby, Bradley & Co., 1847).

2219. Croy, Homer. Let's name the town for me. Saturday evening post 218:6, June 8, 1946.

2220. Cumings, Samuel. The western pilot; containing charts of the Ohio River and of the Mississippi, from the mouth of the Missouri to the Gulf of Mexico; accompanied with directions for navigating the same, and a gazetteer; or description of the towns on their banks, tributary streams, etc. also a variety of matter interesting to travelers, and all concerned in the navigation of those rivers; with a table of distances from town to town on all the above rivers. Corrected by Capts. Charles Ross & John Klinefelter. Cincinnati, J. A. & U. P. James, 1854. 140p.

Earlier editions 1825, 1829, 1832, 1834, 1838, 1840, 1843, 1848.

A revised and altered edition of the author's Western navigator. "Cumings' editions of the 'Navigator' and 'Pilot' were amplifications of The navigator of Zadock Cramer without acknowledgment of the main source of their material."—Joseph Sabin, Dictionary of books relating to America 5:126.

2221. Delanglez, Jean. The Jolliet lost map of the Mississippi. Mid-America 28:67-144, April 1946.

The nomenclature of Jolliet's lost map, p. 97-139.

2222. —— El Rio del Espíritu Santo; an essay on the cartography of the Gulf Coast and the adjacent territory during the sixteenth and seventeenth centuries. Ed. by Thomas J. McMahon. New York, 1945. 182p. (United States Catholic Historical Society. Monograph series, 21)

Much of this monograph appeared in Mid-America 25:189-219, 231-49, July, Oct. 1943; 26:62-84, 138-64, 192-220, Jan.-July 1944.

An inquiry, through a study of maps, of what knowledge the best-informed geographers of the period seem to have had of the Mississippi, and, in particular, whether the river labeled Rio del Espíritu Santo on these maps is the Mississippi itself. Concludes that the Mississippi is not the Rio del Espíritu Santo. Contains a table of nomenclature on four early Spanish maps of the Gulf of Mexico.

2223. Dunn, Jacob Piatt. Names of the Ohio River. Indiana magazine of history 8:166-70, Dec. 1912.

2224. Finnie, W. Bruce. Ohio Valley localisms: topographical terms, 1750-1800. American speech 38:178-87, Oct. 1963.

A list of terms with citation of source in which used.

2225. —— Topographic terms in the Ohio Valley, 1748-1800. University, Ala., published for the [American Dialect] Society by Univ. of Alabama Press, 1970. 119p. (American Dialect Society publication no. 53)
Bibliography: p. 114-19.
Review: W. P. H. Nicolaisen, Names 23:44-45, March 1975.

2226. Haines, Elijah Middlebrook. Indian names; In Rufus Blanchard, The discovery and conquests of the Northwest. Wheaton [Ill.], Blanchard, 1879. p. 589-98.
Also in edition published: Chicago, Cushing, Thomas & Co., 1880. p. 475-84.

2227. Jakle, John A. Salt-derived place names in the Ohio Valley. Names 16:1-5, March 1968. map.

2228. James, Uriah Pierson. James' river guide: containing descriptions of all the cities, towns, and principal objects of interest on the navigable waters of the Mississippi Valley. Illus. with forty-four maps. Rev. ed. Cincinnati, U. P. James, 1871. 128p.
Also published 1856, 1858, 1860, 1869.
Earlier editions published by George Conclin with title A book for all travelers. Conclin's new river guide (see no. 2216).

2229. Kelton, Dwight H. Ancient names of rivers, lakes, etc. Pioneer Society of the State of Michigan. Collections 6:349-51. 1884.
The various names and sources for bodies of water in the northern part of the Middle West.

2230. McDermott, John Francis. The French impress on place names in the Mississippi Valley. Illinois State Historical Society. Journal 72:225-34, Aug. 1979. map.

2231. Read, William Alexander. A Vernerian sound-change in English. Englische Studien 47:169-74. 1913.
A study of the pronunciation and spelling of Missouri and Mississippi.

2232. Schultz, William Eben. The Middle West; changes in the term applied to the geographical section commonly known as the Middle West. American speech 12:316, Dec. 1937.

2233. Stennett, William H. A history of the origin of the place names connected with the Chicago & North western and Chicago, St. Paul, Minneapolis & Omaha railways, comp. by one who for more than 34 years has been an officer in the employ of the system. Chicago, 1908. 201p.
2d ed. 1908.

2234. Thompson, T. P. Origin of the various names of the Mississippi River. Louisiana Historical Society. Publications 9:92-95. 1916.
The names traced in chronological order from early maps and relations of the beginnings of American history.

2235. Voorhis, Ernest. Historic forts and trading posts of the French and of the English fur trading companies. Ottawa, Dept. of the Interior, National Development Bureau, 1930. 188p.
Alphabetical list of forts and posts, p. 28-181.
"A few of these establishments were located on what is now territory of the United States."—Pref.
Includes map of Mississippi and Ohio valleys showing chain of historic French forts.

2236. Wright, Muriel H. The naming of the Mississippi River. Chronicles of Oklahoma 6:529-31, Dec. 1928.

MISSOURI

2237. Adams, Bonnie Lee. The tree that named the Ozarks. Ford times 59:19, Aug. 1966.

The name for the region is derived from Bois Aux Arcs, the name given to a tree by French-Canadian explorers.

2238. Adams, Orvyl Guy. Place names in the north central counties of Missouri. Thesis (M.A.) Univ. of Missouri, 1928.

Includes Carroll, Chariton, Livingston, Linn, Macon, Grundy, Sullivan, Adair, Mercer, Putnam, and Schuyler counties.

2239. Atchison, Anne Eliza. Place names of five west central counties of Missouri. Thesis (M.A.) Univ. of Missouri, 1937.

Includes Jackson, Lafayette, Platte, Clay, and Ray counties.

2240. Beck, Lewis Caleb. A gazetteer of the states of Illinois and Missouri; containing a general view of each state, a general view of their counties, and a particular description of their towns, villages, rivers, &c., &c. With a map, and other engravings. Albany, Printed by C. R. & G. Webster, 1823. 352p.

Reprinted: New York, Arno Press, 1975.

2241. Bell, Margaret Ellen. Place names of the southwest border counties of Missouri.

Thesis (M.A.) Univ. of Missouri, 1933.

Includes Wright, Webster, Christian, Douglas, Ozark, Taney, Stone, Barry, and McDonald counties.

Includes manuscript on McDonald County names by Vance Randolph.

2242. Bess, Charles E. Podunk in southeast Missouri. American speech 10:80, Feb. 1935.

2243. Bloody Island. Missouri historical review 26:389-91, July 1932.

Dueling place in the Mississippi River opposite St. Louis.

2244. Broadhead, G. C. Sniabar. Kansas City review of science and industry 5:23-24, May 1881.

A creek.

2245. Campbell, Robert Allen. Campbell's gazetteer of Missouri; from articles contributed by prominent gentlemen in each county of the state, and information collected and collated from official and other authentic sources, by a corps of experienced canvassers, under the personal supervision of the editor. Rev. ed. St. Louis, R. A. Campbell, 1875. 796p.

First published 1874.

2246. Cruz, Humberto. Confusion rises in never-never land of street names. Kansas City times Nov. 2, 1967, p. 1A, 12A.

Duplication of street names in Kansas City metropolitan area.

2247. Discord about a great name. New York times Jan. 3, 1933, p. 22, col. 4.

Editorial on pronunciation of Missouri, following talk by Allen Walker Read before Linguistic Society of America.

2248. Doolittle, Mo., meets the General himself at its formal dedication under his name. New York times Oct. 12, 1946, p. 10, col. 2.
Formerly Centerville.

2249. Drums in old Mizzou. Time 72:38, Sept. 1, 1958.
Naming the new road to the Missouri University stadium in Columbia, Mo., and the furor it caused.
The Chamber of Commerce proposed to name it Caniff in honor of Milton Caniff, cartoonist, creator of the character Miss Mizzou in the comic strip Steve Canyon. This produced much comment, both favorable and unfavorable, much of which illustrates various principles of place-naming.
References to some of the newspaper articles on this controversy follow:

"Gutter tactics" hit by head of C. of C. Columbia Missourian July 29, 1958, p. 1-2.
Delugach, Al. Bard and comic strip author involved in street name fuss. Kansas City star Aug. 10, 1958, p. 1, 19A.
Decorum of M. U. city shaken by "Miss Mizzou." Columbia Missourian Aug. 11, 1958, p. 8.
Suggests a way to honor Don Faurot. Kansas City star Aug. 13, 1958, p. 10D.
"No name" publicity. Columbia Missourian Aug. 14, 1958, p. 4.
Editorial.
Capacity crowd expected at street-naming meeting. Columbia Missourian Aug. 16, 1958, p. 1.
Street of no name. Columbia Missourian Aug. 20, 1958, p. 4.
Editorial; picture.
Providence wins out over Caniff. Kansas City star Sept. 3, 1958, p. 1.
"Caniff obituary." Columbia Missourian Sept. 4, 1958, p. 4.
Editorial.
Council selects Providence as inner loop compromise. Columbia Missourian Sept. 9, 1958, p. 1.
Letters to the editor. Columbia Missourian July 29, 1958, p. 4; Aug. 5, p. 4; Aug. 6, p. 4; Aug. 7, p. 3; Aug. 19, p. 4; Aug. 26, p. 4; Aug. 28, p. 4.

2250. Eaton, David Wolfe. How Missouri counties, towns and streams were named. Columbia, State Historical Society, 1916-18. 5v.
Reprinted from the Missouri historical review 10:197-213, 263-87, April, July 1916; 11:164-200, 330-47, Jan., April-July 1917; 13:57-74, Oct. 1918.

2251. Elliott, Katherine. Place-names of six northeast counties of Missouri.
Thesis (M.A.) Univ. of Missouri, 1938.
Includes Marion, Shelby, Lewis, Knox, Clark, and Scotland counties.

2252. Ewing, Martha Kennedy. Place-names in the northwest counties of Missouri.
Thesis (M.A.) Univ. of Missouri, 1929.
Includes Buchanan, Clinton, Caldwell, Daviess, DeKalb, Andrew, Holt, Atchison, Nodaway, Worth, Gentry, and Harrison counties.

2253. Gazetteer and business directory of the new Southwest. Embracing all of that region of country—including counties, towns, and cities—contiguous to the St. Louis and San Francisco Railway, its divisions and branches, located in southwest Missouri, southeastern Kansas, the eastern portion of the Indian country, and the northwest section of Arkansas. In which is included an abridged directory of leading business houses of St. Louis. St. Louis, United States Directory Pub. Co., 1881. 224p.

2254. Hamlett, Mayme Lucille. Place-names of six southeast counties of Missouri.
Thesis (M.A.) Univ. of Missouri, 1938.
Includes Pemiscot, Scott, Dunklin, New Madrid, Mississippi, and Stoddard counties.

2255. Harding, Samuel Bannister. Life of George R. Smith, founder of Sedalia, Mo., in its relation to the political, economic, and social life of southwestern Missouri, before and during the Civil War. Sedalia, Mo., Privately printed, 1904. 398p.
The name Sedalia: p. 291.

2256. Harrison, Eugenia Lillian. The place-names of four river counties in eastern Missouri.
Thesis (M.A.) Univ. of Missouri, 1943.
Includes Franklin, Lincoln, St. Charles, and Warren counties.

2257. How Randolph County was named. Missouri historical review 26:215, Jan. 1932.

2258. Johnson, Bernice Eugenia. Place-names in six of the west central counties of Missouri.
Thesis (M.A.) Univ. of Missouri, 1933.
Includes Bates, Cass, Henry, Johnson, St. Clair, and Vernon counties.

2259. Kansas City, North, may get new name. Kansas City star March 24, 1961, p. 1, 2A.

2260. Kiel, Herman Gottlieb. The centennial biographical directory of Franklin County, Missouri. Washington, D.C., 1925. 444p.
Includes a list of geographical names, and a list of post offices.

2261. Lee, Fred L. Town of Kansas named at town meeting. Jackson County Historical Society. Journal 10:4-6, Fall 1967.
Renamed Kansas City in the Charter of 1889.

2262. Lee, Linda. Daisy, Defiance, Solo, and other unusual Missouri place names. Bittersweet 7:45, Spring 1979.

2263. Leech, Esther Gladys. The place-names of Pike County, Missouri; In Robert Lee Ramsay, Introduction to a survey of Missouri place-names. Columbia, Univ. of Missouri, 1934. p. 60-124.
Bibliography: p. 121-24.

2264. —— Place-names of six east central counties of Missouri.
Thesis (M.A.) Univ. of Missouri, 1933.
Includes Randolph, Monroe, Audrain, Montgomery, Ralls, and Pike counties.

2265. Leland, J. A. C. Indian names in Missouri. Names 1:266-73, Dec. 1953.
Etymology of the Indian names selected from Ramsay, Our storehouse of Missouri place names (see no. 2284).

2266. McDermott, John Francis. Sun or Beausoleil Island? A hidden origin in a place name. American speech 32:155-56, May 1957.
Once a stopping place for the fur trader Eugene Pourée dit Beausoleil and therefore incorrectly named (i.e., translated) by William Clark and others, 1804- .

2267. Maddux, Teresa. Peculiar, Bourbon, and Competition and other unusual place names. Bittersweet 3:2, Winter 1976.

2268. March, David. Sobriquets of Missouri and Missourians. Missouri historical review 72:243-61, April 1978.

2269. Meyer, Jeanne. Missouri's names born of humor, frustration, hope. News and tribune, Jefferson City. Dec. 4, 1977.

A note on the state place-name survey directed by Adolf Schroeder, with comments on some of the unusual names.

2270. Missouri. Magazine of American history 29:299, March 1893.
The source and significance of the name Missouri as given by the Indians.

2271. Missouri counties, past and present. Missouri historical review 34:498-506, July 1940.
Includes origin of names.

2272. The Missouri state gazetteer and business directory, containing full and complete descriptions of the cities, towns and villages, with the names and address of the merchants, manufacturers, professional men, etc. etc. St. Louis, Sutherland & McEvoy, 1860. 781p.

2273. Mottaz, Mabel Manes. Laclede County's unusual names. Ozarks mountaineer 15:11, July 1967.
Includes some names from Pulaski and Camden counties.

2274. Myers, Robert Lee. Place-names in the southwest counties of Missouri.
Thesis (M.A.) Univ. of Missouri, 1930.
Includes Barton, Jasper, Newton, Cedar, Dade, Lawrence, Polk, and Greene counties.

2275. O'Brien, Anna. Place-names of five central southern counties of Missouri.
Thesis (M.A.) Univ. of Missouri, 1939.
Includes Dallas, Laclede, Texas, Dent, and Shannon counties.

2276. Origin of Franklin County names. Republican tribune, Union (Mo.), Aug. 15, 1919.

2277. Overlay, Fauna Robertson. Place-names of five south central counties of Missouri.
Thesis (M.A.) Univ. of Missouri, 1943.
Includes Benton, Camden, Hickory, Morgan, and Pettis counties.

2278. Pace, Nadine. Place-names in the central counties of Missouri.
Thesis (M.A.) Univ. of Missouri, 1928.
Includes Callaway, Boone, Howard, Cole, Moniteau, Cooper, and Saline counties.

2279. Peterson, Karl L. Legendary frontier names identify growing list of Midwestern reservoirs. Kansas City star June 28, 1964, p. 2G.
Map on p. 1G.

2280. Picinich, Donald George. A pronunciation guide to Missouri place names. Rev. by Robert Lee Ramsay. Columbia, Mo., 1951. 32p. (University of Missouri bulletin, v. 52, no. 35. Journalism series, no. 126)
1st ed. 1951. 24p. (University of Missouri bulletin, v. 52, no. 3. Journalism series, no. 121)

2281. Place names: poverty of invention is some proof of gratitude. Missouri Historical Society. Bulletin 23:236-40, April 1967.
Signed: Antiquary. Reprinted from the Missouri intelligencer, Franklin, Mo., April 29, 1823.
The author illustrates his idea by discussing the names and prominence of some of the individuals for whom places are named.

2282. Pottenger, Cora Ann. Place-names of five southern border counties of Missouri.

Thesis (M.A.) Univ. of Missouri, 1945.
Includes Howell, Oregon, Ripley, Carter, and Butler counties.

2283. Pronunciation of "Missouri." Missouri historical review 26:387-89, July 1932.

2284. Ramsay, Robert Lee. Our storehouse of Missouri place names. Columbia, Univ. of Missouri, 1952. 160p. (Missouri handbook no. 2) (University of Missouri bulletin, v. 53, no. 34. Arts and science series, 1952, no. 7)
Review: Hobart M. Lovett, Names 1:61-62, March 1953.

2285. —— Place-name paragraphs, published in the Sunday editions of the St. Louis Globe-Democrat May 26, 1946 to September 21, 1947; with an article on the "Place names in Lawrence County" from the Centennial number of the Lawrence Chieftain, Mt. Vernon, Mo. July 24, 1947. 36 ℓ.
Photostatic reproduction of a scrapbook, Missouri University Library.

2286. —— The place names of Boone County, Missouri. Gainesville, Fla., American Dialect Society, 1952. 52p. (American Dialect Society. Publication, no. 18)
Review: Mayme L. Hamlett, Names 1:218, Sept. 1953.

2287. —— The place names of Franklin County, Missouri. Columbia, Mo., 1954. 55p. (University of Missouri studies, v. 26, no. 3)
Most of the material used in this study was published in preliminary form in the Washington Missourian July 5-Nov. 1, 1951.

2288. —— Progress in the survey of Missouri place-names. Missouri Academy of Science. Proceedings 7:55-65, Oct. 25, 1941.
Survey was begun in 1928. 13 theses completed, covering 90 of 114 counties with remaining counties assigned and in progress.

2289. —— Some secrets of Jefferson County place names. Missouri Historical Society. Bulletin 10:8-26, 406, Oct. 1953, April 1954.
Most of the material used in this study was published in preliminary form in the Jefferson republic, De Soto, March 29-July 12, 1951.

2290. —— The study of Missouri place-names at the University of Missouri. Missouri historical review 27:132-44, Jan. 1933.
"A report of progress made in the study of Missouri place-names. Five theses include a total of 47 counties and over 3,500 place-names."—Griffin.

2291. —— ; Allen Walker Read, & Esther Gladys Leech. Introduction to a survey of Missouri place-names. Columbia, Univ. of Missouri, 1934. 124p. (University of Missouri studies; a quarterly of research. v. 9, no. 1)
Bibliography of literary sources: p. 39-59.
Bibliography for Pike County place-names: p. 121-24.
An important document in place-name studies; not only an outline of the outstanding university program but also a model to be followed in other states.
Review: American speech 9:304-06, Dec. 1934; Beiblatt zur Anglia 47:69, March 1936.

2292. Read, Allen Walker. Plans for the study of Missouri place-names. Missouri historical review 22:237-41, Jan. 1928.

2293. —— Pronunciation of the word "Missouri." American speech 8:22-36, Dec. 1933.
Reprinted in part in Frank Luther Mott, ed. Missouri reader (Columbia, Univ. of Missouri Press, 1964), p. 17-21.
Includes many references to newspaper articles.

2294. Reference update, a rose by any other name. Missouri State Library. Show-me libraries 29:10-12, Nov. 1977.
Popular article on many intriguing place-names in the state.

2295. Ross, Mildred E. Nodaway County, Missouri. Maryville, Mo., 1959. 64p. (Northwest Missouri State College studies, v. 23, no. 3, Aug. 1, 1959) (Northwest Missouri State College bulletin, v. 53, no. 8)
Appendix I: Historical guide to the towns: p. 56-63.

2296. Sauer, Carl O. Origin of the name "Ozark." Missouri historical review 22:550, July 1928.
Reprinted from his The geography of the Ozark highland of Missouri (Chicago, Univ. of Chicago Press, 1920), p. 5.

2297. Schroeder, Walter A. Panther Hollow and Dead Elm School: plant and animal place names in Missouri. Missouri historical review 73:321-47, April 1979. maps.

2298. Schultz, Gerard. Geographical names of Miller County. Missouri historical review 25:540-41, April 1931.
From Miller County autogram, Tuscumbia, Aug. 28, 1930.

2299. Shoemaker, Floyd Calvin. Missouri, the name. Missouri historical review 38:199-202, Jan. 1944.
From his Missouri and Missourians (Chicago, Lewis Pub. Co., 1943), 1:1-3.

2300. Some lost counties of Missouri. Missouri historical review 26:89-91, Oct. 1931; 27:169-70, Jan. 1933.
Why some of the proposed names were changed before they were accepted.

2301. Squires, Monas N. Missouri's abbreviation: Mo. Missouri historical review 26:84-85, Oct. 1931.
"Uncritical."—A. W. Read.

2302. Switzler, William F. The real meaning of the word Missouri. Missouri historical review 17:231-32, Jan. 1923.
From the Boonville democrat Oct. 22, 1897, and the Kansas City star Aug. 27, 1922.
A note by J. Walter Fewkes was published in Missouri historical review 17:377-78, April 1923.

2303. There are many queerly named towns in Missouri and Kansas. Kansas City star Aug. 1, 1937.

2304. Town names reveal much state history. St. Louis post-dispatch Sept. 21, 1919.

2305. U.S. 88th Congress, 1st session. House. A bill to provide that the Bull Shoals Dam and the Bull Shoals Reservoir, White River Basin in Missouri and Arkansas shall hereafter be known as the "Harry S. Truman Dam" and the "Harry S. Truman Reservoir." H. R. 1094. Jan. 9, 1963. Washington, 1963. 2p.
Introduced by Mr. Hull and referred to the Committee on Public Works.

2306. Van Brunt, Henry. Many of city's streets were named after trees. Kansas City star August 14, 1955, p. 6D.

2307. Van Duyn, Mona. A small excursion. Poetry 120:103-04, May 1972.
A poem on the interesting place-names in Missouri.

2308. Vaughan, Bill. The case for Missour-uh. The Midwest motorist April 1976, p. 6-8.
Including: And the case for Missour-ee, by Martin Quigley.

2309. Vogel, Virgil J. The origin and meaning of "Missouri." Missouri Historical Society. Bulletin 16:213-22, April 1960.
An examination of the early sources on the name of the Indians and the river.

2310. Weakley, Janet. Missouri names. St. Louis globe-democrat July 8, 1945.

2311. Weber, Frank Thomas Ewing. Place-names of six south central counties of Missouri.
Thesis (M.A.) Univ. of Missouri, 1938.
Includes Miller, Pulaski, Osage, Maries, Phelps, and Gasconade counties.

2312. Welty, Ruth. Place names of St. Louis and Jefferson County.
Thesis (M.A.) Univ. of Missouri, 1939.

2313. Wetmore, Alphonso. Gazetteer of the State of Missouri. With a map of the state. To which is added an appendix, containing frontier sketches, and illustrations of Indian character. With a frontispiece, engraved on steel. St. Louis, C. Keemle, 1837. 382p.
Reprinted: New York, Arno Press, 1975.

2314. The Word "Missouri." Missouri historical review 34:87-93, Oct. 1939.
"A study of the various meanings suggested for the word since Father Marquette's time. 'Muddy Water' as one of these is discredited in favor of 'town of the large canoes.'"—American speech.

2315. Zimmer, Gertrude Minnie. Place-names of five southeast counties of Missouri.
Thesis (M.A.) Univ. of Missouri, 1944.
Includes Ste. Genevieve, St. François, Washington, Iron, and Crawford counties.

MONTANA

2316. Baker, Marcus. Survey of the northwestern boundary of the United States, 1857-1861. U.S. Geological Survey. Bulletin 174:58-61, 1900.
Indian names of camps, stations, rivers, etc., along the 49th parallel in Washington, Idaho, and Montana. Based on the work George Gibbs did for the Smithsonian Institution.

2317. Brower, Jacob Vradenberg. Geographic names; In his The utmost waters of the Missouri River. American Geographical Society. Bulletin 28:390-91. 1896.
Origin of place-names in the region of the source of the Missouri River.

2318. Bue, Olaf J. A guide to pronunciation of place names in Montana. Missoula, Bureau of Press & Broadcasting Research, School of Journalism, Montana State Univ., 1959. 28p.

2319. Chamberlain, Alexander F. Geographic terms of Kootenay origin. American anthropologist n.s. 4:348-50, April-June 1902.
"Concerned with names of places, camp-sites, and stations along the 49th parallel in British Columbia, Washington, Idaho and Montana. These names which seem to have been taken from the language of the Kootenay Indians of this region are mentioned in the reports on the boundary survey. The meanings and etymologies are given where possible."—Price.

2320. Cheney, Roberta Carkeek. Montana place names. Montana, the magazine of western history 20:48-61, Jan. 1970. maps.

2321. —— Names on the face of Montana: the story of Montana's place names. [Missoula, Univ. of Montana, 1971]. xix, 275p. maps. (University of Montana publication in history)
Bibliography: p. 265-68.
Review: Kelsie B. Harder, Names 23:46-47, March 1975.

2322. Childears, Lucille. Montana place name records. Western folklore 13:47-50, Jan. 1954.

2323. —— Montana place names from Indian myth and legend. Western folklore 9:263-64, July 1950.

2324. Grinnell, George Bird. Some Indian stream names. American anthropologist n.s. 15:327-31, April-June 1913.
Names of the Gros Ventres of the Prairie Indians, and the Pawnee Indians.

2325. Holtz, Mathilde Edith & Katharine Isabel Bemis. Some Blackfeet legends and Indian names; In their Glacier National Park, its trails and treasures. New York, Doran, 1917. p. 191-207.

2326. Keller, Kathryn M. Mount Oberlin. Ohio cues (Maumee Valley Historical Society) v. 15, no. 2, p. 2, Nov. 1965.
Mountain in Glacier National Park named for Oberlin College by faculty member Lyman B. Sperry.

2327. Koch, Elers. Geographic names of western Montana and northern Idaho. Oregon historical quarterly 49:50-62, March 1948.

2328. McClintock, Walter. The old North trail; or, Life, legends and religion of the Blackfeet Indians. London, Macmillan, 1910. 539p.
An Indian recounts to the author the Blackfeet names for rivers, mountains, and other landmarks along the trail, near Helena, Mont., p. 437-40.

2329. McDavid, Raven I., Jr. Hidden "Hell" in "Helena." American speech 26:305-06, Dec. 1951.

2330. Mansfield, Michael Joseph. Proposed change of name of Hungry Horse Dam. Congressional record v. 109, no. 33, p. 3293, March 4, 1963.
From Hungry Horse Lake to Truman Lake or Truman Reservoir.

2331. Montana. Historical Society. The changing place-names of Glacier National Park; In its Blackfeet man: James Willard Schultz. Helena, 1961. (Montana heritage series, no. 12) p. 18-20.
Schultz's endeavors to restore the Indian names, reproduced from Signposts of adventure.

2332. The Montana almanac. 1957- . Missoula, Montana State Univ.
Origin of Montana place-names, an alphabetical list scattered at intervals throughout the various editions.

2333. Mundt, Karl E. Two Mobridges in two states. Congressional record 105:16816-17, Sept. 7, 1959.
South Dakota, and new town in Montana. Includes origin of name.

2334. Omundson, Don Bert. A study of place names in Missoula County, Montana. Thesis (M.S.) Montana State Univ., 1961.

2335. Pemberton, W. Y. Changing the name of Edgerton County. Montana. Historical Society. Contributions 8:323-27. 1917.
Reasons for changing the name to Lewis and Clark County.

2336. Rowe, Jesse Perry. The origin of some Montana place names. Missoula, The Author, n.d. p. 260-313.

2337. Saindon, Bob. The river which scolds at all others: an obstinate blunder in nomenclature. Montana, the magazine of western history 76:2-7, July 1976.
It is the Milk River, not the Marias, which should carry the Indian name Ah-mah-tah- ru-shush-sher which translates "the river which scolds at all others."

2338. Sanders, Wilbur Edgerton. Montana: organization, name, and naming. The word, its significance, derivation, and historical use. Montana. Historical Society. Contributions 7:15-60. 1910.

2339. Schultz, James Willard. Indian names in Glacier Park. Outlook 143:442-44, July 28, 1926.
Gives briefly some of the Blackfeet and Kutenai Indian names for places in the park.

2340. —— Signposts of adventure; Glacier National Park as the Indians know it. Boston, Houghton, 1926. 224p.
Contents: Introductory; Blackfeet Indian names of the topographical features of Glacier National Park upon its east side; Kutenai Indian names of the topographical features of the west side of Glacier National Park.

2341. Territory of Montana. Montana. Historical Society. Contributions 6:171. 1907; also U.S. Congress. Congressional globe, 38th Congress, 1st session, 1863-64, p. 1168-69, 2510.
Memorial from Territory of Idaho asks that eastern portion of the territory be organized into a new territory to be called Jefferson Territory. Considerable debate about whether the new territory should be named Jefferson, Douglas, Idaho, or Montana. James M. Ashley's proposal of Montana won out.

2342. U.S. Board on Geographic Names. Decisions. Place names, Glacier National Park, Mont. March 6, 1929. Washington, Govt. Print. Off., 1929. 18p.

2343. U.S. 88th Congress, 1st session. Senate. A bill to designate the lake to be formed by the waters impounded by the Clark Canyon Dam in the State of Montana as Hap Hawkins Lake. S. 142. Jan. 14 (legislative day, Jan. 9), 1963. Washington, 1963. 1p.
Introduced by Mr. Metcalf and Mr. Mansfield and referred to the Committee on Public Works.
Subsequent documents relating to this bill were published as follows:

U.S. 88th Congress, 1st session. Senate. Designating the lake to be formed by the waters impounded by the Clark Canyon Dam, Mont., as Hap Hawkins Lake. Report no. 274, to accompany S. 142. June 19, 1963. Calendar no. 255. Washington, 1963. 4p.
Submitted by Mr. Metcalf, from the Committee on Public Works, without amendment.

—— [Reprint of the original bill, June 19, 1963, to accompany the report. Report no. 274 and Calendar no. 255 added] 1p.

U.S. 88th Congress, 1st session. House. An act to designate the lake to be formed by the waters impounded by the Clark Canyon Dam in the State of Montana as Hap Hawkins Lake. S. 142. In the House of Representatives June 24, 1963. Washington, 1963. 1p.

Referred to the Committee on Interior and Insular Affairs. Passed the Senate June 20, 1963.

2344. —— Senate. Joint resolution to designate the lake to be formed by the waters impounded by the Canyon Ferry Dam, Montana, "Lake Townsend." S. J. Res. 121. Sept. 24, 1963. Washington, 1963. 1p.
Introduced by Mr. Mansfield and Mr. Metcalf and referred to the Committee on Interior and Insular Affairs.
In honor of the city of Townsend and the man for whom it was named, an official of the Northern Pacific Railway Company.

2345. Wolle, Muriel Vincent Sibell. Montana pay dirt; a guide to the mining camps of the Treasure State. Denver, Sage Books, 1963. 436p.
Bibliography: p. 411-16.

NEBRASKA

2346. Abbott, N. C. Lincoln, name and place. Nebraska State Historical Society. Publications 21:8-133. 1930.

2347. Brashier, Mary. Alias a river; behind a river lies a priceless heritage. Outdoor Nebraska 37:12-13, 24, Dec. 1959.
Discusses French, Spanish, and Indian names for the Platte River and other rivers in Nebraska.

2348. Broadcast tale of dead cities—Ghost towns of Box Butte County. Alliance news March 12, 1931.

2349. Campbell, I. C. G. The Weeping Water legend; an anthology and commentary. Weeping Water, Neb., Chamber of Commerce, 1964. 36p.
Legends relating to the origin of the name of Weeping Water, Neb.

2350. Changing Missouri coming back to Rockport--Old river town forgotten for fifty years. Omaha world-herald Oct. 20, 1912.

2351. Chase, Carroll & Richard McP. Cabeen. The first hundred years of United States territorial postmarks, 1787-1887. Nebraska Territory. American philatelist 59:430-39, 609-17, Feb., April 1946.
Includes a list of post offices, with notes on the origin of some of the names.

2352. Christensen, Arved. A pronunciation guide to Nebraska place names, prepared by Arved Christensen, Wayne B. Wells, Nanci Debord, under the supervision of Paul Schupbach. Lincoln, Univ. of Nebraska, Radio Section, Dept. of Speech, School of Fine Arts, 1953. 48p. (University of Nebraska publication no. 183)

2353. County names, changes made news in early days. Lincoln (Neb.) Sunday journal and star May 30, 1954, p. 12F.

2354. Crowther, Charles L. The pocket gazetteer of the State of Nebraska, with a complete list of counties and principal towns in the same, population, banks, hotels, halls, churches, attorneys at law. Also, a valuable index and original railroad guide to Nebraska, etc., etc. Lincoln, Journal Co., state printers, 1882. 72p.

2355. Early settlers had mania for laying out town sites in Dakota County. Eagle, South Sioux City, Aug. 25, 1932.

2356. Eight Mile Grove fades into mists of pioneer past. Nebraska State journal, Lincoln, May 5, 1935.

2357. Fairclough, G. Thomas. Notes on some unusual street names in Nebraska City. American speech 34:70-71, Feb. 1959; 37:157-58, May 1962.
Refers to article ibid. 20:177, Oct. 1945.

2358. Fitzpatrick, Lilian Linder. Nebraska place-names. Lincoln, 1925. 166p. (University of Nebraska studies in language, literature and criticism, no. 6)
Bibliography: p. 148-52.
Review: American speech 1:46-48, Oct. 1925; Michigan history magazine 10:643-46, Oct. 1926.

2359. —— Nebraska place names [new ed.]. Including selections from The origin of the place-names of Nebraska, by J. T. Link. Ed., with an introduction, by G. Thomas Fairclough. Lincoln, Univ. of Nebraska Press, 1960. 227p. (A Bison book, BB 107)
Fitzpatrick's work, first published 1925, is reprinted in full, with two pages of errata added. The selections from Link's work, published 1933, include the name of the state, the state's natural features, and some miscellaneous cultural features.
Fairclough says that this edition brings together the most significant work that has been done in the study of Nebraska place-names.
Review: William Coyle, Ohio historical quarterly 70:184-85, April 1961. Contrasts Nebraska names with those in Ohio; Thomas M. Pearce, Journal of American folklore 75:76-77, Jan.-March 1962.

2360. Fontenelle, one of oldest towns. Arlington review-herald Sept. 29, 1910.

2361. Gibson, Ron. Possible rift over lake name waning. Lincoln (Neb.) evening journal Sept. 9, 1960, p. 26.
Proposals that the lake to be created by the Red Willow Dam near McCook be named for Senators Hugh Butler and George Norris.

2362. Gilmore, G. H. Ghost towns in Cass County, Nebraska. Nebraska history magazine 18:181-84, July-Sept. 1937.

2363. Gilmore, Melvin Randolph. The aboriginal geography of the Nebraska country. Mississippi Valley Historical Association. Proceedings 6:317-31, 1912-13.
Aboriginal names of streams and places with an appended list of some place-names as applied by the Dakota, Omaha, and Pawnee, and identified by the English name for the same place.

2364. —— Some Indian place names in Nebraska. Nebraska State Historical Society. Publications 19:130-39. 1919.
Read before the Association of American Geographers, Chicago, Dec. 29, 1914.

2365. Green, Norma Kidd. Ghost counties of Nebraska. Nebraska history 43:253-63, Dec. 1962.

2366. Hamilton, William. Indian names and their meaning. Nebraska State Historical Society. Transactions and reports 1:73-76. 1885.
Appended is a list of Indian names of streams and localities contributed by Henry Fontenelle.
Includes Sac names.

2367. Herman, Dick. That Devil's Nest name is as old as Nebraska. Lincoln evening journal and Nebraska State journal July 4, 1962.
Name of a real-estate development in Knox County; also other locations in the United States involving the word devil.

2368. How to say "Beatrice" depends on location. Lincoln Sunday journal and star June 2, 1963, p. 7B.

2369. Jones, Alf D. Origin of the name Omaha, according to the Indian tradition. Nebraska State Historical Society. Transactions and reports 4:151-52. 1892.

2370. Kistler, Richard C. Discontinued depots of Nebraska, 1919-1967. Lincoln, Neb., Railroad Station Historical Society [1970] 19p. (Railroad station monograph no. 1)

Published as a supplement to v. 3, no. 1 of the Society's Bulletin.

Alphabetical lists, by station, naming railroad, date discontinuation authorized, and date station closed, abandoned, moved, etc.

2371. Lee, Wayne C. Nebraska's name changers. Western folklore 25:122-24, April 1966.

The names of a great many towns in Nebraska have been changed from their original ones.

2372. Link, John Thomas. The origin of the place names of Nebraska (The toponomy of Nebraska). Lincoln, Printed by authority of the State of Nebraska, 1933. 186p. (Nebraska. Geological Survey. Bulletin 7, 2d ser.)

Issued also as the author's thesis (Ph.D.) Univ. of Nebraska, 1932, under title: The toponomy of Nebraska. Selections also reprinted in Lilian Linder Fitzpatrick, Nebraska place-names (see no. 2358).

Bibliography: p. 161-70.

2373. Lost towns of Nebraska. Nebraska State journal, Lincoln, March 27, 1910.

2374. Many defunct Richardson County towns tell tale of pioneer ambition. Nebraska State journal, Lincoln, June 30, 1935.

2375. Mattes, Merrill J. Chimney Rock on the Oregon Trail. Nebraska history 36:1-26, March 1955.

Reviews early travelers' descriptions and notes various names used.

2376. —— Hiram Scott, fur trader. Nebraska history 26:127-62, July-Sept. 1945.

A speculative biography of the man for whom Scotts Bluff was named.

2377. Meredith, Mamie. A Nebraska "Podunk." American speech 19:74-75, Feb. 1944.

The town of Brock, Neb., formerly known as Podunk.

2378. Miller, John C. Ghost towns in Otoe County. Nebraska history magazine 18:185-89, July-Sept. 1937.

2379. Nebraska. Laws, statutes, etc. A joint resolution to designate Nebraska in a popular sense, The Tree Planters State; In Nebraska. Laws, statutes, etc. The compiled statutes of the State of Nebraska, 1881. 7th ed. With amendments 1882 to 1895. Lincoln, Neb., State Journal Co., 1895. p. 441. (Chap. 119. Sen. file no. 270)

2380. Nebraska cities and towns. Omaha Sunday world-herald May 30, 1954, Centennial section no. 7. 16p.

An alphabetical listing of Nebraska's incorporated places together with the origins of their names. To be used with caution.

2381. Nebraska in the making. Elkhorn Valley mirror, Norfolk, Neb., v. 1, no. 35, Oct. 14, 1926.

2382. "Nebraska place-names" tells when a crick becomes a stream. Summer Nebraskan (Univ. of Nebraska) July 11, 1961, p. 2.
Popular article based on Lilian Linder Fitzpatrick, Nebraska place-names (see no. 2358).

2383. Nebraska town, county names add up to confused picture. Lincoln (Neb.) star Sept. 11, 1958, p. 10.
Duplication of names causes the confusion.

2384. Neol, Richard. Street names in Waverly. Names 2:276. Dec. 1954.
Town in Lancaster County named in honor of Sir Walter Scott's historical novel. Six east-west avenues named for other Waverly novels, six north-south streets named for trees.

2385. Neu, Irene. The alphabet along the railroad. California folklore quarterly 5:200, April 1946.
On the Burlington between Lincoln and Kearney.

2386. New towns in a new state. Nebraska State journal, Lincoln, Feb. 21, 1909.

2387. The Old river towns. 3p.
Typescript in Nebraska Historical Society Library.

2388. Omaha's name. Omaha world-herald Nov. 22, 1925.

2389. Pangle, Mary Ellen. Place-names in Nebraska. Journal of American history 26:177-88. 1932.
Bibliography: p. 187-88.

2390. Perkey, Elton A. Perkey's names of Nebraska locations. Nebraska history 58:537-49, 1977; 59:84-149, 259-97, 438-72, 1978.

2391. Phillips, Hazel Spencer. Invincible gambler; folklore. Lebanon, Ohio, Warren County Historical Society, n.d. [4]p. (Folklore series, no. 9)
"Information furnished by Mrs. Thomas Bamber, and Harry B. Allen, Cozad, Nebraska, whose research inspired Mari Sandoz' book Gamblin' Man's Son."
John Jackson Cozad, who established Cozaddale, Ohio, and Cozad, Neb.

2392. Place names. Michigan history magazine 10:643-46, Oct. 1926.
The significance of some of the unusual Nebraska names.

2393. Potts, Aartje. Omaha street nomenclature.
Thesis (M.A.) Univ. of Nebraska, 1931.

2394. Ramsey, Basil S. From what source did Cass County derive its name? Plattsmouth journal March 6, 1913.

2395. Rapp, William F. Discontinued post offices of Nebraska. Crete, Neb., J-B Pub. Co., 1967. 11p.
A list of post offices that have been discontinued as of November 1, 1966. Name of post office and county in which it was located are given. For some, the date of discontinuation is given, and for a very few, the date of establishment. Includes such names as Trouble, Cherry County; Biscuit, Holt County; and Spud, Sioux County.

2396. —— The post offices of Nebraska, part 1: territorial post offices. Crete, Neb., J-B Pub. Co. [c1971]. 15p. maps.

2397. Roberts, Martha G. Omaha's namesake: Omaja, Cuba. Omaha world-herald Nov. 27, 1955, Magazine, p. 24G.

In 1906 a homesick railroad foreman from Omaha, Neb., began using the name Omaha in his daily reports. The name was kept for the first settlement in 1906 at Omaja (pronounced Omaha) by the family of Cornelio Plant, Mormons coming from England.

2398. Savage, James W. The christening of the Platte. Nebraska State Historical Society. Transactions and reports 3:67-73. 1892.

2399. Solitary ghosts. Nebraska history magazine 18:189-91, July-Sept. 1937.

Supplementary to the articles by G. H. Gilmore and J. C. Miller in the same issue.

2400. Story of DeSoto, one time river boom town. Omaha world-herald Oct. 4, 1925.

2401. Taylor, Norm. Nebraska can give Texas run for title of "Brag Capital." Lincoln (Neb.) Sunday journal and star Sept. 11, 1960, p. 1B, 7B.

Boastful town titles, such as The Best Little City Out West, Home of Famous Men.

2402. Towns of the past are now cornfields. Omaha world-herald Feb. 27, 1910.

2403. True, M. B. C. County names. Nebraska State Historical Society. Transactions and reports 4:141-44. 1892.

Brief notes about the counties that were named for the presidents and other eminent men. Also suggests names that might be used in the future.

2404. Turpin, Ted. Surprising thing about Surprise is how early town got its name. Lincoln (Neb.) evening journal Dec. 14, 1961.

2405. U.S. Federal Writers' Project. Nebraska. Origin of Nebraska place names. Comp. by the Federal Writers' Project, Works Progress Administration, State of Nebraska; sponsored by the Nebraska State Historical Society. Lincoln, 1938. 28p.

2406. What's in a street name? Commissioners will decide. Lincoln (Neb.) Sunday journal and star Oct. 27, 1963.

Problem of whether to give a traffic artery traversing both the northern part of the city of Lincoln and the county a single street name, and, if so, which name of the at least seven names now in use.

NEVADA

2407. Ashbaugh, Don. Nevada's turbulent yesterday; a study in ghost towns. [Los Angeles], Westernlore Press, 1963. 346p. (Westernlore ghost town series, 1)

2408. Averett, Walter R. Directory of southern Nevada place names. Rev. ed. Las Vegas, 1962. 114p.

Also published in a facsimile edition by the Arthur H. Clark Company, Glendale, Calif.

1st ed. 1956. 40ℓ.

Bibliography: p. 111-14.

Includes towns, railroad sidings, topographic features, springs and waterholes, mines, and some ranches. Special attention to obscure or forgotten names.

2409. Brown, Thomas Pollok. Elko, Nevada. Western folklore 9:378-79, Oct. 1950.

2410. Carlson, Helen Swisher. Influence of nineteenth-century Nevada railroads on names along the line. Western folklore 15:113-21, April 1956.

2411. —— Mine names on the Nevada Comstock lode. Western folklore 15:49-57, Jan. 1956.

2412. —— Names of mines on the Comstock.
Thesis (M.A.) Univ. of Nevada, 1955.
Much of this thesis was published as a series of articles in the Reno evening gazette May 9-24, 1955.

2413. —— Nevada. Western folklore 14:44-49, Jan. 1955.
In the Names and places section. A survey of bibliographical aids.

2414. —— Nevada place names: a geographical dictionary, with foreword by Charlton Laird. Reno, Univ. of Nevada Press, 1974. 282p.
Review: T. M. Pearce, Names 23:45-46, March 1975; Margaret M. Bryant, American speech 49:287-89, Fall-Winter 1974.

2415. —— Nevada place names: origin and meaning.
Thesis (Ph.D.) Univ. of New Mexico, 1959. Dissertation abstracts 20:2791, 1960.

2416. Chase, Carroll & Richard McP. Cabeen. The first hundred years of United States territorial postmarks, 1787-1887. Nevada Territory. American philatelist 56:586-94, June 1943.
Includes list of post offices, with notes on some names.

2417. Chatham, Ronald Lewis. Nevada town names.
Thesis (M.S.) Sacramento State College, 1956.

2418. —— & Paul F. Griffin. How Nevada towns were named; Nevada history has left its mark on the nomenclature of the state. Nevada highways and parks v. 17, no. 2, p. 26-31, 1957.
From the research paper of the authors.

2419. Fox, Theron. Nevada treasure hunters ghost town guide. Includes 1881 fold-in map of Nevada with glossary of 800 place names, 1867 map of Nevada. Handy reference to locating old mining camps, ghost town sites, mountains, rivers, lakes, camel trails, abandoned roads, springs and water holes. San Jose, Calif., 1961. 24p.

2420. Frickstad, Walter Nettleton. A century of Nevada post offices, 1852-1957, by Walter N. Frickstad and Edward W. Thrall, with the collaboration of Ernest G. Meyers. Oakland, Calif., 1958. 40p.

2421. Gibby, Patricia Martin. Deeth and Disaster in Nevada. Western folklore 11:42, Jan. 1952.
Some place-names.

2422. Grieder, T. G. Beowawe: a Nevada place name. Western folklore 19:53-54, Jan. 1960.
In Paiute Beowawe means "great posterior."
See also More on Beowawe, a Nevada place name, by K. W. Clarke, ibid. 20:112, April 1961.

2423. Hall, Eugene Raymond. Mammals of Nevada. Berkeley, Univ. of California Press, 1946. 710p.
Gazetteer: p. 650-69.

2424. Huggins, Dorothy H. Elko, Nevada. Western folklore 8:370, Oct. 1949.
cf. George Rippey Stewart article, ibid. 9:156, April 1950.

2425. Leigh, Rufus Wood. Nevada place names, their origin and significance. Sponsors: Southern Nevada Historical Society, Las Vegas; Lake Mead Natural History Association, Boulder City [Salt Lake City?, 1964]. 149p.
Bibliography: p. 143-44.

2426. Linsdale, Jean M. The birds of Nevada. Berkeley, Cooper Ornithological Club, 1936. 145p. (Pacific coast avifauna no. 23)
List of localities: p. 14-22.

2427. McVaugh, Rogers & F. R. Fosberg. Index to the geographical names of Nevada. [Washington, D.C., 1941] 3 pts. (216ℓ) (U.S. Bureau of Plant Industry. Division of Plant Exploration and Introduction. Contributions toward a flora of Nevada, no. 29. June 1, 1941)
Work Projects Administration of Nevada, Projects O.P. 65-2-04-13, W.P. 658; O.P. 165-2-04-21, W.P. 752. Collaborator, University of Nevada.

2428. Nevada. Constitutional Convention, 1864. Official report of the debates and proceedings. San Francisco, F. Eastman, printer, 1866. p. 33-35.
In convention the year before, the name Nevada was chosen for the state after consideration of Washoe, Esmeralda, and Humboldt. Move to change to Washoe in this session was defeated.

2429. —— Department of Highways. Planning Survey Division. Directory of geographic names in Nevada. [Carson City], 1971. 192p. maps.
Prepared in cooperation with the Federal Highway Administration.
Review: Thomas L. Clark, Names 20:208-09, Sept. 1972.

2430. Ohmert, Audrey Winifred. The significance of the nomenclature in Washoe County, Nevada. Nevada Historical Society. Biennial report 2:82-95. 1909-10.

2431. Paher, Stanley W. Nevada ghost towns and mining camps. Berkeley, Howell-North Books, 1970. 492p. maps.
Bibliography: p. 481-83.
Records the histories of more than 575 towns and settlements that are now entirely abandoned or that have dwindled in importance.
Review: Fred and Harriet Rochlin, Journal of the West 10:167, Jan. 1971.

2432. Palmer, Theodore Sherman. Place names of the Death Valley region in California and Nevada. Los Angeles, Dawson's Book Shop, 1948. 80p.
Result of National Park Service project.
Review: Katherine Karpenstein, Names 1:62-63, March 1953.

2433. Patterson, Edna B. Who named it? History of Elko County place names. Elko, Nev., Warren L. and Mary J. Monroe, in cooperation with the Elko Independent, 1964. 92p.
Also appeared in Northeastern Nevada Historical Society. Bulletin 1977, no. 2, p. 3-48.

2434. The Significance of the nomenclature in Churchill, Douglas, Lyon, Ormsby, and Storey counties. Nevada Historical Society. Biennial report 3:169-223. 1911-12.
Prepared by students in fulfillment of thesis requirements in the History Department of the State University.
Churchill County, by Vera Ellen Hasch; Douglas, Ormsby, and Storey counties, by Cora Mildred Cleator; Lyon County, by Florence Leslie Bray.

2435. Stewart, George Rippey. Buffalo Meadows, Nevada. Western folklore 7:174, April 1948.

2436. —— Elko, Nevada. Western folklore 9:156, April 1950.
In answer to Dorothy H. Huggins's article, ibid. 8:370, Oct. 1949.

2437. Taylor, Jock. Comstock mystery man. Westways 41:11, March 1949.
"On Ebenezer Fenimore ('Old Virginia') alleged by Dan de Quille in the Territorial enterprise, July 20, 1881, to have named Virginia City."—Griffin, Writings on American history.

2438. Territory of Nevada; In Hubert Howe Bancroft, History of Nevada, Colorado and Wyoming. San Francisco, History Co., 1890. p. 150-51; also in U.S. Congress. House. Journal, 35th Congress, 1st session, 1857-58, p. 789; U.S. Congress. Congressional globe, 36th Congress, 2d session, 1860-61, p. 120, 897, 1334, 1362.
Delegate Crane wrote to his constituents from Washington in Feb. 1858 that a territorial government was about to be established under name of Sierra Nevada. On May 12, 1858, a bill was introduced to organize the Territory of Nevada. Bills were again introduced in 1860 and 1861, and passed March 2, 1861, organizing the new Territory of Nevada out of the western portion of Utah, then known as the Washoe Mines.

2439. U.S. Writers' Program. Nevada. Origin of place names: Nevada. Nevada State Dept. of Highways, sponsor, and State Dept. of Education, co-sponsor. Reno, 1941. 79p.

NEW ENGLAND

2440. Achorn, Erik. Geographical and place names taken from "A map of the most inhabited part of New England . . . Nov. 29, 1774." Essex Institute. Historical collections 89:275-87, July 1953.

2441. Baylies, Francis. The original of local and other names, a letter from Hon. Francis Baylies to Hon. P. W. Leland. Brooklyn, 1879. 24p. (Elzevir Club series, no. 1)
Most of the names are of Massachusetts.

2442. Berry, A. B. New England's lost city found. Magazine of American history 16:290-92, Sept. 1886.
"The discussion pertains to the origin of the word and the discovery of the location by Prof. Horsford. The city is Norumbega."—Price.

2443. Bolton, Charles Knowles. The real founders of New England: stories of their life along the coast, 1602-1628. Boston, F. W. Faxon Co., 1929. xiv, 192p. maps. (Useful reference ser., no. 38)
Reprinted: Baltimore, Genealogical Pub. Co., 1974.
Early settlements and their founders, p. 166-77; Early names, p. 183-84.

2444. Buchanan, Milton Alexander. Notes on Portuguese place-names in northeastern America; In Estudios hispánicos, homenaje a Archer M. Huntington. Wellesley, Mass., 1952. p. 99-104.
Principally Newfoundland; also Labrador, Nova Scotia, New England coast.

2445. Bushnell, David Ives. New England names. American anthropologist n.s. 13:235-38, April 1911.
"Contains a copy of a document giving the Indian names of rivers along the New England coast, and the names of the chiefs whose villages occupied their shores. The

document is now in the British Museum and was probably written in the early part of the 17th century."—Griffin.

2446. De Costa, B. F. The lost city of New England. Magazine of American history 1:14-20, Jan. 1877.
The source and meaning of Norumbega, a name that has ceased to exist. Raises the question whether such a city as described did exist.

2447. Dorson, Richard Mercier. Jonathan draws the long bow. Cambridge, Mass., Harvard Univ. Press, 1946. 274p.
Local legends: p. 138-87. Legends that owe their interest to specific landmarks and places.
Place names: p. 188-98. Place-names in New England that are related to local legends.

2448. Douglas-Lithgow, Robert Alexander. Dictionary of American-Indian place and proper names in New England; with many interpretations, etc. Salem, Salem Press, 1909. 400p.
List of Abnaki words (Maine and New Hampshire): p. 387-91.
List of Massachusetts, or Natick, Indian words: p. 393-96.
Bibliography: p. 397-400.

2449. Ganong, William Francis. The origin of the place-names Acadia and Norumbega. Royal Society of Canada. Proceedings and transactions 3d ser. v. 11, sec. 2, p. 105-11. 1917.
"Presents evidence drawn from early maps and records of explorations."—Griffin. See also Ganong's article, Norumbega, ibid. v. 25, sec. 2, p. 200-02, 1931, in which he concludes that it was the Indian name for the country between Narragansett Bay and New York, or, more specifically, was used by the Indians of Narragansett Bay for their country.

2449a. Gersuny, Carl. Industrial toponomy and territorial divisions of labor. Connecticut onomastic review 1:35-40. 1979.
Names of streets that indicate the type of industry located thereon, and of industrial parks.

2450. Hayward, Edward F. The names of New England places. New England magazine n.s. 13:345-48, Nov. 1895.
A general article citing the origin of names in the New England states.

2451. Hayward, John. The New England gazetteer; containing descriptions of all the states, counties and towns in New England. Alphabetically arranged. 14th ed. Concord, N.H., I. S. Boyd & W. White; Boston, J. Hayward, 1841. 528p.
1st-9th ed. published 1839; a later ed. published Boston, Parker, Elliott & Co., 1856. 704p.

2452. Huden, John Charles. Indian place names of New England. New York, Museum of the American Indian, Heye Foundation, 1962. 408p. (Contributions from the Museum of the American Indian, Heye Foundation, v. 18)
Bibliography: p. 387-94.
Review: Hamill Kenny, Names 12:234-38, Sept.-Dec. 1964; Gordon M. Day, American anthropologist 65:1198-99, Oct. 1963; Wilcomb E. Washburn, New England quarterly 36:525-26, Dec. 1963; Meredith F. Burrill, Professional geographer n.s. 16:43, Jan. 1964; Philip Wagner, Linguistic folklore, Journal of American folklore 79:386-87, April-June 1966.

2453. Leighly, John. New England town names derived from personal names. Names 18:155-74, Sept. 1970.

Information on all the namings of incorporated towns in the six New England states from 1620 to 1860. Includes 1553 namings, of which 1399 were in effect at the end of 1860. The author classifies the names into those derived from personal names (28 percent), transferred British place-names (54 percent), names borrowed from places outside Britain and New England (5 percent), and other.

2454. Masta, Henry Lorne. Abenaki Indian legends, grammar and place names. Victoriaville, P.Q., La Voix des Bois-Francs, 1932. 110p.
The meaning of Indian names of rivers, lakes, etc., p. 81-105.

2455. Matthews, Albert. The name "New England" as applied to Massachusetts. Colonial Society of Massachusetts. Publications 25:382-90. 1924.

2456. Mitchell, Edwin Valentine. It's an old New England custom. New York, Vanguard Press, 1946. 277p.
To adopt peculiar place names: p. 215-52.

2457. The New England gazetteer. 1902. Boston, Sampson, Murdock & Co., 1902. p. 1637-1828.
The gazetteer portion of the New England business directory and gazetteer published separately.

2458. The New England gazetteer, comprising a concise description of the cities, towns, county seats, villages, and postoffices. Boston, Sampson, Davenport & Co., 1885. 182p.

2459. Nicolaisen, W. F. H. Celtic place names in America, B.C. Vermont history 47:148-60, Spring 1979.
A critique of a thesis by Barry Fell: "Fell, for the reasons adduced . . . has failed to demonstrate that there are ancient Celtic place names in New England."

2460. Prince, Tomas. The vade mecum for America: or A companion for traders and travellers: containing I. An exact and useful table, shewing the value of any quantity of any commodity. II. A table of simple and compound interest. III. The names of the towns and counties in the several provinces and colonies of New-England, New-York and the Jersies; as also the several counties in Pennsilvania [sic], Maryland and Virginia; together with the time of the setting of their courts. IV. The time of the general meeting of the Baptists and Quakers. V. A description of the principle [sic] roads from the mouth of Kennebeck-River in the north-east of New England to James-River in Virginia. VI. A correct table of the Kings and Queens of England. Together with several other instructive tables in arithmetick, geography, &c. To which is added, the names of the streets in Boston. Collected & composed with great care & accuracy. Boston, Printed by S. Kneeland & T. Green for D. Henchman, & T. Hancock, 1732. 220p.
Attributed to Thomas Prince. cf. Charles Evans, American bibliography, no. 3598.

2461. Rafn, Carl Christian. Derivation from the Icelandic of Indian names. Massachusetts Historical Society. Proceedings 8:194-97, Feb. 1865.
"Cites some Indian names in the New England region and suggests that their origin may have been from words of the ancient Norsemen. Interprets the possible relation between the names in this country and those in the Scandinavian countries."--Price.

2462. Rounds, Stowell. A note on place names in New England. Names 6:124-25, June 1958.
Use of Street in names of hamlets or settlements.

2463. Russell, Francis. Place names in New England. Nineteenth century and after 140:284-88, Nov. 1946.

2464. Savage, James. A list of the ancient Indian names of our modern towns, &c.; In John Winthrop, The history of New England from 1630 to 1649. Boston, Phelps & Farnham, 1825-26. 2:392-95.

2465. Shulsinger, Stephanie Cooper. What's in a place name? Yankee 36:50-53, June 1972.
269 New England place-names with meanings sampled from "best known sources."

2466. Sleeper, Myron O. Indian place names in New England. Massachusetts Archaeological Society. Bulletin 10:89-93, July 1949.

2467. Stone, Stuart B. New England names. Journal of education (Boston) 81:19, 48, Jan. 7, 14, 1915.
Brief notes concerning the source of some New England place-names.

2468. Tooker, William Wallace. The significance of John Eliot's Natick and the name Merrimac; with historical and ethnological notes. New York, F. P. Harper, 1901. 56p. (The Algonquian series, no. 10)
First essay "Read before the American Association for the Advancement of Science, Section H, 1897, and reprinted in the American anthropologist 10:281-87, Sept. 1897. Now reprinted with additions."—p. 5.
Second essay appeared originally in the American antiquarian 21:14-16. 1899.

2469. True, Nathaniel Tuckerman. Collation of geographical names in the Algonkin language. Essex Institute. Historical collections 8:144-49, Sept. 1868.
Also published separately. 6p.

2470. Tuttle, Charles W. Communication on geographical names. Massachusetts Historical Society. Proceedings 16:377-79, Nov. 1878.
Explains the significance of Piscataqua River.

2471. —— The Piscataqua River. Magazine of New England history 1:207, Oct. 1891.
Views on the derivation and meaning of the Indian name.

2472. Verrill, Alpheus Hyatt. Indian names and their meanings; In his The heart of old New England. New York, Dodd, 1936. p. 284-91.

2473. Walker, Joseph B. The valley of the Merrimack. New Hampshire Historical Society. Collections 7:414-15. 1863.
Indicates different ways of spelling the name Merrimack and the origin of Monomack as applied to the valley.

2474. Webb's New England railway and manufacturers' statistical gazetteer; containing an interesting sketch of every station, village and city on each railroad in New England, together with a statistical, historical and biographical account of their representative manufacturing establishments. Providence, Providence Press Co., 1869. 568p.

NEW HAMPSHIRE

2475. Alden, Timothy. Indian names of White Hills and Piscataqua River. Massachusetts Historical Society. Collections 2d ser. 2:266-67. 1814.

2476. Ballard, Edward. Indian mode of applying names. New Hampshire Historical Society. Collections 8:446-52. 1866.

With particular reference to New Hampshire. Includes a list of Indian names connected with the valley of the Merrimack, and their meanings.

2477. Brennan, James F. What was the origin of the name of our town? American Catholic Historical Society. Records 26:25-35, March 1915.
Also published separately. 7p.
Peterborough, N.H.

2478. Burt, Frank H. The nomenclature of the White Mountains. Appalachia 13:359-90, Dec. 1915; 14:261-68, June 1918.
Bibliography 13:389-90.

2479. Charlton, Edwin Azro. New Hampshire as it is. Claremont, N.H., Tracy & Sanford, 1855. 592p.
3d ed. rev. with an appendix containing additions and corrections for the gazetteer. Claremont, Kenney, 1857. 594, 4p.
Part II, A gazetteer.

2480. Coffin, F. Parkman. Indian names on the Piscataqua River, Great Bay and its tributary streams. New Hampshire archeologist no. 11, p. 5-8, Oct. 1962.

2481. Colby, Fred Myron. The nomenclature of some New Hampshire towns. Magazine of history 11:145-49, March 1910.

2482. Day, Gordon M. The name Contoocook. International journal of American linguistics 27:168-71, April 1961.
Analysis of this name borne by a lake, a river, and a village in southern New Hampshire.

2483. Edmands, J. Rayner. Topographical contributions. Appalachia 5:121-28, June 1888.
Further comments on the system of nomenclature submitted by the Committee on Nomenclature in the article, Nomenclature of the White Mountains (see no. 2501).

2484. Farmer, John. A catechism of the history of New-Hampshire, from its first settlement to the present period; for the use of schools and families. 2d ed. Concord, Hoag & Atwood, 1830. 108p.
The Appendix contains "A list of the most considerable towns in New-Hampshire; their former name, the time they were settled."

2485. —— & Jacob B. Moore. A gazetteer of the State of New-Hampshire. Embellished with an accurate map of the state, and several other engravings, by Abel Bowen. Concord, J. B. Moore, 1823. 276p.

2486. Fay, Charles E. Our geographical nomenclature. Appalachia 3:1-13, June 1882.
Presidential address, general remarks on nomenclature in New Hampshire.

2487. Fogg, Alonzo J. The statistics and gazetteer of New-Hampshire. Containing descriptions of all the counties, towns and villages, statistical tables, with a list of state officers, etc. Concord, D. L. Guernsey, 1874. 674p.

2488. Green, Samuel Abbott. Observations on the names of certain villages in Massachusetts and New Hampshire. Massachusetts Historical Society. Proceedings 2d ser. 10:465-67, Feb. 1896.
Also published separately, Boston, 1896. 3p.
Use of Harbor away from the coastline. Includes Mason Harbor and Dunstable Harbor.

2489. —— Some Indian names. Massachusetts Historical Society. Proceedings 2d ser. 4:373-74, May 1889.
Also published separately, 1889. 3p.
South Eggenocke, Southheaganock, and Souhegan; also Pennichuck.

2490. Hammond, Otis G. New Hampshire county names. Magazine of history 9:48-50, Jan. 1909.

2491. Hancock, Mary Louise. The mountains of New Hampshire, a directory locating the mountains and prominent elevations. Concord, New Hampshire State Planning and Development Commission, 1949. 145p.

2492. Hayward, John. A gazetteer of New Hampshire, containing descriptions of all the counties, towns, and districts in the state; also of its principal mountains, rivers, waterfalls, harbors, islands, and fashionable resorts. To which are added, statistical accounts of its agriculture, commerce and manufactures. Boston, J. P. Jewett, 1849. 264p.

2493. Hunt, Elmer Munson. New Hampshire town names and whence they came. Peterborough, H. H., Noone House, William L. Bauhan, publisher [1971, c1970] xxi, 282p. maps.
Bibliography: p. 260-63.
Incorporates the great majority of a series of articles that the author wrote for a regular column in the Manchester (N.H.) union leader.
Review: Sterling A. Stoudemire, Names 20:140-41, June 1972.

2494. —— & Robert A. Smith. The English background of some of the Wentworth town grants. Historical New Hampshire Nov. 1950, p. 1-52.
The English source of many New Hampshire town names.

2495. Kearsarge. Historical magazine 9:28-29, Jan. 1865.
The various forms of the name with derivation and meaning.

2496. Martin, Lawrence. Who named Mount Washington? Geographical review 28:303-05, April 1938.
"Points out that although the name was given to Mount Washington, in New Hampshire, some time prior to 1792, the date and occasion of the naming have not been established."—Griffin.

2497. Mason, Ellen McRoberts. The North Conway Mount Kearsarge. Granite monthly 47:72-74, Feb.-March 1915.
Concerning proposed change of name to Pequawket.

2498. Merrill, Eliphalet & Phinehas Merrill. Gazetteer of the State of New-Hampshire. Comp. from the best authorities. Exeter, Printed by C. Norris & Co. for the authors, 1817. 218p.

2499. New Hampshire. Secretary of State. Manual for the General Court. no. 1- . 1889- .
Each year includes a record of grants. A list gives original names, many of which are now obsolete, and present names. Includes corporate history of the towns, with origin and changes of name.

2500. —— State Planning and Development Commission. Communities, settlements, and neighborhood centers in the State of New Hampshire. An inventory prepared by the State Planning and Development Commission, Concord, New Hampshire. Concord, 1937. 55p.

2501. Nomenclature of the White Mountains. Appalachia 1:7-11, June 1876.
Report of the Committee on Nomenclature of the Appalachian Mountain Club, suggesting a system that might be applied.

2502. The Origin of some New Hampshire mountain names. Historical New Hampshire 11:1-28, April 1955.

2503. Smith, Robinson V. New Hampshire Indians have gone but their names at least remain. Historical New Hampshire 8:32-36, Oct. 1952.

2504. U.S. Board on Geographic Names. Mount Kearsarge and Mount Pequawket, New Hampshire: historical notes relating to the conflicting names of Mount Kearsarge and Mount Pequawket, New Hampshire, submitted to the United States Geographic Board at the suggestion of Senator J. H. Gallinger, together with the decision of the Board in regard thereto. Comp. by David M. Hildreth, topographer, Post Office Department, member, United States Geographic Board. Washington, Govt. Print. Off., 1916. 14p. (64th Congress, 1st session, Senate doc. no. 307)
The U.S. Geographic Board decided that Kearsarge was the proper name of the mountain located in Merrimack County and Pequawket of the one in Carroll County.

NEW JERSEY

2505. Amboy, Kill van Kull, Arthur Kill. Magazine of American history 1:197-98, March 1877.
A reply to an inquiry, p. 129, for the meaning of these names.

2506. Becker, Donald William. Indian place-names in New Jersey. Cedar Grove, N.J., Phillips-Campbell Pub. Co., 1964. 111p.
Bibliography: p. 101-03.

2507. Berlin, N.J. is opposed to changing its name. New York times Oct. 11, 1944, p. 23, col. 4.

2508. Bisbee, Henry Harold. Place names in Burlington County, New Jersey. Riverside, N.J., Burlington County Pub. Co., 1955. 115p.
Review: Pennsylvania magazine of history and biography 80:270-71, April 1956.

2509. —— Sign posts: place names in history of Burlington County, New Jersey. Willingboro, N.J., Alexia Press, 1971.
Bibliography: p. 271-80.

2510. Borough of Ho-Ho-Kus insists on hyphens; tells Farley it knows how to spell name. New York times Dec. 28, 1939, p. 23, col. 4-5.

2511. Boucher, Jack E. Place names of that portion of Old Gloucester County that became Atlantic County in the year 1837 as of the year 1834. Atlantic County Historical Society. Yearbook 5:77-86, Oct. 1965.
Compiled from Thomas Francis Gordon's History and gazetteer of New Jersey, Trenton, 1834.

2512. Boyer, Charles Shimer. The origin and meaning of place names in Camden County. Camden, 1935. 16p. (Camden County Historical Society. Camden history, v. 1, no. 8)
Reprinted from West Jersey press of May 23, 30, and June 6, 13, 1935.

2513. Collins, Thomas E. A town by any other name. The Searcher 5:105. 1968.
A list of changes in names of New Jersey towns.

2514. De Costa, B. F. Cabo de arenas; or, The place of Sandy Hook in the old cartology. New England historical and genealogical register 39:147-60, April 1885.

A study of various names used on old maps for the geographical feature now called Sandy Hook. Includes a table giving the names appearing on many old maps for Sandy Hook, Connecticut River, Narragansett Bay, Cape Cod, and Cape Breton.

2515. Dryfoos, Susan. Sources of place names in the state. New York times May 7, 1972, p. 102.

Article based on Federal Writers' Project, New Jersey, a guide to its present and past, and Donald W. Becker's Indian place names in New Jersey.

2516. Dulles name to live. New Jersey boulevard will be a memorial. Kansas City times May 28, 1959.

The Dumont Borough Council voted to change the name of Sunnyside Blvd. to Dulles Blvd. in honor of John Foster Dulles.

2517. Dunlap, Arthur Ray. Barnegat. American speech 13:232-33, Oct. 1938.

2518. —— & Clinton Alfred Weslager. Toponomy of the Delaware Valley as revealed by an early seventeenth-century Dutch map. Archeological Society of New Jersey. Bulletin 15-16:1-13, Nov. 1958.

Bibliography: p. 5-6.

2519. —— Two Delaware Valley Indian place names. Names 15:197-202, Sept. 1967.

Recently discovered data make possible an analysis of Queonemysing (Pa.) and Mageckqueshou (N.J.).

2520. Early names of Dover. New Jersey Historical Society. Proceedings n.s. 5:128. 1920.

2521. Eno, Joel Nelson. New Jersey county names. Magazine of history 25:111-13, Sept.-Oct. 1917.

2522. GI village named "Distomo." New York times June 10, 1946, p. 3, col. 4; June 24, p. 33, col. 5.

Community for veterans opposite the airport in Atlantic City.

2523. Gannett, Henry. A geographic dictionary of New Jersey. Washington, Govt. Print. Off., 1894. 131p. (U.S. Geological Survey. Bulletin no. 118)

Issued also as House miscellaneous doc. v. 9, 53d Congress, 3d session.

2524. Gansberg, Martin. Elmwood Park makes a name for itself. New York times April 15, 1973, p. 80.

Voters in November 1972 referendum changed city name from East Patterson to Elmwood Park to distinguish it from Patterson, N.J., across the river.

2525. Gordon, Thomas Francis. A gazetteer of the State of New Jersey. Comprehending a general view of its physical and moral condition, together with a topographical and statistical account of its counties, towns, villages, canals, rail roads &c., accompanied by a map. Trenton, D. Fenton, 1834. 266p.

Reprinted: Cottonport, La., Polyanthos, Inc. 1973.

Review of the reprint edition: Kelsie B. Harder, Names 24:229-30, Sept. 1976.

2526. —— Indian names, with their signification; In John W. Barber & Henry Howe. Historical collections of the State of New Jersey. New York, Tuttle, 1844. p. 512.

2527. Hampton, George. Places and place names of Cumberland County. Vineland historical magazine 9:156-63, Jan. 1924.

2528. Harshberger, John William. The vegetation of the New Jersey pine barrens: an ecologic investigation. Philadelphia, Sower, 1916. 329p.
Geographic place names: p. 9-11.
Names indicative of some local peculiarity with special reference to the flora.

2529. Heckewelder, John Gottlieb Ernestus. Names given by the Lenni Lenape or Delaware Indians to rivers, streams and places in the now states of New Jersey, Pennsylvania, Maryland, and Virginia. Pennsylvania German Folklore Society. Publications 5:1-41. 1940.
Published also in American Philosophical Society. Transactions 4:351-96. 1834; Historical Society of Pennsylvania. Bulletin 1:121-35, 139-54 June, Sept. 1847; Moravian Historical Society. Transactions 1872:275-333; published separately: Bethlehem [Pa.], H. T. Claude, printer, 1872. 58p.; and in his A narrative of the mission of the United Brethren among the Delaware and Mohegan Indians. Cleveland, Burrows Bros., 1907. p. 523-66.

2530. Hoboken. Magazine of American history 4:312, 468, April, June 1880.
Discussion of the possible derivation of the name.

2531. Levittown name change set. New York times Dec. 25, 1963, p. 53.
To Willingboro, effective Feb. 1, 1964.

2532. Lobdell, Jared C. Some Indian place names in the Bergen-Passaic area. New Jersey Historical Society. Proceedings 84:265-70, Oct. 1966.

2533. Mrs. Brisbane bars the use of name for new street. New York times Nov. 17, 1938, p. 19, col. 3.
Asks Point Pleasant officials not to name new street for her husband, Arthur Brisbane.

2534. Nelson, William. Indian words, personal names, and place-names in New Jersey. Washington, 1902. p. 183-92. (Anthropologic miscellanea)
Reprinted from American anthropologist n.s. 4:183-92, Jan.-March 1902.
An "alphabetical list of [Delaware] Indian personal and place-names in New Jersey taken from New Jersey records relating to land transfers prior to 1703. In the original records, 'New Jersey archives, v. 21,' quite a number of the Indian place-names are followed by English interpretations." This list gives the original names and locations of the places.

2535. —— The Indians of New Jersey: their origin and development; manners and customs; language, religion and government. With notices of some Indian place names. Paterson, Press Print. & Pub. Co., 1894. 168p.
Delaware Indians.

2536. New Jersey. Department of Transportation. An alphabetical listing of local places and incorporated municipalities in the State of New Jersey, showing their incorporated titles and the county in which each is located. [Trenton], 1971. 53p.
Also published 1962, 1964, and 1968.

2537. Northern Jersey names vary from sublime to ridiculous, noble community titles blush beside Hogwallow, Teetertown and Cat Swamp. New York times Dec. 4, 1927, sec. 11, p. 6, col. 6-8.

2538. Pei, Mario. Faraway places with strange sounding names. Saturday review 51:64-65, Feb. 10, 1968.
Examples of colorful American and British place names, river names, state-line town names, and New Jersey place-names.

2539. Pennington, Mary V. Tracing Teaneck. New York times Oct. 10, 1935, p. 24, col. 6.
On derivation of Bogota and Teaneck.

2540. Philhower, Charles A. The origin and meaning of the name Amboy and the word Lenape. Archaeological Society of New Jersey. Bulletin 10:9-10, May 1955.

2541. Place names, Gloucester County, New Jersey. Gloucester County Historical Society. Publications. Special number, p. 66-78. 1964.

2542. Salem County Historical Society. Place names of Salem County, N.J. Salem, N.J. 1964. 85p. (Publications, v. 2, no. 4)
Lists both the long-forgotten names and places as well as the present communities, villages, streams, and roads.

2543. Salter, Edwin. Origin and signification of geographical names in the counties of Monmouth and Ocean and their vicinity. New Jersey Historical Society. Proceedings 2d ser. 4:18-26. 1875-77.

2544. Schmidt, Hubert G. Some Hunterdon place names, historical sketches about communities and localities in Hunterdon County, New Jersey. Flemington, D. H. Moreau, 1959. 32p.

2545. Sheppard, Cora June. How it got that name; places in Cumberland County. Vineland historical magazine 23:52-56, April 1938.
"Brief notes on the origin of place names."—Griffin.

2546. Stewart, George Rippey. Professor Stewart comments on "Hoere(n)kil." American speech 19:215-16, Oct. 1944.
In correction of the article by A. R. Dunlap, An early place name puzzle: "Hoere(n)-Kil," ibid., 19:112-14, April 1944, the origin of the word is given, and its location in New Jersey rather than in Delaware.

2547. Union may again be "Connecticut Farms." New York times July 15, 1946, p. 25, col. 1.

2548. U.S. Army Signal Training Command and Fort Monmouth. Fort Monmouth history and place names, 1917-1961. Fort Monmouth, N.J. [1961?]. 89p.

2549. U.S. Writers' Program. New Jersey. The origin of New Jersey place names. Comp. by workers of the Writers' Program of the Work Projects Administration in the State of New Jersey. Sponsored by New Jersey State Library Commission. n.p., 1939. 41p.
Indian place-names bibliography: 3d prelim. leaf.
Reissued: New Jersey Public Library Commission, 1945. 33p.

2550. Vermeule, Cornelius C. Some early New Jersey place-names. New Jersey Historical Society. Proceedings n.s. 10:241-56, July 1925; 11:151-60, April 1926.

2551. Weslager, Clinton Alfred. Dutch explorers, traders, and settlers in the Delaware Valley, 1609-1664. In collaboration with A. R. Dunlap. Philadelphia, Univ. of Pennsylvania Press, 1961. 329p.
Dutch maps and geographical names: p. 215-32.
Includes a list of Dutch names in the Delaware Valley.

2552. —— Robert Evelyn's Indian tribes and place-names of New Albion. Archeological Society of New Jersey. Bulletin 9:1-14, Nov. 1954.

Nine proper nouns mentioned in a letter by the explorer Robert Evelyn discussed and compared with contemporary accounts and maps.

2553. Will honor late publisher. New York times Nov. 25, 1945, p. 24, col. 5.
Five-point intersection to be named Press Plaza in honor of J. Lyle Kinmouth, late publisher of the Asbury Park Press.

2554. Wolfe, Theodore F. More local aboriginal names; some information of great interest regarding the origin and meaning of the names of familiar localities. Iron era, Dover, N.J. June 17, 1892.

2555. —— Origin of the name Succasunna. New Jersey Historical Society. Proceedings n.s. 9:334-40, Oct. 1924.
Originally published in the Iron era, Dover, N.J. Feb. 27, 1891, with additions in the Dover index March 19, 1909.

2556. —— Some local aboriginal names; another valuable contribution to Indian nomenclature. Iron era, Dover, N.J. Nov. 6, 1891.

2557. Zinkin, Vivian. Names of estates in the Province of West Jersey. Names 24:237-52, Dec. 1976.

2558. —— Place names of Ocean County, New Jersey: 1609-1849. Toms River, N.J., Ocean County Historical Society. 1976. 214p. maps.
Bibliography: p. 184-211.
Review: Kelsie B. Harder, Names 25:101-02, June 1977.

2558a. —— Some difficulties encountered in making a place name study. Connecticut onomastic review 1:85-94, 1979.
Special problems encountered in the author's studies of New Jersey names.

2559. —— A study of the place-names of Ocean County, New Jersey, 1609-1849.
Thesis (Ph.D.) Columbia University, 1968. Dissertation abstracts 29:1883A, Dec. 1968.

2560. —— Surviving Indian town names in West Jersey. Names 26:209-19, Sept. 1978.

2561. —— The syntax of place-names. Names 17:181-98, Sept. 1969.
An extract from the author's Ph.D. dissertation, A study of the place-names of Ocean County, New Jersey, 1609-1849.
An analysis of 311 names cited from 1703 through 1789.

NEW MEXICO

2562. Barker, Elliott Speer. What's in a name?; In his Beatty's Cabin: adventures in the Pecos high country. Albuquerque, Univ. of New Mexico Press, 1953. p. 151-62.

2563. Barker, S. Omar. Place names—pleasant and puzzling. New Mexico magazine 34:30, 46, 48, Aug. 1956.
Comments on this article in the Mail bag, ibid. 34:5, 56, Oct. 1956.

2564. —— Road map riddles. New Mexico magazine 40:20-21, 38, May 1962.
Meaning and pronunciation of New Mexico place-names.

2565. Brothers, Mary Hudson. Place names of the San Juan basin. Western folklore 10:165-67, April 1951.

2566. Brown, Frances Rosser. How they were named. New Mexico magazine 13:27, 41-42, Aug. 1935; 13:28, 37-38, Sept. 1935; 13:28, 39-41, Oct. 1935.

2567. —— The Spanish had a name for them. New Mexico magazine 20:14, 29-30, Oct. 1942.
Mountains.

2568. Bryan, Howard. Off the beaten path. Albuquerque tribune Sept. 5, 1957, p. 22.
Origin of Albuquerque and other New Mexico names, some of Moorish or Arabic origin resulting from Moors on Coronado's expedition, according to Rev. Fr. Julius Hartmann.
Other place-name information appeared in this column: Jan. 3, 1955; Jan. 24, 1955; Jan. 31, 1955; and June 4, 1955.

2569. —— Some colorful place names in New Mexico. Western folklore 15:285-86, Oct. 1956.
Reprinted from Albuquerque tribune June 4, 1956.

2570. Burnham, Lucy S. New Mexico place-names: Fruitland, The Meadows, Burning Hill. Western folklore 10:74-75, Jan. 1951.

2571. Carlson, Helen Swisher. Truth or Consequences, New Mexico. Western folklore 16:125-28, April 1957.
New name of Hot Springs, derived from radio program.
The voters decided on Jan. 13, 1964, by a vote of 891 to 752, to keep the new name.—New York times Jan. 15, 1964, p. 17.

2572. Cassidy, Ina Sizer. New Mexico place name studies. Western folklore 14:121-23, April 1955.

2573. —— New Mexico place names—Taos. El Palacio 61:296-99, Sept. 1954.

2574. —— The story of Sapello, or "Seat Joe." Western folklore 12:286-89, Oct. 1953.
Origin of Sapello, N.Mex.

2575. —— Taos, New Mexico. Western folklore 8:60-62, Jan. 1949.

2576. Chant, Elsie Ruth. The naming of Tucumcari. New Mexico folklore record 3:36-37. 1948-49.

2577. Chapman, Hank. New Mexico place names tongue twisters. Denver post June 2, 1968, Roundup, p. 34.

2578. Chávez, Angelico, Fray. The Albuquerque story. New Mexico magazine 34:18-19, 50-51, Jan. 1956.

2579. —— Albuquerque, what does it mean? New Mexico magazine 34:12, 48, July 1956.

2580. —— Aztec or Nahuatl words in New Mexico place-names. El Palacio 57:109-12, April 1950.

2581. —— Don Fernando de Taos. Western folklore 8:160, April 1949.

2582. —— Neo-Mexicanisms in New Mexico place names. El Palacio 57:67-79, March 1950.

2583. —— New Mexico place-names from Spanish proper names. El Palacio 56:367-82, Dec. 1949.
Spanish colonial families whose names became attached to the land.

2584. —— New Mexico religious place-names other than those of saints. El Palacio 57:23-26, Jan. 1950.

2585. —— Saints' names in New Mexico geography. El Palacio 56:323-35, Nov. 1949.

2586. Crocchiola, Stanley Francis Louis. The grant that Maxwell bought, by F. Stanley, [pseud.] [Denver, World Press, 1952]. 256p.
Living towns of the Grant: p. 159-201.
Ghost towns of the Grant [including rivers, canyons, parks, mesas, lakes, ranches]: p. 203-35.
Includes origin of some names.

2587. Dike, Sheldon Holland. New Mexico territorial postmark catalog. Albuquerque, Dikewood Corp., 1965. 71p.

2588. —— The territorial post offices of New Mexico. Albuquerque, Dikewood Corp., 1958. [57] ℓ.
Originally published in New Mexico historical review 33:322-27, Oct. 1958; 34:55-69, 145-52, 203-26, 308-09, Jan.-Oct. 1959.
A listing of 1175 post offices covering the period up to Jan. 6, 1912. Includes dates of establishment, discontinuance (in some cases after 1912), re-establishment, name changes, and chronological county location.

2589. Forrest, Earle Robert. Missions and pueblos of the old Southwest. Cleveland, Arthur H. Clark Co., 1929. 2v.
Spanish mission names in Arizona and New Mexico, with their English equivalents, 1:333-35.

2590. 44,000 postmasters will hear about Truth or Consequences. Albuquerque tribune April 3, 1950, p. 6.
New name for Hot Springs.

2591. Gatschet, Albert Samuel. The navel in local names. American anthropologist 6:53-54, Jan. 1893.
Includes ruin Hálona, one of the Seven Cities of Cibola, on south bank of Zuni River.

2592. Hale, Edward Everett, Jr. French place-names in New Mexico. French review 3:110-13, Nov. 1929.
Also reprinted separately. 6p.

2593. Hardeman, Nicholas P. Camp sites on the Santa Fe trail in 1848 as reported by John A. Bingham. Ed. by Nicholas P. Hardeman. Arizona and the West 6:313-19, Winter 1964.

2594. Harrington, John Peabody. The ethnogeography of the Tewa Indians. U.S. Bureau of American Ethnology. Annual report 29:29-636. 1907-08.
Bibliography: p. 585-87.
Includes the derivation and meaning of geographical terms and place-names in the Tewa language.

2595. —— Haák' o, original form of the Keresan name of Acoma. El Palacio 56:141-44, May 1949.

2596. —— Name of Zuñi Salt Lake in Alarcon's 1540 account. El Palacio 56:102-05, April 1949.

2597. —— Old Indian geographical names around Santa Fe, New Mexico. American anthropologist n.s. 22:341-59, Oct.-Dec. 1920.
Also reprinted separately.

2598. —— Olivella River. El Palacio 56:220-22, July 1949.
On the name'O`gha'p'oo`ghe`, meaning Olivella River, applied in the Tewa language to the part of Santa Fe Creek on which Santa Fe stands.

2599. Heck, Lewis. [Letter requesting information as to form of name of a mountain, Chicoma Peak or Tschicoma Peak]. New Mexico magazine 36:5, Jan. 1958.

2600. Hewett, Edgar L. Origin of the name Navaho. American anthropologist n.s. 8:193, Jan.-March 1906.
The tribal designation is derived from the Tewa Indian pueblo of Navahú, meaning "the place of great planted fields."

2601. Hill, Robert T. Descriptive topographic terms of Spanish America. National geographic magazine 7:291-302, Sept. 1896.
Prepared for reports to Director of U.S. Geological Survey on geography of Texas-New Mexico region.
Terms cover topographical features such as protuberances or mountain forms, plains, declivities, streams, and stream valleys.

2602. Hodge, F. W. Early Spanish bungling of Indian names. Western folklore 9:153-54, April 1950.

2603. —— The name "Navaho." Masterkey (Southwest Museum, Los Angeles) 23:78, May 1949.
A Tewa pueblo near Santa Clara.

2604. —— Pueblo names in the Oñate documents. New Mexico historical review 10:36-47, Jan. 1935.

2605. Jenkinson, Michael. Ghost towns of New Mexico: playthings of the wind. Photographs by Karl Kernberger. Albuquerque, Univ. of New Mexico Press, 1967. 156p.

2606. Jett, Stephen C. An analysis of Navajo place-names. Names 18:175-84, Sept. 1970.
Many official place-names in northeastern Arizona, northwestern New Mexico, and southeastern Utah are of Navajo origin, either by Anglicization of the Navajo names or by translation. Most Navajo place designations describe features of the natural landscape.

2607. Jones, Fayette Alexander. Old mines and ghost camps of New Mexico. Fort Davis, Tex., Frontier Book Co., 1968. 214p.
Reprinted from the author's New Mexico mines and minerals, (Santa Fe, New Mexico Bureau of Immigration, 1905), some of which was published as Old mining camps of New Mexico, 1854-1904 (Santa Fe, Stagecoach Press, 1964. 92p.).
Includes origin of names.

2608. Jones, William M. Origin of the place-name Taos. Anthropological linguistics v. 2, no. 3, p. 2-4. 1960.

2609. Land of Enchantment investigated. The New Mexican, Santa Fe, Oct. 10, 1954.
Background of the nickname The Land of Enchantment used on auto license plates.

2610. Looney, Ralph. Haunted highways: the ghost towns of New Mexico. New York, Hastings House, 1968. 220p.
Bibliography: p. 213-14.

2611. McHarney, Caryl. What's in a name? Nowhere in the Southwest are place titles more expressive than in New Mexico where three cultures met and mingled. Denver post Dec. 4, 1955, Empire magazine, p. 31.

2612. Martinez, Velma. Names under the sun. New Mexico magazine 36:24, 46-47, April 1958.

2613. Meleski, Patricia F. Echoes of the past: New Mexico's ghost towns. With photos by R. P. Meleski. Albuquerque, Univ. of New Mexico Press, [1972]. xi, 254p.
Bibliography: p. 246-47.
Includes 43 towns with some place-name information.
Review: Felix D. Almaraz, Jr. Journal of the West 13:153, Jan. 1974.

2614. Mirkowich, Nicholas. A note on Navajo place names. American anthropologist n.s. 43:313-14, April-June 1941.
Lists Navajo names still in use for a few places in Arizona and New Mexico.

2615. Mitchell, L. B. The meaning of the name Albuquerque. Western folklore 8:255-56, July 1949.

2616. Myers, Lee. Military establishments in southwestern New Mexico: stepping stones to settlement. New Mexico historical review 43:5-48, Jan. 1968.

2617. New Mexico Folklore Society. Place-name Committee. New Mexico place-name dictionary. 1st-3rd collection. 1949-51. Albuquerque, 1949-51. 3 pts.
Each annual collection lists from 138 to 334 names.

2618. —— Report for 1950-51. New Mexico folklore record 7:25-26. 1952-53.
Signed by Ina Sizer Cassidy, chairman.

2619. Pearce, Thomas M. "Albuquerque" reconsidered. Western folklore 16:195-97, July 1957.

2620. —— Loving and Lovington: two New Mexico towns. Western folklore 8:159-60, April 1949.

2621. —— The lure of names. New Mexico quarterly 32:161-77, Autumn-Winter 1962-63.
Includes geographical names in New Mexico, p. 167-72.

2622. —— New Mexico place-name dictionary. Western folklore 8:257-59, July 1949.
Discussion of the first collection.

2623. —— The New Mexico place-name dictionary: a polyglot in six languages. Names 6:217-25, Dec. 1958.

2624. —— New Mexico place names: a geographical dictionary. Ed. by T. M. Pearce, assisted by Ina Sizer Cassidy and Helen S. Pearce. Albuquerque, Univ. of New Mexico Press, 1965. xv, 187p.
Bibliography: p. 183-85.
Review: Margaret M. Bryant, Names 14:186-88, Sept. 1966; New Mexico magazine 44:35, May 1966; William Bright, Western folklore 26:140-43, April 1967.

2625. —— Religious place names in New Mexico. Names 9:1-7, March 1961.

2626. —— Second collection, New Mexico place-name dictionary. Western folklore 9:372-78, Oct. 1950.

2627. —— Some Indian place names of New Mexico. Western folklore 10:245-47, July 1951.
From the New Mexico place-name dictionary, third collection.

2628. Rainwater, John R. [Letter regarding spelling of San Augustine Plains]. New Mexico magazine 36:5, Aug. 1958.

2629. Reeve, Frank D. Early Navaho geography. New Mexico histosical review 31:290-309, Oct. 1956.
Fixing the location of certain geographic terms (Cebolleta, Navaho, and Piedra Alumbre or Lumbre) is partly a matter of defining words.

2630. Schilling, Frank A. Military posts of the old frontier: Arizona, New Mexico. Historical Society of Southern California. Quarterly 42:133-49, June 1960.
Includes origin and changes of names.

2631. Sherman, James E. & Barbara H. Sherman. Ghost towns and mining camps of New Mexico. Norman, Univ. of Oklahoma Press, [1975]. x, 270p. maps.
Bibliography: p. 259-61.
Review: Watson Parker, Journal of the West 14:149, Oct. 1975; Helen Blumenschein, Western historical quarterly 6:449-50, Oct. 1975.

2632. Simons, Katherine. Street names of Albuquerque. American speech 17:209-10, Oct. 1942.

2633. Sleight, Frederick W. A problem of clarification in ethnographic nomenclature. El Palacio 56:295-300, Oct. 1949.
Names of peaks in the Jemez Range.

2634. Standley, Paul Carpenter. The type localities of plants first described from New Mexico. A bibliography of New Mexican botany. Washington, Govt. Print. Off., 1910. p. 143-246. (Smithsonian Institution. United States National Museum. Contributions from the United States National Herbarium, v. 13, pt. 6)
Descriptive list of type localities: p. 151-74.

2635. Sullinger, James H. N. M. town to vote again on name. Hot controversy springs up again in Truth or Consequences. Denver post (Western Slope ed.) Aug. 17, 1967, p. 32.

2636. "T or C" backers win vote; suit indicated. Denver post (Western Slope ed.) Aug. 20, 1967, p. 38.
Regarding change of name of Truth or Consequences.

2637. Thatcher, Harold F. & Mary Hudson Brothers. Fabulous La Plata River. Western folklore 10:167-69, April 1951.

2638. Trager, George L. The name of Taos, New Mexico. Anthropological linguistics v. 2, no. 3, p. 5-6. 1960.

2639. Van Valkenburgh, Richard F. & Frank O. Walker. Old placenames in the Navaho country. Masterkey (Southwest Museum, Los Angeles) 19:89-94, May 1945.
Contains a list giving the popular, Spanish, and Navaho names, location, etc.

2640. Where is Reyes Linares? Folklore Society needs 100 more place names to complete listing. The New Mexican, Santa Fe, Jan. 4, 1959, p. 5.
Plea for information needed to complete the Dictionary of New Mexico place names.

2641. White, Marjorie Butler. What's in a name? New Mexico magazine 38:10-11, 40-42, July 1960.

2642. White, Rose P. New Mexico place names: Roosevelt County. Western folklore 9:63-65, Jan. 1950.
Dead Negro Draw and Nigger Hill.

2643. —— The town of Portales, New Mexico. Western folklore 8:158-59, April 1949.

2644. Who knows the name of New Mexico park? Kansas City star Feb. 14, 1960, sec. F, p. 6.
Pancho Villa State Park suggested for new state park established at Columbus, N.Mex., to commemorate the 1916 raid by the army of Pancho Villa.

2645. Whole town "Jumping up and down" over proposal. Hot Springs herald March 30, 1950, p. 1.
Proposed change of Hot Springs to Truth or Consequences.

2646. Williamsburg plans vote May 23 on Hot Springs name. Hot Springs herald April 6, 1950, p. 1.
To use name for a city addition changed by original city to Truth or Consequences.

2647. Woods, Dora Elizabeth Ahern. Ghost towns and how to get to them, by Betty Woods. Maps by M. T. Williams. Scene: New Mexico. Time: the present. Santa Fe, N.Mex., Press of the Territorian, 1964. 36p. (Western Americana series, no. 4)
Includes, in addition, Lucien A. File's copyrighted list of ghost towns, p. 34-36.

2648. Wooton, Elmer Ottis & Paul Carpenter Standley. Flora of New Mexico. Washington, Govt. Print. Off., 1915. 794p. (Smithsonian Institution. United States National Museum. Contributions from the United States National Herbarium, v. 19)
Geographic index: p. 755-71.

2649. Young, Robert W. & William Morgan. Navajo place names in Gallup, New Mexico. El Palacio 54:283-85, Dec. 1947.

NEW YORK

2650. Adirondack town looks for a name; iron mining community born of war. New York times Sept. 13, 1942, p. 21, col. 1. Suggested Dalliba for Maj. James Dalliba, founder of iron industry at Morish. Correct spelling of his name given ibid. Sept. 15, 1942, p. 21, col. 3.

2651. Alvarez, Grace de Jesus C. The Cuba of New York State: a study in Hispanic toponymy of the Empire State. Little Valley, N.Y., Straight Pub. Co., [c1970]. 48p. map.
Bibliography: p. 43-47.
Review: Elsdon C. Smith, Names 20:151, June 1972.

2651a. Alvarez-Altman, Grace. Spanish place names in the Empire state (New York); In Northeast Regional Names Institute. Names, Northeast, ed. by Murray Heller. Saranac Lake, N.Y., North Country Community College Press, 1979. p. 45-53. (Publication I)

2652. Ames, C. H. Poke-o-Moonshine. Forest and stream 56:503, June 29, 1901.
Reply to Raymond Smiley Spears, ibid. p. 484 (see no. 2808).

2653. Armbruster, Eugene L. Gazetteer of Long Island. n.d. 7v.
Manuscript in the possession of the late Long Island historian's family (263 Eldert St., Brooklyn, N.Y.). It includes a detailed listing of bays, rivers, towns, and other geographical names with information on the origin of these names.

2654. Asher, Georg Michael. A bibliographical and historical essay on the Dutch books and pamphlets relating to New-Netherland and to the Dutch West-India Company and to its possessions in Brazil, Angola, etc. as also on the maps, charts, etc. of New Netherland . . . Comp. from the Dutch public and private libraries and from the collection of Frederik Muller in Amsterdam. Amsterdam, N. Israel, 1960. 234, 22, 23p.
1st ed. 1854-67. 2v.
List of names on the maps: 23p. at end.

2655. Ashokan. Olde Ulster 4:327, Nov. 1908.

2656. Auser, Cortland P. Westchester place names: strata of folk-life and history. New York folklore quarterly, 24:44-49, March 1968.

2657. Barker, Elmer Eugene. Origin of name Bouquet River. Reveille 1:1, 4, April 1957.

2658. —— That name—Marcy. Cloud splitter 11:10, Nov.-Dec. 1948.

2659. Bates, Erl. Place names of New York. (Cornell rural school leaflet 22, no. 1:111-24, Sept. 1928).
Interpretation of Indian names and words erroneously considered Indian in derivation.

2660. Beacon (N.Y.) High School. Sophomore English Class. History and legends of Beacon and vicinity. 1921.
The name Poughkeepsie, p. 22-23.

2661. Beauchamp, William Martin. Aboriginal place names of New York. Albany, New York State Education Dept., 1907. 333p. (New York State Museum. Bulletin 108. Archeology 12)
Reprinted: Detroit, Grand River Books, 1971.
List of authorities: p. 271-78.

2662. —— Indian names in New-York, with a selection from other states, and some Onondaga names of plants, etc. Fayetteville, N.Y., printed by H. C. Beauchamp, 1893. 148p.

2663. Beecher, Willis J. Geographical names as monuments of history. Oneida Historical Society. Transactions 5:9-23. 1889-92. (Publications no. 17)
Those of the ancient country of the Iroquois, with comparison of the country just east of the Iroquois.

2664. Benson, Egbert. Dutch names of places; Dutch names of streets. Halve maen (Holland Society of New York) 19:6, July 1944; 19:3, Nov. 1944.
Excerpts from articles written by Egbert Benson (1743-1833) on the nomenclature of the Dutch in Niew Amsterdam, contributed by Hevlyn Dirck Benson, a descendant.

2665. —— Memoir, read before the Historical Society of the State of New York, December 31, 1816. 2d ed. with notes. Jamaica, H. C. Sleight, 1825. 127p.

1st ed. New-York, W. A. Mercein, 1817. 72p.

Also reprinted from a copy, with the author's last corrections, in New York Historical Society. Collections 2d ser. 2:77-148. 1848. Also published separately, New York, Bartlett & Welford, 1848. 72p.

On the names of places in New York State.

2666. Biondi, Mary H. & Nina W. Smithers. From Podunk to ZIP code 13652: place names in St. Lawrence County. New York folklore quarterly 21:40-48, March 1965.

2667. Board of Geographic Names. New York. State Museum. Museum bulletin 173:43-58, Nov. 1, 1914.

Notice of the creation of the Board, with citation from the law. Includes a glossary, prepared by the Board, of place-names of Albany, Rensselaer, and Schenectady counties.

2668. Boewe, Charles. Mt. Rafinesque. Names 10:58-60, March 1962.

Origin of name of this hill near Troy, N.Y.

2669. Bolton, Reginald Pelham. Aboriginal place-names of the county of Westchester. New York, 1942. 67p.

2670. —— Indian paths in the great metropolis. New York, Museum of the American Indian, Heye Foundation, 1922. 280p. (Indian notes and monographs. Miscellaneous, no. 23)

Index of stations on the maps: p. 220-41.

An enlargement of the list in author's New York City in Indian possession. (New York, Museum of the American Indian, Heye Foundation, 1920 [Indian notes and monographs, v. 2, no. 7]), p. 302-18.

2671. Bouck, Roland O. Unusual spellings of "Schoharie." Schoharie County historical review 13:21, Oct. 1949.

Reprinted: ibid. 31:24, Fall-Winter 1967.

16 different spellings found in E. B. O'Callaghan, Documents relating to the colonial history of the State of New York.

2671a. Brown, Betsy. What's in a street name? New York times Feb. 25, 1979, sec. 22, p. 6.

Westchester County, N.Y.

2672. Byrne, Thomas E. Horseheads streets: how they were named. Chemung historical journal 13:1629-31, Sept. 1967.

2673. Carson, Russell Mack Little. Peaks and people of the Adirondacks. Garden City, N.Y., Doubleday, Page, 1927. 269p.

History of the names of the peaks.

2674. Clark, Joshua Victor Hopkins. Onondaga; or, Reminiscences of earlier and later times. Syracuse, Stoddard, 1849. 2v.

Ancient aboriginal names of lakes, streams, and localities in Onondaga County and vicinity, with their meanings, 1:322-26.

2675. Cocks, George William. Old Matinecock. Nassau County historical journal 22:1-11, Fall 1961.

2676. Coles, Robert R. Indian and other place-names. Long Island forum 34:94-97, June 1971.

General article drawn from William Wallace Tooker's work.

2677. —— Long Island's Indian names. Long Island forum 20:145-46, Aug. 1957.
Indian names for Long Island.

2678. —— Some Matinecock place-names. Long Island forum 17:207, 218, Nov. 1954.

2679. Colorful rites at lake naming. Knickerbocker press, Albany, Aug. 11, 1936.
The naming of Durant Lake.

2680. Constitution Island; origin of its name—neighboring landmarks. American Scenic and Historic Preservation Society. Annual report 29:123-25. 1924.

2681. Cooper, Susan Fenimore. The Hudson River and its early names. Magazine of American history 4:401-18, June 1880.
Traces the historical origin and meaning of the names applied to the Hudson River by different explorers and settlers.

2682. Cotterell, Harry. Oddly named towns. New York times Dec. 18, 1927, sec. 3, p. 5.

2683. Crocker, Elizabeth L. Yesterdays in and around Pomfret, N.Y. Fredonia, N.Y., 1960-63. v. 1-4.

2684. De Camp, L. Sprague. Pronunciation of upstate New York place-names. American speech 19:250-65, Dec. 1944.
Includes 13 pages of names with phonetic spelling for each name.

2685. DeKay, James Ellsworth. Indian names of Long Island. Oyster Bay, 1851. 12p.

2686. Derivation of Indian names. Historical magazine 2:149, May 1858.
The origin and meaning of Wading River, Quogue, and Peacock Neck on Long Island.

2687. Disturnell, John. A gazetteer of the State of New York: comprising its topography, geology, mineralogical resources, civil divisions, canals, railroads and public institutions; together with general statistics; the whole alphabetically arranged. Also, statistical tables, including the census of 1840; and tables of distances. With a new township map of the state. 2d ed. Albany, C. van Benthuysen, 1843. 479p.
1st ed. Albany, 1842.

2688. Douglas, Edward Morehouse. Gazetteer of the lakes, ponds, and reservoirs of the State of New York. Washington, Map Information Office, Board of Surveys and Maps, 1928. 45p.
1st ed. 1926. 44p.

2689. —— Gazetteer of the mountains of the State of New York. Washington, Map Information Office, Board of Surveys and Maps, 1930. 36p.
1st ed. 1927. 36p.

2690. Drake, Leora Wilson. Kanestio; Canisteo, Steuben County; place names in New York State. Yesteryears no. 5:5-8, Oct. 1958.

2691. Dutch proper names in Ulster. Olde Ulster 3:239-42, Aug. 1907.

2691a. Edwards, John. A road by any other name. New York times Sept. 9, 1979, sec. 21, p. 18.
Long Island, N.Y.

2692. Eno, Joel Nelson. A tercentenary history of the towns and cities of New York; their origin, dates, and names, 1614-1914. New York State Historical Association. Proceedings 15:225-64. 1916.

2693. Fillmore, Millard. Inaugural address. Buffalo Historical Society. Publications 1:1-15. 1879.
On the name Buffalo.

2694. First to name square for Truman. New York times Oct. 22, 1945, p. 19, col. 6.
Town Lake, N.Y.

2695. Flick, Alexander Clarence. New York place names. New York, Columbia Univ. Press, 1937. p. 291-332.
Reprinted from New York State Historical Association. History of the State of New York. v. 10.
Bibliography: p. 330-32.
Classified as Indian, French, Dutch, British, German, Revolutionary, classical, New England, institutional, and nature.

2696. Flint, Martha Bockee. Early Long Island, a colonial study. New York, G. P. Putnam's Sons, 1896. 549p. map.
Reprinted as Long Island before the Revolution. Port Washington, Ira J. Friedman, 1967.
A study of names: p. 60-75.

2697. The Founding of the Nieuw Dorp, or Hurley. Olde Ulster 1:257-64, Sept. 1905.

2698. French, John Homer. Gazetteer of the State of New York; embracing a comprehensive view of the geography, geology, and general history of the state, and a complete history and description of every county, city, town, village, and locality with full tables of statistics. 10th ed. Syracuse, R. P. Smith, 1861. 739p.
Eds. 6-8 published 1860.
Reprinted: Port Washington, Ira J. Friedman, 1969.

2699. Gatschet, Albert Samuel. Origin of the name Chautauqua. Glen Echo Chautauqua 1:12, Aug. 1891.

2700. Giles, Dorothy. Polopel Island: Hudson River place-name. New York folklore quarterly 11:125-28, Summer 1955.
Suggests explanation of the Dutch name of the island in the Hudson River east of Storm King.

2701. Gilette, Frieda A. Caneadea: Indian place names in New York State. Yesteryears no. 3:20-21, Feb. 1958.

2702. Gordon, Thomas Francis. Gazetteer of the State of New York: comprehending its colonial history; general geography, geology, and internal improvements; its political state; a minute description of its several counties, towns, and villages. With a map of the state, and a map of each county, and plans of the cities and principal villages. Philadelphia, Printed for the Author, 1836. 801p.

2703. Graham, Hugh P. Cohoes: place names in New York State. Yesteryears no. 4:19, July 1958.

2704. —— Podunk: place names in New York State. Yesteryears no. 6:14, Feb. 1959.

2705. Great Sacandaga Lake. York state tradition 22:51, Fall 1968.
Name of the largest man-made lake in New York State, Sacandaga Reservoir, changed to Great Sacandaga Lake.

2706. Greeson, Philip E., George E. Williams & F. Luman Robison. Instructions for data storage: characteristics of New York lakes, Part I--gazetteer of lakes, ponds, and reservoirs. Albany, State of New York, Water Resources Commission. 1969. 28p. (Report of investigation R1-4)

2707. Haas, Dorothy M. Place names of northern New York. North country life 9:42-44, Fall 1955.

2708. Hadaway, William S. Identification of "Dobbs Ferry." Westchester County Historical Society. Quarterly bulletin 9:16-19, Jan. 1933.

2709. Hale, Edward Everett, Jr. Dialectical evidence in the place-names of eastern New York. American speech 5:154-67, Dec. 1929.
Dutch and English words with definitions of such terms as borough, brook, brush, etc. used for parts of place-names.
Errors in Dutch corrected by A. E. H. Swaen, ibid. 5:400, June 1930.

2710. Hall, Basil. Names on the state. York state tradition 22:51-52, Spring 1968.
Reprinted from the author's Travels in North America in 1827 and 1828.
Comments on his reactions to the classical and other place-names in New York State.

2711. Hanford, Franklin. On the origin of the names of places in Monroe County, New York. Scottsville, I. Van Hooser, printer, 1911. 54p. (Publications of the Scottsville Literary Society, no. 5)
Reprinted in Rochester Historical Society. Publication fund series 5:49-77. 1926.

2711a. Harder, Kelsie B. Sticks and stones and onomastic bones; In Northeast Regional Names Institute. Names, Northeast, ed. by Murray Heller. Saranac Lake, N.Y., North Country Community College Press, 1979. p. 35-44. (Publication I)
Concerned with some names "connected with minor archeological events, with landmarks, or with other slightly askew situations."

2712. Harris, George Henry. Aboriginal occupation of the lower Genesee country. Rochester, 1884. 96p.
Chapter 5, p. 32-36, Indian place-names of the Genesee area.

2713. —— Notes on the aboriginal terminology of the Genesee River. Rochester Historical Society. Publications 1:9-18. 1892.

2714. Hauptman, Herbert C. Adirondack place names. High spots 9:16-17, Jan. 1932.

2715. —— By their names. High spots, the yearbook of the Adirondack Mountain Club 1939:72-76.
Names in the Adirondacks.

2716. Hawley, L. F. The Chadakoin River. Names 3:32-33, March 1955.
Naming the outlet of Chautauqua Lake.

2716a. Heller, Murray. Adirondack settlement names: Mount Pisgah revisited; In North Central Names Institute. Papers, ed. by Lawrence E. Seits. Sugar Grove, Ill., Waubonsee Community College, 1980. p. 101-08. map.

2717. Henry, Mellinger Edward. Old Hudson River town names. Journal of American folklore 56:290, Oct.-Dec. 1943.

2718. Historical notice of Kingston and Rondout. Olde Ulster 8:353-61, Dec. 1912.
Origin and meaning of Rondout appear in footnote on p. 356. In Ibid. 9:8-10, Jan. 1913, in continuation of above article, are given former names of Rondout: The Strand, Kingston Landing, and Bolton.

2719. Hough, Franklin Benjamin. Gazetteer of the State of New York, embracing a comprehensive account of the history and statistics of the state. With geological and topographical descriptions, and recent statistical tables. Albany, A. Boyd, 1872. 745p.

2720. How Old Forge (N.Y.) was named. Forest and stream 72:892, June 5, 1909.
Short note on the forge used by John Brown (1734-1803).

2721. How the counties got their names. New York (State) Secretary of State. Manual for the use of the Legislature of the State of New York. 1932- .
A list appearing in each issue from 1932 on.

2722. Howell, William Thompson. The Hudson Highlands. New York, Lenz & Riecker, 1933-34. 2v.
Place-names: 2:1-31.

2723. Hudson's River. Magazine of American history 8:513-14, July 1882.
Explains the origin of various names for the Hudson River.

2724. Hull, Raymond. Names on the land in St. Lawrence County. North country life 6:32-35, Winter 1952.

2725. Indian name for Elmira. Chemung historical journal 2:199-200, Sept. 1956.

2726. Ingraham, Joseph C. To Connecticut; New England Thruway to open direct route from Bronx to Rhode Island. New York times Oct. 5, 1958, sec. 2, p. 23, col. 1-4.
Includes list of historic names decided on by the New York Legislature for the Thruway and its extensions, such as the Iroquois Trail, the Mohican Path, etc.

2727. Jones, Nathan W. The Esopus Indians and their language. Olde Ulster 1:70-75, March 1905.
Place-names given by the Minsi Indians, a tribe of the Delaware Confederacy.

2728. Kalkoen Hoek. Olde Ulster 2:338, Nov. 1906.
The name applied to Turkey Point by the Dutch.

2729. Ketchum, William. The origin of the name of Buffalo. Read before the Buffalo Historical Society, April 7, 1863. Buffalo Historical Society. Publications. 1:17-42. 1879.
Includes letters on the name from Asher Wright and Nathaniel T. Strong.

2730. Langhans, Rufus S. Place names in the Town of Smithtown: their location, origin, and meaning. Smithtown, Smithtown Library, 1961. 28p. map. (Smithtown Library. Handley series, no. 2)
Bibliography: p. 28.

2731. Lederer, Richard M., Jr. The place names of Westchester County, New York. Harrison, N.Y., Harbor Hill Books, 1978. 192p.

Bibliography: p. 179-88.
Includes more than 2200 topographic features and localities.

2732. Leete, Charles Henry. A study in geographic names. 12p.
Reprint from Herald-recorder, Potsdam, N.Y., March 1927.

2733. Local names from the Dutch. Olde Ulster 4:90-92, March 1908.

2734. Lost town of Gates found by woman. Albany evening news Feb. 3, 1936.
Gates Township in Saratoga County.

2735. Lounsbury, Floyd G. Iroquois place-names in the Champlain Valley; In Interstate Commission on the Lake Champlain basin. Report. Albany, 1960. p. 21-66. (New York State. Legislative document [1960], no. 9)
Reprinted: Albany, University of the State of New York. State Education Dept., [1972?]. p. 23-66.
Based on historical and linguistic research.
Review: C. G. Holland, International journal of linguistics 29:178-80, April 1963.

2736. Low, Edward. Postal service manual, containing the names of post offices, locals and counties, in the State of New York, arranged alphabetically. Tables of distances from the state capital to the several county seats; also, new postal regulations, rates of domestic postage, foreign postage tables, money order offices, state railroad index, and other postal information adapted to the wants of business men throughout the state. Rev. and corr. to August 1872. Albany, Van Benthuysen Print. House, 1872. 108, [113]p. map.

2737. Maar, Charles. Origin of the classical place names of central New York. New York State Historical Association. Quarterly journal 7:155-68, July 1926.
William M. Beauchamp's comment, p. 167-68.
"The author places the responsibility for the assignment of the classical names of the different regions in New York on Simeon De Witt, a surveyor for the state."—Price.
Cf. note: E. E. Hale, Classical names in New York State. American speech 3:256, Feb. 1928.

2737a. McGoff, Michael Francis. Computer-oriented onomastic surveys: the toponyms of New York State. Binghamton, State Univ. of New York, 1981. 371p.

2738. McKaig, Thomas H. Place names of western New York. Niagara frontier 1:61-68, Autumn 1954.

2739. McKelvey, Blake. Names and traditions of some Rochester streets. Rochester History 27:1-22, July 1965.

2740. McKnight, Nellie. Incongruous names; information on the naming of New York towns is sought. New York times Feb. 15, 1928, p. 22, col. 6.
On name Athens, N.Y., and others.
Author's second letter appeared ibid. March 4, 1928, sec. 3, p. 5, col. 6, mentioning Robert Harper, early secretary of the State Land Board, who had a hand in assigning classical names.

2741. Manley, Seon. Long Island discovery. Garden City, Doubleday & Co., 1966. x, 318p.
Brief discussion of a few Indian place-names, Of Indians and place names, p. 28-42.

2742. Manuel Gonzales, the Spaniard. Olde Ulster 6:172-76, June 1910.
Origin of Sam's Point; Shawangunk Mountains; and The Spanish Mine, near Ellenville, p. 175.

2743. Maxwell, Mary Ellis. Camillus: place names in New York State. Yesteryears no. 5:1-4, Oct. 1958.

2744. Metropolitan area loses one of its Central Parks. New York times Oct. 3, 1936, p. 2, col. 5.
Central Park, Long Island, changed to Bethpage.

2745. Miller, C. Henriette. Aboriginal place names in Columbia County. n.p., n.d., 5p.
"This chapter from my book is intended for those who have not read Ruttenber, O'Callaghan, or Beauchamp, but who would be well informed."

2746. Miller, Philip Schuyler. By guess and by gosh. Ad-i-ron-dac 10:6-7, March-April 1946.
The problem of tracing the real story of Adirondack place-names.

2747. —— Those poetic red men. Cloud splitter 5:4-5, March 1942.
There were older, authentic Indian names for Adirondack landmarks, but current Indian names were given by the guides.

2748. —— Why the Bouquet? Ad-i-ron-dac 11:4-5, Jan.-Feb. 1947.
Source of name of Bouquet River.

2749. Milliken, Charles F. Ontario County place names. New York. State Museum. Museum bulletin 253:103-10, July 1924.
An alphabetical list of names which contains brief notes on the meaning of the name and the location of the place.

2750. Mills, Borden H. Charles Fenno Hoffman's Indian place names. Ad-i-ron-dac 12:4-7, July-Aug. 1948.
"Quotes passage from Hoffman's Vigil of faith (1845) reproduced in Kachesco, a legend of the sources of the Hudson (1873) and comments on 26 place names included therein."—Writings on American history.

2751. —— Who was John? Cloud splitter 11:4-6, Jan.-Feb. 1948.
Reprinted in Ad-i-ron-dac 15:97-98, 100, Sept.-Oct. 1951.
Johns Brook was probably named for John Gibbs.

2752. Minton, Arthur. Names of real-estate developments. Names 7:129-53, 233-55, Sept.-Dec. 1959; 9:8-36, March 1961.
Most development names cited are from Long Island.

2753. Morgan, Lewis Henry. League of the Ho-dé-no-sau-nee, or Iroquois. New ed. with additional matter. Ed. and annotated by Herbert M. Lloyd. New York, Dodd, 1904. 2v. in 1.
Also published 1901 in 2v. in an edition of 30 copies only.
1st ed. Rochester, 1851. 477p.
Schedule explanatory of the Indian map, giving the corresponding English and Indian names of places, with their meaning: 2:127-39.
Later printings of this title are as follows:

2754. —— League of the Ho-de-no-sau-nee, or Iroquois. New Haven, Human Relations Area Files, 1954. 2v. (Behavior science reprints)

2755. —— League of the Iroquois. Introd. by William N. Fenton. New York, Corinth Books, 1962. 477p. (The American experience series. AE 12)

2756. Morris, Robert T. Niagara. Saturday review of literature 8:776, 820, June 4, July 2, 1932.

In brief form the author interprets Niagara Falls as meaning "the-waterfall-that-causes-women-to-exclaim 'Gosh!'"

2757. Mountain lake honors Durant. Albany evening news Aug. 11, 1936.

2758. The Name of Katskill, or Kaaterskill. Olde Ulster 9:309-14, Oct. 1913.

2759. The Name of Kingston and its predecessors. Olde Ulster 1:266-68, Sept. 1905.

2760. Name sources of townships of Monroe County. Monroe republican, Rochester, May 1, 1930.

2761. Names of places on Long Island, and their derivations. Historical magazine 9:31, Jan. 1865.

Gives the place-names of Jamaica, Hoppogues, and Comac with derivations and meanings.

2762. The Naming of Troy. Great traditions of Rensselaer County 1:[6-14], Jan. 1964.

Also street names in Troy with sketches of three men for whom streets were named.

2763. New York Historical Society. Report of the aboriginal names and geographical terminology of the State of New York. Part I—Valley of the Hudson. Made to the New York Historical Society, by the committee appointed to prepare a map, etc., and read at the stated meeting of the Society, February, 1844. By Henry R. Schoolcraft, chairman. New York, The Society, 1845. 43p.

Published from the Society's Proceedings 1844:77-115. Additional note in the Proceedings p. 119-20.

The report is based on an historical summary of the Indian tribes, including comments on the sources of their place-names, a map showing the location of the tribes after their dispersal, and terminology of the ancient site of Albany.

Comment on the work of the committee appears under title Indian names in American penny magazine 1:322, June 28, 1845.

2764. New York (State) Division of Archives and History. Geographic names; In New York (State) University. Annual report of the Education Department v. 40, pt. 1, p. 282. 1942-43.

Brief list of names of Adirondack peaks with origin.

2765. New York State Board of Geographic Names. American Geographical Society. Bulletin 46:365. 1914.

A report of the law, chap. 187, 1913, creating the Board. The personnel of the new board is listed in Bulletin 47:47. 1915.

2766. Norris, W. Glenn. The origin of place names in Tompkins County. Ithaca, N.Y., 1951. vii, 56p. maps. (DeWitt Historical Society of Tompkins County. Publication no. 6)

2767. Noyes, Marion F., ed. A history of Schoharie County. Richmondville, N.Y., Richmondville phoenix, 1954. 130p.

Schoharie County place-names: p. 106-14.

2768. Obsolete names of New York. American historian and quarterly genealogical record 1:30-36, 66-73, 113-17, 154-60, July 1875-April 1876.
The four issues of the magazine, all that were published, carried the alphabetical series through "Guy Johnson's patent."

2769. Obsolete towns and villages. New York civil list, 1855-88.
Each issue carries a list of towns and villages with changed names.

2770. O'Callaghan, Edmund Bailey. Indian names of places on the Hudson River. Historical magazine 3:218, July 1859.
"Designates the location of the places and is an extract from the Book of patents, New York."—Price.

2771. Origin of names of New York State counties. New York (State) University. Bulletin to the schools 10:122-23, 158, 170-71, 202, 252, Jan. 15-May 15, 1924.
Compiled by the Committee on Geographic Names, which assumed the duties of the former State Board of Geographic Names.

2772. Origin of place names on the Hudson River. n.d. 7p.
Typewritten manuscript in New York State Library, Albany.

2773. Osborne, Chester G. South Shore inlets and place names. Long Island forum 33:88-90, 116-18, June, July 1970.
Origin of the names.

2774. Paltsits, Victor Hugo. The classic nomenclature of western New York. Magazine of history 13:246-49, May 1911.
"Simeon DeWitt who surveyed the western section of the state has been blamed for bestowing classical place-names on localities. This exonerates him from the heinous deed, and places the responsibility on a committee of four men."—Price.

2775. Parker, Arthur Caswell. Indian episodes of New York State; a drama-story of the Empire State. A booklet of added information about the pictorial map by this name. Rochester, Rochester Museum of Arts and Sciences, 1935. 35p.
Notable Indian names: p. 32-33.

2776. —— Origin and pronunciation of the place name Mahopack. Mahopack weekly March 13, 1929.

2777. Petri, Pitt. The postal history of western New York: its post offices, its postmasters [Buffalo, N.Y., c1960]. 272p. maps.
Includes Genesee, Wyoming, Orleans, Niagara, Erie, Chautauqua, Cattaraugus, and Allegany counties.

2778. Philes, George Philip. "The godfather of the christened West", who was he? Ithaca, N.Y., DeWitt Historical Society of Tompkins County, Inc., 1961.
Written circa 1889, published anonymously in the Daily journal July 9, 1895, in protest of Harold Mack's proposal to change the name of Ithaca.
Philes documents the responsibility for naming 27 townships in the Military Tract erroneously ascribed to Simeon DeWitt.

2779. Place-names in Albany region. Halve Maen 38:8, Jan. 1964; 39:13, Jan. 1965.
Signed: E. R. V. K.

2780. Pollard, Ray F. A jaunt amongst Schoharie County place names and nicknames. Schoharie County historical review 14:25-28, Oct. 1950.

2781. —— Names and nicknames in Schoharie County. Schoharie County historical review 23:21-22, Spring 1959.

Names and nicknames of communities, roads, hills, turns, creeks, and points.

2782. Prince, John Dyneley. Some forgotten Indian place-names in the Adirondacks. Journal of American folklore 13:123-28, April-June 1900.

Reprinted in his Fragments from Babel (New York, Columbia Univ. Press, 1939), p. 165-71.

Derivation, pronunciation, and meaning of names from the Abnaki dialect.

2783. Pritchard, Georgiana. On the Erie Canal. New York folklore quarterly 10:45-47, Spring 1954.

On the origin of certain nicknames and place-names.

2783a. Read, Allen Walker. The quality of decisions by the United States Board on Geographic Names in northern New York; In Northeast Regional Names Institute. Names, Northeast, ed. by Murray Heller. Saranac Lake, N.Y., North Country Community College Press, 1979. p. 60-66. (Publication I)

2784. Reinstein, Julia Boyer. Cheektowaga: place names in New York State. Yesteryears no. 4:38-39, July 1958.

2785. Reynolds, Helen Wilkinson. In regard to the repetition of place names. Dutchess County Historical Society. Year book 18:54-57. 1933.

2786. —— Kromme Elleboog; a seventeenth century place-name in the Hudson Valley. Dutchess County Historical Society. Year book 18:58-68. 1933.

2787. —— Place-names again; something about Staatsburgh-Stoutsburgh-Stoutenburgh and Hyde Park. Dutchess County Historical Society. Year book 19:24-31. 1934.

2788. —— Poughkeepsie; the origin and meaning of the word. Poughkeepsie, 1924. 93p. (Dutchess County Historical Society. Collections v. 1)

Review: American speech 1:46-48, Oct. 1925.

2789. Ruttenber, Edward Manning. Atkarkarton-Atharhacton. Olde Ulster 3:270-74, Sept. 1907.

2790. —— Footprints of the red men. Indian geographical names in the valley of Hudson's River, the valley of the Mohawk, and on the Delaware: their location and the probable meaning of some of them. Pub. under the auspices of the New York State Historical Association. Newburgh, Newburgh Journal Print, 1906. 241p.

Included in New York State Historical Association. Proceedings v. 6. 1906.

2791. Sawyer, Donald J. The story of Bull Run. New York folklore quarterly 14:105-06, Summer 1958.

Legend behind a Fulton County place-name.

2792. Schoolcraft, Henry Rowe. Aboriginal nomenclature. Knickerbocker, or New York monthly magazine 58:109-14, Aug. 1861.

Origin of Indian names such as Neversink, Sing Sing, Poughkeepsie, etc.

2793. Schuyler, Elizabeth. Reasons for calling New York the Empire State. New York State Historical Association. Proceedings 15:280-88. 1916.

2794. Scott, Charles. Shawangunk, its meaning and origin. Olde Ulster 1:19-20, Jan. 1905.

2795. Scott, John A. Odd town names; explanation of classical designations in New York State. New York times Feb. 19, 1928, sec. 3, p. 5, col. 3.

2796. Scribner, Lynette Langer. North country place names. Ad-i-ron-dac 19:32-33, March-April 1955.

2797. —— Some Lake Champlain place names. Ad-i-ron-dac 19:50, May-June 1955.

2798. Sea-Cove Beach renamed. New York times Feb. 26, 1956, p. 65, col. 1.
The town of Oyster Bay renamed Sea-Cove Beach, in Sea Cliff and Glenwood Landing, the Harry Tappen Beach, to honor Mr. Tappen, who served as town supervisor for twenty years.

2799. Shaw, Ann. What's in a name? New York folklore quarterly 14:305-08. 1958.
Significance of some place-names in Westchester County.

2800. Simms, Jeptha R. Indian names. Historical magazine 3d ser. 1:120-21, Feb. 1872.
The origin and meaning of several aboriginal place-names in the region of the Mohawk Valley.

2801. Skilton, Frank Avery. Military township of Milton original name of the territory known at present as Ghoa. Advertiser-journal, Auburn, Aug. 21, 1925.

2802. Smith, Agnes Scott. The Dutch had a word for it. New York folklore quarterly 2:165-73, Aug. 1946.
Includes some Dutch place-names.

2803. Smith, Dorothy Guy. Strange names of school districts. New York folklore quarterly 1:152-59, Aug. 1945.
More schoolhouses, ibid. 2:64-65, Feb. 1946.
Cf. also J. C. Storms's article, no. 2810.

2804. Smith, James L. Erin: place names in New York State. Yesteryears no. 5:12, Oct. 1958.

2805. Sources of Wyoming County place names. Historical Wyoming 1:21-22, Nov. 1947.

2806. Spafford, Horatio Gates. A gazetteer of the State of New York: embracing an ample survey and description of its counties, towns, cities, villages, canals, mountains, lakes, rivers, creeks, and natural topography, with an appendix. Albany, B. D. Packard; Troy, The Author, 1824. 624p.
1st ed. Albany, 1813. 334p.

2807. Spears, Raymond Smiley. Adirondack place names. Forest and stream 56:403, May 25, 1901.

2808. —— Poke-o-Moonshine. Forest and stream 56:484, June 22, 1901.
Possible derivation of the name.
Cf. C. H. Ames's article, ibid. 56:503, June 29, 1901.

2809. Stevens, Ruth Perry. Oswego Township, Tioga County: place names in New York State. Yesteryears no. 4:23-26, July 1958.

2810. Storms, J. C. Why "Doodletown"? New York folklore quarterly 3:58-59, Spring 1947.

On a school district name.
Cf. Dorothy Guy Smith's article, no. 2803.

2811. Streets named for American artists in growing Munsey Park district. New York times Aug. 29, 1937, sec. 12, p. 1, col. 2-3.

2812. Strong, Kate Wheeler. Some strange old place-names. Long Island forum 15:109, 116, June 1952.

2813. Sugrue, Francis. Joy in Babylon: U.S. approves Sampawams as name of creek. Board on Geographic Names yields to campaign of letter writing; two weekly papers cite Huntington 1694 charter as authority. New York herald tribune Oct. 28, 1948.
Formerly popularly known as East Creek.

2814. Swaen, A. E. H. Dutch place-names in Eastern New York. American speech 5:400, June 1930.
Corrects errors in article by Edward Everett Hale, Jr., ibid. 5:154-67, Dec. 1929.

2815. Tallman, Wilfred B. Place names. South of the mountains (Tappan Zee Historical Society) v. 4, no. 1, Jan.-March 1960.
Covers Hudson River localities.

2816. Tappan, New York. Magazine of American History 8:51, Jan. 1882.
Using information in documents relating to the colonial history of New York, v. 13, this article adds a new interpretation of the origin of the name.

2817. Thompson, Benjamin Franklin. The Indian names of Long Island. New York Historical Society. Proceedings 1845:125-31.

2818. Thompson, H. H. Adirondack nomenclature. Field and stream 10:286-87, July 1905.
A plea for better names for the streams, lakes, and ponds of New York.

2819. —— "What's in a name?"—"Millions in it." American angler 4:199-200, Sept. 29, 1883.
Signed: H. H. T.
The aquatic nomenclature of New York State, with special reference to the streams, lakes, and ponds of the North Woods.

2820. Thompson, Harold William. Body, boots and britches. Philadelphia, Lippincott, 1940. 530p.
Place-names: p. 449-80.
History, humor, and beauty in New York State's place-names. Includes a list of Indian names with meanings as given by various authorities.

2821. Thull, Beulah Bailey. Dictionary of place names of Rensselaer County 1609-1971. [Troy, 1971]. 20 ℓ.

2822. Tianderra. Magazine of American history 18:83, July 1887.
Interprets the source of the names Tianderra and Ticonderoga.

2823. Tooker, William Wallace. The Indian names for Long Island, with historical and ethnological notes. New York, F. P. Harper, 1901. 49p. (The Algonquian series, no. 4)
Published originally in Brooklyn daily eagle almanac 1888:55-56; 1889:25-26; 1890:35-37.
Reprinted in Archaeologist 2:171-78, June 1894.

2824. —— Indian place-names in East-Hampton Town, L.I., with their probable significations; In East Hampton, N.Y. Records. Sag-Harbor, 1887-1905. 4:i-x.
Also published separately, Sag-Harbor, J. H. Hunt, 1889. x p.

2825. —— Indian place-names on Long Island. Brooklyn daily eagle almanac 1904, p. 409-410.

2826. —— The Indian place-names on Long Island and islands adjacent, with their probable significations; ed., with an introduction by Alexander F. Chamberlain; published for the John Jermain Memorial Library. New York, G. P. Putnam's Sons, 1911. 314p.
Reprinted: Port Washington, N.Y., I. J. Friedman, 1962. xxviii, 314p. (Empire State historical publications, 6)
Bibliography: p. 303-14.
Review: American historical review 17:410-11, Jan. 1912; Dial 51:346, Nov. 1, 1911.
Review of 1962 reprint edition: Hamill Kenny, Names 13:58-61, March 1965.

2827. —— Some Indian fishing stations upon Long Island, with historical and ethnological notes. New York, F. P. Harper, 1901. 62p. (The Algonquian series, VII)
Read before the American Association for the Advancement of Science, Section H, 1894, and published in the Brooklyn eagle almanac for 1895.

2828. —— Some Indian names of places on Long Island, N.Y. and their correspondences in Virginia, as mentioned by Capt. John Smith and associates. Magazine of New England history 1:154-58, July 1891.

2829. —— Some supposed Indian names of places on Long Island. Long Island magazine 1:51-54, May 1893.
Names that have been misinterpreted or misunderstood.

2830. Trumbull, James Hammond. Indian names of places on Long Island, derived from esculent roots. Magazine of American history 1:386-87, June 1877.

2831. —— Long Island Indians. Magazine of American history 1:330, May 1877.
The origin and meaning of the former names Punksole or Punk's Hole for what is now Manorville.

2832. Tucker, Louis Leonard. Letter [explaining functions of the New York State Committee on Geographic Names]. New York times May 3, 1970, sec. 4, p. 15.
The author, chairman of the committee, cites its refusal to change Sucker Lake or Smoky Point in reply to recent letters on changing place-names.

2833. Tuomey, Douglas. What's in a name? Long Island forum 23:29-30, Feb. 1960.
The derivation of some of the odd names given to points on Long Island by the early settlers.

2834. Tuxedo Club, Tuxedo Park, N.Y. Report to the executive committee of the Tuxedo Club, from the committee appointed to examine into the original historical names of the Tuxedo region; together with a copy of the manuscript map of this portion of New York and New Jersey, made for Washington in the years 1778-1779. New York, 1888. 7p.

2835. Tyler, Alberta V. Cochecton: place names in New York State. Yesteryears no. 4:11-13, July 1958.

2836. Van Dyne, Maud. Canadice: place names in New York State. Yesteryears no. 4:14-15, July 1958.

2837. Van Epps, Percy M. The place names of Glenville; In Glenville, N.Y. Historian. Report 1:1-4. 1926.
Also in New York State Historical Association. Quarterly journal 9:272-78, July 1928.

2838. Van Voris, Arthur H. Aboriginal place names in Schoharie County. Schoharie County historical review 17:3-8, May 1953.

2839. Ver Nooy, Amy. Place-names and folklore in Dutchess County. New York folklore quarterly 20:42-47, March 1964.

2840. Wallkill. Olde Ulster 1:183, June 1905.

2841. The Wallkill. Olde Ulster 6:341-43, Nov. 1910.

2842. Want towns hyphenated, Ardsley, Croton and Hastings ask "-on-Hudson" spelling. New York times April 10, 1948, p. 15.
Favorable decision: U.S. Board on Geographic Names. Decision list no. 4801, p. 11.

2843. Warner, Anne. The counties of the Empire State. New York folklore quarterly 12:292-93, Winter 1956.
The counties arranged in a song, used by New York children to learn them.

2844. Weise, A. J. Paanpaack the site of Troy, N.Y. Magazine of American history 1:682-83, Nov. 1877.
Origin and source of Paanpaack or Pontpacht which was later changed to Troy.

2845. Wells, Charles F. Streets with celestial names. New York folklore quarterly 15:169-71, Autumn 1959.
Streets in Oswego, N.Y., originally named for constellations, later changed.

2846. Whalen, George E. Dover, and how it got its name. Dutchess County Historical Society. Year book 33:38-41. 1948.

2847. What's in a name? Harper's weekly 4:147, March 10, 1860.
Why have we not retained the Indian names? Why was the classical dictionary spilt all over western New York?

2848. White, William Pierrepont. New York classical names due to Governor Clinton. New York times Feb. 26, 1928, sec. 3, p. 5, col. 1-2.
Clinton presided at meeting in 1790 which supplied designations for towns in bonus grants to soldiers.
Followed by letter of Robert E. Moody in regard to part played by the commissioners of the New York Land Office and quoting from John Franklin Jameson, The American Revolution considered as a social movement (Princeton, N.J., Princeton Univ. Press, 1926. p. 64-65).

2849. Wright, Albert Hazen. Simeon DeWitt and Military Tract township names. Ithaca, N.Y., pub. by The Author for DeWitt Historical Society of Tompkins County, 1961. 17p.

New York City

2850. Any name would do, just so it's 6th Ave. New York times June 4, 1966, p. 31, col. 1.
City Councilman Joseph Modugno offers compromise bill changing name of the avenue to Sixth Avenue of the Americas.

2851. Arciniegas, German. America's avenue. Letter. New York times Dec. 13, 1965, p. 38, col. 3.
Former Minister of Education of Colombia opposes restoration of name Sixth Avenue.

2852. Ashley, Leonard R. N. So Ho, No Ho, Lo Ho, and just So So: the commercial and cultural implications of some New York City neighborhood names. Canadian Society for the Study of Names. Onomastica 55:14-26, June 1979.

2853. Back to Sixth Avenue. Editorial. New York times Dec. 4, 1965, p. 30, col. 2.
Supports Councilman Paul O'Dwyer's bill to restore name Sixth Avenue to the Avenue of the Americas.

2854. Badillo selects Sound View as name for area in Bronx. New York times Sept. 3, 1967, p. 41, col. 2.

2855. Berger, Meyer. About New York. New York times Dec. 18, 1939, p. 20, col. 3-4.
Early names for New York streets.

2856. Birss, John Howard. "Mannahatta." American speech 9:154-55, April 1934.
Notes on the appearance of the word.

2857. Blumengarten, Jeannette G. Flatbush place-names. January 1960. 84p.
Thesis (M.A.) Brooklyn College, 1960. On file in the College Library, the Brooklyn Public Library, and the Long Island Historical Society Library.

2858. Bowen, Croswell. Topics: in search of Sixth Avenue. New York times April 1, 1970, p. 44, col. 3-6.
Recalls the 1945 name change to the Avenue of the Americas and assesses the improvement to the image of the former Sixth Avenue.

2859. Breasted, Mary. Street name change stirs a tempest in melting pot. New York times May 4, 1976, p. 39.
Change of Graham Avenue, Brooklyn, to Avenue of Puerto Rico set aside by Mayor Beame who approved designation of Haym Salomon Square in Queens, and change of Weir Creek Park, The Bronx, to Bicentennial Veterans Memorial Park.

2860. Brinley, C. Coapes. The origin of street names of old West Brighton. Staten Island historian 20:1-4, Jan.-March 1959.

2861. Bryant, Margaret M. Some Indian and Dutch names reflecting the early history of Brooklyn. Names 20:106-10, June 1972.

2862. Call it Sixth Avenue, Council bill urges. New York times Dec. 4, 1965, p. 33.
Councilman Paul O'Dwyer files a bill to restore former name to the Avenue of the Americas.

2863. Change of name of Bedloe's Island, N.Y., to Liberty Island. U.S. Congress. Congressional record v. 102, pt. 9, p. 11539, July 2, 1956.
S. J. Res. 114 passed by the Senate.

2864. Changing the name of Bedloe's Island in New York Harbor to Liberty Island. U.S. Congress. Congressional record v. 102, pt. 10, p. 14029-30, July 23, 1956.
Remarks in the House on S. J. Res. 114. Passed.

2865. City draws borders for 87 neighborhoods. Districts mapped as a step to meeting particular needs. New York times July 16, 1962, p. 25.

Designation of neighborhoods in New York City for planning purposes, and consideration of historic names for these communities, such as The Village, Bushwick, Tottenville, etc.

2866. Council would honor MacArthur by renaming East River Drive. New York times April 11, 1942, p. 15, col. 3.
New York City.

2867. Crane, Frank W. History written in street names. New York times Feb. 22, 1942, sec. 10, p. 1, col. 5, p. 2, col. 5.

2868. Davis, William Thompson. Staten Island names; ye olde names and nicknames. With map by Charles W. Leng. New Brighton, Natural Science Assoc., 1896. 76p. (Proceedings of the Natural Science Association of Staten Island, v. 5, no. 5, Special no. 21, March 14, 1896)

2869. —— Supplement to Staten Island names; ye olde names and nicknames. New Brighton, Natural Science Assoc., 1903. 91p. (Proceedings of the Natural Science Association of Staten Island, v. 8, no. 25, Special no. 23)

2870. Devine, Thomas. "Sixth Avenue" preferred. New York times Oct. 8, 1962, p. 22.
A letter to the editor comments on the difficulty in accepting the new name Avenue of the Americas in New York City.

2871. Douglas, Verne. New York City incorrect. New York times Feb. 22, 1945, p. 26, col. 7.
Letter pointing out that correct name of the post office is New York, N.Y.

2872. Dunshee, Kenneth Holcomb. As you pass by. New York, Hastings House, 1952. 270p.
A directory of forgotten streets [in New York City]: p. [272-78].

2873. Eardeley, James W. A system of street nomenclature for Greater New York. 1932. 170p.
Manuscript in New York Public Library, Local History Division.

2874. Early names of city's streets were descriptively conferred. New York times Nov. 11, 1928, sec. 10, p. 22, col. 7.
Such streets in New York City as Pie Woman's Lane.

2875. Eno, Joel Nelson. New York county names. Magazine of history 22:76-82, 127-30, 166-69, March-May 1916; 23:11-15, 126-28, July, Sept. 1916.

2876. Field, Thomas Warren. Indian, Dutch and English names of localities in Brooklyn. Brooklyn. Common Council. Manual 1868:459-70.
Reprinted in his Historic and antiquarian scenes in Brooklyn and its vicinity (Brooklyn, 1868; p. 49-60), with note calling attention to errors in orthography and signification.

2877. Fowler, Glenn. That Avenue gets an "A" for effort; "Rip Van Winkle" ignorers of Avenue of the Americas given ninepin award. New York times April 2, 1965, p. 37, col. 8.
Twentieth anniversary of Mayor Fiorello H. LaGuardia's action to change the name of Sixth Avenue.

2878. Frigand, Sidney J. New York street names. City said to hold its own with Paris in nomenclature. New York times Feb. 19, 1962, p. 30.

This letter to the editor, in reply to the Topics column of Feb. 6 (In Paris a street keeps its name), lists unusual names.

2879. Gay, Alva A. "Madison Avenue." American speech 34:232, Oct. 1959.
"A name not only for the large advertising and public relations companies with offices on Madison Avenue, New York, but also, more generally, for all national advertising," p. 232.

2880. Geographic Board rules Liberty Island is Bedloe's. New York times Jan. 3, 1940, p. 19, col. 2; editorial Jan. 4, 1940, p. 22, col. 4.

2881. Goldstone, Harmon H. Letter opposing public zeal for changing well-established place names. New York times March 16, 1970, p. 42, col. 5.
Goldstone was chairman of the New York City Landmarks Preservation Committee. Examples cited: The Avenue of the Americas, Franklin Delano Roosevelt Drive, and Blackwell's Island, which became Welfare Island in 1921.

2882. Gotham. New Yorker 41:19-20, Aug. 7, 1965.
Nickname for New York.

2883. Greenwich intersection named "Village Square." New York times Nov. 4, 1939, p. 15, col. 2.
Changed from Jefferson Market Square, New York City.

2884. Haber, Richard. Gravesend place-names. May 1964. xliii, 239p.
Thesis (M.A.) Brooklyn College, 1964. On file in the College Library, the Brooklyn Public Library, and the Long Island Historical Society Library.

2885. Henlein, Millard. Sixth Avenue a memory. Letter in reply to Ira Howel Wallach. New York times July 23, 1964, p. 26, col. 6.
Executive vice-president of the Avenue of the Americas Association, notes the improved and impressive character of the avenue since its name change.

2886. Hoffman, Henry B. Changed house numbers and lost street names in New York of the early nineteenth century and later. New York Historical Society. Quarterly bulletin 21:67-92, July 1937.

2887. How famous downtown streets in New York got their names. Brooklyn eagle April 15, 1917.

2888. Hurst, Fannie. Return to Sixth Avenue. Letter. New York times Dec. 18, 1965, p. 28, col. 6.
Approves restoration of name Sixth Avenue to the Avenue of the Americas.

2889. In Paris a street keeps its name. New York times Feb. 6, 1962, p. 34, col. 3.
In the Topics column, the street-naming customs of Paris are contrasted with those of New York City.
For reply, see Sidney J. Frigand, New York street names, ibid. Feb. 19, 1962, p. 30.

2890. Indians, animals and history. New York times Feb. 27, 1961, p. 26L, col. 3.
In the Topics column. Theories concerning the origin of the name Coney Island.

2891. An Inquiry into the who's, whens, whys and hows of naming streets in this great city. New York times April 25, 1937, sec. 4, p. 9, col. 1.
Describes the work of the Aldermanic Committee on Public Thoroughfares, which is the street-naming body for New York City.

2892. Irving and "Gotham." New York times Dec. 4, 1962, p. 40.
The Topics column, devoted to the nickname Gotham for New York City, first used by Washington Irving in Salmagundi (New York, D. Longworth, 1807-08).

2893. It was once "Bronck's Land." Americana 6:1021-22, Oct. 1911.
Origin of the name Bronx.

2894. It's Elk Street now, not Elm. New York times Feb. 17, 1939, p. 14, col. 5.
Elm St. changed to Elk, New York City.

2895. It's still Sixth Avenue to many, but not to its newest tenants. New York times Sept. 23, 1962, p. 18R.
New prestige businesses on the avenue are using the new name Avenue of the Americas.

2896. Johnston, Laurie. Bronx street is named to honor slain Entebbe-raid commander. New York times June 13, 1977, p. 33.
Lt. Col. Yehonatan Netanyahu, the New York-born commander killed in the raid July 3, 1976.

2897. Kaufman, Michael T. Council weighs making Staten Island official. New York times Aug. 28, 1974, p. 31M.

2898. Leighten, George R. On fitting a name to a street. New York times magazine Oct. 21, 1945, p. 16, 53-54.
Reviews attempts to change street names in New York City.

2899. Letters on names for numbered avenues, New York City. New York times Dec. 1, 1937, p. 22, col. 6; Dec. 4, p. 16, col. 7; Dec. 7, p. 24, col. 7; Dec. 9, p. 24, col. 7.

2900. Liberman, Elaine A. Williamsburgh place-names. January 1965. 69p.
Thesis (M.A.) Brooklyn College, 1965. On file in the College Library, the Brooklyn Public Library, and the Long Island Historical Society Library.

2901. Liberty Isle irks Mr. Curran. New York times Aug. 8, 1941, p. 17, col. 4; editorial, Aug. 9, p. 14, col. 2; letter, Aug. 14, p. 16, col. 7; bill offered, Aug. 15, p. 19, col. 2.
Congress proposes to change name of Ellis Island to Liberty Isle.

2902. Ludwig, John Warner. Alphabet of greatness: Manhattan's street names. New York, 1961. 264 ℓ.
Typescript. Copy in New York Public Library.

2903. —— Street names of Manhattan and the stories they tell. New York, 1953. 170 ℓ.
Typescript. Copy in the New York Public Library.

2904. McNamara, John. History in asphalt: the origin of the Bronx street and place names. Harrison, N.Y., Harbor Hill Books, c1978. 528p.

2905. —— Two G's or not two G's—that is the question. Names 13:69-72, March 1965.
Throg's, Throgg's, Throg's—variant spellings used in the Point, Neck, and Bridge and in other names, in the New York City area.

2906. Marlowe, Nicholas. Bedford-Stuyvesant place-names. January 1963. 69p.
Thesis (M.A.) Brooklyn College, 1963. On file in the College Library, the Brooklyn Public Library, and the Long Island Historical Library.

2907. Minsky, Pearl G. Canarsie place-names. January 1963. 116p.
Thesis (M.A.) Brooklyn College, 1963. On file in the College Library, the Brooklyn Public Library, and the Long Island Historical Society Library.

2908. Moscow, Henry. The street book, an encyclopedia of Manhattan's street names and their origins. New York, Hagstrom Co., 1978. 119p. maps.
Review: Kelsie B. Harder, Names 28:87-88, March 1980.

2909. Name of 6th Ave. to be changed to the Avenue of the Americas. New York times Sept. 21, 1945, p. 23, col. 3; Sept. 25, p. 24, col. 7; Sept. 29, p. 17, col. 7; Sept. 30, sec. 8, p. 1, col. 5; Oct. 3, p. 21, col. 1; Oct. 4, p. 22, col. 3; Oct. 22, p. 16, col. 2.
New York City.

2910. Naming of streets for veterans scored. New York times July 27, 1938, p. 15, col. 4.
Mayor of New York refuses to sign bills calling for changes.

2911. O'Brien, Michael J. The story of old Leary Street, or Cortland Street—the Leary family in early New York history. American Irish Historical Society. Journal 15:112-17, April 1916.
Various names by which Cortland St. has been known, with some history of the family for whom it was at one time named.

2912. Old city streets recalled by deal. New York times March 14, 1937, sec. 14, p. 1, col. 1, p. 4, col. 3; letters March 20, p. 18, col. 7; March 30, p. 22, col. 7.
Lower East Side in New York.

2913. Old names for old streets. New York times March 17, 1930, p. 22, col. 6.
Editorial on New York City.

2914. Old street names to be retained in Queens section. New York times Sept. 27, 1967, p. 49, col. 1.
Old names to be retained in Douglas Manor, not to be replaced with numbers.

2915. On re-naming street and schools. American city 60:116, Dec. 1945.
Comments, including an amusing editorial from the New York times, on the proposed change of New York's Sixth Avenue to Avenue of the Americas.

2916. Pastore, John O. Change in name of Bedloe's Island in New York Harbor to Liberty Island. U.S. Congress. Congressional record v. 102, pt. 1, p. 229-30, Jan. 9, 1956.
Remarks on introduction in the Senate of S.J. Res. 114.

2917. Pearlman, Archie. East New York place-names. June 1965. 100, viii p.
Thesis (M.A.) Brooklyn College, 1965. On file in the College Library, the Brooklyn Public Library, the Long Island Historical Society Library, and New York Municipal Reference Library.

2918. Plaza to be named for Cadman. New York times May 10, 1939, p. 25, col. 1.
Brooklyn Bridge Plaza to be changed to S. Parkes Cadman Plaza.

2919. Post, John J. Old streets, roads, lanes, piers and wharves of New York, showing the former and present names, together with a list of alterations of streets,

either by extending, widening, narrowing or closing. New York, R. D. Cooke, 1882. 76p.
In three parts: (1) Former name and present name or location, (2) Present name and former name, (3) Street alterations.

2920. Rashkin, Henry. Bay Ridge place names. August 1960. 47p.
Thesis (M.A.) Brooklyn College, 1960. On file in the College Library, the Brooklyn Public Library, and the Long Island Historical Society Library.

2921. Rhodes, Jerome. The form of street addresses. American speech 33:116-17, May 1958.
Omission of Street in Manhattan but not in other boroughs of New York.
Cf. articles by Allan F. Hubbell, ibid. 32:233-34, Oct. 1957, and G. Thomas Fairclough, ibid. 33:299-300, Dec. 1958.

2922. Ricard, Herbert F. The origin of community names in Queens Borough; In New York (City) Borough of Queens. Historian. Annual report 1:5-15. 1944.

2923. Rubel, Tamara K. Place names in Brooklyn Heights. May 1963. 73p.
Thesis (M.A.) Brooklyn College, 1963. On file in the College Library, the Brooklyn Public Library, and the Long Island Historical Society Library.

2924. Schmauch, W. W. Thoroughfares of the world—the highways and byways of New York. Economy spectator 2:1, 3, March 10, 1931; 2:1, 4, April 10, 1931.
The changes in names in old New York.

2925. Schoolcraft, Henry Rowe. Indian names of the islands and bay of New York; In Denton, Daniel. A brief description of New York. New ed. New York, William Gowans, 1845. p. 23-27.
Reprinted from Broadway journal 1:138-39, March 1845.

2926. Scott, Charles R. What's in a name, "Bowling Green." Telephone review 7:315-18, Nov. 1916.
History of the area from which a new telephone exchange name was adopted.

2927. Sherman, Herman. Red Hook place-names. June 1965. 102p.
Thesis (M.A.) Brooklyn College, 1965. On file in the College Library, the Brooklyn Public Library, the Long Island Historical Society Library, and the New York Municipal Reference Library.

2928. Shulman, David. Coney Island's name. New York times Sept. 26, 1938, p. 16, col. 6-7.

2929. Smith, Thelma E. The islands of New York City. New York Public Library. Municipal Reference Library. Notes 36:97-102, 122-23, June, Sept. 1962.

2930. Square honors Col. Conroy. New York times Feb. 11, 1945, p. 6, col. 1.
Law signed designating as Col. J. Gardiner Conroy Square the intersection of Flatbush, St. Mark's, and Sixth aves. in Brooklyn.

2931. Straus, Nathan. Memorials—to whom? Art news 60:25, April 1961.
Editorial. Most of the text of an address over Station WMCA, New York, citing examples of the system of naming highways and other public improvements in New York City for people, and suggesting creation of a Commission of Memorials charged with the responsibility of selecting the individuals to be honored.

2932. [Streets named for literary figures in New York City] New York Public Library. Municipal Reference Library. Notes 36:12-14, Jan. 1962.
In the Knickerbocker scrapbook column.

2933. Tooker, William Wallace. Indian names of places in the Borough of Brooklyn, with historical and ethnological notes. New York, F. P. Harper, 1901. 53p. (The Algonquin series, no. 2)
From Brooklyn eagle almanac 1893:58-60, with corrections and additions.

2934. —— The origin of the name Manhattan, with historical and ethnological notes. Map. New York, F. P. Harper, 1901. 75p. (The Algonquian series, no. 1)
From Brooklyn eagle almanac for 1897, rev. and enl.

2935. Tottenville recovers its name. Americana 5:1195, Dec. 1910.
Post-Revolutionary name restored and maintained because of historic sentiment.

2936. Ulmann, Albert. Historic events as street names. New York times Aug. 2, 1946, p. 18, col. 6.
Use in New York City.

2937. —— A landmark history of New York; also the origin of street names and a bibliography. New ed. New York, Appleton, 1903. 285p.
1st ed. 1901. 285p. Reprinted: Port Washington, N.Y., Ira J. Friedman, [1969].
Origin of street names: p. 258-67.

2938. —— A landmark history of New York, including a guide to commemorative sites and monuments. New York, Appleton-Century, 1939. 440p.
Origin of street and place names: p. 421-31.

2939. U.S. Congress. Senate. Committee on Interior and Insular Affairs. Change in name of Bedloe's Island . . . Report to accompany S.J. Res. 114. June 26, 1956. Washington, 1956. 4p. (U.S. 84th Congress, 2d session. Senate. Report no. 2356. Calendar no. 2380)
Includes references to the disapproval of the change by the Board on Geographic Names.

2940. U.S. 84th Congress, 2d session. Senate. Joint resolution to change the name of Bedloe's Island in New York Harbor to Liberty Island. S.J. Res. 114. Jan. 9, 1956. Washington, 1956. 2p.
Introduced by Mr. Pastore and referred to the Committee on Interior and Insular Affairs.
Proposes a more appropriate name for the island on which stands the Statue of Liberty and on which the American Museum of Immigration will be built.

2941. U.S. Laws, statutes, etc. Joint resolution to change the name of Bedloe's Island in New York Harbor to Liberty Island. Public law 936. (United States statutes at large. 84th Congress. 2d session. 1956. v. 70, p. 956, Chapter 902)
S.J. Res. 114 became law Aug. 3, 1956.
Newspaper articles that tell the story of this change follow, in chronological order:
Senators favor naming Bedloe's "Liberty Island." New York times June 7, 1956, p. 9, col. 4.
A Senate Interior subcommittee adopted a joint resolution to change the name of Bedloe's Island to Liberty Island. Includes list of previous names of the island.

"Liberty Island." New York times June 8, 1956, p. 24, col. 3.
Editorial in support of the proposed change.

Bedloes Island change backed. New York times June 27, 1956, p. 14, col. 5.
The Senate Interior and Insular Affairs Committee approved changing name.

Liberty Island bill advances. New York times July 3, 1956, p. 16, col. 8.
The Senate passed and sent to the House legislation to change the name of Bedloe's Island to Liberty Island.

Bedloes Island bill gains. New York times July 7, 1956, p. 15, col. 4.
The bill to change the name won the approval of a House Interior subcommittee.

Bedloes bill delayed. New York times July 11, 1956, p. 31, col. 1.
Several committee members and the Budget Bureau opposed the change, contending it would outdate maps and charts of New York harbor. U.S. Board on Geographic Names also opposed.

Statue of Liberty site is voted a new name. New York times July 24, 1956, p. 27, col. 6.
House of Representatives passed and sent to the President the Senate-approved resolution to change the name of Bedloe's Island to Liberty Island. Lists previous names.

It's Liberty Island now. New York times Aug. 4, 1956, p. 17, col. 1.
President Eisenhower signs bill giving new name to Bedloe's Island.

Topics of the Times. New York times Aug. 24, 1956, p. 18, col. 4.
Reports unfavorable comments of a citizen on the change from Bedloe's to Liberty Island.

Statue of Liberty celebrates at 70. New York times Oct. 29, 1956, p. 31, col. 6.
Includes mention of the commemoration of the official change of name to Liberty Island by the unveiling of a plaque, presented by the Downtown Manhattan Association.

Nevins, Allan. Epic of Liberty Island. New York times Oct. 28, 1956, sec. 6, p. 15, 67-69.
A review of the history of immigration, occasioned by the renaming of Bedloe's Island to Liberty Island.

2942. Wall, Alexander J. Blackwell's Island. New York Historical Society. Quarterly bulletin 5:35-42, July 1921.
Reprinted in part in Valentine's manual of old New York 8:341-52. 1924.
Reviewing the Society's protest of the change by New York City to Welfare Island.

2943. Wallach, Ira. Where's Sixth Avenue? Letter. New York times July 10, 1964, p. 28, col. 6.
Confusion because Sixth Avenue was renamed the Avenue of the Americas.

2944. Weisman, Carl M. Brooklyn from Breukelen and Bruijkleen. Names 1:39-40, March 1953.

2945. Williams, John D. Place names in Sea Gate, Coney Island, Brighton Beach and Manhattan Beach. August 1964. 92p.
Thesis (M.A.) Brooklyn College, 1964. On file in the College Library, the Brooklyn Public Library, and the Long Island Historical Society Library.

NORTH CAROLINA

2946. Abenethy, Edgar. Unusual names. State magazine 10:14-15, Jan. 30, 1943.

2947. Battle, Kemp Plummer. Glimpses of history in the names of our counties. North Carolina booklet 6:27-48, July 1906.

2948. —— The names of the counties of North Carolina and the history involved in them. Winston, W. A. Blair, 1888. 38p.

2949. —— North Carolina county names. Magazine of history with notes and queries 7:208-22, April 1908.

2950. Cooper, Elizabeth Scott. How Ocracoke got its name. North Carolina folklore 4:19-21, Dec. 1956.
The legend of the name in ballad form.

2951. Cumming, William Patterson. Naming Carolina. North Carolina historical review 22:34-42, Jan. 1945.
Reprinted without the footnotes: Names in South Carolina 9:14-18, Winter 1962.
Part of a study made with the aid of a grant from the Social Science Research Council.

2952. Edwards, Richard. Statistical gazetteer of the states of Virginia and North Carolina; embracing important topographical and historical information, from recent and original sources with the results of the last census, in many cases to 1855. Richmond, Published for the proprietor, 1856. 601p.

2953. Fink, Paul M. Smoky Mountains history as told in place-names. East Tennessee Historical Society. Publications 6:3-11. 1934.

2954. —— That's why they call it . . . The names and lore of the Great Smokies. Jonesboro, Tenn., P. M. Fink, 1956. 20p.

2955. —— & Myron H. Avery. The nomenclature of the Great Smoky Mountains. East Tennessee Historical Society. Publications 9:53-64. 1937.
Abstracted under the title Arnold Guyot's explorations in the Great Smokies. Appalachia 2:253-61, Dec. 1936.
A major portion of the names either originated with or were confirmed as a result of Arnold Guyot's exploration of the region in the period 1856-60.

2956. Fish, Frederic F. A catalog of the inland fishing waters of North Carolina. Raleigh. [North Carolina Division of Inland Fisheries]. 1968. 312p.
Reprinted: Raleigh, N.C., Graphic Press, c1969. xliii, 188p. maps.
Includes every known fresh-water stream as well as every known lake exceeding 25 acres in area which is open to public fishing.

2957. Gatschet, Albert Samuel. Onomatology of the Catawba River basin. American anthropologist n.s. 4:52-56, Jan.-March 1902.
Also issued separately.

2958. Here's how to start a name collection. Chicago tribune Dec. 1, 1957, pt. 6, p. 12.
Different categories found in North Carolina.

2959. [Hudson, A. P.]. Buncombe—talking to Buncombe. North Carolina folklore 5:23, Dec. 1957.
Popular etymology of the place-name.

2960. Jackson, Sarah Evelyn. Place-names in Ashe County, North Carolina. Names 26:96-105, March 1978.

2961. Jacocks, W. P. Bertie County stream names and their origins. Bertie County Historical Society. Chronicle 6:3-4, Oct. 1958.

2962. Lanman, Charles. The Catawba country of North Carolina. Magazine of history 19:92-100, Aug.-Sept. 1914.

Contains source and significance of names of the Ginger Cake Mountain and Roan Mountain in North Carolina.

2963. Lawrence, R. C. Many changes in names. State magazine 11:6, March 16, 1944.

2964. Lindbergh Drive no longer, New York times June 14, 1941, p. 19, col. 4.
Lindbergh Drive, Charlotte, changed to Avon Ave.

2965. Mason, Robert L. A famous landmark is in dispute, two states contend over changing the name of Mt. Collins. New York times Aug. 31, 1930, sec. 8, p. 9, col. 2-4.
Mount Kephart desired for peak in Smoky Mountains National Park, but U.S. Board on Geographical Names refused.

2966. Mook, Maurice A. Algonkian ethnohistory of the Carolina Sound. Washington Academy of Science. Journal 34:181-97, June 15, 1944. map.
Early Algonkian tribes and towns shown on the map, and discussed in the article.

2967. Naming of places in the Carolinas. Names in South Carolina 14:36-41, Winter 1967.
Unsigned article reprinted from The Southern and western monthly magazine and review, Dec. 1845.

2968. Peak named for Cammerer, Smoky Mountain ridge also honors park director. New York times Feb. 25, 1942, p. 24, col. 2.
Great Smoky Mountains National Park peak named for Arno B. Cammerer.

2969. Powell, William Stevens. The North Carolina gazetteer. Chapel Hill, Univ. of North Carolina Press, [1968]. xviii, 561p. maps.
Includes origin and meaning of names, when available.
Review: Byrd Howell Granger, Names 17:312-14, Dec. 1969.

2970. Quinn, David Beers, ed. The Roanoke voyages, 1584-1590, documents illustrating the English voyages to North America under the patent granted to Walter Raleigh in 1584. London, The Hakluyt Society, 1955. 2v. (Hakluyt Society works, 2d ser. v. 104)
Part C. Commentary on the map of Raleigh's Virginia [part 2], p. 852-72.
Algonquian place-names in Virginia and North Carolina north and south of the swamp which marks the present state line between the two states.

2971. Reeves, Paschal. Thomas Wolfe's "Old Catawba." Names 11:254-56, Dec. 1963.
Thomas Wolfe's fictional name for North Carolina. Derivation of Catawba.

2972. Reynolds, Thurlow Weed. Born of the mountains. [Highlands? N.C., 1964]. 179p.

2973. —— High lands. [Highlands? N.C., 1964]. 178p.
Review of both titles: Kelsie B. Harder, Names 13:133-35, June 1965.
Both books include extensive material on names in the mountains of North Carolina and adjacent states.

2974. Shellans, Herbert. Table d'hote. Towns, counties and places, North Carolina. Names 11:270-71, Dec. 1963.
Names of places listed in the form of a menu for breakfast, luncheon, and dinner.

2975. —— Tarheel place names. North Carolina folklore 4:28-32, Dec. 1956.

2976. "Tar Heels." American speech 1:355, March 1926.
An explanation, in a talk by Maj. William A. Graham, April 25, 1915, of how North Carolinians came to be called by that name.

2977. U.S. Board on Geographic Names. Decisions. No. 28, June 30, 1932. Great Smoky Mountains National Park, North Carolina and Tennessee. Washington, Govt. Print. Off., 1934. 46p.

2978. U.S. Writers' Program. North Carolina. How they began—the story of North Carolina county, town and other place names, comp. by workers of the WPA Writers' Program of the Work Projects Administration in the State of North Carolina. Sponsored by North Carolina Dept. of Conservation & Development, Raleigh, N.C. New York, Harian Publications, 1941. 73p.

2979. Weslager, C. A. Place names on Ocracoke Island. North Carolina historical review 31:41-49, Jan. 1954.

2980. What's in a name, being a continuation of the origin of various place names in counties of North Carolina. State magazine 11:3, March 18, 1944.

2981. Wilburn, Hiram C. Judaculla place-names and the Judaculla tales. Southern Indian studies 4:23-26, Oct. 1952.
Deals with the geographical location and the meaning of natural features and objects that owe their names and stories to the mythological life and activities of the giant Judaculla.

2982. Wilson, E. W. Names in the mountains. State magazine 10:4, March 13, 1943.

NORTH DAKOTA

2983. "Beaver Lodge"—how an oilfield gets its name. Wall Street journal May 12, 1952, p. 1.
In Williams County.

2984. Bessasson, Haraldur. Icelandic place names in Manitoba and North Dakota. Linguistic Circle of Manitoba and North Dakota. Proceedings 2:8-10, May 1960.

2985. Gilmore, Melvin Randolph. Meaning of the word Dakota. American anthropologist n.s. 24:242-45, April-June 1922.
The author considers Dakota to be a derivative of the same root as the Omaha endakutha, and he believes that both words should be taken in the sense "peculiar people" rather than in the sense "friends."

2986. Hughes, Dorothy J. Coined town-names of North Dakota. American speech 14:315, Dec. 1939.

2987. Reid, Russell. Name origins of North Dakota cities, towns and counties. North Dakota history 13:118-43, July 1946.
Based on data gathered by the North Dakota Federal Writers' Project. Contains names of the counties, and place-names A-C; apparently no more published.

2988. Spokesfield, Walter Earnest. The history of Wells County, North Dakota, and its pioneers, with a sketch of North Dakota history and the oregin [sic] of the place names. Valley City, N.D., 1929. 804p.

2989. The State Geographic Board report on North Dakota. North Dakota historical quarterly 2:53-56, Oct. 1927.

"Describes the work of the Board and discusses the 'Seven chief places of historical interest in North Dakota' and 'Places of greatest interest in North Dakota.'"—Price.

2990. Thompson, Roy. The naming of Cando. North Dakota. State Historical Society. Collections 3:321-23. 1910.
"This name is an illustration of a coined word, 'Can-do.' It proved that a small group of men could locate and name, in spite of the opposition of the settlers, the county seat of Towner County, North Dakota."—Price.

2991. Williams, Mary Ann Barnes. Origins of North Dakota place names. Washburn, N.D., Bismarck tribune, 1966. 354p.
"The chief aim has been to find the origin of the name of places white men have established and named—not geographical names nor Indian villages, although the location and facts of historical significance are often included."
Index: Janice Liddle, Index to Mary Ann Barnes Williams' Origins of North Dakota place names. Fargo, Institute for Regional Studies, North Dakota State Univ., 1977. 56p. map.

2992. —— Origins of North Dakota place names: Benson, Cavalier, Pembina, Ramsey, Walsh counties. Washburn, N.D., 1961. 56p.

2993. —— Origins of North Dakota place names: Cass and Barnes counties. Washburn, N.D., 1959. 20p.

2994. —— Origins of North Dakota place names: McLean and Burleigh counties. Washburn, N.D., 1959. 26p.

2995. —— Origins of North Dakota place names: Morton, Mercer, Oliver, Grant, Sioux counties. Washburn, N.D., 1959. 34p.

2996. —— Origins of North Dakota place names: Stutsman, Wells, Foster, Eddy, Kidder counties. Washburn, N.D., 1959. 32p.

2997. —— Origins of North Dakota place names: Ward, Renville, Burke, Mountrail counties. Washburn, N.D., 1959. 22p.

OHIO

2998. Armstrong, J. R. A table of post offices in Ohio, arranged in alphabetical order by counties, giving the name of the townships and towns as they were March 1, 1851, and an alphabetical list of towns which differ in name from the post office. Also, a list of foreign rates of postage, and a table of distributing post offices in the United States. Columbus, printed by Scott & Bascom, 1851. 85p.
Reprinted: Columbus, Richard Nevins, 1861. 136p.

2999. Baker, James W. How our counties got their names. [Columbus, Ohio, Franklin County Historical Society, Center of Science and Industry, 1963]. Unpaged. (Jim Baker's historical handbook series, v. 1)
First published in the Columbus dispatch.
Reprinted: [Worthington, Ohio, Pioneer Press, c1972]. 48 ℓ. maps.

3000. Bauman, Robert F. When the Maumee was called the Tawa. An analysis of river terminology during the last quarter of the 18th century. Northwest Ohio quarterly 28:60-87, Spring 1956.

3001. Borkowski, Joseph A. Sandusky—Indian or Polish origin? Polish American studies 25:6-9, 1968.

Wyandotte Indian name, Sandesti, "at the cold water," rather than named for Sadowski, a Polish pioneer.

3002. Chabek, Daniel J. Ohio names and whence they came. Indians, French, British and American pioneers all helped to provide state with its picturesque nomenclature. Cleveland plain dealer March 7, 1937. p. 8.

3003. Connor, E. Margaret. County named for an English island. Ohio Genealogical Society. Report 5:1, Feb. 1965.
Guernsey County.

3004. Cottingham, Kenneth. The influence of geology in Ohio place-names. Ohio journal of science 49:34-40, Jan. 1949.

3005. Coyle, William. A classification of Ohio place-names. Ohio state archaeological and historical quarterly 60:273-82, July 1951.

3006. Dale, Mrs. T. D. Historical, picturesque and appropriate names for streets and public properties, a paper read before the New Century Historical Society and Woman's Centennial Association, February 22, 1897. Marietta, Woman's Centennial Assoc., 1897. 68p.
Proposal for the names of Marietta's streets.

3007. Davis, Harold E. Indian place names in Ohio.
Dictionary containing several hundred names, in preparation. The author is associated with American University, Washington, D.C.

3008. Dickoré, Marie. Newton first named Mercersburg. Historical and Philosophical Society of Ohio. Bulletin 8:65-67, Jan. 1950.

3009. Dudley, Helen M. The origin of the name of the town of Worthington. Ohio state archaeological and historical quarterly 52:248-59, July-Sept. 1943.

3010. Durbin, Mildred G. Naming the Buckeye State. American forests and forest life 33:585-86, Oct. 1927.

3011. Errett, Russell. Indian geographical names. Magazine of western history 2:51-59, 238-46, May, July 1885.
Names of Algonkin (principally Delaware) and Iroquois origin in Pennsylvania and Ohio. p. 51-59 deal principally with the river names Ohio and Allegheny.

3012. Farrar, William M. Why is Ohio called the Buckeye State? Ohio archaeological and historical quarterly 2:174-79, June 1888.

3013. Fitak, Madge R. Place names directory: northeast Ohio. Columbus, Div. of Geological Survey, 1976. 41p. (Information circular no. 45)
Includes all place-names of 13 counties appearing on the topographic maps issued by the U.S. Geological Survey.

3014. Fitzgerald, Roy G. Ohio's counties; why so named? Historical and Philosophical Society of Ohio. Bulletin 10:157, April 1952.

3015. —— Warren County named for General Warren. Historical and Philosophical Society of Ohio. Bulletin 10:241, July 1952.

3016. Green, James A. The map of Hamilton County. Columbus, F. J. Heer Print. Co., 1926. 33p.

Reprinted from the Ohio archaeological and historical quarterly 35:291-321, April 1926.
Discusses names on the map of Hamilton County.

3017. Heinke, Ed. Here's how Fly town got its name. Daily record, Wooster, Feb. 27, 1980. p. 17.

3018. Herring, Simon Edward. Postal history of Logan County, Ohio. Columbus, Ohio, Rhodopress Publications, 1959. 14p.
(Rhodopress publication no. 2)

3019. Hume, Edgar Erskine. The naming of the City of Cincinnati. Ohio state archaeological and historical quarterly 44:81-91, Jan. 1935.

3020. Hunt, William Ellis. Meaning of the names Muskingum, Tuscarawas, and Walhonding; In his Historical collections of Coshocton County, Ohio, 1764-1876. Cincinnati, Clarke, 1876. p. 162-63.

3021. Italy in Ohio. New York times July 23, 1943, p. 16, col. 4.

3022. Jack, Walter. Origin of the names of Ashtabula County townships. Ashtabula County Historical Society. Quarterly bulletin 9:[2-5], March 15, 1962.

3023. Jenkins, Warren. The Ohio gazetteer and traveller's guide; containing a description of the several towns, townships, and counties, with their water-courses, roads, improvements, mineral productions, etc. etc., together with an appendix, or general register; embracing tables of roads and distances; of post offices, their location and distance from the capital of the state and of the United States; of works of internal improvement; of the several officers of state, their residence, etc.; of the colleges and their officers; of banks, their officers and capital, etc. Rev. ed. with a second appendix, containing the census of the state for 1840, as taken by order of Congress. Columbus, Isaac N. Whiting, 1841. 578p.
1st ed. 1837. 546p. Also published 1839.
"Jenkins' Gazetteer is a continuation of Kilbourn's gazetteers, discontinued in 1834, but is almost entirely rewritten, and contains many additions and corrections."--Peter Gibson Thomson, A bibliography of Ohio (Cincinnati, The Author, 1880).

3024. Johnston, John. Names of the rivers by the Shawanoese; In his Account of the present state of the Indian tribes inhabiting Ohio, in a letter from John Johnston, United States agent of Indian affairs at Piqua, to Caleb Atwater. American Antiquarian Society. Transactions and collections 1:297-99. 1820.

3025. Kaib, H. Thomas. Fussy mapmakers erase Ohio towns, but most still exist, many still charming. Cleveland plain dealer Oct. 22, 1978, sec. 2, p. 8.
Based on a study by William L. Flinn concerning the shift of population away from the rural areas and, in some cases, a return, thus restoring what might have become a ghost town.

3026. —— Ohio's ould sod, namesake hamlets and a special day. Cleveland plain dealer March 19, 1979.
Irish place-names.

3027. Keller, Kathryn M. Indian place names. Ohio cues 15:3, Oct. 1965, 15:5, Jan. 1966.

3028. Kenny, Laurence J. There's a glory in the name "Ohio." Mid-America 37:184-86, July 1955.

3029. Keyerleber, Karl. On the naming of streets. Cleveland plain dealer Jan. 27, 1953.
Street names in Cleveland.

3030. Kilbourn, John. The Ohio gazetteer, or, Topographical dictionary; being a continuation of the work originally comp. by the late John Kilbourn. 11th ed. rev. and enl. by a citizen of Columbus. Columbus, Scott & Wright, 1833. 512p.
1st ed. 1816; 3d ed. 1817; 5th ed. 1818; 6th ed. 1819; 7th ed. 1821; 8th ed. 1826; 9th ed. 1829; 10th ed. 1831.

3031. Laughlin, Emma E. A study of the origin of place names of Belmont County, Ohio, with some early history. Barnesville, Ohio, 1941. 41p.

3032. Lindsey, David. New England origins of Western Reserve place names. American speech 30:243-55, Dec. 1955.

3033. —— Ohio's Western Reserve, the story of its place names. Cleveland, Press of Western Reserve University and the Western Reserve Historical Society, 1955. 111p.
Limited to inhabited places: cities, townships, and villages. Does not account for the names of rivers, lakes, or other geographic features.
Review: William D. Overman, Names 3:261-63, Dec. 1955; Ohio historical quarterly 65:97-98, Jan. 1956.

3034. —— Place names in Ohio's Western Reserve. Names 2:40-45, March 1954.

3035. Lotspeich, C. M. Cincinnati. American speech 1:226, Jan. 1926.
How Cincinnati escaped being called Losantiville.

3036. McDavid, Raven I., Jr. Notes on the pronunciation of Ohio. Names 23:147-52, Sept. 1975.

3037. McFarland, R. W. The Chillicothes. Ohio archaeological and historical quarterly 11:230-31, Oct. 1902.
Identifies five different towns with this Indian name.

3038. McGunagle, Fred. Towns don't exist—but they won't go away. Cleveland press Dec. 9, 1972, p. A7.
Ghost towns.

3039. Mahr, August C. Indian river and place names in Ohio. Ohio historical quarterly 66:137-58, April 1957.
Indian name Ohio does not mean "the Beautiful River."

3040. Martin, Maria Ewing. Ohio, 1803-1903; "origin of its names." New Straitsville, Ohio, 1903. 16p.

3041. —— Origin of Ohio place names. Ohio archaeological and historical quarterly 14:272-90, July 1905.

3042. Morgan, F. A. Names for new land, Guernsey, Belmont, Noble, and Monroe counties. How the counties, towns, townships, streams, and highways were named, and of early families who named them. Quaker City, Home Towner Printing, 1978. 27p. map.

3043. Naming the streets. Historical and Philosophical Society of Ohio. Bulletin v. 4, no. 3, Sept. 1946, p. 23.
Refers to the second ordinance of Cincinnati, which relates to naming the streets and alleys of the town.

3044. Ohio. Auditor's Office. A short history of Ohio land grants. Prepared for the schools of Ohio. [Columbus], 1965. 40p.
How Ohio counties got their names: p. 36-40.
1st ed.: [1959?]

3045. Ohio. Department of Natural Resources. Division of Water. Gazetteer of Ohio streams, comp. by J. C. Krolczyk. Columbus, 1954. 175p. maps.

3046. Ohio Turnpike Commission. The stories behind the Ohio Turnpike service plaza names. n.p., The Commission, 1955. Unpaged.
The names are related to pertinent name information in the immediate area.

3047. Overman, William Daniel. Ohio place names; the origin of the names of over 500 Ohio cities, towns and villages. Akron, The Author, 1951. 86p.

3048. —— Ohio town names. Names 1:115-17, June 1953.

3049. —— Ohio town names. Introd. by William T. Utter. Akron, Atlantic Press, 1958, c1959. 155p.
The origin of the names of more than 1200 Ohio cities, towns, and villages.
Review: G. R. Stewart in Names 7:261-65, Dec. 1959.

3050. Overton, Julie M. The towns and townships of Greene Co., Ohio. Xenia, Ohio, Greene County Historical Society, 1975.
Unpaged. map.

3051. Peters, Walter August. Place names. Cleveland plain dealer Feb. 15, 18, 20, 22, 25, 27, 29, 1924.
A series on the place-names of Greater Cleveland.

3052. —— The street names of Cleveland and vicinity. Western Reserve University bulletin v. 30, no. 7, July 1927. 62p.
Contents: Names of the first stratum, 1792-1853; The second stratum, 1853-1906; The third stratum, 1906-1925; The growth of compounds; The prefixes; The suffixes.

3053. Phillips, Hazel Spencer. Invincible gambler: folklore. Lebanon, Ohio, Warren County Historical Society, n.d. [4]p. (Folklore series, no. 9)
"Information furnished by Mrs. Thomas Bamber, and Harry B. Allen, Cozad, Nebraska, whose research inspired Mari Sandoz' book Gamblin' Man's Son."
John Jackson Cozad, who established Cozaddale, Ohio, and Cozad, Neb.

3054. —— Place names of Warren County, Ohio. Lebanon, Ohio, Warren County Historical Society, 1965. Unpaged.

3055. Phillips, Josephine E. The naming of Marietta. Ohio state archaeological and historical quarterly 55:106-37, April-June 1946.

3056. Raup, Hallock Floy. Names of Ohio's streams. Names 5:162-68, Sept. 1957.

3057. —— The names of Ohio's streams. Ohio conservation bulletin 20:10-11, 27, July 1956.

3058. —— A preliminary study of geographic names in Ohio. Ohio State Archaeological and Historical Society. Museum echoes 22:86-88, Nov. 1949.
Has 35,000 cards on geographic names of places, natural features, state parks and forests, and miscellaneous features in the State of Ohio. Eventually the cards will be transferred to the U.S. Board on Geographic Names.—American Dialect Society, Committee on Place Names, Dec. 1962.

3059. —— The standardization of spelling in Ohio settlement and stream names of Indian origin. Names 15:8-11, March 1967.

3060. Redfield's Ohio railway gazetteer, travelers' guide, and express and shippers' directory, embracing a complete alphabetical gazetteer and travelers' guide. Indianapolis, D. A. Redfield, 1865. 94p.

3061. Rhoades, Rendell. Notes on the post offices of Highland County, Ohio. Columbus, Ohio, Rhodopress Publications, 1958. 8p.

3062. —— The post offices of Butler County, Ohio. Columbus, Ohio, Rhodopress Publications, 1959. 12p.

3063. —— The post towns of Clinton County, Ohio. Columbus, Rhodopress Publications, 1959. 16p.

3064. Richmond, Winthrop Edson. Place-names in Franklin County, Ohio. Ohio state archaeological and historical quarterly 53:135-59, April-June 1944.
Also published separately, 1944. 24p.
Thesis (M.A.) Ohio State Univ., 1940.

3065. Rideout, Mrs. Grant. Origin of Put-in-Bay. Inland seas 3:195-96, July 1947.

3066. Rodgers, Elizabeth G. 'Chagrin—whence the name? 2d ed. Chagrin Falls, Ohio, The Author, [1980].
First edition 1976.

3067. Ross, Edna. Some Logan County place-names. Ed. by Kelsie B. Harder. Chillicothe, Ohio Valley Folk Research Project, Ross County Historical Society, 1962. 8 ℓ. (Ohio Valley folk publications, n.s. no. 96)
Bellefontaine, Degraff, Quincy, Spring Hills, and Loganville.

3068. Rust, Orton Glenn. A short account of Clark County, Ohio, place names. 2d ed. Chillicothe, Priv. pub. R. E. Craver & D. K. Webb, 1951. 4 ℓ.

3069. Scholl, John William. Shull's Road. Ohio state archaeological and historical quarterly 55:293-94, July-Sept. 1946.
A letter to the editor gives reasons why Shell's Road on a road map of Montgomery County should be Shull's Road.

3070. Seamster, Frances Pryor. The place-names of Muskingum County, Ohio. 59p.
Thesis (M.A.) Ohio State Univ., 1965.

3071. Sones, William. Why would anybody name a river the Chagrin? Cleveland plain dealer April 17, 1977. Magazine section.
Names in the Cleveland area.

3072. Sprague, Stuart Seely. The name's the thing: promoting Ohio towns during the era of good feelings. Names 25:25-35, March 1977.
Lots in over 100 new towns were offered for sale between 1815 and 1819, with 56 percent of these towns named for other cities by their promoters to ensure the sales by the promoters of the instant cities.

3073. Taylor, Edward Guy. The origin of place-names in Perry County, Ohio. 41ℓ.
Thesis (M.A.) Ohio State Univ., 1952.

3074. The Towns called Chillicothe. Ohio archaeological and historical quarterly 12:167-79, April 1903.
A criticism by J. B. F. Morgan of R. W. McFarland's article, The Chillicothes, and McFarland's reply, reprinted from the Chillicothe news-advertiser of Jan. 7 and Feb. 2, 1903.

3075. Troyer, Clarence. It's all in the name. Daily record, Wooster, Ohio. March 4, 1975.
The origin of village names in Holmes and Coshocton counties.

3076. —— What's in a village name? Daily record, Wooster, Ohio, Sept. 3, 1974, p. 31; Sept. 19, 1974, p. 12.
Place name histories for towns in Holmes and Tuscarawas counties, Ohio.

3077. Waite, Frederick Clayton. Place names in Lake County and vicinity. 1939.
Mounted newspaper clippings from the Willoughby news herald, in the Cleveland Public Library.

3078. —— Sources of the names of the counties of the Western Reserve. Ohio state archaeological and historical quarterly 48:58-65, Jan. 1939.
Bibliography: p. 65.

3079. Webb, David Knowlton. Index to Ohio place names; survey may aid industries and defense. Chillicothe, Chillicothe gazette. 1950. 3p.
Folder reprinted from the Sesquecentennial edition of the Chillicothe gazette, Oct. 10, 1950.

3080. —— & Emily A. Webb. A list of Ohio place name variations. Chillicothe, Published privately, 1951. Unpaged.

3081. The World in Ohio; a philatelist takes postmaster-eye view of odd Buckeye place names. Cleveland plain dealer May 27, 1956, Pictorial magazine p. 18.

3082. Your county's link with Ohio's history. Ohio schools 41:34-35, 38-39, Nov. 1963.
The origin of the county names.

OKLAHOMA

3083. Brackett, Walter L. Place-names of five northeast counties of Oklahoma. 1943.
Thesis (M.A.) Univ. of Tulsa, 1943.

3084. Brewington, Eugene H. Place names in Oklahoma, their derivation, origin and present status. Oklahoma City, Okla., The Author, 1956. Unpaged.

3085. Chase, Carroll & Richard McP. Cabeen. The first hundred years of United States territorial postmarks, 1787-1887. Indian Territory. American philatelist 60:206-20, 902-07, 914-21, Dec. 1946, Aug. 1947; 61:449-55, 468-70, 547-57, March-April 1948.
Includes list of post offices to 1887, with notes on some names.

3086. Encyclopedia of Oklahoma. [Oklahoma City, 1912]. v. 1.
Editor: v. 1, Emmet Starr.
Gives location (by county) and origin of place-names.

3087. Foreman, Grant. Early post offices of Oklahoma. Chronicles of Oklahoma 6:4-25, 155-62, 271-98, 408-44, March-Dec. 1928; 7:7-33, March 1929.
A list showing name, location, beginning date, and first postmaster, grouped by boundaries of the Indian tribes, and later by counties of Oklahoma Territory.

3088. Gannett, Henry. A gazetteer of Indian Territory. Washington, Govt. Print. Off., 1905. 70p. (U.S. Geological Survey. Bulletin no. 248)

3089. Gazetteer and business directory of the new Southwest. Embracing all of that region of country—including counties, towns and cities--contiguous to the St. Louis and San Francisco Railway, its divisions and branches, located in southwest Missouri, southeastern Kansas, the eastern portion of the Indian country, and the northwest section of Arkansas. In which is included an abridged directory of leading business houses in St. Louis. St. Louis, United States Directory Pub. Co., 1881. 224p.

3090. Geary, its name and founding. Chronicles of Oklahoma 37:245, Summer 1959.

3091. Gibson, Arrell Morgan. Early mining camps in northeastern Oklahoma. Chronicles of Oklahoma 34:193-202, Summer 1956.

3092. Gould, Charles Newton. Oklahoma place names. Norman, Univ. of Oklahoma Press, 1933. 146p.
Unpublished revision in manuscript collection, University of Oklahoma Library.
Review: American speech 9:66-67, Feb. 1934.

3093. Holloway, O. Willard. Origin of place names at Fort Sill, Oklahoma. Fort Sill, U.S. Army Artillery and Missile School Library, 1957. 11p. (USA A&MS Library. Special bibliography no. 13)
Rev. ed. 1959. 12 ℓ.

3094. Jeffords, Gladys Wheeler & Lena Lockhart Daugherty. Oklahoma's fabulous Indian names. Muskogee, Okla., American Print. Co., 1962. 27p.
Oklahoma place names: p. 16-27.

3095. Meaning of the Creek Indian name Eufaula. Chronicles of Oklahoma 40:310-11, Autumn 1962.
A city in Alabama and Oklahoma.

3096. Morgan, Buford. Place-names in the Wichitas. Great Plains journal 17:49-103. 1978.
Wichita Mountains.

3097. Morris, John Wesley. Ghost towns of Oklahoma. Norman, Univ. of Oklahoma Press, 1977. 229p. maps.
Brief sketches of 130 communities.
Review: Odie B. Faulk, Journal of the West 18:111, Jan. 1979.

3098. Mulhall was first called Alfred. Chronicles of Oklahoma 36:213, Summer 1958.

3099. Nye, Wilbur Sturtevant. Place names on the Fort Sill reservation; In his Carbine and lance; the story of old Fort Sill. Norman, Univ. of Oklahoma Press, 1937. p. 417-19.
Gives derivation.

3100. Oklahoma place-names file.
Card file prepared at the Oklahoma City Public Library.

3101. Origin of county names in Oklahoma. Chronicles of Oklahoma 2:75-82, March 1924.

3102. Shirk, George H. First post offices within the boundaries of Oklahoma. Chronicles of Oklahoma 26:178-244, Summer 1948.
List, p. 185-244, includes material on names. Includes Oklahoma Territory, p. 237-44.

3103. —— First post offices within the boundaries of Oklahoma. Chronicles of Oklahoma 30:38-104, Spring 1952.
List of offices and postmasters in the Territory, 1889-1907.

3104. —— Oklahoma place names, foreword by Muriel H. Wright. 2d ed., rev. and enl. Norman, Univ. of Oklahoma Press, 1974. xix, 268p. maps.
Bibliography: p. 267-68.
Review of 1st edition: Edward C. Ehrensperger, Names 14:241-44, Dec. 1966.

3105. Signorelli, Gaspare & Tom J. Caldwell. Indian Territory mail. [Brooklyn?], 1966. 160ℓ.
Contains lists under the headings: The army outposts, The Indian agencies, and Postmark listing.

3106. Tahlequah, Okla. Sequoyah Vocational School. Some Oklahoma place names; or, What's in a name? by the Sooners (grade five). Tahlequah, Okla., n.d. Unpaged.

3107. Taylor, Nat M. How Lookeba got its name. Chronicles of Oklahoma 38:325, Autumn 1960.

3108. Thoburn, Joseph B. The naming of the Canadian River. Chronicles of Oklahoma 6:181-85, June 1928.
"The author believes this river was named by voyageurs from Canada."—Price.

3109. Town named for Gene Autry. New York times Nov. 6, 1941, p. 12, col. 6.
Berwyn changed to Gene Autry.

3110. Townsend, A. C. Indian Territory ghost towns. Chronicles of Oklahoma 21:44-45, March 1943.

3111. U.S. 88th Congress, 1st session. House. Joint resolution designating the navigation channel and canal portion of the Arkansas River navigation and multiple purpose project as the "Robert S. Kerr Seaway." H.J. Res. 82. Jan. 9, 1963. Washington, 1963. 1p.
Introduced by Mr. Edmondson and referred to the Committee on Public Works.
Subsequent documents relating to this joint resolution, and a bill introduced in the Senate, were published as follows:

U.S. 88th Congress, 1st session. Senate. A bill to change the name of Short Mountain Lock and Dam and Reservoir in the State of Oklahoma to Robert S. Kerr Lock and Dam and Reservoir. S. 1173. March 25, 1963. Washington, 1963. 1p.
Introduced by Mr. Monroney and Mr. Edmondson and referred to the Committee on Public Works.

U.S. 88th Congress, 1st session. House. Designating the Short Mountain Lock and Dam and Reservoir, Oklahoma, as the Robert S. Kerr Lock and Dam and Reservoir. Report no. 220, to accompany H.J. Res. 82. April 22, 1963. Washington, 1963. 4p.
Submitted by Mr. Davis, from the Committee on Public Works, with amendments, changing the title of the joint resolution and the name to Robert S. Kerr Lock and Dam and Reservoir.

— [Reprint of the original joint resolution, April 22, 1963, with amendments, to accompany the report. Report no. 220 and House Calendar no. 49 added]. 2p.

U.S. 88th Congress, 1st session. Senate. Joint resolution to change the name of Short Mountain Lock and Dam and Reservoir in the State of Oklahoma to Robert S. Kerr Lock and Dam and Reservoir. H.J. Res. 82. In the Senate May 8, 1963. Washington, 1963. 1p.

Referred to the Committee on Public Works. Passed the House of Representatives May 6, 1963.

— Changing the name of the Short Mountain Lock and Dam and Reservoir, Oklahoma, to the Robert S. Kerr Lock and Dam and Reservoir. Report no. 273, to accompany H.J. Res. 82. June 19, 1963. Calendar no. 254. Washington, 1963. 3p.

Submitted by Mr. McNamara, from the Committee on Public Works, without amendment. Includes favorable comments of the Bureau of the Budget and the Dept. of the Army on identical bill S. 1173.

— [Reprint of the joint resolution, June 19, 1963, to accompany the report. Report no. 273 and Calendar no. 254 added]. 1p.

3112. Wilson, Raymond R. Place-names of six northeast counties of Oklahoma. 1940.

Thesis (M.A.) Univ. of Tulsa, 1940.

3113. Wright, Muriel H. Atoka, a place name in Oklahoma. Chronicles of Oklahoma 43:345-46, Autumn 1965.

3114. — History of Oklahoma emblems, the name Oklahoma. Chronicles of Oklahoma 35:349-50, Autumn 1957.

3115. — The name "Ferdinandina" located on the Arkansas River. Chronicles of Oklahoma 41:157-59, Summer 1963.

3116. — The naming of Oklahoma. Chronicles of Oklahoma 39:335-37, Autumn 1961.

Includes reference to the suggested Territory of Lincoln, in Congressional bills soon after the Civil War.

3117. — Some geographic names of French origin in Oklahoma. Chronicles of Oklahoma 7:188-93, June 1929.

The French traders and trappers gave names to many of the streams and mountains in Oklahoma.

3118. Young, Della I. Names in old Cheyenne and Arapahoe Territory and the Texas Panhandle. Texas Folk-lore Society. Publications 6:90-97. 1927.

OREGON

3119. Abbott, Walter H. Preservation of Indian names. Oregon Historical Society. Quarterly 12:361-68, Dec. 1911.

A plea for the use of Indian names in Oregon.

3120. Axford, Harold. How some Portland areas got their names. Oregon journal, Portland, July 17, 1960.

3121. Barker, M. A. R. Klamath texts. Berkeley, Univ. of California Press, 1963. 197p. (University of California publications in linguistics, v. 30)

Klamath place names with map: p. 189-97. Largely adapted from Leslie Spier, Klamath ethnography (University of California publications in American archaeology and ethnology, v. 30, 1930). 92 new place-names added. 45 additional place-names are included in the Dictionary (published separately).

3122. Barry, James Neilson. Early Oregon forts, a chronological list. Oregon historical quarterly 46:101-11, June 1945.

3123. Barton, J. Tracy. "Amelia" and "Shirt Tail Gulch" in Mormon Basin. Oregon historical quarterly 43:228-31, Sept. 1942.

Information on these two place-names was obtained by the author from his grandfather and grandmother, pioneer settlers of that region.

3124. Berlin, Ore., to take the name of Distomo. New York times Oct. 5, 1944, p. 1, col. 1.

Editorial p. 22, col. 3; Berlin, Ore., rebels at change of name to Distomo. New York times Oct. 11, 1944, p. 23, col. 3; Berlin, Ore., votes not to become Distomo. New York times Oct. 12, 1944, p. 15, col. 2.

3125. Bowman, Florence Read. How Silverton got its name. Genealogical Forum of Portland, Oregon. Monthly bulletin 14:67-68, Feb. 1965.

3126. Bracher, Frederick. "Ouaricon" and Oregon. American speech 21:185-87, Oct. 1946.

Additional evidence based on various editions of Lahontan's Nouveaux voyages which supports George Rippey Stewart's findings reported in his article The source of the name "Oregon" (see no. 3174).

3127. Butterfield, Grace & J. H. Horner. Wallowa Valley towns and their beginnings. Oregon historical quarterly 41:382-85, Dec. 1940.

The origin of the name of the towns of Joseph, Wallowa, and Lostine is included with a brief account of their early history.

3128. Carney, Bobette. Aloha man disputes story on naming town. Beaverton Valley news Nov. 10, 1960.

Early Aloha, Ore., history.

3129. Chase, Carroll & Richard McP. Cabeen. The first hundred years of United States territorial postmarks, 1787-1887. Oregon Territory. American philatelist 56:360-75, March 1943.

Includes list of post offices, with notes on some names.

3130. Clark, Malcolm H. "Oregon" revisited. Oregon historical quarterly 61:211-19, June 1960.

"A minority report" to article by Vernon F. Snow ibid. 60:439-47, Dec. 1959.

3131. Corning, Howard McKinley. Historical place name sketches. Oregon journal, Portland, May 25-Aug. 17, 1950.

3132. Dorsey, James Owen. The gentile system of the Siletz tribes. Journal of American folk-lore 3:227-37, July-Sept. 1890.

Ancient villages and names of tribes living on the Siletz reservation.

3133. Elliott, Thomas Coit. Jonathan Carver's source for the name Oregon. Oregon Historical Society. Quarterly 23:53-69, March 1922.

"Associates the name used by Major Rogers with the French word for storm, ouragan."—McArthur.

3134. —— The mysterious Oregon. Washington historical quarterly 22:289-92, Oct. 1931.

Discusses four theories: (1) that the name was invented by Maj. Robert Rogers; (2) that it was an Indian word; (3) that it was the French word ouragan; (4) that it was Rogers's corruption of the Indian "Ouinipigon," the earliest form of the name Winnipeg.

3135. —— Oregon Inlet, Roanoke Island. Oregon historical quarterly 32:281-82, Sept. 1931.

Directing attention to a curious literary error concerning the name Oregon.

3136. —— The origin of the name Oregon. Oregon Historical Society. Quarterly 22:91-115, June 1921.

This article supplements the article The strange case of Jonathan Carver and the name Oregon (see no. 3137).

3137. —— The strange case of Jonathan Carver and the name Oregon. Oregon Historical Society. Quarterly 21:341-68, Dec. 1920.

"The name Oregon was used in a book by Jonathan Carver, published in London in 1778, entitled, 'Travels through the interior parts of North America,' as applied to the 'River of the West.' The writer here gives the results of his researches regarding Carver and his book, and suggests sources for Carver's use of the name Oregon."—Griffin.

3138. Galvani, William H. Origin of the name of Oregon. Oregon Historical Society. Quarterly 21:336-40, Dec. 1920.

Presents the theory that Oregon is a natural linguistic transformation from Aragon, a name that might very likely have been used by early Spanish settlers.

3139. Gatschet, Albert Samuel. The Klamath Indians of southwestern Oregon. Contributions to North American ethnology v. 2, pt. 1, p. xxvii-xxxii. 1890.

Contents: Topographic list of camping places, on Klamath Marsh, along Williamson River, around Upper Klamath Lake; Eminences around Upper Klamath Lake; Camping places in Sprague River valley, and the Modoc country.

3140. Glassley, Ray Hoard. Letters to the editor. Oregon historical quarterly 59:255-59, Sept. 1958.

History of the names of some of Oregon's outstanding geographic features—the Willamette River and its tributaries.

3141. Holladay, railway tycoon of early day, gave town name. Seaside signal Aug. 24, 1950.

After Ben Holladay's Seaside Hotel.

3142. Holman, Frederick V. Oregon counties; their creations and the origins of their names. Oregon Historical Society. Quarterly 11:1-81, March 1910.

Condensed in Magazine of history 13:119-22, March 1911.

3143. Judson, Lewis. Street names of Salem. Marion County history 5:17-20, June 1959.

3144. Ketchum, Verne L. The naming of Mount Hood. Mazama 13:42-45, Dec. 1931.

3145. Kraft, Walter C. Heceta: a name with a split personality. Names 7:256-60, Dec. 1959.

Discusses two quite different pronunciations for two landmarks on the Oregon coast named for the Spanish explorer Bruno Heceta.

A footnote to above, by John Lyman, ibid. 8:87, June 1960.

3146. Landis, Robert L. Post offices of Oregon, Washington, and Idaho. Portland, Ore., Patrick Press, 1969, 89, 98, 55, 9p.
Includes "Post offices of the Railway Mail Service," 1906, for Oregon, Washington, Idaho, and Alaska.

3147. Larson, Douglas W. & John R. Donaldson. A compilation of the named lakes in Oregon, with bibliography. Corvallis, Dept. of Fisheries and Wildlife, Oregon State Univ. [1971]. 125p. map. (Oregon State University, Corvallis. Water Resources Research Institute WRRI-8)
Bibliography: p. 113-25.

3148. Lewis, William S. Some notes and observations on the origin and evolution of the name Oregon as applied to the River of the West. Washington historical quarterly 17:218-22, July 1926.
Indian origin of the river now named the Columbia.

3149. Lyman, H. S. Indian names. Oregon Historical Society. Quarterly 1:316-26, Sept. 1900.
Aboriginal place-names of the lower Columbia and Willamette rivers.

3150. McArthur, Lewis Ankeny. Earliest Oregon post offices as recorded at Washington. Oregon historical quarterly 41:53-71, March 1940.
Records from the Division of Postmasters' Appointments at the Post Office Dept. in Washington, D.C. Entries by county, from March 9, 1847 to 1855.

3151. —— Oregon geographic names. 4th ed. rev. and enl. by Lewis L. McArthur. Portland, Oregon Historical Society, 1974. 835p.
1st ed. 1928. 450p.; 2d ed. 1944. 581p.; 3d ed. 1952. 686p.
Originally published in Oregon historical quarterly 26:309-423, Dec. 1925; 27:131-91, 225-64, 295-363, 412-47. 1926; 28:65-110, 163-224, 281-306, March-Sept. 1927. Six supplements to the 1st ed. were published ibid. 43:299-317, Dec. 1942; 44:1-18, 176-218, 286-312, 339-60. 1943; 45:42-74, March 1944. Additions after 1944 were published ibid. 46:332-52, Dec. 1945; 47:61-98, 196-216, 329-57, 441-64. 1946; 48:34-42, 68-85, 254-63, 322-31. 1947; 49:63-72, 137-47, 222-43, 299-305. 1948; 50:51-53, 134-38, March-June 1949.
Review of 1st ed.: Canadian historical review 10:169-70, June 1929; David W. Hazen, Oregon historical quarterly 29:211-13, June 1928.
Review of 2d ed.: W. Kaye Lamb, British Columbia historical quarterly 9:170-71, April 1945.
Review of 4th ed.: Robert M. Rennick, Names 24:57-58, March 1976.

3152. —— Oregon place names; pen and ink illustrations by Marilyn Campbell. Portland, Binfords & Mort for the Oregon journal, 1944. 109p.
An abridgment of the author's Oregon geographic names (see no. 3151).

3153. Martinson, Tom L. Wendling, Oregon: ephemeral place but persistent name. Places 2:23-25, July 1975. maps.

3154. Meyers, J. A. Oregan—River of the slaves or River of the West. Washington historical quarterly 13:282-83, Oct. 1922.
"Reasons for thinking that the name Oregon originated from a typographical error in Jonathan Carver's 'Travels through the interior parts of North America in 1766-1768.'"—Price.

3155. Middleton, Lynn. Place names of the Pacific northwest coast: origins, histories, and anecdotes in bibliographic form about the coast of British Columbia, Washington, and Oregon. Victoria, B.C., Elldee Pub. Co., 1969. 226p. maps.
Also published: Seattle, Superior Pub. Co. [1970, c1969].

An alphabetical list, giving location and origin of name, often enlivened with anecdotes and stories of the men and ships involved.

3156. Mills, Hazel E. Two Oregon place name items of 1851 and 1856. Western folklore 11:214-16, July 1952.
New names for towns, rather than repetition of old names used elsewhere, and Willamette, etc.

3157. Mills, Randall Vause. Districts and sections in Eugene, Oregon. Western folklore 11:213-14, July 1952.

3158. —— Notes on Oregon place names. Western folklore 10:316-17, Oct. 1951.

3159. —— Place-name notes from the "Oregon spectator." Western folklore 9:60-63, Jan. 1950.
Published Oregon City, 1846- .

3160. Minto, John. Minto Pass: its history and an Indian tradition; In his Rhymes of early life in Oregon and historical and biographical facts. Salem, Ore., Statesman Pub. Co., 1915?. p. 33-40.
This chapter reprinted from the Quarterly of the Oregon Historical Society, v. 4, no. 3, Sept. 1903.
Original names in Independence Valley: p. 38-39.

3161. Monaghan, Robert R. Pronunciation guide to Oregon place names. Eugene, Oregon Assoc. of Broadcasters, 1961. 81p.
Review: John R. Krueger, Names 10:192-94, Sept. 1962.

3162. The Naming of Mount Hood. Geographical journal 75:173, Feb. 1930.

3163. Oregon Geographic Names Board. Minutes. Portland, 1914?- .

3164. Payne, Edward R. Oregon territorial post offices and handstamped postal markings. Oregon historical quarterly 60:475-88, Dec. 1959.
A draft of this article appeared in the April 1959 Western express, quarterly of the Western Cover Collector's Society.
Includes list of post offices with county now in, date established, and whether discontinued, name changed, or current.

3165. Payne, Edwin R. Oregon territorial postmarks. American philatelist 64:531-32, April 1951.
List of post offices. Additions to Carroll Chase-Richard McP. Cabeen's U.S. territorial postmarks, ibid. 55:360-75, March 1943.

3166. Pioneer's name selected for proposed new city: Ben Holladay, Old West's king of transportation, top choice of committee. Parkrose-East County enterprise March 15, 1961.
Tentative limits of the proposed east Multnomah County city are described in the March 22 issue of the same paper, and the Beaverton Valley news editorializes on the proposed city on March 30.

3167. Place names and their origin. U.S. Writers' Program. Oregon. Oregon oddities May 15, 1940, p. 1-4.
Based on research in the meanings and origins of the state's geographic names by the Oregon Writers' project of the WPA.

3168. Rees, John E. Oregon—its meaning, origin and application. Oregon Historical Society. Quarterly 21:317-31, Dec. 1920.

The word Oregon is derived from a Shoshone Indian expression meaning "The River of the West," originating from two Shoshone words Ogwa, "river," and Pe-on, "west," or Ogwa Pe-on.

3169. Scott, H. W. Not Majoram: the Spanish word "Oregano" not the original of Oregon. Oregon Historical Society. Quarterly 1:165-68, June 1900.

3170. Snow, Vernon F. From Ouragan to Oregon. Oregon historical quarterly 60:439-47, Dec. 1959.
University of Oregon historian evaluates latest interpretation of controversial name.
See also article by Malcolm H. Clark, ibid. 61:211-19, June 1960.

3171. Spier, Leslie. Klamath ethnography. Berkeley, Univ. of California Press, 1930. 338p. (University of California publications in American archaeology and ethnology, v. 30)
Settlements: p. 10-21. Lists of Klamath settlement names, with maps.
For additional material based on this, see M. A. R. Barker, Klamath texts, no. 3121.

3172. Steel, William Gladstone. The mountains of Oregon. Portland, D. Steel, 1890. 112p.
Contains several sections on the names of mountains in Oregon and Washington.

3173. Stewart, George Rippey. Ouaricon revisited. Names 15:166-68, Sept. 1967.
The author traces work on the subject of the name Oregon since the publication of his article "The source of the name Oregon" in American speech April 1944, and the effect of his idea on this work. The original article is reprinted following his new article, p. 169-72.
Reply by Virgil J. Vogel, ibid. 16:136-40, June 1968.

3174. —— The source of the name "Oregon." American speech 19:115-17, April 1944.
From Ouaricon on the Carte générale de Canada of Lahontan's Nouveaux voyages dans l'Amérique Septentrionale, 1709.

3175. Stone, Joan. Polk County geographic names. Dallas, Ore., Dallas Chamber of Commerce, 1972. 17p.

3176. Strozut, George G. Hayesville should have been named Stephensville. Marion County history 4:17-20, June 1958.

3177. Swing, William. St. Johns district gets name from hermit. Portland Oregonian Jan. 22, 1961.
James John, member of the Bidwell-Bartleson immigrant party of 1841, platted St. Johns, which won official city status in May 1865.

3178. Trumbull, James Hammond. Oregon, the origin and meaning of the name. Magazine of American history 3:36-38, Jan. 1879.
Suggests that Carver did not invent the name Oregon, but that he gave the Algonkin equivalent of the name by which he had reason to believe the tribes living near it designated in their unknown language their "fair river" or "belle rivière."

3179. U.S. Board on Geographic Names. Decisions. No. 32, January 4, 1933. Crater Lake National Park, Oregon. Washington, Govt. Print. Off., 1934. 6p.

3180. U.S. Work Projects Administration. Pennsylvania. Geographic names in the coastal areas of California, Oregon and Washington. Comp. under the supervision of the Coast and Geodetic Survey. Washington, 1940. 94p.

3181. Vogel, Virgil J. Oregon: a rejoinder. Names 16:136-40, June 1968.
Reply to George R. Stewart (ibid. 15:166-72, Sept. 1967) regarding theories on the origin of the name Oregon.

3182. Wandering town settles at last. Omaha world-herald April 22, 1956.
Shevlin, Ore., a portable lumbering community, has now taken roots.

3183. Witter, Janet Waldrow. Place names in Clackamas County.
Thesis (M.S.) Reed College, 1962.

PENNSYLVANIA

3184. Alotta, Robert I. Street names of Philadelphia. Philadelphia, Temple Univ. Press, 1975. xii, 158p., 9 ℓ.
Bibliography: p. 155-58.
Alphabetical arrangement with essays on toll roads, numbered streets, and the streets of William Penn's period.
Review: Richard Tyler, Pennsylvania magazine of history and biography 100:561-62, Oct. 1976.

3185. Ammon, John A. Internal Affairs Department aids in quest for derivation of Butler County school name. Pennsylvania. Dept. of Internal Affairs. Monthly bulletin v. 24, no. 6, p. 9-10, May 1956.
Moniteau, from Missouri.

3186. Another Levittown studies possibility of changing name. New York times Nov. 24, 1963, p. 24.
Action stems from success of Levittown, N.J., in changing its name to Willingboro.

3187. Anspach, Marshall R. Origin of place names in Lycoming County. Now and then 15:560-62, Jan. 1968.

3188. Badenoch, Alex. Past and present place names and post offices of Forest County, Pennsylvania. Tionesta, Pa., Forest Press, Inc., 1976. 52p.
Review: Kelsie B. Harder, Names 25:100-01, June 1977.

3189. Beck, Herbert H. The San Domingo Creek, how it was named. Lancaster County Historical Society. Papers 54:63-64. 1950.
On Saunders Lovington, Negro immigrant from Santo Domingo, who died in Lititz, Pa., in 1844.

3190. Bertin, Eugene P. Origins of Lycoming County place names. Now and then 7:202-07, Jan. 1944.

3191. Buck, William J. An enquiry into the origin of the names of places in Bucks County. American notes and queries 1:88-95, March 1, 1857.

3192. Clark, John S. Selected manuscripts of General John S. Clark, relating to the aboriginal history of the Susquehanna, ed. by Louise Welles Murray. Athens, Pa., 1931. 150p. (Publications of the Society for Pennsylvania Archaeology, v. 1)
Bibliography: p. 133-35.
Contents: pt. I. The Carantouan sites of Champlain's "Voyages" and their identification. pt. II. The Andastes or Susquehannocks. pt. III. Indian names and Susquehannock forts.

3193. The "Commonwealth" and the "Keystone State." Greater Pittsburgh 32:9, Oct. 1950.
Why Pennsylvania is called the Keystone State and designated as a Commonwealth.

3194. Davison, Elizabeth M. More about the naming of Wilkinsburg. Western Pennsylvania historical magazine 25:174-80, Sept.-Dec. 1942.

3195. Dedicates Curie Avenue. New York times Jan. 23, 1940, p. 22, col. 3.
Eve Curie dedicates a Philadelphia street to the memory of her parents.

3196. Demorest, Rose. Names of our streets. Carnegie magazine 27:27-28, Jan. 1953.
On the origin of the names of some Pittsburgh streets.

3197. Denton, W. O. How another Enola was named. Faulkner facts and fiddlings 9:113-14, Winter 1967.
Origin of the name of Enola, Pa., which may have been the source of the name of Enola, Ark.

3198. Donehoo, George Patterson. The changing of historic place names; with an introduction and glossary of some historic names changed or misspelled in Pennsylvania, by Henry W. Shoemaker. Pub. under the auspices of the Pennsylvania Alpine Club. Altoona, Tribune Press, 1921. 14p.
"A protest against the unnecessary change of names of places. Includes a partial list of historic place names, changed or misspelled, in Pennsylvania."—Griffin.

3199. —— A history of the Indian villages and place names in Pennsylvania, with numerous historical notes and references. With an introduction by the Hon. Warren K. Moorehead. Harrisburg, Telegraph Press, 1928. 290p.
Reprinted: Baltimore, Gateway Press, 1977.
Bibliography: p. 288-90.
Appendix A: Villages in New York, destroyed by Gen. Sullivan's army, during 1799.
Review of reprint edition: Kelsie B. Harder, Names 28:93-94, March 1980.

3200. Dubbs, Paul M. Where to go and place-names of Centre County; a collection of articles from the Centre daily times, comp. and pub. during 1959-1960. State College, Pa., Centre daily times, 1961. 157p.
A listing and discussion of more than 300 place-names.

3201. Dunlap, Arthur Ray & C. A. Weslager. Two Delaware Valley Indian place names. Names 15:197-202, Sept. 1967.
Recently discovered data makes possible an analysis of "Queonemysing" (Penn.) and "Mageckqueshou" (N.J.).

3202. Errett, Russell. Indian geographical names. Magazine of western history 2:51-59, 238-46, May, July 1885.
Names of Algonkin (principally Delaware) and Iroquois origin in Pennsylvania and Ohio. p. 51-59 deal principally with the river names Ohio and Allegheny.

3203. Espenshade, Abraham Howry. Pennsylvania place names. State College, Pa. Pennsylvania State College, 1925. 375p. (Studies in historical and political science, no. 1)
Reprinted: Detroit, Gale Research Co., 1969; Baltimore, Genealogical Pub. Co., 1970.
List of books consulted: p. 341-45.
Review: American speech 1:451-52, May 1926; Max Förster, Zeitschrift für Ortsnamenforschung 4:94-100. 1928.

3204. Fairclough, G. Thomas. The style of street names. American speech 33:299-300, Dec. 1958.
In Scranton, Pa., Street and Avenue are always used following the name.
Refers to Jerome Rhodes's article, ibid. 33:116-17, May 1958.

3205. Feared "Slippery Rock." New York times July 27, 1939, p. 21, col. 7.
Motorists mistake Slippery Rock name sign for warning.

3206. Fenton, William N. Place names and related activities of the Cornplanter Senecas. Pennsylvania archaeologist 15:25-29, 42-50, 88-96, 108-18. 1945; 16:42-57, April 1946.

3207. Franklin, Walter M. Impress of early names and traits. Lancaster County Historical Society. Papers 3:45-53. 1968.

3208. Fretz, A. Henry. Bucks County place names. Pennsylvania. Dept. of Internal Affairs. Monthly bulletin 21:7-15, 29-32, Feb. 1953; 21:18-24, 29-32, March 1953; 21:23-32, April 1953; 21:26-31, May 1953; 21:31-32, June 1953.

3209. Froke, Marlowe D. & Warren G. Bodow. Pronunciation guide to place names in Pennsylvania. [Harrisburg] Pennsylvania, Assoc. of Broadcasters, 1962. 86 ℓ.

3210. Gibson, Gail E. Historical evidence of the buffalo in Pennsylvania. Pennsylvania magazine of history and biography 93:151-60, April 1969. map.
Although lacking physical evidence, there is still literary evidence in the journals of British army officers of the existence of buffalo and the resulting buffalo place-names in southwestern Pennsylvania.

3211. Gordon, Thomas Francis. A gazetteer of the State of Pennsylvania. Part first, general description of the state; geological construction, canals and rail-roads, bridges, revenue, expenditures, public debt, &c. Part second, counties, towns, cities, villages, mountains, lakes, rivers, creeks, &c., alphabetically arranged. To which is added a table of all the post offices in the state, their distances from Washington and Harrisburg, and the names of the post masters. Philadelphia, T. Belknap, 1832. 508p.
Reprinted, with a new introduction by Mary K. Meyer: New Orleans, Polyanthos, 1975.
Review of reprint edition: Kelsie B. Harder, Names 24:229-30, Sept. 1976.

3212. Grumbine, Lee Leight. The origin and significance of our township names. Lebanon County Historical Society. Historical papers and addresses 1:121-33. 1899.
Also published separately.
Lebanon County names.

3213. Hamilton, Hugh. Sir William Penn: his proprietary province and its counties; those of the Commonwealth of Pennsylvania, with the chronology, etymology and genealogy of the counties. Retiring address of Hugh Hamilton, president (1919) of the Federation of Pennsylvania Historical Societies; delivered at Harrisburg, Pa., January 15th, 1920. Harrisburg, Press of Central Print. & Pub. House, 1920. 14p.

3214. Harding, Julia Morgan. Names of Pittsburgh streets, their historical significance; In Daughters of the American Revolution. Allegheny County, Pa. Fort Duquesne and Fort Pitt. n.p., Reed & Witting Press, 1907. p. 40-47.

3215. Heckewelder, John Gottlieb Ernestus. Names given by the Lenni Lenape or Delaware Indians to rivers, streams and places in the now states of New Jersey, Pennsylvania, Maryland, and Virginia. Pennsylvania German Folklore Society. Publications 5:1-41. 1940.
Published also in American Philosophical Society. Transactions 4:351-96. 1834; Historical Society of Pennsylvania. Bulletin 1:121-35, 139-54, June, Sept. 1847; Moravian Historical Society. Transactions 1872:275-333; published separately: Bethlehem [Pa.], H. T. Claude, printer, 1872. 58p.; and in his A narrative of the mission of the United Brethren among the Delaware and Mohegan Indians. Cleveland, Burrows Bros., 1907. p. 523-66.

3216. Heisey, M. Luther. Indian names of local interest with their origin and meaning. Lancaster County Historical Society. Journal. 76:169-72, Trinity 1972.

3217. Hobbs, Herrwood E. The origin of the names of towns and townships in Schuylkill County. Historical Society of Schuylkill County. Publications 6:43-53. 1947.

3218. Hotchkin, Samuel Fitch. A pocket gazetteer of Pennsylvania arranged by counties. Philadelphia, L. R. Hamersly & Co., 1887. 174p.

3218a. Hudson, Richard L. Jim Thorpe, Pa., has grave problem of name dropping; Pennsylvania town still spars over losing its title to Olympic athlete. Wall Street journal Oct. 10, 1979, p. 1, 34.

The town that changed its name from Mauch Chunk when the athlete's body was buried in the town is now divided over a return to the original name.

3219. Huidekoper, A. Indian and French history in western Pennsylvania. Magazine of American history 1:683-85, Nov. 1877.

Changes in place-names in western Pennsylvania due to historical causes.

3220. Kay, John L. & Chester M. Smith, Jr. Pennsylvania postal history. Lawrence, Mass., Quarterman Publications, c1976. 564p. map.

Review: Elsdon C. Smith, Names 24:216, Sept. 1976.

3221. Kenny, Hamill. Settling Laurel's business. Names 9:160-62, Sept. 1961.

The origin of Laurel in the Pennsylvania and West Virginia place-name Laurel Hill.

3222. McKirdy, James. Origin of the names given to the counties in Pennsylvania. Western Pennsylvania historical magazine 8:37-58, 104-19, 159-75, 235-56, Jan.-Oct. 1925.

Also published separately, 76p.

Bibliography: p. 74-76.

3223. MacReynolds, George. Place names in Bucks County, Pennsylvania, alphabetically arranged in an historical narrative. 2d ed. Doylestown, Bucks County Historical Society, 1955. 454p.

1st ed. 1942. 474p.

An 80p. pamphlet was issued to members of the Society in 1941 for suggestions and additions.

3224. Mahr, August C. How to locate Indian places on modern maps. Ohio journal of science 53:129-37, May 1953.

Delaware or Lenni Lenape Indian names for Pennsylvania localities, from Rev. Johannes Roth's diary, 1772.

3225. Martin, George Castor. Indian names of nearby streams. n.p., Martin & Allardyce, 1911. 4p.

Vicinity of Philadelphia.

3226. Maxwell, Hugh M. Mt. Gretna—origin of the name. Lebanon County Historical Society. Papers and addresses 2:100-03. 1901.

3227. Meiser, Gloria Jean & George W. Meiser. Elusive place names in Berks County. Historical review of Berks County 35:92-95, 1970.

3228. Miller, Ernest C. More place names in Warren County, Pennsylvania. Western Pennsylvania history magazine 57:43-49, Jan. 1974.

3229. —— Place names in Warren County, Pennsylvania. Western Pennsylvania history magazine 54:15-36, 167-80, Jan.-April 1971.
Bibliography: p. 179-80.

3230. Morley's "Conshohockens" make Conshohocken mad. New York times Nov. 26, 1939, p. 38, col. 7.
Citizens protest use of name as expletive in Christopher Morley's book Kitty Foyle.

3231. Morton, John S. A history of the origin of the appellation Keystone State, as applied to the Commonwealth of Pennsylvania; together with extracts from many authorities relative to the adoption of the Declaration of Independence. To which is appended the new constitution of Pennsylvania. Philadelphia, Claxton, Remsen & Haffelfinger, 1874. 190p.
A compilation of newspaper articles and other material in relation to the theory that Pennsylvania was called the Keystone State from the fact that, by the casting of the vote of one of her delegates in the Continental Congress (John Morton), the unanimous adoption of the Declaration of Independence was secured.

3232. The Naming of Obelisk. Historical Society of Montgomery County. Bulletin 6:177-78, April 1948.

3233. Origin of Delaware County names. Delaware County Historical Society. Bulletin 10:2, Nov. 1957; 11:2, Jan. 1958.
Names of farms or country houses in the neighborhood of Philadelphia.

3234. Origin of some Somerset County names. Pennsylvania. Dept. of Internal Affairs. Monthly bulletin 10:31-32, Nov. 1942.

3235. Pearce, Ruth L. Welsh place-names in southeastern Pennsylvania. Names 11:31-43, March 1963.

3236. Pennsylvania. Historical Society. Historical map of Pennsylvania, showing the Indian names of streams, and villages, and paths of travel; the sites of old forts and battle-fields; the successive purchases from the Indians; and the names and dates of counties and county towns; with tables of forts and proprietary manors; ed. by P. W. Sheafer and others. Philadelphia, Historical Society of Pennsylvania, 1875. 26p.

3237. —— State Geographic Board. Decisions, 1923-1926. Altoona, Times Tribune Press, 1926. 8p.
List of changes, compiled by G. H. Ashley, the Secretary, in April 1926, was published in American speech 21:163-64, Dec. 1926.

3238. —— State University. Department of Agricultural Economics and Rural Sociology. Alphabetical listing of cities and towns of Pennsylvania and their county locations. University Park, 1961. 38p.

3239. Pennsylvania Historical Review. Gazetteer, post-office, express and telegraph guide. City of Philadelphia. Leading merchants and manufacturers. New York, Historical Pub. Co., 1886. 292p.

3240. Pillsbury, Richard. The street name systems of Pennsylvania before 1820. Names 17:214-22, Sept. 1969.

3241. Pinkowski, Edward. Chester County place names. Rev. and enl. Philadelphia, Sunshine Press, 1962. 288p.
1st ed. 1955. 230p.

3242. Prowell, George R. Pennsylvania county names. Magazine of history 10:130-36, Sept. 1909; 12:210-19, Oct. 1910; 19:231-38, Dec. 1914.
Concluded in 24:234-35, May-June 1917 by Joel N. Eno.

3243. Raasch, Henry David. Northampton County, Pennsylvania, whence went our place name. Northamptonshire past and present 4:85-89. 1967/68.
Named for Northamptonshire in England.

3244. Randel, William Peirce. The place names of Tioga County, Pennsylvania. American speech 14:181-90, Oct. 1939.

3245. Roberts, Charles R. Place names of Lehigh County and their origin. Lehigh County Historical Society. Annual proceedings 1936:5-12.

3246. Roberts, John M. & Son, Pittsburgh. The story behind the names of western Pennsylvania counties. Pittsburgh, 1948. 55p.
Reprinted from advertisements in the Pittsburgh sun-telegraph.

3247. Russ, William A., Jr. The export of Pennsylvania place names. Pennsylvania history 15:194-214, July 1948.
On the transplanting of Pennsylvania names to the South and West, as a result of the Delaware migration (ca. 1765).

3248. Schawacker, Erwin W., Jr. Street and road names in Chester County, Pennsylvania. American speech 43:40-50, Feb. 1968.
The 2712 names of streets in Chester County, Pa., illustrate new patterns in street-naming emerging in suburban areas.

3249. Scott, Joseph. A geographical description of Pennsylvania; also of the counties respectively; in the order in which they were established by the Legislature. With an alphabetical list of the townships in each county; and their population in 1800. Philadelphia, Printed by Robert Cochran, 1806. 147p.

3250. Shain, Samson A. Old Testament place names in Berks and neighboring counties. Historical review of Berks County 28:51-52, Spring 1963.

3251. —— Old Testament place names in Lancaster County. Lancaster County Historical Society. Journal 67:184-93, Autumn 1963.
A chapter in book Rabbi Shain is writing on Old Testament place-names in Pennsylvania.

3252. Shaw, L. C. & W. F. Busch. Pennsylvania gazetteer of streams. Harrisburg, Dept. of Environmental Resources, 1970. (Water resources bulletin no. 6)

3253. Shoemaker, Henry Wharton. Place names and altitudes of Pennsylvania mountains, an address at the quarterly meeting of the Wyoming Historical and Geological Society, Wilkes-Barre, Pennsylvania, Friday evening, March 9, 1923. Altoona, Times Tribune Press, 1923. 15p.

3254. Snyder, Charles Fisher. Township names of old Northumberland County, their origin and meaning. Northumberland County Historical Society. Proceedings and addresses 8:195-248. 1936.

3255. Spieler, Gerhard G. Pennsylvania Dutch place names. Pennsylvania Dutchman 5:5-6, Nov. 1953.

3256. Stevenson, David B. The place names of Centre County, Pennsylvania: a geographical analysis.
Thesis (M.A.) Pennsylvania State Univ., 1969.

3257. Township names in Delaware County. Delaware County Historical Society. Bulletin 11: [2], March 1958.

3258. U.S. 88th Congress, 1st session. House. A bill to designate the reservoir on the Shenango River above Sharpsville, Pennsylvania, as the George Mahaney Reservoir. H.R. 7368. July 1, 1963. Washington, 1963. 1p.
Introduced by Mr. Weaver and referred to the Committee on Public Works.

3259. Ward, Townsend. Suggestions regarding the production of a correct geographical and historical map of Pennsylvania. Philadelphia, 1875. 7p.
Includes Indian names.

3260. Weslager, Clinton Alfred. Dutch explorers, traders, and settlers in the Delaware Valley, 1609-1664. In collaboration with A. R. Dunlap. Philadelphia, Univ. of Pennsylvania Press, 1961. 329p.
Dutch maps and geographical names: p. 215-32.

3261. Yoder, Don. Local place names: folk-cultural questionnaire no. 14. Pennsylvania folklife 19:47-48, Winter 1969-70.
A questionnaire, with examples given, requests information about local Pennsylvania names: valleys, mountains, streams, farms, fields, villages, post offices, churches, hotels, pronunciation and abbreviation, etymology and place-name lore.

RHODE ISLAND

3262. Best, Mary Agnes. The town that saved a state, Westerly. Westerly, Utter Co., 1943. 283p.
Some general comments on diversity of opinion about the naming of Rhode Island: p. 42-43.

3263. Bicknell, Thomas Williams. Place names in Rhode Island; In his The history of the state of Rhode Island and Providence Plantations. New York, American Historical Society, 1920. 3:1200-09.
Includes Indian names, p. 1207-09.

3264. Brigham, Clarence Saunders. Seventeenth century place-names of Providence Plantations, 1639-1700. Providence, 1903. 28p.
Reprinted from Rhode Island Historical Society. Collections 10:373-400. 1902.

3265. Chapin, Howard M. Glocester, R.I. Rhode Island Historical Society. Collections 26:64-65, April 1933.
Why it is spelled without the "u."

3266. Clapp, Roger Tillinghast. How Acid Factory Brook got its name. Rhode Island history 5:97-104, Oct. 1946.

3267. Cocumcussoc. Rhode Island Historical Society. Collections 28:25, Jan. 1935.
Meaning of the word as contained in a letter from William B. Cabot which appeared in the Evening bulletin of Oct. 3, 1934.

3268. Colorful town not on map. Lincoln (Neb.) evening journal Oct. 21, 1959, p. 19i.
Colorful names in the township of Richmond, which itself does not appear on a map.

3269. Gannett, Henry. A geographic dictionary of Rhode Island. Washington, Govt. Print. Off., 1894. 31p. (U.S. Geological Survey. Bulletin no. 115)
Issued also as House miscellaneous doc. v. 27, 53d Cong., 2d sess.

3270. Haley, John Williams. "The Old Stone Bank" history of Rhode Island. Providence, Providence Institution for Savings, 1944. 4:205-10.
Streets and squares of Providence.

3271. Howland, Benjamin B. The streets of Newport, R.I. Magazine of New England history 2:77-93, April 1892.

3272. The Influence of birds on Rhode Island nomenclature. Rhode Island Historical Society. Collections 31:72-75, July 1938.

3273. Kohl, J. G. How Rhode Island was named. Magazine of American history 9:81-93, Feb. 1883.

3274. List of Indian and other names of places. Rhode Island Historical Society. Collections 3:302-07. 1835.

3275. The Meaning of Indian place names. Rhode Island Historical Society. Collections 22:33-38, April 1929.
An interview with William B. Cabot.
"Notes regarding Algonquin place names in Rhode Island."—Griffin.

3276. Millward, Celia. Place-name generics in Providence, R.I., 1636-1736. Names 19:153-66, Sept. 1971.
Lists the topographical generics and their meanings; shows some of the ways in which written records can be employed in toponymic studies; and suggests how the naming practices of early Providence may provide valuable information about the general language of the settlers and the attitudes of the settlers toward their environment.

3277. —— Universals in place-name generics. Indiana names 3:48-53, Fall 1972.
Includes examples from Rhode Island.

3278. Miner, George L. The possible origin of the name Point Judith. Rhode Island Historical Society. Collections 13:103-04, July 1920.
On the possibility of Roger Williams having named the point after Lady Judith Barrington.

3279. Mussolini Street in retreat. New York times Jan. 11, 1942, p. 14, col. 6.
Providence considers renaming Mussolini St. Russo St.

3280. The Name Rhode Island. Rhode Island Historical Society. Collections 20:81, July 1927.

3281. Parsons, Charles W. Town-names in Rhode Island. Rhode Island Historical Society. Proceedings 1886-87:42-51.

3282. Parsons, Usher. Indian names of places in Rhode-Island: collected by Usher Parsons, M.D., for the R.I. Historical Society. Providence, Knowles, Anthony & Co., printers, 1861. 32p.
Narraganset names.

3283. Pease, John Chauncey & John Milton Niles. A gazetteer of the states of Connecticut and Rhode-Island. Written with care and impartiality, from original and authentic materials. Consisting of two parts. With an accurate and improved map of each state. Hartford, Printed and pub. by William S. Marsh, 1819. 389p.

3284. Preston, Howard W. Providence street names. Rhode Island Historical Society. Collections 20:69-79, July 1927.
Lists established 1772 and 1805.

3285. Rhode Island gazetteer. Providence, Providence journal-bulletin, 1964. 116p.
The official gazetteer of Rhode Island compiled by the Rhode Island Geographic Board and the United States Geographic Board, published in 1932, served as the basis for this new gazetteer.

3286. Rhode Island Historical Society. Committee on Rhode Island Geographical and Historic Names in the Indian Language. Report on Indian names in Rhode Island. Rhode Island Historical Society. Proceedings 1890-91:71-79.
Proposes general rules for the application, spelling, pronunciation, etc., of Indian names.

3287. Rider, Sidney Smith. The lands of Rhode Island as they were known to Caunounicus and Miantunnomu when Roger Williams came in 1636. An Indian map of the principal locations known to the Nahigansets and elaborate historical notes. Providence, The Author, 1904. 297p.
Concerning the Indian names of places on these lands and the meanings of the same, p. 45-58.

3288. —— Sowams, now Warren, the first Indian name of a location known to the Plymouth settlers, 16th of March, 1620-1. Book notes, consisting of literary gossip, criticisms of books and local historical matters connected with Rhode Island 23:57-63, 65-70, 73-79, 81-87, 97, April 7-June 16, 1906.

3289. Stevens, Mana Lyman. Newport streets. Newport Historical Society. Bulletin 67:1-13, Dec. 1928.

3290. Tooker, William Wallace. Indian geographic names, and why we should study them, illus. by some Rhode Island examples. Rhode Island Historical Society. Publications n.s. 5:203-15, Jan. 1898.

3291. Trumbull, James Hammond. Indian local names in Rhode Island. Book notes, consisting of literary gossip, criticisms of books and local historical matters connected with Rhode Island 29:65-68, April 27, 1912.

3292. Tyler, Clarice E. Topographical terms in the seventeenth century records of Connecticut and Rhode Island. New England quarterly 2:383-401, July 1929.
"These terms provide some interesting illustrations of changes in the English language."—Griffin.

3293. U.S. Board on Geographic Names. Official gazetteer of Rhode Island. Comp. by the Rhode Island Geographic Board in cooperation with the United States Geographic Board. Washington, Govt. Print. Off., 1932. 95p.
Includes names recommended for adoption as well as obsolete ones. Review: New York times Jan. 9, 1933, p. 18, col. 3-4.

SOUTH CAROLINA

3294. Anderson, Sallie B. Plantation names near Stateburg. Names in South Carolina 13:31-36, Nov. 1966; 14:23-27, Winter 1967.

3295. —— Some Clarendon County names. Names in South Carolina 15:32-36, Winter 1968; 16:31-36, Winter 1969; 17:30-33, Winter 1970.

3296. Bass, Robert Duncan. Some names in Britton's Neck. Names in South Carolina 24:19-21, Winter 1977.
Marion County.

3297. Benton, John T. Names and places on Cooper River. Names in South Carolina 12:201-11, Winter 1965.
Berkeley County.

3298. Bigham, John A. Calhoun County place names. Names in South Carolina 27:13-15, Winter 1980.

3299. Bonham, Milledge Louis. Notes on place names. American speech 1:625, Aug. 1926.
In South Carolina and Louisiana.

3300. Boykin, Hope. Plantations in lower Kershaw County, part I; Kings County names, part II. Names in South Carolina 16:45-49, Winter 1969; 17:35-39, Winter 1970. maps.

3301. Bull, Elias B. Coastal island names. Names in South Carolina 16:22-30, Winter 1969. maps.

3302. —— Community and neighborhood names in Berkeley County. Names in South Carolina 11:149-57, Winter 1964; 12:211-19, Winter 1965; 13:37-44, Nov. 1966; 14:29-32, Winter 1967.

3303. —— The islands of the littoral. Names in South Carolina 17:11-15, Winter 1970; 18:24-28, Winter 1971.

3304. —— Old postal routes, 1855. Names in South Carolina 23:34-38, Winter 1976.
Information on the names included in a Charleston Mercury postal advertisement, Feb. 14, 1855.

3305. Bull, Gertrude C. Georgetown street names, 1734-1970. Names in South Carolina 17:15-21, Winter 1970.

3306. Chappell, Buford S. Names—old, new, and forgotten—along Monticello Road and Little River. Names in South Carolina 21:15-19, Winter 1974.

3307. Cohen, Hennig. A colonial topographical poem. Names 1:252-58, Dec. 1953.
A study of South Carolina place-names, especially rivers, mentioned in the poem "C. W. in Carolina to E. J. at Gosport."

3308. Coleman, Foster D. & Joe A. Dennis. Inventory of lakes in South Carolina ten acres or more in surface area. Cayce, South Carolina Water Resources Commission, 1974. 221p. maps. (Report no. 119)

3309. Cumming, William Patterson. Naming Carolina. North Carolina historical review 22:34-42, Jan. 1945.
Reprinted without the footnotes: Names in South Carolina 9:14-18, Winter 1962.
Part of a study made with the aid of a grant from the Social Science Research Council.

3310. Davis, Ted M. Place names in and around Walhalla. Names in South Carolina 12:194-97, Winter 1965.

3311. Derrick, Barbara. A name for a state. South Carolina magazine 13:12, 23-24, Aug. 1950.
Origin of Palmetto State, 1776.

3312. Dunbar, Gary S. A southern geographical word list. American speech 36:[293]-96, Dec. 1961.
Glossary of regional topographic terms: cow pen, hog crawl, etc.

3313. Duncan, Alderman. Extinct place names. Names in South Carolina 25:17, Winter 1978.

3314. —— Feminine place names. Names in South Carolina 18:32-36, Winter 1971.

3315. —— Place names of Scottish origin. Names in South Carolina 26:19-21, Winter 1979.

3316. Eisiminger, Sterling. South Carolina nicknames. Names in South Carolina 26:22-24, Winter 1979.

3317. Floyd, Viola Caston. Lancaster County place names. Names in South Carolina 15:39-42, Winter 1968.

3318. Gandee, Lee R. Some Lexington County place names. Names in South Carolina 8:14-20, Winter 1961.

3319. Gasque, Thomas J. A rhyme, and a reason for naming our rivers. Names in South Carolina 15:57-62, Winter 1968.
Refers to Martin V. Moore's The rhyme of the southern rivers (Nashville, M. E. Church Pub. House, 1897), 107p.

3320. Gatschet, Albert Samuel. Onomatology of the Catawba River basin. American anthropologist n.s. 4:52-56, Jan.-March 1902.

3321. Gibert, Anne C. Abbeville District towns and plantations on the Savannah. Names in South Carolina 20:34-37, Winter 1973.

3322. Harrelson, William L. Ancient ferryman on Little Pee Dee. Names in South Carolina 20:23-29, Winter 1973.
Names along the Little Pee Dee River, primarily in Marion County.

3323. Hartley, Dan Manville. Streets of Barnwell. Names in South Carolina 17:45-49, Winter 1970.

3324. Henderson, P. F. Some Aiken County names. Names in South Carolina 7:14-19, Winter 1960.

3325. Hensley, Cornelia H. Some early place names in lower Richland [County]. Names in South Carolina 13:16-26, Nov. 1966.

3326. Hewell, Marion McJ. Some Greenville names. Names in South Carolina 10:130-33, Winter 1963.

3327. Hicks, Theresa M. Streams of Florence County. Names in South Carolina 19:32-35. Winter 1972. map.

3328. Idol, John L. Street names in Pendleton. Names in South Carolina 27:26-27, Winter 1980.

3329. Johnson, Nexsen B. Some Williamsburgh County names. Names in South Carolina 16:36-40, Winter 1969.

3330. Kibler, James & Rene LaBorde. South Carolina post offices, 1867. Names in South Carolina 20:46-49, Winter 1973.

3331. Kinard, James C. Place names in Newberry County. Names in South Carolina 11:48-52, Winter 1964.

3332. LaBorde, Rene. Correct mispronunciation of some South Carolina names. Names in South Carolina 23:38-40, Winter 1976.
Revised from the author's article in The State, Columbia, S.C., July 25, 1976, p. 2E. Correct pronunciation in South Carolina, however.

3333. Lachicotte, Alberta Morel. Georgetown plantation names. Names in South Carolina 3:9-14, Winter 1956.
Georgetown County.

3334. McClendon, Carlee T. Names of plantations and homes in Edgefield County. Names in South Carolina 11:166-70, Winter 1964.

3335. McColl, Eleanor T. Place names in Marlboro County. Names in South Carolina 16:12-19, Winter 1969.

3336. McDavid, Raven I., Jr. & Raymond K. O'Cain. South Carolina county names: unreconstructed individualism. Names 26:106-15, March 1978.
Includes information on the county seat names and comparative data from other states.

3337. McIver, Petrona. Some towns and settlements of Christ Church Parish. Names in South Carolina 13:46-50, Nov. 1966.
Charleston County.

3338. Mackintosh, Robert H., Jr. Historic names in York County (c.1760-1860). Names in South Carolina 24:32-37, Winter 1977. map.

3339. May, Carl H. Spartanburg County names. Names in South Carolina 25:20-22, Winter 1978.

3340. Moffatt, James S., Jr. Place names of the Abbeville area. Names in South Carolina 5:2-8, Winter 1958.

3341. Morrall, John Fripp & Thomas M. Stubbs. The original streets of Beaufort Town. Part 1. Names in South Carolina 16:43-45, Winter 1969.
Continued: Beaufort expands. Ibid. 17:50-53, Winter 1970.

3342. Moses, Herbert A. Some street names in Sumter. Names in South Carolina 14:42-44, Winter 1967.

3343. Names in South Carolina. v. 1- . 1954- .
Editor: Claude Henry Neuffer.
Published by the Dept. of English, University of South Carolina.
Reissue of volumes 1-12, 1954-1965, bound with index.
Review: Kelsie B. Harder, Names 16:194-95, June 1968.
Index to volumes 19-24, 1972-1977. Comp. by Rene LaBorde Neuffer. Columbia, Dept. of English, University of South Carolina, 1978. 24p.
Review of v. 12, 1965: Thomas Pyles, Georgia review 20:370-71, Fall 1966.

3344. Naming of places in the Carolinas. Names in South Carolina 14:36-41, Winter 1967.
Unsigned article reprinted from The Southern and western monthly magazine and review Dec. 1845.

3345. Neuffer, Claude Henry. Alleys, lanes, and courts of Charleston. Names in South Carolina 12:197-201, Winter 1965.

3346. —— The Bottle Alley song. Southern folklore quarterly 29:234-38, Sept. 1965.
Origin of the name of the alley in Charleston, with material about the song in which it is featured.

3347. —— Calhoun County plantations of St. Matthew's Parish near the Congaree-Santee River. Names in South Carolina 12:224-28, Winter 1965.

3348. —— Folk etymology in South Carolina place names. American speech 41:274-77, Dec. 1966.

3349. —— Names in South Carolina: a study of its origin and development. University of South Carolina magazine 1:14-15, 25, Summer 1965.

3350. —— Names reveal the man and the land. South Carolina librarian 6:10-12, March 1962.
Sources of names in the state.

3351. —— Notes on names. Names in South Carolina v. 1- . 1954- .
An extensive article in each issue containing miscellaneous material on names assembled from correspondence and other sources.

3352. —— The origin and development of a state onomastic periodical. Names 16:127-29, June 1968.
About Names in South Carolina.

3353. —— Place names related to the Lords Proprietors and their associates. The State, Columbia, S.C. Oct. 1969.
Prepared for the tricentennial of South Carolina, special edition.

3354. —— Rich source of picturesque names. The State, Columbia, S.C. 75th anniversary edition, Feb. 13, 1966, p. 7A.

3355. —— S.C. place names: from Gobbler's Knob to Whooping Island. South Carolina magazine 31:23-26, Feb. 1967.
Primarily about the publication Names in South Carolina.

3356. —— & Irene Neuffer. The name game: from Oyster Point to Keowee. Illus. by Bob & Faith Nance. [Columbia], Sandlapper Press, [1972]. viii, 60p.
Juvenile literature describing the origins of various place-names in South Carolina.
Review: Elsdon Coles Smith, Names 21:122-23, June 1973.

3357. O'Bannon, Joyce S. Disappearing place names in Barnwell County. Names in South Carolina 18:41-49, Winter 1971.

3358. —— Names in Barnwell County. Names in South Carolina 15:10-18, Winter 1968.

3359. O'Cain, Raymond K. Some place names here and there in Orangeburg County. Names in South Carolina 13:51-57, Nov. 1966.

3360. Owens, Tony J. Cherokee place-names in Upper South Carolina. Names in South Carolina 27:28-30, Winter 1980.

3361. Pearson, Bruce L. On the Indian place-names of South Carolina. Names 26:58-67, March 1978.
230 names of Indian origin, "confined mainly to rivers and streams or to communities or plantations."

3362. —— Savannah and Shawnee: same or different? Names in South Carolina 21:19-22, Winter 1974; 23:20-22, Winter 1976.
Dealing with the derivation of these two words in relation to Indians, the articles throw light on the name of the Savannah River.

3363. Peeples, Robert E. H. Old Hilton Head Island names. Names in South Carolina 19:38-53, Winter 1972.

3364. Pickens, Andrew Lee. Dictionary of Indian place names in upper South Carolina. Greenwood, S.C., 1937. 10p. (South Carolina natural history no. 51-53)

3365. —— Indian place-names in South Carolina. Names in South Carolina 8:3-7, Winter 1961; 9:20-24, Winter 1962; 10:35-40, Winter 1963.

3366. Pruett, Jean. Camden street names. Names in South Carolina 26:10-15, Winter 1979.

3367. Robinson, Lynn C. Street names in Orangeburg. Names in South Carolina 24:24-26, Winter 1977.

3368. Salley, A. S., Jr. Formation of counties in South Carolina. Names in South Carolina 20:29, Winter 1973.

3369. Simons, Katherine Drayton Mayrant. Place names on or near the Cooper River. Names in South Carolina 7:77-79, Winter 1960; 8:88-89, Winter 1961.
Berkeley County.

3370. —— South Carolina island place names. Names in South Carolina 11:163-65, Winter 1964.

3371. Smith, Henry A. M. Some forgotten towns in lower South Carolina. South Carolina historical and genealogical magazine 14:134-46, July 1913.

3372. Stubbs, Thomas M. More about Sumter street names. Names in South Carolina 15:43-47, Winter 1968.

3373. Terry, George D. Eighteenth century plantation names in Upper St. John's, Berkeley. Names in South Carolina 26:15-19, Winter 1979. map.

3374. Thomas, Charles E. Some Fairfield County names of plantations and houseseats. Names in South Carolina 12:228-33, Winter 1965.

3375. U.S. Writers' Program. South Carolina. Palmetto place names. Comp. by workers of the Writers' Program of the Work Projects Administration in the State of South Carolina. Sponsored and pub. by the South Carolina Education Association. Columbia, Sloane Print. Co., 1941. 158p.
Reprinted: Spartanburg, S.C., Reprint Co., 1975.

3376. Ware, Owen. How Montmorenci got its name. South Carolina magazine 12:34-35, Feb. 1949.
"Story of Count Achille de Caradeux in the Vale of Montmorency (formerly Conway's Valley) S.C., from 1840 to some time before 1870, and subsequent renaming of the village of Pole Cat."—Writings on American history.

3377. Watson, Harry L. Greenwood County place names. Names in South Carolina 7:7-10, Winter 1960.
Reprinted from the Index-journal, Greenwood, S.C., July 7, 1935.

3378. Welborn, George E. Some Pickens County names. Names in South Carolina 11:158-62, Winter 1964.

3379. Williams, Horace G. Anderson County place names. Names in South Carolina 10:118-27, Winter 1963; 11:175-81, Winter 1964.

SOUTH DAKOTA

3380. Black Hills names. South Dakota historical collections 6:273-74. 1912.
A letter from Valentine T. McGillycuddy, dated 1908, explaining the origin of many names in the Black Hills region, reprinted from the Rapid City journal.

3381. Clay County Historical Society. Clay County place names, comp. by the Historic Sites Committee, Lloyd R. Moses, editor. Vermillion, S.D., Clay County Historical Society, c1976. 202p. maps.
Review: Jan M. Dykshorn, North Dakota history 44:35-36, Winter 1977; Robert F. Karolevitz, South Dakota history 7:69-70, Winter 1976; Edward C. Ehrensperger, Names 24:305-06, Dec. 1976.

3382. Colorful names in Black Hills originated in days of frontier gold rush. Christian Science monitor July 11, 1952, p. 6C.

3383. Diller, Aubrey. Pawnee House: Ponca House. Mississippi Valley historical review 36:301-04, Sept. 1949.
Missouri River trading post, 1790s.

3384. Distad, Lucile. A study of place-names in Mellette County, South Dakota.
Thesis (M.A.) Univ. of South Dakota, 1943.

3385. Frybarger, Marjorie L. A study of place-names in Meade County, South Dakota.
Thesis (M.A.) Univ. of South Dakota, 1941.

3386. Gilmore, Melvin Randolph. Meaning of the word Dakota. American anthropologist n.s. 24:242-45, April-June 1922.
The author considers Dakota to be a derivative of the same root as the Omaha endakutha, and he believes that both words should be taken in the sense "peculiar people" rather than "friends."

3387. Hamburg, James F. Papertowns in South Dakota. Journal of the West 16:40-42, Jan. 1977. map.
At least 34 towns were surveyed into blocks and lots in which buildings or at most a very few were erected.

3388. —— Postmasters' names and South Dakota place-names. Names 21:59-64. 1973.

Contains lists of post offices by county with name of first postmaster for whom they were named.

3389. Hanson, Agnes J. A study of place-names in Kingbury County, South Dakota.
Thesis (M.A.) Univ. of South Dakota, 1940.

3390. Harlow, Dana D. A study of place-names in Spink County, South Dakota.
Thesis (M.A.) Univ. of South Dakota, 1944.

3391. Holland, Ann J. A study of place-names in Sanborn County, South Dakota.
Thesis (M.A.) Univ. of South Dakota, 1942.

3392. Hutcheson, Floyd E. A study of place-names in Davison County, South Dakota.
Thesis (M.A.) Univ. of South Dakota, 1944.

3393. James, Leta May. A study of place-names in Beadle County, South Dakota.
Thesis (M.A.) Univ. of South Dakota, 1939.

3394. Jones, Mildred McEwen. Supplement [Derivation of local place names]; In her Early Beadle County, 1879 to 1900. Huron, S.D., 1961. p. 97-104.

3395. Kleinsasser, Anna. A study of place-names in Charles Mix County, South Dakota.
Thesis (M.A.) Univ. of South Dakota, 1938.

3396. Molumby, Joseph A. A study of place-names in Clark County, South Dakota.
Thesis (M.A.) Univ. of South Dakota, 1939.

3397. Mundt, Karl E. Two Mobridges in two states. Congressional record 105:16816-17, Sept. 7, 1959.
South Dakota, and new town in Montana. Includes origin of name.

3398. Parker, Watson, & Hugh K. Lambert. Black Hills ghost towns. Chicago, Swallow Press, 1974. 215p.
1st ed.: Norman, Okla., 1964. 36 ℓ.
Bibliography: p. 214-15.
Review: George Ernest Webb, Arizona and the West 17:86-87, Spring 1975; Allen C. Ashcraft, Journal of the West 14:146-47, April 1975; Gary D. Olson, Western historical quarterly 6:450, Oct. 1975.
A gazetteer of more than 600 towns.

3399. Place names and post offices. Wi-iyohi (South Dakota Historical Society) 6:1-6, April 1952; 6:3-6, May 1952; 6:3-6, June 1952; 6:3-6, July 1952; 6:3-6, Aug. 1952.
List of more than 1900 early South Dakota post offices, with location in a present county, date of founding, and the first and last date the name was found on a map.

3400. Sneve, Virginia Driving Hawk. Dakota's heritage, a compilation of Indian place names in South Dakota. Sioux Falls, S.D., Brevet Press, 1973. xi, 74p.

3401. Snyder, Mary P. A study of place-names in Turner County, South Dakota.
Thesis (M.A.) Univ. of South Dakota, 1940.

3402. South Dakota. Legislature. Legislative manual. 190?- . Pierre.
Some issues compiled by Dept. of Finance.
Each issue contains a list of county names with origin of name.

3403. South Dakota. State College of Agriculture and Mechanic Arts. What's that name? South Dakota names most often mispronounced, [by] Judy A. Wheeler and George H. Phillips. Rev. ed. Brookings, 1963. [10] ℓ.

3404. U.S. 88th Congress, 1st session. Senate. A bill to change the name of Fort Randall Reservoir in the State of South Dakota to Lake Francis Case. S. 130. Jan. 14 (legislative day, Jan. 9), 1963. Washington, 1963. 1p.
Introduced by Mr. Mundt and referred to the Committee on Public Works.
In honor of the late Senator of South Dakota.
Subsequent documents relating to this bill were published as follows:

U.S. 88th Congress, 1st session. Senate. Changing the name of Fort Randall Reservoir, Missouri River, S. Dak., to Lake Francis Case. Report no. 266, to accompany S. 130. June 19, 1963. Calendar no. 247. Washington, 1963. 3p.
Submitted by Mr. McNamara, from the Committee on Public Works, without amendment.

—— [Reprint of the original bill, June 19, 1963, to accompany the report. Report no. 266 and Calendar no. 247 added]. 1p.

U.S. 88th Congress, 1st session. House. An act to change the name of Fort Randall Reservoir in the State of South Dakota to Lake Francis Case. S. 130. In the House of Representatives June 24, 1963. Washington, 1963. 1p.
Referred to the Committee on Public Works. Passed the Senate June 20, 1963.

—— Changing the name of Fort Randall Reservoir, Missouri River, S. Dak., to Lake Francis Case. Report no. 567, to accompany S. 130. July 22, 1963. Washington, 1963. 3p.
Submitted by Mr. Davis, from the Committee on Public Works, without amendment.

—— [Reprint of the act, July 22, 1963, to accompany the report. Report no. 567 and House Calendar no. 107 added]. 1p. An identical bill was introduced in the House as follows:

U.S. 88th Congress, 1st session. House. A bill to change the name of Fort Randall Reservoir in the State of South Dakota to Lake Francis Case. H.R. 1578. Jan. 10, 1963. Washington, 1963. 1p.
Introduced by Mr. Berry and referred to the Committee on Public Works.

3405. —— —— A bill to change the name of the Big Bend Reservoir in the State of South Dakota to Lake Sharpe. S. 131. Jan. 14 (legislative day, Jan. 9), 1963. Washington, 1963. 1p.
Introduced by Mr. Mundt and referred to the Committee on Public Works.
In honor of M. Q. Sharpe, the late Governor of South Dakota.
Subsequent documents relating to this bill were published as follows:

U.S. 88th Congress, 1st session. Senate. Changing the name of Big Bend Reservoir, S. Dak., to Lake Sharpe. Report no. 269, to accompany S. 131. June 19, 1963. Calendar no. 250. Washington, 1963. 3p.
Submitted by Mr. McNamara, from the Committee on Public Works, without amendment.

—— [Reprint of the original bill, June 19, 1963, to accompany the report. Report no. 269 and Calendar no. 250 added]. 1p.

U.S. 88th Congress, 1st session. House. An act to change the name of the Big Bend Reservoir in the State of South Dakota to Lake Sharpe. S. 131. In the House of Representatives June 24, 1963. Washington, 1963. 1p.
Referred to the Committee on Public Works. Passed the Senate June 20, 1963.

— Changing the name of Big Bend Reservoir, S. Dak., to Lake Sharpe. Report no. 568, to accompany S. 131. July 22, 1963. Washington, 1963. 3p.

Submitted by Mr. Davis, from the Committee on Public Works, without amendment.

— [Reprint of the act, July 22, 1963, to accompany the report. Report no. 568 and House Calendar no. 108 added]. 1p.

An identical bill was introduced in the House as follows:

U.S. 88th Congress, 1st session. House. A bill to change the name of the Big Bend Reservoir in the State of South Dakota to Lake Sharpe. H.R. 1577, Jan. 10, 1963. Washington, 1963. 1p.

Introduced by Mr. Berry and referred to the Committee on Public Works.

3406. U.S. Writers' Program. South Dakota. South Dakota place names, enl. and rev. Comp. by workers of the Writers' Program of the Work Projects Administration in the State of South Dakota. Sponsored by the Department of English, University of South Dakota. Vermillion, Univ. of South Dakota, 1941. 689p.

Reprinted: South Dakota geographic names. Sioux Falls, S.D., Brevet Press, 1973. 639p.

Bibliography: p. 679-84.

A preliminary series of pamphlets was issued in 1940. These, together with new material, form the one-volume edition of the complete work. The project was supervised by Dr. Edward C. Ehrensperger, Head of the English Dept., who also conducted the graduate research program which produced a number of place-name theses.

TENNESSEE

3407. Bible, Jean. Town named for first lady. Dandridge, Tenn., bears Martha Washington's maiden name. New York times June 11, 1961, p. XX 13.

3408. Chase, Carroll & Richard McP. Cabeen. The first hundred years of United States territorial postmarks, 1787-1887. Territory of the United States south of the River Ohio. American philatelist 58:203-07, Dec. 1944.

Includes list of post offices, with notes on the proposed state of Franklin and some names.

3409. Coppock, Paul R. History in Memphis street names. West Tennessee Historical Society. Papers 11:93-111. 1957.

3410. Fink, Paul M. Smoky Mountains history as told in place-names. East Tennessee Historical Society. Publications 6:3-11. 1934.

3411. — Some east Tennessee place names. Tennessee Folklore Society. Bulletin 7:40-50, Dec. 1941.

3412. — That's why they call it . . . The names and lore of the Great Smokies. Jonesboro, Tenn., P. M. Fink, 1956. 20p.

3413. — & Myron H. Avery. The nomenclature of the Great Smoky Mountains. East Tennessee Historical Society. Publications 9:53-64. 1937.

An abstracted account under the title, Arnold Guyot's explorations in the Great Smokies, in Appalachia 2:253-61, Dec. 1936.

A major portion of the names either originated with or became confirmed as a result of Arnold Guyot's exploration of the region in the period 1856-1860.

3414. Flowers, Paul. Place names in Tennessee. West Tennessee Historical Society. Papers 14:113-23. 1960.

3415. Fullerton, Ralph O. Place names of Tennessee. Nashville, Tennessee. Dept. of Conservation, Division of Geology, 1974. 421p. (Bulletin no. 73)
Review: Kelsie B. Harder, Names 23:124, June 1975.
A list of place-names, county by county with location keyed to the quadrangle maps of the state.

3416. Irwin, Ned. The legend of Eve Mills. Tennessee Folklore Society. Bulletin 14:28-30, June 1948.
Monroe County.

3417. Kay, Donald. Municipal British-received place names in Tennessee. Appalachian journal 2:78-80. 1974.

3418. McWhorter, A. W. Classical place names in Tennessee. Word study 9:7-8, Nov. 1933.

3419. Martin, Daniel S. A guide to street naming and property numbering. Nashville, Tennessee State Planning Commission, 1951. 47p. (Publication no. 230)

3420. Mason, Robert L. A famous landmark is in dispute, two states contend over changing the name of Mt. Collins. New York times Aug. 31, 1930, sec. 8, p. 9, col. 2-4.
Mount Kephart desired for peak in Smoky Mountains National Park, but U.S. Board on Geographical Names refused.

3421. Montgomery, James R. The nomenclature of the upper Tennessee River. East Tennessee Historical Society. Publications 28:46-57. 1956.

3422. Morris, Eastin. The Tennessee gazetteer, or topographical dictionary; containing a description of the several counties, towns, etc. To which is prefixed a general description of the state, and a condensed history from the earliest settlements down to the convention in 1834. With an appendix, containing a list of the practising attorneys at law in each county; principal officers of the general and state governments; times of holding courts; and other valuable tables. Nashville, W. H. Hunt & Co., 1834. 178p.

3423. Ordoubadian, Reza. Rutherford County: a study in onomastics. 250p.
Thesis (Ph.D.) Auburn Univ. 1968. Dissertation abstracts 29:890A, Sept. 1968.
The names are discussed under the six classifications established by George R. Stewart in his A classification of place-names. Names 2:1-13, March 1954.

3424. Patton, Eugene E. First territory named for Washington. D.A.R. magazine 86:139-40, 251, Feb. 1952.
Washington District, N.C. (the later State of Tennessee), established Dec. 3, 1776.

3425. Peak named for Cammerer, Smoky Mountain ridge also honors Park director. New York times Feb. 25, 1942, p. 24, col. 2.
Great Smoky Mountains National Park peak named for Arno B. Cammerer.

3426. Starnes, D. T. Bulls Gap and some other related place names. Names 14:41-42, March 1966.

3427. Swint, Henry Lee. Ezekiel Birdseye and the free state of Frankland. Tennessee historical quarterly 3:226-36, Sept. 1944.

Proposals for creating a new nonslave state, to be called Frankland, from the mountain counties of Tennessee, Virginia, North Carolina, and Georgia.

3428. Tennessee blue book. Nashville, Secretary of State.
The origin of county names—a section in each issue 1961-62 to date, including the Special edition for young readers.

3429. U.S. Board on Geographic Names. Decisions. No. 28, June 30, 1932. Great Smoky Mountains National Park, North Carolina and Tennessee. Washington, Govt. Print. Off., 1934. 46p.

3430. U.S. 88th Congress, 1st session. Senate. A bill to change the name of the lake formed by Kentucky Dam. S. 462. Jan. 23 (legislative day, Jan. 15), 1963. Washington, 1963. 2p.
Introduced by Mr. Kefauver and Mr. Gore and referred to the Committee on Public Works.
To change the name from Kentucky Lake to Tennessee-Kentucky Lake.
An identical bill was introduced in the House as follows:

U.S. 88th Congress, 1st session. House. A bill to change the name of the lake formed by Kentucky Dam. H.R. 4254. Feb. 26, 1963. Washington, 1963. 2p.
Introduced by Mr. Murray and referred to the Committee on Public Works.

3431. Williams, Samuel C. The first territorial division named for Washington. Tennessee historical magazine n.s. 2:153-64, April 1932.
Priority of the county of Washington, N.C. (now in the State of Tennessee) as the first locality in the United States to bear the name of Washington.

TEXAS

3432. Aarts, Dorothy. Ghost towns of the republic of Texas. n.p., 1939. 22p.

3433. "Abused Spanish" place names in Texas. American speech 19:238, Oct. 1944.
Signed: C. D. P.
Bunavista, Tex., a name which is a "fermentation of petroleum industry and abused Spanish."

3434. Anderson, John Q. From Flygap to Whybark: some unusual Texas place names. Texas Folklore Society. Publications 31:73-98. 1962.
Bibliography: p. 95-98.

3435. —— Texas stream names. Texas Folklore Society. Publications 32:112-47. 1964.
Bibliography: p. 132-34.

3436. Aschbacher, Frances M. Pronouncing directory of cities, towns, and counties in Texas. San Antonio, The Author, 1953. 32p.

3437. Bartholomew, Ed Ellsworth. 800 Texas ghost towns. Fort Davis, Tex., Frontier Book Pub. 1971. 105p. map.
Alphabetical list, locates town, and gives brief history and present condition.

3438. Benson, Nettie Lee. San Saba. Southwestern historical quarterly 51:88-89, July 1947.

3439. Bolton, Herbert Eugene. The native tribes about the East Texas missions. Texas State Historical Association. Quarterly 11:249-52, April 1908.
Full treatment of the name Texas.

3440. Bryson, Artemisia Baer. Contrasting American names compared with the Spanish names found in Texas. American speech 3:436, June 1928.

3441. Cameron, Minnie B. County of Bexar. Southwestern historical quarterly 53:477-79, April 1950.
Corrects material in correspondence of Mrs. Cameron, ibid. 49:275, Oct. 1946.

3442. Carlisle, Mrs. George F. The origin of some of the Dallas street names. Local History and Genealogical Society [Bulletin] 3:16, May 1957.

3443. Clover, Margaret G. The place-names of Atascosa County, Texas. Austin, 1952. 229 ℓ.
Thesis (M.A.) Univ. of Texas, 1952.
Bibliography: 203-18.
A collection of the current and past place-names of Atascosa County, arranged alphabetically with origin of the names.

3444. Coltharp, Lurline H. Bilingual onomastics: a case study. In Paul R. Turner, ed., Bilingualism in the Southwest. Tucson, Univ. of Arizona Press, c1973. p. 131-40.
Deals with the specific problems that a bilingual city, El Paso, with its English and Spanish names, has in naming streets.

3445. Curtis, Albert. Fabulous San Antonio. San Antonio, Naylor, 1955. 287p.
San Antonio street names: p. 280-87.

3446. Curtis, Rosalee M. Texas counties named for South Carolinians. Names in South Carolina 20:39-46, Winter 1973. map.

3447. Davis, Jeff. Around the plaza. San Antonio light June 9, 1936.
A newspaper article on curious geographical names in Texas.

3448. Dienst, Alex. The naming of Metheglin Creek, Bell County. Texas Folk-lore Society. Publications 3:208-09. 1924.

3449. Dobie, James Frank. How the Brazos River got its name. Texas Folk-lore Society. Publications 3:209-17. 1924.

3450. —— Stories in Texas names. Southwest review 21:125-36, 278-94, 411-17, Jan., April, July 1936.
Also in J. F. Dobie, ed., Straight Texas (Hatboro, Pa., Folklore Associates, 1966), p. 1-78; reprint of Texas Folklore Society. Publications no. 13, c1937.
Sources: p. 70-78.
"Folk origins of many Texas place names."—American speech.

3451. Edwards, Roy. Cut'n Shoot, Texas. Western folklore 18:33-34, 1959.
Legends about this name, not a town, but a community and a state of mind.

3452. El Paso streets and how they were named. El Paso County Historical Society. Password 13:33-34, Summer 1968.

3453. Emmett, Chris. Shanghai Pierce: a fair likeness. Norman, Univ. of Oklahoma, 1953. 326p.
"There shall be no town naming to the exclusion of my perpetuity": p. 110-18.
Railroad stations named for members of the Telferner, Hungerford, and Pierce families.

3454. Fulcher, Walter. The way I heard it: tales of the Big Bend. Ed. with introduction and notes by Elton Miles. Austin, Univ. of Texas Press, 1959. 87p.
Places, names, and what happened: p. 30-52.
Presents new information on many Big Bend place names.

3455. Fulmore, Zachary Taylor. The history and geography of Texas as told in county names. Rev. ed. Austin, S. R. Fulmore, 1926. 225p.
1st ed. 1915. 312p.

3456. ——— Austin, Steck Co., 1935. 312p. (Original narratives of Texas history and adventure)
A facsimile reproduction of the original edition of 1915.

3457. Gannett, Henry. A gazetteer of Texas. 2d ed. Washington, Govt. Print. Off., 1904. 177p. (U.S. Geological Survey. Bulletin no. 224. Series F, Geography, 36)
1st ed. 1902. 162p. (Bulletin no. 190. Series F, Geography, 28)

3458. Geiser, Samuel Wood. Ghost-towns and lost-towns of Texas, 1840-1880. Texas geographic magazine 8:9-20, Spring 1944.
Works cited: p. 20.
Lists more than a thousand towns.

3459. Gibson, Freda. Local place names. West Texas Historical and Scientific Society. Publications 1:37-41. 1926. (Sul Ross State Teachers College. Bulletin 21)

3460. Gill, Donald Artley. A linguistic analysis of the place names of the Texas Panhandle. Commerce, Tex., 1970. 288 ℓ.
Thesis (Ph.D.) East Texas State Univ., 1970. Abstract: Dissertation abstracts 31A:2366, Nov. 1970.
Bibliography: 273-88.

3461. —— Texas Panhandle place names of Spanish origin. In South Central Names Institute. Ethnic names. Commerce, Tex., Names Institute Press, 1978. p. 37-47. (Publication 6)
References: p. 44-47.

3462. Gilpin, George H. Street-names in San Antonio: signposts to history. Names 18:191-200, Sept. 1970.

3463. Glasgow, William J. On the confusion caused by the name El Paso. El Paso Historical Society. Password 1:65-67, May 1956.

3464. Gray, Glenn Arthur. Gazetteer of streams of Texas. Washington, Govt. Print. Off., 1919. 267p. (U.S. Geological Survey. Water-supply paper 448)

3465. Gray, Jo Anne. Place-names of the Texas Coastal Bend. Commerce, Tex., 1962. 209 ℓ.
Thesis (M.A.) East Texas State College, 1962.
Selected bibliography: 196-204.

3466. Greear, Yvonne E. Antelope, buffalo, deer and tiger in the street: a brief history of Corpus Christi, Texas, street names. In South Central Names Institute. They had to call it something. Commerce, Tex., Names Institute Press, 1974. p. 55-63. (Publication 3)

3467. —— The name of the game: street names. In South Central Names Institute. Labeled for life. Commerce, Tex., Names Institute Press, 1977. p. 29-33. (Publication 5)

3468. The Handbook of Texas. Walter Prescott Webb, editor-in-chief, H. Bailey Carroll, managing editor, Llerena B. Friend, Mary Joe Carroll, Louise Nolen, editorial assistants. Austin, Texas State Historical Assoc., 1952. 2v.
Includes origin of name and other information about many Texas place-names.

3469. Hayes, Lois Ercanbrack. Place names in Concholand. Commerce, Tex., 1969. 115 ℓ.
Thesis (M.A.) East Texas State Univ., 1969.
Selected bibliography: 111-15.
Concholand is the eight-county area touching the Concho River.

3470. —— Place names of Concholand. In South Central Names Institute. Of Edsels and Marauders. Commerce, Tex., Names Institute Press, 1971. p. 51-57. (Publication 1)

3471. Hayes, Robert M. East Texas miscellany. Dallas morning news July 8, 1960, sec. I, p. 15.
Texas town names: Slocum, Cash, and Po-Boy.

3472. Haynes, Harry. Death of early towns in Washington County: what changes time has wrought. Dallas morning news Aug. 17, 1902, p. 4, col. 4-5.

3473. —— Towns gone: some places in Washington County of which nothing but dim memory remains, the sites even having been lost. Dallas morning news Sept. 12, 1902, p. 6, col. 6-7.

3474. —— Towns of Washington County: origin, date and reason of establishment, and how the names were suggested. Dallas morning news Sept. 1, 1902, p. 6, col. 6-7.

3475. Hill, Frank P. Plains names. Panhandle-Plains historical review 10:36-47. 1937.
Bibliography: p. 47.

3476. Hill, Robert T. Descriptive topographic terms of Spanish America. National geographic magazine 7:291-302, Sept. 1896.
Prepared for reports to Director of U.S. Geological Survey on geography of Texas-New Mexico region.
Topographical features as protuberances or mountain forms, plains, declivities, streams, and stream valleys.

3477. Home city has Nimitz Parkway. New York times Dec. 24, 1944, p. 18, col. 3.
Fredericksburg, Tex., street named for Admiral Chester W. Nimitz.

3478. Jones, Nancy N. Pronunciation patterns of place names in northeast Texas. Commerce, Tex., 1967. 219 ℓ.
Thesis (M.A.) East Texas State Univ., 1967.
Selected bibliography: 216-19.

3479. Jordan, Terry G. The origin of motte and island in Texan vegetational terminology. Southern folklore quarterly 36:121-35, June 1972. maps.
The Texas use of three terms, grove, island and motte (or mott), to mean a clump of trees in a prairie.

3480. Kay, Donald. Texas: British through and through. Indiana Place-Name Survey. Newsletter 4:2-6. 1974.
A handlist of Texas municipal place-names and British equivalent place-names.

3481. Kemp, Mrs. Jeff T. Significance and origin of the names of the rivers and creeks of Milam County. Cameron, Tex., n.d. 6p.
An address based on the author's thesis (M.A.) Univ. of Texas, 1929.

3482. King, Dick. Ghost towns of Texas. San Antonio, Naylor, 1953. 140p.

3483. Knight, Ona. Street names of Palestine. Junior historian (Texas) 9:19-21, 23, March 1949.
Sketches of persons after whom streets were named.

3484. McCampbell, Coleman. Texas history as revealed by town and community name origins. Southwestern historical quarterly 58:91-97, July 1954.
A sampling of names taken from The handbook of Texas. Austin, Texas State Historical Assoc., 1952. 2v.

3485. McGregor, Stuart. Spanish-named Texas streams. Dallas news March 29, 1961, p. 3.

3486. Madison, Virginia & Hallie Stillwell. How come it's called that? Place names in the Big Bend country. Rev. ed. New York, October House, 1968. 129p. maps.
1st ed.: Albuquerque, Univ. of New Mexico Press, 1958.
Review of 1st ed.: Madison S. Beeler, Journal of American folklore 74:178-80, April-June 1961.

3487. —— Place names in the Big Bend of Texas. Western folklore 14:200-05, July 1955.

3488. Martin, George Castor. Some Texas stream and place names. San Antonio, N. Brock, 1947. 15p.

3489. Massengill, Fred I. Texas towns; origin of name and location of each of the 2148 post offices in Texas. An interesting compilation of nomenclature running the whole gamut of human interest and sympathies, including religion, history, sports, ranch life and personalities all properly classified for your convenience, entertainment and to add to the sum total of useful knowledge. Terrell, Tex., 1936. 222p.

3490. Morgan, Paul. Texas ballads and other verses. Dallas, Tardy Pub. Co., 1934. 173p.
Introduction (place names of Texas): p. 9-51.

3491. Murley, Olga Chadwell. Texas place names: voices from the historic past in a goodly land. Commerce, Tex., 1966. 73 ℓ.
Thesis (M.A.) East Texas State Univ., 1966.
Selected bibliography: 71-73.

3492. Norvell, Claudia W. Texas. Dallas, Southwest Press, 1933. 79p.
A search for the meaning of the name Texas through a study of the Indians of Texas.

3493. Olsen, Frank N. Tales of Texas cities. Dallas morning news June 28, 1970, Magazine sec., p. 19.
Exotic names of Texas towns and cities.

3494. Origin of the name of Texas. Magazine of American history 7:67, 149, July, Aug. 1881; 8:145-46, 158, 167, Feb., March 1882.
"A discussion of the source and significance of the name with various interpretations by different authors."—Price.

3495. Origins of names of Texas cities, towns, mountains, rivers and physiographic divisions. Texas almanac and state industrial guide 1936:109-18.
A revision and amplification of a list of cities and towns published in Texas almanac 1926:338-46.

3496. Payne, L. W., Jr. How medicine mounds of Hardeman County got their names. Texas Folk-lore Society. Publications 3:207-08. 1924.

3497. —— Indian Bluff on Canadian River. Texas Folk-lore Society. Publications 3:205-06. 1924.
Legend in name.

3498. Place-names. West Texas Historical and Scientific Society. Publication 8:18-22. 1938.

3499. Pope, Harold Clay. The lighter side of Texas place naming. Western folklore 13:125-29, April 1954.

3500. —— Western history in Texas names. True West 3:29-31, Sept.-Oct. 1955.

3501. Price, Armstrong. Place names in Texas. Texas geographic magazine 8:31-34, Autumn 1944.

3502. Rutherford, Phillip Roland. Place-name study of five East-Central Texas counties. Commerce, Tex., 1964. 161 ℓ.
Thesis (M.A.) East Texas State College, 1964.
Bibliography: 158-61.

3503. Sanders, John Barnette. The postoffices and post masters of Nacogdoches County, Texas, 1845-1930. Center, Tex., 1964. 12p.

3504. —— The postoffices and post masters of Panola County, Texas, 1845-1930. Center, Tex., 1964. 12p.

3505. —— The postoffices and post masters of Sabine County, Texas, 1845-1930. Center, Tex., 1964. 7p.

3506. —— The postoffices and post masters of San Augustine County, Texas, 1845-1930. Center, Tex., 1964. 6p.

3507. —— The postoffices and post masters of Shelby County, Texas, 1845-1930. Center, Tex., 1964. 16p.

3508. Sebree, Mac. What's in a name? Just about everything. Austin (Tex.) statesman Feb. 14, 1959, p. 3.
How U.S. oil fields get their names; picturesque examples.

3509. Shields, Carla Sue Smith. Spanish influences on East Texas place names and vocabulary. Commerce, Tex., 1966. 70 ℓ. map.
Thesis (M.A.) East Texas State Univ., 1966.
Bibliography: 68-70.

3510. Smith, Victor J. How Dead Horse Canyon got its name. Texas Folk-lore Society. Publications 3:209. 1924.

3511. Somes, Evelyn. Some place names and Mexican superstitions of the Balmorhea neighborhood. West Texas Historical and Scientific Society. Publications 2:53-54. 1928 (Sul Ross State Teachers College. Bulletin, extra no., Jan. 1, 1928)

3512. Sperry, Omer E. Place names. West Texas Historical and Scientific Society. Publications 8:18-22. 1938. (Sul Ross State Teachers College. Bulletin v. 19, no. 4)
Within area of proposed Big Bend National Park.

3513. Stokes, George M. A guide to the pronunciation of Texas towns. Waco, The Author, c1977. xii, 141p.

3514. Strecker, John Kern. Animals and streams; a contribution to the study of Texas folk names. Waco, Tex., Baylor Univ., 1929. 23p. (Contributions to folk-lore, no. 2)

3515. Strickland, Rex W. Ghost towns of Texas. Southwestern historical quarterly 47:410, April 1944.

3516. Tarpley, Fred. 1001 Texas place names. Austin, Univ. of Texas Press, 1980. 236p.

3517. —— Place names of northeast Texas. Commerce, Tex., East Texas State Univ., Education Research and Field Services, 1969. xxi, 245p.
Gives origin of name for those found on the current general county maps of the Texas Highway Department for 26 counties in northeast Texas.
Review: Lalia P. Boone, Names 18:318-20, Dec. 1970.

3518. —— Principles of place-name studies outlined. Humanities in the South, newsletter of the Southern Humanities Conference no. 32, p. [3-4], Fall 1970.
Texas names are used as illustrations in the ten broad categories of origins of place-names.

3519. Texas. Agricultural & Mechanical University. Texas Agricultural Extension Service. Texas pronunciation guide for unusual names. College Station, Tex., n.d. 26p.
Preface signed: R. B. Hickerson and W. N. Williamson.

3520. —— State Highway Department. Planning Survey Division & U.S. Federal Highway Administration. Bureau of Public Roads. Listing of Texas cities, towns, communities, and railroad stations by counties. n.p., 1967. 21 ℓ.

3521. Texas counties and their names. Fort Worth Genealogical Society. Genealogical Society bulletin 8:12, 15, March; 8:7-10, April; 8:7-10, May; 8:7-10, June; 8:5-7, July; 8:5-6, Aug.; 8:12-13, Sept.; 8:7-10, Oct. 1965.

3522. Texas towns of historic interest that have been abandoned or remain small towns today. "Ghost" towns and "lost" towns. Texas almanac and state industrial guide 1936:119-24.

3523. Tilloson, Cyrus. Place names of Nueces County. Frontier times 26:175-78, April 1949.

3524. Tolbert, Frank X. At "Sanphilop" by the Brazos. Dallas morning news Oct. 25, 1959, sec. III, p. 1.
Pronunciation of Sanfelipe.—American speech.

3525. —— Dialogue heard in city of Cuney. Dallas morning news Oct. 30, 1960, p. 1-18.
"The all-Negro town of Cuney was named for Norris Wright Cuney, Negro Republican leader."—American speech.

3526. —— Earl of Clarendon inspired the name? Dallas morning news July 11, 1961, sec. IV, p. 1.
Origin of the name Clarendon.—American speech.

3527. —— Last rail stop on way to Hades. Dallas morning news Feb. 10, 1959, sec. 4.
The Texas place names Ditty-Waw-Ditty and Cheesy (Chiesa).

3528. —— Nixon, Kennedy look good to Little Hope. Dallas morning news Oct. 30, 1960, p. 1-15.
"On the name of the Texas town, Little Hope."—American speech.

3529. —— A phantom fort in Jones County. Dallas morning news Nov. 8, 1960, sec. 4, p. 1.
The origin of the name of Fort Phantom Hill, Texas.—American speech.

3530. —— Why does Montell always count 75? Dallas morning news April 24, 1961, sec. IV, p. 1.
On the Texas town named after Capt. Charles S. de Montel.—American speech.

3531. Town renamed Truman; was Mesquite Tap, Texas. New York times Nov. 23, 1945, p. 9, col. 2.

3532. Tuerk, Richard. Names in and around Mulberry Bend. In South Central Names Institute. The scope of names. Commerce, Tex., Names Institute Press, 1979.

3533. Two place-name pronunciations. American speech 4:156-57, Dec. 1928.
Staunton, Va., and Houston, Tex.

3534. U.S. 88th Congress, 1st session. House. A bill to designate the McGee Bend Dam and Reservoir on the Angelina River, Texas, as the Sam Rayburn Dam and Reservoir. H.R. 7594. July 16, 1963. Washington, 1963. 1p.
Introduced by Mr. Brooks and referred to the Committee on Public Works.
Subsequent documents relating to this bill were published as follows:

U.S. 88th Congress, 1st session. House. Designating the McGee Bend Dam and Reservoir on the Angelina River, Texas, as the Sam Rayburn Dam and Reservoir. Report no. 581, to accompany H.R. 7594. July 25, 1963. Washington, 1963. 2p.
Submitted by Mr. Davis, from the Committee on Public Works, without amendment.

—— [Reprint of the original bill, July 25, 1963, to accompany the report. Report no. 581 and House Calendar no. 112 added]. 1p.

U.S. 88th Congress, 1st session. Senate. An act to designate the McGee Bend Dam and Reservoir on the Angelina River, Texas, as the Sam Rayburn Dam and Reservoir. H.R. 7594. In the Senate August 6, 1963. Washington, 1963. 1p.
Referred to the Committee on Public Works. Passed the House of Representatives August 5, 1963.

3535. U.S. 88th Congress, 1st session. House. Joint resolution to designate the lake to be formed by the waters impounded by Sanford Dam, Canadian River project, Texas, as "Lake Meredith." H.J. Res. 442. May 20, 1963. Washington, 1963. 1p.
Introduced by Mr. Rogers and referred to the Committee on Interior and Insular Affairs.
Reintroduced in the 89th Congress, 1st session, as H.J. Res. 95.
In honor of A. A. Meredith.

3536. U.S. Federal Writers' Project. Texas. Dallas guide and history.
Unpublished manuscript in Dallas Public Library.
Street names, O pioneers: p. 549-59. Includes an alphabetical list with source of each name.

3537. Van Demark, Harry. Texas county names. Texas monthly 5:309-15, April 1930.

3538. Walter, Ray A. The town of Mexia. Southwestern historical quarterly 62:108-09, July 1958.
Origin of name.

3539. What's in a name. Texas municipalities 10:160, Nov. 1923.
Comment on and analyses of a series of articles running in the Dallas news, Sunday supplement, on How Texas towns got their names.

3540. Wheat, Jim. More ghost towns of Texas. [Garland, Tex., Lost & Found, 1971]. 44p.
Bibliography: p. 44.

3541. Williams, J. W. Ghost towns in the Wichita Falls area. Southwestern historical quarterly 47:311-12, Jan. 1944.

3542. Williamson, Lela. How Devil's River received its name. West Texas Historical and Scientific Society. Publications 1:43. 1926. (Sul Ross State Teachers College. Bulletin 21)

3543. Willis, Roystein E. Ghost towns of the south plains. Lubbock, 1941. 82p. Thesis (M.A.) Texas Technological College.

3544. Young, Della I. Names in the old Cheyenne and Arapahoe Territory and the Texas Panhandle. Texas Folk-lore Society. Publications 6:90-97. 1927.

UTAH

3545. Bero, John A. Utah place names. Utah humanities review 2:79-80, Jan. 1947.
Only five cities in Utah derive their names from the Book of Mormon, and only four have Biblical names.

3546. Chamberlin, Ralph V. Place and personal names of the Gosiute Indians of Utah. American Philosophical Society. Proceedings 52:1-13, Jan. 1913.

3547. Gannett, Henry. A gazetteer of Utah. Washington, Govt. Print. Off., 1900. 43p. (U.S. Geological Survey. Bulletin no. 166)

3548. Hunt, Charles B. Geology and geography of the Henry Mountains region, Utah. Washington, Govt. Print. Off., 1953. 234p. (U.S. Geological Survey. Professional paper, no. 228)
Derivation of place names: p. 21-24.

3549. Jett, Stephen C. An analysis of Navajo place-names. Names 18:175-84, Sept. 1970.
Many official place-names in northeastern Arizona, northwestern New Mexico, and southeastern Utah are of Navajo origin, either by Anglicization of the Navajo names or by translation. Most Navajo place designations describe features of the natural landscape.

3550. Judd, Neil M. On some names in Natural Bridges National Monument. National parks magazine 41:16-19, Oct. 1967.

3551. Leigh, Rufus Wood. Five hundred Utah place names, their origin and significance. Salt Lake City, Deseret News Press, 1961. 109p.

A pocketbook excerpted from his full-length book manuscript, Indian, Spanish, and government survey place names of the Great Basin and Colorado plateaus.

3552. —— Lake Bonneville, its name and history. Utah historical quarterly 26:150-59, April 1958.

Excerpt from a book manuscript, Place names of the Great Basin and Colorado plateaus.

3553. Marling, William. From one spot in Utah. Harper's magazine 252:4, Jan. 1976.

Oddities in the names given by the pioneers.

3554. Phillips, Maxine Brown. The strange new language of a magic land. Denver post March 14, 1965, Empire magazine, p. 6-9.

An article on the Glen Canyon National Recreation Area with emphasis on the place-names in it.

3555. Roylance, Ward Jay. Derivation of county names; In his Materials for the study of Utah's counties. Salt Lake City, 1962. p. 17-18.

Extracted from Facts about Utah (Utah Tourist & Publicity Council, 1962), 4th printing, rev.

3556. Thompson, Grant & Don Dunn. Udy Hot Springs: a bogey. Western folklore 18:166, April 1959.

3557. U.S. Board on Geographic Names. Decisions. No. 38, Decisions rendered April 4, 1934. Zion National Park, Utah. Washington, Govt. Print. Off., 1934. 6p.

3558. U.S. 88th Congress, 1st session. Senate. Joint resolution to designate the lake to be formed by the waters impounded by the Flaming Gorge Dam, Utah, and the recreation area contiguous to such lake in the states of Wyoming and Utah, as "O'Mahoney Lake and Recreation Area." S. J. Res. 17. Jan. 15, 1963. Washington, 1963. 2p.

Introduced by Mr. McGee and others and referred to the Committee on Interior and Insular Affairs.

Subsequent documents relating to this joint resolution, and related joint resolutions introduced in the House, were published as follows:

U.S. 88th Congress, 1st session. House. Joint resolution to designate the lake to be formed by the waters impounded by the Flaming Gorge Dam, Utah, and the recreation area contiguous to such lake in the states of Wyoming and Utah, as "O'Mahoney Lake and Recreation Area." H.J. Res. 293. Feb. 28, 1963. Washington, 1963. 2p.

Introduced by Mr. Aspinall and referred to the Committee on Interior and Insular Affairs.

U.S. 88th Congress, 1st session. Senate. Designating the lake to be formed by the waters impounded by the Flaming Gorge Dam, Utah, in the states of Wyoming and Utah, as "Lake O'Mahoney." Report no. 279, to accompany S.J. Res. 17. June 19, 1963. Calendar no. 260. Washington, 1963. 5p.

Submitted by Mr. Jackson, from the Committee on Interior and Insular Affairs, with amendments, as recommended by the Dept. of the Interior, to restrict the name to the lake, and designate it as Lake O'Mahoney.

—— [Reprint of the original joint resolution, June 19, 1963, with amendments, to accompany the report. Report no. 279 and Calendar no. 260 added] 2p.

U.S. 88th Congress, 1st session. House. Joint resolution to designate the lake to be formed by the waters impounded by the Flaming Gorge Dam, Utah, as "Ashley Lake." H.J. Res. 604. July 31, 1963. Washington, 1963. 1p.

Introduced by Mr. Burton and referred to the Committee on Interior and Insular Affairs.

In honor of William Henry Ashley (1778-1838), a fur trader, explorer, and Congressman.

—— Providing designations for the lake to be formed by the waters impounded by Flaming Gorge Dam. Report no. 879, to accompany S.J. Res. 17, Oct. 30, 1963. Washington, 1963. 4p.

Submitted by Mr. Rogers, from the Committee on Interior and Insular Affairs, with amendments, that that portion of the lake in Utah be known as Lake Ashley and the portion in Wyoming as Lake O'Mahoney. Two members of the Committee dissented. The Committee considered S.J. Res. 17, H.J. Res. 293, and H.J. Res. 604 simultaneously.

—— [Reprint of S.J. Res. 17, Oct. 30, 1963, with amendments, to accompany the report. Report no. 879 and House Calendar no. 161 added]. 2p.

3559. U.S. Writers' Program. Utah. Origins of Utah place names. 3d ed. Comp. and written by Utah Writers' Project, Work Projects Administration. Sponsored and pub. by Utah State Dept. of Public Instruction. Salt Lake City, 1940. 47p. (American guide series)

1st ed. 1938. 29p.; 2d ed. 1938. 36p.; comp. and written by U.S. Federal Writers' Project. Utah.

3560. Utah Tourist and Publicity Council. Facts about Utah. 2d printing rev. Salt Lake City, 1959. 114p.

Frequently reprinted, revised.

Counties, with origin of name: p. 46-52.

VERMONT

3561. Abbott, Susie A. Place names in Peacham. Vermont quarterly n.s. 20:291-94, Oct. 1952.

3562. Allen, Morse S. Connecticut and Vermont town names. Vermont history n.s. 22:273-78, Oct. 1954.

Influence of Connecticut.

3563. Billings, Agnes B. Ripton—the derivation of the name. Vermont history n.s. 22:305, Oct. 1954.

3564. Caldwell, Renwick K. The man who named Vermont. Vermont history n.s. 26:294-300, Oct. 1958.

Dr. Thomas Young.

3565. Changes in town names, from Thompson's Gazetteer, p. 200, 1842 edition. Vermont quarterly n.s. 21:239, July 1953.

3566. Clement, John. Naming Vermont in 1763? Vermont Historical Society. Proceedings n.s. 1:83-92. 1930.

"An examination of the Sherburne town records with a map of Killington and Rutland, dated 1774."—Griffin.

3567. Colby, Elbridge. How Bristol Pond became Winona Lake. Vermont history n.s. 36:150-04, Summer 1968.
Bibliographical footnotes.

3568. Crèvecoeur, Michel-Guillaume St. Jean de. Letters to Ethan Allen, 31 May, and 17 July 1785; In Vermont. Governor and Council, Records. Montpelier, 1875. v.3, p.386-90.
Lists his suggestions for naming settlements and civil divisions to be established including those adopted: St. Johnsbury (for his alias, Hector St. John), Vergennes, and Danville. Allen's reply giving the action of the Legislature, 2d March, 1786: p.391-92.

3569. Dale, George N. Place names in northeastern Vermont. Vermont quarterly n.s. 21:145-48, April 1953.

3570. —— Towns in Essex County named for famous men. Vermont quarterly n.s. 20:204-07, July 1952.

3571. Dean, James. An alphabetical atlas, or, Gazetteer of Vermont; affording a summary description of the state, its several counties, towns, and rivers. Calculated to supply, in some measure, the place of a map; and designed for the use of offices, travellers, men of business, &c. Montpelier, Printed by Samuel Goss for the author, 1808. 43p.

3572. George, Noah J. T. A pocket geographical and statistical gazetteer of the State of Vermont. Embellished with diagrams. To which is prefixed a particular description of the City of Washington, and a large number of statistical tables of the United States. Comp. from the most recent authorities and personal observation. Haverhill, N.H., S. T. Goss, 1823. 264p.

3573. Hartwell, Florence B. Old names of Vermont towns. Vermont history n.s. 24:71-72, Jan. 1956.

3574. Hayward, John. A gazetteer of Vermont: containing descriptions of all the counties, towns, and districts in the state, and of its principal mountains, rivers, waterfalls, harbors, islands, and curious places. To which are added statistical accounts of its agriculture, commerce and manufactures; with other useful information. Boston, Tappan, Whittemore & Mason, 1849. 216p.

3575. Huden, John Charles. Historical Champlain maps. Vermont history n.s. 27:34-40, 85-87, 191-93, Jan.-July 1959.
Includes identification of names on early maps and modern names that correspond with the map names.

3576. —— Indian place-names in Vermont. Vermont history n.s. 23:191-203, July 1955.
Additional Indian place-names, ibid. n.s. 24:168-69, April 1956.

3577. —— Indian place names in Vermont. Burlington, Vt., The Author, 1957. 32p. (Monograph no. 1)
Review: Hamill Kenny, Names 6:119-23, June 1958; G. M. Day, New England quarterly June 1958, p. 273-74.

3578. —— Iroquois place-names in Vermont. Vermont history n.s. 25:66-76, Jan. 1957.

3579. Hudson, Verne R. The naming of Marshfield, Vt. Vermont history n.s. 23:56-57, Jan. 1955.

3580. Johnston, Thesba N. & others. Vermont town names and their derivations. Vermont quarterly n.s. 20:260-78, Oct. 1952; 21:10-16, 101-17, 188-99, Jan.-July 1953.

3581. Leighly, John. Gallic place-names for Vermont, 1785. Names 21:65-74, June 1973.

Reprinted in Vermont history 42:12-21, Jan. 1974.

Discussion of St. Jean de Crèvecoeur's suggestions to Ethan Allen for place-names in Vermont commemorating French assistance in the American Revolution.

3582. Lounsbury, Floyd C. Iroquois place-names in the Champlain Valley. Albany, University of the State of New York. State Education Dept. [1972?] 23-66p.

Reprinted from the Report of the New York-Vermont Interstate Commission on the Lake Champlain Basin, 1960. Legislative document (1960), no. 9, p. 23-66.

3583. McAleer, George. A study in the etymology of the Indian place name, Missisquoi. Worcester, Mass., Blanchard Press, 1906. 102p.

Bibliography: p. 101-02.

"In his little volume will be found all that is known of the history of the word, with the opinions and discussions of all authorities from the earliest to the most recent,—practically every etymology that has ever been suggested is recorded, and the list of them is an object lesson in the difficulties as well as the 'ease' of etymologizing."—Review of historical publications relating to Canada 11:199. 1906.

In the Review of historical publications relating to Canada (15:92. 1910) McAleer is criticized for a further study, The etymology of Missisquoi. Addenda. (Worcester, Mass., The Author, 1910. 39p.), as being careless in references and etymologies.

3584. Morrissey, Charles T. The name of the game is toponymy. Vermont life 29:20-22, Spring 1975.

3585. The Name, Vermont. Vermont history 41:78-81. 1973.

3586. Palermo, Joseph. The mythical etymology of the name of Vermont, trans. by Maurice Kohler. Vermont history 41:78-79. Spring 1973.

Translation of the author's L'etymologie mythique du nom du Vermont. Romance notes 3:188-89, Autumn 1971.

H. N. Muller III, The name of Vermont; an afterword. Vermont history 41:79-81, is in disagreement with the thesis of Joseph Palermo as presented in the translation.

3587. Prentice, E. Parmalee. A name and its meaning. Vermont quarterly n.s. 19:30-34, Jan. 1951.

Equinox Mountain.

3588. Roberts, Gwilym R. Where did Poultney get its name. Vermont Historical Society. News and notes 11:82, July 1960.

3589. Rouillard, Eugène. Missisquoi, origine et signification de ce nom. Société de Géographie de Québec. Bulletin 4:248-51, oct. 1910.

About the name of a bay of Lake Champlain in Quebec and a river in northern Vermont.

3590. Rubicam, Harry C. Grafton, Vt.—the source of its name. Vermont history n.s. 22:54, Jan. 1954.

3591. Slawson, George Clarke; Arthur W. Bingham, & Sprague W. Drenan. The postal history of Vermont. New York, Collectors Club, 1969. 308p. maps. (Collectors Club handbook no. 21)

3 Bibliographical footnotes.
The post offices of Vermont: p. 182-222. Gives town, county, date of establishment, and history of its existence and name.

3592. Swift, Esther Munroe. Vermont place-names: footprints of history. Brattleboro, Vt., Stephen Greene Press, 1977. 701p. maps.
Bibliography: p. 615-20.
Review: H. Gardiner Barnum, Vermont history 45:252-54, Fall 1977; Eugene Green, Names 26:116-17, March 1978.

3593. Thompson, Zadock. A gazetteer of the State of Vermont; containing a brief general view of the state, a historical and topographical description of all the counties, towns, rivers, &c. Montpelier, Pub. by E. P. Walton and The Author, 1824. 310p.
Reprinted in the author's History of Vermont (Burlington, Chauncey Goodrich, 1842); also in 1853 ed.

3594. Vermont. New England historical and genealogical register 16:346, Oct. 1862.
Naming of Vermont.

3595. Ward, Merlin B. Moretown, Vt.—the source of its name. Vermont history n.s. 22:54, Jan. 1954.

VIRGINIA

3596. Ashton, Betty Parker. Rapidan or Rapid Anne? Name of river is puzzling. Richmond times-dispatch Nov. 1, 1959, p. D-3, col. 1-3.

3597. Barbour, Philip L. Chickahominy place names in Captain John Smith's True relation. Names 15:216-27, Sept. 1967.
Deals with the Indian nomenclature of the Chickahominy River basin in 1607. The guest editor of this issue, Hamill Kenny, raises several questions, p. 225-26.

3598. —— The earliest reconnaissance of Chesapeake Bay area: Captain John Smith's map and Indian vocabulary. Virginia magazine of history and biography 79:280-302, July 1971.
Bibliography: p. 283-84.
The Indian place-names recorded by Capt. Smith in his writings and on his map are listed, roughly located, and where possible analyzed. Most are in the language called Powhatan, one of the Central-Eastern group of the Algonkian family. Names are mainly in Virginia and Maryland with a few in Delaware and Pennsylvania.

3599. Berkely, Francis L. "Purton." Virginia magazine of history and biography 43:150-52, April 1935.
Origins and associations of the name of an estate in Gloucester County.

3600. Biggs, Thomas H. Geographical and cultural names in Virginia. Charlottesville, Virginia Division of Mineral Resources, 1974. 374p. map. (Information circular, no. 20)
Review: P. Burwell Rogers, Names 23:215-16, Sept. 1975.
An index to the names appearing on the 805 U.S. Geological Survey maps of the state.

3601. Bristol, Roger P. Approved place names in Virginia, an index to Virginia names approved by the United States Board of Geographic Names from 1970 through 1973. Charlottesville, Univ. of Virginia, 1974. 14p. (Virginia Place Name Society. Occasional paper no. 18)

3602. —— Greene County place names. Charlottesville, Univ. of Virginia, 1974. 27p. (Virginia Place Name Society. Occasional paper no. 17)

3603. Brown, Alexander Crosby. Wolf Trap, the baptism of a Chesapeake Bay shoal. Virginia magazine of history and biography 59:176-83, April 1951.

3604. Burrill, Meredith F. Terminology of Virginia's geographic features. Virginia Geographical Society. Bulletin 9:12-20, March 1957.

3605. Butts, Marshall W. Place names of early Portsmouth. A publication of the Portsmouth, Virginia, American Revolution Bicentennial Committee. Portsmouth, Portsmouth Public Schools Printshop, 1973. vii, 32p. map.
Review: P. Burwell Rogers, Names 22:75-76, June 1974.

3606. Cocke, Charles Francis. Parish lines, Diocese of Southern Virginia. Richmond, Virginia State Library, 1964. 287p.
Names of counties and parishes: p. 235-46. Includes origin.

3607. —— Parish lines, Diocese of Southwestern Virginia. Richmond, Virginia State Library, 1960. 196p. maps. (Virginia State Library. Publication no. 14)
Bibliography: p. 179-80.
Counties in the Diocese with location of parishes and churches: p. 153-78.

3608. Cridlin, William Broadus. A history of colonial Virginia, the first permanent colony in America, to which is added the genealogy of the several shires and counties and population in Virginia from the first Spanish colony to the present time. Pageant ed. Richmond, Williams Print. Co., 1923. 181, 13p.
Plantations, shires, counties by date of foundation, and source of name.

3609. Crouch, Kenneth Elwood. Bedford has one of several schools named for women. Bedford (Va.) bulletin-democrat June 25, 1964, p. 6.
Includes origin of the name of Staunton River.

3610. —— The Hocomawananch River. Bedford, Va., 1957. 6 ℓ.
Reprinted from the Oct. 3, 1957 issue of the Bedford (Va.) democrat.
Is the river which is to be dammed Roanoke or Staunton? Earlier reference to a name for the river is the Indian name Hocomawananch.

3611. —— The names of the streams and mountains in Bedford County, Virginia. Bedford, Va., 1959. 6 ℓ.
From the Bedford (Va.) democrat issue of May 7, 1959, with title: Bedford's streams, mountains have many picturesque names.

3612. —— New map of post-annexation Bedford adds many streets. Bedford (Va.) democrat Oct. 13, 1960, sec. 2, p. 2.
Names of new streets in the town added by Jan. 1960 annexation, and some changes of names within the town due to that annexation.

3613. —— Place names of Bedford County, their origins and outside associations. Bedford (Va.) bulletin-democrat Jan. 31, 1963, sec. 3, p. 6; Feb. 7, sec. 2, p. 4; Feb. 14, sec. 3, p. 5; Feb. 21, sec. 2, p. 6.

3614. —— Research on Moneta's name leads to Italy, Indian tribe. Bedford (Va.) bulletin-democrat Oct. 24, 1963, p. 6.
Theory of origin of this place-name in Bedford community.

3615. —— Should it be Huddleston or Huttleston? Some history. Bedford (Va.) bulletin-democrat Sept. 6, 1962, sec. 2, p. 1, col. 1-2.

More on the same, under title Huttleston Rogers stories evoke interest of family, ibid. Sept. 13, 1962, p. 5.

Station on the old Virginia Railway named for its builder, H. Huttleston Rogers, but misspelled.

3616. —— Spelling Chamblissburg poses problem for many. Bedford (Va.) bulletin-democrat May 24, 1978, p. 5B

The post office was established in the store of William Chambliss in 1827.

3617. —— Street names in the town of Bedford, Virginia. Bedford, Va., 1958. 3 ℓ.
Reprinted from the Bedford (Va.) democrat issues of Dec. 11 and 23, 1958.

3618. —— That name Staunton River: official views and history. Bedford (Va.) bulletin-democrat Sept. 5, 1963, p. 6.

Historical background concerning the name of the river which makes Staunton River High School a suitable name for a new school on the south side of Bedford County.

3619. Dashiell, Segar Cofer. Local place names are peculiar but colorful, ancient, approved. Newport News (Va.) daily press, Aug. 14, 1964, p. 14.

Place-names in Isle of Wight County.

3620. Dramatic history of Albemarle is reflected in quaint names. Charlottesville Daily progress, July 1, 1937, p. 7.

3621. Edwards, Richard. Statistical gazetteer of the states of Virginia and North Carolina; embracing important topographical and historical information, from recent and original sources. With the results of the last census, in many cases to 1855. Richmond, Pub. for the proprietor, 1856. 601p.

Earlier edition: Richmond, 1855. 469p. Did not include North Carolina.

3622. Evans, Cerinda W. Newport News, origin of the name. Virginia magazine of history and biography 55:31-44, Jan. 1947.

3623. —— On how Buckroe got its name. (Letter to the editor). Newport News (Va.) daily press, April 24, 1966, p. 4.

3624. —— Third Earl of Southampton gave name to City of Hampton. Newport News (Va.) daily press, Dec. 15, 1957, p. D1.

3625. —— Whence Tangier? (Letter to the editor). Newport News (Va.) daily press, Aug. 3, 1958, p. D2.

The naming of Tangier Island in the upper Chesapeake Bay.

3626. First town named Washington. New York times May 30, 1949, p. 26.

Claim of Washington, Va., surveyed and plotted by George Washington, Aug. 4, 1749.

3627. Gannett, Henry. A gazetteer of Virginia. Washington, Govt. Print. Off., 1904. 159p. (U.S. Geological Survey. Bulletin no. 232, Ser. F, Geography, no. 40; also as House doc. no. 727, 58th Congress, 2d session)

Reprinted with the author's West Virginia gazetteer, Baltimore, Genealogical Pub. Co., 1975. 159, 164p.

3628. Gerard, William R. Some Virginia Indian words. American anthropologist n.s. 7:222-49, April-June 1905.

Derivation and meaning of some place-names in Virginia with the author's answer to a criticism of his opinions by William Wallace Tooker in Oct.-Dec. 1904 issue.

3629. —— The Tapehanek dialect of Virginia. American anthropologist n.s. 6:313-30, April-June 1904.
Deals with the derivation of the language and some place-names.
Criticized by William Wallace Tooker, ibid. Oct.-Dec. 1904.

3630. Gilliam, Charles Edgar. Ajacan, the Algonkian name for Hampton Roads, Virginia. Names 6:57-59, March 1958.

3631. —— The Algonquian term—Ajacan—its Indian and Spanish meaning. Archeological Society of Virginia. Quarterly bulletin 12:[2-11], Dec. 1957.

3632. —— Ethnic significance of the term: Appomattoc. Archeological Society of Virginia. Quarterly bulletin 7:[11-12], March 1953.
Concerned only with the use of this term within the area of the Powhatan tribal country Appomattoc.

3633. —— Geoethnology—Apamatuck (Mattica) and/or Appamattucks: the chief villages of the Appomattoc, 1607-1691. Archeological Society of Virginia. Quarterly bulletin 4:[8-9], June 1950.
Earlier spellings and meaning of the name Appomattox.

3634. —— "Harrican" in colonial Virginia records. Virginia magazine of history and biography 50:337-44, Oct. 1942.
References in colonial records to variant spellings of Hurricane as a place-name.

3635. —— Indicated portals of safe entry into Appomattoc. Archeological Society of Virginia. Quarterly bulletin 7:14-15, June 1953.

3636. —— Pagan Creek: ethnology of name. Archeological Society of Virginia. Quarterly bulletin 14:9, March 1960.

3637. —— The Potomac debate. Names 15:242, Sept. 1967.
Disagrees with the meaning "place of trade" or "emporium" especially if trade was in buffalo skins or steatite.

3638. —— Tsenakcommacah. Archeological Society of Virginia. Quarterly bulletin 9:4-7, March 1955.
Meaning of the name.

3639. Gordon, James W., Jr. French place-names in Virginia.
Thesis (M.S.) Univ. of Virginia, 1933. "Deposited in the Virginia room of the University Library; one copy may be borrowed."--American speech.

3640. —— French place names in Virginia. Charlottesville, Virginia Place Name Society, 1975. 20ℓ. (Occasional paper no. 19)

3641. Green, Bennett Wood. How Newport's News got its name: Cui Bono? Richmond, W. E. Jones, 1907. 142p.

3642. —— Word-book of Virginia folk-speech. Richmond, W. E. Jones' Sons, 1912. 530p.
Includes Virginia names of places.

3643. Gritzner, Janet H. Seventeenth century generic place-names: culture and process on the Eastern Shore. Names 20:231-39, Dec. 1972.
Summarizes the results of a study to identify the various cultural processes involved in naming all of the peninsula east of Chesapeake Bay.

3644. Hall, Virginius Cornick, Jr. Virginia post offices, 1789-1859. Virginia magazine of history and biography 81:49-97, Jan. 1973.

Listed from the official post office lists, 1798-1837, and other references.

Virginia Place Name Society. Newsletter, no. 5 (May 1978, p. 6) adds 54 that were not given county locations.

3645. Hanson, Raus McDill. Virginia place names: derivations, historical uses. Verona, Va., McClure Press, 1969. 253p.

Includes notes gathered from long-time residents regarding the origins of many of the 1000 names listed.

Review: P. Burwell Rogers, Names 17:306-11, Dec. 1969; Eugene Green, Names 20:207-08, Sept. 1972.

The author's notes for a future supplement have been deposited in the Manuscripts Department of Alderman Library, University of Virginia with other Virginia Place Name Society records.

3646. Heckewelder, John Gottlieb Ernestus. Names given by the Lenni Lenape or Delaware Indians to rivers, streams and places in the now states of New Jersey, Pennsylvania, Maryland, and Virginia. Pennsylvania German Folklore Society. Publications 5:1-41. 1940.

Published also in American Philosophical Society. Transactions 4:351-96. 1834; Historical Society of Pennsylvania. Bulletin 1:121-35, 139-54, June, Sept. 1847; Moravian Historical Society. Transactions 1872:275-333; published separately: Bethlehem [Pa.], H. T. Claude, printer, 1872. 58p.; and in his A narrative of the mission of the United Brethren among the Delaware and Mohegan Indians. Cleveland, Burrows Bros., p. 523-66.

3647. Hench, Atcheson L. Virginia county names. American speech 19:153, April 1944.

In Piedmont, Va., the custom is to omit the word county whenever the speaker wishes to.

3648. Hiden, Martha Woodroof. How justice grew: Virginia counties, an abstract of their formation. Williamsburg, Virginia, 350th Anniversary Celebration Corp., 1957. 101p. (Jamestown 350th anniversary historical booklet, no. 19)

Bibliography: p. 79.

Includes the naming of the counties.

3649. A Hornbook of Virginia history. Richmond, Virginia State Library, 1965. (Virginia State Library Publications no. 25)

Chapters entitled The counties of Virginia, p. 13-30, and The cities of Virginia, p. 31-38, contain comments on the origin of the names.

3650. Hummel, Ray Orvin. A list of places included in 19th century Virginia directories. Richmond, Virginia State Library, 1960. 153p. (Virginia. State Library. Publications, no. 11)

3651. Johnson, Thomas Cary. How Albemarle got its name. Magazine of Albemarle County history 16:20-24. 1957-1958.

3652. Kemper, Charles E. Home names in the Valley. Virginia magazine of history and biography 45:353-56, Oct. 1937.

A partial list, with brief notes, of names of the homes of prominence in the Valley of Virginia, given and used before the Civil War.

3653. Kennedy, Joe. They're all around, but what are their names? Roanoke (Va.) times and world news Aug. 28, 1979, Sec. C, p. 1, 6. map.

Mountains in the Roanoke area.

3654. Kinnier, C. L. The renaming of Arlington streets. Arlington historical magazine 1:41-51, Oct. 1959.

Describes the work of Arlington's Street Names Committee, appointed in 1932, and the system worked out for relieving confusion in street and highway names in Arlington County.

3655. Long, Charles Massie. Virginia county names; two hundred and seventy years of Virginia history. New York, Neale Pub. Co., 1908. 207p.

Authorities consulted: 1 page at end.

3656. Lynchburg, Va. Ordinances, etc. Ordinance naming and describing streets of the city of Lynchburg, Va., amended to August 26, 1958. n.p., 1958. 66p.

3657. McJimsey, George Davis. Topographic terms in Virginia. New York, Columbia Univ. Press, 1940. 151p. (American speech. Reprints and monographs, no. 3)

Appeared serially in American speech 15:3-38, 149-79, 262-300, 381-419. 1940.

Bibliography of works cited: p. 141-47.

"A topographic term is not a place name: it is not a proper name used to designate a specific topographic feature. It is merely a word or phrase applied to a group of topographic features which possess essentially the same characteristics. This study is concerned with proper names only when they supply significant topographic information."--Introd.

cf. Henry Bosley Woolf, The DAE and topographic terms. American speech 17:177-78, Oct. 1942, which records words from McJimsey's list not found in the Dictionary of American English.

3658. Martin, Joseph. A new and comprehensive gazetteer of Virginia, and the District of Columbia. To which is added a History of Virginia from its first settlement to the year 1754: with an abstract of the principal events from that period to the independence of Virginia, written expressly for the work by a citizen of Virginia [W. H. Brockenbrough]. Charlottesville, J. Martin, 1836. 636p.

Also published 1835, and at Richmond without date under title: A comprehensive description of Virginia and the District of Columbia.

3659. Milbourne, Mrs. V. S. The founding of Luray and the origin of its name. William and Mary College quarterly historical magazine 2d ser. 10:142-44, April 1930.

3660. Miller, Mary R. Place-names of the Northern Neck of Virginia: a proposal for a theory of place-naming. Names 24:9-23, March 1976.

Based on her study of the names of the counties of Westmoreland, Northumberland, Richmond, and Lancaster, five periods are suggested: Indian; English, the age of autocracy; the age of nostalgia in which settlers transplanted names from the homeland; the romantic age glorifying the common man, usually a local figure; and the age of public indifference and of governmental authorization.

3661. Moore, J. Brewer & Bruce S. Trant. Street renaming is no cinch, but it solves a lot of problems, as the colorful experience of Portsmouth, Va., demonstrates. American city 77:82-84, Aug. 1962.

3662. The New Newport News. Richmond times-dispatch Sept. 13, 1957, p. 12.

On the place-name.

3663. Origin of the name of Newport News. William and Mary College quarterly historical magazine 9:233-37, April 1901.

3664. Percy, Alfred. Old place names, West Central Piedmont and Blue Ridge Mountains. Madison Heights, Va., Percy Press, 1950. 22, 5p.

3665. Presnall, Clifford C. Names of waters bordering the Northern Neck. Northern Neck of Virginia historical magazine v. 21, no. 1, p. 33-34, n.d.

3666. Quarles, Garland R. The streets of Winchester, Virginia: the origin and significance of their names. Winchester, Va., Farmers and Merchants National Bank, n.d. 47p.

3667. Quinn, David Beers, ed. The Roanoke voyages, 1584-1590, documents illustrating the English voyages to North America under the patent granted to Walter Raleigh in 1584. London, Hakluyt Society, 1955. 2v. (Hakluyt Society works, 2d ser., v. 104)

Part C. Commentary on the map of Raleigh's Virginia [part 2], p. 852-72.

Algonquian place-names in Virginia and North Carolina north and south of the swamp which marks the present state line between the two states.

3668. Raitt, Nathan S. The "whys" of the word; place names of Virginia. Virginia Association of Assessing Officers. News-bulletin 1961, no. 4, p. 5.

3669. Rawlings, James Scott. Virginia's colonial churches: an architectural guide together with their surviving books, silver & furnishings. Richmond, Garrett & Massie, 1963. xi, 286p.

Each discussion of the 48 colonial churches includes the origin of the name of the parish.

3670. Robinson, Morgan Poitiaux. Virginia counties: those resulting from Virginia legislation. Virginia. State Library. Bulletin 9:1-283. 1916.

Includes the origin of the county names.

3671. Rogers, P. Burwell. Changes in Virginia names. American speech 31:21-24, Feb. 1956.

Names of persons and places undergoing changes in pronunciation.

3672. —— Indian names in tidewater Virginia. Names 4:155-59, Sept. 1956.

3673. —— Place names on the Virginia peninsula. American speech 29:241-56, Dec. 1954.

Between the James and the York rivers.

3674. —— Tidewater Virginians name their homes. American speech 34:251-57, Dec. 1959.

A study of patterns in naming homes.

3675. —— Virginia counties. Charlottesville, Univ. of Virginia, Oct. 1972. 10p. (Virginia Place Name Society. Occasional paper no. 16)

A history of the names and changes.

The extensive place-name papers of the late Mr. Rogers have been placed in the collection of the Virginia Place Name Society in the Manuscript Division of the Alderman Library of the University of Virginia.

3676. Sheppard, Harvey. Town name changes in Virginia. Virginia Postal History Society, Way markings. Feb. 1972, Nov. 1972.

3677. Some Virginia names and their meanings. Virginia magazine of history and biography 11:317-21, Jan. 1904.

3678. A Street is named for Harmon Killebrew. Kansas City times June 18, 1959, p. 28.

A street in Springfield, Va., was named for the baseball player.

3679. [Street names of Fredericksburg, Va.]. New York times Jan. 22, 1960, p. 26.
A full Topics of the Times column.

3680. Tanner, Douglas W. From the Albemarle bookshelf: Charlottesville's royal namesake, Britain's Queen Charlotte. Magazine of Albemarle County history v. 33-34:173-80, 1975-76.
Includes reference to other places named for the Queen, e.g., Charlotte, N.C.

3681. —— Madison County place names. Charlottesville, Univ. of Virginia, 1978. xiv, 119p. map. (Virginia Place Name Society. Occasional publication no. 21)

3682. —— Place name research in Virginia: a handbook. Charlottesville, Univ. of Virginia, 1976. 52p. (Virginia Place Name Society. Occasional publication no. 20)
A comprehensive manual for the Virginia survey of place-names with lists of terms, standard designators and bibliographical aids.

3683. Tooker, William Wallace. Derivation of the name Powhatan. American anthropologist n.s. 6:464-68, July-Sept. 1904.
"The generally accepted etymology and translation as given by the late Dr. Trumbull for the word Powhatan, 'falls in a stream,' is erroneous."—Price.

3684. —— The Kuskarawaokes of Captain John Smith. American anthropologist 6:412-13, Oct. 1893.
The derivation and meaning of the name Roanoke.

3685. —— Meaning of some Indian names in Virginia. William and Mary College quarterly historical magazine 14:62-64, July 1905.

3686. —— The names Chickahominy, Pamunkey, and the Kuskarawaokes of Captain John Smith; with historical and ethnological notes. New York, F. P. Harper, 1901. 90p. (The Algonquian series, no. 9)
1st essay from American anthropologist 8:257-63, July 1895, with additions and corrections.
2d essay also published in American antiquarian 17:289-93, Sept. 1895.
3d essay from American anthropologist 6:409-14, Oct. 1893.

3687. —— The Powhatan name for Virginia. Lancaster, Pa., New Era Print. Co., 1906. p. 23-27.
Reprinted from the American anthropologist n.s. 8:23-27, Jan.-March 1906.

3688. —— Some Indian names of places on Long Island, N.Y. and their correspondence in Virginia, as mentioned by Capt. John Smith and associates. Magazine of New England history 1:154-58, July 1891.

3689. —— Some more about Virginia names. American anthropologist n.s. 7:524-28, July-Sept. 1905.
Reprinted separately, 1905.
Adds further information to the etymology of names given in the author's answer to William R. Gerard, ibid. Oct.-Dec. 1904.

3690. —— Some Powhatan names. American anthropologist n.s. 6:670-94, Oct.-Dec. 1904.
A criticism of the opinions of William R. Gerard as found ibid. April-June 1904.

3691. Trumbull, James Hammond. Indian names in Virginia. Historical magazine 2d ser. 7:47-48, Jan. 1870.

3692. Two place-name pronunciations. American speech 4:156-57, Dec. 1928.
Staunton, Va., and Houston, Tex.

3693. U.S. Board on Geographic Names. Decisions. No. 35. Decisions rendered April 5, 1933. Shenandoah National Park, Virginia. Washington, Govt. Print. Off., 1934. 13p.

3694. —— Decisions. No. 36. Decisions rendered April 5, 1933. Names in the vicinity of Shenandoah National Park, Virginia. Washington, Govt. Print. Off., 1934. 4p.

3695. Virginia. Division of Planning and Economic Development. Index of the surface waters of Virginia. Rev. March 1951. n.p., 1951. 59ℓ.

1st ed. 1949.

Lists the names and approximate locations of the surface waters of Virginia.

Kenneth E. Crouch has added to a few copies two typewritten sheets of additions and corrections for Bedford County.

3696. —— Division of Water Resources. Index of the surface waters of Virginia. Rev. Jan. 1960. Richmond, 1960. 66p.

Incorporates the additions for Bedford County made by Kenneth E. Crouch.

3697. —— University. Library. Approved place names in Virginia: an index to Virginia names approved by the United States Board on Geographic Names through 1969, comp. by Mary Topping and other members of the Reference staff of the University of Virginia Library. Charlottesville, Univ. Press of Virginia, 1971. 167p.

An alphabetical list giving identification, location, and date of decision by the United States Board.

3698. Virginia Place Name Society. Newsletter. no. [1]- , May 1972- . Charlottesville, Va.

Information on the Virginia place-name survey, requests for information, and other notes.

3699. —— Occasional papers, no. 1- . Charlottesville, Univ. of Virginia, 1961- .

1961, no. 1, Feb. 17. A preliminary bibliography of Virginia place-names literature, by Gary S. Dunbar. 12 ℓ.

1961, no. 2, Sept. 20. Virginia place names, 1676. [Reproduction of a portion of Notes to accompany a facsimile of John Speed's A map of Virginia and Maryland, 1676, published by the McGregor Library, Univ. of Virginia, 1961]. 8 ℓ.

1961, no. 3, Dec. Analysis of Virginia place-names as to origin, by John E. Manahan. 8 ℓ.

1962, no. 1, Jan. 30. Some notes on bison in early Virginia, by Gary S. Dunbar [including list of buffalo place-names on U.S. Geological Survey topographic sheets]. Addenda to Virginia place-name bibliography. 10 ℓ.

1962, no. 2, June 18. Ah Sid, by N. Harvey Deal. Yellow Jacket town, by Chas. Edgar Gilliam. A note on the place-name Blacks and Whites (present Blackstone, Va.), by Virginia Jordan. 13 ℓ.

1962, no. 3. For this number, members received copies of Index of the surface waters of Virginia, by Virginia. Division of Water Resources (see no. 3696).

1962, no. 4, Aug. 8. Meadow Branch, the stream east of Monticello, lately called Tufton Branch, with some notes on the nearby surface waters, by J. C. Wyllie. 7ℓ.

1963, no. 1, March 25. Manassas Gap, by David Alan Williams. 7ℓ.

1963, no. 2, Oct. 8. Totier Creek, a first-families-of-Albemarle place name, by John Cook Wyllie. 10 ℓ.

1964, no. 10, Oct. 7. The mountains of Virginia, comp. from a card list in the Division of Water Resources and arranged for publication by Brad Gunter, Lee W. Finks, and N. Harvey Deal. 40ℓ.

1966, no. 11, Jan. 25. British origins of names of some old Virginia homes, by John E. Manahan. Richmond's Kissing Lane, by Atcheson L. Hench. 8 ℓ.

1967, no. 12, Feb. 10. The first names of Virginia, by P. Burwell Rogers. 14 ℓ.

1967, no. 13. Index to Green Peyton's A map of Albemarle County, Virginia, by Mary Catherine Murphy and others. 23 ℓ.

1969, no. 14. Prospectus. 18p.

1971, no. 15. Approved place names in Virginia, by Virginia. University Library (see no. 3697).

1972, no. 16. Virginia counties, by P. Burwell Rogers (see no. 3675).

1974, no. 17. Greene County place names, by Roger P. Bristol (see no. 3602).

1974, no. 18. Approved place names in Virginia, by Roger P. Bristol (see no. 3601).

1975, no. 19. French place names in Virginia, by James W. Gordon, Jr. (see no. 3640).

1976, no. 20. Place name research in Virginia, by Douglas W. Tanner (see no. 3682).

1978, no. 21. Madison County place names, by Douglas W. Tanner (see no. 3681).

3700. Virginians name new city. New York times June 28, 1962, p. 29.

The new city, to be named Chesapeake, became official on Jan. 1, 1963, with the merger of South Norfolk and Norfolk County.

WASHINGTON

3701. Baker, Marcus. Survey of the northwestern boundary of the United States, 1857-1861. U.S. Geological Survey. Bulletin 174:58-61. 1900.

Indian names of camps, stations, rivers, etc., along the 49th parallel in Washington, Idaho, and Montana. Based on the work George Gibbs did for the Smithsonian Institution.

3702. Bechly, Ernst Carl. Map of Washington Territory west of the Cascade Mountains (as of 1870), being a composite of maps of 1859, 1865, and 1870. Showing counties, forts, Indian reservation, roads, R.R. surveys, trails, etc., including data when created or founded, also meaning of words. Chehalis, Wash., 1952. map 125 x 92 cm.

3703. Bowman, J. A. Washington nomenclature. A study. Washington historical quarterly 1:5-13, Oct. 1906.

3704. Brier, Warren J. How Washington Territory got its name. Pacific Northwest quarterly 51:13-15, Jan. 1960.

3705. Chamberlain, Alexander F. Geographic terms of Kootenay origin. American anthropologist n.s. 4:348-50, April-June 1902.

"Concerned with names of places, camp-sites, and stations along the 49th parallel in British Columbia, Washington, Idaho, and Montana. These names which seem to have been taken from the language of the Kootenay Indians of this region are mentioned in the reports on the boundary survey. The meanings and etymologies are given where possible."—Price.

3706. Chase, Carroll & Richard McP. Cabeen. The first hundred years of United States territorial postmarks, 1787-1887. Washington Territory. American philatelist 61:871-74, Aug. 1948; 62:362-69, 686-91, Feb., June 1949; 63:43-50, 276-85, Oct. 1949, Jan. 1950.

Includes list of post offices to 1887, with notes on a few names.

3707. Colbert, Mildred. Naming and early settlement of Ilwaco, Washington. Oregon historical quarterly 47:181-95, June 1946.

3708. Collins, Josiah. Tacoma vs. Rainier. Nation 56:329-30, May 4, 1893.

3709. Connelly, Dolly. Mighty Joe Morovits: real-life Bunyan. Sports illustrated 18:52-57, Jan. 7, 1963.
Story of the mountain man whose name is immortalized in landmark names.

3710. Conover, C. T. Many Puget Sound names were given by Wilkes Porter. Seattle times Nov. 22, 1956.

3711. Conover, Charles Tallmadge. Mount Rainier or Mount Tacoma? Brief summary of the essential facts in this historic controversy. National magazine 48:223-24, 237-38, June 1919.

3712. [Coones, S. F.]. Dictionary of the Chinook jargon, as spoken on Puget Sound and the Northwest, with original Indian names for prominent places and localities, with their meanings. Seattle, Lowman & Hanford Stationery & Print. Co., [1891]. 38p.

3713. Correspondence relative to the Indian names of the great mountain. Mount Rainier or Tacoma. Conducted by Mr. Benjamin L. Harvey. Washington State Historical Society. Publications 2:440-64. 1907-14.

3714. Costello, Joseph A. The Siwash, their life legends, and tales; Puget Sound and Pacific Northwest. Seattle, Calvert Co., 1895. 169p.
Seattle names included.

3715. Craven, Arthur J. Mount Baker--its name and first explorer. Mazama 6:33-44, Dec. 1920.

3716. Davidson, George. The name "Mt. Rainier." Sierra Club bulletin 6:87-99, Jan. 1906.
Proposed reasons on which the club accepted Mount Rainier.

3717. Denman, A. H. Mount Tacoma--its true name. Congressional record 72:10871-73, June 16, 1930.
Historical article on the origin of the Indian name Tacoma for Mount Rainier.

3718. —— The name. Tacoma, Mt. Tacoma Club, 1924. 10p.
In connection with the effort to change the name of Mount Rainier.

3719. —— The name of Mount Tacoma; urging the official removal from America's most sublime mountain of the name Rainier and the perpetuation by official adoption of the original Indian name therefor in its most appropriate, euphonious and generally accepted form—Tacoma. Embodying also the research of Judge James Wickersham and the "brief" of John B. Kaiser, S. W. Wall, Benjamin L. Harvey, W. N. Allen and Walter J. Thompson. Tacoma, Rotary Club, Kiwanis Club, etc., 1924. 93p.
The "brief" also issued separately; see no. 3782.

3720. Eells, Myron. Aboriginal geographic names in the State of Washington. American anthropologist 5:27-35, Jan. 1892.

3721. Egan, Clifford L. Joel Barlow's suggestion to rename the Columbia. Oregon historical quarterly 74:268-70, Sept. 1973.
The name of the river should honor Meriwether Lewis, the explorer, according to Joel Barlow's proposal sent in a letter to Thomas Jefferson, Jan. 13, 1807.

3722. Fish, Byron. Ranger named many state peaks, streams. Seattle times Dec. 5, 1955, p. 22.
Work of Albert Hale Sylvester of U.S. Geological Survey and U.S. Forest Service. cf. Sylvester's article on his work in American speech 18:241-52, Dec. 1943.

3723. —— Some peaks' names picturesque; others just plain "Baldies." Seattle times Nov. 22, 1955, p. 4.

3724. Francis, DeWitt C. Derivation of Washington State town names. Puyallup, Wash., Valley Press, 1971. 28p.

3725. Gibbs, Rafe. The mountain with two names. American mercury 30:39-40, June 1955.
Mount Rainier.

3726. Gudde, Erwin Gustav. Okanagan place names. Western folklore 8:161-62, April 1949.
Refers to article by A. G. Harvey, Okanagan place names, no. 4255.

3727. Hanford, Thaddeus. The local nomenclature of the Territory. Washington standard Jan. 13, 1866, p. 1; Jan. 27, p. 1.
Signed: Philopatris.
Prefers Indian names; also recommends the name Tacoma for the Territory.

3728. Hanson, Howard A. The naming of Elliott Bay. Shall we honor the chaplain or the midshipman? Pacific Northwest quarterly 45:28-32, Jan. 1954.
Bay on which Seattle is located. Named for Midshipman Elliott rather than for Chaplain, both of Wilkes expedition, 1841.

3729. Hazeltine, Jean. The discovery and cartographical recognition of Shoalwater Bay. Oregon historical quarterly 58:251-63, Sept. 1957.

3730. Himes, George Henry. Tyrrell's name should be saved. Washington historical quarterly 10:182-84, July 1919.
Justifies Tyrrell for the prairie in Thurston County rather than Hawk's Prairie.

3731. Hitchman, Robert. Color names, surnames, and place names. Western folklore 9:372, Oct. 1950.

3732. —— Corruption of French names in Lewis County, Washington. Western folklore 9:156-57, April 1950.

3733. —— The Irishman in name-origin stories. Western folklore 8:366, Oct. 1949.
Discounts Irishman's connection with naming of Osoyoos and Okanogan ("spelled thus on most maps").

3734. —— Sedro-Wooley, Washington. Western folklore 8:369-70, Oct. 1949.
Skagit County.

3735. —— Venturesome stories lie behind the names on the frontierland they called Washington. American heritage 4:42-43, 65-67, Summer 1953.

3736. Indians named Puyallup, and this is why! Chicago tribune Dec. 18, 1955, pt. 6, p. 10.

3737. Kids to rename streets of town. Denver post Nov. 11, 1964, p. 12.
Because of confusion in the names of streets in Milton, Wash., students in fifth and sixth grades were asked to rename the streets, using consecutive numbers one way and alphabetical names the other.

3738. Kingston, C. S. Juan de Fuca Strait: origin of the name. Pacific Northwest quarterly 36:155-66, April 1945.

3739. Kitsap County history: a story of Kitsap County and its pioneers, comp. by the Kitsap County Historical Society Book Committee, Evelyn T. Bowen and others. Silverdale, Wash., The Society, 1977. 730p.
Appendix: Origin of the geographical names in the county. 12p.

3740. Landes, Henry. A geographic dictionary of Washington. Olympia, F. M. Lamborn, public printer, 1917. 346. (Washington. Geological Survey. Bulletin no. 17)

3741. Landis, Robert L. Post offices of Oregon, Washington, and Idaho. Portland, Ore., Patrick Press, 1969. 89, 98, 55, 9p.
Includes post offices of the Railway Mail Service, 1906, for the three states and Alaska.

3742. A List of mountain peaks and altitudes of the State of Washington; Prominent mountain passes in Washington. Mountaineer 1:141-46, Nov. 1908.

3743. Löfgren, Svante. Swedish place names of Washington State. American Swedish Historical Foundation. Chronicle 3:17-27, Autumn 1956-Winter 1956-57.
Originally written for Svenska posten, Seattle.

3744. Lummis, Charles Fletcher. Editorials on changing the name of Mt. Rainier. Out west 23:367-68, 494-95, Oct., Nov. 1905.

3745. McAdie, Alexander. Mt. Rainier or Mt. Tacoma—which?; In his Alexander McAdie, scientist and writer. Charlottesville, Va., M. R. B. McAdie, 1949 [i.e., 1950]. p. 183-86.
Reprinted from Sierra Club bulletin 9:95-98, June 1913.
Supports George Davidson's argument that the name Rainier should not be changed.

3746. McArthur, Lewis Ankeny. Early Washington post offices. Washington historical quarterly 20:129-33, April 1929.
A few Washington offices included in the book of Oregon records in the Post Office Dept. For period Jan. 1850-Sept. 1853.

3747. McDonald, Lucile. Explorers of 1791 gave many Spanish names to San Juans. Seattle times Nov. 6, 1955, p. 2.

3748. —— Vaughn named for settler of 1852. Seattle Sunday times Sept. 7, 1958.

3749. Meany, Edmond Stephen. Dropping the "h" from Port Townsend. Washington historical quarterly 24:49-52, Jan. 1933.
Origin and history of the name.

3750. —— Indian geographic names of Washington. Seattle, Hyatt-Powells School, 1908. 20p.

3751. —— Name of Mount Saint Helens. Washington historical quarterly 15:124-25, April 1924.

3752. —— Origin of geographical names in the San Juan Archipelago. Seattle post-intelligencer June 6, 1915, Magazine section p. 4.

3753. —— Origin of geographical names in the vicinity of Seattle. Seattle post-intelligencer May 30, 1915, Magazine section p. 4.

3754. —— Origin of Point Defiance and other names on Puget Sound. Seattle post-intelligencer May 23, 1915, part 6, p. 4.

3755. —— Origin of Washington geographic names. Seattle, Univ. of Washington Press, 1923. 357p.
Originally published in Washington historical quarterly v. 8-14, 1917-23.
Reprinted: Detroit, Gale Research Co., 1968.
Review: American speech 1:397, April 1926; American historical review 29:614-15, April 1924.

3756. —— Place names and elevations in Mount Rainier National Park; In his Mount Rainier, a record of exploration. New York, Macmillan, 1916. p. 302-25.
This list is not included in his book, Origin of Washington geographic names.

3757. —— Three cities of Washington, origin of their names. Seattle, Univ. of Washington Press, n.d. 7p.
Reprinted from the Washington historical quarterly.
The three cities are Seattle, Spokane, and Tacoma.

3758. —— Vancouver's discovery of Puget Sound; portraits and biographies of the men honored in the naming of geographic features of northwestern America. New York, Macmillan, 1915. 344p.

3759. Meeker, Ezra. Who named Tacoma? Address to the Washington Historical Society, at Tacoma, January 22, 1904. n.p., 1905. 8p.
Thomas W. Prosch in an address to the Washington Historical Society, at Tacoma, October 4, 1905 (p. 4-8), points out many errors and misstatements in Meeker's paper.

3760. Merriam, Clinton Hart. Shall the name of Mount Rainier be changed? Statement by C. Hart Merriam before the United States Geographic Board, May 11, 1917. Washington, Govt. Print. Off., 1917. 10p.
Opposes the proposal to change the name to Mount Tacoma.

3761. Middleton, Lynn. Place names of the Pacific northwest coast: origins, histories, and anecdotes in bibliographic form about the coast of British Columbia, Washington, and Oregon. Victoria, B.C., Elldee Pub. Co., 1969. 226p. maps.
Also published: Seattle, Superior Pub. Co., [1970].

3762. Mount Rainier keeps its name. New York times June 13, 1937, sec. 10, p. 25, col. 3.

3763. Oliphant, J. Orin. Notes on early settlements and on geographic names of eastern Washington. Washington historical quarterly 22:172-202, July 1931.
Forms an appendix to Edmond Stephen Meany's Origin of Washington geographic names (see no. 3755), although Oliphant was interested in assembling data relating to early settlements in one area of Washington.

3764. Olympia (Wash.) Chamber of Commerce. The great myth--"Mount Tacoma"; Mount Rainier and the facts of history. Issued by the Olympia Chamber of Commerce and the Thurston County Pioneer and Historical Society. Olympia, 1924. 31p.

3765. Petite, Irving. Adventures in state names; Anna Cortez is Anacortes. Seattle argus May 3, 1957.

3766. —— How names do change! Seattle times July 31, 1955, p. 7.
Street-name changes in Seattle.

3767. Phillips, James Wendell. Washington State place names. Rev. and enl. Seattle, Univ. of Washington Press, 1976. 167p. maps.
1st ed. 1971.

Bibliography: p. 165-67.
Review of 1st ed.: Francis Lee Utley, Names 21:267-69, Dec. 1973.
Review of 2d ed.: Kelsie B. Harder, Names 25:241-42, Dec. 1977.
A journalistic account with some newer names established since 1923 when Edmond S. Meany's book was published.

3768. Piper, Charles Vancouver. Flora of the State of Washington. Washington, Govt. Print. Off., 1906. 637p. (Smithsonian Institution. United States National Museum. Contributions from the United States National Herbarium, v. 11)
Geographical index: p. 619-22.

3769. Powell, J. V., William Penn and others. Place names of the Quileute Indians. Pacific Northwest quarterly 63:104-12, July 1972. map.
Contains table of Quileute names with their meaning and current name.

3770. Prosch, Thomas Wickham. McCarver and Tacoma. Seattle, Lowman & Hanford Print. Co., 1906. 198p.
History of naming the city of Tacoma, p. 162-67.

3771. —— Seattle and the Indians of Puget Sound. Washington historical quarterly 2:303-08, July 1908.
Claims that the city was named for Chief Seattle, not Sealth.

3772. Reese, Gary Fuller. Origin of geographic names of Tacoma—Pierce County, Washington. Tacoma, Tacoma Public Library, 1974. 99p.

3773. Relander, Click. Geographic names and nomenclature; In his Drummers and dreamers. Caldwell, Idaho, Caxton Printers, 1956. p. 286-319.
Pertaining to the Columbia River and the adjoining area from Pasco to Vantage, Wash., including Wanapum names of old native villages, campsites, and landmarks.
Review: Walter C. Kraft, Names 5:186-87, Sept. 1957.

3774. Rundell, Hugh A. Washington names; a pronunciation guide of Washington State place names. 2d ed. Pullman, Wash., Radio Station KWSC and the Extension Service, Institute of Agricultural Sciences, Washington State University, 1959. 78 ℓ.
Includes counties and cities.

3775. Smith, Charles Wesley. The naming of counties in the State of Washington. Seattle, 1913. 15p. (Bulletin of the University of Washington. University studies, no. 6)
Reprinted from the Magazine of history 10:9-16, 79-85, July, Aug. 1909.

3776. Smith, Francis E. Pacific coast place names in the State of Washington. Americana 20:23-30, Jan. 1926.

3777. Snowden, Clinton A. Mount Tacoma or Mount Rainier; In his History of Washington. New York, Century House Co., 1909. 4:249-54.
Long controversy over the name of the peak Rainier is impartially reviewed.

3778. Snyder, Warren Arthur. Southern Puget Sound Salish: texts, place names, and dictionary. Sacramento, Calif., Sacramento Anthropological Society, Sacramento State College, 1968. vi, 199p. map. (Sacramento Anthropological Society. Paper no. 9)
Bibliography: p. 198-99.
"place names section includes information on use and population. . . ."
Review: Pamela Amoss, Journal of American linguistics 37:134, April 1971.

3779. Steel, William Gladstone. The mountains of Oregon. Portland, D. Steel, 1890. 112p.
Contains several sections on the names of mountains in Oregon and Washington, particularly on the name Tacoma.

3780. Strong, William Duncan. Wakemap: a Columbia River site mispronounced. American antiquity 21:410, April 1956.
This Indian archaeological site should be given the Indian rather than the anglicized pronunciation.

3781. Sylvester, Albert Hale. Place-naming in the Northwest. American speech 18:241-52, Dec. 1943.
An account by the retired supervisor of the Wenatchee National Forest of his assignment of names to topographical features in the Forest. A rare and entertaining firsthand account.

3782. Tacoma. Justice to the Mountain Committee. Brief submitted to the United States Geographic Board urging the official removal from America's most sublime mountain of the name Rainier and the perpetuation by official adoption of the original Indian name therefor in its most appropriate, euphonious and generally accepted form—Tacoma. May 2, 1917. Tacoma, The Committee, 1917. 77, 24p.
Authorities consulted: p. 72-77.
Proceedings of the Tacoma Academy of Science, Feb. 8, 1893, paper by Hon. James Wickersham: "Is it 'Mt. Tacoma,' or 'Rainier'?" 24p. at end.

3783. Tacoma or Rainier? Americana 18:474-77, Oct. 1924.

3784. Taylor, William H. Mount Si Trail dedicated. Washington historical quarterly 22:213-15, July 1931.
Story of Josiah Merritt, "Uncle Si," for whom the mountain was named.

3785. Territory of Washington; In Meany, Edmond Stephen. History of the State of Washington. New York, Macmillan, 1924. p. 156-58; also in U.S. Congress. Congressional globe, 32d Congress, 2d session, 1852-53, p. 540-42, 1039, 1046.
Bill introduced for organization of Territory of Columbia. After discussion on name it was passed as Territory of Washington.

3786. Thompson, Albert W. The early history of the Palouse River and its names. Pacific Northwest quarterly 62:69-76, April 1971.

3787. Todd, C. C. Origin and meaning of the geographic name Palouse. Washington historical quarterly 24:190-92, July 1933.
"A modification of the Indian tribal name, Palloatpallahs."--Griffin.

3788. U.S. Board on Geographic Names. Before the United States Geographic Board, in the matter of the proposal to change the name of Mount Rainier. Statement of C. T. Conover, representing numerous citizens of the State of Washington in favor of retaining the present name, and oral presentation by C. T. Conover and Victor J. Farrar, May 2, 1917. Statement of C. Hart Merriam, a member of the United States Geographic Board, before said body, May 11, 1917. The decision, May 11, 1917. Addenda: statement by John Muir, statements by Dr. C. M. Buchanan, statement by Edwin Els, statement by H. B. McElroy. Seattle, Lowman & Hanford Co., 1924. 74p.
1st ed. 1917. 58p.

3789. —— Decisions. No. 29, June 30, 1932. Mount Rainier National Park, Washington. Washington, Govt. Print. Off., 1934. 14p.

3790. —— Decisions on Washington place names. Washington historical quarterly 10:79-80, 185-89, Jan., July 1919.

3791. —— Report of United States Geographic Board on S.J. Res. 64, a joint resolution to change the name of "Mount Rainier" to "Mount Tacoma" and for other purposes. Washington, Govt. Print. Off., 1924. 8p.

3792. U.S. Work Projects Administration. Pennsylvania. Geographic names in the coastal areas of California, Oregon and Washington. Comp. under the supervision of the Coast and Geodetic Survey. Washington, 1940. 94p.

3793. Washington. State Board on Geographic Names. Guidelines for the Washington State Board on Geographic Names. [Rev. ed. Olympia, 1976]. folder.
The Board was created by law April 25, 1973 (Chapter 177).

3794. Waterman, Thomas Talbot. An essay on geographic names in the State of Washington. American anthropologist n.s. 24:481-83, Oct.-Dec. 1922.
An unfavorable review of Edmond Stephen Meany's article in the Washington historical quarterly v. 8, 1917.

3795. —— The geographical names used by the Indians of the Pacific coast. Geographical review 12:175-94, April 1922.

3796. Wickersham, James. Is it "Mt. Tacoma" or "Rainier"; what do history and tradition say? Tacoma, Puget Sound Print. Co., 1893. 16p. (Tacoma Academy of Science. Proceedings, February 6, 1893)
2d ed., Tacoma, News Pub. Co., 1893. 34p.
Also included in Tacoma. Justice to the Mountain Committee. Brief submitted to the United States Geographic Board . . . (see no. 3782).

3797. Wood, Robert L. Across the Olympic mountains: the Press expedition, 1889-90. Seattle, The Mountaineers and the Univ. of Washington Press, 1967. 220p. maps.
Nomenclature of the Press Exploring Expedition: p. 215-20.
List of names given by men of the expedition to natural features in the Olympic Mountains, with origin of the names.

WEST VIRGINIA

3798. Ball, Frank. Place names in W. Va. Preacher changed the name to Poca-to-Hell-you-go. The West Virginia hillbilly 17:1, July 12, 1975.

3799. —— West Virginia: state with funny names. The West Virginia hillbilly 17:1, 10, July 5, 1975.

3800. Bowman, E. L. Origin of counties given for entire state. Glenville democrat June 12, 1930.

3801. Braake, Alex L. What's in a name: the three Charlestowns. West Virginia history 30:351-57, July 1968.
Of the three early towns bearing the name, one became Charles Town, 1912.

3802. Carpenter, Charles. Our place names. West Virginia review 6:422, 440, Aug. 1929.

3803. Chrisman, Lewis H. The origin of place names in West Virginia. West Virginia history 7:77-88, Jan. 1946.

3804. —— The origin of the names of the county seats of West Virginia. West Virginia review 8:44-45, 62, Nov. 1930.

3805. Counties of West Virginia take names from early statesmen. Cumberland (Md.) evening times June 20, 1939.

3806. Gannett, Henry. A gazetteer of West Virginia. Washington, Govt. Print. Off., 1904. 164p. (U.S. Geological Survey. Bulletin no. 233, Ser. F, Geography no. 41; also as House doc. no. 728, 58th Congress, 2d session)

Reprinted with the author's Virginia gazetteer, Baltimore, Genealogical Pub. Co., 1975. 159, 164p.

Review: Otis K. Rice, West Virginia history 36:327-28, July 1975.

3807. Indian names—early geography of West Virginia. West Virginia. Dept. of Archives and History. Biennial report 1:251-68. 1904-06.

Includes Indian names of West Virginia rivers, and the names of places on early maps.

3808. Johnston, Ross B. U.S. Board accedes to West Virginia wishes. West Virginia history 16:48, Oct. 1954.

Tygart Valley and Tygart Valley River.

3809. Kenny, Hamill. Cheat River and the "Horn papers." American speech 28:65-66, Feb. 1953.

3810. —— Settling Laurel's business. Names 9:160-62, Sept. 1961.

The origin of Laurel in the Pennsylvania and West Virginia place-name Laurel Hill.

3811. —— The synthetic place name in West Virginia. American speech 15:39-44, Feb. 1940.

3812. —— West Virginia place names, their origin and meaning including the nomenclature of the streams and mountains. Piedmont, W. Va., Place Name Press, 1945. 768p.

Reprinted in 1960 by the West Virginia University Library in a special limited edition for West Virginia schools.

Review: E. G. Gudde, American speech 21:206-08, Oct. 1946.

3813. Laidley, W. S. Former names of West Virginia towns. West Virginia historical magazine quarterly 3:255, July 1903.

List of 21 changed names.

3814. Mahr, August C. Shawnee names and migrations in Kentucky and West Virginia. Ohio journal of science 60:155-64, May 1960.

The migration of the western half of the Shawnee Nation from the Cumberland River eastward through the wilderness later called Kentucky can be traced by place-names of Shawnee origin.

3815. Maxwell, Claude W. Indian names in West Virginia. West Virginia review 2:286, 291, May 1925.

3816. Miller, Aaron. How Kettle Run was named. West Virginia folklore 10:4-5, Fall 1959.

3817. Myers, Sylvester. The counties of West Virginia; In his History of West Virginia. Wheeling, 1915. 2:1-14.

3818. —— Rivers of West Virginia and how they were named; In his History of West Virginia. Wheeling, 1915. 2:395-408.
From West Virginia archives and history.

3819. Names of Gilmer County towns have interesting origin. Glenville pathfinder Dec. 27, 1934.

3820. Norona, Delf. Wheeling; a West Virginia place-name of Indian origin. Moundsville, W. Va., West Virginia Archeological Society, 1958. 38p. (West Virginia Archeological Society. Publication series no. 4) (Wheeling, W.Va., Oglebay Institute. Mansion Museum Committee. Publication no. 1)

3821. Price, R. N. Place names in Pocahontas County, West Virginia. Pocahontas times, Marlinton, March 28, 1940.

3822. Randolph, Jennings. Dogbone and other towns represent strength in America--place names present quaint and original quality of life in West Virginia. Congressional record 116:41683, Dec. 15, 1970.

3823. Summers, George W. State place names honor many noted Virginians. Charleston (W.Va.) daily mail Nov. 5, 1939.

3824. West, Roy A. West Virginia place names. West Virginia folklore 3:15-16, Fall 1952.

3825. West Virginia. Constitutional Convention, 1861-1863. Debates and proceedings. Huntington, Gentry Bros., 1939?. 1:81-107.
The debate was on the first section of the constitution, which read: The State of Kanawha shall be and remain one of the United States of America. Move to strike out Kanawha, debated and carried. Moved to insert Alleghany, Columbia, New Virginia, West Virginia. These motions withdrawn and a vote taken by roll call, each answering with name preferred. Results: West Virginia, 30; Kanawha, 9; Western Virginia, 2; Allegheny, 2; Augusta, 1.

3826. —— University. School of Journalism. Pronunciation guide to West Virginia place names. Morgantown, 1951. 51p.
Foreword signed: Paul Krakowski.

WISCONSIN

3827. Ahnapee's new name. Milwaukee sentinel Aug. 13, 1897.

3828. Banta, George. The significance of "Neenah." Wisconsin magazine of history 5:419-20, June 1922.
"Neenah was originally a Winnebago village and its name was Wee-nah-pe-ko-ne, which was modified into 'Neenah.'"—Griffin.

3829. Barton, Albert O. Where Wisconsin names originated. Wisconsin archeologist n.s. 26:84-85, Dec. 1945.

3830. Bisson, Camille. Eau Claire and Eau Galle rivers. Wisconsin magazine of history 16:216-18, Dec. 1932.
The story of the early names of the rivers.

3831. Bleyer, Henry W. Derivation of the name Milwaukee. Magazine of western history 6:509-11, Sept. 1887.

3832. Brunson, Alfred. Wisconsin geographical names. Wisconsin. State Historical Society. Annual report and collections 1:110-15. 1854.

3833. Calkins, Hiram. Indian nomenclature of northern Wisconsin, with a sketch of the manners and customs of the Chippewas. Wisconsin. State Historical Society. Annual report and collections 1:119-26. 1854.
Contains Chippewa names of streams, falls, and rapids.

3834. Cassidy, Frederic Gomes. Dane County place-names. Madison, Univ. of Wisconsin Press, 1968. xvii, 245p.
Reprint with corrections of the author's The place-names of Dane County, with a foreword by Robert L. Ramsay. 1947. 255p. (Publication of the American Dialect Society no. 7)
Bibliography: p. 229-45.
Review of 1st ed.: Einar Haugen, Wisconsin magazine of history 31:209-11, Dec. 1947; A. R. Dunlap, American speech 23:52-55, Feb. 1948.
Review of reprint: Edward C. Ehrensperger, Names 17:239-41, Sept. 1969.

3835. —— Folklore in place-names. Badger folklore 1:21-22, April 1948.

3836. —— "Koskonong," a misunderstood place-name. Wisconsin magazine of history 31:429-40, June 1948.
Applied to parts of Dane County, 1820- .

3837. —— The names of Green Bay, Wisconsin. Names 21:168-78, Sept. 1973.
A historical survey of the Indian, French, and English names applied to the bay.

3838. —— The naming of the "Four Lakes." Wisconsin magazine of history 29:7-24, Sept. 1945.
Dane County.

3839. Chapelle, Ethel Elliott. The why of names in Washburn County. Birchwood, Wis., 1965. 72p.

3840. Cole, Harry Ellsworth. Baraboo and other place names in Sauk County, Wisconsin. Baraboo, Wis., Baraboo News Pub. Co., 1912. 50p.

3841. Derleth, August. Country places. Wisconsin tales and trails 1:25, Spring 1960.
A poem on Wisconsin's place-names.

3842. Doty, J. D. Indian names in Wisconsin. National intelligencer, Washington, Dec. 19, 1840, p. 2.
From the New York American.
Pleads for standardized spelling of Indian names, and appends a list of Wisconsin names.

3843. Eaton, Conan Bryant. The naming; a part of the history of Washington Island. Sturgeon Bay? Wis., 1966. 32p. maps. (The island series)
Review: Kelsie B. Harder, Names 16:64, March 1968.

3844. The Egg war. Wisconsin then and now 10:8, Oct. 1963.
Origin of the name Egg Harbor as recalled by Elizabeth Baird in v. 14 of the Wisconsin historical collections.

3845. Engel, Harold A. Wisconsin place names: a pronouncing gazetteer. Madison, Univ. of Wisconsin, Univ. Extension, WHA [1969]. 52p.
1st ed. 1938; 2d ed. 1948.
Provides preferred pronunciation recommended by residents of the areas concerned.

3846. Gard, Robert Edward & Leland George Sorden. The romance of Wisconsin place names. Assisted by Margaret Kelk, Helen Smith, and Maryo Gard. New York, October House, 1968. 144p. (A Wisconsin House book)

Review: Virgil J. Vogel, Wisconsin magazine of history 53:57-58, Autumn 1969 (cites many errors); Kelsie B. Harder, Michigan history 53:259-63, Fall 1969; Frederic G. Cassidy, Names 18:231-34, Sept. 1970.

3847. —— What's in a name? Wisconsin tales and trails 6:13-14, Autumn 1965.

Stories of some Wisconsin place-names.

3848. —— Wisconsin lore: antics and anecdotes of Wisconsin people and places. New York, Duell, Sloan & Pearce, 1962. 308p.

An appendix of place names: p. 335-68.

A selection of Wisconsin names, with their origins.

3849. Hathaway, Joshua. Indian names. State Historical Society. Annual report and collections 1:116-18. 1854.

12 names in the Chippewa language, with meanings and etymologies.

3850. The History in our county names. Badger history for boys and girls 3:10-13, 28, Feb. 1950.

3851. How the names came, story of Wisconsin and their titles. Milwaukee sentinel Dec. 1895.

3852. Hunt, John Warren. Wisconsin gazetteer, containing the names, location, and advantages of the counties, cities, towns, villages, post offices, and settlements, together with a description of the lakes, water courses, prairies, and public localities, in the State of Wisconsin. Alphabetically arranged. Madison, B. Brown, printer, 1853. 255p.

3853. An Indian love story. Wisconsin then and now 15:8, Jan. 1969.

From the book by Carl Quickert, The story of Washington County.

The town of Mequon was named for an Indian maiden.

3854. Indian names of our Wisconsin lakes. Wisconsin archeologist n.s. 4:164-65, July 1925.

An effort should be made to recover from present members of tribes as many as possible of the aboriginal designations, now largely unknown.

3855. Kellogg, Louise Phelps. Memorandum on the spelling of "Jolliet." Wisconsin magazine of history 1:67-69, Sept. 1917.

Prepared for submission to the Committee on State Affairs of the Wisconsin Assembly in April 1917. As a result, the bill which provided that the name Joliet be given to a state park at the mouth of the Wisconsin River was amended by substituting the spelling Jolliet.

3856. —— Organization, boundaries and names of Wisconsin counties. Madison, The Society, 1910. p. 183-231.

From Wisconsin. State Historical Society. Proceedings 57:183-231. 1909.

3857. Kuhm, Herbert W. Indian place-names in Wisconsin. Wisconsin archeologist 33:1-157, March-June 1952.

An alphabetical list.

3858. Legler, Henry Eduard. Origin and meaning of Wisconsin place-names; with special reference to Indian nomenclature. Wisconsin Academy of Sciences, Arts and Letters. Transaction 14:16-39. 1903.

Bibliography: p. 36-39.

3859. McGraw, Peter A. A German footnote to Cassidy's Place-names of Dane County, Wisconsin. American speech 48:150-53, Spring-Summer 1973.
The German Kölsch dialect names in the county.

3860. Naming of Wisconsin and Iowa. Annals of Iowa 3d ser. 27:323-24, April 1946.
Naming of the territories described in a letter from Sen. George W. Jones, Iowa, to Charles Aldrich, curator of the Iowa Historical Department, in 1896.

3861. Nichols, Phebe Jewell. Wisconsin—what does it mean? América indígena 8:171-76, July 1948.
On the Menominee origin of the name.

3862. Nicollet, Joseph Nicolas. The journals of Joseph N. Nicollet: a scientist on the Mississippi headwaters, with notes on Indian life, 1836-37. Trans. from the French by André Fertey. Ed. by Martha Coleman Bray. St. Paul, Minnesota Historical Society, 1970. 288p. maps.
Names of lakes and streams: p. 225-41.
An alphabetical list of modern names for lakes and rivers, with, in columns opposite, the name as found in the Journals, on the 1836, 1837, and 1843 maps, and in other Nicollet notes.
Review: Raphael N. Hamilton, Wisconsin magazine of history 54:223-24, Spring 1971.

3863. Origin of name Wisconsin. Annals of Iowa 3d ser. 31:367, July 1952.

3864. Origin of the word "Winnequah." Wisconsin magazine of history 1:196-97, Dec. 1917.
An explanation for the source of the name given to the point projecting into Lake Monona.

3865. Reddick, G. H. People and places of Forest County. Badger folklore 3:11-13. 1951.

3866. Rouillard, Eugène. Les Îles des Douze Apôtres. Société de Géographie de Québec. Bulletin 12:40, janv. 1918.

3867. Rudolph, Robert S. Wood County place names. Madison, Univ. of Wisconsin Press, 1970. 121p. map.
Bibliography: p. 114-21.
An alphabetical list of current and former places giving location, variant spellings, changes in name, and origin.
Review: Marvin Carmony, Names 20:62-63, March 1972.

3868. Schafer, Joseph. Testing traditions--I. Naming Wisconsin valley towns. Wisconsin magazine of history 7:238-42, Dec. 1923.
Avoca, Muscoda, Boscobel.

3869. Scott, Margaret Helen. The place names of Richland County, Wisconsin. Richland Center, Wis., Richland County Publishers, 1973. 53p.

3870. Skinner, Alanson Buck. Some Menomini place names in Wisconsin; In his Material culture of the Menomini. New York, Museum of the American Indian, Heye Foundation, 1921. (Indian notes and monographs. Miscellaneous, no. 20) p. 382-90.
List obtained from John V. Satterlee.
Some of these names were published in the Wisconsin archeologist 18:97-102, Aug. 1919.

3871. Smith, Alice E. Stephen H. Long and the naming of Wisconsin. Wisconsin magazine of history 26:67-71, Sept. 1942.
Origin and earliest use of word Wisconsin for the territory.

3872. Smith, Huron H. Indian place names in Wisconsin. Milwaukee. Public Museum. Yearbook 10:252-66. 1930.
A list giving derivation and meaning, with several authorities quoted for each name.

3873. Some very odd names; Wisconsin towns that are badly handicapped. Milwaukee sentinel Jan. 3, 1897.

3874. Stuart, Donna Valley. What's in a name, 18 counties have Indian names. Wisconsin then and now 17:6-7, Sept. 1970.
Gives translations and meanings.

3875. Taube, Edward. The name "Wisconsin." Names 15:173-81, Sept. 1967.
Study is based on the belief that the form beginning M- is the correct one and concludes that the meaning is "at the great point."

3876. Taylor, Stephen. How Mineral Point came by its sobriquet of "Shake-rag-under-the-hill." Wisconsin. State Historical Society. Collections 2:486. 1856.

3877. That's diggin' pretty deep. Wisconsin then and now 11:[8], Dec. 1964.
Names of towns and diggings in the mining country, in the form of a sonnet, from a pamphlet entitled The home of the Badgers, by Oculus [Josiah Bushnell Grinnell]. Milwaukee, Wilshire & Co., 1845. 36p.

3878. Thwaites, Reuben Gold. Badger Indian names. Milwaukee sentinel Oct. 5, 1898.

3879. —— Origin of the term "Badger." Wisconsin. State Historical Society. Proceedings 1907:303-04.
Explanation as given by Moses M. Strong in the State journal, Madison, Dec. 10, 1879.

3880. Thwaites, Mrs. Reuben Gold. Indian nomenclature in Wisconsin. Milwaukee sentinel June 9, 1898.
Classified as distinctive names derived from fish, birds, animals, water, etc.

3881. Towns shed colorful names to gain dignity in Wisconsin. Peoria (Ill.) star Feb. 15, 1939.

3882. U.S. Board on Geographic Names. Decisions. No. 33, October 4, 1933. Names in Sawyer County, Wisconsin. Washington, Govt. Print. Off., 1934. 10p.

3883. U.S. Federal Writers' Project. Wisconsin. Wisconsin Indian place-name legends. Wisconsin centennial issue. Dorothy Moulding Brown. Madison, D. M. Brown, 1948. 30p. (Wisconsin folklore publications)
Published in 1936 under title: Wisconsin Indian place legends. 50p.

3884. U.S. Post Office Department. A list of all known post offices in the Territory and State of Wisconsin, from the first P.O. established, December 1821 to October 1917, over 3500 P.O.'s in all, copied from the records of the State Historical Society, Madison, Wis., derived from U.S. P.O. Dept. files. Also a list of all Wisconsin counties, with dates of organization or change. Milwaukee, 1948. 37ℓ. map.
Printed under the auspices of the Wisconsin Postal History Group of the Wisconsin Federation of Stamp Clubs.

3885. Verwyst, Chrysostom. Geographical names in Wisconsin, Minnesota, and Michigan having a Chippewa origin. Wisconsin. State Historical Society. Collections 12:390-98. 1892.
"Cites distortions of names and the source and significance of the correct terminations."—Price.

3886. —— A glossary of Chippewa Indian names of rivers, lakes and villages. Acta et dicta 4:253-74, July 1916.
These names are mostly of the Chippewa language though a considerable number of them are from other Algic dialects.

3887. Vogel, Virgil J. Wisconsin's name: a linguistic puzzle. Wisconsin magazine of history 48:181-86, Spring 1965.
Discussion and evaluation of known theories of the origin and meaning of the name, and adds another theory to the list.
Comments by Donald C. Chaput, and reply by Virgil J. Vogel, ibid. 49:352-53, Summer 1966.
Comments by Mrs. E. A. Hackbarth, reply by Vogel, and Editor's note, ibid. 50:165-66, Winter 1967.

3888. What's in a name. Hobbies 57:28, May 1952.
Name changes in Wisconsin.

3889. What's in a name? Wisconsin tales and trails v. 1, no. 1- Spring 1960- .
A section on Wisconsin place-names that continued for a number of issues.

3890. Wheeler, Everett Pepperrell. Geographical names of Chippewa origin.
Manuscript in possession of the State Historical Society of Wisconsin.

3891. White, H. H. French and Indian names in Wisconsin. Sheboygan Falls news May 1898.
Reprinted in the Carnival edition of the Milwaukee sentinel May 1898.

3892. Wisconsin. State Conservation Department. Inventory of mapped lakes. Madison, 1964. 29p.

3893. —— Wisconsin lakes. Madison, 1964. 67p. (Publication no. 218-64)
Includes every named lake.

3894. Wisconsin. State Historical Society. List of post offices in Wisconsin.
A file of 4000 cards lists the names of all post offices in Wisconsin, and a chronological listing from the first in 1821 to the end of 1917. Available in the Society's Manuscript Division.

3895. Witherell, B. P. H. Reminiscences of the Northwest, XV. Indian names. Wisconsin. State Historical Society. Collections 3:337. 1857.

3896. Woodbury, Jack E. Names, names, names. Badger history 12:8-9, Sept. 1958.

3897. Worthing, Ruth Shaw. The history of Fond du Lac County as told by its place names. 2d ed. Fond du Lac, 1979.

WYOMING

3898. Bass, Mabel. What's in a name. Annals of Wyoming 32:164-66, Oct. 1960.
Jay Em, named for Jim Moore.

3899. Bonney, Orrin H. & Lorraine Bonney. Guide to the Wyoming mountains and wilderness areas. 2d ed. Denver, Sage Books, 1965. 528p. maps.

1st ed. 1960. 389p. Parts of this edition dealing with the mountains were also issued separately.

"There is nothing else in print which gives the origin of place names in the Wyoming mountains as this does."--Annals of Wyoming.

3900. Brock, J. Elmer. How the Chugwater got its name. Westerners. Denver Posse. Brand-book v. 7, no. 5, p. 10, May 1951.

3901. Carter, W. A. List of names in Uinta County, Wyoming. July 1929.
Manuscript in the State Historical Department of Wyoming.

3902. Chittenden, Hiram Martin. The Yellowstone National Park. Cincinnati, Clarke, 1895.

The various editions of this contain a chapter on geographic names in Yellowstone Park, and a map index giving the names in the park.

3903. Christiansen, Cleo. Sagebrush settlements. Lovell, Wyo., Mountain States Print. Co., 1967. 122p.

Origin of names of counties and towns.

3904. Clough, Wilson Ober. Some Wyoming place names. Southern folklore quarterly 7:1-11, March 1943.

3905. —— Some Wyoming place names. Somewhat enlarged from a paper read before the Western Folklore Conference, University of Denver, July 9, 1942. n.p., 1943. 22p.

3906. —— Wyoming's earliest place names. Annals of Wyoming 37:211-20, Oct. 1965.

Geographic features named by explorers and fur traders, especially from 1800 to 1847.

3907. Edwards, Elsa Spear. Geographic names, Sheridan County, Wyoming. June 1929.

Manuscript in the State Historical Department of Wyoming.

3908. Emery, Raymond C. A dictionary of Albany County place names. 115p.
Thesis (M.S.) Univ. of Wyoming, 1940.

3909. Fenwick, Robert W. Casper to mark Indian battle that gave misspelled name. Denver post July 25, 1965, p. 14.

Named for Lt. Caspar Collins, who died in an Indian battle 100 years ago.

3910. Frémont, John Charles. [Letter]. Annals of Wyoming 30:173-74, Oct. 1958.
Letter to Herman G. Nickerson acknowledging Legislature's designation of his name to a county, March 22, 1884.

3911. Hagen, Mary. Turn left at Spring Creek. American forests 70:30-31, 57-59, Sept. 1964.

Names of streams in Wyoming.

3912. Hebard, Grace Raymond. Early history of Wahakie County, Wyoming. 1924.
Manuscript in the State Historical Department of Wyoming.

3913. How Powder River shibboleth began. Wyoming tribune July 17, 1931.

3914. How Rawlins was named. Wyoming tribune July 28, 1931.

3915. Jackson Hole correct way to say it. Pinedale roundup Dec. 19, 1929.

3916. King, Norman D. Old Wyoming postoffices. Annals of Wyoming 29:157-59, Oct. 1957.
Origins of the names.

3917. Lacy, Bessie Elizabeth. Place names [in Fremont County]; In Wyoming. University. Extension Classes Dept. Fremont County and its communities. 1952. p. 67-71.

3918. Linford, Dee. Wyoming stream names. 2d ed., rev. and enl. by Neal L. Blair, Judy Hosafros, assistant. Cheyenne, Wyoming Game & Fish Dept., 1975. xviii, 75p. (A bicentennial publication)
1st ed. 1944.
Originally published in parts in the Wyoming wild life magazine; reprinted: Bulletin no. 3, Wyoming Game and Fish Commission, 1944; Annals of Wyoming 15:163-74, 254-70, 413-16, April, July, Oct. 1943; 16:71-74, Jan. 1944.

3919. McDermott, John D. The search for Jacques Laramee: a study in frustration. Annals of Wyoming 36:169-74. 1964.
The search for Jacques (probably Joseph) Laramee, a French Canadian from whom the name of Laramie was derived, is inconclusive.

3920. Massicotte, E. Z. Le nom géographique Laramie. Bulletin des recherches historiques 40:730-31. 1934.
A note on the origin of the name. Lists various people called Laramie, including French traders, 1788-1810, but does not determine the one for whom the city was named.

3921. Mokler, Alfred James. Wyoming Board compiled a list of geographic names. Casper tribune herald Feb. 9, 1930.

3922. Our mountains bear their names. Pinedale roundup Aug. 25, 1932.

3923. Owen, William O. The naming of Mount Owen. Annals of Wyoming 5:72-77, Oct. 1927-Jan. 1928.

3924. Pence, Mary Lou & Lola M. Homsher. The ghost towns of Wyoming. New York, Hastings House, 1956. 242p.

3925. Place names of Natrona County and their derivation as told by a historian. Manuscript in the State Historical Department of Wyoming.

3926. Powder River nothing else. Wyoming tribune Dec. 3, 1928.

3927. Ridings, Reta W. Wyoming place names, comp. from clippings in University of Wyoming library. 1940. 77p.
Manuscript in the University library.

3928. Seminoe Range is not namesake of Seminole Indians. Wyoming tribune Feb. 19, 1922.

3929. Sioux Indians claim they name Rawhide Buttes. Lusk herald July 4, 1929.

3930. Tale of the Crazy Woman, Wyoming. Omaha world-herald Jan. 22, 1929.

3931. Tensleep named by Indian tribe. Wyoming tribune Dec. 2, 1931.

3932. Territory of Wyoming; In Hubert Howe Bancroft, History of Nevada, Colorado and Wyoming. San Francisco, History Co., 1890. p. 739-40; also in U.S. Congress. Congressional globe, 38th Congress, 2d session, 1864-65, p. 116; 40th Congress, 2d session, 1868, p. 1143, 2792-2802, 4322, 4344-45, 4352, 4380.

The first bill to provide temporary government for the Territory of Wyoming, introduced in Congress in 1865, rested in committee. In 1868 there was considerable discussion about choice of name: Lincoln, Cheyenne, Shoshonee, and Arapaho also being proposed. James M. Ashley defended Wyoming.

3933. Titus, C. L. Derivation of name, Telephone Canyon. March 13, 1930.

Letter to the Wyoming State Historian which is in the State Historical Department of Wyoming.

3934. U.S. Board on Geographic Names. Decisions. No. 8, Decisions rendered June 3, 1931. Grand Teton National Park, Wyoming. Washington, Govt. Print. Off., 1931. 5p.

3935. —— Decisions. Yellowstone National Park, Wyoming, May 7, 1930. Washington, Govt. Print. Off., 1930. 26p.

3936. —— Decisions rendered Aug. 10, 1937: Yellowstone National Park, Wyoming. Washington, Govt. Print. Off., 1938. 11p.

3937. U.S. 88th Congress, 1st session. Senate. Joint resolution to designate the lake to be formed by the waters impounded by the Flaming Gorge Dam, Utah, and the recreation area contiguous to such lake in the states of Wyoming and Utah, as "O'Mahoney Lake and Recreation Area." S.J. Res. 17. Jan. 15, 1963. Washington, 1963. 2p.

Introduced by Mr. McGee and others and referred to the Committee on Interior and Insular Affairs.

Subsequent documents relating to this joint resolution, and related joint resolutions introduced in the House, were published as follows:

U.S. 88th Congress, 1st session. House. Joint resolution to designate the lake to be formed by the waters impounded by the Flaming Gorge Dam, Utah, and the recreation area contiguous to such lake in the states of Wyoming and Utah, as "O'Mahoney Lake and Recreation Area." H.J. Res. 293. Feb. 28, 1963. Washington, 1963. 2p.

Introduced by Mr. Aspinall and referred to the Committee on Interior and Insular Affairs.

U.S. 88th Congress, 1st session. Senate. Designating the lake to be formed by the waters impounded by the Flaming Gorge Dam, Utah, in the states of Wyoming and Utah, as "Lake O'Mahoney." Report no. 279, to accompany S.J. Res. 17. June 19, 1963. Calendar no. 260. Washington, 1963. 5p.

Submitted by Mr. Jackson, from the Committee on Interior and Insular Affairs, with amendments, as recommended by the Dept. of the Interior, to restrict the name to the lake, and designate it as Lake O'Mahoney.

—— [Reprint of the original joint resolution, June 19, 1963, with amendments to accompany the report. Report no. 279 and Calendar no. 260 added]. 2p.

U.S. 88th Congress, 1st session. House. Joint resolution to designate the lake to be formed by the waters impounded by the Flaming Gorge Dam, Utah, as "Ashley Lake." H.J. Res. 604, July 31, 1963. Washington, 1963. 1p.

Introduced by Mr. Burton and referred to the Committee on Interior and Insular Affairs.

In honor of William Henry Ashley (1778-1838), a fur trader, explorer, and Congressman.

—— Providing designations for the lake to be formed by the waters impounded by Flaming Gorge Dam. Report no. 879, to accompany S. J. Res. 17. Oct. 30, 1963. Washington, 1963. 4p.

Submitted by Mr. Rogers, from the Committee on Interior and Insular Affairs, with amendments, that that portion of the lake in Utah be known as Lake Ashley and the portion in Wyoming as Lake O'Mahoney. Two members of the Committee dissented. The Committee considered S.J. Res. 17, H.J. Res. 293, and H.J. Res. 604 simultaneously.

—— [Reprint of S.J. Res. 17, Oct. 30, 1963, with amendments, to accompany the report. Report no. 879 and House Calendar no. 161 added]. 2p.

3938. Urbanek, Mae Bobb. Wyoming place names. 3d ed. rev. Boulder, Colo., Johnson Pub. Co., 1974. 236p. maps.

1st ed.: 1967. 223p.

A comprehensive list of names of cities, counties, rivers, mountains, etc., with information about the place and name.

3939. Wyoming place names. Annals of Wyoming 14:158-61, 227-39, 322-24, April, July, Oct. 1942; 15:85-90, Jan. 1943.

3940. Wyoming 75th Anniversary Commission. Wyoming, the 75th year. Official publication. Douglas, Wyo., 1965. 138p.

Much of this booklet is devoted to the counties of Wyoming, giving date organized and origin of name.

3941. Yochelson, Ellis L. Monuments and markers to the territorial surveys. Annals of Wyoming 43:113-24. 1971.

Includes names of geographic features named for the government explorers of the western territories, Ferdinand Vandeveer Hayden, Clarence King, George Montague Wheeler and John Wesley Powell.

CANADA

GENERAL

3942. Armstrong, George Henry. The origin and meaning of place names in Canada. Toronto, Macmillan, 1930. 312p.
Reprinted, 1972.
Authors and works consulted: p. 312.
Review: Canadian historical review 12:319-20, Sept. 1931.

3943. Assiniwi, Bernard. Lexique des noms Indiens en Amérique. 1, Noms géographiques; 2, Personnages historiques. Montréal, Lemeac, 1973. 2v.
Review: Marcel Trudel, Revue d'histoire de l'Amérique française 29:97-99, juin 1975.

3944. Association of Dominion Land Surveyors. Memorandum, prepared by the Executive Committee, in accordance with a resolution regarding geographical nomenclature and orthography in Canada, March 15th and 16th, 1886. Association of Dominion Land Surveyors. Report of proceedings 5:49-60. 1888.
Also printed separately: Montreal, J. Lovell & Son, 1888. 12p.
Suggests ways to correct errors through compilation of a geographical dictionary by the Surveyor General, and in so doing follow the recommended system of nomenclature.

3945. Audet, Francis J. Variations des noms géographiques du Canada. Société de Geographie de Québec. Bulletin 15:290-301. 1921; 16:19-36. 1922.
Gives past and present names.

3946. Baker, Edna. Prairie place names. Toronto, Ryerson Press, 1928. 28p. (The Ryerson Canadian history readers no. 3)
"One of a series of readers designed to present historical facts to young Canadians."—Price.

3947. Barbeau, Marius. Legend and history in the oldest geographical names of the St. Lawrence. Canadian geographical journal 61:2-9, July 1960.
Reprinted: Inland seas 17:105-13, Summer 1961.

3948. —— Légende et histoire dans les plus anciens noms géographiques du Saint-Laurent. Congrès international de toponymie et d'anthroponymie. 3d, Brussels, 1949. v. 2, Actes et mémoires. 1951. p. 404-11.

3949. —— Les noms les plus anciens sur la carte du Canada. Revue trimestrielle canadienne 35:243-55, automne. 1949.
Based on 16th-century maps.

3950. —— Les plus anciens noms du Saint-Laurent. Revue de l'Université Laval 3:649-57, avril 1949.

3951. Barr, William. New Wales, New Denmark, or New Yorkshire? The Musk-ox no. 15, p. 67-70. 1975. maps.
"Area lying inland of the western and southwestern coasts of Hudson Bay does not enjoy a single regional name, but is divided between the provinces of Ontario, Manitoba, and possibly Saskatchewan, and the Keewatin District of the Northwest Territories."

3952. The Bay of Fundy. Historical magazine 10:321, Oct. 1866.
A note on the origin of the name Fundy.

3953. Bedard, Avila. La traduction des noms géographiques. Le parler français (Société du Parler Français au Canada) 13:263-72, fév. 1915.
The author criticizes the translation into English names that were originally French.

3954. Bell, Charles Napier. Some historical names and places of the Canadian North-west. A paper read before the Society on the evening of 22d January, 1885. Winnipeg, Manitoba Free Press Print, 1885. 8p. (Manitoba. Historical and Scientific Society. Transactions no. 17)

3955. Bourinot, John George. Canadian historic names. Canadian monthly 7:289-300, April 1875.
Considers the effect of Indian nomenclature and legends of different localities on present-day English names.

3956. Brant-Sero, J. Ojijateckha. Indian place names in Mohawk, collected by J. O. Brant-Sero and Chief Alexander Hill. Toronto. Ontario Provincial Museum. Annual archaeological report 1898:171-72.
A list of Canadian and American names with their Indian equivalents.

3957. Brochu, Michel. Normes et principes généraux de toponymie. Québec, Les Éditions Ferland, 1962. 16p.
General principles of writing and presenting place-names, with examples in French.

3958. Bryant, Margaret M. After 25 years of onomastic study. Names 24:30-55, March 1976.
A survey of onomastic study in the United States and Canada during the first 25 years of the American Name Society.

3959. Buchanan, Milton Alexander. Notes on Portuguese place-names in north-eastern America; In Estudios hispánicos, homenaje a Archer M. Huntington. Wellesley, Mass., 1952. p. 99-104.
Principally Newfoundland; also Labrador, Nova Scotia, New England coast.

3960. Burns, E. L. M. Their name is Mud. Beaver outfit [i.e., volume] 267:14-19, June 1936.
A member of the Geographic Board of Canada describes something of the procedure and problems of straightening out the confusion of duplicate and trite names for lakes, streams, and mountains.

3961. Burwash, Armon. Concerning a few well known Indian names. Toronto. Ontario Provincial Museum. Annual archaeological report 1913:34-36.

3962. —— Concerning some Indian place-names in Canada. Ottawa naturalist 32:153-55, Feb. 1919.
Indicates source of name by tribe.

3963. Buyniak, Victor O. Early Doukhobor villages and their names. Canadian Society for the Study of Names. Onomastica 57:1-9, June 1980.

3964. Campbell, Frank W. Canada post offices, 1755-1895. Lawrence, Mass. Quarterman Publications, [1972]. [12], 191p.
List of post offices with date of establishment and of discontinuance or change of name, for all provinces except Newfoundland.
Review: James Montagnec, Canadian geographical journal 87:39, July 1973.

3965. Canada. Bureau of Statistics. Standard geographical classification manual; a working manual. 2d interim ed. Ottawa, 1968. 4v.
Contents: Quebec; Maritime Provinces; Western provinces; Ontario.
A manual of classification of geographical names by means of punched-card system.

3966. —— Department of Mines and Technical Surveys. Geographical Branch. Selected bibliography of Canadian toponymy. Ottawa, 1964. 27p. (Its Bibliographical series, no. 30)

3967. —— Geographic Board. Nomenclature of the mountains of western Canada, approved on the 2nd April, 1918. Ottawa, J. de L. Taché, 1918. 4p. map.
Also published in its report 16:33-34. 1917/19.

3968. —— —— Report, containing all decisions. v. 1-19. 1898-1927. Ottawa.
No. 1-11, 1898-1912, Supplement to the Annual report of the Dept. of Marine and Fisheries. Marine; no. 12-19, 1913-27, Supplement to the Annual report of the Dept. of the Interior.
Reports for 1898-1919/21 issued in the Sessional papers of the Parliament.
Some reports are cumulative from 1898.
Supplements to the various reports were published in the Canada gazette from time to time and were incorporated in the next report.
Review: Review of historical publications relating to Canada 16:125-26. 1912; of v. 1, Henry Gannett, National geographic magazine 10:519-20, Nov. 1899.

3969. —— Permanent Committee on Geographical Names. Information circular. no. 1-26. July 22, 1963-June 20, 1968.
Issued irregularly.
Contains miscellaneous news items, reprints of papers and articles.
The Geographic Board of Canada was created by Order in Council, 1897. The name was changed to Canadian Board on Geographic Names, 1948. In 1961 the name was changed to Permanent Committee on Geographical Names. Membership and functions are defined by Order in Council P.C. 1969-1458.

3970. —— —— Principles and procedures. Rev. 1976. Ottawa, Surveys and Mapping Branch, Dept. of Energy, Mines and Resources, 1976. 9p.
The French edition is bound in at reverse position, 9p.
Earlier editions: 1963; by the Board on Geographic Names 1948.

3971. Canadian Broadcasting Corporation. A guide to the pronunciation of Canadian place names. Rev. ed. Toronto, 1959. 32p.
Originally appeared as part of the CBC's Handbook for announcers, published 1942.

3972. Canadian Institute of Onomastic Sciences. Onomastics—a neglected discipline in Canada; a memorandum presented to the MacDonald Senate Committee on Research, in Ottawa, June 30, 1968, by J. B. Rudnyćkyj on behalf of the Institute. Canadian Institute of Onomastic Sciences. Onomastica 38:6-12, 1969.

3973. —— Proceedings, no. 1-9, 1967-75; In its Onomastica no. 36, 1968, no. 38, 1969, no. 42, 1971, no. 44, 1972, no. 49, 1974, no. 50, 1976.

3974. Canadian Permanent Committee on Geographical Names. Canadian geographical journal 91:47-48, Sept. 1975.

3975. Canadian Society for the Study of Names. The name gleaner. v. 1- , Sept. 1976- .

The news bulletin of the Society.

3976. —— Onomastica. no. 1- . 1951- .

No. 1, 1951-35, 1968, published by the Ukrainian Free Academy of Sciences; no. 36, 1968-50, 1976, by the Canadian Institute of Onomastic Sciences.

Onomastica includes organizational information and scholarly papers in the field of international name studies with primary interest in Canadian studies.

3977. Canoma; news and views concerning Canadian toponymy, comp. by the Secretariat of the Canadian Permanent Committee on Geographical Names. v. 1- , July 1975- .

Restricted distribution.

3978. Caron, Abbé Ivanhoe. Les noms géographiques de la Rivière Ottawa in 1686. Société de Géographie de Québec. Bulletin 11:4-10, janv. 1917.

3979. Carrière, Gaston. Essai de toponymie oblate canadienne. Revue de l'Université d'Ottawa 28:364-94, 522-31, juil./sept.-oct./déc. 1958; 29:92-108, 233-46, janv./mars-avril/juin 1959.

3980. Chicanot, E. L. A mine of any other name would sound more sweet; a plea for reform in the matter of Canadian nomenclature. Canadian mining journal 57:598-99, Nov. 1936.

3981. Corry, J. H. Some Canadian cities; meaning and origin of names. Canadian geographical journal 26:297, June 1943; 27:17, 263, July, Dec. 1943; 28:40, Jan. 1944.

3982. Daviault, Pierre. Les noms de lieux au Canada. Royal Society of Canada. Transactions 3d ser. v. 42, sec. 1, p. 42-52, May 1948.

Discussion of this article by W. H. Alexander in Western folklore 8:259-60, July 1949.

3983. Delaney, Gordon F. Commercial usages in Canadian toponymy. Canadian Society for the Study of Names. Onomastica 51:16-19, June 1977.

The problem of correctly applying place-names in commercial publications, such as atlases, in a bilingual country.

3984. —— Current problems in Canadian geographic nomenclature. Canadian surveyor 9:6-12, Jan. 1947.

3985. —— Language problems in Canadian toponymy; In Henri Dorion, ed., Les noms de lieux et le contact des langues. Québec, Les Presses de l'Université Laval, 1972. p. 302-33.

3986. —— Problems in cartographic nomenclature. Canadian surveyor 16:254-63, Nov. 1962.
Summary in French on p. 263.
Discusses the desirability of a more serious and systematic approach to map nomenclature on the part of cartographers. Gives examples of difficulties caused by the existence of several languages in an area.

3987. Denys, Nicolas. The description and natural history of the coasts of North America (Acadia). Trans. and ed., with a memoir of the author, collateral documents, and a reprint of the original by Wm. F. Ganong. Toronto, Champlain Society, 1908. 625p.
Extensive place-name footnotes.

3988. Desbois, Paul. Noms géographiques. Société de Géographie de Québec. Bulletin 7:180-83, 215-23, 285-91, mai-sept. 1913.
Notes on the origin and correct form of certain geographical names.

3989. Donovan, Frank P., Jr. Named for railroad presidents. Railroad magazine Feb. 1965, p. 24-27.
Communities in the United States and Canada that were named for railroad presidents.

3990. Dorion, Henri. La problematique choronymique des régions multilingues; In Henri Dorion, ed., Les noms de lieux et le contact des langues, avec la collaboration de Christian Morissonneau, Publié pour le Centre International de Recherches sur le Bilinguisme, et le Groupe d'Étude de Choronymie et de Terminologie Géographique. Québec, Les Presses de l'Université Laval, 1972. p. 9-41.
Review: Kelsie B. Harder & Conrad M. Rothrauff, Names 21:201-04, Sept. 1973.

3991. —— New perspective in choronymic research. Canoma 1:4-7. 1975.

3992. —— & Louis Edmond Hamelin. De la toponymie traditionnelle à une choronymie totale. Cahiers de géographie de Québec 10:195-211, sept. 1966.
Also in Geographical bulletin 9:141-57, 1967. English version in Canoma 2:6-9. 1976.
Proposal to employ the term choronymy for the science of place-names, as more inclusive than toponymy.

3993. —— Louis Edmond Hamelin, & Fernand Grenier. Liste des choronymes canadiens dans l'atlas du monde contemporain. Édition préliminaire. Québec, 1967. 110ℓ. (Groupe d'études choronymiques et terminologiques. Publication no. 3)
Statement of the principles of a new French toponymy for Canada, followed by a list of choronyms.

3994. —— & Louise Laperrière-Monaghan. Research possibilities in onomastics. Québec, Institut de Géographie, Université Laval, 1976. 81p.
Review: Kelsie B. Harder, Names 25:38-39, March 1977.

3995. Douglas, Robert. Meaning of Canadian city names. Ottawa, F. A. Acland, 1922. 21p.
Reprinted from Canada. Geographic Board. Report 17:34-52. 1919/21.
Translation: Histoire des noms de quelques cités canadiennes. Société de Géographie de Québec. Bulletin 17:242-49, 304-15, sept., nov. 1923; 18:33-41, janv. 1924; reprinted separately: Ottawa, F. A. Acland, 1923. 22p.

3996. —— Notes on mountain nomenclature; coming of age of the Geographic Board of Canada. Canadian alpine journal 10:32-37. 1919.

3997. —— The place-names of Canada. Scottish geographical magazine 36:154-57, July 15, 1920.
Discusses the principles which underlie a system of nomenclature for Canada.

3998. Drolet, Jean-Paul. Developments in Canadian toponymy, 1972-1977. Canoma 3:2-3, July 1977.
Also published in United Nations Conference on the Standardization of Geographical Names, 3d, Athens, 1977. Canada. Ottawa, 1978. p. 61-63.
French version: p. 217-20.

3999. —— Progress report on the standardization of geographical names in Canada; In United Nations Conference on the Standardization of Geographical Names. 1st, Geneva, 1967. Report on Canadian participation. Ottawa, 1968. p. 10-12.

4000. Fairclough, G. Thomas. Toward a systematic classification of street name patterns in the U.S.A. and Canadian cities: a progress report; In South Central Names Institute. They had to call it something. Commerce, Tex., Names Institute Press, 1974. p. 65-76. (Publication 3).

4001. Fletcher, Roy Jackson. Settlements of northern Canada, a gazetteer and index. Edmonton, Boreal Institute for Northern Studies, Univ. of Alberta, 1975. Unpaged. maps. (Occasional publication, no. 11)
Includes: Yukon and Northwest Territories, Labrador, Ungava, Quebec, and Newfoundland in a single alphabetical list of settlements.

4002. Florin, Lambert. A guide to western ghost towns. Seattle, Superior Pub. Co., [1967]. 96p. maps. (A Superior travel book)
Includes more than 400 towns in the western states of the United States and Canada.

4003. Fraser, J. Keith. Canadian Permanent Committee on Geographical Names. Geographical bulletin (Canada. Dept. of Mines and Technical Surveys. Geographical Branch) 21:130-34, May 1964.
A brief history of the organization and work of the Committee and its predecessors, with a list of guiding principles for place-names.

4004. —— Canadian Permanent Committee on Geographical Names; In United Nations Conference on the Standardization of Geographical Names. 1st, Geneva, 1967. Report on Canadian participation. Ottawa, 1968. p. 31-33.

4005. —— The history and foundations of the Canadian Permanent Committee on Geographical Names. Ukrainian Free Academy of Sciences. Onomastica 35:11-17, 1968.

4006. —— Place names of the Hudson Bay region; In Canada. Dept. of Energy, Mines and Resources. Science, history, and Hudson Bay. Ottawa, 1968. 2v. 1:236-62.
Also reprinted separately: Ottawa, Surveys and Mapping Branch, Dept. of Energy, Mines and Resources, 1970. p. 236-61. (Reprint no. 29)

4007. —— Problems of domestic standardization of geographical names; In United Nations Conference on the Standardization of Geographical Names. 1st, Geneva, 1967. Report on Canadian participation. Ottawa, 1968. p. 21-30.

4008. —— The realistic approach to geographical names in Canada. Cahiers de géographie de Québec 10:235-39, sept. 1966.

4009. —— & R. Disipio. Gazetteer of Canada; In United Nations Conference on the Standardization of Geographical Names, 1st, Geneva, 1967. Report on Canadian participation. Ottawa, 1968. p. 37-44.

4010. Frémont, Donatien. Des noms français pour nos centres français. Société de Géographie de Québec. Bulletin 16:222-24. 1922.
Plea to preserve the significant French names of western Canada.

4011. Ganong, William Francis. Crucial maps in the early cartography and place-nomenclature of the Atlantic coast of Canada. With an introduction, commentary, and map notes by Theodore E. Laying. Toronto, Univ. of Toronto Press in co-operation with the Royal Society of Canada, 1964. 511p. (Royal Society of Canada. Special publications no. 7)
Reprint of material originally published in Royal Society of Canada. Proceedings and transactions 3d ser. v. 23, sec. 2, p. 135-75; v. 24, sec. 2, p. 135-88; v. 25, sec. 2, p. 169-203; v. 26, sec. 2, p. 125-79; v. 27, sec. 2, p. 149-95; v. 28, sec. 2, p. 149-294; v. 29, sec. 2, p. 101-29; v. 30, sec. 2, p. 109-29; v. 31, sec. 2, p. 101-30. 1929-37.
"Traces the evolution of the cartography and place-nomenclature of the Atlantic coast of Canada, with the associated parts of Newfoundland and New England, from the time of the first discoveries down to the inauguration of our modern geography by Champlain, 1526-1600."—Griffin. Discusses in particular the Cosa map of 1500; the Third decade, 1520-1530, the Homem maps, and the Fagundes voyages; maps of Maggiolo, 1527, and Verrazano, 1524 and 1529; maps of 1535 to 1542; the compiled or composite maps from 1526 to 1600; the geography and cartography of the Cartier voyages; the Mercator world chart of 1569; and Transition from the Mercator chart to the cartographical works of Champlain.
Review: W. Gillies Ross, Cahiers de géographie 10:371-72, sept. 1966.

4012. —— The history of certain geographical names; In his The cartography of the Gulf of St. Lawrence, from Cartier to Champlain. Royal Society of Canada. Proceedings and transactions v. 7, sec. 2, p. 51-55. 1889.

4013. Gaubert, H. Baptêmes géographiques: la baie d'Hudson. Geographica 96:2-8. 1959.
Place-names from the explorations of Henry Hudson.

4014. Guinard, Joseph Étienne. Les noms indiens de mon pays. Leur signification, leur histoire. Montréal, Éditions Rayonnement [1960]. 197p.

4015. Hamelin, Louis Edmond. Classement des noms de lieux du Canada; In Mélanges de géographie: physique, humaine, économique, appliquée, offerts à M. Omer Tulippe. Gembloux, Éditions J. Ducolot, [1967]. v. 1, 617-27.
Also in Études de linguistique franco-canadienne: communications présentées au XXXIVe Congrès de l'Association canadienne-française pour l'avancement des sciences, Québec, nov. 1966. Québec, Les Presses de l'Université Laval, 1967. p. 153-63.
Four major classes: I. Classification génétique de la toponymie non-indigène; II. Classification linguistique; III. Classification spatiale; IV. Stratification chronologique.

4016. —— Noms de régions. Cahiers de géographie de Québec 10:253-62, sept. 1966. maps.

4017. —— & Henri Dorion. Le Groupe d'Études de Choronymie et de Terminologie Géographique. (G.E.C.E.T.). Cahiers de géographie de Québec 13:366-72, déc. 1969.

4018. Hamilton, P. St. C. Origin of Canadian place names. MacLean's magazine 38:35, Aug. 1, 1925.

4019. Hamilton, William Baillie. The Macmillan book of Canadian place names. Toronto, Macmillan of Canada, c1978. 340p.

Bibliography: p. 333-40.
Arranged by province, the names have been included for the major centers of population; the most important physical features; significant historical places; and those of human interest.
Review: Kelsie B. Harder, Names 26:287, Sept. 1978.

4020. Harder, Kelsie B. Canadian contributions to the American Name Society. Ukrainian Free Academy of Sciences. Onomastica 35:22-26, 1968.

4021. —— Illustrated dictionary of place names, United States and Canada. New York, Van Nostrand Reinhold Co., 1976. 631p.
Bibliography: p. 627-31.
Review: Eugene B. Vest, Names 24:315-16, Dec. 1976; Manfred Hanowell, Beiträge zur Namenforschung N.F. 12:303-05. 1977.

4022. Harrington, John Peabody. Our state names. Smithsonian Institution. Annual report 1954:373-88.
Reprinted as: Smithsonian Institution. Publication 4205. 1955.
Includes Canadian names of Indian origin: p. 387-88.

4023. Harris, Lewis J. Mapping the land of Canada. Geographical journal 138:131-38, June 1972. map.
Place names and gazetteers: p. 135-36, describes work and publications of the Canadian Permanent Committee on Geographical Names, 1967-1972.

4024. Harrisse, Henry. The discovery of North America; a critical, documentary, and historic investigation, with an essay on the early cartography of the New World, including descriptions of two hundred and fifty maps or globes existing or lost, constructed before the year 1536; to which are added a chronology of one hundred voyages westward, projected, attempted, or accomplished between 1431 and 1504; biographical accounts of the three hundred pilots who first crossed the Atlantic; and a copious list of the original names of American regions, caciqueships, mountains, islands, capes, gulfs, rivers, towns, and harbours. London, H. Stevens & Son; Paris, H. Welter, 1892. 802p.
Reprinted: Amsterdam, N. Israel, 1961. 802p.
Geographical index, p. 751-84.

4025. Hawkes, Arthur. Town christeners in the West. Canadian magazine 37:72-78, May 1911.
"Some interesting examples of the origin of place-names in Canada, especially along the railroad lines."—Price

4026. Hoffman, Bernard G. Cabot to Cartier, sources for a historical ethnography of northeastern North America, 1497-1550. [Toronto] Univ. of Toronto Press, [1961]. xii, 287p. maps.
Bibliography: p. 229-63.
Complementary to and an evaluation of much the same material in William Francis Ganong, Crucial maps in the early cartography and place-nomenclature of the Atlantic coast of Canada (Toronto, n.p., 1964).

4027. Holmer, Nils Magnus. Indian place names in North America. Cambridge, Harvard Univ. Press, 1948. 44p. (American Institute in the University of Upsala. Essays and studies on American language and literature)
Reprinted: Nendeln, Kraus Reprint, 1973.

4028. How, D. Who called it that? Devout Indians and loyal Englishmen; stray Portuguese and footloose Frenchmen—they all left a mark on our map. MacLean's magazine 61:19, 31-32, July 1, 1948.

4029. Indian place names in western Canada. Canadian pictorial 10:18-19, June 1915.
Signed: Max McD.

4030. Johnson, George. Place-names of Canada, read before the Ottawa Scientific Society, Dec. 3rd, 1897. Ottawa, E. J. Reynolds, 1898. xxxvii p.
Also published in Ottawa Literary and Scientific Society. Transactions 1:27-62. 1897-98.

4031. —— Place-names of Canada: Selkirk. Canadian magazine 13:395-406, Sept. 1899.
Names commemorating the Earl of Selkirk.

4032. —— Place-names of Canada: the Carletons. Canadian magazine 12:289-95, Feb. 1899.
Places, streets, etc., named in memory of Sir Guy Carleton.

4033. Jolicoeur, T. & J. Keith Fraser. Geographical features in Canada named for surveyors. Ottawa, Geographical Branch, Dept. of Mines and Technical Surveys, 1966. 50p. (Gazetteer of Canada. Special supplement no. 2)

4034. Jones, Cyril Meredith. Indian, pseudo-Indian place names in the Canadian West. Ukrainian Free Academy of Sciences. Onomastica 12:1-19. 1956.

4035. Kelton, Dwight H. Indian names of places near the Great Lakes. Detroit, Mich., Detroit Free Press, 1888. 55p.
Most of the names are derived from the Ojibway, Cree, and Delaware languages.
Review: A. S. Gatschet, Journal of American folk-lore 2:69, Jan.-March 1889; D. G. Brinton, American antiquarian 11:68, Jan. 1889.

4036. Kerfoot, Helen. Surveyors general: their recognition in Canadian landscape feature names. Canoma 4:11-17, Dec. 1978.
French version included.

4037. Kirkconnell, Watson. Canadian toponymy and the cultural stratification of Canada. Ukrainian Free Academy of Sciences. Onomastica 7:1-16. 1954.

4038. —— Scottish place-names in Canada; a paper delivered at the third annual meeting of Canadian Institute of Onomastic Sciences, York University, Toronto, June 13, 1969. Canadian Institute of Onomastic Sciences and Ukrainian Free Academy of Sciences. Onomastica 39:1-32. 1970.
A study based on maps of Scotland and of the provinces of Canada, and on the surnames of Scotland, culminating in a list of 1200 Scottish place-names.

4039. Krahn, Cornelius. Mennonite names of persons and places. Mennonite life 15:36-38, Jan. 1960.
In North and South America.
For a complete list of Mennonite villages, see article "Villages" in v. 4 of Mennonite encyclopedia. 1959.

4040. Krawchuk, Peter. Ukrainian place names in Canada. Ukrainian Canadian Nov. 1968, p. 7-9.
In the provinces of Manitoba, Saskatchewan and Alberta.

4041. Lacourcière, Luc. Toponymie canadienne; In Société du Parler Français au Canada. Études sur le parler français au Canada. Québec, Les Presses de l'Univ. Laval, 1955. p. 199-220.
Observations on Canadian place-names.

4042. LaHam, Mary. Gazetteer production and names processing at the federal level in Canada; In United Nations Conference on the Standardization of Geographical Names, 3d, Athens, 1977. Canada. Ottawa, 1978. p. 147-49.
French version: p. 309-11.

4043. Lanos, J. M. What's in a name? Queen's quarterly 17:44-57, July-Sept. 1909.
A plea for regeneration in name giving in the United States and Canada. Deals largely with place-names in western Europe, showing how beautiful and appropriate is the terminology used by the Anglo-Saxons, Northmen, and Celts.

4044. Laurent, Joseph. Etymology of Indian names by which are designated certain tribes, towns, rivers, lakes, etc.; In his New familiar Abenakis and English dialogues. Quebec, Printed by L. Brousseau, 1884. p. 205-22.

4045. Leechman, Douglas. The father of place names. Beaver outfit [i.e., volume] 285:24-30, Autumn 1954.
Robert Bell, 1841-1917, of Geological Survey, named more than 3000 topographic features.

4046. Loveless, Edna. Geographic names. Canadian surveyor 8:21-23, April 1946.
Meaning of a few names.

4047. Macfarlane, James. An American geological railway guide, giving the geological formation at every railroad station, with altitudes above mean tide-water, notes on interesting places on the routes, and a description of each of the formations. 2d ed., rev. and enl. New York, Appleton, 1890. 426p. map.
Lists of places with their altitudes on all the railroads in the United States and Canada in the 1880s.

4048. MacLean, John. Bungay and others. Beaver 4:397-99, Aug. 1924.
Indian place-names on the prairies.

4049. MacMillan, Donald Baxter. Eskimo place names and aid to conversation. Washington, Hydrographic Office, U.S. Navy, 1943. 154p. (H. O. Miscel. no. 10,578)
A list of Eskimo names, with meaning, found on northern maps and charts, for Labrador, Hudson Bay, Baffin Land, Greenland, Ellesmere Land, p. 7-77.

4050. Maheux, A. Les noms de lieux. Société de Géographie de Québec. Bulletin 16:234-39. 1922.
General survey of the subject--the act of commemorating historical and religious persons or natural locations.

4051. Masta, Henry Lorne. Abenaki Indian legends, grammar and place names. Victoriaville, P.Q., La Voix des Bois-Francs, 1932. 110p.
The meaning of Indian names of rivers, lakes, etc., p. 81-105.

4052. Matthews, Constance Mary Carrington. Place names of the English-speaking world. London, Weidenfeld & Nicholson, [1972]. xi, 370p.
Also published: New York, Scribner, [c1972].
Part 3: The New World. The approach to the New World; The American colonies; the United States; Canada: p. 163-231.
Review: Kelsie B. Harder, Names 21:112-14, June 1973.

4053. Maurault, Joseph Pierre Anselme. Histoire des Abenakis, depuis 1605 jusqu'à nos jours. [Sorel, Qué.], Imprimé à l'atelier typographique de la "Gazette de Sorel," 1866. 631p.
A list of place-names in Maine and Canada, with significations, in introduction p. ii-vii.

4054. Meadows-Wood, P. D. Canadian city names. United empire n.s. 13:651-53, Oct. 1922.

4055. Miller, Emile. Nos noms de lieux. Société de Géographie de Québec. Bulletin 4:205-07, sept. 1910.
Many places have been named after saints.

4056. Munro, Michael R. Native toponyms of excessive length. Canoma 4:25-29, Dec. 1978.
French version included.
"Any corruption of a name either through translation or contraction contravenes the purpose and principles of the Canadian Permanent Committee on Geographical Names."

4057. Naming new towns big task in Canada. New York times Nov. 18, 1934, sec. 8, p. 12, col. 3.
In choosing place-names near international boundary, Canada cooperates with U.S. Geographic Board. Brief description of work of Canadian Geographic Board.

4058. No passport for Canada. New York times June 16, 1940, sec. 10, p. 24.
Origin of some place-names.

4059. Origine de quelques noms canadiens. Bulletin des recherches historiques 11:145, 183, 215, 242, 269, 277, 309, mai-oct. 1905; 12:77, mars 1906.
A list giving brief notes on origin of names.

4060. Pacifique de Valiguy, O. F. M. Le pays des Micmacs. Liste de 2500 noms géographiques des Provinces Maritimes (l'ancienne Acadie), de la Gaspésie et de Terreneuve en langue micmaque avec la signification quand elle est connue, les noms correspondants en anglais ou en français et de copieuses notes historiques et géographiques; contient cinq cartes régionales, selon les anciens districts. Montréal, l'Auteur, 1934; In his Études historiques et géographiques. Ristigouche, Co. Bonaventure, 1935. p. 175-321.
Also reprinted separately: Montréal, l'Auteur, 1934. p. 176-321.
Originally published in Société de Géographie de Québec. Bulletin 21:111-17, 165-85. 1927; 22:43-55, 140-45, 270-77. 1928; 23:37-45. 1929; 25:96-106. 1931; 27:51-64. 1933; 28:105-47. 1934. The book corrects many typographical errors that appeared in the articles.
Includes place-names with English equivalents.

4061. Palmer, P. E. By any other name. Canadian geographical journal 36:149-51, March 1948.
Wide variety of generic and proper names given to similar physical features.

4062. —— The Canadian Board on Geographical Names. Names 1:79-84, June 1953.
A brief summary of the organization and work of the Board, by the chairman.

4063. Patterson, R. M. Names and the unnamed spaces. Canadian magazine 74:13, 30, July 1930.
Too often place-names are ugly and pointless.

4064. Pease, Mary Agnes. There's something in a name. MacLean's magazine 52:65, April 15, 1939; 52:49, May 1, 1939; 52:77, May 15, 1939; 52:49, June 1, 1939; 52:49, June 15, 1939.
Series of articles on whys and wherefores of Canadian place-names. Includes Canada, Nova Scotia, New Brunswick, Prince Edward Island, and St. Lawrence River.

4065. Poirier, Jean. Aperçu général sur la toponymie canadienne française. Onoma 17:262-66. 1972/73.
Report of onomastic activities in Canada.

4066. —— Terminology and choronymy. Canoma 3:1-5. 1977.
French version included.

4067. —— La toponyme Lacolle et son dérivé anglais Cole. Revue géographique de Montréal 25:163-67. 1971.
A résumé was published in Canadian Institute of Onomastic Sciences. Onomastica 42:26-28. 1971.

4068. Price, Esther Frances. Guide to material on place-names in the United States and Canada. Urbana, Ill., 1934. 250p.
Thesis (M.A.) Univ. of Illinois, 1934. On file in the University Library.

4069. Prowse, George Robert Farrar. Exploration of the Gulf of St. Lawrence, 1499-1525. Winnipeg, 1929. 23p.
List of place-names: p. 21-23.

4070. Prud'homme, L. A. Dans l'ouest canadien. Société de géographie de Québec. Bulletin 5:136-39, mars 1911.
Lakes, rivers, portages, and forts.

4071. Quinn, David B. & Jacques Rousseau. Les toponymes amérindiens du Canada chez les anciens voyageurs anglais, 1591-1602. Cahiers de géographie de Québec 10:263-77, sept. 1966.

4072. Rayburn, Alan. English geographical names in Canada with generic terms of French origin. Canadian cartographer 7:88-104, Dec. 1970.
Reprinted separately: Ottawa, Surveys and Mapping Branch, Dept. of Energy, Mines and Resources, 1971. p. 88-104. (Reprint no. 35)

4073. —— Geographical names of Amerindian origin in Canada. Names 15:203-15, Sept. 1967; 17:149-58, 1969.
Presents some of the more prominent populated places and physical features with names originating from Amerindian languages. The guest editor of the Sept. 1967 issue, Hamill Kenny, questions some of the meanings (p. 214-15).

4074. —— The placement of dispersed community names on medium- and large-scale maps. Canadian cartographer 5:18-24, June 1968. maps.
Proposal for a new method of placement of names of dispersed (rural) communities on maps. Determination of their names and areas is function of Canadian Permanent Committee on Geographical Names.

4075. —— The possessive and the apostrophe in geographical names. Canadian Society for the Study of Names. Onomastica 57:19-28, June 1980.

4076. —— Reflections of Greece in Canadian toponymy. Canoma 3:7-8, July 1977.
Published also in United Nations Conference on the Standardization of Geographical Names, 3d, Athens, 1977. Canada. Ottawa, 1978. p. 159-61.
French version: p. 321-23.

4076a. —— ed. Selected toponymic articles on the history and geography of Canada, published on the occasion of the XIV International Congress of Onomastic Sciences, Ann Arbor, Michigan, Aug. 23-29, 1981. Onomastica 59/60:1-52, June/Dec. 1981.
26 articles quoted in part or abstracted.

4077. Read, Allen Walker. The rivalry of names for the Rocky Mountains of North America. International Congress of Onomastic Sciences, 10th, Vienna, 1969. Proceedings 1:207-22.
Bibliography: p. 221-22.
Traces the names applied to the mountain system from earliest record until the present designation became fixed.

4078. Reade, John. The history of Canadian geographical names. New Dominion monthly 11:344. 1873.
Also in Maple leaves, Quebec, 1873.

4079. —— The testimony of names of places. Rose-Belford's Canadian monthly 1:602-04, Nov. 1878.
The source of some of the names in North America.

4080. Reynolds, Horace. Fish names land. Christian Science monitor Dec. 11, 1957, p. 8.
"The Basque word baccallaóa (Spanish bacallao), meaning codfish, may have come from the Indians. It once was the name of all the French territory north of the St. Lawrence."—American speech.

4081. Robinson, Percy James. Potier—places aux français (from Mss. in Municipal Library, Montreal). Bulletin des recherches historiques 48:365-68, déc. 1942.
Indian names with French equivalents in Potier's list.

4082. Roe, Frank Gilbert. Buffalo place-names; In his The North American buffalo. Toronto, Univ. of Toronto Press, 1951. p. 817-28.
Also miscellaneous references in index: Place-names.

4083. Rouillard, Eugène. L'invasion des noms sauvages. Bulletin du parler français au Canada 7:162-70, janv. 1909; 8:97-100, nov. 1909.

4084. —— Un nom géographique: la Baie des Chaleurs. Société de Géographie de Québec. Bulletin 9:210-11. 1915.
Plea for name to be recognized as it was historically known, instead of the proposed translation Chaleur Bay.

4085. —— Noms sauvages; étymologie. Québec, É. Marcotte, 1905. 17p.
Reprinted from Bulletin du parler français au Canada.

4086. —— Quelques noms géographiques. Société de Géographie de Québec. Bulletin 11:91-95, mars 1917.
The history and origin of the Baie du Tonnerre, Rivière Dalmas, French names in the Baie James, Tracadie.

4087. Roy, Pierre Georges. D'où vient le nom de "Nouvelle France"? Société de Géographie de Québec. Bulletin 12:79-80, mars 1918.

4088. —— Quelques forts du régime français. Bulletin des recherches historiques 54:5-14, 35-46, janv.-fév. 1948.

4089. —— Quelques noms de France. Société de Géographie de Québec. Bulletin 12:57-58, janv. 1918.

4090. Rudnyćkyj, Jaroslav Bohdan. Canadian place names of Ukrainian origin. 3d ed. Ukrainian Free Academy of Sciences. Onomastica 2:1-88. 1957.
In Ukrainian. The Ukrainian forms are accompanied by the transliterated English form.

A partial English version of this appeared in the author's Studies in onomastics. no. 15, 1958.
Review: Yar Slavutych, Names 6:254-55, Dec. 1958.

4091. —— Classification of Canadian place-names. Congrès international de sciences onomastiques. 4th, Uppsala. Mémoires. 1952. v. 2, pt. 2, p. 453-57.
Also reprinted separately, and in Ukrainian Free Academy of Sciences. Onomastica 15:7-11, 1958.

4092. —— Etymological formula in onomastics. Cahiers de géographie de Québec 10:213-18, sept. 1966.
2d rev. ed. published in Ukrainian Free Academy of Sciences. Onomastica 33:5-10, 1967.
Presents a methodology of research for the etymological explanation of names. Concludes that there is a need for an etymological dictionary of Canadian geographical names which would follow his formula.

4093. —— Names in contact: Canadian pattern; In Henri Dorion, ed., Les noms de lieux et le contact des langues. Québec, Les Presses de l'Université Laval, 1972. p. 293-301.

4094. —— Onomastics--a neglected discipline in Canada. Canadian Institute of Onomastic Sciences. Onomastica 38:6-12, 1969.

4095. —— Slavic toponymic neologisms in Canada. Canadian Slavonic papers 1:89-92, 1956.
An abstract included in International Congress of Onomastic Sciences, 5th, Salamanca, 1955. Program and communications p. 66.
Descriptive names, abbreviated names, other forms of names.

4096. —— Studies in onomastics. Ukrainian Free Academy of Sciences. Onomastica no. 11, 15.
No. 11, Canadian Slavic namelore; in Ukrainian with English summary. The author presents a full scheme of the types of namelore illustrating his theoretical classification with the material gathered among Slavic settlers in Canada, in 1949-55.
No. 15, includes among other papers, the author's Classification of Canadian place names, p. 7-11, and Toponymic neologisms in Canada, p. 12-16.
Review of no. 15: Yar Slavutych, Names 8:61-62, March 1960.

4097. —— Toward standardizing place names. Winnipeg free press June 13, 1972, p. 22.
Report on the work of and Canada's participation in the United Nations Conference on standardization of geographical names, London, May 10-31, 1972.

4098. —— ed. Ukrainian-Canadian folklore. Texts in English translation. Winnipeg, Ukrainian Free Academy of Sciences, 1960. 232p. (Ukrainica occidentalia, v. VII [5])
Short articles on origin of various place-names, p. 174-83.

4099. Scadding, Henry. Sir Joseph Banks again. Queen Charlotte and some local names, a supplemental note. Toronto, 1890?. 4p.

4100. —— Some lapsed names in Canadian local nomenclature. Canadian Institute. Proceedings n.s. 1:33-38. 1898.

4101. Scargill, M. H. Onomastica UVAN. Ukrainian Free Academy of Sciences. Onomastica 35:5-8. 1968.
Highlights in the publications of the Academy's Onomastica series.

4102. —— Ten years of Onomastica, 1951-1961. Ukrainian Free Academy of Sciences. Onomastica 21:5-8. 1961.

4103. Sebert, L. Geographic place names. Canadian surveyor 15:113-17, March 1960.
Principles of transliteration and representation on maps of place-names in Canada and elsewhere.

4104. Shepherd, Paul. Too many Pine lakes, a story of the troubles dogging the Geographic Board of Canada. Forest and outdoors 44:24-25, July 1948.
Repetition of names.

4105. Sherwin, Reider Thorbjorn. The Viking and the red man; the Old Norse origin of the Algonquin language. New York, Funk & Wagnalls, 1940-48. 5v.
Algonquin place names: 1:254-310; 2:162-78; 3:155-61; 4:172-208; 5:170-99.
Bibliography of principal sources of Algonquin place names: 1:331; 2:191.

4106. Sims, A. G. Canadian airmen on the map. Canadian geographical journal 91:28-33, Nov. 1975. map.
Includes: C. F. Stevenson, A list of geographical place names connected with Canada's aviation history. p. 29.

4107. Skinner, Charles M. Some odd names of places across the border. Current literature 25:41, Jan. 1899.
An extract from his Myths and legends beyond our borders. Gives origin and meaning.

4108. Skinner, L. B. Map nomenclature. Canadian surveyor 12:274-77, July 1954.
The story behind the names, including work of the Canadian Board on Geographical Names.

4109. Slavutych, Yar. Slavic contribution to Canadian toponymy. Canoma 3:5-6, July 1977.
Also published in United Nations Conference on the Standardization of Geographical Names, 3d, Athens, 1977. Canada. Ottawa, 1978. p. 71-72.
French version: p. 227-28.

4110. Smart, Michael B. National standardization—exonyms: a national policy for the bilingual treatment of geographical names on Canadian maps; In United Nations Conference on the Standardization of Geographical Names, 3d, Athens, 1977. Canada. Ottawa, 1978. p. 73-91.
French version: p. 229-50.

4111. —— Toponymy and the technological imperative. Canoma 1:1-3. 1975.

4112. Sprague, Marshall. The great gates; the story of the Rocky Mountain passes. Boston, Little, Brown, 1964. 468p. maps.
Bibliography: p. 356-64.
A roster of passes: p. 371-456. A list including altitude, location, and in many cases, origin of name.

4113. Stevenson, A. A new Inuit orthography for geographical names; In United Nations Conference on the Standardization of Geographical Names, 3d, Athens, 1977. Canada. Ottawa, 1978. p. 67-70.
French version: p. 223-26.

4114. Stevenson, C. F. A list of named glaciological features in Canada. Ottawa, Geographical Branch, Dept. of Mines and Technical Surveys, 1964. vii, 14p. (Gazetteer of Canada. Special supplement no. 1)

4115. Stewart, George Rippey. Names of wild animals for natural features in the United States and Canada. Revue internationale d'onomastique 12:282-92, déc. 1960.
Estimated that about 40,000 natural features in the United States bear the names of wild animals; in Canada, about 10,000.

4116. Strathglass, Allan. Odd Canadian place names. MacLean's magazine 40:17, 76-77, June 1, 1927.

4117. Stursberg, Peter. The strange place names of Canada. Saturday night, Canada's magazine of business and contemporary affairs 76:17-18, Aug. 19, 1961.

4118. Tanguay, C. Étude sur les noms. Royal Society of Canada. Proceedings and transactions 1st ser. v. 1, sec. 1, p. 119-29. 1883.

4119. Thomson, D. Walter. There's magic in a name. MacLean's magazine 41:3-5, 54, June 1, 1928.

4120. United Nations Conference on the Standardization of Geographical Names, 1st, Geneva, 1967. Report on Canadian participation. Ottawa, 1968. 138p.

4121. United Nations Conference on the Standardization of Geographical Names, 2d, London, 1972. General report of Canada's participation in and of the work of the Conference. Ottawa, 1973.

4122. United Nations Conference on the Standardization of Geographical Names, 3d, Athens, 1977. Canada. Ottawa, Canadian Permanent Committee on Geographical Names, 1978. 323p. maps.
French version: p. 163-323.

4123. U.S. Board on Geographic Names. Decisions on names in Canada. August 1953. Washington, Dept. of the Interior, 1953. 78p. (Its Cumulative decision list no. 5304)
Changes in Canada: 1953- , Gazetteer supplement, Sept. 1971; In U.S. Board on Geographical Names. The Americas. Washington, Sept. 1971. p. 29-34.
Canada was included in the Board's Decision lists: 4301 (July 1943-Oct. 1943); 4404, 4406-4407 (April, June-July 1944); 4701-4703 (Jan.-March 1947); 4801-4806 (Jan.-June 1948); 4905-4906 (May-June 1949); 5007 (Nov. 1950).

4124. Van Steen, Marcus. Our heritage of fascinating place-names. Imperial oil review 43:9-11, April 1959.

4125. Voorhis, Ernest. Historic forts and trading posts of the French and of the English fur trading companies. Ottawa, Dept. of the Interior, National Development Bureau, 1930. 188p. map.
Alphabetical list of forts and posts, p. 28-181.
"A few of these establishments were located on what is now territory of the United States."—Pref.
Includes map of Mississippi and Ohio valleys showing chain of historic French forts.

4126. Walton, Ivan H. Origin of names on the Great Lakes. Names 3:239-46, Dec. 1955.
Names of the lakes and their connecting waterways, with some mention of surrounding territory.

4127. Whitcher, A. H. Geographical nomenclature. n.p., 1893. p. 67-72.
Reprinted from Proceedings of the Association of Dominion Land Surveyors.

4128. Wilkinson, Ron. Labelling the land: Canada needs 2,000,000 more place names. Canadian geographical journal 87:12-19, July 1973.
Concerns the work of the Canadian Permanent Committee on Geographical Names and the many unnamed features in Canada.

4129. Williams, Glyndwr. East London names in Hudson Bay. East London papers, a journal of history, social studies and the arts 7:23-30, July 1964. map.

4130. Wintemberg, W. J. The Crimean War and some place names of Canada. Royal Society of Canada. Proceedings and transactions 3d ser. v. 21, sec. 2, p. 71-79. 1927.
Place- and street names which perpetuate the names of battles, cities, fortresses and also some of the officers' names.

4131. —— Early names of the Ottawa River. Royal Society of Canada. Proceedings and transactions 3d ser. v. 32, sec. 2, p. 97-105. 1938.

4132. —— Yeo, W. B. Canada's curious usage of Italian place names. Canadian geographic 98:58-61, Feb./March 1979.

4133. —— Canada's Italian names. Canoma 4:11-15. 1978.
French version included.

4134. —— The generic term coulée. Canoma 2:7-8, Dec. 1976.
French version included.

4135. —— Toponymy research at the federal level in Canada; In United Nations Conference on the Standardization of Geographical Names, 3d, Athens, 1977. Canada. Ottawa, 1978. p. 143-45.
French version: p. 305-07.

4136. Zyla, Wolodymyr T. J. B. Rudnyćkyj as an onomatologist; In Canadian Institute of Onomastic Sciences. Onomastica 50:12-23, 1976.
A similar paper appeared in Onoma 19:422-31, 1973.

GAZETTEERS

4137. Allen, William Frederick. Gazetteer of railway stations in the United States and the Dominion of Canada. Designating telegraph, express, post, and money-order offices, with the population. Also, a list of the counties and county towns of the several states, with the date at which the several courts are held, together with much other valuable statistical information. Comp. from information obtained from official sources. Philadelphia, National Railway Publication Co., 1874. 412p.

4138. Bouchette, Joseph. The British dominions in North America; or, A topographical and statistical description of the provinces of Lower and Upper Canada, New Brunswick, Nova Scotia, the islands of Newfoundland, Prince Edward, and Cape Breton. Including considerations on land-granting and emigration; and a topographical dictionary of Lower Canada: to which are annexed the statistical tables and tables of distances. London, Longman, Rees, Orme, Brown & Green, 1831. 2v.
v. 2 published by H. Colburn and R. Bentley.
Also published 1832, without the "Topographical dictionary of Lower Canada" found in the edition of 1831.
The "Topographical dictionary of the Province of Lower Canada" also published separately (see no. 4615).

4139. Canada. Permanent Committee on Geographical Names. Gazetteer of Canada. Supplement. no. 1-20. Decisions of the Canadian Permanent Committee on Geographical Names, Jan./June 1963-July/Dec. 1972. Ottawa, Dept. of Mines and Technical Surveys, Geographical Branch, 1964-1973.
No. 7-20 published by Dept. of Energy, Mines and Resources, 1966-1973.

4140. — Post Office Dept. Canada official postal guide, comprising the chief regulations of the Post Office, rates of postage and other information, together with an alphabetical list of post offices in Canada. Quebec, etc., 1855- .
Title varies: 1855-73, List of post offices in Canada; 1875-78, Canadian official postal guide.

4141. — — Canada official postal guide, 1952. Part II. List of post offices in Canada arranged alphabetically, corrected to 1st Dec. 1950. Ottawa, 1952. 194p.

4142. — — List of post offices in Canada. Liste des bureaux de poste du Canada. Oct. 1, 1954- . (Loose-leaf)
Formerly included in Canada official postal guide.
Kept up to date by monthly supplements.

4143. — — Table of post offices in Canada and the name of the postmasters, on the 1st of January, 1854. Quebec, Printed by Lovell & Lamoureux, 1854. 75p.

4144. Davenport, Bishop. A history and new gazetteer, or geographical dictionary of North America and the West Indies. Comp. from the most recent and authentic sources. A new and much improved ed. New York, S. W. Benedict & Co., 1842. 592p.
Earlier editions published in Baltimore, Philadelphia, and Providence, 1832, 1833, 1835, 1836, 1838 under title A new gazetteer.

4145. — A pocket gazetteer, or Traveller's guide through North America and the West Indies; containing a description of all the states, territories, counties, cities, towns, villages, seas, bays, harbors, islands, capes, railroads, canals, &c. connected with North America, and the West Indies, to which is added a large amount of statistical information, relating to the population, revenue, debt, and various institutions of the United States. Comp. from the most recent and authentic sources. Baltimore, Plaskitt & Co., 1833. 468p.
Also published in Trenton, N.J.
Other editions published 1834, 1838.

4146. Forbes, H. A. Gazetteer of northern Canada and parts of Alaska and Greenland. Ottawa, Geographical Bureau, 1948. 75ℓ.

4147. Lovell's gazetteer of the Dominion of Canada, containing the latest and most authentic descriptions of over 14,850 cities, towns, villages and places in the provinces of Ontario, Quebec, Nova Scotia, New Brunswick, Prince Edward Island, Manitoba, British Columbia, Alberta, Saskatchewan, and the new districts of the Northwest territories, Yukon, Franklin, Mackenzie, Keewatin, and Ungava; together with Newfoundland; besides general information, drawn from official sources, as to names, locality, extent, etc., of over 3,000 lakes and rivers; with a table of routes. Ed. with an intro. by G. Mercer Adam. 4th issue, carefully rev. Montreal, J. Lovell and Son, 1908. 973p.
1st ed. published under title Lovell's gazetteer of British North America. Montreal, 1873. 2v.
Also published: Montreal, 1881. 533p.; Montreal, 1895. 675p.

4148. McAlpine's gazetteer of Nova Scotia, New Brunswick, Prince Edward Island and Newfoundland; a geographical and historical data of provinces and cities—location of towns, villages and hamlets—barristers, hotels, express offices and banks. Halifax, McAlpine Pub. Co., 1911. 649p.

Also published 1904, 1133p., under title McAlpine's Maritime and Newfoundland gazetteer for Nova Scotia, New Brunswick, Prince Edward Island, and the island of Newfoundland.

4149. The North-American and the West-Indian gazetteer. Containing an authentic description of the colonies and islands in that part of the globe, shewing their situation, soil produce, and trade; with their former and present condition. Also an exact account of the cities, towns, harbours, ports, bays, rivers, lakes, mountains, number of inhabitants, &c. Illus. with maps. 2d ed. London, G. Robinson, 1778. 218p.
1st ed. London, G. Robinson, 1776. 220p.

4150. Rowell, George P. & Co. George P. Rowell & Co.'s gazetteer, containing a statement of the industries, characteristics, population and location of all towns in the United States and British America, in which newspapers are published. New York, G. P. Rowell & Co., 1873. 243p.

4151. Upham, Warren. Altitudes between Lake Superior and Rocky Mountains. Washington, Govt. Print. Off., 1891. 229p. (U.S. Geological Survey. Bulletin no. 72)
By places along railway lines, including supplementary lists, with indexes for Hills and mountains; Lakes; Towns and stations.

4152. White, G. D. On first looking into the Gazetteer of Canada. Canadian forum 39:80-81, July 1959.
Comments on some of the names listed.

4153. White, James. Altitudes in the Dominion of Canada. By James White assisted by George H. Ferguson. 2d ed. Ottawa, Published by Mortimer Co., for Canada Commission for Conservation, 1915. 603p.
1st ed., by James White, Ottawa, S. E. Dawson, 1901. 266p. For the Geological Survey of Canada.
Supplemented by the author's Dictionary of altitudes in the Dominion of Canada (see no. 4154).
Arranged by order of stations under names of railroads.

4154. —— Dictionary of altitudes in the Dominion of Canada. 2d ed. Ottawa, Published by Mortimer Co., for Canada Commission for Conservation, 1916. 251p.
1st ed. Ottawa, S. E. Dawson, 1903. 143p. For the Dept. of the Interior.
Supplements the author's Altitudes in the Dominion of Canada (see no. 4153).
Arranged alphabetically under provinces and territories.

4155. White, William. Post office gazetteer of the Dominion of Canada; comp. from official records, by permission of the Postmaster General. Montreal, J. Lovell, 1872. 174p.

THE NAME CANADA

4156. Buchanan, Milton Alexander. Early Canadian history. Royal Society of Canada. Transactions 3d ser. v. 42, sec. 2, p. 31-57, May 1948.
The name Canada, p. 52-53. Concludes "Cartier's definition of the word must be accepted."

4157. Canada. Historical magazine and notes and queries concerning the antiquities, history and biography of America 1:153, 188, 217, 315, 349, May-Nov. 1857; 2:23-24, Jan. 1858; 3:192, June 1859.
In the Notes and queries column.
Various explanations of the origin of the word.

4158. Dauzat, Albert. Le nom du Canada. Revue internationale d'onomastique 3:81-82, juin 1951.

4159. Davies, B. On the origin of the name "Canada." Canadian naturalist and geologist 6:430-32, Dec. 1861.

4160. Elliott, Aaron Marshall. On the word "Canada." British American magazine 1:490-93, 1863.

4161. —— Origin of the name "Canada." Modern language notes 3:327-45, June 1888.

Elliott's theory, which traces the word to a Spanish origin, is disposed of by Walter Bell Scaife, Historical notes on certain geographical names (see no. 4167).

4162. Falconer, Robert. What is implied in the term Canadian. English review 41:595-604, Oct. 1925.

The history of Canada has given the term Canadian a distinctive meaning, more suitable than the name American as used by inhabitants of the United States.

4163. Johnson, Alexander. Origin of the name of Canada; In his Our semi-jubilee and Canada. Royal Society of Canada. Proceedings and transactions 2d ser. 12:lxi-lxiii. 1906.

4164. Lanctot, Gustave. Nouvelle-France ou Canada. Revue d'histoire de l'Amérique française 14:171-72, sept. 1960.

4165. Masters, D. C. A name for the Dominion. Mitre 54:23-26, Trinity 1947.

Controversy over name before passing of the British North America Act.

4166. O Tupona. Newsweek 30:46, Oct. 20, 1947; 30:2, Nov. 3, 1947.

Names that were considered for Canada. Based on article by D. C. Masters (see no. 4165).

4167. Scaife, Walter Bell. Historical notes on certain geographical names. Canada; In his America: its geographical history, 1492-1892. Baltimore, Johns Hopkins Press, 1892. p. 83-88.

Disposes of theory advanced by Aaron Marshall Elliott, Origin of the name "Canada" (see no. 4161), that the name Canada originated from a Spanish word, and traces use of the name on maps from 1548 to 1630.

4168. Skelton, Isabel. The name "Canada." Canadian magazine of politics, science, art and literature 57:312-14, Aug. 1921.

4169. Velyhorskyi, Ivan. The term and name "Canada." Winnipeg, Ukrainian Free Academy of Sciences, 1955. 30p. (Ukrainian Free Academy of Sciences. Series: Onomastica, no. 10)

In Ukrainian with summary in English.

ALBERTA

4170. Alberta. Dept. of Public Health. Division of Vital Statistics. Geographical code for Alberta. Alphabetical list of place names, showing census divisions, provincial municipalities, statistical publication areas. Issued in collaboration with Vital Statistics Section, Dominion Bureau of Statistics. Edmonton, n.d. 39p.

Keyed to census of June 1, 1956.

4171. Alberta's place-names of colorful origin. Within our borders March 1, 1954.

4172. Canada. Department of the Interior. Dominion Parks Branch. Through the heart of the Rockies and Selkirks, by M. B. Williams. Ottawa, 1921. 105p.

Place names and altitudes in Rocky Mountains Park: p. 91-95; in Yoho Park: p. 95-97; in Glacier Park: p. 97-99; in Mount Revelstoke Park: p. 100. The first two are from a paper by James White, read before the Royal Society of Canada, 1916; the last two are from Arthur O. Wheeler, The Selkirk Mountains (see no. 4318).

Same in 2d ed. 1924. 110p. p. 95-104.

In 4th ed. 1929. 112p.: Place names and altitudes in Banff Park: p. 97-101; in Yoho Park: p. 101-03; in Glacier Park: p. 103-05; in Mount Revelstoke Park: p. 106.

4173. —— Geographic Board. Place names of Alberta. Pub. for the Geographic Board by the Dept. of the Interior. Ottawa, F. A. Acland, printer, 1928. 138p.

4174. —— Permanent Committee on Geographical Names. Gazetteer of Canada. Alberta. 2d ed. Ottawa, Surveys and Mapping Branch, Dept. of Energy, Mines and Resources, 1974. xliii, 153p. maps.

1st ed.: Canada. Board on Geographical names. Gazetteer of Canada. Alberta. 1958. 96p.

Review: Eric J. Holmgren, Alberta history 24:31-32, Spring 1976.

4175. Chipeniuk, R. C. Lakes of the Lac La Biche District. Lac La Biche, Alta., The Author, 1975. 318p. map.

Includes information on the names.

4176. Chrapka, George. How Hairy Hill got its name. Alberta folklore quarterly 2:34, March 1946.

4177. Comfort, D. J. William McMurray, the name behind the fort. Alberta history 23:1-5, Autumn 1975.

Fort McMurray, trading post, later town.

4178. Dawson, George M. Blackfoot names of a number of places in the North-west Territory, for the most part in the vicinity of the Rocky Mountains. Canada. Geological Survey. Report of progress 1882-84:158c-167c.

Names in the list were received from J. C. Nelson, who with A. P. Patrick was engaged in the surveys. Names in the vicinity of the Bow and the Belly rivers, now in Alberta Province.

4179. Dempsey, Hugh Aylmer. Blackfeet place-names. Alberta historical review 4:29-30, Summer 1956.

4180. —— Indian names for Alberta communities. Calgary, Glenbow-Alberta Institute, 1969. 19p. (Glenbow-Alberta Institute. Occasional paper no. 4)

English names are listed, with the names the Indians gave them after they had been established and named by the English.

Review: Maurice A. Mook, Names 18:311-13, Dec. 1970.

4181. Edmonds, W. Everard. Broad horizons. Toronto, Musson, 1919. 224p.

Place names in southern Alberta, historical sketch: p. 173-78.

4182. Edmonton (Alta.) City Planning Dept., Zoning Branch. Place names of Edmonton. [Edmonton], 1974. [52]ℓ.

Includes subdivisions and neighborhoods, streets and roads, freeways, parks and ravines, and schools.

4183. Edmonton Regional Planning Commission. Regional planning: origin of place names. Edmonton, The Commission, 1964. 6ℓ.

4184. Edwards, Ralph W. Mount Eisenhower. Canadian geographical journal 32:59-62, Feb. 1946.
Mountain renamed in honor of Gen. Eisenhower.

4185. Former Stony Plain County name becomes Parkland after contest. Within our borders April 1969, p. 7.

4186. Fryer, Harold. Ghost towns of Alberta. Langley, B.C., Stagecoach Pub. Co., 1976. 200p. map.
Includes early forts.

4187. Gardner, James. Mountain place names and the Lake Louise Club. Alberta historical review 18:12-17, Spring 1970.
The Club, formed in 1894 by Yale University students, was an informal mapping and exploration group responsible for the toponymy of Lake Louise and nearby areas in the Canadian Rocky Mountains.

4188. Godsal, F. W. Origin of the name Crow's Nest Pass. Canadian alpine journal 12:184-85. 1922.

4189. —— Origin of the name Kicking Horse Pass. Canadian alpine journal 14:136. 1924.

4190. Holmgren, Eric J. Geographic Board of Alberta. Progress made in the standardization of geographical names—Province of Alberta; In United Nations Conference on the Standardization of Geographical Names. 1st, Geneva. 1967. Report on Canadian participation. Ottawa, 1968. p. 45-47.

4191. —— Some observations on place-names in the Canadian Rockies. Canadian Society for the Study of Names. Onomastica 52:6-11, Dec. 1977.
A brief historical sketch of the naming process from Indian times to the present.

4192. —— & Patricia M. Holmgren. Over 2,000 place names of Alberta. 3d ed. Saskatoon, Sask., Western Producer Prairie Books, 1976. 301p. maps.
1st ed. 1972; 2d ed. 1973.

4193. How Wetaskiwin received its name. Alberta folklore quarterly 2:13-14, March 1946.

4194. Indian names in Alberta. Native people, Alberta Native Communication Society 13:8, Oct. 10, 1980.

4195. MacGregor, James G. Who was Yellowhead? Alberta historical review 17:12-13, Autumn 1969.
Offers a theory about identification of the person for whom Yellowhead Pass was named.

4196. Mardon, Ernest G. Community names of Alberta. Lethbridge, Alta., Univ. of Lethbridge, [1973]. 223p. map.
Review: Alan Rayburn, Canadian geographical journal 88:44, May 1974 (numerous errors, too great reliance on the work of Robert Douglas); Hugh A. Dempsey, Alberta historical review 22:29-30, Spring 1974 ("so many errors").

4197. —— The history of place names in southern Alberta. Canadian Institute of Onomastic Sciences. Onomastica 43:5-23. 1972.

4198. Mike Mountain Horse. Medicine Rock, Lethbridge. Alberta folklore quarterly 1:133, Dec. 1945.

4199. Rudnyćkyj, Jaroslav Bohdan. Onomastic aspects of the Rocky Mountains in Canada. International Congress of Onomastic Sciences. 10th, Vienna, 1969. Proceedings 1:117-22.

4200. Sanford Evans Statistical Service. Alberta place guide. Winnipeg, 1951. 68p.

Lists cities, towns, villages, and rural municipalities and improvement districts, with locations.

4201. Stanley, George F. G. The naming of Calgary. Alberta history 23:7-9, Summer 1975.

Includes information from Scottish sources on the meaning of the name which comes from Gaelic.

4202. Thorington, J. Monroe. An interpretation of some old map names in the vicinity of the Kananaskis Pass. Canadian Alpine journal 13:245-50. 1923.

Further comment, by A. O. Wheeler, ibid. p. 250-51.

Some names of mountains on early maps that cannot be identified.

4203. Tyrrell, Joseph Burr. Report on a part of northern Alberta and portions of adjacent districts of Assiniboia and Saskatchewan; In Canada. Geological and Natural History Survey. Annual report 1886, pt. E.

Appendix IV. Cree and Stoney Indian names for places within the area of the accompanying map, p. 172-76.

4204. White, James. Place-names in the Rocky Mountains between the 49th parallel and the Athabaska River. Royal Society of Canada. Proceedings and transactions 3d ser. v. 10, sec. 2, p. 501-35. 1916.

4205. Williams, Mabel Berta. Origin of name of Jasper National Park; In Canada. Dept. of the Interior. Dominion Parks Branch. Jasper National Park. Ottawa, F. A. Acland, 1928. p. 7-8.

Place names and altitudes: p. 145-62.

4206. —— Place names and altitudes; In Canada. Dept. of the Interior. Dominion Parks Branch. Waterton Lakes National Park, Alberta, Canada. Ottawa, F. A. Acland, 192?. p. 44-45.

4207. Yeo, W. B. Geographic names in the vicinity of Banff. Canoma 3:6-13. 1977.

BRITISH COLUMBIA

4208. Aikens, Kathleen A. The Peachland story. Okanagan Historical Society. Annual report 37:73-79. 1973.

4209. Akrigg, George Phillip Vernon. British Columbia place names. Western folklore 12:44-49, Jan. 1953.

Bibliography: p. 48-49.

A survey of the work done in the study of British Columbia place-names.

4210. —— & Helen B. Akrigg. 1001 British Columbia place names. 3d ed. Vancouver, Discovery Press, 1973. xii, 195p. map.
1st ed. 1969; 2d ed. 1970.
Review of 1st ed.: Alan Rayburn, Canadian geographical journal 81:v-vi, July 1970. Reply to review: Jost, T. P. About a very valuable book, and not so valuable review. Revue de l'Université d'Ottawa 41:153-56, janv.-mars. 1971.
Review of 2d ed.: Fred Tarpley, Names 20:151-52, June 1972.

4211. Atkinson, Reginald N. Changes in Okanagan place-names. Okanagan Historical Society. Report 15:21-24. 1951.

4212. Audet, Francis J. Noms géographiques francais en Colombie anglaise. Société de Géographie de Québec. Bulletin 16:80-82. 1922.

4213. Balf, Mary Burch. Why that name? Place names of Kamloops District. [Kamloops, B.C.], Kamloops Museum, 1978. 48p.

4214. Bilbao, Pedro. When Spaniards sailed the north Pacific. Américas 15:13-18, Jan. 1963. map.
Place-names of Spanish origin along the Alaskan and British Columbia coasts.

4215. Boas, Franz. Geographical names of the Kwakiutl Indians. New York, Columbia Univ. Press, 1934. 83p. (Columbia University contributions to anthropology, v. 20)
Reprinted: New York, AMS Press [1969].
Reprinted in part: Hymes, Dell H., ed., Language in culture and society; a reader in linguistics and anthropology. New York, Harper & Row [1964]. p. 171-81.

4216. Brent, Maria. Indian place names. Okanagan Historical Society. Report 13:20-21. 1949.
Vernon District.

4217. British Columbia. Department of Health and Welfare. Division of Vital Statistics. Geographical code for British Columbia; alphabetical list of place names, showing school districts, registration districts, statistical publication areas. Victoria, [1967]. vi, 74p.

4218. —— Department of Provincial Secretary. Chief Electoral Officer. List of polling divisions, settlements, post offices, railway stations, and landings. Rev. ed. Victoria, 1972. 20p. map.

4219. —— Lands Department. Geographic Division. Geographical gazetteer of British Columbia. Victoria, Printed by C. F. Banfield, 1930. 291p.

4220. Brown, Harrison. Admirals, adventurers and able seamen; forgotten stories about places on our British Columbia coast and how they got their names. [Vancouver, B.C., Keystone Press, 1953]. 30p. map.

4221. Buckland, F. M. Kelowna—its name. Okanagan Historical Society. Report 6:45, 1935; 17:100, 1953.
6:45, 1935, reprinted from v.1. 1925.

4222. Burrard, Gerald. The naming of Burrard Inlet. British Columbia historical quarterly 10:143-49, April 1946.
See also article by W. Kaye Lamb, no. 4269.

4223. Butler, David. The rise and fall of Hedley. Okanagan Historical Society. Annual report 37:109-11. 1973.

4224. Campbell, Norman. Place names of Renfrew County. [Pembroke, 1943]. 23ℓ.

4225. Canada. Department of the Interior. Dominion Parks Branch. Through the heart of the Rockies and Selkirks, by M. B. Williams. Ottawa? 1921. 105p.
Place names and altitudes in Rocky Mountains Parks: p. 91-95; in Yoho Park: p. 95-97; in Glacier Park: p. 97-99; in Mount Revelstoke Park: p. 100. The first two are from a paper by James White, read before the Royal Society of Canada, 1916; the last two are from Arthur O. Wheeler, The Selkirk Mountains (see no. 4318).
Same in 2d ed. 1924. 110p. p. 95-104.
In 4th ed. 1929. 112p.: Place names and altitudes in Banff Park: p. 97-101; in Yoho Park: p. 101-03; in Glacier Park: p. 103-05; in Mount Revelstoke Park: p. 106.

4226. —— Permanent Committee on Geographical Names. Gazetteer of Canada: British Columbia. 2d ed. Ottawa, Geographical Branch, Dept. of Energy, Mines and Resources, 1966. 739p.
1st ed. 1953. 641p., published by Canada. Board on Geographical Names.

4227. Canadian Federation of University Women. Prince George Branch. Prince George, British Columbia: street names A-Z. [Prince George] 1970. 50p. map.
Includes local subdivision and park names.

4228. Canadian peaks named for "Big 3." New York times Nov. 15, 1944, p. 6.
Peaks north of Finlay River in the northeastern corner of the Peace River block and British Columbia have been named after Roosevelt, Churchill, and Stalin.

4229. Captain Vancouver named many places. Wildlife review 7:24, Summer 1974.

4230. Central Carrier country: British Columbia, Canada. [Fort St. James, B.C.], Summer Institute of Linguistics, 1974. [19]p. maps.
Takulli Indian names.

4231. Chamberlain, Alexander F. Geographic terms of Kootenay origin. American anthropologist n.s. 4:348-50, April-June 1902.
Names of places, camp-sites, and stations along the 49th parallel in British Columbia, Washington, Idaho, and Montana.

4232. Chamberlin, Rollin T. Cariboo Mountains, a correction. Geographical Society of Philadelphia. Bulletin 26:121-22, April 1928.
A derogatory article on the Geographic Board of Canada because it changed several names given to peaks in the Cariboo Mountains. The author and Allen Carpe made the first ascents.

4233. Corner, Ray. Glenmore. Okanagan Historical Society. Annual report 35:124-25. 1971.

4234. Crane, Charles Allen. Vernon, Enderby and O'Keefe. Okanagan Historical Society. Report 8:14. 1939.

4235. Daly, Reginald A. The nomenclature of the North America Cordillera between the 47th and 53d parallels of latitude. Geographical journal 27:586-606, June 1906.
Bibliography: p. 604-06.
A systematic nomenclature is needed for this vast mountain system. Varying definitions used for mountain ranges, systems, etc. are included.

4236. Dalzell, Kathleen E. The Queen Charlotte Islands—Book 2 of places and names. [Prince Rupert, B.C., Dalzell Books, 1973]. 472p. maps.
Review: D. F. Pearson, Canadian geographical journal 88:42, May 1974.

4237. Dawson, George M. Notes on the Shuswap people of British Columbia. Royal Society of Canada. Proceedings and transactions v. 9, sec. 2, p. 3-44. 1891.
List of 220 place-names.

4238. Deaville, Alfred Stanley. The colonial postal system and postage stamps of Vancouver Island and British Columbia, 1849-1871; a sketch of the origin and early development of the postal service on the Pacific seabord of British North America. Printed by authority of the Legislative Assembly. Victoria, B.C., Printed by C. F. Danfield, 1928. 210p. (Archives of British Columbia. Memoir no. VIII)

4239. Emery, Don. Mineola. Okanagan Historical Society. Annual report 34:36-39. 1970.

4240. Firth, Major. Geographical place names in British Columbia. Canadian surveyor 9:2-6, April 1948.

4241. Florin, Lambert. Ghost town El Dorado. Seattle, Superior Pub. Co., 1968. 192p. maps. (The western ghost town series)
Includes towns in 11 western states of the United States and in British Columbia.

4242. —— Ghost town trails. Maps and drawings by David C. Mason. Seattle, Superior Pub. Co., 1963. 192p.
Bibliography: p. 190.
A roster of known ghost towns: p. 191-92.
Includes western states of the United States and British Columbia.

4243. Foote, Elsie. Kettle River. Okanagan Historical Society. Report 9:68. 1941.

4244. Ford, Helen, Dorrit Macleod & Gene Joyce. Place names of the Alberni Valley. [Port Alberni, B.C.], Alberni District Museum and Historical Society, c1978. 84p. map.

4245. Fotheringham, Alan. Place names enliven B.C. scene. Denver post May 18, 1969, Roundup, p. 43.

4246. Gibson, Rex. What's in a name? Canadian alpine journal 38:82-84. 1955.
Principles for naming mountains in British Columbia.

4247. Goodfellow, John C. Princeton place names; a paper read before the Similkameen Historical Association, July 26th, 1936. Okanagan Historical Society. Report 7:10-16. 1937.

4248. Graham, Clara Lucy Drake. This was Kootenay. Vancouver, Evergreen Press, 1964. 270p.
Some Kootenay place-names: p. 265-69.

4249. Gudde, Erwin Gustav. Okanagan place names. Western folklore 8:161-62, April 1949.
Refers to article by A. G. Harvey, Okanagan place names (see no. 4255).

4250. Haggen, R. W. Origin of place names in Boundary District, B.C. 1945.
Manuscript in British Columbia Provincial Archives, Victoria.

4251. Hamilton, Basil G. Naming of Columbia River and the Province of British Columbia. [Cranbrook, B.C.], Cranbrook courier, [1921]. 16p.

4252. Hamp, E. On mountains among the Kwakiutl. In International Congress of Onomastic Sciences. 10th, Vienna, 1969. Proceedings 2:131-35.
Considers the "extent the land forms played an onomastic part in the life of the people, and more specifically to what extent and in what way they named the mountains."

4253. Harbron, John D. Spaniards on the coast, the eighteenth century Spanish explorers left many place names that are found in British Columbia today. Beaver outfit [i.e., volume] 288:4-8, Summer 1957.

4254. Harvey, A. G. The mystery of Mount Robson. British Columbia historical quarterly 1:207-26, Oct. 1937.

4255. —— Okanagan place names: their origin and meaning. Okanagan Historical Society. Report 12:193-223. 1948.

4256. —— The place name Armstrong. Okanagan Historical Society. Report 13:153-55. 1949.
Later information than that in his article ibid. 12:197. 1948.

4257. An Historical gazetteer of Okanagan--Similkameen. Okanagan Historical Society. Report 22:123-69. 1958.
A second article appeared, Looking back to the Historical gazetteer, in ibid. 22 (1958).
Two corrections, an addition, and a comment ibid. 23:97-98. 1959.

4258. Hull, Anthony Hardinge. Spanish and Russian rivalry in the north Pacific regions of the New World, 1760-1812. [Tuscaloosa, Ala.], 1966. 272ℓ. maps.
Thesis (Ph.D.) Univ. of Alabama.
Bibliography: 251-72.
Selected place names, north Pacific region, showing present and past localities: 237-46.

4259. Jost, T. P. Rev. A. G. Morice, discoverer and surveyor, and the problems of the proper geographical names in north central British Columbia. Revue de l'Université d'Ottawa 37:463-76, juil.-sept. 1967.

4260. Kennard, H. B. Indian place names. Okanagan Historical and Natural History Society. Report 3:16-17. 1929.

4261. Kenyon, Carla. Faulder, B.C. Okanagan Historical Society. Report 38:74. 1974.

4262. Kerfoot, Helen & W. B. Yeo. Chief geographer's place name survey, 1905-1909. I. British Columbia. Canoma 4:1-10. 1978.
French version included.

4263. Kerr, James. British Columbia coast names; their significance today. National review 124:229-32, March 1945.

4264. —— British Columbia place names. Canadian geographical journal 2:153-70, Feb. 1931.

4265. —— The coast names of British Columbia. United empire 39:296-97, Nov.-Dec. 1948.

4266. Knowles, J. B. Origins of Kelowna street names. Okanagan Historical Society. Report 18:93-97. 1954.

4267. Laing, F. W. Geographical naming record, established and other names. 1938.
Manuscript in British Columbia Provincial Archives, Victoria.

4268. —— Scotty Creek and Scottie Creek. Okanagan Historical Society. Report 9:56-63. 1941.

4269. Lamb, W. Kaye. Burrard of Burrard's Channel. British Columbia historical quarterly 10:273-79, Oct. 1946.
Disagrees with theory advanced in Gerald Burrard's article, ibid. 10:143-49, April 1946.

4270. Longstaff, F. V. Captain George Vancouver, 1792-1942; a study in commemorative place-names. British Columbia historical quarterly 6:77-94, April 1942.
The history of the place-names that commemorate Capt. George Vancouver.

4271. Lucas, E. A. The place names of British Columbia. Canadian forum 1:209-11, April 1921.

4272. Manning, Helen B. Cariboo place names. 1943.
Manuscript in University of British Columbia. Dept. of History, Vancouver.

4273. Martin, Ged. The naming of British Columbia. Albion 10:257-63, Spring 1979.

4274. Martin, Stuart J. Vernon street-names. Okanagan Historical Society. Report 13:156-61. 1949.

4275. Meany, Edmond Stephen. The name of Mount Robson a puzzle. Washington historical quarterly 19:20-30, Jan. 1928.

4276. Meek, R. J. Spanish explorers left their mark on Canada. Saturday night 63:20, Oct. 4, 1947.
Names on the west coast and adjacent islands commemorate the Spanish explorers.

4277. Melvin, George H. Post offices in the Okanagan and surrounding area. Okanagan Historical Society. Report 30:248-55. 1966.

4278. —— Post offices of British Columbia. Vernon, B.C., The Author, 1972. 1v, 189p.
2400 post offices which existed between 1858 and 1971, including origin of the names, opening, closing and name changing dates, and spelling variations.

4279. Middleton, Lynn. Place names of the Pacific Northwest coast; origins, histories and anecdotes in bibliographic form about the coast of British Columbia, Washington and Oregon. Victoria, B.C., Elldee Pub. Co., 1969. 226p. maps.
Also published: Seattle, Superior Pub. Co. [1970]. 226p. maps.

4280. Morice, A. G. The northern interior of British Columbia and its maps. Royal Canadian Institute. Transactions 12:25-39. 1920.
The author writes of the deplorable state of the official maps and the application of names on them.

4281. Mount Keogan named for pioneer. Okanagan Historical Society. Report 20:24-25. 1956.
Michael Keogan.

4282. Mountain pathfinder founder of Princeton. Okanagan Historical Society Annual report 37:27-32. 1973.

4283. A Mountain renamed. Okanagan Historical Society. Report 30:144. 1966.
A mountain near Penticton changed from Nigger Toe Mountain to Mount Nkwala, the Indian personal name.

4284. Nanaimo Senior High School. Nanaimo, B.C. Nanaimo past and present. [Nanaimo, 1962]. 18ℓ.
Place-names of the Nanaimo area.

4285. —— Place names of Vancouver Island. [Nanaimo, 1958]. 20ℓ.

4286. Nelson, Denys. Place names of the delta of the Fraser. 2v.
Typewritten manuscript in the University of British Columbia Library, Vancouver.

4287. —— Some origins of place names of greater Vancouver. Museum notes (Art, Historical and Scientific Association of Vancouver, B.C.) 3:5-10, Sept. 1928.

4288. New, Donald A. Voyage of discovery: Gulf Island names and their origins. Galiano, B.C., The Author, 1966. 18p. map.

4289. New names on the international boundary. Geographical journal 62:234-35, Sept. 1923.
A glacier and several peaks.

4290. Norris, L. Some place names. Okanagan Historical Society. Report 2:33-37. 1927; 4:31-32. 1930; 6:133-58. 1935; 8:50-53. 1939; 17:118-24. 1953.

4291. Parsons, Alberta & Barbara Lawrence. Keremeos, a history. Okanagan Historical Society. Annual report 36:50-58. 1972.

4292. Pearson, John. Land of the Peace Arch. Cloverdale, B.C., Surrey Centennial Committee, [1958]. xii, 159p. maps.
A history of Surrey including a chapter on place-names.

4293. Pemberton, C. C. Discovery and naming of the Strait of Juan de Fuca. British Columbia Historical Association. Report and proceedings 4:33-36. 1929.

4294. Phillips, Ivan E. This heavenly Summerland. Okanagan Historical Society. Report 35:27. 1971.
Summerland got its name from the words of the Summerland hymn.

4295. Place names. Okanagan Historical Society. Report 21:40. 1957.

4296. Place names—their significance. The year book of British Columbia, ed. R. E. Gosnell. 1897:74-83.

4297. Post offices in the Okanagan and surrounding area. Okanagan Historical Society. Report 30:248-55. 1966.

4298. Richthofen, Erich Freiherr von. The Spanish toponyms of the British Columbia coast, with sideglances at those in the states of Washington, Oregon and Alaska. Ukrainian Free Academy of Sciences. Onomastica 26:1-22. 1963.

4299. Rosoman, Graham. The naming of Enderby. Okanagan Historical Society. Report 6:219. 1935.

4300. Rudnyćkyj, Jaroslav Bohdan. Onomastic aspects of Rocky Mountains in Canada. In International Congress of Onomastic Sciences. 10th, Vienna, 1969. Proceedings 1:117-22.

4301. —— The origin and meaning of the oronym Mount Poletica on the British Columbia Alaska boundary. Canadian Society for the Study of Names. Onomastica 55:1-3, June 1979.
Named for Russian minister to the United States and commission member for the Alaskan boundary negotiations with Great Britain in 1824.

4302. Sanford Evans Statistical Service. British Columbia place guide. Winnipeg, 1951. 70p.
Lists cities, towns and villages, census subdivisions and municipal districts, with locations.

4303. Schell, Ruth. Penticton streets. Okanagan Historical Society. Report 26:96-99. 1962.

4304. Schultz, James Willard. Signposts of adventure: Glacier National Park as the Indians know it. Boston, Houghton Mifflin, 1926. 224p.
Contents: Introductory: Blackfeet Indian names of the topographical features of Glacier National Park upon its east side; Kutenai Indian names of the topographical features of the west side of Glacier National Park.

4305. Sismey, Eric D. Falkland, B.C. Okanagan Historical Society. Annual report 40:64-65. 1976.

4306. —— Myncaster, B.C. Okanagan Historical Society. Annual report 37:104. 1973.

4307. —— Okanagan--what does it mean? Okanagan Historical Society. Report 28:96-97. 1964.

4308. Spence, Terry. B.C. yesterday. Burnaby, Forest Lawn, [1969]. [51]ℓ.
Brief histories of British Columbia place-names.

4309. Stewart, D. K.; G. B. Latimer & H. H. Whitaker. Penticton street names honouring old-timers. Okanagan Historical Society. Report 15:198-202. 1951.

4310. Tassie, G. C. Some place-names. Okanagan Historical Society. Report 10:34-38. 1943.

4311. Taylor, Wendy. Place names of the B.C. coast. B.C. outdoors 34:32-33, 35-37, Feb. 1978.

4312. Thorington, J. Monroe. The climber's guide. Canadian alpine journal 38:85. 1955.
To naming mountains in British Columbia.

4313. Wagner, Henry Raup. The cartography of the northwest coast of America to the year 1800. Berkeley, Univ. of California Press, 1937. 2v.
Reprinted: Amsterdam, N. Israel, 1968. 2v. in 1.
Place-names still in use: 2:371-422.
Obsolete place-names: 2:423-525.
Bibliography: 2:527-43.

4314. Walbran, John T. British Columbia coast names, 1592-1906; to which are added a few names in adjacent United States illustrations. Ottawa, Published by Govt. Print. Bureau for Geographic Board of Canada, 1909. 546p.
Reprinted: Vancouver, The Library's Press, 1971. 546p.; Seattle, Univ. of Washington Press, 1972. 546p.
Review: Review of historical publications relating to Canada 14:115-18. 1910.

4315. Wamboldt, Beryl. Enderby and district: from wilderness to 1914. Okanagan Historical Society. Annual report 33:31-48. 1969.

4316. Watson, Robert. Victoria's early names. Beaver outfit [i.e., volume] 263:32, June 1932.

4317. West, Robert. Mountain names in Mt. Revelstoke Park. Canadian alpine journal 42:49. 1959.

4318. Wheeler, Arthur O. The Selkirk Mountains; a guide for mountain climbers and pilgrims. Winnipeg, Stovel Co., 1912. 191p.
Source of name is given for all geographical points mentioned.

4319. White, James. Place-names in the Rocky Mountains between the 49th parallel and the Athabaska River. Royal Society of Canada. Proceedings and transactions 3d ser. v. 10, sec. 2, p. 501-35. 1916.

4320. —— Place names in vicinity of Yellowhead Pass. Canadian alpine journal 6:143-58. 1914-15.
"Numerous names and their derivations have been investigated by the author who also discusses the interpretations by other authors."—Price.

4321. Wolfenden, Madge. The naming of Holland Point. British Columbia historical quarterly 18:117-21, Jan.-April 1954.

MANITOBA

4322. Bessasson, Haraldur. A few specimens of North American-Icelandic. Scandinavian studies 39:115-46, May 1967.
Includes Icelandic place-names, p. 137-42.

4323. —— Icelandic place names in Manitoba and North Dakota. Linguistic Circle of Manitoba and North Dakota. Proceedings 2:8-10, May 1960.

4324. Bowsfield, Hartwell. Place names. Manitoba pageant 6:19-21, Sept. 1960.
General essay on Manitoba place-names.

4325. Canada. Geographic Board. Place-names of Manitoba. Pub. for the Geographic Board by the Dept. of the Interior. Ottawa, J. O. Patenaude, acting King's Printer, 1933. 95p.

4326. —— Permanent Committee on Geographical Names. Gazetteer of Canada: Manitoba. 2d ed. Ottawa, Surveys and Mapping Branch, Dept. of Energy, Mines and Resources, 1968. 93p. map.
1st ed. 1955. 60p., published by Canada. Board on Geographic Names.

4327. Carlyle-Gordge, Peter. Streetfighting in St. Norbert. MacLean's magazine 92:19, Jan. 15, 1979.
The Winnipeg City Council changed eight English street names to French names in suburban St. Norbert over the objection of some residents.

4328. Cole, George E. Flin Flon—the name; alliteration and music blend in making a good name for a great mine. Canadian mining journal 70:63-71, March 1949.
Origin of the name.

4329. Davies, W. A. A brief history of the Churchill River. The Musk-ox 15:30-38. 1975. map.
A list of fur-trade posts and historic features found within and adjacent to the Churchill River basin.

4330. Dzatko, O. Names tell a story. Ukrainian Canadian May 1970, p. 36-37.

4331. Hall, Frank. How Manitoba got its name. Manitoba pageant 15:3-16, Winter 1970.

4332. Ham, Penny. Place names of Manitoba. Saskatoon, Western Producer Prairie Books, 1980. 160p.

4333. Hislop, Mary. The streets of Winnipeg. Winnipeg, T. W. Taylor, 1912. 46p.

4334. McKay, Henry. What's in the name of Manitoba. Beaver outfit [i.e., volume] 261:102, Dec. 1930.
Derived from Cree word meaning "the spirits' narrows."

4335. Magnusson, Kristiana. Place-names of Breiðuvik District-Hnausa. Icelandic Canadian 32:33-37, Summer 1975; 33:38-44, Autumn 1975.

4336. —— Place-names of New Iceland. Canada west magazine 7:20-24, Spring 1977.

4337. Manitou Baa. Beaver outfit [i.e., volume] 287:54, Summer 1956.
Meaning of name for lake.
Disagrees with George H. Armstrong's definition in his The origin and meaning of place names in Canada (see no. 3942).

4338. Munro, Michael R. The Pas to Churchill on the Hudson Bay Railway. Canoma 4:1-10, Dec. 1978. maps.
French version included.
Naming the stations along a rail line built 1924-31.

4339. —— The treatment of toponyms in Manitoba from languages without an alphabet. In United Nations Conference on the Standardization of Geographical Names, 3d, Athens, 1977. Canada. Ottawa, 1978. p. 151-57.
French version: p. 313-20.

4340. Prud'homme, L. A. Le nom de Manitoba. Revue canadienne n.s. 8:23-26, juil. 1911.
The origin of the name is not in the language of the Salteaux who now surround Lake Manitoba, but in the Sioux word Minnetoba, which signifies "water-prairie."

4341. Rouillard, Eugène. Le nom de Manitoba. Société de Géographie de Québec. Bulletin 9:310-11. 1915.
Traces name to aboriginal sources.

4342. Rudnyćkyj, Jaroslav Bohdan. Manitoba: mosaic of place names. With an introd. by Watson Kirkconnell. Winnipeg, Canadian Institute of Onomastic Sciences, 1970. 221p. maps.
The origin, history and meaning of the province's place-names, primarily those of populated places.

Review: Elsdon C. Smith, Names 19:58-59, March 1971.

An abbreviated version of Watson Kirkconnell's Introduction to this book appeared in Canadian Institute of Onomastic Sciences. Onomastica 44:3-10, 1972.

4343. —— Mosaic of Winnipeg street names. Canadian Institute of Onomastic Sciences. Onomastica 48:1-333. 1974.

Credits for information are given to the publication of Mary Hislop. The streets of Winnipeg (see no. 4333) and articles by Harry Shave in the Winnipeg free press and by Vince Leah in the Winnipeg tribune.

4344. —— Slavic geographical names in Manitoba. Canadian Institute of Onomastic Sciences. Onomastica 45:1-24. 1974. map.

4345. Sanford Evans Statistical Service. Manitoba place guide. Winnipeg, 1951. 53p.

Lists cities, towns, villages, rural municipalities and local government districts, airports and landing strips, with locations.

4346. Tyrrell, Joseph Burr. Algonquian Indian names of places in northern Canada. Royal Canadian Institute. Transactions 10:213-31, May 1914.

Reprinted separately: Toronto, Univ. Press, 1915; Toronto, Canadiana House, 1968.

List of Indian names collected during extensive travels, with meanings of the names, the current names on maps, and the location of the places.

Manitoba and District of Patricia, Ontario.

Review: Review of historical publications relating to Canada 19:208. 1914.

MARITIME PROVINCES

4347. Bourgeois, François. Les noms géographiques dans les Provinces Maritimes. Société de Géographie de Québec. Bulletin 7:336-52, nov. 1913.

4348. Cormier, Clément. L'origine et l'histoire du nom Acadie, avec un discours sur d'autres noms de lieu acadiens. Académie ukrainienne libre de sciences. Onomastica 31:1-16. 1966.

Part 1 was published in Societe Historique Acadienne. Les cahiers 2:58-60. 1962.

Part 2 discusses (in English) the name of Saint John, N.B., and the River Saint John.

4349. Dawson, Samuel Edward. The Saint Lawrence basin and its border-lands, being the story of their discovery, exploration and occupation. London, Lawrence & Bullen, 1905. 451p.

Also published under the title The Saint Lawrence, its basin & border-lands: New York, Stokes, 1905. 451p.

The origin and meaning of the word Acadia: p. 249-50.

4350. DeGrâce, Eloi. Noms géographiques de l'Acadie. Moncton, N.B., Société Historique acadienne, c1974. 256ℓ.

4351. Froidevaux, Henri. Origine du mot "Acadie." Société des Américanistes de Paris. Journal n.s. 12:267-68. 1920.

4352. Ganong, William Francis. An organization of the scientific investigation of the Indian place-nomenclature of the Maritime Provinces of Canada. Royal Society of Canada. Proceedings and transactions 3d ser. v. 5, sec. 2, p. 179-93; v. 6, sec. 2, p. 179-99; v. 7, sec. 2, p. 81-106; v. 8, sec. 2, p. 259-93; v. 9, sec. 2, p. 375-448. 1911-15.

In addition to material on specific words, includes a summary of "methods of exact scientific analysis." The Indian groups are Micmac, Maliseet, Passamaquoddy, a division of the Maliseets, and the Penobscots.

4353. —— An organization of the scientific investigation of the Indian place-nomenclature of the Maritime Provinces of Canada, a paper read at the Royal Society, May 1915. Toronto, Canadiana House, 1968. p. 375-448.
Reprinted from Royal Society of Canada. Proceedings and transactions 3d ser. 1915.

4354. —— The origin of the place-names Acadia and Norumbega. Royal Society of Canada. Proceedings and transactions 3d ser. v. 11, sec. 2, p. 105-11. 1917.
Based on early maps and records of explorations. See also author's article Acadia, ibid. v. 25, sec. 2, p. 202-03. 1931, which develops argument stated ibid. v. 9, sec. 2, p. 439-48. 1915.

4355. McAlpine, C. D. The gazateer [sic] of the Maritime Provinces, for 1878-79. Containing routes for summer travel through the towns of Nova Scotia, New Brunswick, Cape Breton, and P. E. Island. Saint John, C. D. McAlpine, 1878. 240p.

4356. Pacifique de Valiguy, O. F. M. À propos du mot "Acadie." Société de Géographie de Québec. Bulletin 11:298, sept. 1917.

4357. Rand, Silas Tertius. A first reading book in the Micmac language: comprising the Micmac numerals, and the names of the different kinds of beasts, birds, fishes, trees, &c. of the Maritime Provinces of Canada. Also, some of the Indian names of places, and many familiar words and phrases, trans. literally into English. Halifax, Nova Scotia Print Co., 1875. 108p.
Micmac place-names: p. 81-104.

4358. —— Micmac place-names in the Maritime Provinces and Gaspé Peninsula recorded between 1852 and 1890. Collected, arranged and indexed by Lieut.-Col. Wm. P. Anderson. Ottawa, Printed at the Surveyor General's Office, 1919. 116p.
Publication of the Geographic Board of Canada.

4359. —— Micmac place names in the Maritime Provinces of Canada, copied from Rand's manuscripts, and supplemented by help from other sources; In his Rand's Micmac dictionary from phonographic wordlists. Charlottetown, P.E.I., Patriot Pub. Co., 1902. p. 177-92.

4360. Rayburn, Alan. Acadia, the origin of the name and its geographical and historical utilization. Canadian cartographer 10:25-43, June 1973. maps.

4361. —— Acadie: l'origine du nom et son usage géographique et historique. Canoma 2:1-5. 1976.
Also published separately by the Dept. of Energy, Mines and Resources, 1973.

4362. Rouillard, Eugène. Noms géographiques de la Province de Québec et des Provinces Maritimes empruntés aux langues sauvages; avec carte indiquant les territoires occupés autrefois par les races aborigènes; étymologie, traduction et orthographie. Québec, Marcotte, 1906. 110p. (Publications de la Société du Parler Français au Canada)
Auteurs et ouvrages consultés: p. 5-6.
"A large proportion of the interpretations of New Brunswick place-names in Rouillard's work although credited to Father Bourgeois . . . are identical with those in my earlier work . . . on New Brunswick place-names, and were evidently taken from

that work, though without the customary acknowledgement, by Father Bourgeois."—William Francis Ganong. An organization of the scientific investigation of the Indian place-nomenclature of the Maritime Provinces of Canada. Royal Society of Canada. Proceedings and transactions 3d ser. v. 5, sec. 2, p. 180. 1911.

4363. —— Noms sauvages; étymologie et traduction. Société de Géographie de Québec. Bulletin 5:410-22, nov. 1911; 6:31-42, janv. 1912.
Supplements the author's Noms géographiques published in 1906.

4364. Wightman, F. A. Maritime provincialisms and contrasts—place-names. Canadian magazine of politics, science, art and literature 39:168-72, June 1912.
Indicates in a general way the types of names peculiar to each province and in contrast to the others.

4365. Wilkins, Ernest Hatch. Ar Cadie. Modern language notes 73:504-05, Nov. 1958.
Offers a different explanation of the process by which Arcadie became Acadie from that discussed in the following article.

4366. —— Arcadia in America. American Philosophical Society. Proceedings 101:4-30, Feb. 15, 1957.
A well-documented study tracing the use of the name Arcadia and all its various spellings from earliest maps and journals to place-names in the United States, Canada, and South America today. All derive from the name of a novel Arcadia, by Jacopo Sannazzaro, written ca. 1485.

NEW BRUNSWICK

4367. Bird, Will R. Nova Scotia and New Brunswick names. Maclean's magazine 41:54, 56, 58, 60, 63, June 1, 1928.

4368. Canada. Permanent Committee on Geographical Names. Gazetteer of Canada: New Brunswick. 2d ed. Ottawa, Surveys and Mapping Branch, Dept. of Energy, Mines and Resources, 1972. xlvi, 213p. map.
1st ed. 1956. 84p., published by Canada. Board on Geographical Names.

4369. Folster, David. While visions of reindeer danced in his head. Maclean's 91:20, Dec. 25, 1978.
Nine peaks named for Clement Moore's eight reindeer and St. Nicholas.

4370. Froidevaux, Henri. À propos de Tracadie. Société de Géographie de Québec. Bulletin 12:158, mai 1918.

4371. Ganong, William Francis. Further suggestions upon nomenclature of unnamed or badly named places in New Brunswick. Natural History Society of New Brunswick. Bulletin 4:321-22. 1901.

4372. —— The Geographic Board of Canada. Science n.s. 25:307-08, Feb. 22, 1907.
Criticism of the Board for disregarding local usage and following abstract principles as shown in New Brunswick examples in the Board's sixth report.

4373. —— A monograph of the place-nomenclature of the Province of New Brunswick. Royal Society of Canada. Proceedings and transactions 2d ser. v. 2, sec. 2, p. 175-289. 1896.
Published separately as Contributions to the history of New Brunswick, no. 2, 1896.

Reprinted: Toronto, Canadiana House, 1968.

Includes: An essay toward an understanding of the principles of place-nomenclature; The historical development of the place-nomenclature of New Brunswick; a dictionary of the place-names of New Brunswick; Sources of information.

Supplemented by information appearing in the author's A monograph of historic sites in the Province of New Brunswick ibid. 2d ser. v. 5, sec. 2, p. 213-357. 1899. (Contributions, no. 4); and his A monograph of the origins of settlements in the Province of New Brunswick, ibid. 2d ser. v. 10, sec. 2, p. 3-185. 1904. (Contributions, no. 6)

Also supplemented by his Additions and corrections to monographs on the place-nomenclature, cartography, historic sites, boundaries and settlement-origins of the Province of New Brunswick, ibid. 2d ser. v. 12, sec. 2, p. 3-157. 1906. (Contributions, no. 7)

Essay toward an understanding of the principles of place-nomenclature, and The historical development of the place-nomenclature of New Brunswick, are reprinted in Alan Rayburn, Geographical names of New Brunswick (see no. 4384).

4374. —— The naming of St. Andrews—a miss. Acadiensis 2:184-88, July 1902.

4375. —— Notes on the natural history and physiography of New Brunswick. Natural History Society of New Brunswick. Bulletin 6:199-204. 1910.

The local nomenclature of the Muniac, Miramichi, and Cains rivers.

4376. —— The origin of the major Canadian place-names of Fundy and Miramichi. Royal Society of Canada. Proceedings and transactions 3d ser. v. 20, sec. 2, p. 15-35. 1926.

4377. —— Origin of the place-name Pabineau. Acadiensis 1:88-89, April 1901.

4378. —— The origin of the place-names in Inglewood Manor. Acadiensis 3:7-18, Jan. 1903.

4379. Hind, Henry Youle. A preliminary report on the geology of New Brunswick. Fredericton, G. E. Fenety, printer, 1865. 293p.

Origin of the names of certain rivers and places in New Brunswick, containing a short vocabulary of the Micmac and Milicete languages, p. 257-59. Names of places and rivers derived from the Abenaquis language, p. 260-61.

4380. Kain, S. W. Indian names in New Brunswick. St. John sun Jan. 14, 1886.

A list of the meanings of 20 Indian place-names—Micmac and Maliseet—in Maine and New Brunswick.

4381. New Brunswick. Department of Health and Social Services. Office of Registrar-General. Geographical code for New Brunswick. Alphabetical list of place names, showing counties, provincial municipalities, statistical publication areas. Fredericton, n.d. 24p.

Keyed to the census of June 1, 1956.

4382. New Brunswick Historical Society. Loyalist souvenir; one hundred and fiftieth anniversary of the landing of the Loyalists in the Province of New Brunswick, 1783-1933. Saint John, New Brunswick Historical Society, 1933. 31p.

Some New Brunswick place-names: p. 22-28.

4383. Rayburn, Alan. Characteristics of toponymic generics in New Brunswick. Cahiers de géographie de Québec 16:285-311, sept. 1972.

4384. —— Geographical names of New Brunswick, by Alan Rayburn for Canadian Permanent Committee on Geographical Names. Ottawa, Surveys and Mapping Branch, Dept. of Energy, Mines and Resources, 1975. 304p. (Toponymy study 2)
References: p. 297-304.
Includes William Francis Ganong's An essay toward an understanding of the principles of place-nomenclature, p. 1-9; The historical development of the place-nomenclature of New Brunswick, p. 9-31, published originally in the Royal Society of Canada. Proceedings and transactions. 1896. (see no. 4373)
Review: Eugene Green, Names 24:220-23, Sept. 1976.

4385. Rouillard, Eugène. À travers le Nouveau-Brunswick, quelques vocables géographiques. Société de Géographie de Québec. Bulletin 14:275-92, nov. 1920.

4386. Squires, W. Austin. New Brunswick's hills and mountains. Canadian geographical journal 77:53-57, Aug. 1968.
Describes the work of William Francis Ganong in mapping and naming features in New Brunswick.

NEWFOUNDLAND

4387. Canada. Dept. of Mines and Technical Surveys. Geographical Branch. A list of the place names of the island of Newfoundland with their geographical positions, comp. from the 10-mile map of Newfoundland pub. by the Dept. of Natural Resources, Newfoundland, 1941. Ottawa, 1950. 59ℓ.

4388. —— Permanent Committee on Geographical Names. Gazetteer of Canada: Newfoundland and Labrador. Ottawa, Geographical Branch, Dept. of Energy, Mines and Resources, 1968. 252, 8p. maps.
Gazetteer of Saint-Pierre and Miquelon (France), 8p. at end. Not official.
Review: Henri Dorion, Cahiers de géographie de Québec 26:303-12. 1968.

4389. Cants, Ernesto do. Quem deu o nome ao Labrodor? (Breve estudo) 3d ed. Porto, Officinas do Commercio do Porto, 1907. 23p.
At head of title: Extrahido do Archivo dos acores, 12:353.

4390. Churchill name to be given to river in Canada. Kansas City times Feb. 6, 1965, p. 1.
Hamilton River and its Falls renamed for Sir Winston Churchill.

4391. English, L. E. F. Historic Newfoundland. St. John's, Newfoundland Tourist Development Division, [1969]. 67p.
Place-names of Newfoundland: p. 60-63.

4392. Forbes, Alexander. Notes on place names; In his Northernmost Labrador mapped from the air. New York, American Geographical Society, 1938. p. 236-43.

4393. Harrington, Michael Francis. Newfoundland names. Atlantic advocate 47:71-77, Oct. 1956.
Places named by the English, Irish, and Scottish; French, Spanish, and Portuguese; original Indian names; changes made by the Nomenclature Board.

4394. Harrisse, Henry. Découverte et évolution cartographique de Terre-Neuve et des pays circonvoisins, 1497-1501-1769; essais de géographie historique et documentaire. London, Henry Stevens, Son & Stiles; Paris, H. Welter, 1900. 420p.
La cartographie américano-dieppoise. Nomenclature de La Nouvelle-Écosse: p. 214-22.

Nomenclature chronologique du Labrador, de Terre-Neuve et de la région adjacente depuis la découverte jusqu'à la fin du XVIe siècle: p. 355-66.

4395. Horwood, Harold. Fumigating the map. Atlantic advocate 49:69, April 1959.
Changes in salty Newfoundland place-names made by the Canadian Post Office Dept.

4396. Howley, Michael Francis. Newfoundland name-lore. Newfoundland quarterly v. 32-39, Oct. 1932-March 1940.
Republished from ibid. Oct. 1901-Dec. 1914.

4397. Keenleyside, H. L. Place-names of Newfoundland. Canadian geographical journal 29:255-67, Dec. 1944.

4398. Kirwin, William. Labrador, St. John's and Newfoundland; some pronunciations. Canadian Linguistic Association. Journal 6:115-16, Fall 1960.
Variant pronunciations of these place-names.

4399. —— Lines, coves, and squares in Newfoundland names. American speech 40:163-70, Oct. 1965.
Newfoundland street names.

4400. Le Messurier, Henry William. The early relations between Newfoundland and the Channel Islands. Geographical review 2:449-57, Dec. 1916.
Many place-names on Newfoundland are of Channel Islands origin, proving that an intimate connection existed with the people of the Channel Islands.

4401. —— Newfoundland name lore; the early relations between Newfoundland and the Channel Islands. Newfoundland quarterly 55:7, March; 55:33, Sept.; 55:37, Dec. 1956.
Extracts from Fay, C. R., ed., Old time Newfoundland.

4402. Miffin, Robert James. Some French place names of Newfoundland. American speech 31:79-80, Feb. 1956.

4403. Munn, W. A. Nomenclature of Conception Bay. Newfoundland quarterly 33:14-16, Dec. 1933.

4404. Newfoundland name-lore. Newfoundland quarterly 64:21-24, Winter 1965/66; 65:19-20, Spring 1966.

4405. Newfoundland 1941. Hand book, gazetteer, and almanac; an annual reference book, ed. by J. R. Smallwood. St. John's, Long Brothers, n.d. 324p.
Gazetteer: p. 67-150.

4406. A Nomenclature board for Newfoundland. Geographical journal 92:478-79, Nov. 1938.
A board—to be the ultimate authority in respect to pronunciation and spelling of all place-names—has been provided for through the Nomenclature Board Act, 1938.

4407. Noms géographiques canadiens. Bulletin des recherches historiques 31:268, juil. 1925.
Baie des Châteaux, and Chéticamp.

4408. Pap, Leo. The Portuguese adstratum in North American place-names. Names 20:111-30, June 1972.

Portuguese influence on the formation of place-names in the United States and in Newfoundland and Nova Scotia in Canada, presented as a linguistic contribution to the investigation of naming processes.

4409. Picturesque place names. Newfoundland quarterly 53:3, Sept. 1954.

4410. Place names being changed. Newfoundland quarterly 53:41, March 1954.
Signed: Wayfarer.

4411. Ross, W. Gillies. Exploration and toponymy on the Unknown River, Labrador. Cahiers de géographie de Québec 10:291-99, sept. 1966. maps.

4412. Rouillard, Eugène. Le Cap Chouart. Société de Géographie de Québec. Bulletin 13:54. 1919.
History of name found on 17th- and 18th-century maps of northern coast of Labrador.

4413. —— Toponymie de la côte nord du Saint-Laurent et du Labrador Canadien. Société de Géographie de Québec. Bulletin 7:208-12, juil. 1913.

4414. Rouleau, Ernest. A gazetteer of the island of Newfoundland, based on the maps (1:50,000) of the National topographic system pub. by the Dept. of Mines and Technical Surveys, Ottawa. April 1961. Montreal, 1961. 245ℓ.

4415. —— Index to the geographical names appearing on the map of Labrador. Montreal, Dept. of Mines and Resources of Newfoundland, 1961. 14p.

4416. —— Index to the geographical names appearing on the map of Newfoundland (1955), pub. by the Dept. of Mines and Resources of Newfoundland. Montreal, 1961. 34p.

4417. Seary, Edgar Ronald. The anatomy of Newfoundland place-names. Names 6:193-207, Dec. 1958.
Place-names are being studied systematically, as part of an investigation into Newfoundland linguistics conducted by members of the English Dept. of the Memorial University of Newfoundland.

4418. —— The French element in Newfoundland place names. Canadian Linguistic Association. Journal 4:63-69, Fall 1958.

4419. —— The French element in Newfoundland place names; a paper read before the Canadian Linguistic Association on June 11th, 1958. Winnipeg, 1958. (Ukrainian Free Academy of Sciences. Onomastica 16:1-16)

4420. —— Linguistic variety in the place names of Newfoundland. Canadian geographical journal 65:146-55, Nov. 1962.

4421. —— Place names of the Avalon Peninsula of the island of Newfoundland. Toronto, Pub. for Memorial Univ. of Newfoundland by Univ. of Toronto Press, 1971. xi, 383p. maps. (Memorial University series, 2)
Also published in microfiche by Univ. of Toronto Press, 1971.
Gazetteer and index of place-names: p. 168-300.
Looks at history through a broad, systematic study of the place-names.
Review: Jean-Claude Dupont, Cahiers de géographie de Québec 15:1, 17, Dec. 1971; Alan Rayburn, Names 20:63-64, March 1972.

4422. —— Toponymy of the island of Newfoundland, checklist. St. John's, Memorial Univ. of Newfoundland, 1959-60. 2v.

4423. Story, G. M. Research in the language and place-names of Newfoundland. Canadian Linguistic Association. Journal 3:47-55, Oct. 1957.
Place-names: p. 47-50.

4424. What's in a name? Newfoundland quarterly 53:3, March 1954.

4425. Wheeler, Everett Pepperrell. List of Labrador Eskimo place names. Ottawa, Minister of Resources and Development, 1953. 105p. (National Museum of Canada. Bulletin, no. 131. Anthropological series, no. 34)

4426. White, James. The "Valley River" of Labrador. Geographical journal 70:287-89, Sept. 1927.
Disagrees with assignment of names made in Varick Frizzell, Explorations in the Grand Falls region of Labrador, ibid. 69:332-40, April 1927.

NORTHWEST TERRITORIES

4427. Arctic islands named after Queen Elizabeth. World affairs (Toronto) 19:15, March 1954.
The northern half of Canadian Arctic Archipelago was renamed by Canada the Queen Elizabeth Islands.

4428. Baird, Patrick Douglas. Baffin Island expedition, 1950, a preliminary report. Arctic 3:131-49, Dec. 1950.
New names, p. 149. Adopted by the Canadian Board on Geographical Names.

4429. —— Baffin Island expedition, 1953, a preliminary field report. Arctic 6:227-51, Dec. 1953.
New names, p. 251. Approved by the Canadian Board on Geographical Names.

4430. Becher, Alexander Bridport. The voyages of Martin Frobisher. Royal Geographic Society. Journal 12:1-28. 1842.
A list of places in the area of Frobisher Strait named by Frobisher on his voyage to find the Northwest Passage, p. 16-19.

4431. Bell, Charles Napier. The great lone land, some historical names and places in the North West. Canadian antiquarian and numismatic journal 12:34-51, Jan. 1885.

4432. —— Some historical names and places of the Canadian North-West. Winnipeg, Manitoba Free Press Print, 1885. 8p. (Historical and Scientific Society of Manitoba. Transactions, no. 17)

4433. Boas, Franz. The Central Eskimo. U.S. Bureau of American Ethnology. Report 6:399-675. 1884-85.
Eskimo geographical names used, with English significations: p. 662-66.

4434. —— Ortsnamen. Petermanns Mitteilungen Ergänzungsband 17. 1884-85. Erganzungsheft 80:90-95.
A list of Eskimo place-names in Baffin Island, followed by a list of the English names with Eskimo equivalents.

4435. Bockstoce, John R. & Charles F. Batchelder. A gazetteer of whalers' place-names for the Bering Strait region and the western Arctic. Names 26:258-70, Sept. 1978.
Obsolete and obscure names including several in Yukon Territory.

4436. Canada. Permanent Committee on Geographical Names. Gazetteer of Canada, Répertoire géographique du Canada: Northwest Territories, Territoires du Nord-Ouest. 1st ed. Ottawa, Surveys and Mapping Branch, Dept. of Energy, Mines and Resources, 1980. xlv, 184p. maps.

First published in 1958 as part of Canada. Board on Geographical Names. Gazetteer of Canada: Northwest Territories and Yukon; Provisional edition: Canada. Permanent Committee on Geographical Names. Gazetteer of Canada: Northwest Territories. 1971. 74p.

Communities and localities, Agglomérations et localites: p. 1-4; Physical and cultural features, Éléments physiques et culturels: p. 5-184.

4437. Castonguay, Rachelle. The relevance of native toponymy in illustrating land occupancy in the Canadian North. Canadian Society for the Study of Names. Onomastica 56:1-12, Dec. 1979.

4438. Chipman, Kenneth G. & John R. Cox. Eskimo place names; In Canada. Dept. of Naval Service. Report of the Arctic expedition, 1913-18. Ottawa, F. A. Acland, 1918-28. 11:37B-42B.

Translation and etymology verified by D. Jenness, ethnologist of the expedition.

4439. Debenham, Frank. Place-names in the Polar regions. Polar record 3:541-52, July 1942.

Discussion of origin, difficulties with application of rules and problems resulting from duplication.

4440. Dionne, Jean Claude. Pour un emploi rationnel des termes géographiques appliqués aux littoraux de l'Arctique canadien. Canadian geographer 7:116-30. 1963.

Abstract in English.

A study of topographical maps of Canadian Arctic Archipelago shows a generalized confusion in the use of geographic terms applied to coastal and sea features. An international dictionary defining such terms is needed.

4441. Forbes, H. A. Gazetteer of northern Canada and parts of Alaska and Greenland. Comp. by Squadron Leader H. A. Forbes, R. C. A. F. n.p., 1948. 75p.

Indicates latitude and longitude for each name.

4442. Fraser, J. Keith. Tracing Ross across Boothia. Canadian geographer 10:40-60. 1957. maps.

Features on Boothia Peninsula for which the Sir John Ross expedition of 1829-33 obtained Eskimo names are identified according to modern native usage.

4443. Geographical names in the Canadian North. Arctic 3:72, 195, April, Dec. 1950; 4:144, Sept. 1951; 5:63-64, 132, March, July 1952; 6:280, Dec. 1953; 8:77, Winter 1955; 9:272-75. 1956; 10:61-62, 123-28. 1957; 11:64-66, 127-32, 193-94, 257. 1958; 12:59, 124-28, 183-92, 248-51. 1959; 13:65-66, 142-44, 208, 276. 1960; 14:133-38, 204-08, 269-74. 1961.

Lists official names adopted by the Canadian Board on Geographical Names and gives locations.

4444. Hall, Charles Francis. Narrative of the second Arctic expedition. Washington, Govt. Print. Off., 1879. 644p. (45th Cong., 3d sess. Senate. Ex. doc. 27)

Contains lists of names to accompany sketch maps, as told to Hall by the Innuit who made the map, as follows:

Innuit names of the Northeast coast of Fox Channel, by the Innuit Oong-er-luk: p. 354; Innuit names of Admiralty Inlet, by Oon-er-luk: p. 355; Names around Pond's Bay, by the Innuit Papa: p. 370; Names of King William's Land and the adjacent country, by the Innuit In-nook-poo-zhee-jook: p. 398.

4445. Hamelin, Louis-Edmond. Caracteres et problemes de la choronymie du Nord Canadien. Royal Society of Canada. Proceedings and transactions 4th ser. 10:31-44. 1972.

The insufficient numbers of official choronyms; the deficiencies of existing terms; and the low position accorded to Indian names.

4446. Hammond, Lyle & L. A. C. O. Hunt. Too much geography makes naming havoc! North 21:28-29, Jan.-Feb. 1974.

4447. Hattersley-Smith, G. Northern Ellesmere Island, 1953 and 1954. Arctic 8:2-36, Winter 1955.

New names, p. 33.

4448. Holmer, Nils Magnus. The native place names of arctic America. Names 15:182-96, Sept. 1967; 17:138-48, June 1969.

Confined to Eskimo and Aleutian toponymy, which predominates in the region. Concludes that, even in the toponymy, the peoples of arctic America reveal themselves as speakers of typical Amerindian languages and that Eskimo and Aleutian place-names should not be excluded when dealing with the native names of America.

4449. Johns, Robert E. A toponymy of the Northwest Territories. Musk-ox 6:59-69. 1969.

4450. Kerfoot, Helen. Canada's names in the Hanbury and Upper Thelon area: from Hearne to Cosmos. Canoma 4:16-23. 1978.

French version included.

4451. Manning, Thomas Henry. Eskimo place names of Southampton Island. Geographical journal 88:241-42, Sept. 1936.

Although new English names have proved satisfactory and have been accepted by the Geographic Board of Canada, Eskimo names are used by the inhabitants. A list is included.

4452. —— The Foxe Basin coasts of Baffin Island. Geographical journal 101:225-51, May-June 1943.

New names submitted to the Geographic Board of Canada: p. 248-49.

4453. —— Narrative of a second Defence Research Board expedition to Banks Island, with notes on the country and its history. Arctic 9:3-77. 1956.

Geographical names, p. 66-68. Adopted by the Canadian Board on Geographical Names. Other official names, p. 72-74.

4454. —— Narrative of an unsuccessful attempt to circumnavigate Banks Island by canoe in 1952. Arctic 6:171-97, Oct. 1953.

New names, p. 196-97. Approved by the Canadian Board on Geographical Names.

4455. —— Notes on the coastal district of the eastern Barren Grounds and Melville Peninsula from Igloolik to Cape Fullerton. Canadian geographical journal 28:84-105, Feb. 1943.

New names given by the British Canadian-Arctic Expedition: p. 87.

4456. Markham, Sir Clemente Robert. Life of Admiral Francis Leopold McClintock. London, J. Murray, 1909. 370p.

Appendix C. Place names given by Sir John Ross, Sir William Edward Parry, Admiral McClintock and others to localities in the Canadian Arctic: p. 332-46.

4457. Mary-Rousselière, Guy. Toponymie esquimaude de la région de Pond Inlet. Cahiers de géographie de Québec 10:301-11, sept. 1966. map.
Includes a list of 245 names on Baffin Island, with French translation for each.

4458. Naming of Arctic islands. Arctic 2:125, Sept. 1949.
Prince Charles Island in Foxe Basin, and Mackenzie King Island for the southern part of Borden Island.

4459. Naming of northern weather stations. Arctic 2:125, Sept. 1949.
Four postwar weather stations established jointly by the Canadian and U.S. governments in the Canadian Arctic.

4460. "Nattilik" or "Inuit Nunaga" may show up on maps soon. Lincoln (Neb.) evening journal and Nebraska State journal Nov. 14, 1962, p. 20.
The Northwest Territories to be split in two, the western section to be called the Territory of Mackenzie, the eastern to have a name chosen by the Eskimo inhabitants.

4461. Parry, Sir William Edward. Journal of a second voyage for the discovery of a northwest passage from the Atlantic to the Pacific; performed in the years 1821-22-23, in His Majesty's ships Fury and Hecla, under the orders of Captain William Edward Parry. London, John Murray, 1824. 571p.
Also published: New York, E. Duyckinck, 1824. 464p.
Esquimaux names of places: p. 570-71 (London ed.).

4462. Petitot, Émile Fortuné Stanislas Joseph. On the Athabasca District of the Canadian North-West Territory. Royal Geographical Society. Proceedings n.s. 5:633-55, Nov. 1883.
Contains a number of geographic names.

4463. Prud'homme, L. A. Noms historiques de la langue française au Nord-ouest canadien. Société de Géographie de Québec. Bulletin 9:195-209, 283-93, 348-64, juil.-nov. 1915.

4464. Queen Elizabeth Islands. Polar record 7:334, Jan. 1955.
Summarized from The Times, London, Feb. 6, 1954.
Canadian announcement of designation for the islands which include the Parry and Sverdrup groups.

4465. Rasmussen, Knud Johan Victor. Iglulik and Caribou Eskimo texts. Copenhagen, Gyldendal, 1930. 160p. (Report of the 5th Thule expedition, 1921-24. The Danish expedition to Arctic North America in charge of Knud Rasmussen. v. 7, no. 3)
Iglulik texts. Place-names according to Eskimo sketch maps from the Iglulingmiut: p. 89-99.
Caribou texts. Place-names according to sketch maps from Caribou Eskimos: p. 146-60.

4466. —— Netsilik Eskimos, social life and spiritual culture. Copenhagen, Gyldendal, 1931. 542p. (Report of the 5th Thule expedition to Arctic North America in charge of Knud Rasmussen. v. 8, no. 1-2)
The Seal Eskimos and their country. Eskimo topography: p. 91-113. Around territory of Boothia Isthmus, Netsilik Lake, and Adelaide Peninsula.

4467. Ross, Sir John. Narrative of a second voyage in search of a north-west passage, and of a residence in the Arctic regions during the years 1829, 1830, 1831, 1832, 1833. Including the reports of James Clark Ross and the discovery of the northern magnetic pole. London, A. W. Webster, 1835. 2v.
v. 2 is Appendix, with 120, cxliv, lxiv p.

Place-names are listed in v. 2, p. 3, p. lii-lxiv, in groups as follows: Latitudes and longitudes, from the N.E. Cape to Gulf of Boothia and King William IV Sea; Latitudes and longitudes of places in Baffin's Bay, determined 1818, 1833; Sir Edward Parry's first voyage; Sir Edward Parry's second voyage; From Sir John Franklin's chart; Sir John Franklin's first journey; From Captain Beechy's chart.

4468. Rouillard, Eugène. Chronique de géographie. Société de Géographie de Québec. Bulletin 16:170-71. 1922.
Decision of the Canadian Geographic Board to assign the name Breynat à la Pointe de la Rive, in District of Mackenzie, in honor of bishop thereof.

4469. —— Dans l'extrême Nord du Canada. Société de Géographie de Québec. Bulletin 8:195-200, juil. 1914.

4470. Rowley, Diana. Stefansson Island. Arctic circular 5:46-53, Oct. 1952.
Naming of the Island and discussion of names of adjacent features.

4471. Stevenson, Alex. The romance of northern names. North 13:21-25, July-Aug. 1966.

4472. Sutton, George Miksch. The exploration of Southampton Island, Hudson Bay. Pittsburgh, Pa., Carnegie Institute, 1932-36. 7 pts. (Memoirs of the Carnegie Museum, v. 12)
Includes notes on place-names, in pt. 1, sec. 2, p. 8-23.

4473. Thibert, Arthur. Dictionary; English-Eskimo, Eskimo-English. Ottawa, Research Center of Amerindian Anthropology, Univ. of Ottawa, 1954. 174p.
Geographical names of places in the Arctic: p. 163.

4474. Usher, Peter J. Fur trade posts of the Northwest Territories, 1870-1970. Ottawa, Northern Science Research Group, Dept. of Indian Affairs and Northern Development, 1971. 180p. maps. (NRSG-71-4)
Review: Canadian geographer 17:412. 1973.

4475. White, James. Place-names—Northern Canada. Canada. Geographic Board. Report 9:231-455. 1910.
Also published separately, 1911. 224p.
A partial report of this study, which deals especially with the names conferred by the explorers in the far north, was published in Royal Society of Canada. Proceedings and transactions 3d ser. v. 4, sec. 4, p. 37-40. 1910.
Review: Review of historical publications relating to Canada 16:126. 1912.

4476. Wordie, J. M. An expedition to north west Greenland and the Canadian Arctic in 1937; note on names. Geographical journal 92:415-18, Nov. 1938.
The region was mapped and new names proposed.

4477. Wright, John. South-east Ellesmere Island. Geographical journal 95:278-91, April 1940.
Coastal names: p. 288-89.

NOVA SCOTIA

4478. Bernard, Angel B. Indian place names of Cape Breton. Tawow 1:16-17, Spring 1970.
Includes some on the mainland of Nova Scotia.

4479. Bird, Will R. Nova Scotia and New Brunswick names. Maclean's magazine 41:54, 56, 58, 60, 63, June 1, 1928.

4480. Brown, Thomas J. Place-names of the Province of Nova Scotia. Halifax, Royal Print. & Litho. Ltd., 1922. 158p.
Reprinted: Toronto, Canadiana House, 1969.

4481. Canada. Permanent Committee on Geographical Names. Gazetteer of Canada: Nova Scotia. 2d ed. Ottawa, Surveys and Mapping Branch, Dept. of Energy, Mines and Resources, 1977. xlv, 477p. maps.
1st ed. 1961. 192p., published by Canada. Board on Geographical Names.

4482. Dawson, Robert MacGregor. Nova Scotian place-names. Linguistic Circle of Manitoba and North Dakota. Proceedings 1:10-12, May 1959.

4483. —— Place names in Nova Scotia. A paper read before the Linguistic Circle of Manitoba and North Dakota on May 16th, 1959. Ukrainian Free Academy of Sciences. Onomastica 19:1-16. 1960.

4484. Frame, Elizabeth. A list of Micmac names of places, rivers, etc., in Nova Scotia. Cambridge, Mass., John Wilson and Son, 1892. 12p.
Reprinted: Toronto, Canadiana House, 1968.
Compiled for the library of the Massachusetts Historical Society, and presented at the meeting on June 9, 1892.

4485. Ganong, William Francis. The origin of the East-Canadian place-names Gaspé, Blomidon, and Bras d'Or. Royal Society of Canada. Proceedings and transactions 3d ser. v. 22, sec. 2, p. 249-70. 1928.

4486. Harrisse, Henry. Découverte et évolution cartographique de Terre-Neuve et des pays circonvoisins, 1497-1501-1769; essais de géographie historique et documentaire. London, Henry Stevens, Son & Stiles; Paris, H. Walter, 1900. 420p.
La cartographie américano-dieppoise. Nomenclature de La Nouvelle-Écosse: p. 214-22.
Nomenclature chronologique du Labrador, de Terre-Neuve et de la région adjacente depuis la découverte jusqu'à la fin du XVIe siècle: p. 355-66.

4487. Hill, George W. Nomenclature of the streets of Halifax. Nova Scotia Historical Society. Collections 15:1-22. 1911.

4488. Kirkconnell, Watson. Place-names in Kings County, Nova Scotia. n.p., 1971. 39p.

4489. Maclellan, W. E. Origin of Pictou's name. Dalhousie review 2:251-53, July 1922.

4490. Noms géographiques canadiens. Bulletin des recherches historiques 31:268, juil. 1925.
Baie des Châteaux, and Chéticamp.

4491. Nova Scotia. Department of Mines. Gazetteer of Nova Scotia; a geographical dictionary giving names and locations of places in alphabetical order. Comp. by Eva R. Duncan. Halifax, 1958. 199p.

4492. —— —— Index of geographical names appearing on new map of the Province of Nova Scotia (with addenda of place-names). Halifax, N.S., 1955. 41p.

4493. —— Department of Public Health. Division of Vital Statistics. Geographical code for Nova Scotia. Alphabetical list of place names, showing counties, provincial municipalities, statistical publication areas. Halifax, n.d. 27p.
Keyed to the census of June 1, 1956.

4494. —— Public Archives. Place-names and places of Nova Scotia; with an introd. by Charles Bruce Ferguson. Halifax, N.S., 1967. 751p. maps. (Nova Scotia series, 3).
Reprinted: Belleville, Ont., Mika Pub. Co., 1974.
Review: Alan Rayburn, Names 19:51, March 1971.

4495. Nova Scotian place names. Journal of education for Nova Scotia 4th ser. 2:68-71, Dec. 1931; 3:75-77, 85-89, 103-12, 146-51, 172-75, Jan.-Oct. 1932; 5:101-08, 371-73, April-Oct. 1934; 6:87-92, March 1935.

4496. Pacifique de Valiguy, O.F.M. Cap Breton. Société de Géographie de Québec. Bulletin 27:34-50, janv. 1933.
Includes list of native names (Micmac) with English equivalents.

4497. Pap, Leo. The Portuguese adstratum in North American place-names. Names 20:111-30, June 1972.
A survey of Portuguese influence on the formation of place-names in the United States and in Newfoundland, Labrador, and Nova Scotia in Canada, presented as a linguistic contribution to the investigation of naming processes.

4498. Post office directory for Nova Scotia, shewing the names of every village, settlement and township in the province. London, H.M.S.O., 1850. 33p.

ONTARIO

4499. Baker, R. H. A brief history of names in the County of Haliburton, with the dates of first improvements in county and townships. Ottawa, Public Archives, 1931. 40p.

4500. Banks, Margaret A. Upper and Lower Canada or Canada West and East, 1841-67? Canadian historical review 54:473-82, Dec. 1973.
No uniform official terminology for the constituent parts of the Province of Canada from 1841 to 1849, from then until the end of the union, 1867, Upper and Lower Canada were recognized as correct.

4501. Bannister, J. A. The romance of forgotten towns. Western Ontario historical notes 21:46-76, Sept. 1965.

4502. Barnard, W. A. Ontario names. Sylva, your lands and forest review 12:26-28, Jan.-Feb. 1956.

4503. Bell, Robert. Meanings of Indian geographical names in the country around Sudbury. Canada. Geological Survey. Annual report v. 5, pt. 1, p. 91F-95F. 1890-91.

4504. Black, M. J. L. Place names in the vicinity of Fort William, and Fort William streets. Thunder Bay Historical Society. Annual report 16-17:12-25, 80-83. 1926-28.

4505. Brighty, Isabel McComb. A pilgrimage through the historic Niagara district, including a list of place names. St. Catharines, Lincoln Historical Society, 1932. 12p. (Lincoln Historical Society. Publication no. 1)

4506. Cameron, James M. An introduction to the study of Scottish settlement of southern Ontario--a comparison of place names. Ontario history 61:167-72, Sept. 1969. maps.
A comparison between maps of Scotland and Ontario, as a basis for study of national groupings in Ontario. Settlement took place 1815-35.

4507. Campbell, John S. Why this city is called St. Catharines. Named after Catharine Hamilton, wife of Hon. Robert Hamilton—evidence establishing this reviewed—Miss Merritt's contention shown to be baseless. St. Catharines standard Dec. 14, 1926.

4508. Canada. Board on Geographical Names. Gazetteer of Canada: Southwestern Ontario. Ottawa, 1952. [123]p.

4509. —— Permanent Committee on Geographical Names. Gazetteer of Canada: Ontario. 2d ed. Ottawa, Surveys and Mapping Branch, Dept. of Energy, Mines and Resources, 1974. xxxiii, 823p. map.
1st ed. Dept. of Mines and Technical Surveys. Geographical Branch. Ottawa, 1962. 614p.

4510. —— Surveys and Mapping Branch. List of geographical townships in the Province of Ontario including those designated by letter and number. Rev. to July 15th, 1955. Ottawa, [1955]. 23p.

4511. Canfield, Mrs. Ernest J. Street names of Woodstock; a paper given before Oxford Historical Society 1932. Supplement by Mrs. W. R. Ward. [Woodstock, Ont., Oxford Historical Society, 1970]. 23p.

4512. Charbonneau, Louis. Toponymie de la Province d'Ontario. Société historique du Nouvel-Ontario, Sudbury. Documents historiques, 1:33-42. 1942.

4513. Clark, John S. A study of the word Toronto. Toronto. Ontario Provincial Museum. Annual archaeological report 1899:190-98.

4514. Curry, Frederick C. Fontaine Becancourt. Ontario history 57:99-100, June 1965.
17th-century name on the shore of the St. Lawrence River.

4515. Duff, Louis Blake. Names are pegs to hang history on. Ontario Historical Society. Papers and records 23:223-36. 1926.
Regarding the origin of place-names in Ontario.

4516. —— The romance of our place-names, a series of eight radio addresses, Feb. 20 to April 10, 1934, station CKTB, St. Catharines. Fort Erie, Ont., The Review Co., 1934. 22p.
Indian, French, and English place-names in Ontario.

4517. Eames, Frank. Gananoque, the name and its origin. Gananoque, The Author, 1942. 26p.

4518. Gardiner, Herbert Fairbairn. Nothing but names, an inquiry into the origin of the names of the counties and townships of Ontario. Toronto, G. N. Morang & Co., 1899. 561p.
Review: Canadian magazine 13:484-85, Sept. 1899.

4519. —— Ontario onomatology and British biography. Ontario Historical Society. Papers and records 6:37-47. 1905.
Names of places remind the author of the history of various British families.

4520. A Gazetteer of the Province of Upper Canada, to which is added, an appendix, describing the principal towns, fortifications and rivers in Lower Canada. New York, Prior & Dunning, 1813. 83p.
Based upon Sir D. W. Smyth, A short topographical description of Upper Canada. London, 1799.

4521. Goulet, Louis. French and Indian place-names in Kent and adjoining counties. Kent Historical Society. Papers 3:38-50. 1917.

4522. Hammond, Mrs. A. Names in Wellington County. Western Ontario historical notes 14:24-26, March 1958.

4523. Hartley, Alan H. The expansion of Ojibway and French place-names into the Lake Superior region in the seventeenth century. Names 28:43-68, March 1980.

4524. Herrington, W. S. The origin of some of our local names. Lennox and Addington Historical Society. Papers and records 1:29-41. 1909.

4525. Hewitt, John Napoleon Brinton. Iroquois place-names on the north shore of Lake Ontario; In Percy James Robinson, Toronto during the French regime. Toronto, Ryerson Press, 1933. p. 243.

4526. Highway named for Queen. New York times May 10, 1939, p. 25.
Road between Toronto and Fort Erie to be called Queen Elizabeth's Way.

4527. Hitsman, J. Mackay. They named it Vars. Ontario history 49:138, Summer 1957.
Also mentions nearby town named Kars.

4528. James, C. C. The origin of "Napanee." Ontario Historical Society. Papers and records 6:47-49. 1905.
Early documents show that the original name was Apanee.

4529. Johnson, Henry Smith. Norfolk County place names. 3d ed. Simcoe, Ont., Norfolk Historical Society, 1969. 11p.
1st ed. 1934. 15p.

4530. Johnston, Albert J. Lambton County names and places. 2d ed. rev. n.p., Lambton County Council. 1942. 54p.
1st ed. 1925. 55p.

4531. Jones, Arthur Edward. Identification of the Huron village sites of 1615-1650. Ontario. Bureau of Archives. Report 5:xxxii, 1-266. 1908.
The derivation of the Indian names of Huron villages.

4532. Lapierre, André. Quelques problèmes de contact des langues en toponymie ontarienne. Canadian Society for the Study of Names. Onomastica 58:18-27, Dec. 1980.

4533. Lefcourt, Charles R. A rose by any other name: ethnic conflict in Berlin, Ontario. Keystone folklore quarterly 12:119-26, Summer 1967.
World War I reaction to the name led to a change of the name to Kitchener.

4534. Lendrum, Frank. Moosonee place-names and their origin. The Quarterly (Ontario Northland Railway) 62:7-11. Sept. 1961.

4535. Lewis, Ella N. East Elgin place names. St. Thomas, Printed for the Elgin Historical Society by the Sutherland Press, 1935. 25p.

4536. Macdonald, George F. How Windsor got its name. Essex Historical Society. Papers and addresses 3:33-36, 1921.

4537. McFall, William Alexander. Relations of wars of Europe to the place names of Ontario. n.p., n.d. 7p.

4538. McKay, Ian A. Place names in historical geography. Ontario geography 1:40-44, Jan. 1967. maps.

For reply to this article and McKay's rejoinder, see Rayburn, Alan. Place names in the Kitchener-Stratford area of Ontario as indicators of national origin (see no. 4557).

Examines the association of name and name-giver to evaluate the usefulness of place-names as an indicator of national origin of settlers.

4539. McKenzie, Charles. Cataraqui, 1901. Ontario Historical Society. Papers and records 8:142-46. 1908.

4540. MacLaren, D. H. British naval officers of a century ago. Barrie and its streets—a history of their names. Ontario Historical Society. Papers and records 17:106-12. 1919.

Many streets in Barrie are named in honor of naval officers of the War of 1812-1814.

4541. Marsh, A. W. Place names of Essex County. Essex Historical Society. Papers 1:58-68. 1913.

4542. Middleton, Jesse Edgar. An historical gazetteer of the counties and districts in the Province of Ontario; In his The Province of Ontario, a history, 1615-1927. Toronto, Dominion Pub. Co., 1928. 2:1084-1245.

4543. Mika, Nick & Hilma Mika. Places in Ontario. Belleville, Ont., Mika Pub., 1977. 716p. (Encyclopedia of Ontario, v. 2, pt. 1, A to E)

In preparation: F to Z in 2 parts.

Includes brief historical notes.

4544. Moore, William Francis. Indian place names. Wentworth Historical Society. Papers and records 6:17-24. 1915.

Discussion of a few names but with meanings not endorsed by the authorities.

Review: Review of historical publications relating to Canada 20:191. 1915.

4545. —— Indian place names in Ontario. Toronto, Macmillan, 1930. 48p.

4546. Myers, Frank A. How Little Current got its name. Inland seas 16:119-22, Summer 1960.

Port on northeasterly end of Manitoulin Island.

4547. Names of Niagara Falls, Ontario. Ontario history 43:90-91, April 1951.

4548. Ontario. Department of Lands and Forests. List of geographical townships in the Province of Ontario, including those designated by letter or number. Toronto, 1949. 23p.

4549. —— Geographic Names Board. Naming Ontario, a guide to the collection of geographic names. Toronto, 1977. 22p. maps.

The Board was established by Statute of 1968 (Ontario. Revised statutes, ch. 314. 1975).

The Board has also published its Principles of geographical naming (Toronto, Queen's Printer, 1975).

4550. —— Office of Registrar-General. Geographical code for Ontario. Alphabetical list of place names, showing counties and districts, provincial municipalities, statistical publication areas. Toronto, n.d. 49p.
Keyed to the census of June 1, 1956.

4551. Ottawa may get Finland Ave. New York times March 21, 1940, p. 7.
Residents petition that Wurtemberg St. be changed to Finland Ave.

4552. Peel (Ont.) Regional Municipality Planning Committee. The Ontario Geographic Names Board--feasibility study on urban place names. [Toronto], The Committee, 1977. 8, 10p.
Includes: Principles of geographic naming, and Community names, some cartographic and toponymic problems.

4553. Place names. Thunder Bay Historical Society. Annual report v. 18-19, p. 80-83. 1926-28.
From the Toronto globe, by "A Bystander at the office window."

4554. Priddis, Harriet. The naming of London streets. Read before the London and Middlesex Historical Society, May 16th, 1905. Rev. and corrected up to date, Jan. 9th, 1909. London and Middlesex Historical Society. Papers 1908/09:7-30.
Reprinted: London and Middlesex Historical Society. Centennial review 1967. Publication 16:29-53. 1967.
Includes information on naming of the city of London.

4555. Rannie, William F. Names in Lincoln: a study of street, road and other names in an Ontario town. Lincoln, Ont., W. F. Rannie, 1975. 36p.

4556. Rayburn, Alan. Geographical names of Renfrew County. Ottawa, Geographical Branch, Dept. of Energy, Mines and Resources, 1967. 74p. maps. (Geographical paper no. 40)
Bibliography: p. 62-66.
Review: R. A. Mohl, Names 16:193-94, June 1968.

4557. —— Place names in the Kitchener-Stratford area of Ontario as indicators of national origin. Ontario geography 2:82-88. 1968. map.
An answer to Ian A. McKay, Place names in historical geography.
A rejoinder by Ian A. McKay, in ibid. 2:89-91. 1968.

4558. Read, E. G. History of the County of Carleton. Women's Historical Society. Transactions 4:5-9. 1911.

4559. Reed, T. A. The historic value of street names. Ontario Historical Society. Papers and records 25:385-87. 1929.
Street names in Toronto.

4560. Riddell, William Renwick. Toronto in cartography. Ontario Historical Society. Papers and records 28:143-45. 1932.
List of maps: p. 144-45.
Traces the appearance of the name Toronto in early maps. Includes also the varied terminology of the Great Lakes.

4561. Robinson, Percy James. The Chevalier de Rocheblave and the Toronto purchase. Royal Society of Canada. Proceedings and transactions 3d ser. v. 31, sec. 2, p. 131-52. 1937.
Discussion of a theory of the origin of the name Toronto which gains some support from a fresh examination of the terms of the original Toronto purchase.

4562. —— Huron place-names on Lake Erie. Royal Society of Canada. Transactions 3d ser. v. 40, sec. 2, p. 191-207, May 1946.
A study of Rev. Pierre Potier's list, Huron Mss. Ontario Archives 1920. p. 155.

4563. —— Montreal to Niagara in the seventeenth century, a philological excursion. Royal Society of Canada. Proceedings and transactions 3d ser. v. 38, sec. 2, p. 137-53. 1944.

4564. —— More about Toronto. Ontario history 45:123-27, Summer 1953.

4565. —— Notes on Potier's Huron place-names in the vicinity of Lake Erie, 1745. n.p., n.d. 14p.

4566. —— On the derivation of certain place-names in the Georgian Bay. Royal Canadian Institute. Transactions 10:127-29, May 1915.
Review: Review of historical publications relating to Canada 19:208. 1914.

4567. Rouillard, Eugène. Dans l'Ouest et à Ontario; quelques noms géographiques. Société de Géographie de Québec. Bulletin 14:351-55, janv. 1921.

4568. Roulston, Pauline Jane. Field collection of geographic names in Province of Canada; In United Nations Conference on the Standardization of Geographical Names, 3d, Athens, 1977. Canada. Ottawa, 1978. p. 121-34.
French version: p. 279-94.

4569. —— Place names of Peel: past and present. Cheltenham, Ont., Boston Mills Press, c1978. 79p. maps.
Review: Alan Rayburn, Canadian geographic 98:70-71, Feb./March 1979.

4570. —— Urban community names: some cartographic and toponymic problems. Canoma 4:1-7, Dec. 1976.
French version included.
The purpose is to outline difficulties confronted by the Ontario Geographic Names Board in the handling of urban community names and to develop recommendations that can be used as a basis of discussion by toponymists, cartographers, and others involved in map production.

4571. Sanford Evans Statistical Service. Ontario place guide. Winnipeg, 1951. 251p.
Lists alphabetically cities, towns, villages, and townships, with locations.

4572. Scadding, Henry. A note on the etymology of Ontario. Canadian journal of industry 7:502-08. 1862.

4573. —— Yonge Street and Dundas Street: the men after whom they were named. Canadian journal 2d ser., 15:615-41. 1878.

4574. Sinclair, James. The former names of the Thames River. Ontario Historical Society. Papers and records 17:37-39. 1919.

4575. Smart, Michael B. Generic names in Ontario, the case for retention of the place element in geographical nomenclature; In Henri Dorion, ed. Les noms de lieux et le contact des langues. Québec, Les Presses de l'Univ. Laval, 1972. p. 344-55.

4576. Smith, Raymond A. From Adanac to Zebra: a gazetteer of place-names, past and present, in the Territorial District of Parry Sound. [Parry Sound, Ont.] The Author, 1974. 35p. map.

With some information on the location of now vanished settlements, and an attempt to provide derivations for their names.

4577. Smith, William Henry. Canada: past, present and future. Being a historical, geographical, geological and statistical account of Canada West. Containing ten county maps and one general map of the province, comp. expressly for the work. Toronto, T. MacLear, 1851. 2v.

4578. —— Smith's Canadian gazetteer: comprising statistical and general information respecting all parts of the Upper Province, or Canada West: distance tables; government and district officers and magistrates in each district; list of post offices, with their distances from some of the principal towns; stage and steamboat fares; principal hotels and taverns; rates of toll on the Welland Canal and some of the principal harbours; lists of exports; quantity of crown lands for sale in each township; names and addresses of land agents and forwarders; the leading features of each locality as regards soil, climate, &c., with the average value of land. With a mass of other desirable and useful information for the man of business, traveller, or emigrant. With a map of the Upper Province. Toronto, Pub. for the author by H. & W. Rowsell, 1846. 285p.

Published also 1849. 285p.

Reprinted: Toronto, Coles Pub. Co., 1970. x, 285p.

4579. Smyth, David William. A short topographical description of His Majesty's province of Upper Canada, in North America. To which is annexed a provincial gazetteer. London, W. Faden, 1799. 164p.

2d ed. rev. by Francis Gore. London, W. Faden, 1813. 123p.

Reprinted: Henry Scadding, Canadian local history, the first gazetteer of Upper Canada, with annotations. Canadian journal n.s. 14:55-72, 208-17, 305-08, 367-87, 513-41, 658-74, Nov. 1873-Dec. 1875.

4580. Sulte, Benjamin. The name of Ottawa. Ottawa Literary and Scientific Society. Transactions 1:21-23. 1897-98.

4581. —— Ottawa, ce nom. Societe de Geographie de Quebec. Bulletin 7:352-65, nov. 1913.

4582. —— Le passage de Toronto. Societe de Geographie de Quebec. Bulletin 8:323-28. 1914.

Toronto means "passage that goes from Lake Ontario to Lake Huron."

4583. Tait, George. Street and place names and early reminiscences of Bridgebury. Welland County Historical Society. Papers and records 3:104-13. 1927.

4584. Tyrrell, Joseph Burr. Algonquian Indian names of places in northern Canada. Royal Canadian Institute. Transactions 10:213-31, May 1914.

Reprinted separately: Toronto, Univ. Press, 1915; Toronto, Canadiana House, 1968. 213-31p.

List of Indian names collected during extensive travels, with meanings of the names, the current names on maps, and the location of the places.

Manitoba and District of Patricia, Ontario.

Review: Review of historical publications relating to Canada 19:208. 1914.

4585. Van Dorp, Brother Gerard Francis. A survey of the place names of Waterloo County. London, Univ. of Western Ontario, Dept. of Geography, n.d.

4586. White, James. Place-names in Georgian Bay (including the North Channel). [Toronto, The Society, 1913]. 81p. (Ontario Historical Society. Papers and records, v. 11)

Names given by Bayfield in the survey of 1819-22; the local names given by fishermen and others between 1822 and 1883; and names created by the new survey, 1883-93.

4587. —— Place-names in the Thousand Islands, St. Lawrence River. Pub. by order of Hon. L. P. Brodeur, Minister of Marine and Fisheries of Canada, for the Geographic Board of Canada. Ottawa, Govt. Print. Bureau, 1910. 7p.
Published also in Canada. Geographic Board. Report 9:223-27. 1909-10.
Review: Review of historical publications relating to Canada 15:105. 1910.

4588. Williams, David. The origin of the names of the post offices in Simcoe County. Ontario Historical Society. Papers and records 7:193-236. 1906.
Review: James H. Coyne, Review of historical publications relating to Canada 11:129. 1906.

4589. Williams, W. R. Georgian Bay's Grumbling Point. Inland seas 7:280, Winter 1951.
Grondine Point.

4590. Wintemberg, W. J. Early names of the Grand River, Ontario. Royal Society of Canada. Proceedings and transactions 3d ser. v. 23, sec. 2, p. 125-33. 1929.

4591. —— Origin of the place and stream names of Waterloo County. Waterloo Historical Society. Report 1927:351-80.

4592. —— The place and stream names of Oxford County, Ontario. Ontario Historical Society. Papers and records 22:259-95. 1925.
List of books and maps consulted: p. 259-61.
Includes also archaic forms and names no longer in use, with dates of maps on which these latter are found.

PRINCE EDWARD ISLAND

4593. Bremner, Benjamin. Tales of Abegweit (Prince Edward Island) containing historical, biographical and humorous sketches and selections, collected, ed. and written by Benjamin Bremner, with an appendix of place-names in Prince Edward Island with their origins or meanings. Charlottetown, Irwin Print. Co., 1936. 132p.

4594. Burke, A. E. Who named the Magdalens? Prince Edward Island magazine 2:134-38, July 1900.

4595. Canada. Geographic Board. Place-names of Prince Edward Island, with meanings. Comp. by R. Douglas, Secretary, Geographic Board of Canada. Ottawa, F. A. Acland, 1925. 55p.

4596. —— Permanent Committee on Geographical Names. Gazetteer of Canada: Prince Edward Island. Centennial issue 1873-1973. 2d ed. Ottawa, Surveys and Mapping Branch, Dept. of Energy, Mines and Resources, 1973. xxxv, 35p. map.
Reprinted 1978.
1st ed. Published by Canada. Board on Geographical Names. 1960. 19p.
Introduction in English and French.

4597. Moase, L. M. Louise. 1800-1971, the history of New Annan, Prince Edward Island, comp. for the New Annan Women's Institute. n.p., n.d.
Place-names, p. 9-10.

4598. Prince Edward Island. Dept. of Health and Welfare. Division of Vital Statistics. Geographical code for Prince Edward Island. Alphabetical list of place names, showing counties, provincial municipalities, statistical publication areas. Charlottetown, n.d. 6p.
Keyed to the census of June 1, 1956.

4599. Rayburn, Alan. Geographical names of Prince Edward Island, by Alan Rayburn for Canadian Permanent Committee on Geographical Names. Ottawa, Surveys and Mapping Branch, Dept. of Energy, Mines and Resources, 1973. 135p. map. (Toponymy study no. 1)
Reprinted 1978.
Bibliography: p. 131-35.
Origin and use of more than 1600 names.

QUEBEC

4600. Arnaud, Charles. List of names of places in the Montagnois language. Canada. Dept. of Indian Affairs. Annual report 1884, pt. 1, p. 29-31.
Originally appeared in Annals of the propagation of the faith June 1880.

4601. Arsenault, Yves. Choronymie de la côte de Beaupré. 170p.
Thesis (M.A.) Univ. Laval, 1969.

4602. Audet, Francis J. Le Pointe Mondion; origine du nom. Société de Géographie de Québec. Bulletin 18:155-57, mai 1924.
Attempt to establish Joseph Mondion, from mention in historical records, as one for whom place is named.

4603. Banks, Margaret A. Upper and Lower Canada or Canada West and East, 1841-67? Canadian historical review 54:473-82, Dec. 1973.
No uniform official terminology for the constituent parts of the Province of Canada existed from 1841 to 1849. From then until the end of the union, 1867, Upper and Lower Canada were recognized as correct.

4604. Barbeau, V. De la prononciation du mot Ungava. Revue canadienne de géographie 13:172-73. 1959.

4605. Baudry, René. D'où viennent les noms "Bras d'Or" et "Labrador"? Revue d'histoire de l'Amérique française 6:20-30, juin 1952.

4606. Beauregard, Ludger. Toponymie de la région métropolitaine de Montréal. Québec, Ministère des Terres et Forêts du Québec, Commission de Géographie, 1968. 225p. map. (Étude toponymique, nouv. sér., 2)
Bibliography: p. 200-06.
A study of 672 toponyms from the point of view of their usage, their origin, and their meaning.
Review: Sterling A. Stoudemire, Names 17:238-39, Sept. 1969; Jules Herbillon, Onoma 12:247-48, 1966/67; see also Jacques Rousseau, La toponymie montréalaise. Revue de geographie de Montréal 24:91-96. 1970 (See no. 4794.)

4607. Bedard, Avila. La Commission de Géographie de Québec. Les traductions inopportunes, une motion importante. Société de Géographie de Québec. Bulletin 8:162-64, mai 1914.

4608. Bélanger, Léonidas. Le nom Chicoutimi. Saguenayensia (Chicoutimi) 5:129-32, sept.-dec. 1963.

4609. Bélanger, René. De la Pointe de tous les diables au Cap Grincedents—toponymie historique et actuelle de la Côte-Nord. Québec, Bélisle, 1973. 165p. maps.

4610. —— Nomenclature des noms géographiques indiens de la Côte-Nord. Saguenayensia (Chicoutimi) 1:8-9, janv.-fév. 1959.
Indian names, with corresponding French names in some cases, with meaning.

4611. Bell, Robert. Geographical nomenclature—Bell River. Société de Géographie de Québec. Bulletin 2:257-59. 1893-97.
Nomenclature géographique, La Rivière Bell. Traduction par M. Baillaigre, ibid. p. 259-61.

4612. Bonin, René. Réflexions sur la toponymie chez nous. Action nationale 58:444-55, janv. 1969.
Proposes a return to Amerindian and French sources rather than English for Quebec names.

4613. Bonnelly, Christian. Jurisdictions et normalisation des noms géographiques au Québec. Canoma 3:6-7, July 1977.
Also published in United Nations Conference on the Standardization of Geographical Names, 3d, Athens, 1977. Canada. Ottawa, 1978. p. 295-98.
English version: p. 135-38.

4614. Bouchette, Joseph. A topographical description of the Province of Lower Canada, with remarks upon Upper Canada and on the relative connexion of both provinces with the United States of America. London, W. Faden, 1815. 640, lxxxvi p.
Reprinted: St. Lambert, P.Q., Canada East Reprints, 1973. xv, 640, lxxxvi p. 17ℓ.

4615. —— A topographical dictionary of the Province of Lower Canada. London, Longman, Rees, Orme, Brown, Green, & Longman, 1832. 360p.
Published also: London, H. Colburn and R. Bentley, 1831.

4616. Breton, Yvan. Notes d'observation sur la toponymie de la Rivière Saint-Paul, Côte-Nord. Québec, Univ. Laval, 1967. [18]p.
A manuscript deposited with the Commission de Toponymie, Québec.

4617. Brochu, Michel. Le défi du Nouveau-Québec. Montréal, Éditions du Jour, 1962. 156p.
Toponymie du Nouveau-Québec: p. 125-44. Text is similar to that in his separate publication, Toponymie des côtes du Nouveau-Quebéc.

4618. —— Normes et principes généraux de toponymie. Québec, Éditions Ferland, 1962. 16p.

4619. —— Toponymie des côtes du Nouveau-Québec. Québec, Éditions Ferland, 1961. [31]p.
Similar text appears in his Le défi du Nouveau-Québec (see no. 4617).
New names and changed names for points, capes, bays, etc., along the north shore of New Quebec, with origins of the names.

4620. Cailleux, André. Choronymie planifiée: application au Nouveau-Québec, with English summary. Revue de géographie de Montréal 26:77-87. 1972.
Corrections: ibid. 26:231. 1972.

4621. Canada. Geographic Board. Place-names in Quebec, by James White; In its Report 9:153-219. 1909/10.
Includes lists of expeditions and explorers in northern Canada (1576-1910).
Review: Review of historical publications relating to Canada 16:126. 1912.

4622. —— —— Place-names on Anticosti Island, Que., by Lt.-Col. W. P. Anderson, member Geographic Board of Canada. Ottawa, F. A. Acland, 1922. 15p.
Reprinted from its Report 17:53-65. 1919/21.
Translation: Nomenclature géographique de l'Île Anticosti. Société de Géographie de Québec. Bulletin 18:297-303, nov. 1924; 19:47-50, 94-99, 174-78, janv.-mai 1925.
Includes both accepted and discarded forms.

4623. —— —— Place-names on Magdalen Islands, Que., comp. by R. Douglas, Secretary, Geographic Board of Canada. Ottawa, F. A. Acland, 1922. 11p.
Reprinted from its Report 17:66-74. 1919/21.
Translation: La nomenclature géographique des Îles Madeleine, Province de Québec. Société de Géographie de Québec. Bulletin 19:228-40, 300-05, oct.-déc. 1925.

4624. Cape Diamond à changer pour Cap Diamant. Commerce (Montréal) 66:90, déc. 1964.

4625. Carrière, Gaston. Essai de toponymie oblate canadienne. I. Dans la Province de Québec. Revue canadienne de géographie 11:31-45, janv.-mars 1947.
Later included, with some modifications and corrections, in the author's Essai de toponymie oblate canadienne, in Revue de l'Université d'Ottawa. (see no. 3979)
Lists the places in Quebec which bear names of Oblate Fathers, including date on which name was proclaimed, bibliographical references, and brief history of the patronymic.

4626. Chiasson, Laurent. Latest Arctic pastime: watch the names go by. Financial post 58:1, 4, Oct. 3, 1964.
Names being changed on James Bay, Hudson Bay, Hudson Strait, Ungava Bay.

4627. Clarke, John Mason. The heart of Gaspé; sketches in the Gulf of St. Lawrence. New York, Macmillan, 1913. 292p.
The place-names: p. 259-89.

4628. Demers, Louis Philippe. Rues de Sherbrooke et leur symbole. Sherbrooke's streets and their meaning. Sherbrooke, 1964. 51p.
In French and English.

4629. Desautels, Jacques. Des lacs Culotte, sans compter les Rouges. Magazine Maclean 10:7, janv. 1970.
Brief categorization of the names in the Répertoire géographique du Québec.
English version in Maclean's magazine 61:167-72, Sept. 1969.

4630. Deschamps, Clément E. Liste des municipalités dans la Province de Québec. List of municipalities in the Province of Quebec. Lévis, Mercier & Cie., 1886. 816p.
In French and English in parallel columns.

4631. —— Municipalités et paroisses dans la Province de Québec. Municipalities and parishes in the Province of Québec. Québec, Léger Brousseau, 1896. 1295p.
Text in French and English in parallel columns.

4632. Deschênes, E. B. L'apport de Cartier et de Jean Alfonse dans l'onomastique de la Gaspésie. Bulletin des recherches historiques 40:410-30, juil. 1934.

4633. —— Essai de toponymie gaspésienne. Bulletin des recherches historiques 42:148-73, 200-15, mars-avril 1936.
Reprinted: Revue d'histoire et de traditions populaires de la Gaspésie 15:134-57, juil.-sept. 1977.

4634. Desmeules, J. Divisions administratives et toponymie de la Province de Québec. Cahiers de géographie de Québec 4:369-70, avril-sept. 1960.

4635. Dorion, Henri. Contribution à la connaissance de la choronymie aborigène de la Côte-Nord. Les noms de lieux montagnais des environs de Mingan. Québec, Presses de l'Univ. Laval, 1967. 214 ℓ. maps. (Groupe d'étude de choronymie et de terminologie géographique. [Publication] no. 2)
Montagnais Indian place-names: an inventory (29-208) giving location, current name, translation, explanation, and variant names.

4636. —— Doit-on françiser les noms de lieux du Québec? In Études de linguistique franco-canadienne: Communications presentées au XXXIVe Congrès de l'Association canadienne-française pour l'avancement des Sciences Québec, nov. 1966. Québec, Les Presses de l'Univ. Laval, 1967. p. 165-74.

4637. —— Practical considerations involved in defining the term "geographical name;" In United Nations Conference on the Standardization of Geographical Names, 3d, Athens, 1977. Canada. Ottawa, 1978. p. 103-07.
French version: p. 261-65.

4638. —— Les problèmes de normalization des noms géographiques au niveau subetatique: Le cas du Québec; In International Congress of Onomastic Sciences, 11th, Sofia, 1972. Proceedings.
Abstract: Canadian Institute of Onomastic Sciences. Onomastica 46:18. 1973.

4639. —— Quelques réflexions en marge de deux inventaires toponymiques. Cahiers de géographie de Québec 12:303-13. 1968.
Suggests theories for toponymic studies and criticizes the article by Ludger Beauregard, Toponymie de la région métropolitaine de Montréal. (See no. 4606.)

4640. —— Terre Québec, un pays à nommer. Forces Hydro-Québec 6:4-9, Winter 1969. map.
The work of the toponymist.

4641. —— & Jean Poirier. Lexique des termes utiles à l'étude des noms de lieux. Québec, Presses de l'Univ. Laval, 1975. 162p. (Choronoma, 6)
Bibliography: p. 155-62.

4642. Dubuc, Carl. Pouvons-nous savoir quel est votre nom. Commerce 73:28-29, juil. 1971.
On the names of streets in Montreal.

4643. Dugas, Jean-Yves. Le problème des gentilés au Québec: état de la question et éléments de solution. Canadian Society for the Study of Names. Onomastica 56:25-40, Dec. 1979.

4644. Dulong, G. Le mot morne en canadien francais; In International Congress of Onomastic Science, 10th, Vienna, 1969. Proceedings 1:255-58. map.

4645. The Eastern townships gazetteer and general business directory; a commercial directory and guide to the eastern townships of Canada, containing also much useful information of a miscellaneous character. St. Johns, Smith & Co., 1867. 133p.

4646. Fafard, F. X. Les cantons de la Province de Québec, nomenclature. Québec, 1913. 32p.

4647. Froidevaux, Henri. L'oeuvre de la Commission de Géographie de Québec. Société de Géographie de Québec. Bulletin 11:327-33, nov. 1917.

4648. Ganong, William Francis. The origin of the East-Canadian place-names Gaspé, Blomidon, and Bras d'Or. Royal Society of Canada. Proceedings and transactions 3d ser. v. 22, sec. 2, p. 249-70. 1928.

4649. Gauvreau, Marcelle. La toponymie des Îles de Mingan. Société de Géographie de Québec et de Montréal. Bulletin 2:49-55, avril 1943.

4650. Goyer, Germain, Jr. & Line Croteau. Toponymie ville de Montréal-Est. Montréal-Est, Bibliotheque Municipale, [c1975]. 16p. map.

4651. Gravel, Albert. Une page d'histoire locale; les origines du mot Coaticook et l'expédition de Rogers en 1759. Canada français 12:187-92, nov. 1924.

4652. Grenier, Fernand. Les noms de lieux de la Beauce. Rapport préliminaire de recherches effectuées sous la direction de Fernand Grenier. Québec, Institut de Géographie, Université Laval, 1965. 99 ℓ.
A list of names, by zones, with cartographic source for each.

4653. —— F. Dumont & Jean-Claude Dupont. Inventaire toponymique des îles du Saint-Laurent situées entre Orleans et Anticosti. Québec, Univ. Laval, Travaux de l'Institut de Géographie, 1964. 14:39.

4654. Grenon-Roy, Judith. Aspects pratiques de la différenciation du générique et de l'entité; In Canadian Society for the Study of Names. Onomastica 54:19-24, Dec. 1978.
English version: p. 25-30.

4655. —— The computerization of geographical names: the Quebec experiment; In United Nations Conference on the Standardization of Geographical Names, 3d, Athens, 1977. Canada. Ottawa, 1978. p. 139-42.
French version: p. 299-303.

4656. —— Contribution a la toponymie du Canton de Bagot. Québec, 1972. 213p.
Manuscript deposited at the Commission de Toponymie, Quebec.

4657. —— Le traitement automatisé des noms géographiques: l'expérience du Québec. Canoma 3:3-5, July 1977.

4658. Guay, Réal. Les points cardinaux dans la choronymie québecoise. Canadian Society for the Study of Names. Onomastica 51:7-15, June 1977.

4659. —— Le rang: étude choronymique et son inscription dans le paysage laurentien. n.p., fév. 1972. 82p.
Presents classification of toponyms "de rang."

4660. Guerin, Raymond. Several city street names honor colorful characters. Montreal star Oct. 18, 1969, p. 16.
Popular account of the naming of several Montreal streets.

4661. Headley, W. Significance of Quebec names. Canadian bookman 2:40-41, Jan. 1920.

4662. Hebert, Diane. Toponymiste, juriste, musicien, Henri Dorion parcourt le Québec pour y semer des noms. The name gleaner 5:4-10, March 1980.
English translation by Alan Rayburn: p. 6-10.
An account of the work of a leading toponymist in Quebec, and the state of toponymy in Quebec.

4663. Huden, John Charles. Historical Champlain maps. Vermont history n.s. 27:34-40, 85-87, 191-93, Jan.-July 1959.
Includes identification of names on early maps and modern names that correspond with the map names.

4664. Lacasse, Jean-Paul. Limochoronymie de la frontière Québec-Maine. Canadian Society for the Study of Names. Onomastica 52:1-5, Dec. 1977.

4665. Laflèche, Louis. [Origine des toponymes indiens]. Rapport sur les missions de Diocèse de Québec, avril 1857. p. 100-05.
A brief note reprinted in Courrier du Canada, mai 22, 1857.

4666. Laverdière, Camille. Du choronyme Jaseux ou Jaseur. Revue de géographie de Montréal 24:353-54. 1970.

4667. —— Génériques, spécifiques et genres des potamonymes québecois. Revue de géographie de Montréal 24:265-76. 1970. map.
Various problems arising in Quebec from a poorly defined geographical terminology, as well as from the fact that its choronymy is too often influenced by English.

4668. —— Sur l'emploi de quelques termes géographiques. Naturaliste canadien 88:253-56, oct. 1961.
Proper and improper usage of geographic terms in relation to the Saguenay River.

4669. —— Sur les noms de lieux relevés le long de la nationale 54. Cahiers de géographie de Québec 10:280-89, sept. 1966. map.

4670. —— La toponymie du Nouveau-Québec. Le devoir v. 52, no. 269, no. 283, nov. 17, déc. 4, 1961.
Lettre au Devoir, and L'Opinion du lecteur.
Response by Michel Brochu: Défense et illustration de la toponymie du Nouveau-Québec, ibid. déc. 29, 1961.

4671. Lefebvre, Gilles. Rapport sur la toponymie du Nouveau-Québec: section traitant des toponymes esquimaux. 1964. 20p.

4672. Lemoine, Georges. Dictionnaire français-montagnais avec un vocabulaire montagnais-anglais, une courte liste de noms géographiques et une grammaire montagnaise. Boston, Cabot, 1901. 281, 63p.

4673. Le Vasseur, N. Le suffixe "ville." Société de Géographie de Québec. Bulletin 13:143-47. 1919.
Discussion of the tendency in Canada, and especially in Quebec, to attach "ville" to even insignificant settlements. Lists those in Quebec.

4674. Losique, Serge. Étymologies de quelques oronymes du Québec. In International Congress of Onomastic Sciences. 10th, Vienna, 1969. Proceedings 3:21-33.

4675. McAleer, George. A study of the etymology of the Indian place name, Missisquoi. Worcester, Blanchard Press, 1906. 102p.
Bibliography: p. 101-02.
Review: Review of historical publications relating to Canada 11:199. 1906.
In the Review of historical publications relating to Canada 15:92 (1910), this author is criticized for a further study, The etymology of Missisquoi. Addenda. (Worcester, The Author, 1910. 39p.), as being careless in his references and etymologies.

4676. McGill University. McGill Sub-Arctic Research Laboratory, Montreal. Annual report 1957-58, field research in Labrador-Ungava. n.p., 1959. 88p.
Appendix ii: Proposal for the adoption of a standard nomenclature [names—Labrador-Ungava, Ungava Peninsula, Nouveau-Québec]. p. 77-82.

4677. Macquisten, (?). Registre des rues. Ville de Montréal, Service des Travaux Publics, 1865.

4678. Magnan, Hormisdas. Dictionnaire historique et géographique des paroisses, missions et municipalités de la Province de Québec. Arthabaska, L'Imprimerie d'Arthabask, 1925. 738p.

4679. Manning, Thomas Henry. Explorations on the east coast of Hudson Bay. Geographical journal 109:58-75, July 1947.
List of new names used on accompanying map, and approved by the Geographic Board of Canada: p. 75.

4680. Massicotte, E. Z. Origine des noms de rues et de localités dans la région de Montréal. Bulletin des recherches historiques 27:152, mai 1921; 28:49-50, 114-15, 272-73, fév., avril, sept. 1922; 29:52-53, 77-78, 169-70, fév., mars, juin 1923; 30:175-77, 245-46, juin, août 1924; 31:125-26, avril 1925; 33:485, juil. 1927; 34:731-32, déc. 1928.

4681. Mercier, Jean. Autour de Mena'Sen. Preface de Me Armand Nadeau. Sherbrooke, Apostolat de la Presse, 1964. 224p.
Lists of streets, parks, etc., in Sherbrooke and Ascot-Nord, including origins and changes.

4682. —— L'Estrie. Preface chanoine Lionel Groulx. Sherbrooke, Apostolat de la Presse, 1964. 262p.
First presented as thesis to the University of Montreal.
L'onomastique de l'Estrie: p. 97-257, in two parts—historical names and literary names.

4683. —— Toponymie du Québec. [Québec, Conseil de la vie française en Amérique, 1958?]. 31p.
Nom officiel des municipalités, par Paul Dozois: p. 18-29.
In the interest of more French names in the Province of Quebec.

4684. Montréal, Québec. Répertoire des noms de rues. [Montréal], Service de Planification, 1979. 147p.
Earlier editions published by Service d'Urbanisme, 1963, 1965, 1968.

4685. Montréal, Québec. Service d'Urbanisme. Toponymie, [par Georges-F. Seguin]. 3e ed. Montréal, 1971. 43ℓ. (Bulletin d'information, no. 7)
1st ed. published in 1961 under title: D'où viennent les noms de nos rues?; 2d ed. 1966.
A list explaining the origin of the names of the streets of Montreal.

4686. Morin, Rosaire. Montréal, la plus grande ville française de langue anglaise: la toponymie des rues. Action nationale 56:26-40, sept. 1966.
Against street names of English origin.

4687. Morisset, Georges. À propos de nos Plaines. Mais . . . s'agit-il d' "Abraham" Lincoln? Revue de l'Université Laval 12:55-57, sept. 1957.
Plains of Abraham.

4688. Morrissoneau, Christian. Le Langage géographique de Cartier et de Champlain—choronymie, vocabulaire et perception, avec la collaboration de Henri Dorion. Québec, Les Presses de l'Univ. Laval, 1978. 230p. (Choronoma 17)

4689. —— Noms de lieux et contact des langues, une approche de la choronymie du Québec; In Henri Dorion, ed., Les noms de lieux et le contact des langues. Québec, Les Presses de l'Univ. Laval, 1972. p. 246-92.

4690. —— & Jean-Marc Nicole. La terminologie géographique archaïque et dialectale dans les noms de lieux du Québec. Cahiers de géographie de Québec 16:325-34, sept. 1972.

4691. Notes sur le nom Québec. Bulletin des recherches historiques 19:161-82, juin 1913.
A symposium on what various scholars have said about the origin of the name.
Review: Review of historical publications relating to Canada 18:85. 1913.

4692. O'Bready, Maurice. Qu'attend-on pour reconnaître officiellement le vocable Estrie? Action nationale 54:87-91, sept. 1964.
Wants official recognition of Estrie instead of Eastern.

4693. L'Origine du nom Bic. Bulletin des recherches historiques 33:486-89, juil. 1927.

4694. Ouimet, Séraphin. Le nom de Rivière Lairet. Bulletin des recherches historiques 62:217-18, oct.-déc. 1956.
In response to a comment ibid. 62:117, avril-juin 1956.

4695. Poirier, Jean. La Commission de Géographie du Québec; Ukrainian Free Academy of Sciences. Onomastica 35:18-21. 1968.

4696. —— De la tradition orale en toponymie. Cahiers de géographie de Québec 9:92-96, oct. 1964-mars 1965.
On the value of oral tradition in toponymy, illustrated with names in Quebec.

4697. —— Esquisse de toponymie quebécoise. Revue internationale d'onomastique 3:189-200, sept. 1967.

4698. —— Les êtres surnaturels dans la toponymie amérindienne du Québec. Revue internationale d'onomastique 21:287-300, déc. 1969.

4699. —— Graphie des toponymes esquimaux du Nouveau-Québec; In L'Annuaire de Québec 1964-1965. 47th ed. Québec, Ministère de l'Industrie et du Commerce, n.d.

4700. —— L'origine et la signification de plus anciens noms du Saint-Laurent.
Thesis (Ph.D.) Univ. of Paris. "à venir."

4701. —— Politiques toponymiques du Québec à l'égard des contacts linguistiques; In Henri Dorion, ed. Les noms de lieux et le contact des langues. Québec, Les Presses de l'Univ. Laval, 1972. p. 334-43.

4702. —— Problèmes généraux de toponymie au Québec. Cahiers de géographie de Québec 10:219-33, sept. 1966. maps.

4703. —— La toponyme Île au Ruau. Revue de géographie de Montréal 23:21-26. 1969.
Summaries in English and German.

4704. —— Les toponymes amérindiens encore en usage dans la nomenclature du Québec. Revue de géographie de Montréal 22:133-38. 1968. map.
Summaries in English and German.
Should Amerindian names that have not yet appeared on maps be put on maps? Some problems arise.

4705. —— Les toponymes la Malbaie, au Québec; In International Congress of Onomastic Sciences. 11th. Sofia. 1972. Proceedings.
Abstract: Canadian Institute of Onomastic Sciences. Onomastica 46:19-20. 1973.

4706. —— La toponymie de l'Île d'Orleans. Cahiers de géographie de Québec 6:183-99, avril-sept. 1962. maps.

4707. —— La toponymie historique et actuelle de l'Île d'Orleans. Québec, 1961. xiv, 137p. maps.
Thesis (M.A.) L'Institut de Géographie de Univ. Laval. 1961.
Bibliography: p. vii-xiv.

4708. —— Toponymie; méthode d'enquête. Québec, Presses de l'Univ. Laval, 1965. 165p. maps.
Bibliography: p. 139-43.
Review: Henri Dorion, Cahiers de géographie 10:343-46, sept. 1966; Sterling A. Stoudemire, Names 14:239-40, Dec. 1966.

4709. Poirier, Pascal. Recherches sur l'origine du mot de Québec. Royal Society of Canada. Proceedings and transactions 3d ser. v. 20, sec. 1, p. 93-98. 1926.

4710. Porlier-Bardages, Laure & Lily Tanguay-Desrochers. Répertoire historique et géographique des noms de rues de Sept-Îles. Sept-Îles, La Société Historique du Golfe, 1974. 83p. maps.

4711. Potvin, Damase. Ménage à faire dans notre toponymie. Revue de l'Université Laval 3:309-19, dec. 1948.

4712. Québec. Bureau de la Statistique. Répertoire des municipalités, 1974. Québec, Division de la diffusion des données de recensement, Service de l'information statistique, Ministère de l'Industrie et du Commerce, 1975. 465p.
Published under various titles, 1917- .
Includes: Chronologie des transformations municipales, 1961-74. Érections, annexions, changements de nom, p. 9-36; Liste alphabétique des municipalités et leurs principales correspondances territoriales, p. 37-301; Réserves indiennes et territoires non organisés, p. 302-27; Liste des corporations de comté et des communautés urbaines ou régionales, p. 329-38.
The 1969 edition included: Toponymes populaires, p. 229-54.

4713. —— Commission de Géographie. Guide toponymique du Québec. Québec, Ministère des Terres et Forêts, Commission de Géographie, 1968. 22p. (Étude toponymique, nouv. sér. 1)
Describes the role of the Commission de Géographie and rules of nomenclature.
The Commission de Géographie was succeeded by the Commission de Toponymie in 1977.
Review: Henri Dorion, Cahiers de géographie de Québec 12:470-72, déc. 1968.

4714. —— —— Noms géographiques de la Province de Québec. 3. ed. Québec, Dépt. des Terres et Forêts, 1926. 158p.
1st ed. 1916; 2d ed. 1921.

4715. —— —— Répertoire géographique du Québec. Québec, Ministère des Terres et Forêts, Commission de Géographie, 1969. 701p. (Étude toponymique, nouv. sér. 3)
Published originally in Gazette officielle du Québec March 15, 1969, v. 101, no. 11A, as required by law before the Commission's decisions are final.
Supplemented by decisions published in the Gazette officielle: v. 103, no. 45A, Nov. 1971; v. 104, no. 33A, Aug. 24, 1972; v. 106, no. 9A, May 5, 1974; v. 109, no. 31A, Aug. 8, 1977.
Superseded by 1978 publication (see no. 4729).
Review: Gilbert Maistre, Revue d'histoire de l'amérique-française 23:472, déc. 1969.

4716. ——— Toponymie des principaux reliefs du Québec. Québec, Ministère des Terres et Forêts, Commission de Géographie, 1971. 72p. map. (Étude toponymique, nouv. sér. 4)

Bibliography: p. 67-72.

4717. —— Commission de Toponymie. À propos de noms de lieux. [Québec, n.d.] 10 ℓ.

A publicity pamphlet on the work of the Commission.

The Commission de Toponymie succeeds the Commission de Géographie organized in 1912 and placed under the responsibility of the Ministère de Terres et Forêts in 1920. The new Commission was authorized in the August 1977 Quebec charter of the French language, articles 122-128. The Commission is attached administratively to the Office for the French Language. The following items reflect the mandates of the 1977 charter.

4718. ——— Dossier toponymique de la Côte-Nord. Document préparé à l'occasion de la semaine du français sur la Côte-Nord, 18 au 21 septembre 1979. Québec, La Commission, 1979. 25p.

4719. ——— Dossier toponymique de la région de Montréal. Document préparé à l'occasion du Congrès annuel de la Société canadienne pour l'Étude des Noms, 29 mai au 1er juin 1980. Québec, La Commission, 1980. 61p.

Prepared by Ludger Beauregard and Jean-Yves Dugas.

4720. ——— Dossier toponymique de la région de Québec. Aspect historique et probleme des gentilés. Québec, La Commission, 1980. 30p.

4721. ——— Dossier toponymique de la région de Trois-Rivières. Document préparé à l'occasion de la semaine du français dans la region de Trois-Rivières, 24 mars au 28 mars 1980. Québec, La Commission, 1980. 24p.

4722. ——— Dossier toponymique de l'Outaouais. Document préparé a l'occasion de la semaine du français dans l'Outaouais du 1er au 5 octobre 1979. Québec, La Commission, 1979. 21p.

4723. ——— Dossier toponymique des Cantons-de-l'Est (Estrie). Document préparé à l'occasion de la semaine du français dans les Cantons-de-l'Est (Estrie), 15 au 19 octobre 1979. Québec, La Commission, 1979. 21p.

4724. ——— Dossier toponymique du Bas-Saint-Laurent-Gaspésie. Document préparé à l'occasion de la semaine du français dans le Bas-Saint-Laurent-Gaspésie 5 au 9 novembre 1979. Québec, La Commission, 1979. 23p.

4725. ——— Dossier toponymique du Nord-Ouest. Document préparé à l'occasion de la semaine du français dans le Nord-Ouest, 29 octobre au 2 novembre 1979. Québec, La Commission, 1979. 20p.

Cover-title: Dossier toponymique de l'Abitibi-Temiscamingue, (Nord-Ouest).

4726. ——— Dossier toponymique du Saguenay-Lac-Saint-Jean. Document préparé à l'occasion de la semaine du français au Saguenay-Lac-Saint-Jean, 24 au 28 septembre 1979. Québec, La Commission, 1979. 26p.

4727. ——— Guide toponymique du Québec. Comment choisir, comment écrire, comment faire officialiser un nom de lieu au Québec. Édition provisoire. Québec, La Commission, 1979. 43p.

Instructions for carrying out the provisions of the new French language charter, articles 122-128.

4728. ——— Guide toponymique municipal. Document de travail. Québec, La Commission, 1979. 118p.
Regulations for cities under the new French-language charter on the criteria for the choice of place-names, and other rules which apply to the naming practice.

4729. ——— Répertoire toponymique du Québec, 1978. Québec, La Commission, 1978. xvii, 1199p. map.
Supersedes the Commission de Géographie's Répertoire géographique du Québec, 1969 (see no. 4715), and adds 30,000 names to the 45,000 in the 1969 edition for a total of 75,000.
New names and changes to be published annually in a special supplement of the Gazette officiel.
Review: Alan Rayburn, Canadian geographic 100:73, Feb./March 1980.

4730. —— Dépt. des Colonisation, Mines et Pêcheries. Municipalités, paroisses, cantons, etc. de la Province de Québec de 1896 à 1924, comp. par Odessa Piche. Québec, 1924. lxxviii, 498p.

4731. ——— Vastes champs offerts à la colonisation et à l'industrie. La Gaspésie, Quebéc, 1914. 276p.
Noms géographiques: p. 258-64.

4732. —— Dépt. des Terres et Forêts. Les cantons de la Province de Québec. Comp. par le Service des Arpentages du Ministère des Terres et Forêts. Québec, 1936. 42p.
A list of the cantons with the county in which located.

4733. ——— Dictionnaire des rivières et lacs de la Province de Québec. Québec, 1925. 399p.
Earlier edition by Eugène Rouillard: 1914. 432p. (See no. 4765.)

4734. ——— Répertoire des cantons du Québec. Ministère des Terres et Forêts, Service de l'Arpentage et de la Géodésie. Québec, 1966. 68p. map.
Earlier editions with title: Nomenclature des cantons de la Province de Québec, 1945, 1950, 1952, and 1956.
A list of the cantons with location, date proclaimed, etc.

4735. —— Ministère des Affaires Culturelles. Répertoire des rues de Montréal au XIXe siècle. Montréal, Direction Générale du Patrimoine, 1976. 176p. (Dossier 17)

4736. —— Service du Cadastré. Liste des villes, villages, paroisses et cantons cadastré de la Province de Québec, comp. par A. J. Duchesnay. Québec, 1938. 50ℓ.

4737. ——— Répertoire cadastral du Québec. [Québec], Ministère des Terres et Forêts. [1972?]. 230p.

4738. Richardson, Martha E. Montreal street names. Canadian magazine 18:535-37, April 1902.

4739. Robinson, Percy James. Montreal to Niagara in the seventeenth century, a philological excursion. Royal Society of Canada. Proceedings and transactions 3d ser. v. 38, sec. 2, p. 137-53. 1944.

4740. —— The origin of the name Hochelaga. Canadian historical review 23:295-96, Sept. 1942.
Traces the derivation of the Indian name for Montreal.

4741. —— Some of Cartier's place-names, 1535-1536. Canadian historical review 26:401-05, Dec. 1945.
In the region between Île aux Coudres and Île d'Orleans.

4742. Rouillard, Eugène. À propos de noms sauvages. Société de Géographie de Québec. Bulletin 11:283-85, sept. 1917.

4743. —— L'Abord-à-Plouffe. Société de Géographie de Québec. Bulletin 9:152-54. 1915.

4744. —— Albanel. Société de Géographie de Québec. Bulletin 15:119. 1921.

4745. —— Albert. Société de Géographie de Québec. Bulletin 15:119. 1921.
In honor of Prince Albert (1819-61).

4746. —— Les baies de la Province de Québec. Société de Géographie de Québec. Bulletin 10:231-41. 1916.

4747. —— Betsiamites; quelle est la véritable orthographie de ce nom? Société de Géographie de Québec. Bulletin 13:149-50. 1919.

4748. —— Le canton de Frampton. Société de Géographie de Québec. Bulletin 13:87-89. 1919.
Traces name to Mary Frampton, English writer.

4749. —— Le Canton Michaux. Société de Géographie de Québec. Bulletin 9:58. 1915.
Named for famed scientist.

4750. —— Commission de Géographie. Société de Géographie de Québec. Bulletin 13:95. 1919.
Fafard, and River Macamic.

4751. —— Commission de Géographie de Québec: modifications toponymiques--sommaire des travaux accomplis dans les trois dernières années. Société de Géographie de Québec. Bulletin 10:101-04. 1916.

4752. —— Commission de Géographie. Dénominations de cantons, lacs et rivières. Société de Géographie de Québec. Bulletin 11:41-44, janv. 1917.

4753. —— Commission de Géographie. Les méchins-lacs de la région de l'Abitibi. Société de Géographie de Québec. Bulletin 11:228-30, juil. 1917.

4754. —— Commission de Géographie. Nouveaux cantons. Société de Géographie de Québec. Bulletin 8:73-75, 166-68, mars, mai 1914; 12:85-87, mars 1918.

4755. —— Commission de Géographie. Nouveaux cantons—Rivière Malbaie, Lacs Squateck. Suppression de dénominations sauvages. Société de Géographie de Québec. Bulletin 8:44-45, janv. 1914; 13:47. 1919.

4756. —— Commission de Géographie. Nouveaux cours d'eau. Société de Géographie de Québec. Bulletin 8:233, juil. 1914.

4757. —— La Commission Géographique. Société de Géographie de Québec. Bulletin 5:217-18, mai 1911; 7:42-43, 103, janv., mars 1913; 8:280-82, sept. 1914; 11:100-02, 166-67, mars-mai 1917; 12:235-36, juil. 1918.

4758. —— Le Comté de Chambly et son fondateur. Société de Géographie de Québec. Bulletin 14:110. 1920.
Biographical sketch of military figure for whom site was named.

4759. —— La Côte-Nord du Saint-Laurent et le Labrador canadien. Esquisse topographique, nomenclature des cours d'eau. Québec, Laflamme et Proulx, 1908. 181p.

4760. —— Création d'une Commission Géographique. Société de Géographie de Québec. Bulletin 6:363-64, nov. 1912.
A Commission for Quebec.

4761. —— De l'orthographie des noms de lieu. Société de Géographie de Québec. Bulletin 5:83-87, mars 1911.
Railroad companies have changed names of places without reason.

4762. —— Défendons nous! La langue géographique. Société de Géographie de Québec. Bulletin 12:262-63, sept. 1918.

4763. —— Les deux Lorette. Société de Géographie de Québec. Bulletin 13:108. 1919.
Two villages in Quebec of the same name, one of which was to be changed to Loretteville.

4764. —— Deux points géographiques, Pointe-des Monts et Cap-de-Chatte. Société de Géographie de Québec. Bulletin 4:38-43, fév. 1910.

4765. —— Dictionnaire des rivières et lacs de la Province de Québec. Québec, Département des Terres et Forêts, 1914. 432p.
Also published in Société de Géographie de Québec. Bulletin 7:169-78, 238-48, 303-15, 365-74; 8:18-25, 95-102, 173-80, 220-32, 297-304, 362-71; 9:44-53, 97-104, 166-76, 231-39. 1913-15.

4766. —— Les îles de la Province de Quebéc. Société de Géographie de Québec. Bulletin 10:23-33, 105-15. 1916.

4767. —— Le Lac Abanel. Société de Géographie de Québec. Bulletin 4:66, fév. 1910.
Restoration of above name to lake known as Petit Lac Mistassini.

4768. —— Le Lac Chamouchouan. Société de Géographie de Québec. Bulletin 13:111. 1919.

4769. —— Lac Noir ou Black Lake. Société de Géographie de Québec. Bulletin 15:187. 1921.
Cites desire of Society to see return of French name on maps rather than English.

4770. —— Le Lac Piakouakamy ou Lake Saint-Jean. Société de Géographie de Québec. Bulletin 13:82-83. 1919.
A reprint, with comment, of history of aboriginal name from records of the explorer Normandin.

4771. —— Missisquoi, origine et signification de ce nom. Société de Géographie de Québec. Bulletin 4:248-51, oct. 1910.
About the name of a bay of Lake Champlain in Quebec and a river in northern Vermont.

4772. —— Nomenclature géographique, cours d'eau de l'Abitibi. Société de Géographie de Québec. Bulletin 6:231-34, juil. 1912.

4773. —— Une nomenclature géographique, les nouveaux noms géographiques de l'Abitibi et du Comté de Pontiac. Société de Géographie de Québec. Bulletin 6:156-64, mai 1912.

4774. —— Les noms de gares. Société de Géographie de Québec. Bulletin 11:98-99, mars 1917.

4775. —— Noms de lieux. Cap-de-la-Magdeleine, Rivière, Godbout, Pointe le Heu. Société de Géographie de Québec. Bulletin 11:339-41, nov. 1917.

4776. —— Les noms de villes. Société de Géographie de Québec. Bulletin 11:172, mai 1917.

4777. —— Les noms géographiques dans Québec. Nouvelle-France 12:515-20, nov. 1913.

4778. —— Les noms géographiques de la Province de Québec. Société de Géographie de Québec. Bulletin 15:102-07, 166-70, mars, mai 1921.

4779. —— Noms géographiques de la Province de Québec et des Provinces Maritimes empruntés aux langues sauvages; avec carte indiquant les territoires occupés autrefois par les races aborigènes; étymologie, traduction et orthographie. Québec, Marcotte, 1906. 110p. (Publications de la Société du Parler Français au Canada)
Auteurs et ouvrages consultés: p. 5-6.

4780. —— Les noms géographiques de Québec, conference de M. l'Abbé H. Simard. Société de Géographie de Québec. Bulletin 10:74-75. 1916.
Simard deplored the prevalence of aboriginal names on the map of Canada. Rouillard defends their right through history to a place on the map.

4781. —— Noms sauvages: étymologie et traduction. Société de Géographie de Québec. Bulletin 5:410-22, nov. 1911; 6:31-42, janv. 1912.
"A collection of geographical names of the Province of Quebec and the Maritime Provinces, supplementary to the author's 'Noms géographiques' published in 1906."—Griffin.

4782. —— Nouveaux cantons dans la région du Saint-Maurice. Société de Géographie de Québec. Bulletin 6:364-73. 1912.

4783. —— Nouvelles dénominations géographiques. Société de Géographie de Québec. Bulletin 12:94-95, mars 1918.

4784. —— Parcs des îles du Saint-Laurent. Société de Géographie de Québec. Bulletin 15:247. 1921.

4785. —— Quelques noms géographiques. Société de Géographie de Québec. Bulletin 5:382-86, nov. 1911.
Names by the original explorers.

4786. —— Quelques points géographiques. Société de Géographie de Québec. Bulletin 10:205-08. 1916.
Names in the Gaspé region.

4787. —— Respect aux noms primitifs. Société de Géographie de Québec. Bulletin 3:30-32, déc. 1909.

4788. —— La Rivière des Géants. Société de Géographie de Québec. Bulletin 13:110-11. 1919.

4789. —— Toponymie de la Côte Nord du Saint-Laurent et du Labrador Canadien. Société de Géographie de Québec. Bulletin 7:208-12, juil. 1913.

4790. —— La traduction des noms de lieux. Société de Géographie de Québec. Bulletin 8:352-53, nov. 1914.

4791. —— Le trait d'union dans les noms géographiques. Société de Géographie de Québec. Bulletin 8:87-88, mars 1914.
Use of hyphen and abbreviation in names with St. or Saint.

4792. Rousseau, Jacques. Les noms géographiques du Bic. Société de Géographie de Québec. Bulletin 23:26-36, janv. 1929.
Parish of Bic.

4793. —— La toponymie de l'Île aux Coudres. Société de Géographie de Québec. Bulletin 1:89-100, 106-14, 121-27, oct.-déc. 1942; 2:47-48, mars 1943.

4794. —— La toponymie montréalaise. Revue de géographie de Montréal 24:91-96. 1970.
Criticizes and supplements the article by Ludger Beauregard, Toponymie de la région métropolitaine de Montréal (See no. 4606.)

4795. Roy, Carmen. La littérature orale en Gaspésie. 2e. ed. Ottawa, 1962. 389p. (Musée National du Canada. Bulletin 134. Série anthropologique, no. 36)
1st ed. 1956.
Les noms de lieux dans la tradition (noms géographiques et légendes toponymiques): p. 20-60.

4796. Roy, Pierre Georges. Ce que rappelle le nom Murray Bay. Société de Géographie de Québec. Bulletin 11:226-27, juil. 1917.

4797. —— Les noms géographiques de la Province de Québec. Lévis, Impr. par La Cie de Publication le Soleil, 1906. 514p.
Review: Review of historical publications relating to Canada 11:112-16. 1907.

4798. Rudnyćkyj, Jaroslav Bohdan. Languages in contact and onomastics; In International Congress of Onomastic Sciences, 11th, Sofia, 1972. Proceedings.
Abstract: Canadian Institute of Onomastic Sciences. Onomastica 46:19-20. 1973.

4799. Sanford Evans Statistical Service. Quebec place guide. Winnipeg, 1946. 130p.
To accompany Quebec population maps, 1946.

4800. Savard, Pierre. Sur les noms de paroisses au Québec des origines à 1925. Société canadienne d'Histoire de l'Église Catholique. Sessions d'étude 41:105-13. 1974.
Refers to different periods in which names were related to Irish emigration, and to cycles of Jesuit and Franciscan influence.

4801. Société du Parler Français au Canada. Extrait du livre des délibérations, 9 mai 1907; In United Nations Conference on the Standardization of Geographical Names, 3d, Athens, 1977. Canada. Ottawa, 1978. p. 251-59.
English version: p. 93-101.
The answer of the Society to the Canadian Geographic Board's request concerning the use of two nomenclatures, English and French, in the Province of Quebec.

4802. Tremblay, Victor. Betsiamites. Bulletin des recherches historiques 59:231-33, oct.-déc. 1953.
History of the name, in response to a question ibid. 59:178, juil.-sept. 1953.

4803. Trépanier, Léon. Les rues du vieux Montréal. Montréal, Fides, 1968. 187p.

4804. Vassal, H. List of names of certain places in the Abenakis language. Canada. Dept. of Indian Affairs. Annual report 1884, pt. 1, p. 27-29.
In vicinity of Pierreville.

4805. Viger, Jacques. Rapport sur les chemins, rues, ruelles et ponts de la cité et paroisse de Montréal. Montréal, J. Lovell, 1841.

4806. Wood, William. The place names of Quebec. University magazine (Montreal) 11:220-31, April 1912.
A popular article treating the names in groups, as language, events and people, animals, saints, etc.

4807. Wood, William Charles Henry. Place-names of Quebec. 20p.
Mounted clippings from The Gazette, Montreal, Jan. 6-7, 9-13, 1922, in the New York Public Library.

SASKATCHEWAN

4808. Bereskin, A. I. Cree Indian place names. Saskatchewan archaeology newsletter 4:15-17. 1966.

4809. Canada. Permanent Committee on Geographical Names. Gazetteer of Canada: Saskatchewan. 2d ed. Ottawa, Surveys and Mapping Branch, Dept. of Energy, Mines and Resources, 1969. 173p. map.
1st ed. 1957. 92p. Published by Canada. Board on Geographical Names.

4810. Davies, W. A. A brief history of the Churchill River. The Musk-ox 15:30-38. 1975. map.
A list of fur-trade posts and historic features found within and adjacent to the Churchill River basin: p. 32-33.

4811. Gauthier, Alphonse. Le nom de Radville en Saskatchewan. Bulletin des recherches historiques 59:203, oct.-déc. 1953.

4812. Horsefield, R. B. Saskatchewan place-names believed to be of Cree origin. Lake Cowichan, B.C., The Author, [1963]. 12p.

4813. Johnson, Gilbert. Place names in Churchbridge municipality. Saskatchewan history 6:70-72, Spring 1953.

4814. —— Place names in Langenburg municipality. Saskatchewan history 5:33-34, Winter 1952.

4815. Place names. Saskatchewan history 1:23-24, Spring 1948; 1:21-22, Autumn 1948; 2:28-29, Winter 1949; 2:29, Spring 1949; 3:34-35, Winter 1950; 3:111-12, Autumn 1950; 5:33-34, Winter 1952; 6:70-72, Spring 1953; 9:19-20, Winter 1956.
A section of the periodical, compiled variously by Alex R. Cameron, Bruce Peel, Gilbert Johnson, and others. Includes school-district names and names connected with medical history and the fur trade.

4816. Rouillard, Eugène. Le nom de Qu'appelle. Société de Géographie de Québec. Bulletin 4:64, fév. 1910.

4817. —— Nom géographique. Société de Géographie de Québec. Bulletin 16:52. 1922.
Decision of the Canadian Geographic Board to assign the name Bélanger to a river in Saskatchewan.

4818. Russell, Edmund Thomas Pete. What's in a name: the story behind Saskatchewan place names. Expanded and rev., 3d ed. Saskatoon, Western Producer Prairie Books, 1980. 350p.
1st ed., compiled by the Kelsey Public School, Saskatoon. 1968. 128p.; 2d ed., compiled by the Kelsey Public School, Saskatoon, edited by Edmund Thomas Russell. Saskatoon, 1973. 364p. map. (Prairie books)

4819. Turner, A. R., ed. Documents of western history: Wascana Creek and the "Pile o' Bones." Saskatchewan history 19:111-18, Autumn 1966.
Documentation on the name of the creek.

4820. —— Saskatchewan place names, a mirror held up to history, Saskatchewan history 18:81-88, Autumn 1965.

4821. Tyrrell, Joseph Burr. Report on a part of northern Alberta and portions of adjacent districts of Assiniboia and Saskatchewan. Canada. Geological and Natural History Survey. Annual report 1886, pt. E.
Appendix IV. Cree and Stoney Indian names for places within the area of the accompanying map: p. 172-76.

YUKON

4822. Canada. Permanent Committee on Geographical Names. Gazetteer of Canada Répertoire géographique du Canada: Yukon Territory Territoire du Yukon. 4th ed. Ottawa, Surveys and Mapping Branch, Dept. of Energy, Mines and Resources, 1981. xxxviii, 70p. maps.
First published in 1958 as part of Canada. Board on Geographical Names. Gazetteer of Canada: Northwest Territories and Yukon; Provisional edition of Yukon 1971. 22p.; 3d ed. 1976. 55p.

4823. Coutts, R. C. Yukon: places and names. Sidney, B.C., Gray's Publishing, Ltd., 1980. 294p.

4824. Kennedy name to a mountain. Kansas City times Nov. 21, 1964, p. 2.
Mountain in the Yukon near Alaska to be named Mount Kennedy in memory of President John F. Kennedy.

4825. Phillips, James Wendell. Alaska-Yukon place names. Seattle, Univ. of Washington Press, c1973. 149p. map.
Bibliography: p. 147-49.
A short list with origins and meanings of city, town, and a sampling of remote native (both Eskimo and Indian) village names and name sources for historical or currently significant geographical features.
Review: C. F. Stevenson, Canadian geographical journal 89:44-45, Dec. 1974; Ted C. Hinckley, Montana, the magazine of western history 24:72, Winter 1974; Claus-M. Naske, Pacific Northwest quarterly 65:149, July 1974; Robert M. Rennick, Names 22:78-80, June 1974.

4826. Rouillard, Eugène. Le Mont Logan. Société de Géographie de Québec. Bulletin 13:246. 1919.

Brief note on the mountain named for Sir William E. Logan.

4827. White, James. Place-names--Northern Canada. Canada. Geographic Board. Report 9:231-455. 1910.

Also published separately. 1911. 224p.

A partial report of this study, which deals especially with the names conferred by the explorers in the far north, was published in Royal Society of Canada. Proceedings and transactions 3d ser. v. 4, sec. 4, p. 37-40. 1910.

Review: Review of historical publications relating to Canada 16:126. 1912.

4828. Woodall, Robert G. The postal history of Yukon Territory. [Wimborne, Eng., The Author, 1964]. 156p. maps.

Review: S. A. S., Beaver, outfit [i.e., volume] 295:57, Autumn 1964.

SAINT-PIERRE AND MIQUELON
Territory of France

4829. Canada. Permanent Committee on Geographical Names. Gazetteer of Saint-Pierre and Miquelon (France). Ottawa, Geographical Branch, Dept. of Energy, Mines and Resources, 1968. 8p.

Bound with Canada. Permanent Committee on Geographical Names. Gazetteer of Canada: Newfoundland and Labrador. Ottawa, 1968.

Not an official gazetteer. Compiled from the 1955 maps published by l'Institut Géographique National of France.

4830. Roy, Carmen. Saint-Pierre et Miquelon; une mission folklorique aux îles. 2. ed. Ottawa, Ministère du Nord canadien et des resources nationales, 1966. (Musée national du Canada. Bulletin no. 182. Série anthropologique, no. 57 [i.e. 56])

Les noms de lieux dans la tradition: p. 41-60.

AUTHOR AND PERSONAL NAME INDEX

Numbers listed refer to entries and not to pages.

SUBJECT INDEX

Numbers listed refer to entries and not to pages.